Wildlife
Photographer
of the Year
Diary 2017

David Wright,
13th October 2016.

Published by the Natural History Museum, London

NATURAL HISTORY MUSEUM

The award-winning pictures gathered in this diary have been drawn from the archives of the Wildlife Photographer of the Year competition – the international showcase for the very best nature photography. The competition is owned by the Natural History Museum, London, which prides itself on revealing and championing the diversity of life on Earth.

Wildlife Photographer of the Year is one of the most popular of the Museum's exhibitions. Visitors come not only to see breathtaking imagery, but also to understand some of the threats faced by our planet's animals and plants. Understanding and finding ways of conserving the Earth's biodiversity is at the heart of the Museum's work. This exhibition is one way to share that mission with others, encouraging us to see the environment around us with new eyes.

The Natural History Museum looks after a world-class collection of over 80 million specimens. It is also a leading scientific research institution, with ground-breaking projects in more than 68 countries. About 200 scientists work at the Museum, researching the valuable collections to better understand life on Earth. Every year more than five million visitors, of all ages and levels of interest, are welcomed through the Museum's doors.

2016

JANUARY

wk	M	T	W	Th	F	S	S
1					1	2	3
2	4	5	6	7	8	9	10
3	11	12	13	14	15	16	17
4	18	19	20	21	22	23	24
5	25	26	27	28	29	30	31

FEBRUARY

wk	M	T	W	Th	F	S	S
6	1	2	3	4	5	6	7
7	8	9	10	11	12	13	14
8	15	16	17	18	19	20	21
9	22	23	24	25	26	27	28
10	29						

MARCH

wk	M	T	W	Th	F	S	S
10		1	2	3	4	5	6
11	7	8	9	10	11	12	13
12	14	15	16	17	18	19	20
13	21	22	23	24	25	26	27
14	28	29	30	31			

APRIL

wk	M	T	W	Th	F	S	S
14					1	2	3
15	4	5	6	7	8	9	10
16	11	12	13	14	15	16	17
17	18	19	20	21	22	23	24
18	25	26	27	28	29	30	

MAY

wk	M	T	W	Th	F	S	S
18							1
19	2	3	4	5	6	7	8
20	9	10	11	12	13	14	15
21	16	17	18	19	20	21	22
22	23	24	25	26	27	28	29
23	30	31					

JUNE

wk	M	T	W	Th	F	S	S
23			1	2	3	4	5
24	6	7	8	9	10	11	12
25	13	14	15	16	17	18	19
26	20	21	22	23	24	25	26
27	27	28	29	30			

JULY

wk	M	T	W	Th	F	S	S
27					1	2	3
28	4	5	6	7	8	9	10
29	11	12	13	14	15	16	17
30	18	19	20	21	22	23	24
31	25	26	27	28	29	30	31

AUGUST

wk	M	T	W	Th	F	S	S
32	1	2	3	4	5	6	7
33	8	9	10	11	12	13	14
34	15	16	17	18	19	20	21
35	22	23	24	25	26	27	28
36	29	30	31				

SEPTEMBER

wk	M	T	W	Th	F	S	S
36				1	2	3	4
37	5	6	7	8	9	10	11
38	12	13	14	15	16	17	18
39	19	20	21	22	23	24	25
40	26	27	28	29	30		

OCTOBER

wk	M	T	W	Th	F	S	S
40						1	2
41	3	4	5	6	7	8	9
42	10	11	12	13	14	15	16
43	17	18	19	20	21	22	23
44	24	25	26	27	28	29	30
45	31						

NOVEMBER

wk	M	T	W	Th	F	S	S
45		1	2	3	4	5	6
46	7	8	9	10	11	12	13
47	14	15	16	17	18	19	20
48	21	22	23	24	25	26	27
49	28	29	30				

DECEMBER

wk	M	T	W	Th	F	S	S
49				1	2	3	4
50	5	6	7	8	9	10	11
51	12	13	14	15	16	17	18
52	19	20	21	22	23	24	25
53	26	27	28	29	30	31	

2017

JANUARY

wk	M	T	W	Th	F	S	S
1							1
2	2	3	4	5	6	7	8
3	9	10	11	12	13	14	15
4	16	17	18	19	20	21	22
5	23	24	25	26	27	28	29
6	30	31					

FEBRUARY

wk	M	T	W	Th	F	S	S
6			1	2	3	4	5
7	6	7	8	9	10	11	12
8	13	14	15	16	17	18	19
9	20	21	22	23	24	25	26
10	27	28					

MARCH

wk	M	T	W	Th	F	S	S
10			1	2	3	4	5
11	6	7	8	9	10	11	12
12	13	14	15	16	17	18	19
13	20	21	22	23	24	25	26
14	27	28	29	30	31		

APRIL

wk	M	T	W	Th	F	S	S
14						1	2
15	3	4	5	6	7	8	9
16	10	11	12	13	14	15	16
17	17	18	19	20	21	22	23
18	24	25	26	27	28	29	30

MAY

wk	M	T	W	Th	F	S	S
19	1	2	3	4	5	6	7
20	8	9	10	11	12	13	14
21	15	16	17	18	19	20	21
22	22	23	24	25	26	27	28
23	29	30	31				

JUNE

wk	M	T	W	Th	F	S	S
23				1	2	3	4
24	5	6	7	8	9	10	11
25	12	13	14	15	16	17	18
26	19	20	21	22	23	24	25
27	26	27	28	29	30		

JULY

wk	M	T	W	Th	F	S	S
27						1	2
28	3	4	5	6	7	8	9
29	10	11	12	13	14	15	16
30	17	18	19	20	21	22	23
31	24	25	26	27	28	29	30
32	31						

AUGUST

wk	M	T	W	Th	F	S	S
32		1	2	3	4	5	6
33	7	8	9	10	11	12	13
34	14	15	16	17	18	19	20
35	21	22	23	24	25	26	27
36	28	29	30	31			

SEPTEMBER

wk	M	T	W	Th	F	S	S
36					1	2	3
37	4	5	6	7	8	9	10
38	11	12	13	14	15	16	17
39	18	19	20	21	22	23	24
40	25	26	27	28	29	30	

OCTOBER

wk	M	T	W	Th	F	S	S
40							1
41	2	3	4	5	6	7	8
42	9	10	11	12	13	14	15
43	16	17	18	19	20	21	22
44	23	24	25	26	27	28	29
45	30	31					

NOVEMBER

wk	M	T	W	Th	F	S	S
45			1	2	3	4	5
46	6	7	8	9	10	11	12
47	13	14	15	16	17	18	19
48	20	21	22	23	24	25	26
49	27	28	29	30			

DECEMBER

wk	M	T	W	Th	F	S	S
49					1	2	3
50	4	5	6	7	8	9	10
51	11	12	13	14	15	16	17
52	18	19	20	21	22	23	24
53	25	26	27	28	29	30	31

December – January

WEEK 1

26 Monday

Boxing Day, holiday (Christian)

27 Tuesday

Christmas Day holiday (substitute day) (Christian)

28 Wednesday

29 Thursday

Ice birds

by Jeanine Lovett

This giant iceberg was drifting just off the South Orkney Islands in the Southern Ocean. At some point, it had rolled over, to expose a dazzling underbelly of water-textured layers. Jeanine was watching a flock of Cape petrels soaring, swooping and dipping down over the sea, their long wings catching the updraughts and carrying them at speed. 'The photograph gives the impression that the berg was right beside our ship, but the petrels with their 60-centimetre wingspans show the true scale.'

30 Friday

31 Saturday

New Year's Eve
Hogmanay (Scotland)

1 Sunday

New Year's Day

Another year begins. i wonder what it will bring.

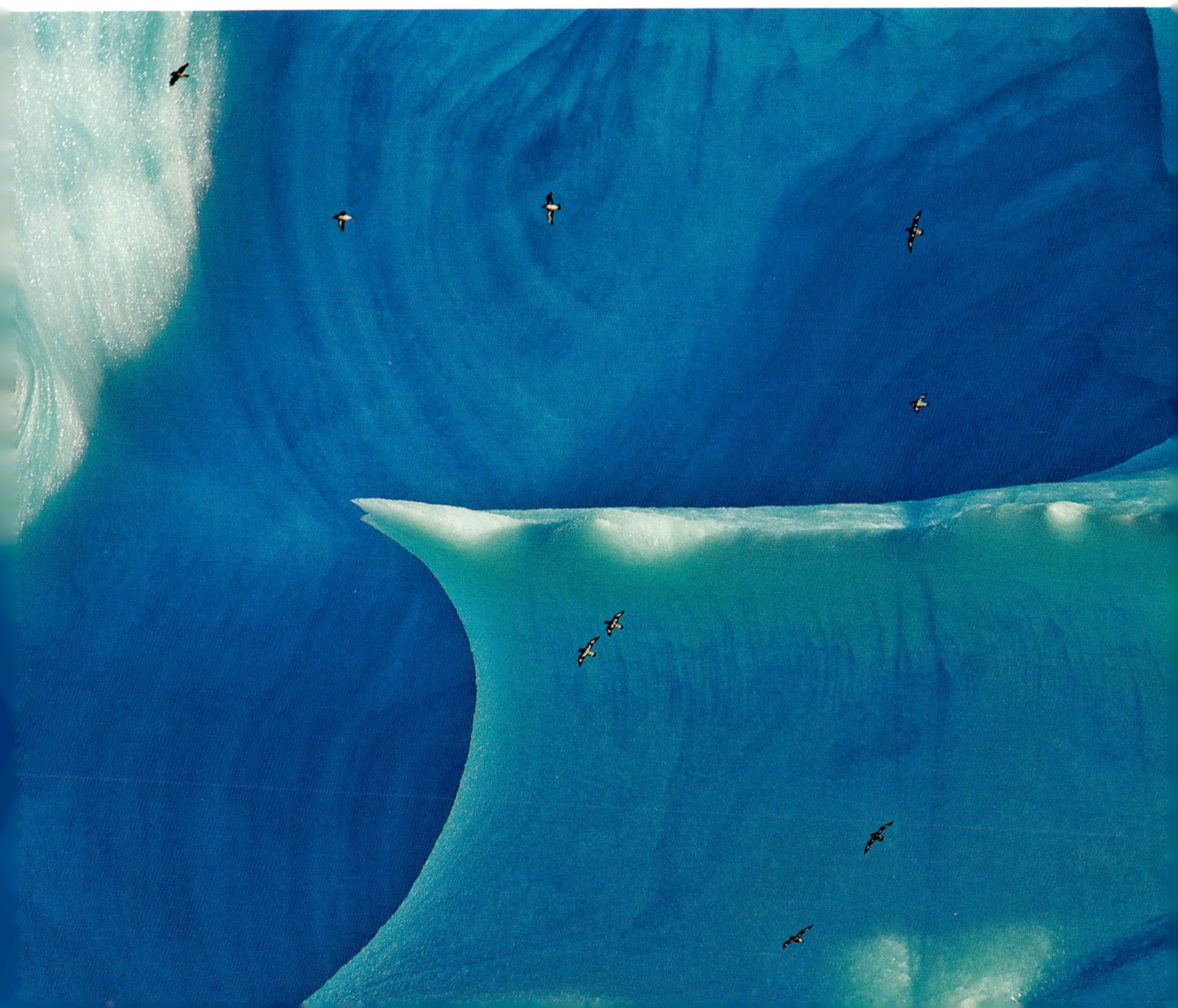

5th – Paignton Zoo; lit from D.I.D.; lit from Donkeys.

Received lit from the Folio Society.

2 Monday

Ordered a book from Folio Society.

New Year's Day holiday (substitute day) (UK, Republic of Ireland)
2nd January holiday (Scotland)

Went to Paignton Zoo again. Posted postcard to Susie. Had my hair cut.

3 Tuesday

New Year's Day holiday (substitute day) (Scotland)

Went to Shaldon Zoo. Bought two more book marks.

4 Wednesday

Did a bit of shopping. Travelled back home. Booked next chiropody appointment.

5 Thursday

Ordered the next book from Wild Sounds, and "The Penultimate Curiosity". Opened post – Xmas cards from Elizabeth Hillman, Sharon and Dick, and Stephan?, lit from D.W.C.T., Orangutan Foundation, letter from Barts;

Great tit poised

by Corentin Graillot Denaix

Corentin took this picture of a great tit on a lichen-covered twig in his garden. Each winter, his father sets up a hide there so that they can watch the birds that come to the bird feeders. Corentin uses it every weekend. 'About ten species visit,' he says. 'Several land on nearby branches, but when it's a blue or a great tit, it stays on the perch a very short time. So you have to take the picture very fast.'

5th. Charged my M. Scooter.

6 Friday

Epiphany (Christian)

Received "The Penultimate Curiosity" from Waterstones. Did some shopping. Met Serin's mother. She told me S. has quite a collection of cards now.

7 Saturday

Received a thank you letter from D.W.C.T., and "Slugs And Snails". No 133 in the New Naturalist Series.

8 Sunday

Julian and Pauline have returned from their holiday. Rang Stephen Norley.

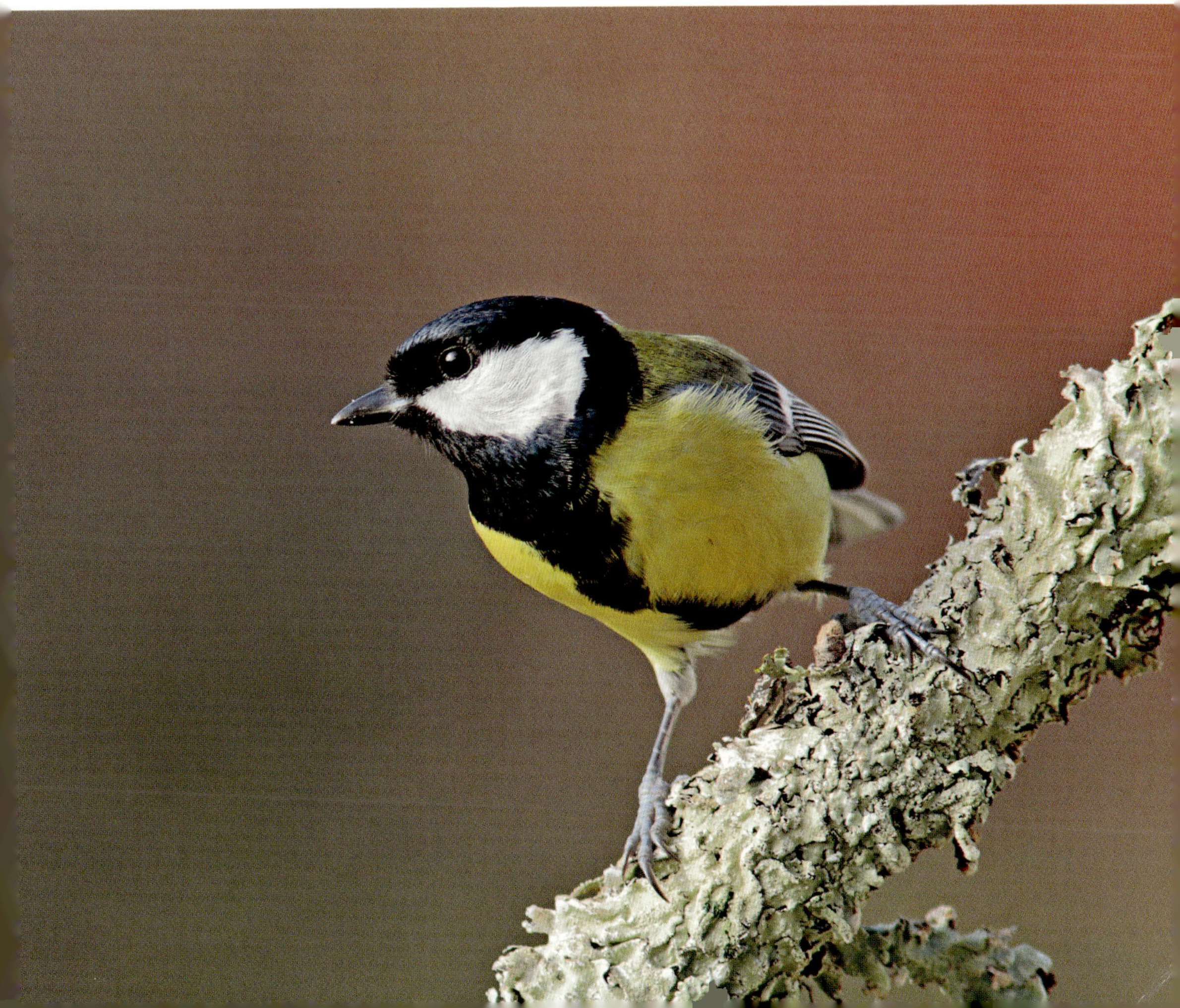

9 Monday

Wrapped up present for Margaret Greenleaf. Received a cheque from Friends Life; details of R.S.P.B. weekend; a thank you letter from D.W.C.T.; a Puzzler Magazine

10 Tuesday

Posted photo frame to Margaret Greenleaf did a little shopping.

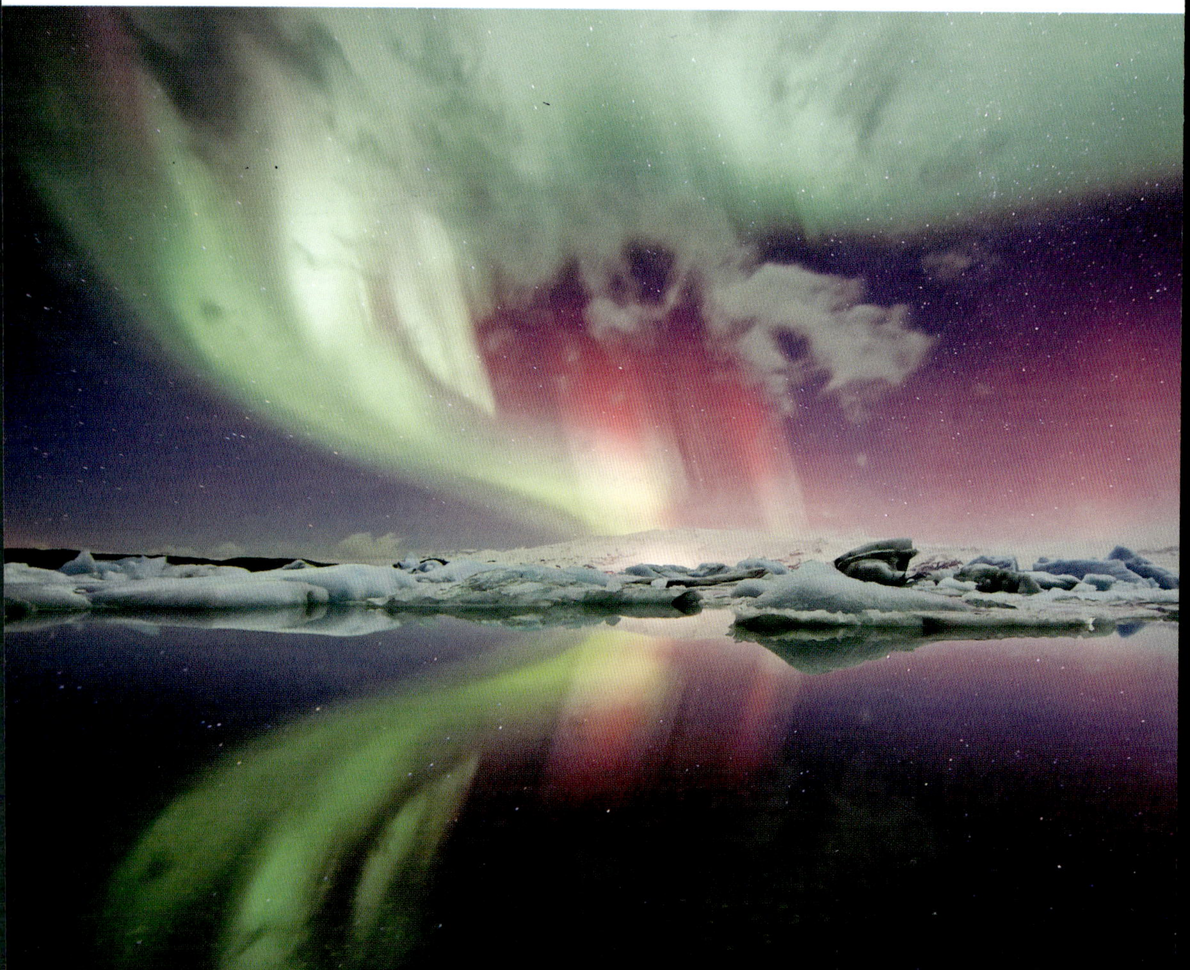

11 Wednesday

Received literature from World Animal Protection, and another Puzzler Magazine. Rang John Reynolds

12 Thursday

Full moon ○

Received "Analects" from the Folio Society. Received a bank statement, and an R.S.P.B. Magazine. Rang Cynthia Blizzard.

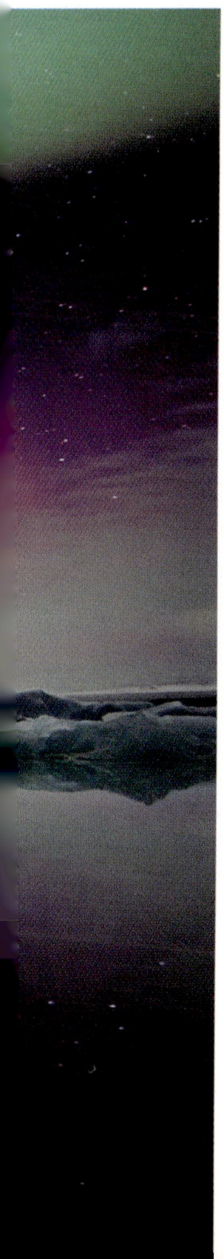

13 Friday

Received the Annual Bulletin of the Société Jersiaise for 2016, and literature from the British Red Cross. Ordered more medication.

14 Saturday 15 Sunday

Received a letter from D.W.C.T., to say that one of my adoptees, a radiated tortoise, has had to be euthanized. I now have a female tortoise as an adoptee instead.

Ice aurora

by Ellen Anon

The plan was to drive out to photograph the northern lights over the icebergs in Jökulsárlón, Iceland. But when Ellen arrived, the sky was thick with clouds. Hours later, the clouds suddenly parted revealing a breathtaking aurora borealis. She grabbed her gear and ran down to the water's edge, feeling fortunate that the aurora became even more intense. 'This was my favourite image – the swirl of the clouds complimenting the unusual colours in the aurora, all mirrored in the lagoon,' says Ellen.

16 Monday

Martin Luther King Day (USA)

Charged my M. Scooter.

17 Tuesday

Received a telephone bill. Did some shopping.

18 Wednesday

19 Thursday

Booked ambulance for Barts. Hospital, for Monday. Received a letter from D.W.C.T., about an adoptee, a pied tamarin.

Resurrection

by Marsel van Oosten

Deadvlei is the white clay bed of an ancient lake in the Namibian Desert. The acacia trees, which must have taken root when there was still moisture some 900 years ago, are all dead. Marsel had an image in his mind but the key ingredient was fog, which occurs only a handful of times a year when hot dry air from the east meets the cold humid air from the west. So it was many years before Marsel got his shot, with the tree illuminated with a flashlight behind the trunk.

20 Friday

Charged my M. Scooter. Rang chemists. I should be able to collect medication tomorrow.

21 Saturday

Received membership card for 2017, from the Société Jersiaise. Did some shopping. Collected medication.

22 Sunday

Prepared things for tomorrow's hospital visit. Rang Stephen Norley. He is going to Cuba on 9th February.

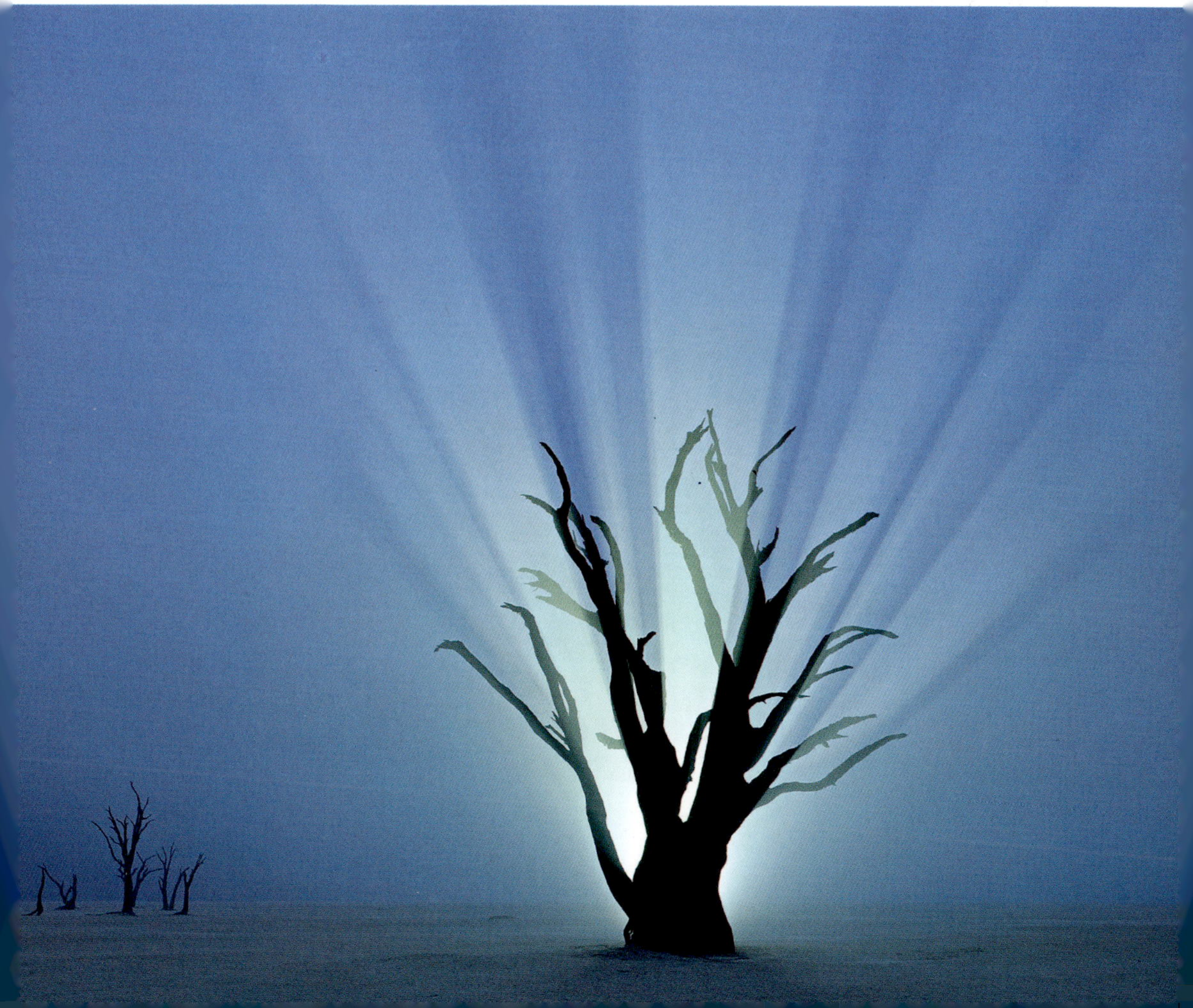

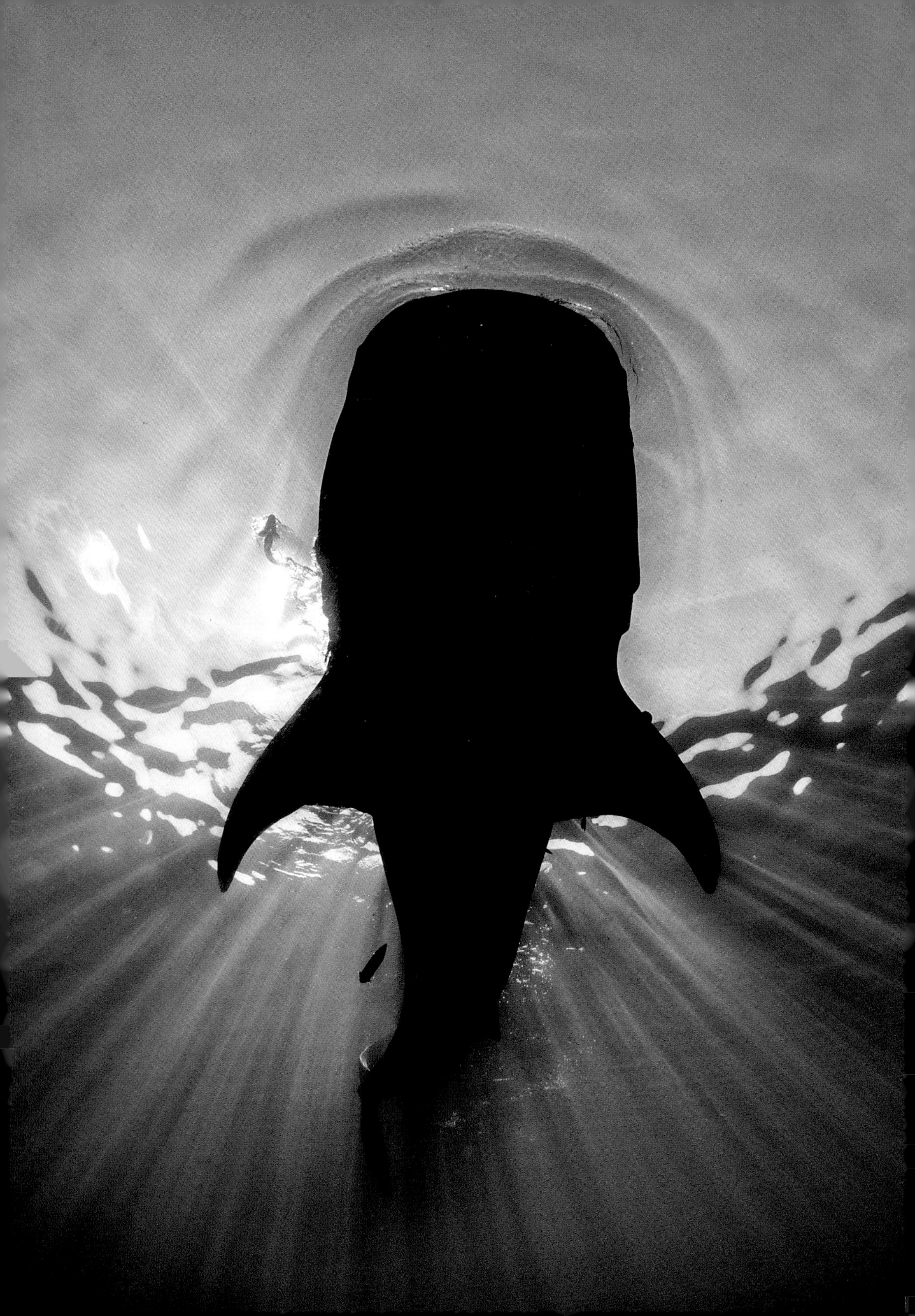

Wed - Received more Eurax Cream.
Rang Stephen Norley

23 Monday

Went to Barts Hospital. My pacemaker is alright. My next appointment is for 21st July, 13.50. Received literature from the Folio Society.

24 Tuesday

25 Wednesday

Burns Night (Scotland)

Received literature about House Insurance; and a letter from Margaret Greenleaf. Annabel's husband have been in an accident in Malawi. Husband has a broken back.

26 Thursday

Australia Day

Julian took the envelope with cheque to pay my house insurance, to post. Wrote a long letter to Margaret Greenleaf.

27 Friday

Received 'Evolve', from the Natural History Museum.

28 Saturday

Chinese New Year (Year of the Rooster)
New moon ●

Changed my mobility scooter.

29 Sunday

Posted a long letter to Margaret Greenleaf telling her about Sheldon Zoo, and the M Scooter at Paignton Zoo. Did some shopping.

Giant with sunbeams

by Alexander Mustard

Alex took this shot in open water in the Caribbean Sea, off Mexico's Yucatán Peninsula, while swimming among a huge aggregation of whale sharks, feasting on millions of tuna eggs. When he spotted the fin of an approaching shark with the sun behind it, he dived down and waited for the eight-metre animal to pass overhead so he could shoot it backlit, with the sunbeams spearing into the water along its flanks.

30 Monday

31 Tuesday

Rang House Insurance people. They haven't received my payment yet.

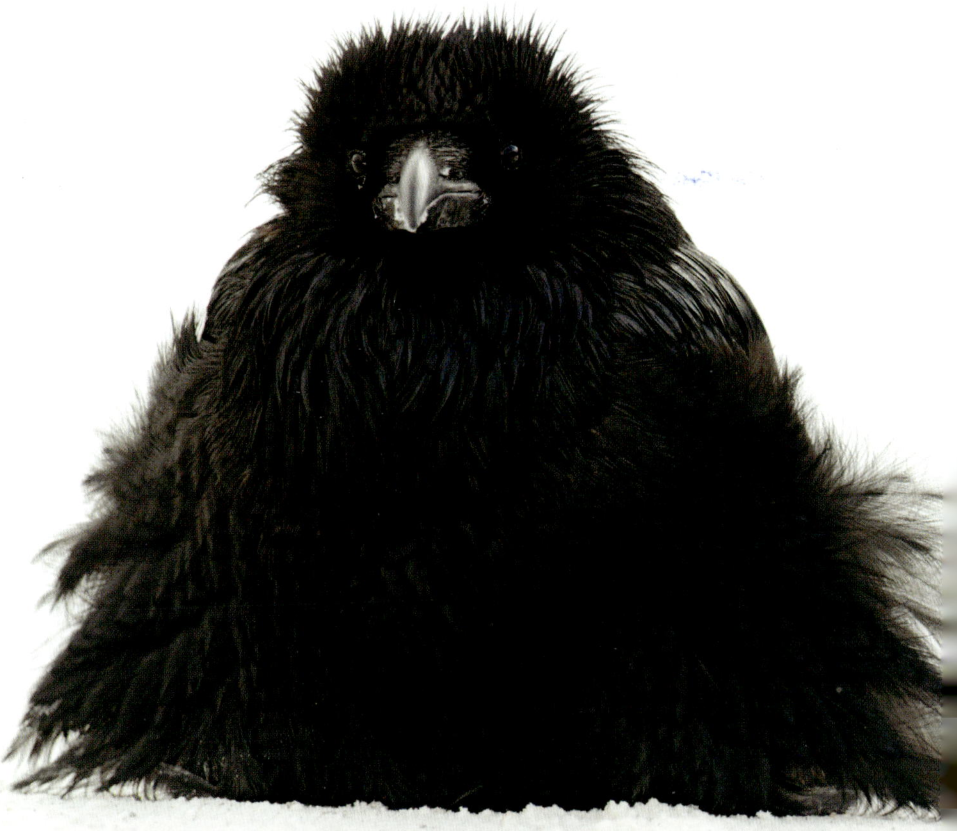

1 Wednesday

2 Thursday

Charged M. Scooter. Rang R. Morrell, but he knows nothing about the Thomas Paine Society anymore. He said he has been in hospital.

3 Friday

Received the Ethical Record for February. Did some shopping.

4 Saturday

Received two Puzzler Magazines.

5 Sunday

Fluff-up

by John E Marriott

A shapeless lump of puffed-up black that's what the figure looked like, squatting in the middle of a snow-covered road in Jasper National Park, Alberta, in the heart of the Canadian Rockies. As John drove slowly towards the feathers, he realised it was a raven. 'I fully expected it to fly off at any moment, but it just sat there, looking as though it had just got out of bed,' he says. 'Looking through the images afterwards, I laughed out loud.'

6 Monday

Ordered more medication. Received literature from the Folio Society.

7 Tuesday

Received a cheque for £54-81 from Friends Life.

8 Wednesday

Received literature from the L.A.C.S. Rang Master Quote. They have received my cheque for House Insurance. Completed form for Telecare. Received more medication

9 Thursday

A swirl of flamingos

by Klaus Nigge

In winter, the 22-kilometre-long estuary of the Ría Celestún on Mexico's Yucatán peninsula attracts thousands of Caribbean flamingos, which congregate here to feed on the microscopic life in the shallow, briny water. These flamingos – the largest and pinkest of the five species – also use their time in the estuary to engage in synchronous courtship dancing as a prelude to breeding. Klaus's aerial shot captures the beauty of pattern, form and colour of the mass aggregation, with the birds appearing as if one organism.

10 Friday

Received a Nat. West Bank statement: House Insurance literature; and literature from D.I.D. Rang, G. Austin, and Simon Jones.

11 Saturday

Full moon ○

Received lit. from the Folio society.

12 Sunday

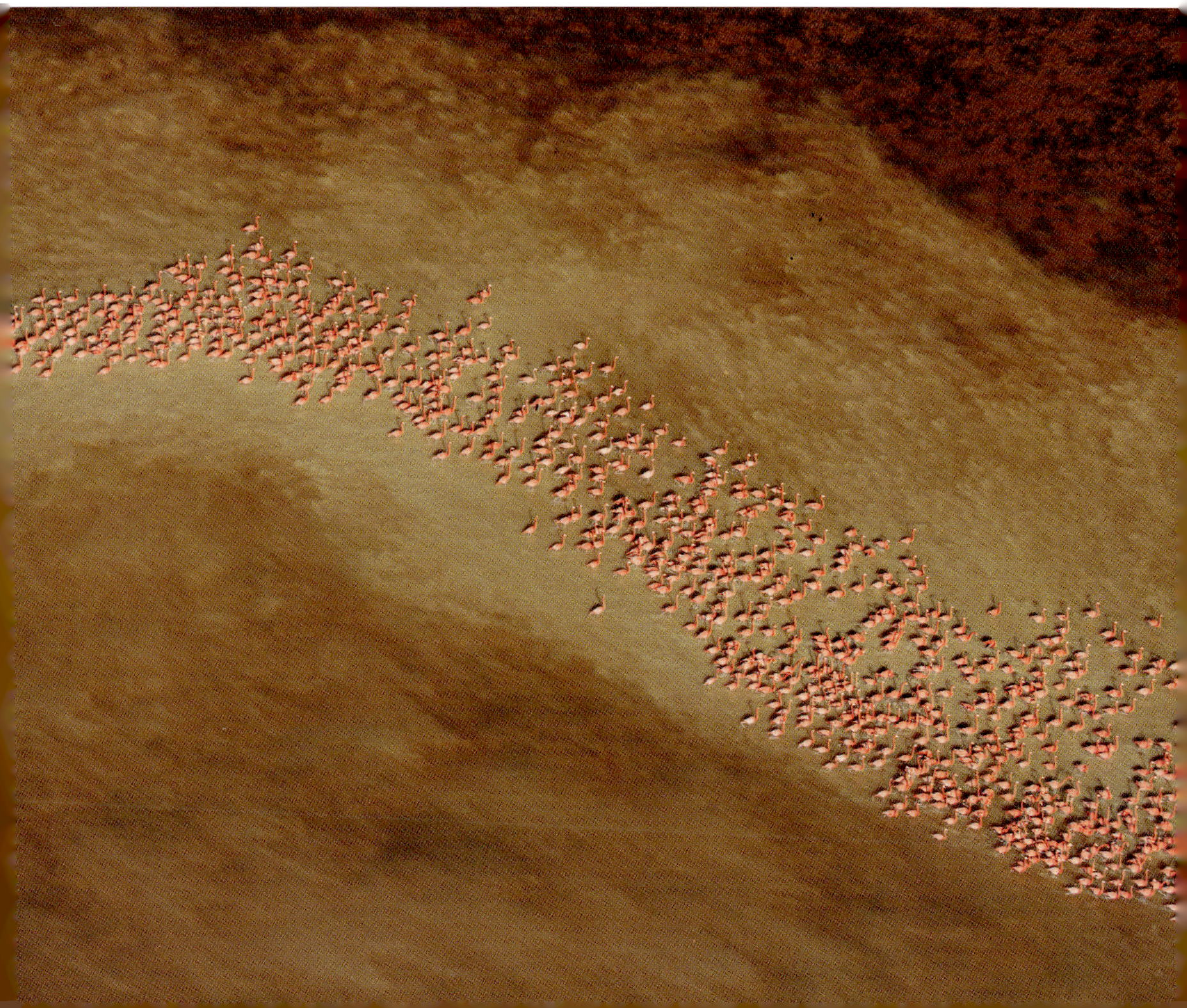

13 Monday

Received an appeal from the Gorilla Organization.

14 Tuesday Valentine's Day

Charged my M. Scooter.
Finished reading "The Penultimate Curiosity."

15 Wednesday

Received literature from the House Insurance people. Posted three letters, and did some shopping.

16 Thursday

Received a phone bill, and a Butterfly Conservation membership card.

True love

by Steve Race

Northern gannets show impressive devotion to each other, pairing for life and returning to the same nest site each year to breed. At the seabird colony on Bempton Cliffs on the Yorkshire coast, Steve has watched gannet behaviour for a number of years. 'Many times I have seen a male offer the female a gift such as a feather or blade of grass', he says. 'But on this occasion I was amazed to see the male give his partner a necklace of red campion.'

17 Friday

Ordered more medication. Received New Humanist for Spring 2017; and literature from World Animal Protection.

18 Saturday

Received Kew Magazine; an N.S.S. Bulletin and other literature; B.H.A. literature; and lit from the Donkey Sanctuary. Charged my M. Scooter.

19 Sunday

Posted a donation to the N.S.S., and tickets for the Donkey Sanctuary raffle. Had my hair cut. Did some shopping.

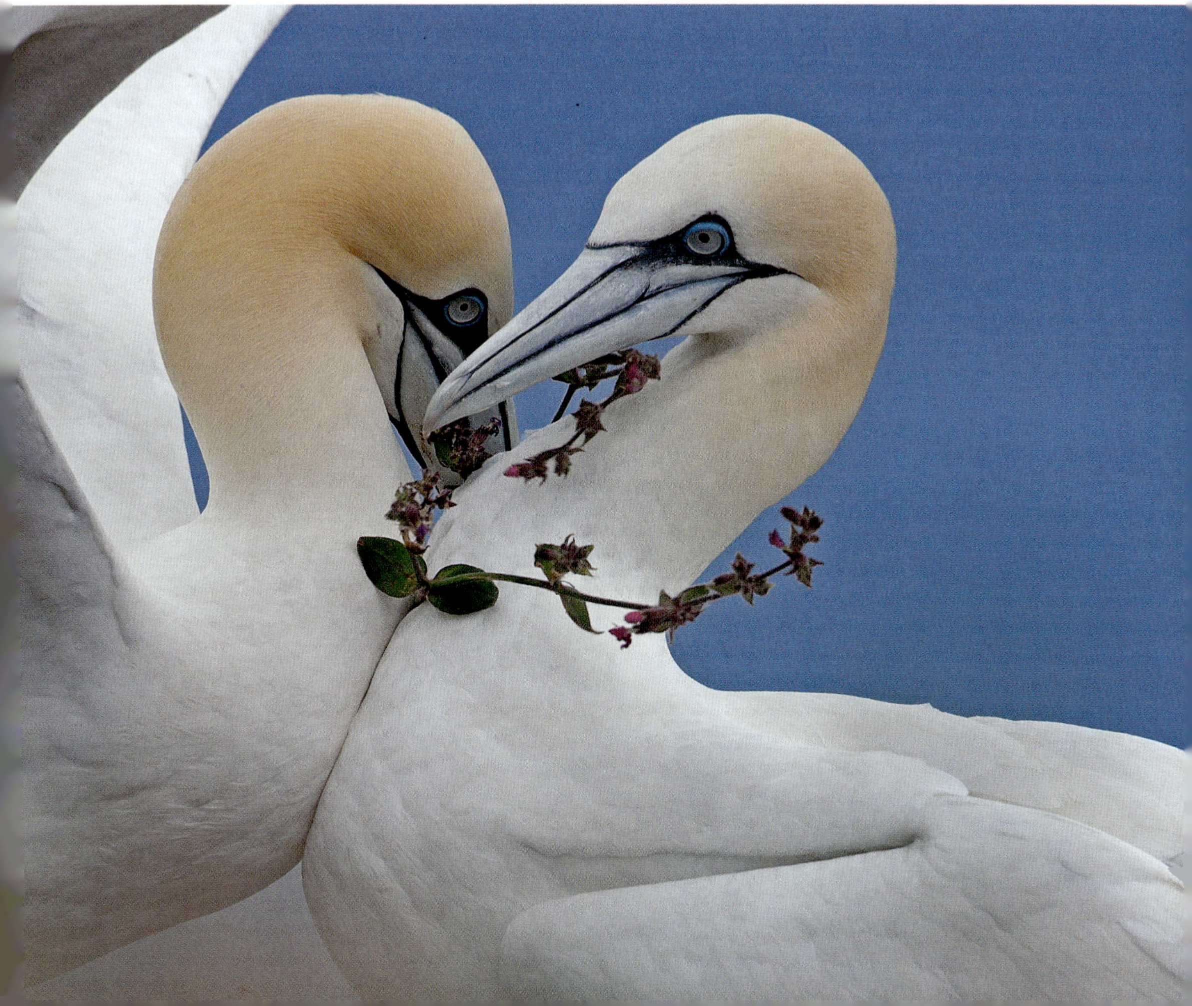

February

20 Monday

George Washington's Birthday (USA)

Received Life Fellows
News from the R.S.P.B

21 Tuesday

Charged my M. Scooter.

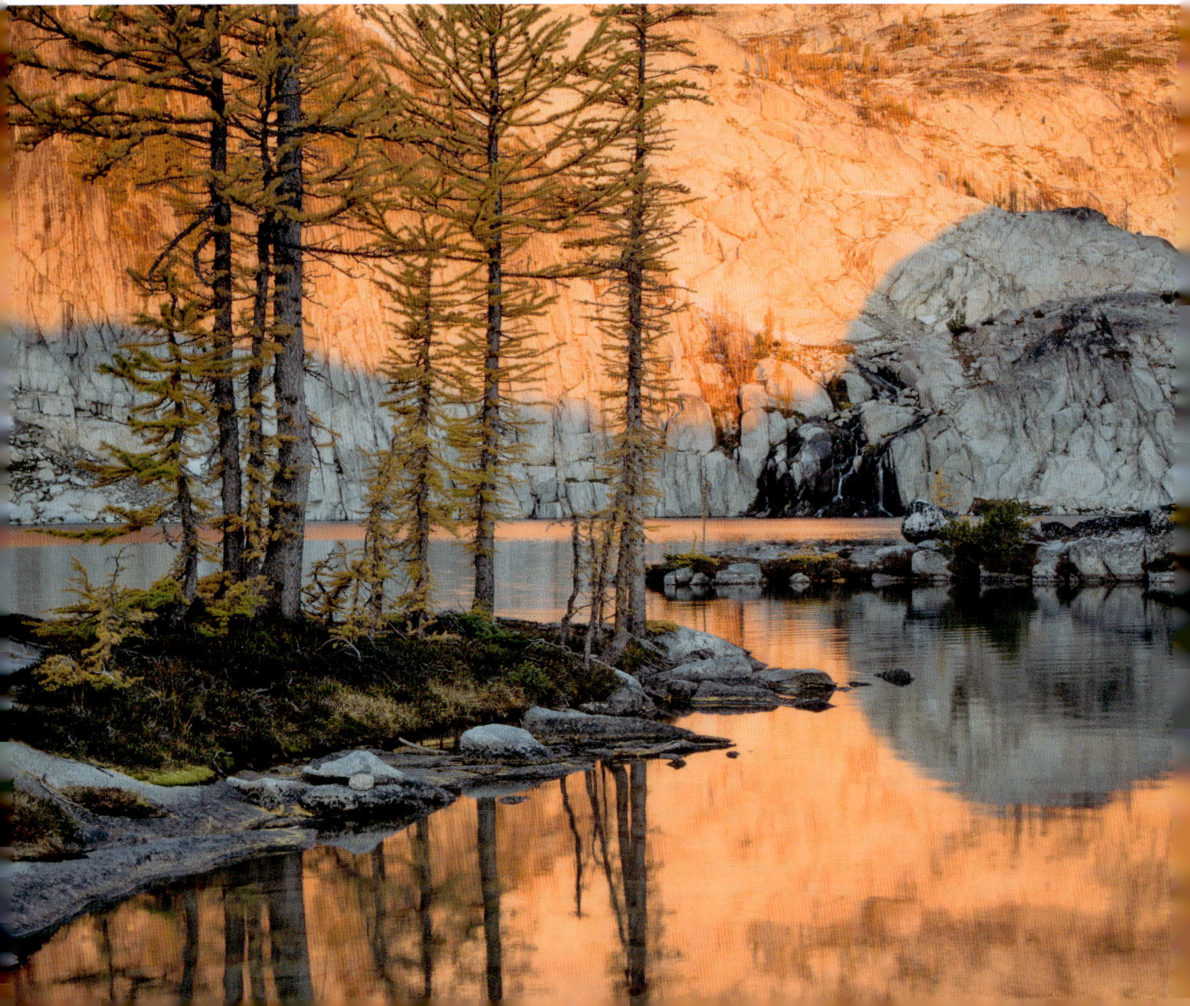

22 Wednesday

Posted donation to R.S.P.B. Did some shopping. Received a call from Paignton foot care.

23 Thursday

Rang Torbay Foot Care, and confirmed date for me to be treated by Anne Marie. Booked a ticket for the Secularist of the Year Function, at the Imperial Hotel.

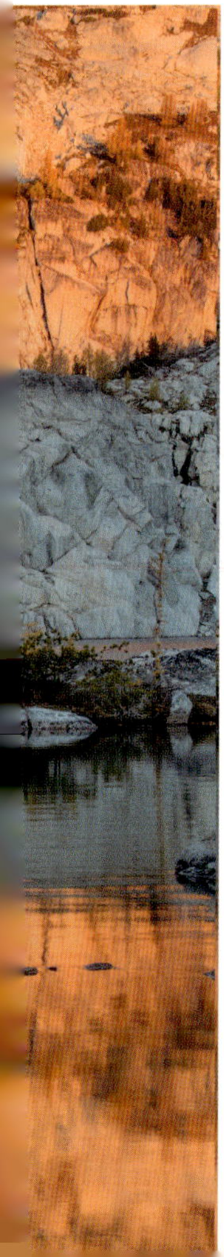

24 Friday

Received literature about voting.

25 Saturday

Received ticket for the S. of the year award on 13th March. Received renewal form from D.I.D.

26 Sunday

New moon ●

The enchantment

by Adam Gibbs

At first, Adam was bothered by the broad strap of shadow on the shoreline opposite. He had hiked to the Enchantments, an area of lakes and tarns in the Alpine Lakes Wilderness in Washington, USA, and had set up camp for a few days. Adam knew he would probably be able to find another, shadow-free viewpoint, but while thinking about moving, the beauty of the overall scene dawned on him and he realised the shadow was a key element of the composition.

27 Monday

Charged my M. Scooter.

28 Tuesday

Shrove Tuesday, Pancake Day (Christian)

Posted cheque to D.I.D., for Annual Sub. Did some shopping.

1 Wednesday

St David's Day (Wales)
Ash Wednesday (Christian)

Received a letter from B.T., about changes in prices, and a letter from Hackney about recycling.

2 Thursday

Received more medication. Julian and Pauline have gone to Yorkshire till a week on Saturday. Received literature from Thames Water.

The greeting

by Richard Packwood

The remains of trees half-submerged in Lake Kariba, the world's largest (by volume) artificial lake, stand sentry around a spit of land along the border between Zambia and Zimbabwe. Attracted to this view of the lake by the surreal atmosphere, Richard began watching a lone elephant splashing around in the water. When he realised that another one was fast approaching along the sand spit and that the two would greet each other, he knew he had the chance of a magical shot.

3 Friday

Received the Ethical Record for March, and a Seabirds Appeal from the R.S.P.B. Paid the R.S.P.B. a £20-00 donation.

4 Saturday

Received two Puzzler Magazines; and magazine from Butterfly Conservation.

5 Sunday

Charged my M. Scooter.

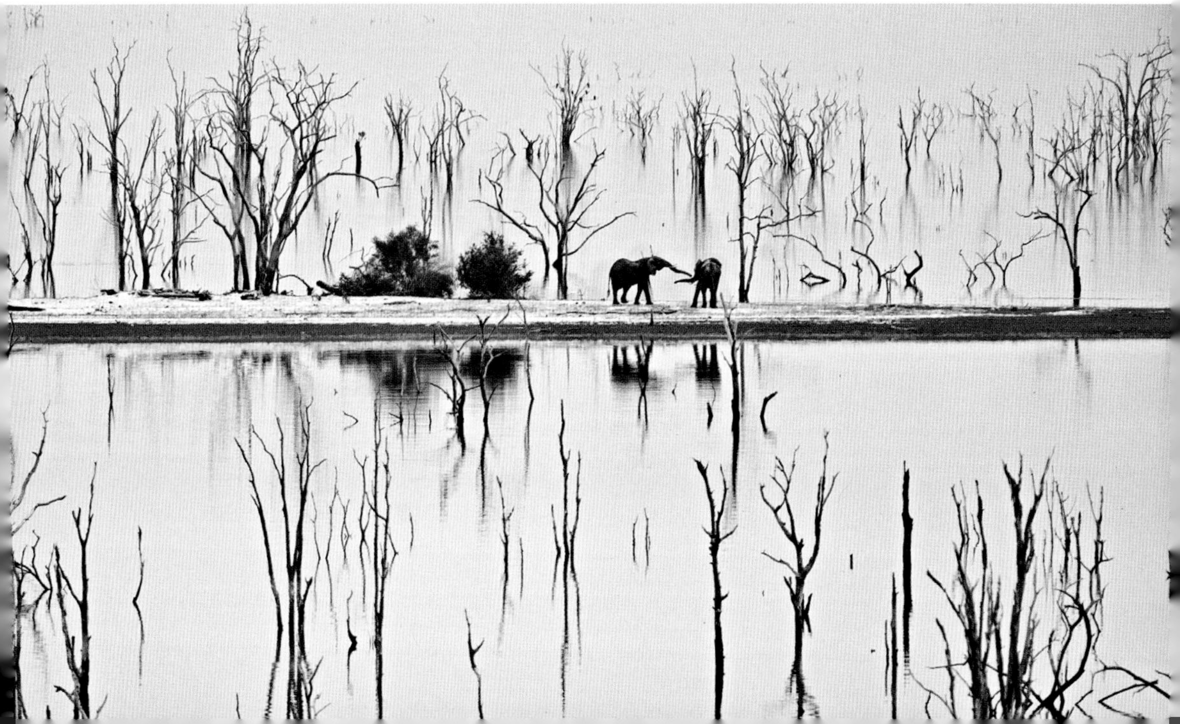

6 Monday

Received literature from Thames Water, and B.H.A. News. Posted form to Butterfly Conservation, telling them that I have mentioned them in my will. Did some shopping.

7 Tuesday

Received a letter from D.I.D., and a cheque for £54-81 from Friends Life.

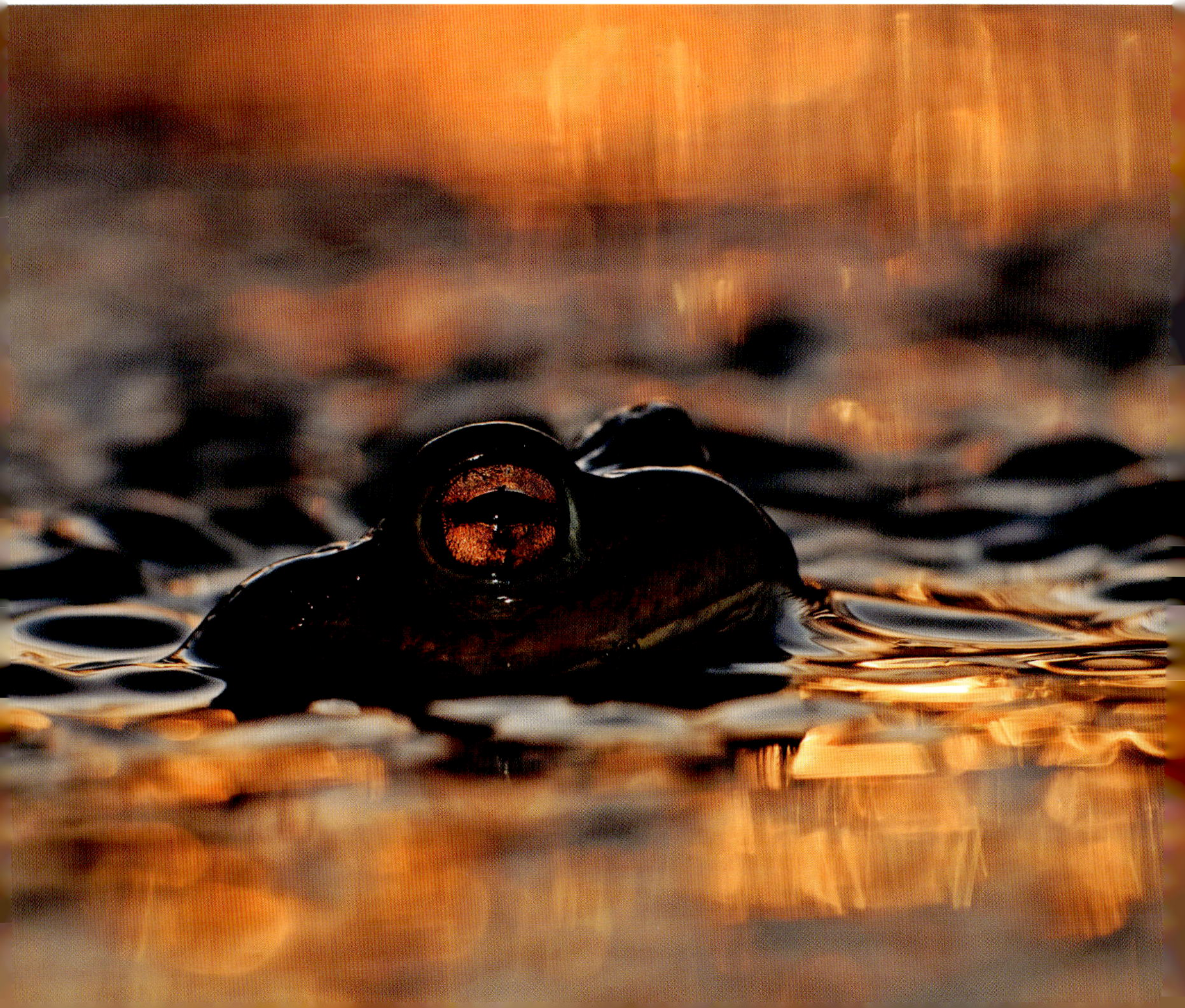

Saturday – charged my M. Scooter. Julian and Pauline haven't returned from Yorkshire.

8 Wednesday

It is thirty years ago today since Mum died. Received a letter from D.I.D., to ask if I am a taxpayer. Rang Stephen Norley.

9 Thursday

Received Raffle tickets from the British Red Cross. Felt rather ill this afternoon.

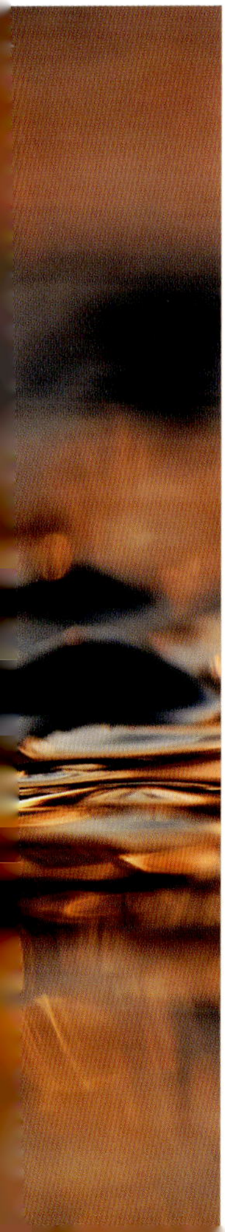

10 Friday

Received two Bank Statements; a thank you letter from The Gorilla Organization; an appeal from L.A.C.S.; and another letter from Thames Water.

11 Saturday

Received details of my Council Tax for the coming year, and a card thanking me for mentioning Butterfly Conservation in my will

12 Sunday

Full moon ○

Rang Julian, Pauline told me he has been ill. Posted three letters. Did some shopping.

Eye of a toad

by Lukasz Bozycki

Early spring sees a pond near Lukasz's home city of Warsaw, Poland, full of mating frogs and a few toads. On this March day, Lukasz shared the pond with them for an evening, sitting in the icy water in his chest-high waders, keeping as still as possible, despite the numbing cold. 'I wanted to find a fresh way of portraying the amphibians', he says, 'at water level.' His prize was 'the glorious pool of sunset colour' and the fiery glow of the toad's eye.

13 Monday

Booked a medical appt. for 10.00 am on Wednesday. Received an appeal from the B.H.A., and literature from the Folio Society. Ordered a book from the Folio Society. Rang the N.S.S.

14 Tuesday

Stephen Norley rang up.

Received a call from N.S.S., giving me two 'phone numbers to ring when I arrive for the S. of the Year function.

15 Wednesday

Posted a donation to the B.H.A. Went to the Health Centre. Was sent to Hom. Hospital for tests. Was admitted to the Acute Care Unit. Was discharged home. Stephen Norley brought me home.

16 Thursday

Stephen Norley took me to Homerton Hospital, to collect my valuables. Received a telephone bill, and "Wildabout" magazine, from the ZSL.

Pelican perspective

by Bence Máté

From his kitchen table, Bence planned the way he would photograph Dalmatian pelicans. He wanted a water-level perspective of them. So he designed and constructed a catamaran-style floating system, incorporating an underwater camera housing and specially positioned lights and flashes, and set off for Lake Kerkini in northern Greece. 'It was a huge buzz', says Bence, 'to find that the contraption actually worked.' Using cables, Bence took photos from a distance away on a boat, monitoring the scene on a screen.

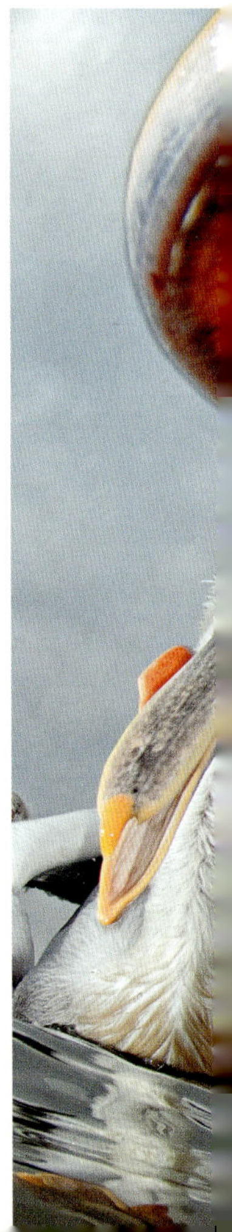

17 Friday

St Patrick's Day, holiday (Ireland)

Received "Lord Peter Views The Body" from the Folio Society. Received literature from the Princess Theatre, Torquay. Received a 'phone call from Keith P. Wood. Ordered more medication.

18 Saturday

Received literature from Thames Water. Received "The Shavian". Charged my M. Scooter.

19 Sunday

Did some shopping. Julian and Pauline have returned. Told Pauline about Shaldon Zoo.

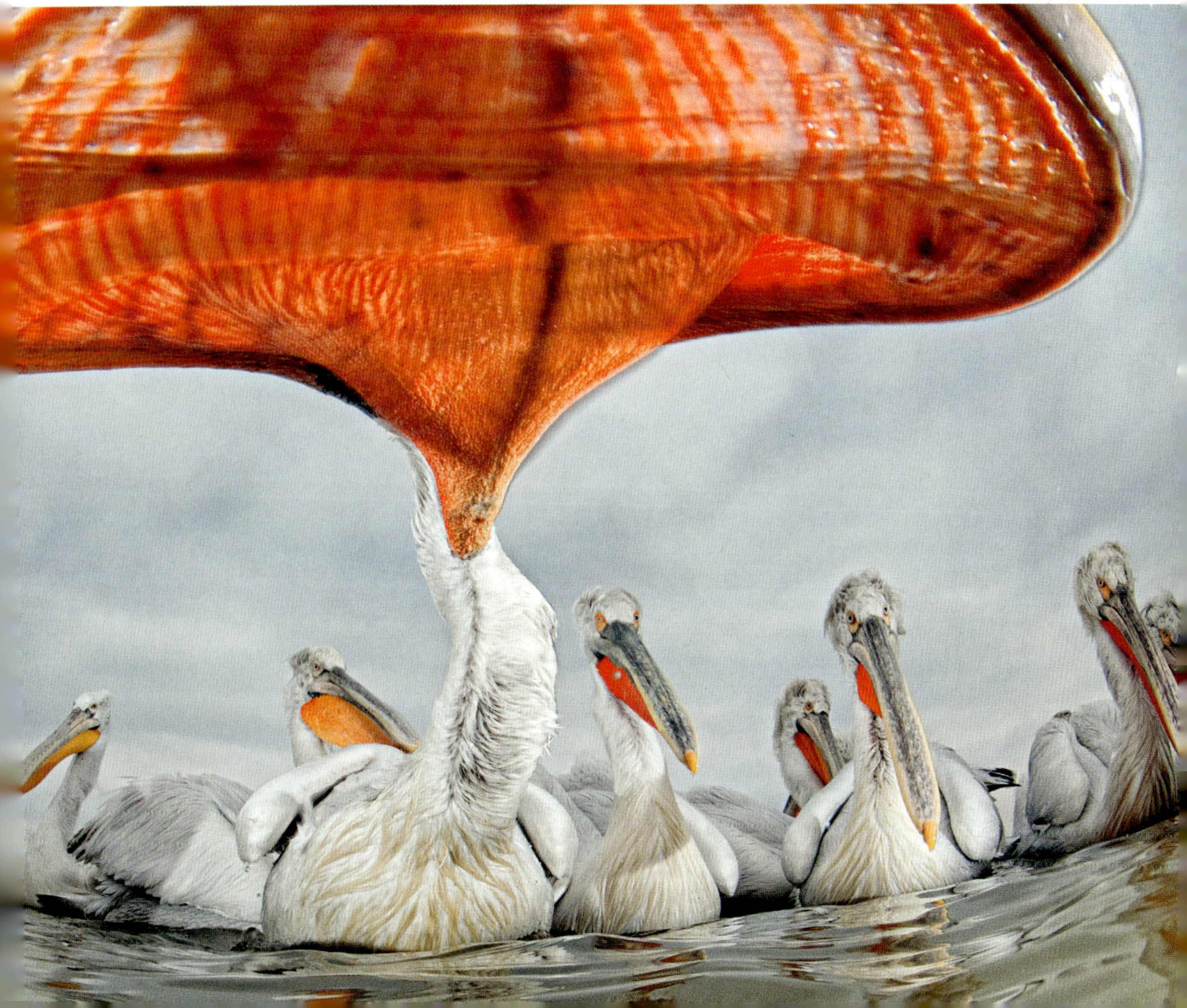

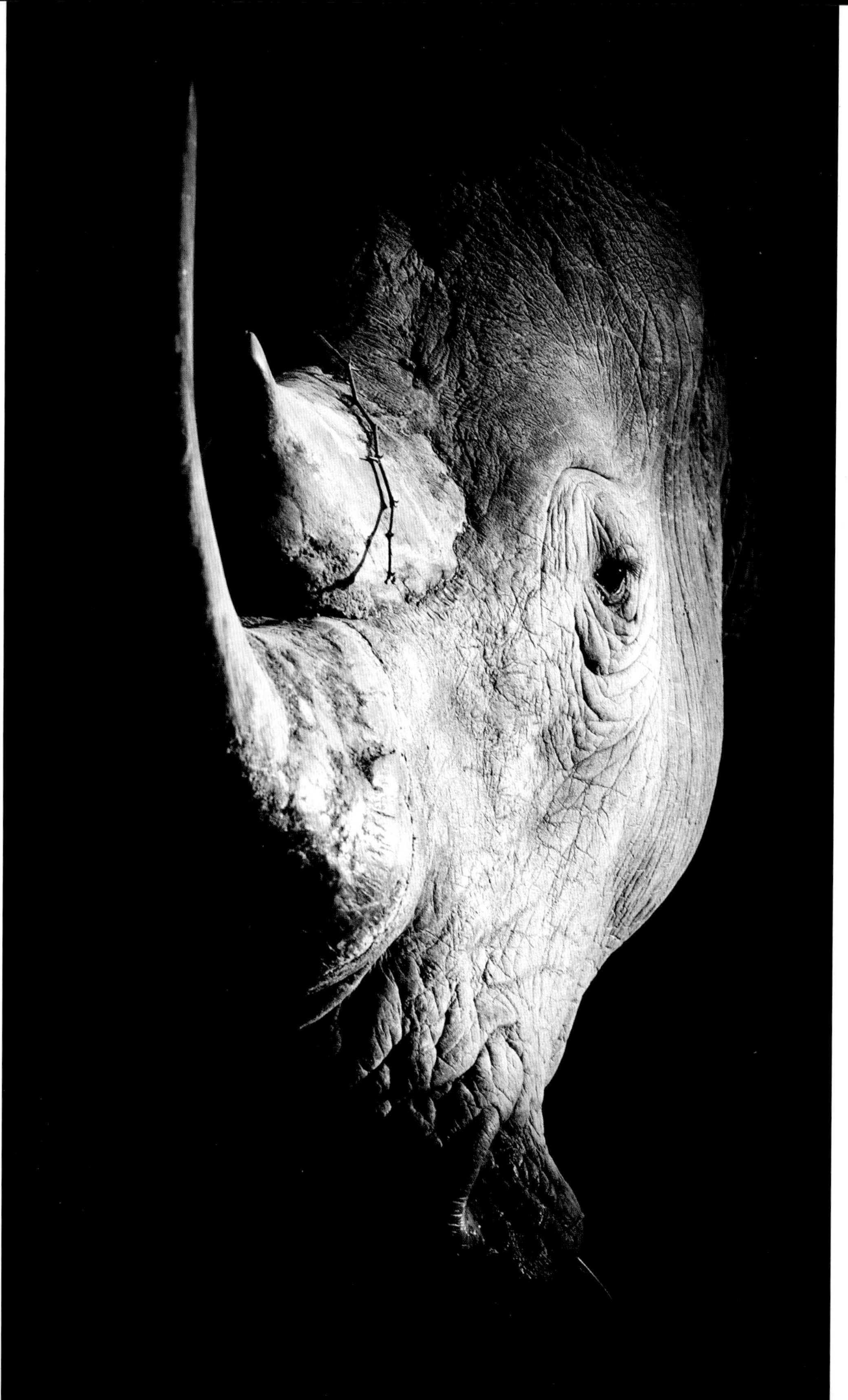

25th - Sat. Met Julian in the street. He said his cancer has spread to his bones.

March

20 Monday

Spring Equinox

Received an invitation to a meeting from the L.A.C.S..

21 Tuesday

22 Wednesday

Received from D.W.C.T., news of Bluey, my adopted frog becoming a father. Rang Wildsounds, but the next N.N. book is not available till May.

23 Thursday

24 Friday

Received a new cheque book, and an appeal from World Animal Protection. Charged my M. Scooter. Received some medication.

25 Saturday

It is twenty years ago today since I first moved to this address. Posted a donation to W.A.P. Did some shopping. Received information about Bandro, and Astrid, a radiated tortoise; and an appeal from Freedom From Torture.

26 Sunday

Mother's Day

British Summertime begins, clocks go forward

Rhino in charge

by Wim van den Heever

The white rhino was clearly feeling a bit edgy. He was the dominant male in this area of the Sabi Sands Game Reserve and well known for his unpredictable temperament when in female company. Without warning, the rhino charged, pulling up at the last minute. Having made his point, he started running back. 'For a second he stopped, turned round, and looked at me,' says Wim, 'just long enough for me to get the shot.'

27 Monday

Received Two Puzzler Magazines; a letter from L.A.C.S., Thanking me for donation; Galapagos Matters Magazine; and letter from B.H.S. Thanking me for donation. Ordered 3 books from Museum Collection. Rang N.H.S. Mus. to order a book, it will be available on 1st June.

28 Tuesday

New moon ●

Rang Ruth, at Twiggers. Donated £30-00 to the G. Con. Trust Appeal. Received a call from Rod. Rang him back. Had my hair cut.

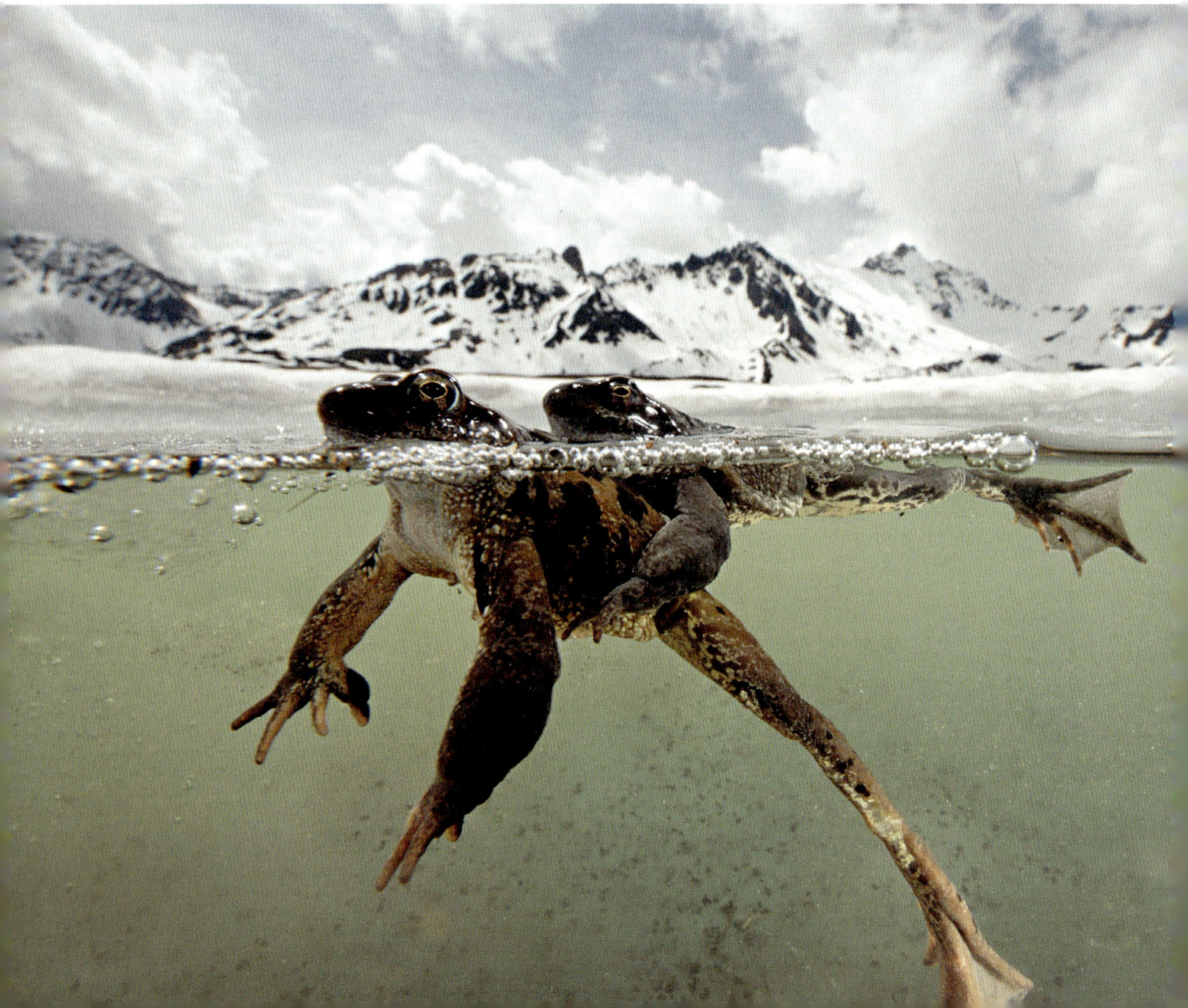

29 Wednesday

Received literature from the Donkey Sanctuary. Rang Stuart Ware. He is going to send me photos of the bust of Charles Bradlaugh.

30 Thursday

Received photos from Stuart Ware; three books from Museum Collection; and a Branch Newsletter from Butterfly Conservation. Did some shopping.

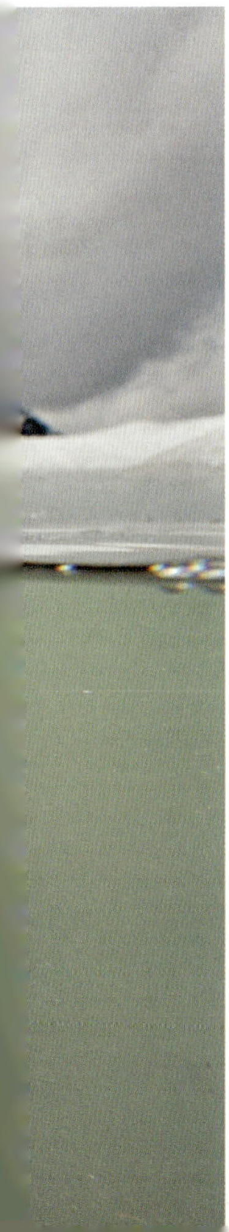

31 Friday

Received a message from Ruth, at Twiggers. Received the Ethical Record for April. Ordered more medication. Ordered a new paperback book from Ruth.

1 Saturday

April Fool's Day

Cut the hedge in the front garden. Charged my Mobility Scooter.

2 Sunday

Posted a donation to Freedom From Torture. Did some shopping.

Cold embrace

by Cyril Ruoso

Cyril couldn't believe his ears. He was 2,000 metres (6,500 feet) up in the French Alps, beside a lake covered with ice, but he could hear the mating rituals of hundreds of common frogs under the ice. Ten days later, the ice began to melt, and the first choristers appeared from hibernation. 'The males jump on anything that moves,' says Cyril. Here, one male is holding onto another as they both wait for a female to show up.

3 Monday

Rang Stuart Ware, and ordered coloured photos. Told Julian that I had found two more keys to my house. Ordered some more cards from Museum Collection. Washed some clothes.

4 Tuesday

Received literature from the Folio Society. Received a letter from the Green Party, to tell me that I need to renew my membership. Posted photos to Stuart Ware, so that he can get coloured ones done; and cheque to Green Party, to become a Life Member.

5 Wednesday

6 Thursday

Charged my M. Scooter.

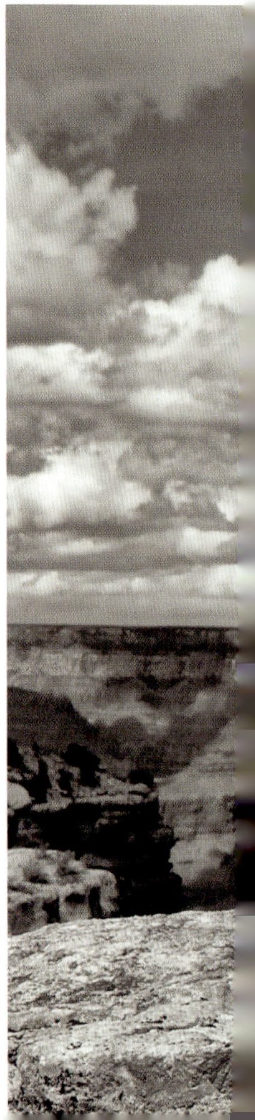

Grand raven

by Chris Aydlett

The raven features a lot in native North American folklore, revered as a deity and regarded as a trickster and even as a mediator between life and death. For visitors to the Grand Canyon in Arizona, this bold, intelligent bird, twice the size of a crow, is a familiar sight. Turning the strong midday light to his advantage, Chris created the shot in black and white, to give the scene impact and boost the metallic gloss of the raven's plumage.

7 Friday

Received my copy of "The Mystery Of A Hansom Cab", and did some shopping. Obtained some medication. Julian and Pauline have gone away again.

8 Saturday

Received a cheque from Friends Life; an appeal from the Green Party; news about the gorillas from D.W.C.T; and cards ordered from the Museum Collection.

9 Sunday

Palm Sunday (Christian)

Received the Yellow Pages. Did some shopping.

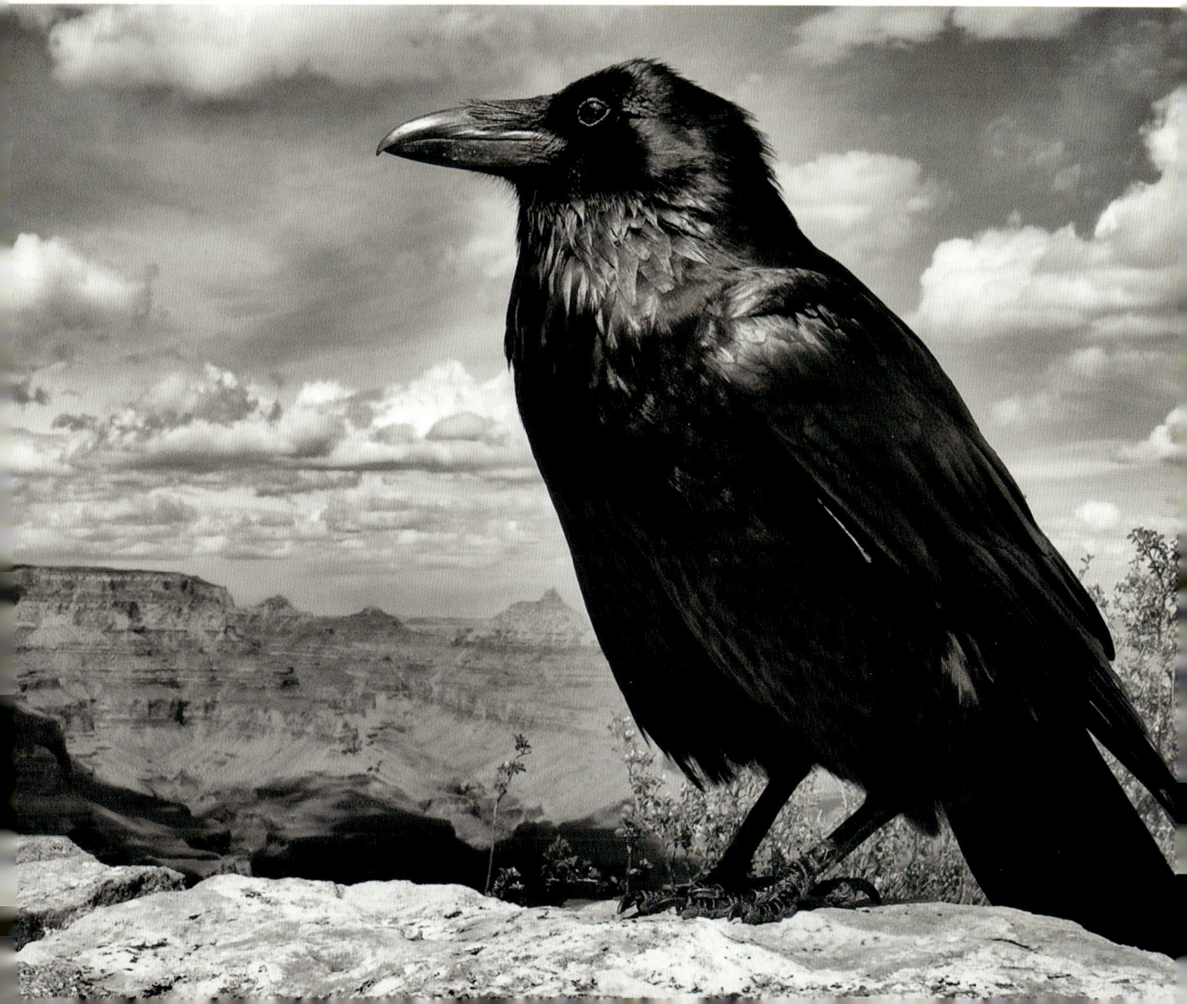

11th (Tues.) – Received lt. about my Nat. West Platinum Account.

April WEEK 16

10 Monday

First day of Passover (Jewish)

Received literature from the Folio Society; and an appeal from the British Red Cross. Ordered two books from the Folio Society. Charged my M. Scooter.

11 Tuesday

Full moon ○

Received a letter from Thames Water about Meters. A message was left for me by Stuart Wane, about the pictures. Posted donations to Green Party, and B. Red Cross. Collected Dermovate, and did some shopping.

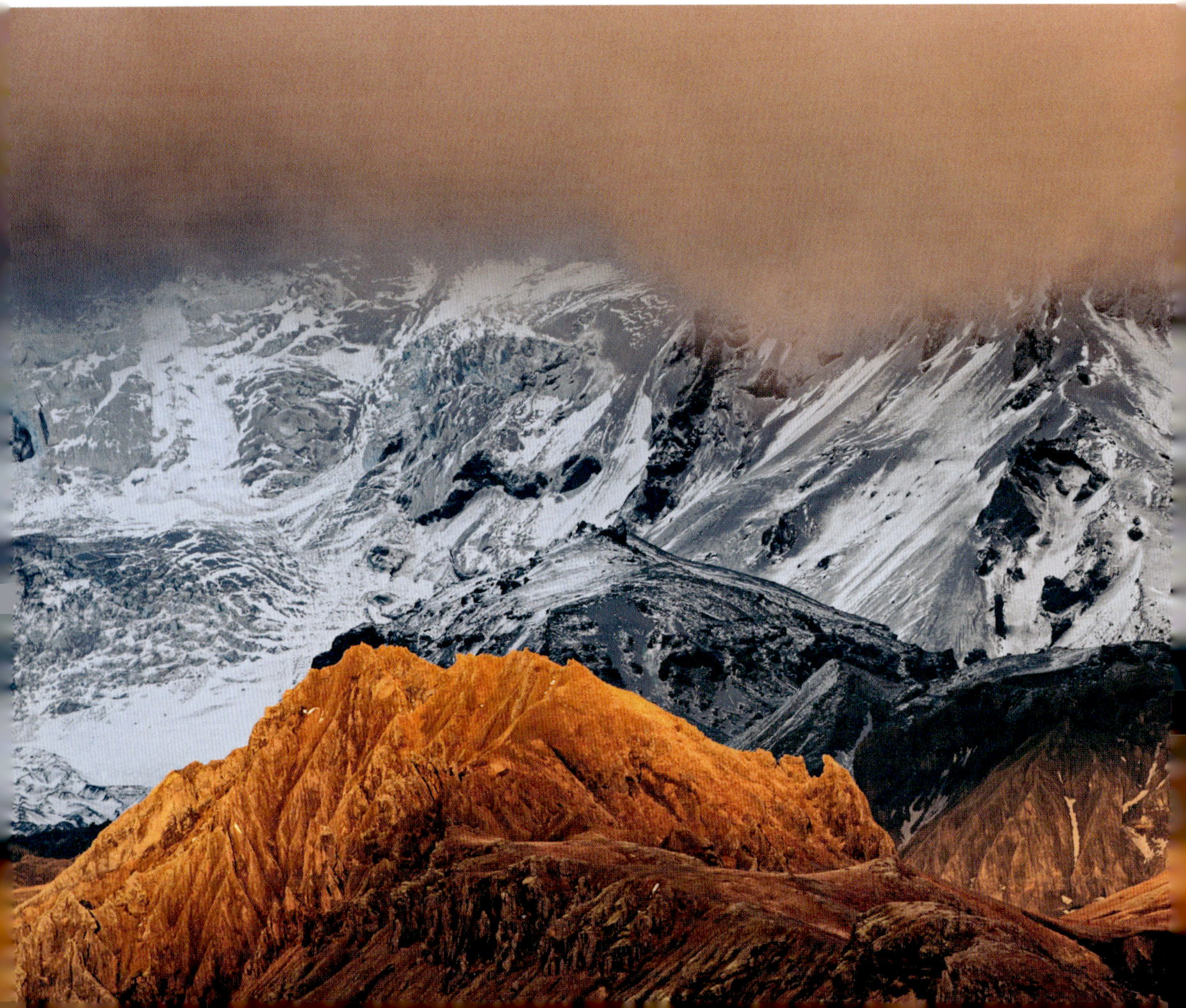

15TH (SAT) Did some shopping.

12 Wednesday

Charged my M. Scooter. Received a statement of my Nat. West Select Platinum Account. Did some shopping. Received two books from Folio Society, "Vermeer", and "Van Gogh". Bought a Birthday card for Seria.

13 Thursday

Maundy Thursday (Christian)

Booked ticket for Paignton.
Rang Blue Waters Lodge. Received a Hackney Recycling Rewards Card; lit from Freedom From Torture; lit from L.A.C.S.; and a Puzzler Magazine.

14 Friday

Good Friday, holiday (Christian)

Rang Julian.

15 Saturday

Received another Puzzler Magazine; ticket for Paignton; literature from Dignity In Dying; and Society Jersiaise Newsletter.

16 Sunday

Easter (Christian)

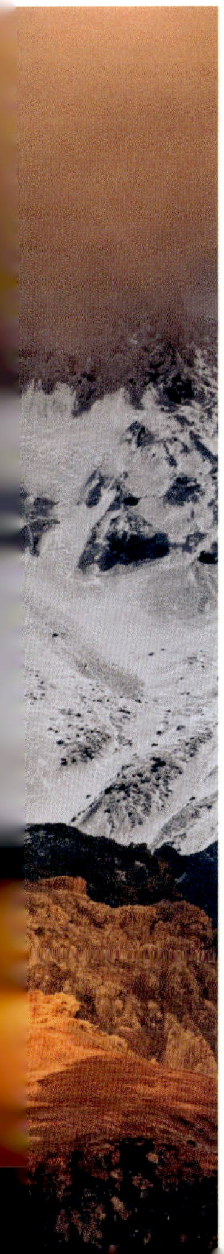

Land of fire and ice

by Erlend Haarberg

Erlend arrived in Iceland on 12 April 2010, two days before the Eyjafjallajökull volcano began to erupt. On the first clear evening after the eruption began, Erlend climbed a nearby mountain and began to photograph the volcanic ash plume. Pausing for a moment, he turned around to look at the mountain ridge behind him. The shaded snow-covered slopes of Thórsmörk were tinged blue by the low-lying clouds, but the lower slopes and the clouds above were lit by the setting sun.

April

WEEK 17

18th Tuesday - Made a £30-00 donation to Galapagos Conservation Trust. Charged my M. Scooter.

17 Monday

Easter Monday, holiday (excl. Scotland) (Christian)

Began packing case. Received a 'phone call from Stephen Norlay.

18 Tuesday

Last day of Passover (Jewish)

Ordered more medication. Received an appeal from the Gal. Conservation Trust. Did some shopping. Received a 'phone call from Stuart Ware, I should receive the Bradlaugh Bust photos tomorrow.

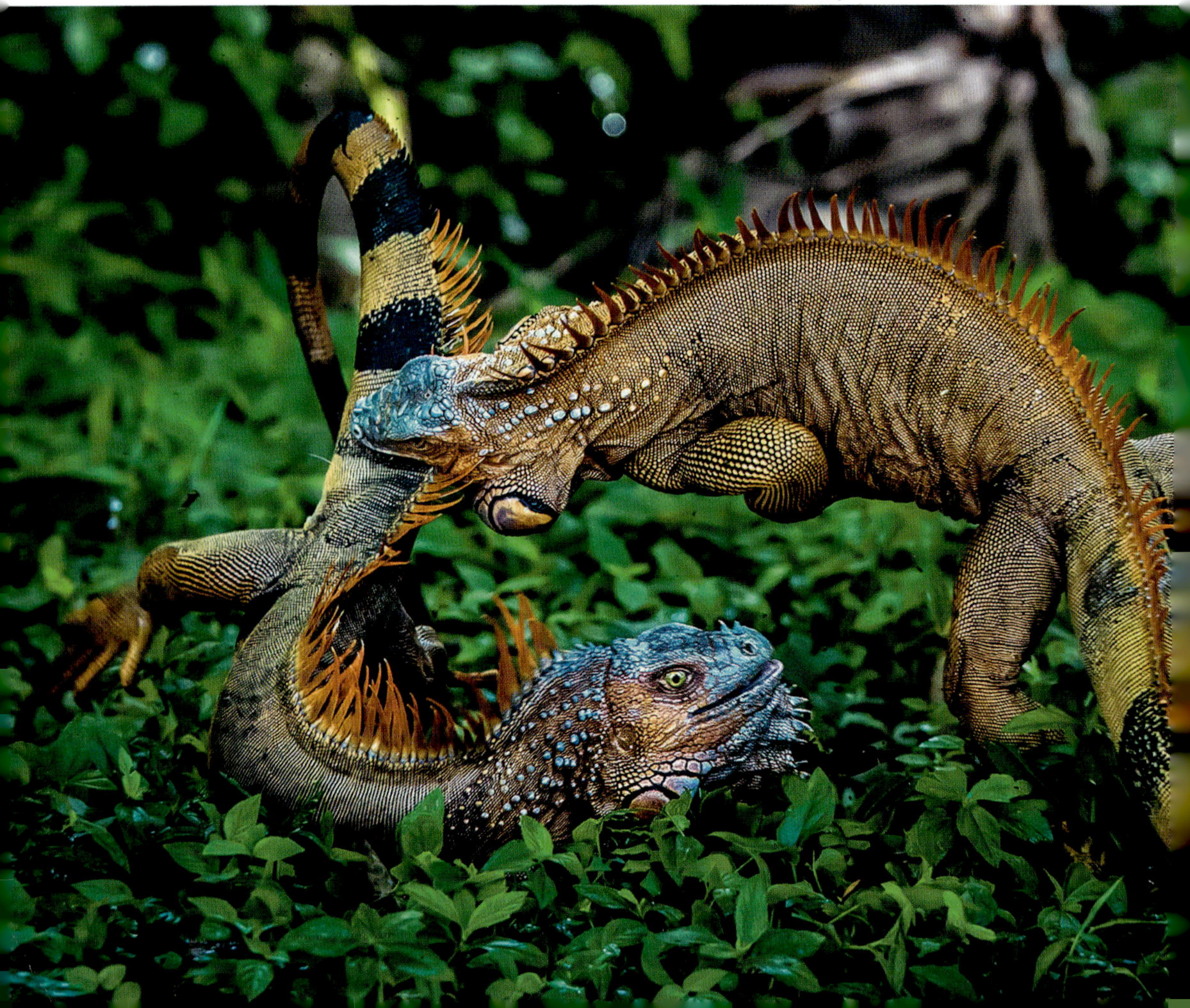

20th - Thursday. - Rang Stephen Nooley.

19 Wednesday

Received colour photos taken at the Bradlaugh Bust event at Port Cullis House. Did some shopping. Prepared present and card for Sian.

20 Thursday

Received a telephone bill; an appeal from World Animal Protection; and news from D.W.C.T. about my adopted Ring-tailed Lemur. The house next door to me is up for sale. Rang Pauline. They are coming back on Sunday.

21 Friday

Queen Elizabeth II's Birthday

Obtained more medication. Did some shopping. Booked return ticket from Paignton.

22 Saturday

Received return tickets from Paignton; and literature from D.W.C.T. Rang Blue Waters Lodge. Paul has had a slight heart attack.

23 Sunday

St George's Day (England)

Julian and Pauline have returned.

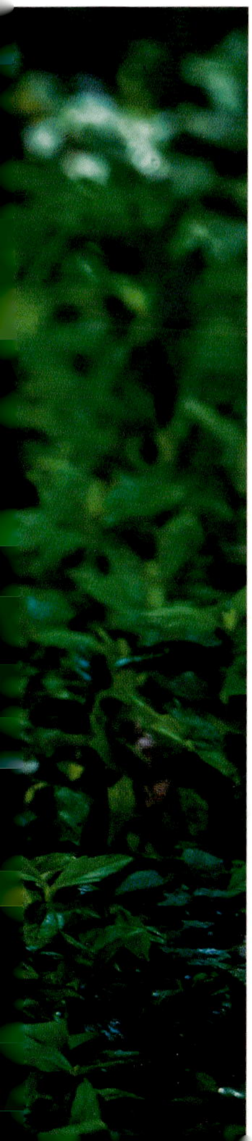

Battle colours

by Gergely Bíró

A loud commotion caught Gergely's attention. He and his friend were paddling down the San Carlos River in Costa Rica when they discovered two male green iguanas, in full breeding colours, locked in a violent battle. These dragon-like reptiles fight with razor-sharp teeth and whip-like tails during territorial disputes. Focusing on the iguanas was a challenge. 'I was trying to hold the camera and the big, heavy telephoto lens in the rocking canoe,' says Gergely. 'We were lucky not to capsize.'

24th – Monday. Booked Assistance for train travel. Received a 'phone

24 Monday

call from S. Health Centre. Appt for Thurs

Received literature from the Folio Society, an appeal from the Gorilla Organisation; and the R.S.P.B. Summer Magazine. Donated £20-00 to the Gorilla organisation.

25 Tuesday

Rang Stuart Ware. He will send black/white photos

Anzac Day (Australia, New Zealand)

Rang Rod. Charged my M. Scooter.

26 Wednesday

New moon ●

Received black and white photos from Stuart Ware. Did some shopping. Had call from Blue Waters Lodge, telling me the cost of holiday. Tried to deliver present and card to Serin. but she wasn't in.

27 Thursday

Posted form for holiday insurance. Had my blood pressure taken at Health Centre. Serin's mother was out again. Received Bank Statement. I should soon receive an organ donor form.

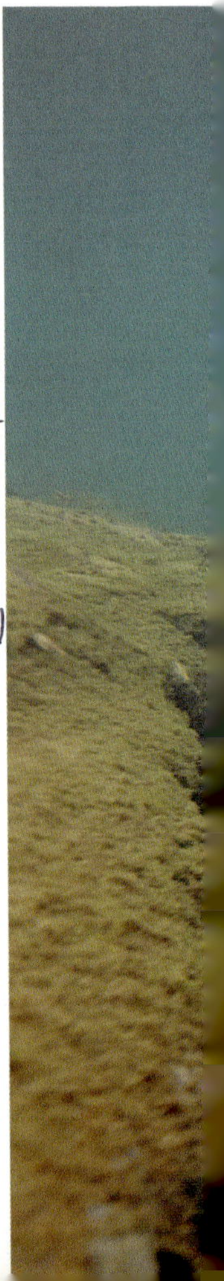

Beavering

by Louis-Marie Préau

'I have never forgotten', says Louis-Marie, 'the first time I saw a European beaver under water delivering a branch to its family.' He is passionate about beavers and has returned to the same spot on the Loire River in France on many occasions to try to photograph what he saw that first time. Finally, he got lucky and photographed this adult dragging a poplar branch back to the dam for its kits. 'It looked like hard work,' says Louis-Marie.

28 Friday

Received the Ethical Record for May-June, and Museum Selection, for Summer. Charged my M. Scooter. Had my hair cut. Gave Selin's present and card to her mother.

29 Saturday

Received a phone call from Andrew, from 6PES.

30 Sunday

Julian is going away tomorrow, till a week on Saturday. Received a telephone book.

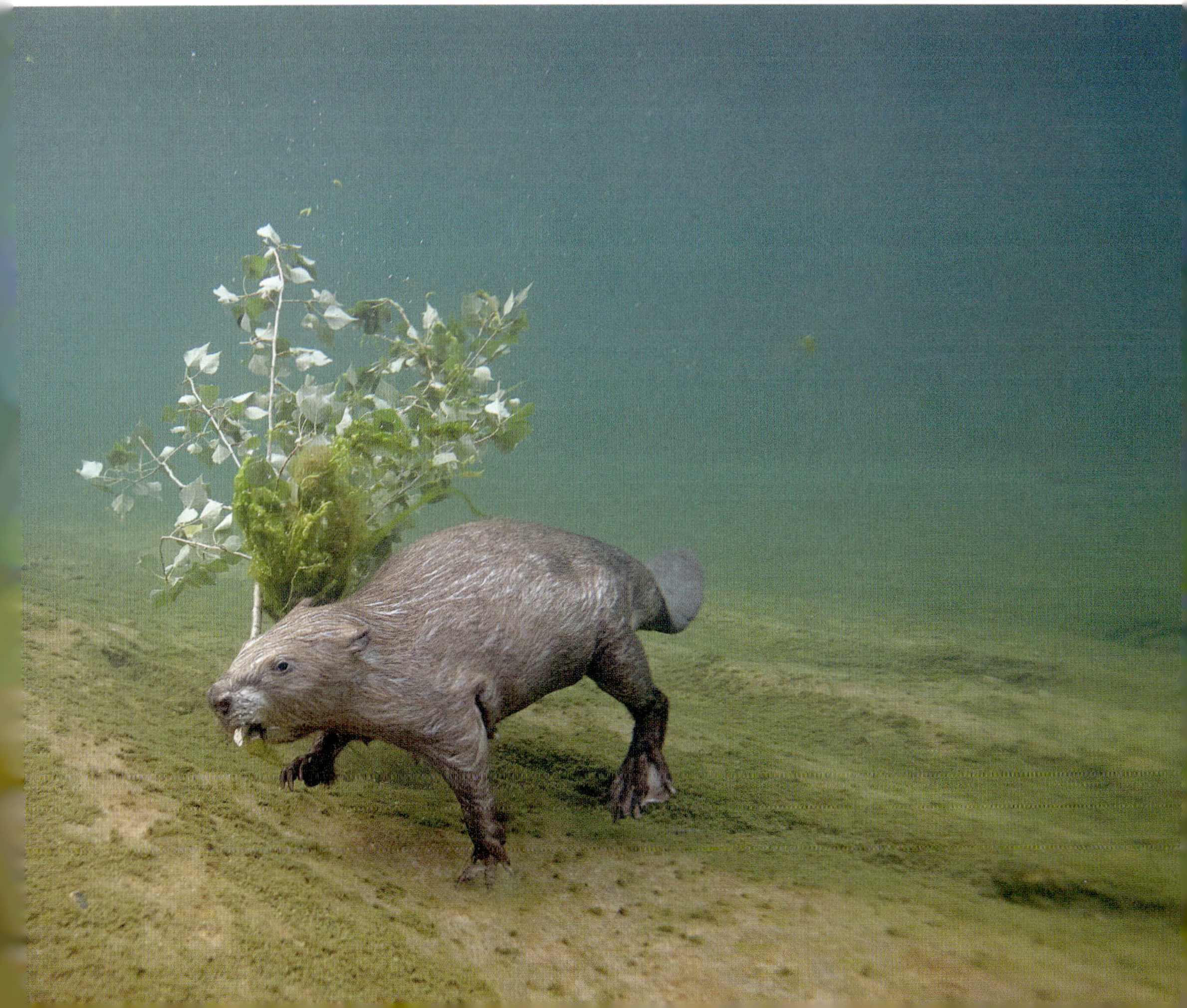

2 – Tuesday – Drew out some money, and did some shopping.

1 Monday

Early May holiday

Julian rang. He is not going away till tomorrow. Charged my mobility scooter.

2 Tuesday

Received Evolve, the Natural History Museum Magazine. Rang them to order a book, but it is not available.

3 Wednesday

Received an appeal from L.A.C.S. Ordered some books and cards from Museum Selection. Finished reading "The Mystery of A Hansom Cab."

4 Thursday

Received a ticket for an Antiquarian Book Fair. Ordered more medication. Posted a donation to L.A.C.S.. Did some shopping.

5 Friday

Received Insurance literature from Rothwell & Towler

6 Saturday

Received literature from the British Red Cross.

7 Sunday

Posted donation to B. Red Cross, and did some shopping. Found an old organ donor card.

Twin hope

by Diana Rebman

The hike to the mountain gorillas was particularly arduous that day. 'Consistent rain made the ground very slippery,' says Diana, 'and the hillside was so steep it felt vertical.' The gorilla group ahead finally settled to feed. 'What made all the physical effort worth it was to see the mother with her two babies.' This is only the fifth set of twins ever to be reported in Rwanda's Volcanoes National Park.

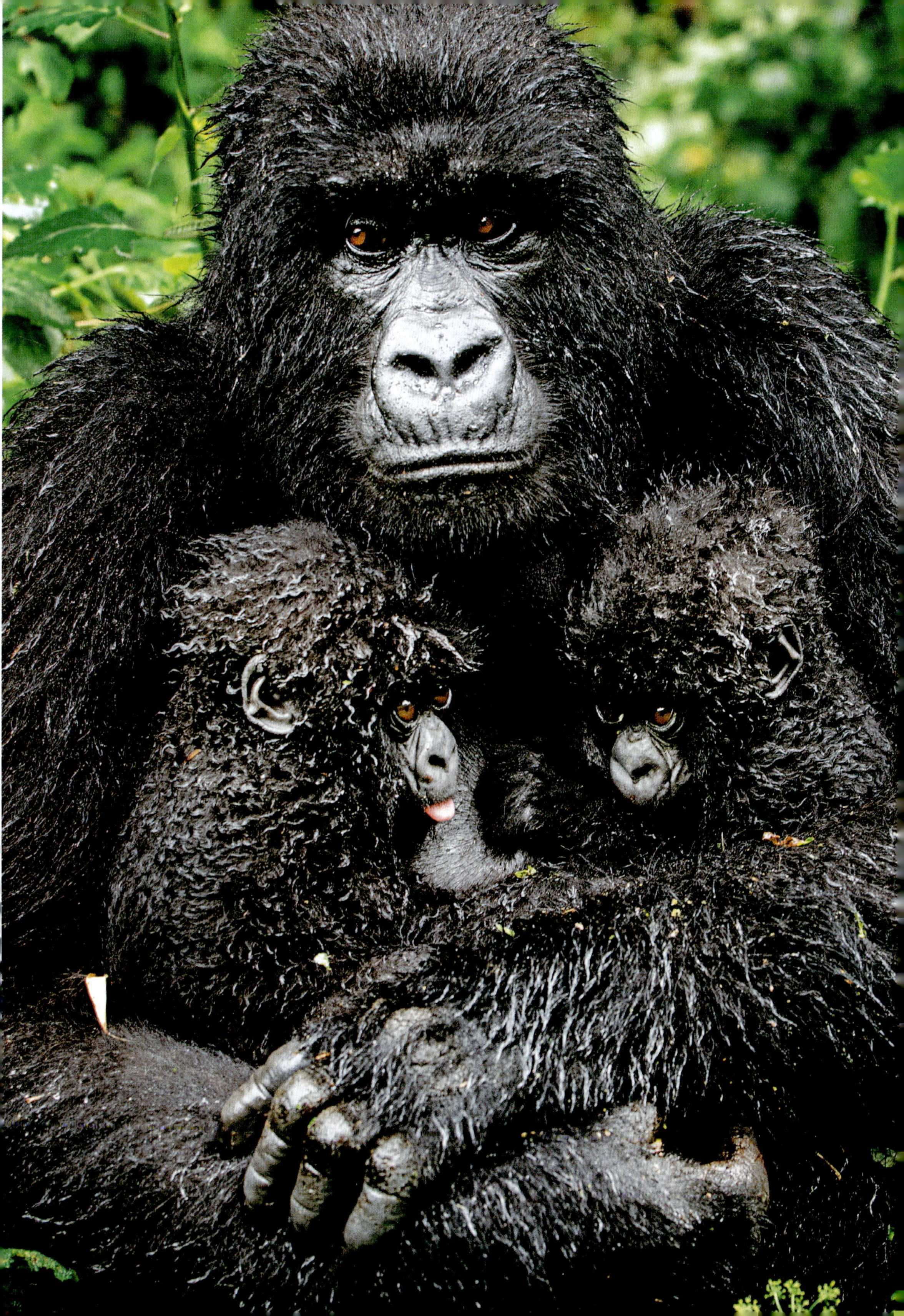

8 Monday

Received a cheque for £54-81, from Friends Life; and literature from World Animal Protection. Rang Stephen Norley, and Barbara Jones.

9 Tuesday

Met Karen, Pauline's friend. Rang Mary Reynolds, and told her my news.

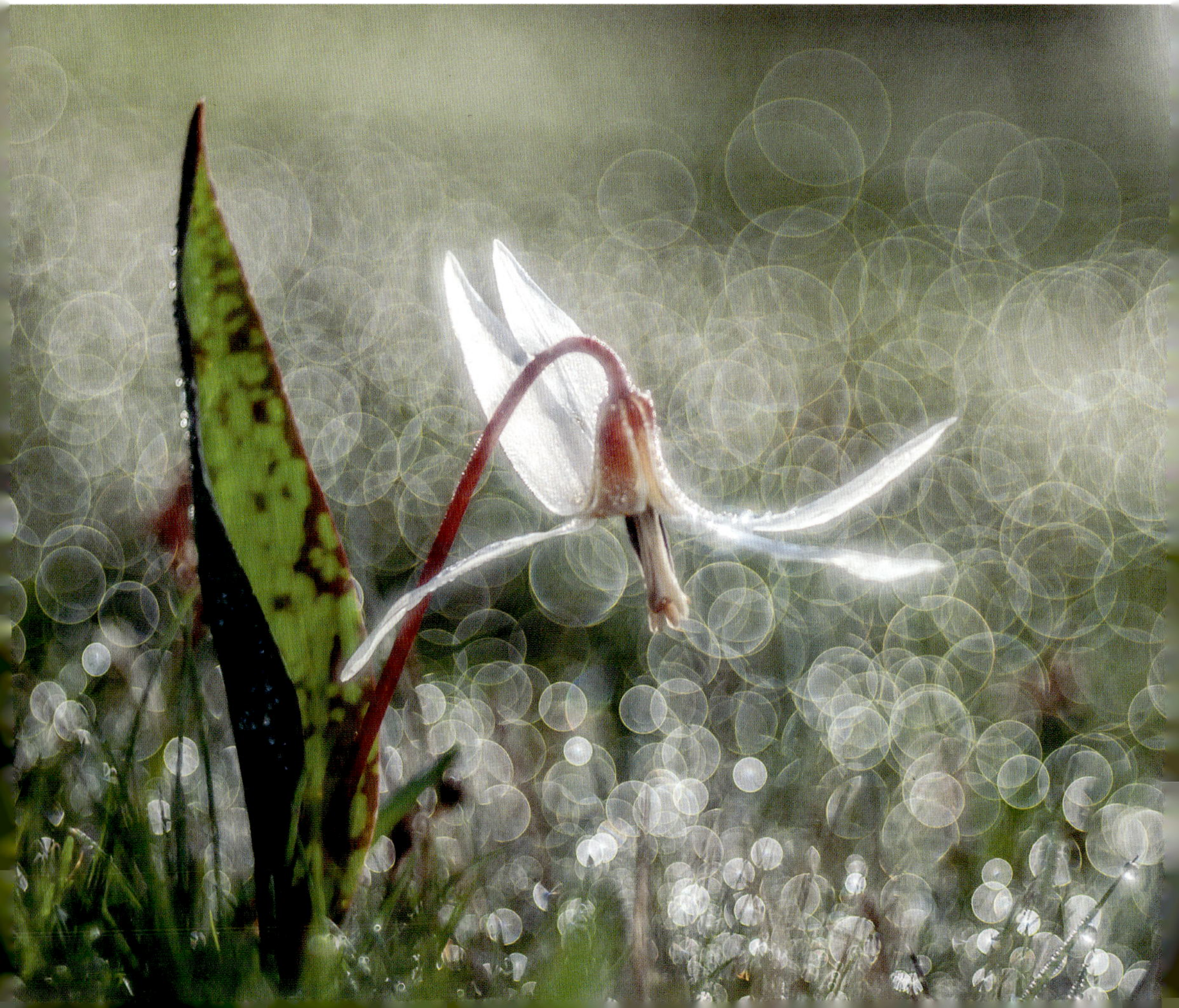

10 Wednesday

Full moon ○

11 Thursday

Received box of items ordered from Museum Selection, and a Nat. West. Bank Statement. Charged my M. Scooter. Posted donation to World Animal Protection. Collected medication. Did some shopping.

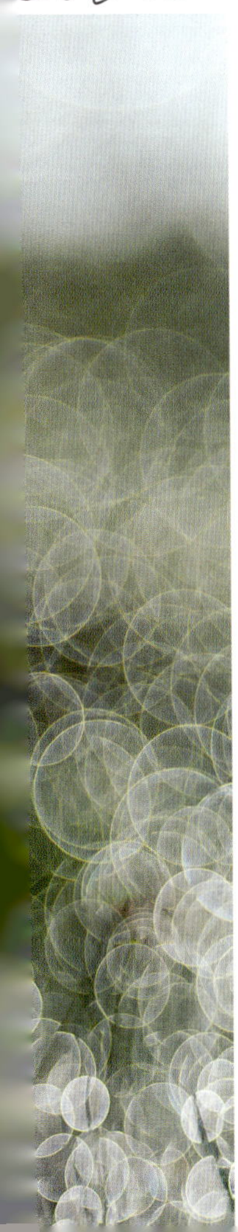

12 Friday

Received literature from the Orang-Utan Foundation. Did some shopping.

13 Saturday

Received a Postal Poll Card. I should receive my vote form around 26th May.

14 Sunday

Julian and Pauline have returned.

Simplicity

by Valter Binotto

A day of rain followed by a clear night left the dog's tooth violets in a meadow near Valter's home in Possagno, Italy, drenched in dew. He set up before dawn, choosing his flower, and as the first rays of sun touched the petals at the right angle, he took the image – one that captures for him some of the magic of the moment. 'The dog's tooth violet is a simple flower, so common that it is often overlooked,' he says.

15 Monday

Gave a donation to, and ordered a book from the Orangutan Foundation.
Received a Puzzler Magazine. Made a telephone entry to a puzzle in the Puzzler.

~~16~~ 17th ~~Tuesday~~

Received a telephone bill; lit from Freedom From Torture; lit from L.A.C.S.; another Puzzler Magazine; news from D.W.C.T., about a R. Fruit Bat; and book, "The Orangutan World" from the Orangutan Foundation; plus a thank you note for my donation.

17 Wednesday

Charged my M. Scooter.
My Electricity Meter was read.

18 Thursday

Received literature from the D.W.C.T.. Posted donations to L.A.C.S., Freedom From Torture; and D.W.C.T..
Did some shopping.

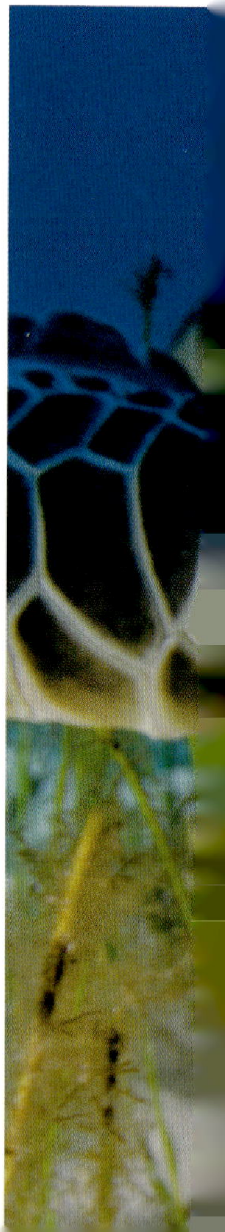

Dive buddy

by Luis Javier Sandoval

The beaches of the Yucatán Peninsula, Mexico, near Cancún are traditional nesting sites for the endangered green turtle. But as Cancún has also grown as a holiday and dive resort, development has reduced the area available to turtles. Today, measures have been taken to ensure that nesting sea turtles go undisturbed, and there is publicity to help local people and resort owners. 'The turtles are so used to seeing people in the water that they think we're just part of the environment,' says Luis.

Saturday – rang Robert Gillmor and had a long conversation with him.

19 Friday

Received a thank-you letter from the British Red Cross; and the New Humanist for Summer 2017. Neil, next door, has borrowed my ladders.

20 Saturday

Received voting papers for the General Election, and "Early Humans," the 134th book in the New Naturalists series.

21 Sunday

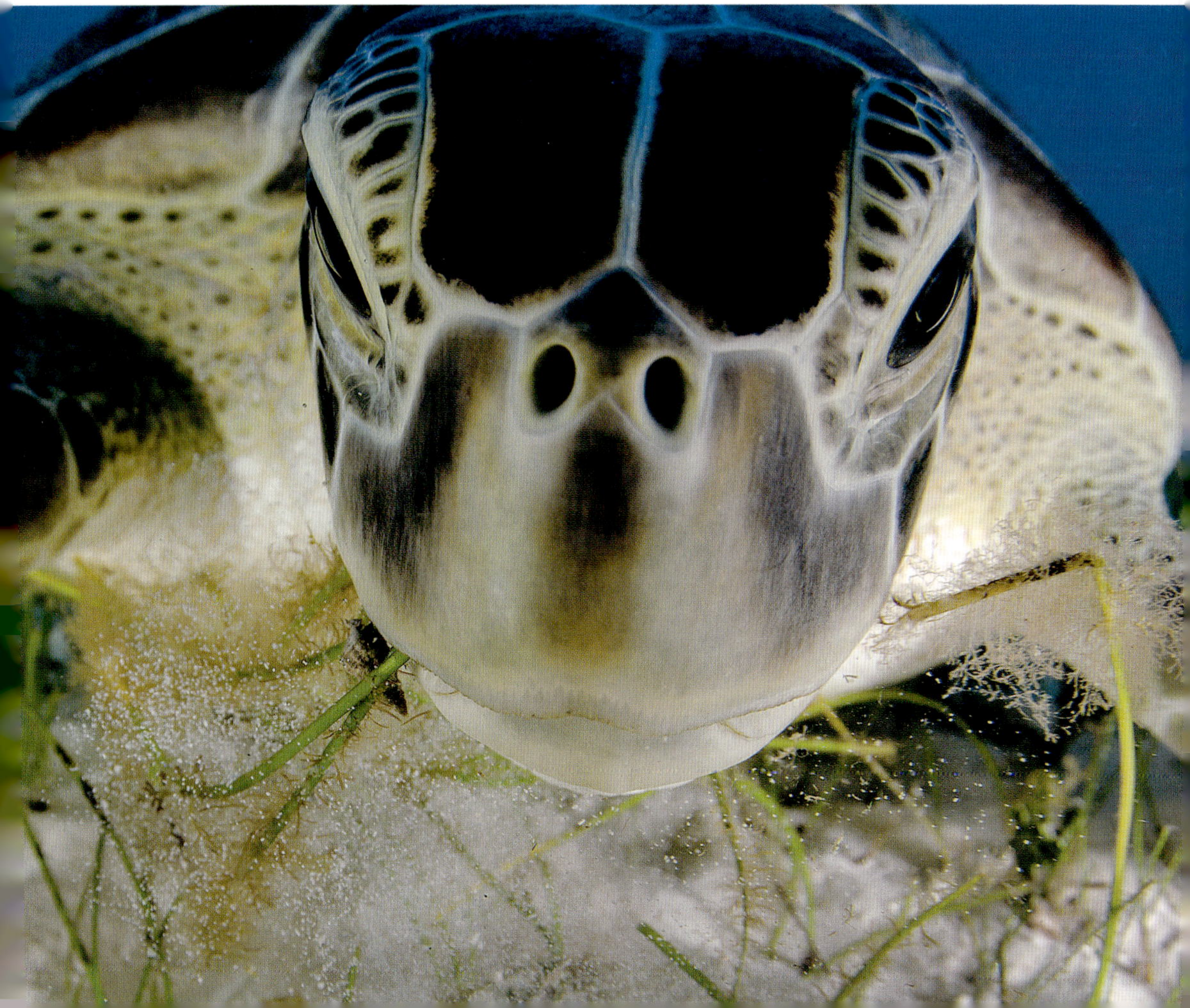

22 Monday

Rang Wild Sounds. The next book is out on 29th June. Told them to wait till I get back from holiday. Received literature from the Folio Society, and from Nat. West Bank. Ordered some books from Folio Society. Charged M. Scooter.

23 Tuesday

Recived a P60 from Friends Life. Did some shopping. Posted my vote. Bought an electric kettle.

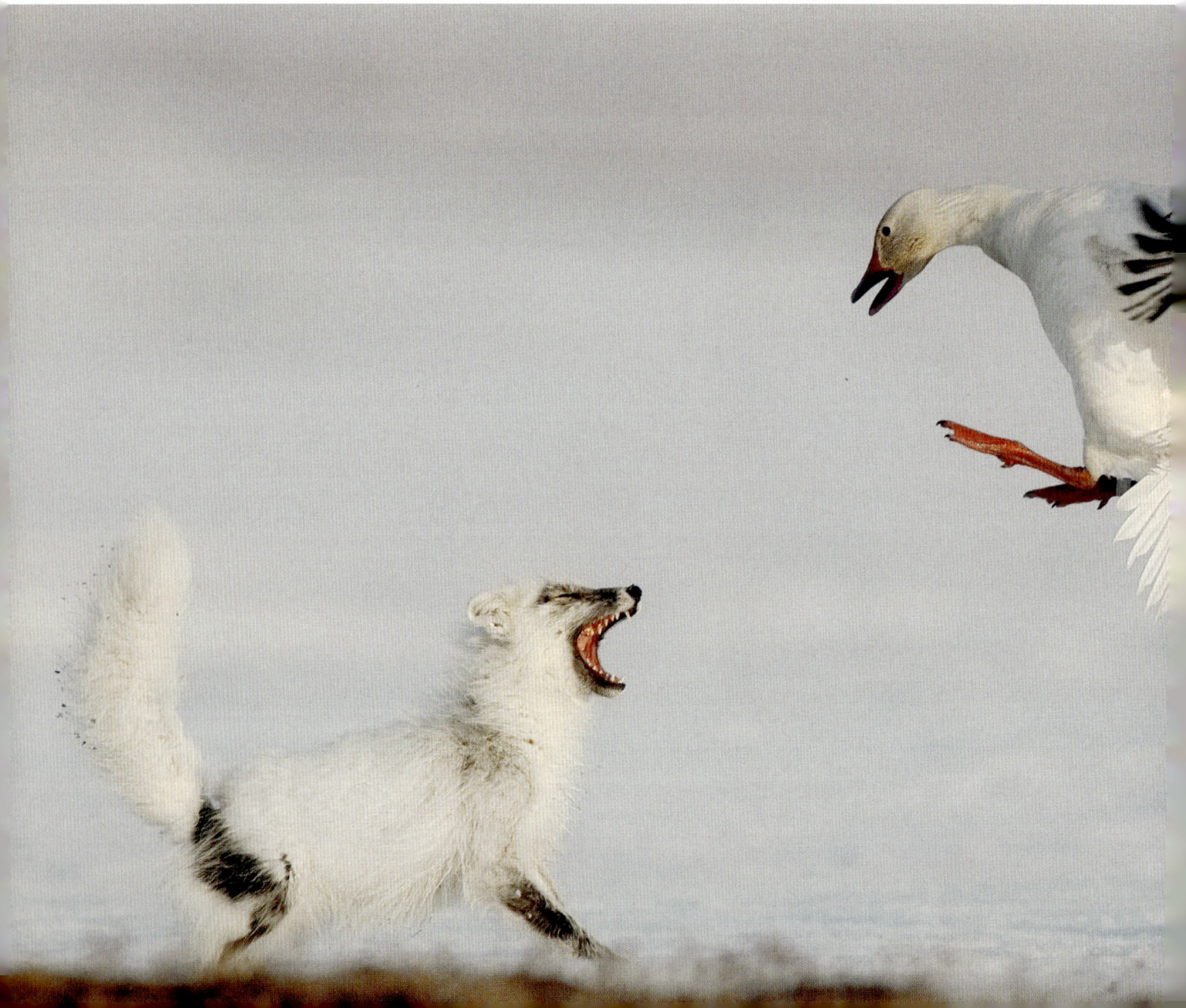

[...]n. 28th — Rang Colin back. Booked Princess Theatre - Mon. 11th September, I shall have to travel each way on Sundays in Sep.

24 Wednesday

25 Thursday

Ascension Day (Christian)
New moon ●

Rang the R.S.P.B. They are going to send me a catalogue, so that I can order a bird table. Received books from Folio Society. Ordered six more books.

26 Friday

Received R.S.P.B. catalogue. Ordered a bird table, and a squirrel baffle

27 Saturday

Ramadan begins (Islamic)

Received a thank-you letter from the L.A.C.S.

28 Sunday

Received a 'phone call from Colin.

The duel

by Sergey Gorshkov

In late May, about a quarter of a million snow geese arrive from North America to nest on the remote Wrangel Island, in northeastern Russia. They form the world's largest breeding colony of snow geese. Arctic foxes take advantage of the abundance of eggs, but a goose is easily a match for a fox. 'The battles were fairly equal,' notes Sergey, 'and I only saw a fox succeed in grabbing an egg on a couple of occasions, despite many attempts.'

29 Monday

Spring holiday (UK, Scotland)

Did some shopping.
Rang Barbara Smoker.

30 Tuesday

Received bird table from R.S.P.B..
Received literature from the Mary Ann Evans Hospice. Charged my M. Scooter

31 Wednesday

Received details of A.G.M., and voting papers from D.I.D.. Posted Birthday card to Barbara Smoker; a donation to the Mary Ann Evans Hospice; and voting paper to D.I.P.. Did a little shopping.

1 Thursday

Received details of A.G.M., and voting papers from the B.H.A., and box of books from the Folio Society.

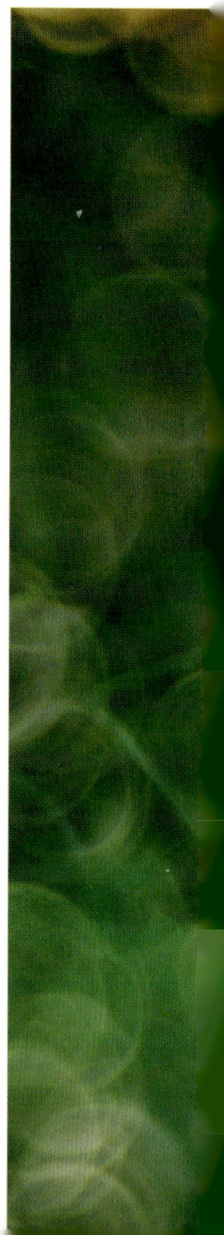

Badger dream scene

by Marc Steichen

For several years Marc has been photographing badgers in May and June at a sett near his home town in Luxembourg. On this early summer evening, the light was fading fast as the first badger emerged from its den to check its surroundings. To capture the warm apricot sun-flare, he made a double exposure, first focusing on the badger and then defocusing to take a softer image, 'creating as dreamy a scene as it was that evening'.

2 - Friday - ordered more medication.

2 Friday

Received literature from Colin about the Agatha Christie Festival, and an appeal from World Animal Protection. Charged my M. Scooter. Ordered Galapagos book from Waterstones. Rang Colin.

3 Saturday

Posted a donation to World Animal Protection. Did some shopping. Received details of B.H.A. AG.M., and news about a pied tamarin from D.W.C.T.

4 Sunday

Pentecost/Whitsun (Christian)

Rang Barbara smoker.

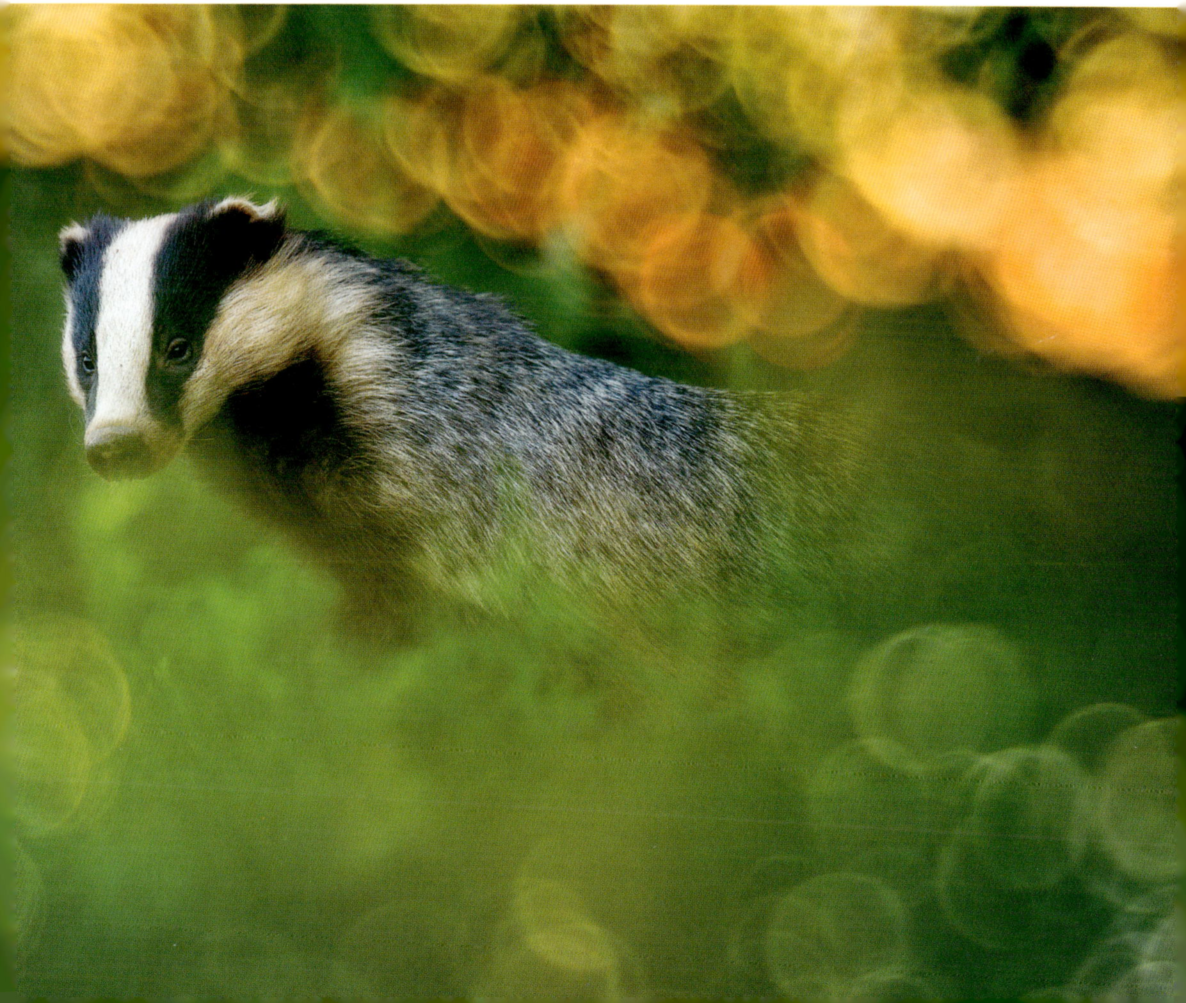

5 Monday

June holiday (Republic of Ireland)

Rang the B.H.A., and offered my apologies for not attending the A.G.M. Booked an appt with Chiropodist for Tues. 11th September. Bought a new washing-up bowl, and obtained more medication.

6 Tuesday

Had my hair cut, and did some shopping.

7 Wednesday

Received an offer from British Gas.

8 Thursday

Received literature from D.I.D. and news of a change from Friends Life. Stephen Norley rang me.

Travelling companions

by Douglas Seifert

Swimming in front of this dugong in the Red Sea are juvenile golden trevallies, riding the pressure waves created by its nose. They use the great mammal as protection from predators and also feed on any small creatures it disturbs. The dugong is a tranquil, slow moving animal, and it used to be an easy target for hunters. These days, it is more at risk from the loss of its seagrass habitat and from encounters with boats and fishing nets.

9 Friday

Full moon ○

Charged my M. Scooter.
Received a cheque from Friends Life, for £54-61; Kew Magazine for Summer; and Museum Selection Magazine

10 Saturday

Received a form to renew my adoption, from the Orang-Utan Foundation, and a Puzzler Magazine. Did some shopping.

11 Sunday

Trinity Sunday (Christian)

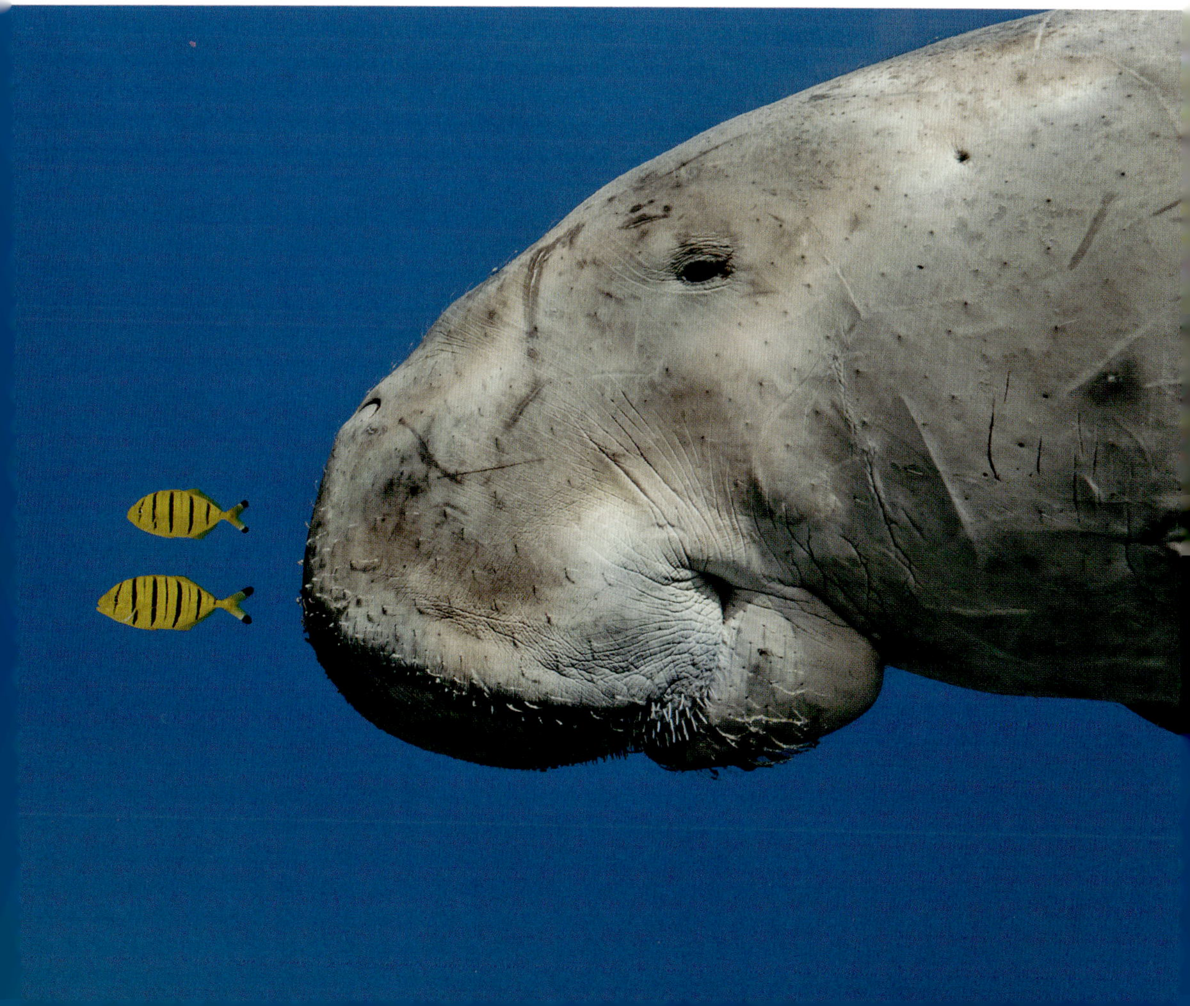

12 Monday

Renewed my adoption of an orang-utan at the O. Foundation. Received news of a young orangutan from the D.W.C.T.. Ordered a book from Kew Gardens. Ordered more medication.

13 Tuesday

Received literature from Nat. West. Bank

14 Wednesday

Received "Pollination Power" from Kew Gardens. Received two Nat. West Bank statements. and an offer for travel insurance; literature from B. Red Cross; and a Puzzler Magazine Washed some clothes.

Thursday — Charged M. scooter again.

15 Thursday

Corpus Christi (Christian)

Received details of my orang adoption, from the O. Foundation; literature from the Folio Society; and literature from Freedom From Torture. Posted entry to the British Red Cross raffle, and entry to the B.H.A. Raffle. Did some shopping.

16 Friday

Received survey from D.I.D.; a telephone bill; literature from B. Red Cross. Posted donation to B. Red Cross. Did some shopping. Received a 'phone call from Nat. His. Museum about book.

17 Saturday

Received literature from Kew Gardens about George Bentham. Rang shop in Islington, and ordered Galapagos book.

18 Sunday

Father's Day

Flowerbow

by Olar Barndõk

When drops of rain in the air refract sunlight in a particular way a rainbow appears in the sky. As the droplets get smaller, the way the light is dispersed changes, and the arc's colours weaken. If there is mist or fog rather than rain, the arc can become almost entirely white. Olar saw this magnificent fogbow on a trip to the Sibillini Mountains National Park in Italy. It was June and the valley was a mass of flowers.

19th - Finished packing my case.

June WEEK 26

19 Monday

Rang Kew Garden. They will send me the pin badge in September. Received another appeal from the Gorilla Organization. Phoned a donation to the Gorilla Organization. Received more medication.

20 Tuesday

Pauline gave me a Birthday Card. Received "Collecting Evolution", from Waterstones.

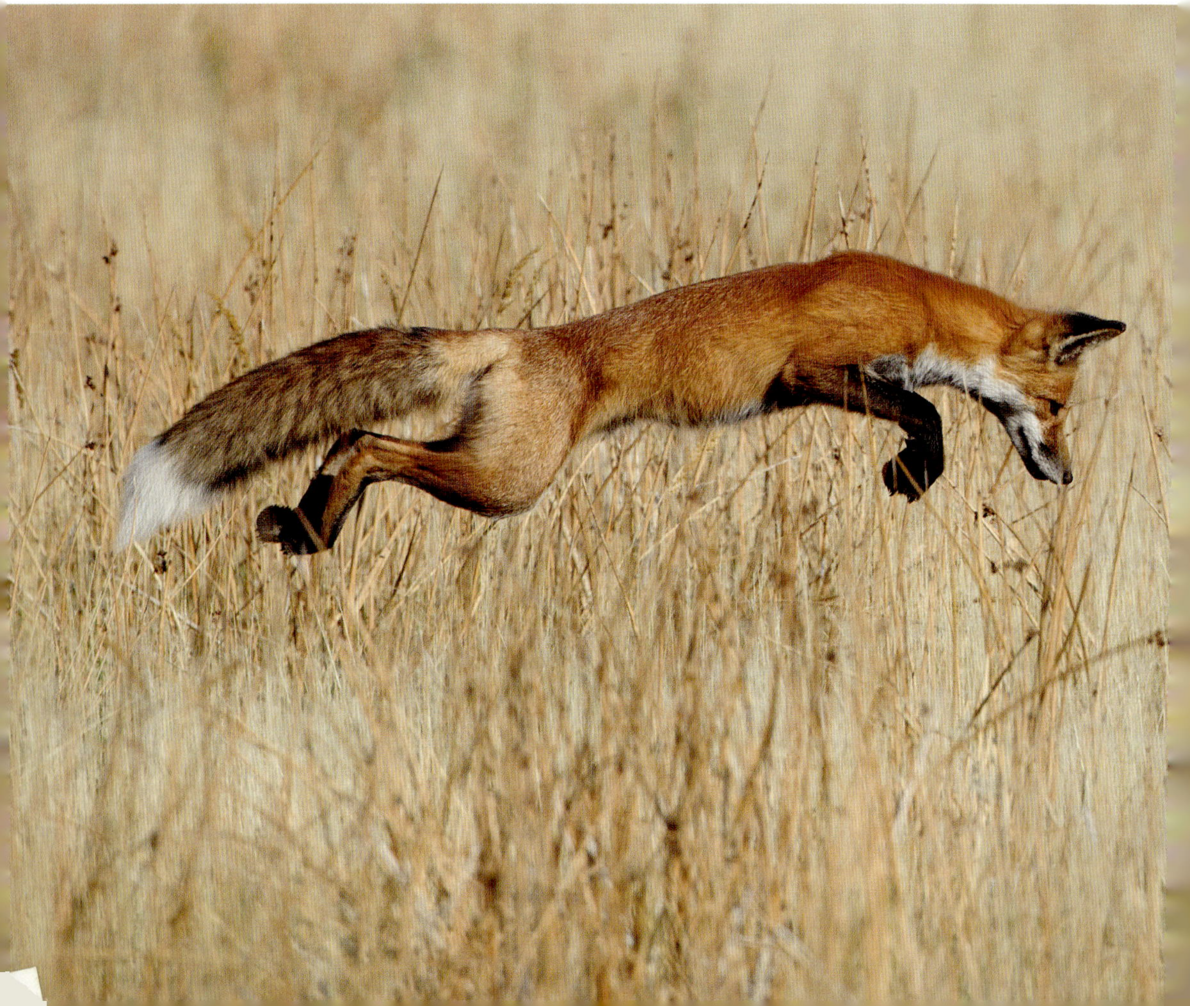

Sat – did a little shopping.

21 Wednesday

Summer Solstice

Received an appeal from the R.S.P.B. for Sherwood Forest, and raffle tickets from L.A.C.S. Made a donation to the R.S.P.B.

22 Thursday

Posted three letters. Did some shopping. Met Serina's Mum.

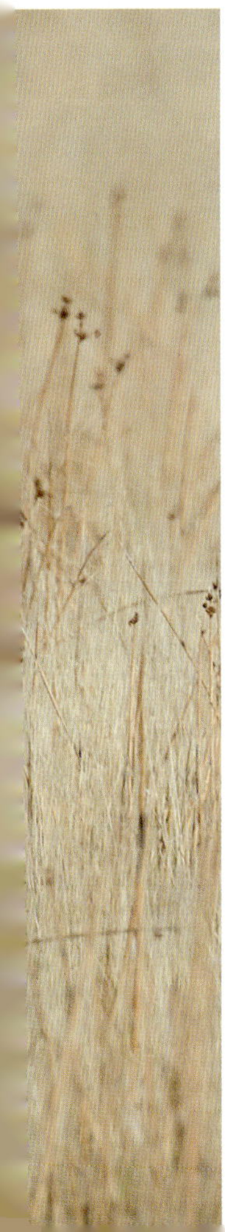

23 Friday

Received literature from the Donkey Sanctuary, and a bulletin and appeal from the N.S.S. David Tribe has died.

24 Saturday

New moon ●

Received literature from the Gas Board, and a Thank you letter from the Gorilla Organization. Julie will ring me on Monday.

25 Sunday

Ramadan ends (Islamic)

Lucky pounce

by Connor Stefanison

'Anticipating the pounce – that was the hardest part,' says Connor, who had come to Yellowstone National Park, Wyoming, USA, in search of wildlife as much as the spectacular landscape. He had found this fox, his first ever, on his last day in the park. It was so absorbed in hunting – it quartered the grassland, back and forth, and then started staring intently at a patch of ground. When it sprung up, Connor got his shot. And when it landed, the fox got his mouse.

26 Monday

Received literature from the Folio Society.

27 Tuesday

Travelled to Paignton.

28 Wednesday

Posted card to Serin. Went to bank. Drew out money and paid in 6 cheques. Went to Torbay Book Shop and bought five books. Also bought a second hand book from cancer research. Had treatment at the Torbay Foot care.

29 Thursday

Went to Paignton Zoo. They now have Parson's Chameleons.

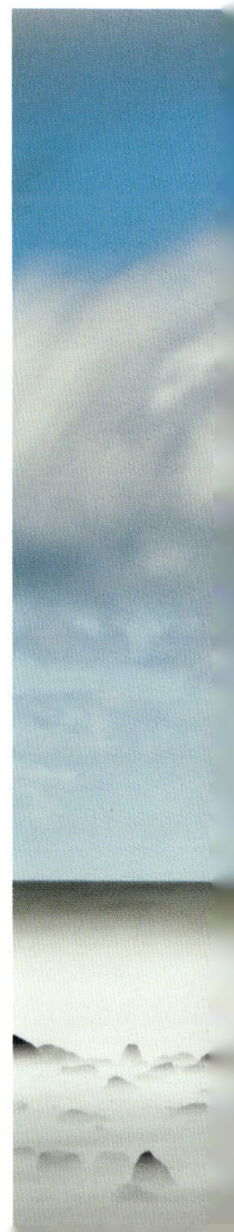

Exposed

by Gerard Leeuw

Blue skies, white clouds and sunshine – perfect for a stroll along the beach of Ameland Island in the Netherlands, but holding little promise for a photographer. There was a strong wind, and as Gerard watched the waves smash against the breakwater, he began to think about the contrast between the wind and water and the solidity of the rocks. A long exposure eliminated movement in the water but exposed the movement of the clouds.

2ND Sunday - Went to Paignton Zoo.
Colin bought me a supper at the Inn On The Green.

30 Friday

Bought a Joanna Trollope book, from the Cancer Research Shop. Colin told me that Thorntons is going to close.

1 Saturday Canada Day

Did not feel too well.

Also received chocolates and a book from Colin and Jackie.

2 Sunday

It is my 70th Birthday
Opened card from Julian and Pauline. Also cards from Colin and Jackie, and Paul and Gillian.

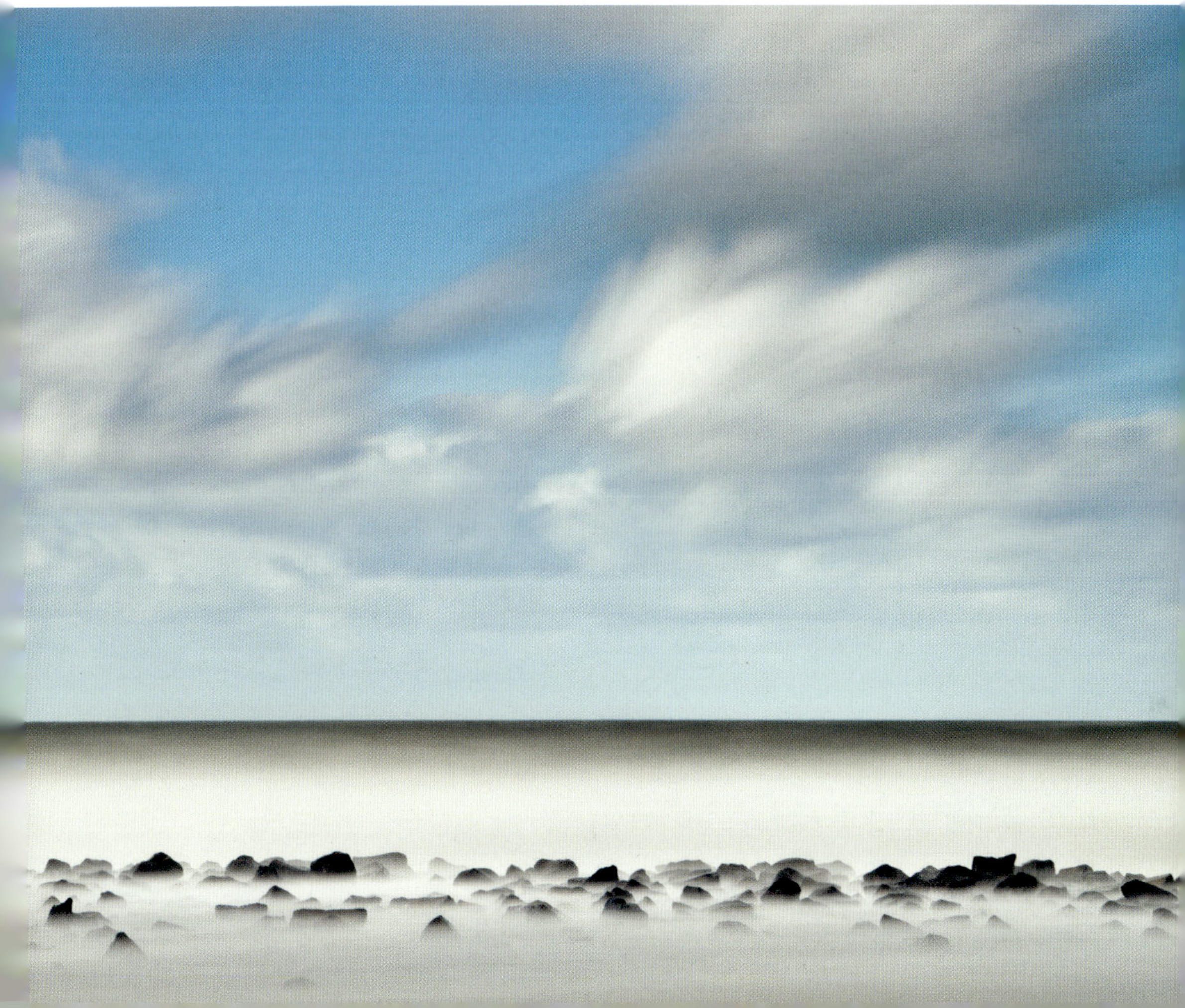

3 Monday

Had my hair cut. Posted a second card to Sevin. Bought a p.b. book from Cancer Research shop.

4 Tuesday

Independence Day (USA)

Posted 10 postcards. Bougt a second-hand book, "Architects of Eternity", from a feline charity shop.

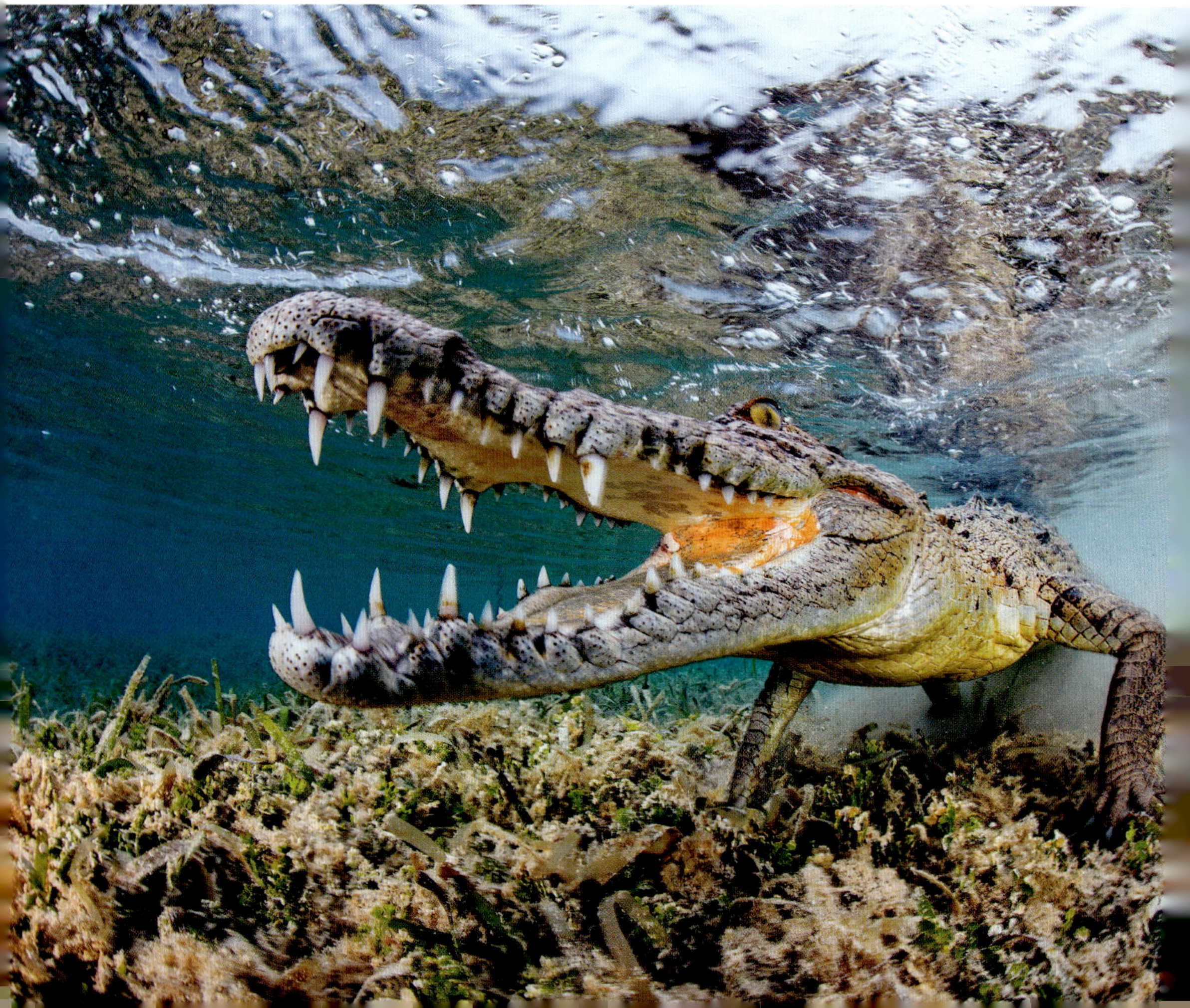

5 Wednesday

Went to Paignton Zoo. Broke my tooth in the restaurant.

6 Thursday

Was taken to Shaldon Zoo. They have had a lot of misfortune with staff health. Bought some photos of animals. Bought a pair of blue shorts.

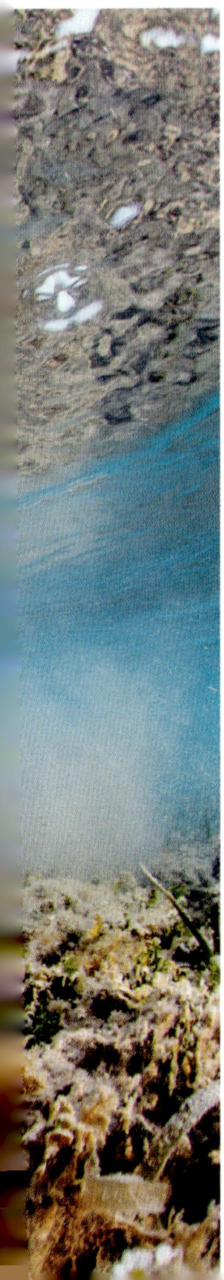

7 Friday

Bought 3 notepads, and another pair of shorts.

8 Saturday

Went to Paignton Zoo.

9 Sunday

Full moon ○

The shy crocodile

by Jordi Chias Pujol

Jordi was diving at Jardines de la Reina, an archipelago off southern Cuba, when he encountered this juvenile American crocodile. 'I so wanted to photograph it,' says Jordi, 'but it was shy, and trying to tempt it to stay with fish and chicken leftovers made no difference.' On the third day, when he slipped into the water, the crocodile just kept watching him, allowing him to take this stunning photograph.

10 Monday

Posted another card to Serin. Went to the Torbay Bookshop, and bought several books, and two sets of book clips and some chocolate. The shop closes in August. Paid my bill to Colin.

11 Tuesday

Travelled back home
Had a 'phone call from the L.A.C.S.

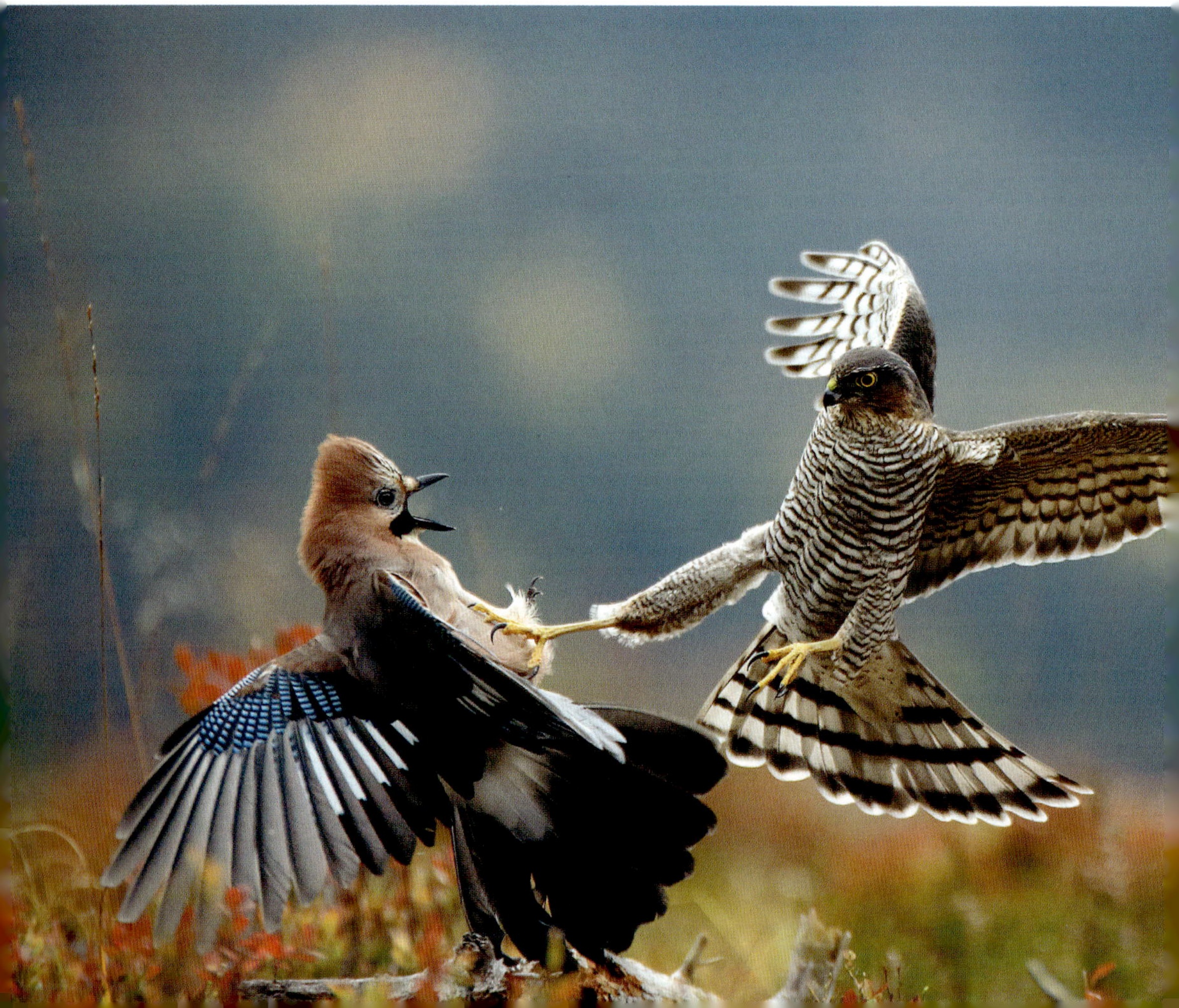

12th — Ordered 2 books from Folio Society; ordered a Mark Haddon Book from
Had a 'phone call from Keith P. Wood.
an appeal from the B.H.A.

12 Wednesday

Battle of the Boyne, holiday (Northern Ireland)

Received ltr from the B.H.A., and an appeal from British Red Cross; Opened other post, — 2 Puzzler Magazines; a Birthday Card from B. Smoker; The Ethical Record; ltr. from Folio Society; Mag. from Butterfly Conservation; thank you letter from Kew Gardens; Museum Collection Mag; two letters from D.W.C.T. — they have hatched a baby Radiated Tortoise; a Nat. West. Bank statement; London Zoo Magazine;

13 Thursday

Received card from J. Greenleaf.
Charged my M.S. scooter. Did some shopping.
Made a donation to the B.H.A.

14 Friday

Received an appeal from Butterfly Conservation. Made a donation to them. Received order from Folio Society. Charged my M. Scooter. Did some shopping. Heard that "D. giving D. Serinus Hum." is available. Ordered it and 2 Ladybird Books.

15 Saturday

St Swithin's Day (Christian)

Received a new Kew Gardens Mem. Card.
Medication was delivered.

16 Sunday

Received "The Pier Falls" by Mark Haddon.

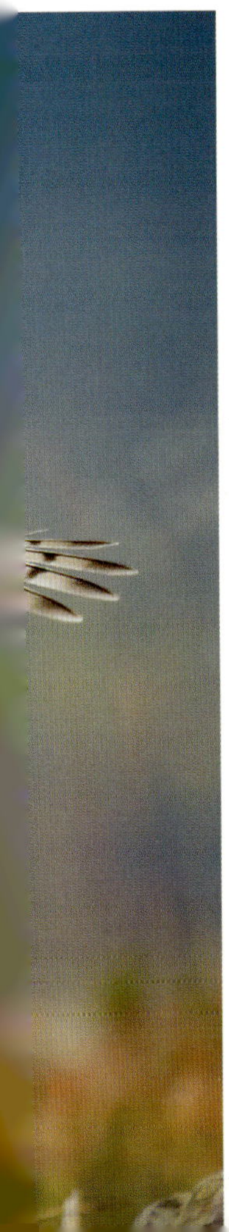

Life in the balance

by Pål Hermansen

When a pair of sparrowhawks started to frequent a feeding station at Pål's hide in Dalen, Norway, he didn't imagine they would catch a jay. They didn't, but they brought their young for hunting practice. Time after time the youngsters' attempts failed. 'So I practised pressing the shutter just before an attack began,' says Pål, and managed to, on this occasion, capture the height of the action, the moment when life truly hangs in the balance.

17 Monday

Changed my M. Scooter. Did some shopping. Julian says he is going aw[ay] next Monday for 5 or 6 weeks.

18 Tuesday

Received a telephone bill. Booked appt. at Barts Hosp. on Frid[ay]. Rang Stephen Norley. He says he will ring me on Monday.

19 Wednesday

Received three books from Waterstones. Did a bit of shopping.

20 Thursday

The encirclement

by Thomas Haider

Large shoals of anchovies are uncommon around Indonesia, so Thomas knew he was witnessing something special when he saw an enormous shoal encircling a rock off Indonesia's West Papua province. As he approached, it separated like a curtain and encircled him in a fountain formation. This revealed a group of longfin batfish close to the rock, and below them fusiliers and jacks. Fish shoal for protection, and predators and potentially dangerous animals would normally be on the outside.

23RD – Julian is not going away tomorrow now, as he is not well.

21 Friday

Went to Barts. Hospital, and had my pace maker checked. It is alright. Received more Dermovate. Rang Norman Bacrac.

22 Saturday

Received a letter from the L.A.C.S. about wills; and the R.S.P.B. magazine for Autumn. Delivered card to Julian. Booked tickets for Paignton. Did some shopping.

23 Sunday

New moon ●

Charged my M. Scooter. Posted raffle ticket stubs to Butterfly Con.

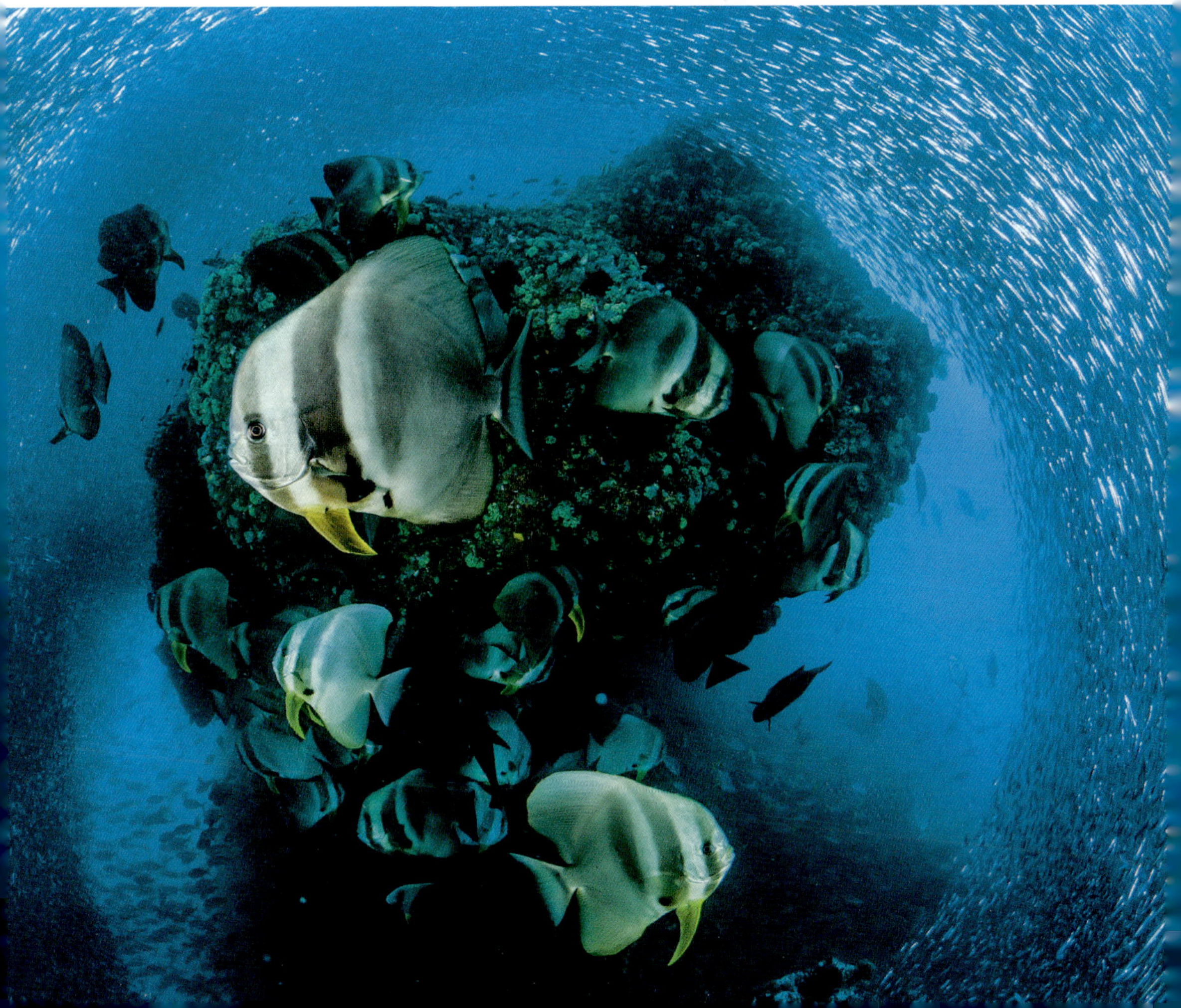

24 Monday

Ordered a book from Folio Society. Received more literature from Folio Society and literature from Electoral Registration Officer.

25 Tuesday

Received tickets for Paignton. Had a call from Stephen Naoley. Rod is on holiday this week.

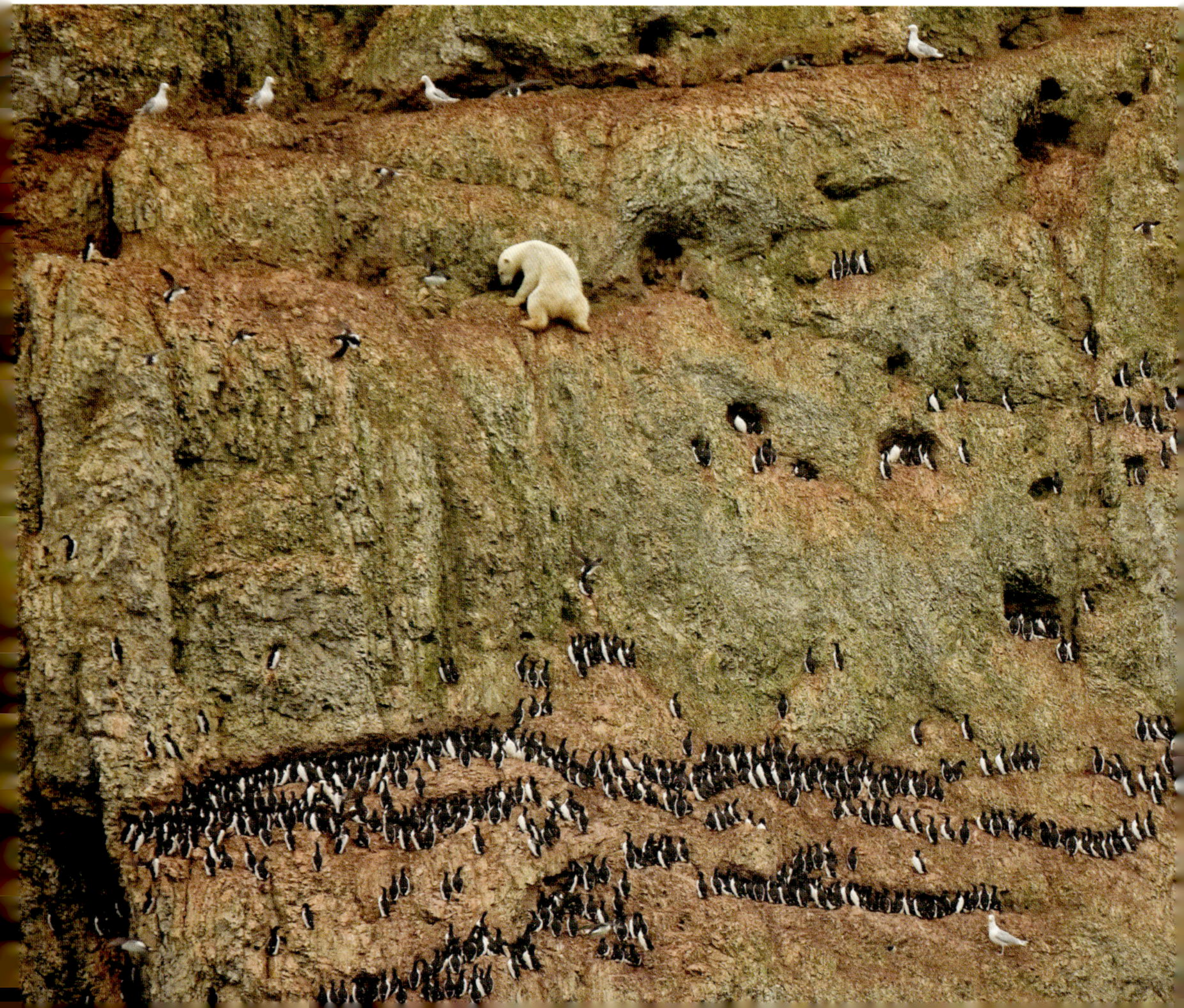

29th – Did some shopping.

26 Wednesday

Received literature from the L.A.C.S.

27 Thursday

Received lit from the Donkey Sanctuary, and voting lit. from the Green Party. Did some shopping. Posted two letters. The remaining piece of my broken tooth has come out.

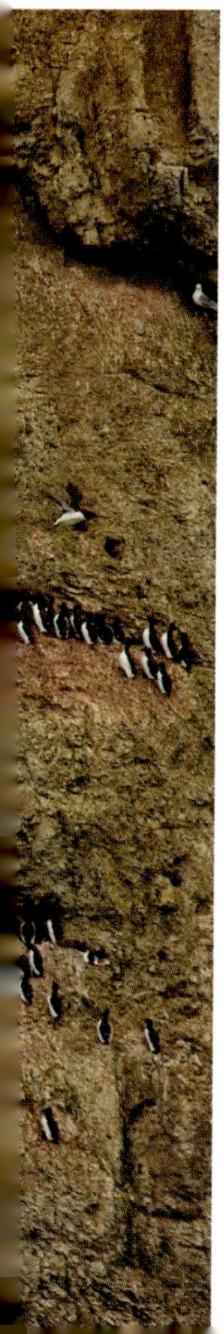

28 Friday

Ordered more medication.

Received "Leviathan" from the Folio Society.

29 Saturday

Received a Puzzler Magazine, and a card from Monica Green. Received a thank-you from Serin.

30 Sunday

Gave bird table to Pauline to sort out.

Perilous pickings

by Jenny E Ross

At first, the white speck looked like a patch of snow on the cliff but Jenny soon realised it was a polar bear. Polar bears rely on a sea-ice platform to catch their prey but in an increasing number of regions, the sea ice now melts completely in summer, forcing the bears ashore. This hungry young male was desperately attempting to climb down the rock face to scavenge eggs from nesting Brünnich's guillemots. Jenny photographed the spectacle in the Russian Arctic National Park.

31 Monday

Received another Puzzler Magazine, and "Evolve" Magazine, from the Nat. His. Museum. The next New Nat. book show arrive next week. Ordered a dinosaur book from the Nat. His. Museum. Received more medication.

1 Tuesday

Charged my M. Scooter.

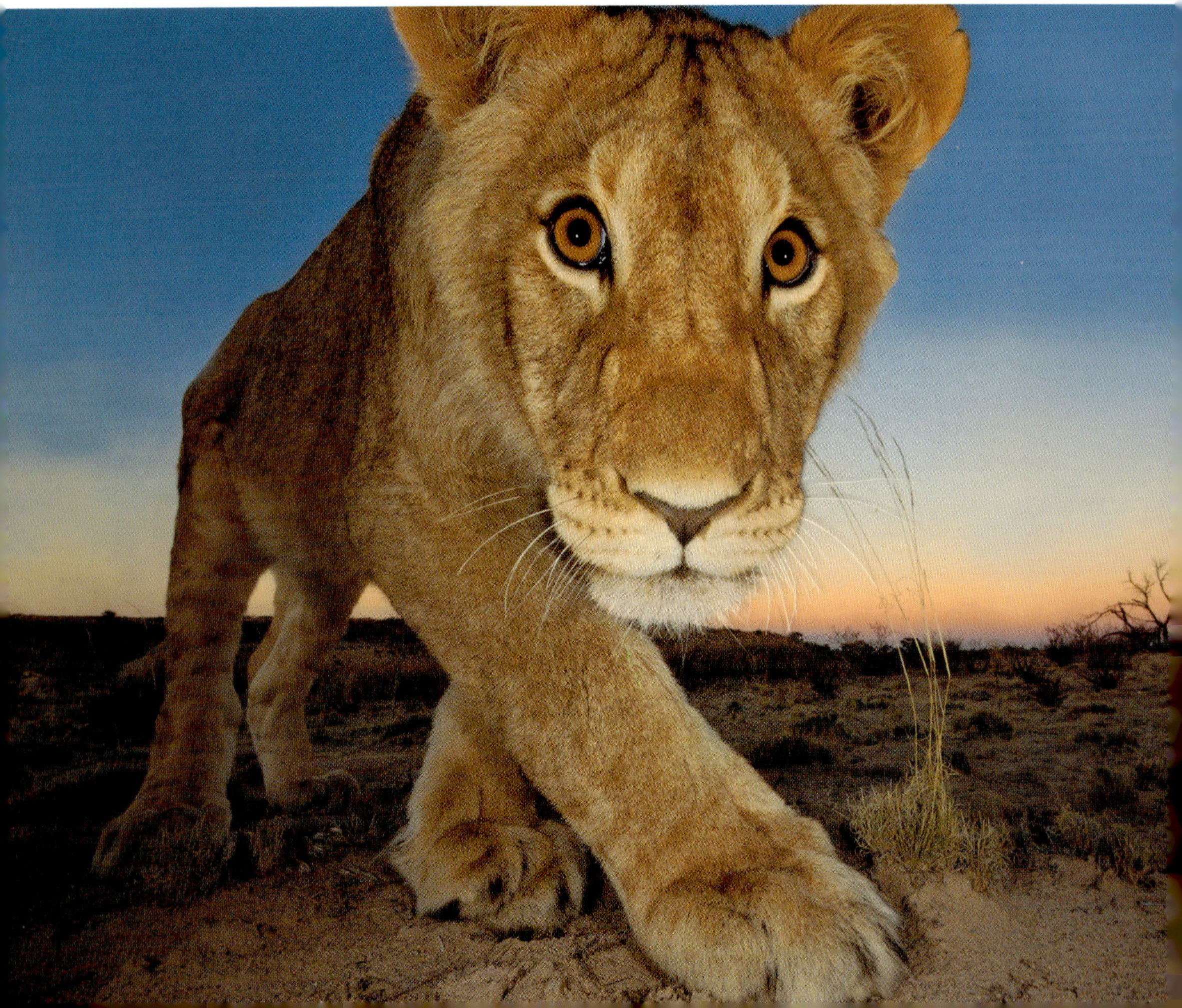

2 Wednesday

Posted form to Rothwell & Towler, and donation to Green Party. Did some shopping. Received No. 135 in the New Naturalist Series: - "Farming and Birds"

3 Thursday

Received Museum Selection Magazine. It is a year ago today since my pacemaker was put in. Did some shopping. Received "Dinosaurs" from the Natural History Museum. Heard from Stephen.

4 Friday

We will go to Rod's, 3.20pm next Wednesday. Received literature from Freedom From Torture.

5 Saturday

Changed my M. Scooter. Received lit from Rothwell & Towler, and info about a flamingo at D.W.C.T. Had my hair cut. Cut the hedge in front garden.

6 Sunday

Curiosity and the cat

by Hannes Lochner

Hannes has spent years perfecting his remote wireless technology to photograph intimate portraits of wild African animals, by night especially. In the Kgalagadi Transfrontier Park in the Kalahari, South Africa, he set up one camera near a waterhole. On this particular evening, he was settled in his vehicle, just as the sun was setting, when a pride of lions arrived. This bold cub gazed into the camera lens as it stepped forwards to sniff the strange object.

7 Monday

Summer holiday (Scotland, Republic of Ireland)
Full moon ○

Charged scooter. Did some shopping.

8 Tuesday

9 Wednesday

Received a Nat. West. Bank Statement; and literature from British Red Cross. Went with S. Norley to see Rod. Sorted out what I am going to do.

10 Thursday

Received another cheque from Friends Life, and a letter from L.A.C.S..

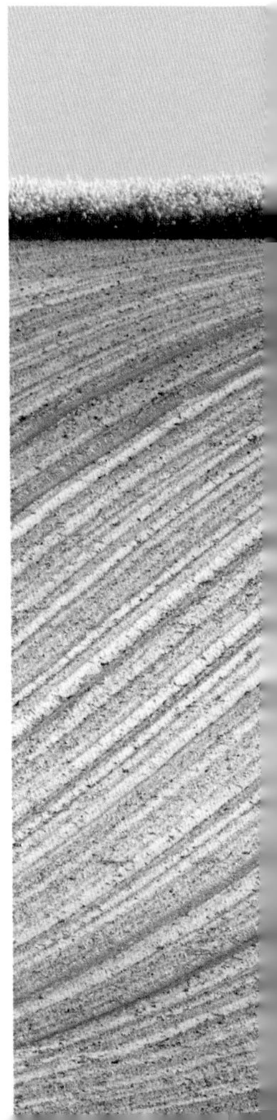

Hare in a landscape

by Robert Zoehrer

This steep, ploughed field, in Burgenland, Austria, with a ribbon of dazzling yellow oilseed rape and a swathe of green, lacked a focus point. As if on cue, a brown hare entered stage right from the grass and sat motionless on the furrowed soil. 'But once I saw the image in black and white,' says Robert, 'not only was the stark geometry highlighted but also the small hare became the centre of the composition rather than being lost among the colour.'

11 Friday

12 Saturday

Received raffle tickets from Gal. Can. Trust. Posted donations to Freedom from Torture, and British Red Cross. Did a little shopping.

13 Sunday

Did some shopping.

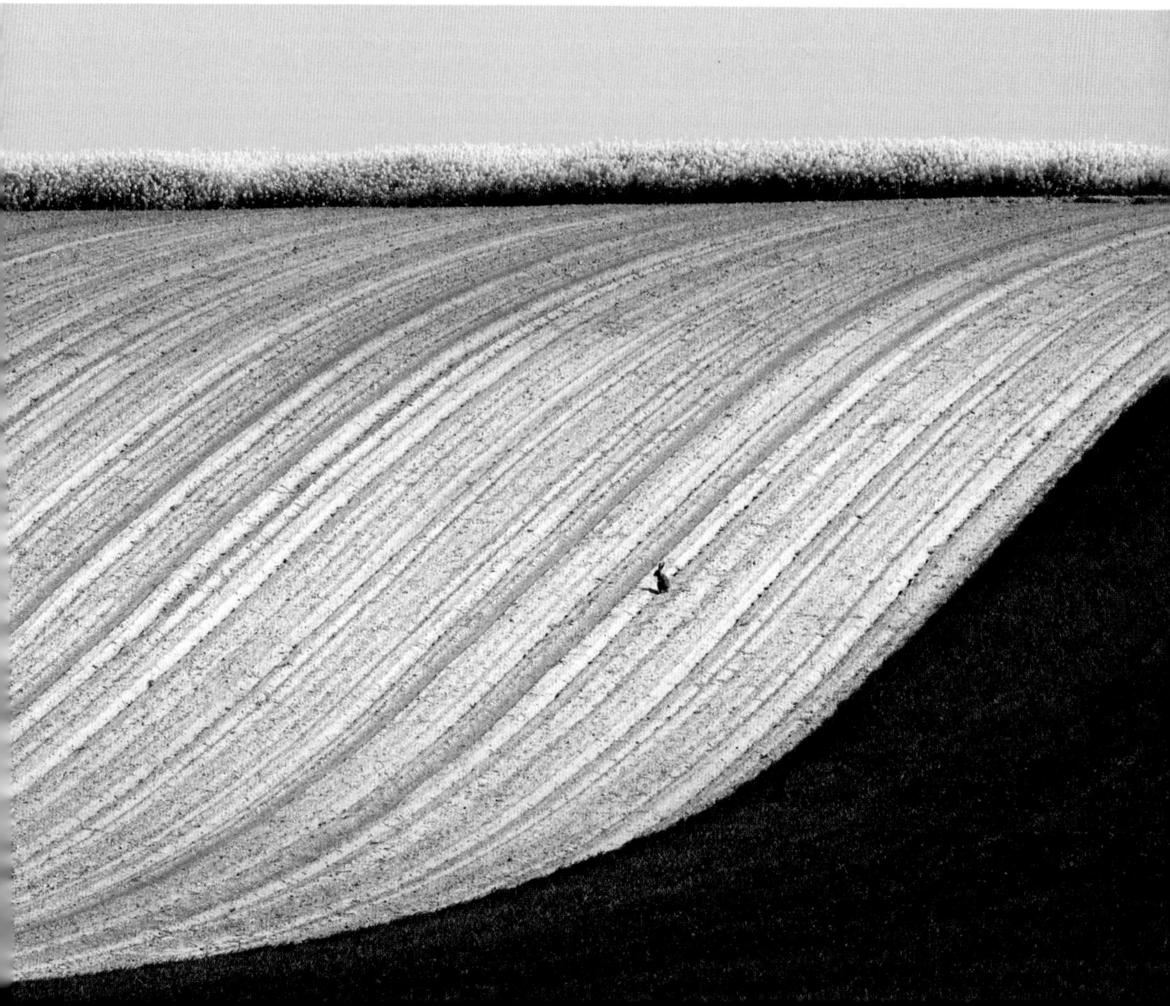

August

14 Monday

Received literature from W.S.P.A.

15 Tuesday

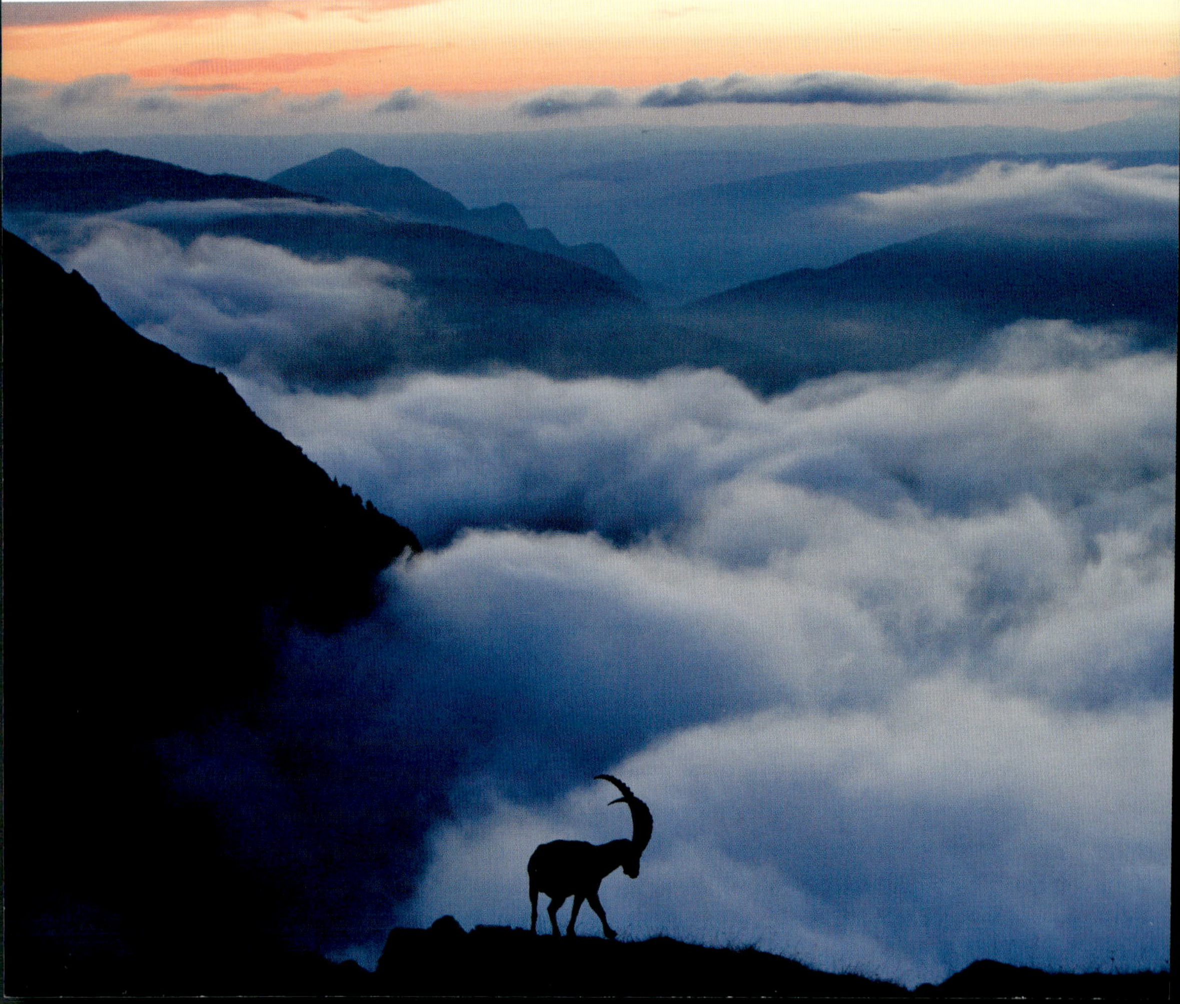

16 Wednesday

Received a telephone bill, and a letter from C.H.E.S. about their A.G.M., on 12th November. Washed some clothes.

17 Thursday

Posted raffle stubs to Ed. Con. Trust. Did a little shopping. Collected Balneum Plus from chemist. Told Sevin's mother about socks. Pauline told me that Julian has been admitted to hospital.

18 Friday

Charged M. Scooter. Did some shopping. Posted donation to W.S.P.A. Received literature from Freedom from Torture, and the New Humanist for Autumn 2017.

19 Saturday

Received a Puzzler Magazine.

20 Sunday

On top of the world

by Jérémie Villet

Jérémie's childhood dream was to climb mountains and see a wild Alpine ibex. In the summer of 2012, he went to the French Alps specifically to look for ibex. He set off on the four-hour climb in good time to catch the sunset, but a thick fog meant it took him several more hours to reach the summit. 'When I emerged from the clouds,' says Jérémie, 'it was like entering a new world.' But the real surprise was to see a male ibex below him.

21 Monday

New moon ●

Received another Puzzler Magazine.

22 Tuesday

Charged M. Scooter. Did a little shopping.

23 Wednesday

Received literature from Freedom From Torture. Charged M. Scooter. Did some shopping. Collected 3 ointments.

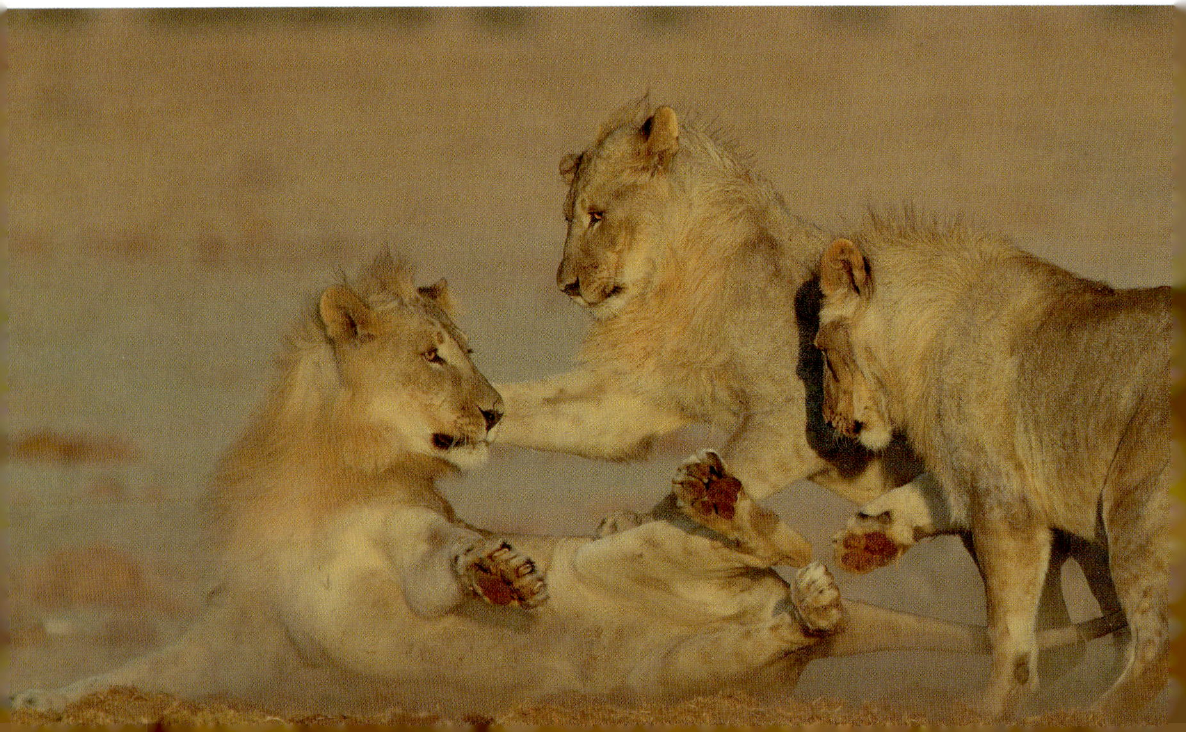

24 Thursday

Booked an appointment to see the doctor next Tuesday.

25 Friday

26 Saturday

Pauline told me that she had some exciting news. She and Julian are getting married! Received a letter from Telecare. Received a thank-you letter from W.A.P. and an appeal from L.A.C.S. Charged M. Scooter.

27 Sunday

Posted a donation to L.A.C.S, and a reply to telecare. Did some shopping.

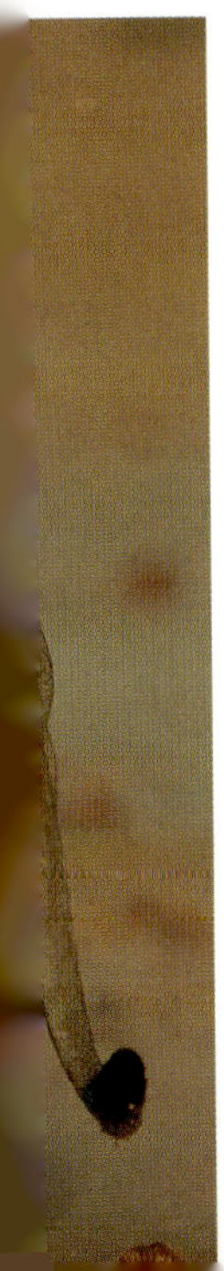

The golden hour

by Lou Coetzer

As the sun came up, a playful mood seemed to infect the whole pride, but these three adolescent males were particularly skittish. Lou was photographing at a remote waterhole in Etosha National Park, Namibia, where the lions had gathered. Now, as the adolescents engaged in an entertaining round of chasing, cuffing, pouncing and wrestling, the scene was bathed in a golden glow. 'It was a rare opportunity', Lou says, 'to see lions in such beautiful light against a simple backdrop.'

28 Monday

Summer holiday (UK)

Charged M. Scooter.

29 Tuesday

Received literature from the Gorilla Organization. Went to health centre, but it ought to be Thursday. Posted raffle stubs and donation to the Gorilla Organizatio

30 Wednesday

Received a letter from B.T. about nuisance calls. Charged M. Scooter.

31 Thursday

Received literature from the B.H.A.. Ordered a book, "Secularism" by Andrew Copson, from Oxford University Press. Went to The Health Centre, and obtained a new prescription.

The magical kokerbooms

by Uge Fuertes Sanz

When he clinched the frame, at the final moment of sunset, Uge was ecstatic. 'I felt this was possibly the most beautiful picture I'd ever created.' He had set up camp in the Giant's Playground in Namibia specifically to photograph the dramatic landscape at night. And as night descended, he felt the enchantment of the place. It wasn't just the dolerite boulders, strewn about like a giant's toys, it was also the otherworldly kokerbooms – giant succulents found only in Namibia and part of South Africa.

1 Friday

Received an R.S.P.B. catalogue, and literature from the British Red Cross. 'Phoned an order to the R.S.P.B. Obtained more medications. Bought rubber gloves. Did some shopping.

2 Saturday

Received diary and Xmas cards from R.S.P.B.; catalogue from Owl Barn. Ordered two books from Culture Vulture Direct.

3 Sunday

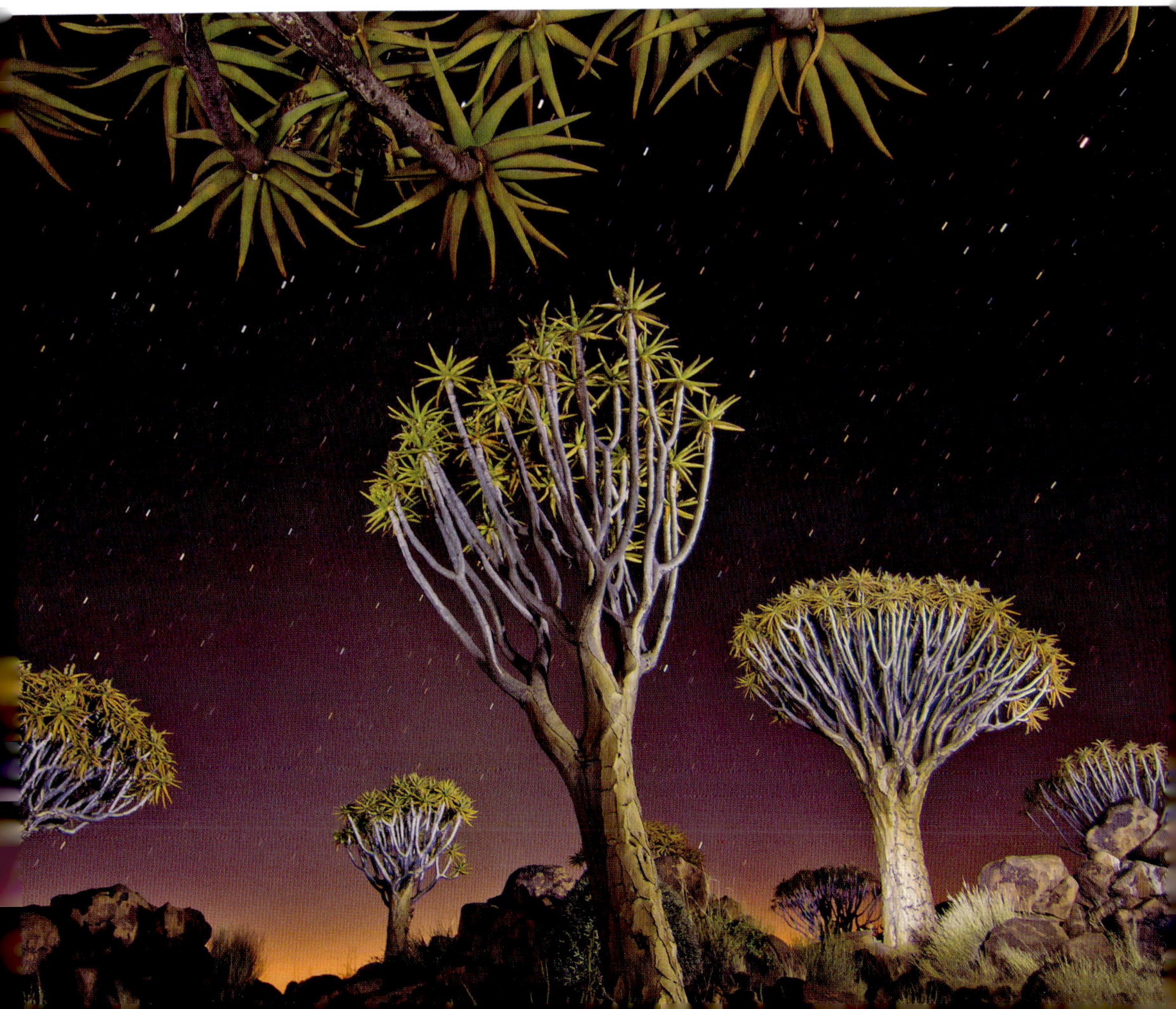

4 Monday

Labor Day (USA)
Labour Day (Canada)

Received a form to renew my subscripti
to Puzzler Magazine. Charged M. Scooter.

5 Tuesday

Received a new Nat. West cheque Book. Rang Nick Dunn. The two sick members of staff are back at the zoo, but another member has died. Had my hair cut, and did some shopping. Posted payment for Puzz subscription.

6 Wednesday

Full moon ○

Received voting literature from the Green Party.

7 Thursday

Received a membership renewal form from the Nat. His. Mus., and a Museum Selection catalogue. Posted subscription to Nat. His Museum.

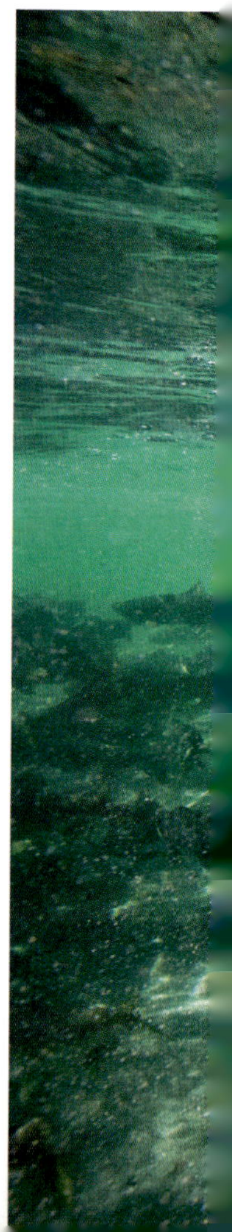

Salmon swipe

by Paul Souders

'I set out to show a salmon's-eye view of a swimming bear swiping at a fish with its huge paws,' says Paul. The location he chose was Katmai National Park in Alaska, and he arrived in time for the late-summer runs of red and chum salmon heading upstream to spawn. Grizzly bears cluster around good fishing spots on the rivers to gorge on salmon, in preparation for the long winter. At shallow points, they wade into the water to try to grab the fish.

Friday – spoke to Margaret Greenleaf.

8 Friday

Received two books from Culture Vulture Direct. Arranged with Shaldon Zoo, to go there on Tuesday 19th. Julian and Pauline are getting married on Friday 29th September. There will be a party the next week.

9 Saturday

Received a cheque for £54-81 from Friends Life; a Folio Catalogue, and lit from British Red Cross. Finished packing bags. Booked taxi for tomorrow.

10 Sunday

Travelled to Paignton.

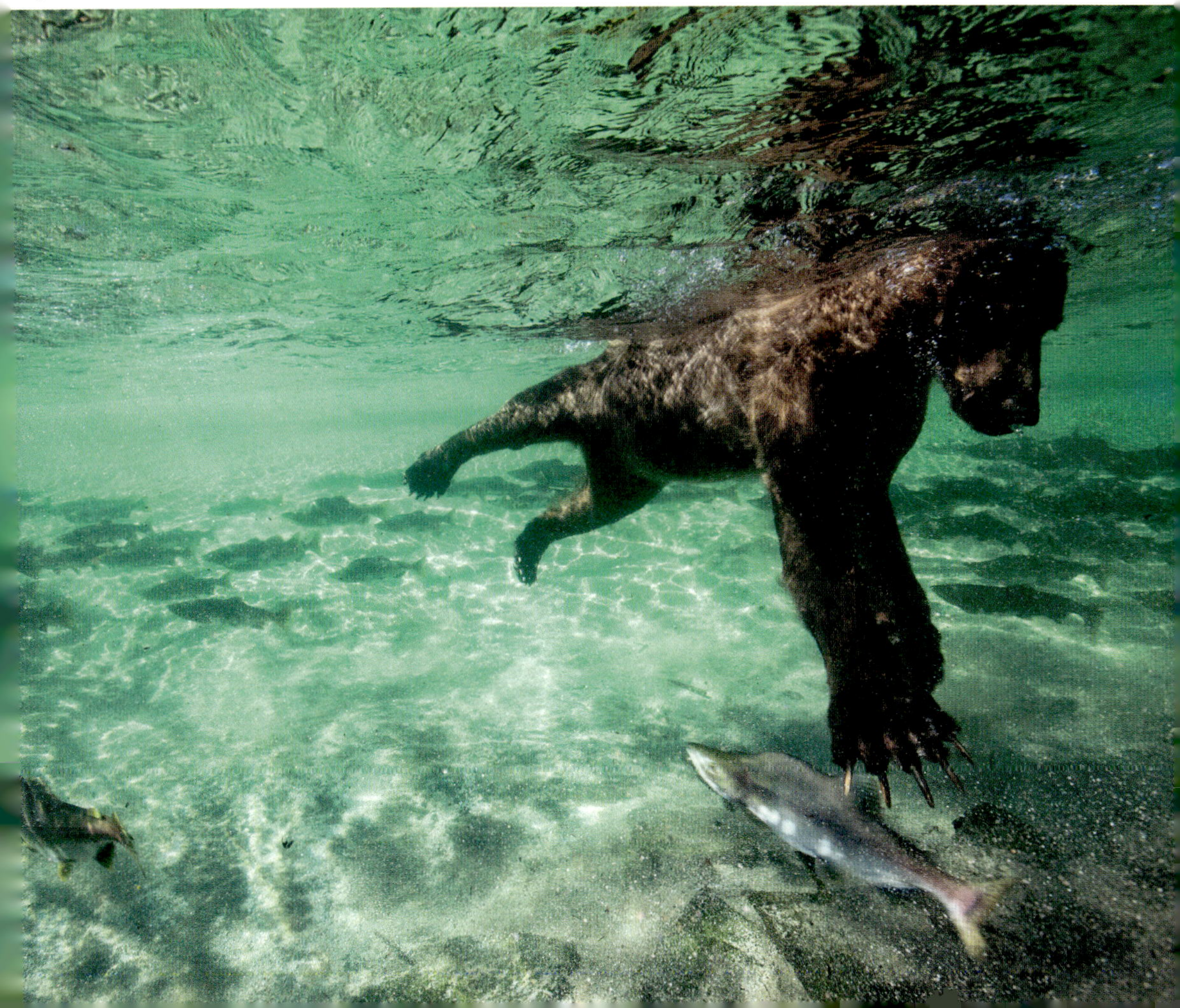

11 Monday

Went to Paignton Zoo. Bought a frog calendar, and 4 post cards.

12 Tuesday

Posted card to Serin. Bought a Wedding card. Had foot treatment. Transferred £10,000-00 into my current bank account, and paid in 3 cheques. Saw "A Judgement in Stone", by Ruth Rendell, at the Princess Theatre, Torquay.

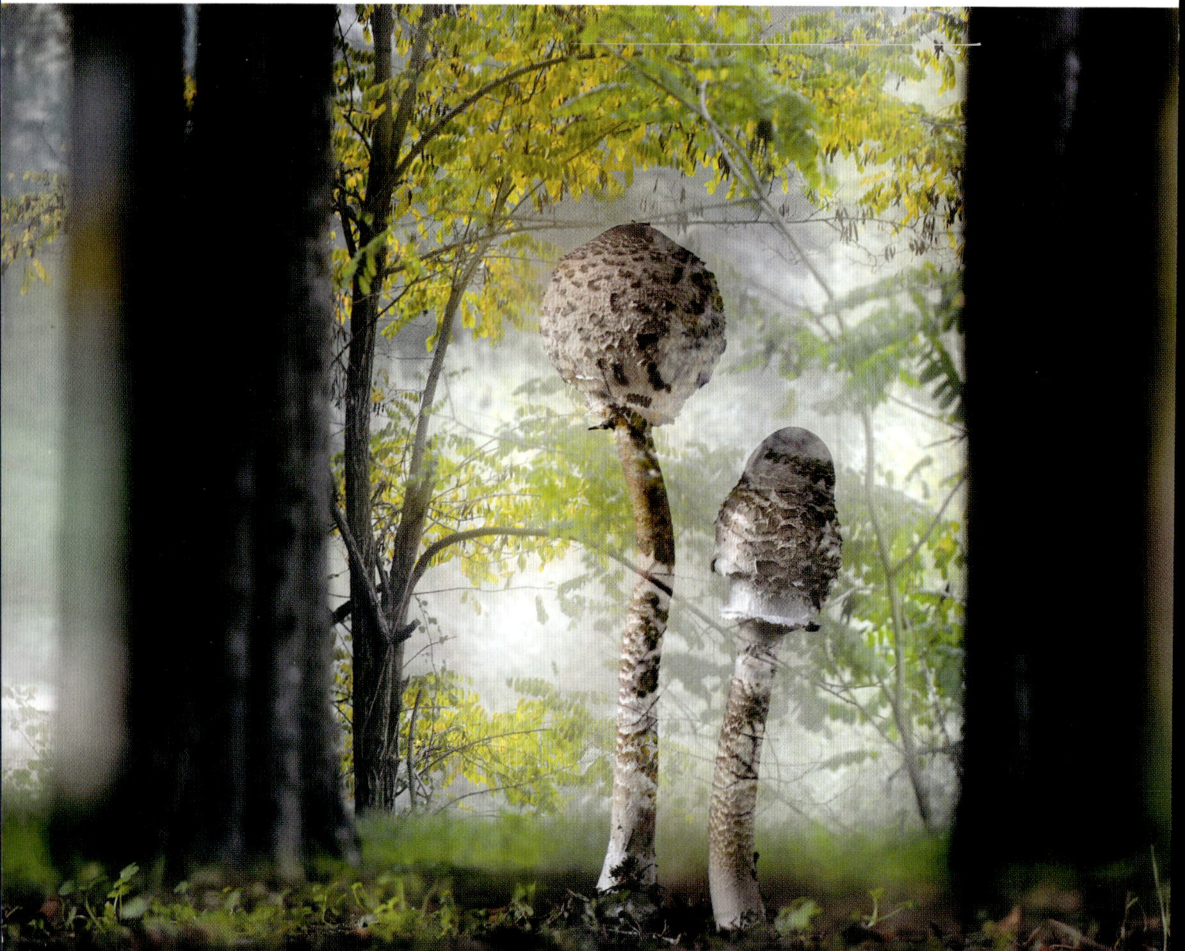

13 Wednesday

Went to Torre Abbey. Bought nine books.

14 Thursday

Went to Torre Abbey again. Bought two more books. Attended two talks. Bought six post cards.

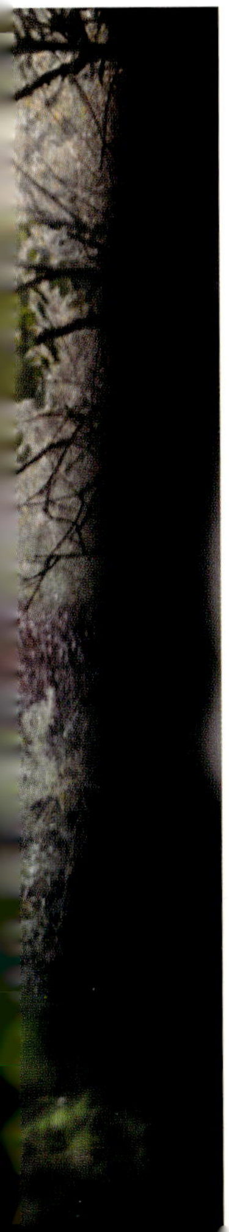

15 Friday

Went to Paignton Zoo again.

16 Saturday

Posted 4 P.C cards. Bought two second-hand books from a charity shop.

Bought three more books.

17 Sunday

Went to Torre Abbey again. Walked around the garden, greenhouse, and building.

Magic mushrooms

by Agorastos Papatsanis

The taller of these two parasol mushrooms is just 30 centimetres. That is tall for a parasol, but their prominence against the tree trunks behind is a slight optical illusion, the result of an in-camera double exposure. Agorastos found the fungi growing in woodland in the Grevena region of Greece, and was fascinated by the subtle browns of the scales of their 'skins' and their relationship to each other. What he wanted to capture was the fairytale feel of the scene.

18 Monday

Bought a small brown teapot, and a shaving mirror from a charity shop. Drew out more money from the bank.

19 Tuesday

Went to Shaldon Zoo. Met Julie, Nic, Claire and Carly. Nic gave me a copy of a painting of Doris, the Loris. They plan to have koalas there, in a few years time. Bought a sm folding stool in Paignton. Bought 8 p. car at Shaldon Zoo, and gave them another donati

20 Wednesday

Rosh Hashanah (at sunset), Jewish New Year

New moon ●

Dined at a Chinese Restaurant in Paignton.

21 Thursday

It is two years ago today since I opened the amphibian room at Shaldon Zoo. Went to Living Coasts. Bought 16 P. cards.

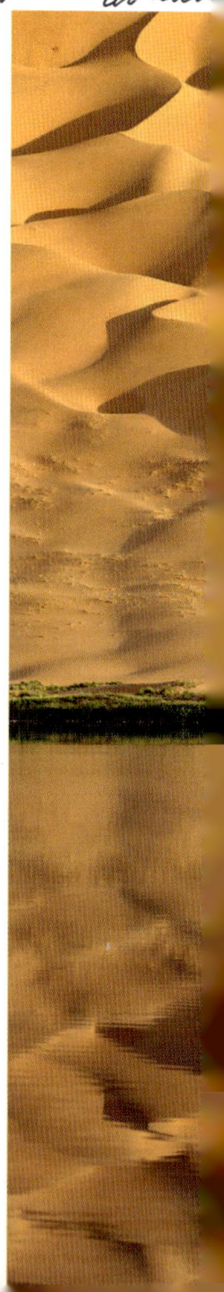

Gobi oasis

by Alessandra Meniconzi

China is second home to Alessandra. She's travelled the country since childhood, visiting the most remote and wild corners, often cycling or hitch-hiking to get there. During a trip to Inner Mongolia, Alessandra travelled to the Alxa Desert Geopark in the Gobi Desert, which has the world's highest stationary dunes and more than 140 spring-fed lakes, and is a centre for the study of desertification. Climbing the highest dune, the oasis scene below took her breath away.

24th – It is 49 years ago today since I first came to London.

22 Friday

Autumn Equinox

Posted another card to Sevin. Confirmed Paignton dates for Xmas - New Years.

23 Saturday

Went to P. Zoo. Bought two books, and a fridge magnet.

24 Sunday

Finished packing. Paid hotel and scooter bills. Travelled back to London. Reached home at 9-45pm.

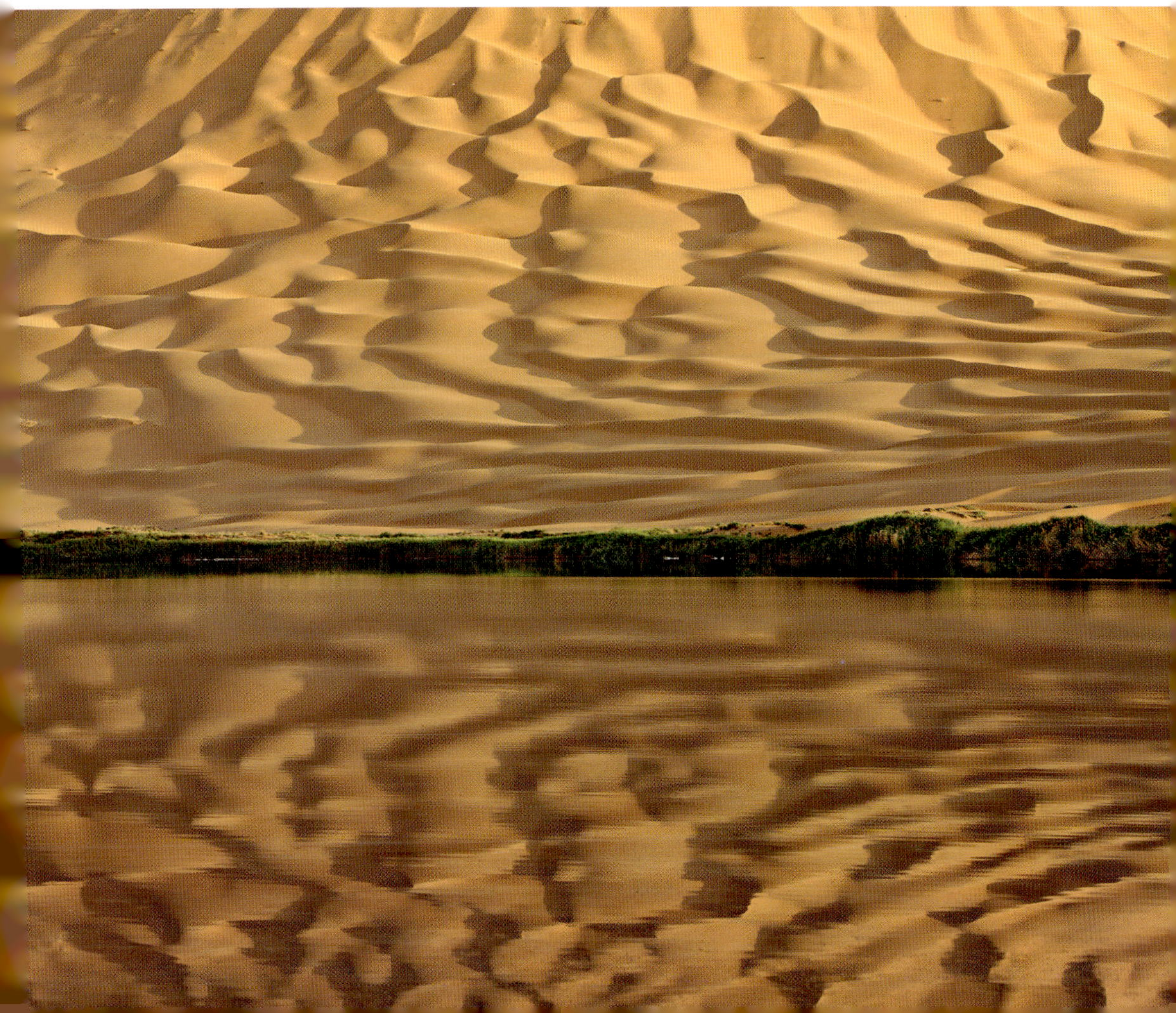

25th. Opened Post

25 Monday

It is twenty years ago today since Stephen died. Ordered three books from the Folio Society. Received an appeal from the B.H.A.; lit from Freedom from Torture; and "Secularism", by Andrew Copson. Made a donation to the B.H.A. Placed an order with Owl Barn. Made a donation to R.S.P.

26 Tuesday

Discovered that the next book in the County Gar series comes out next June. Charged M. Scoote. Ordered another book case.

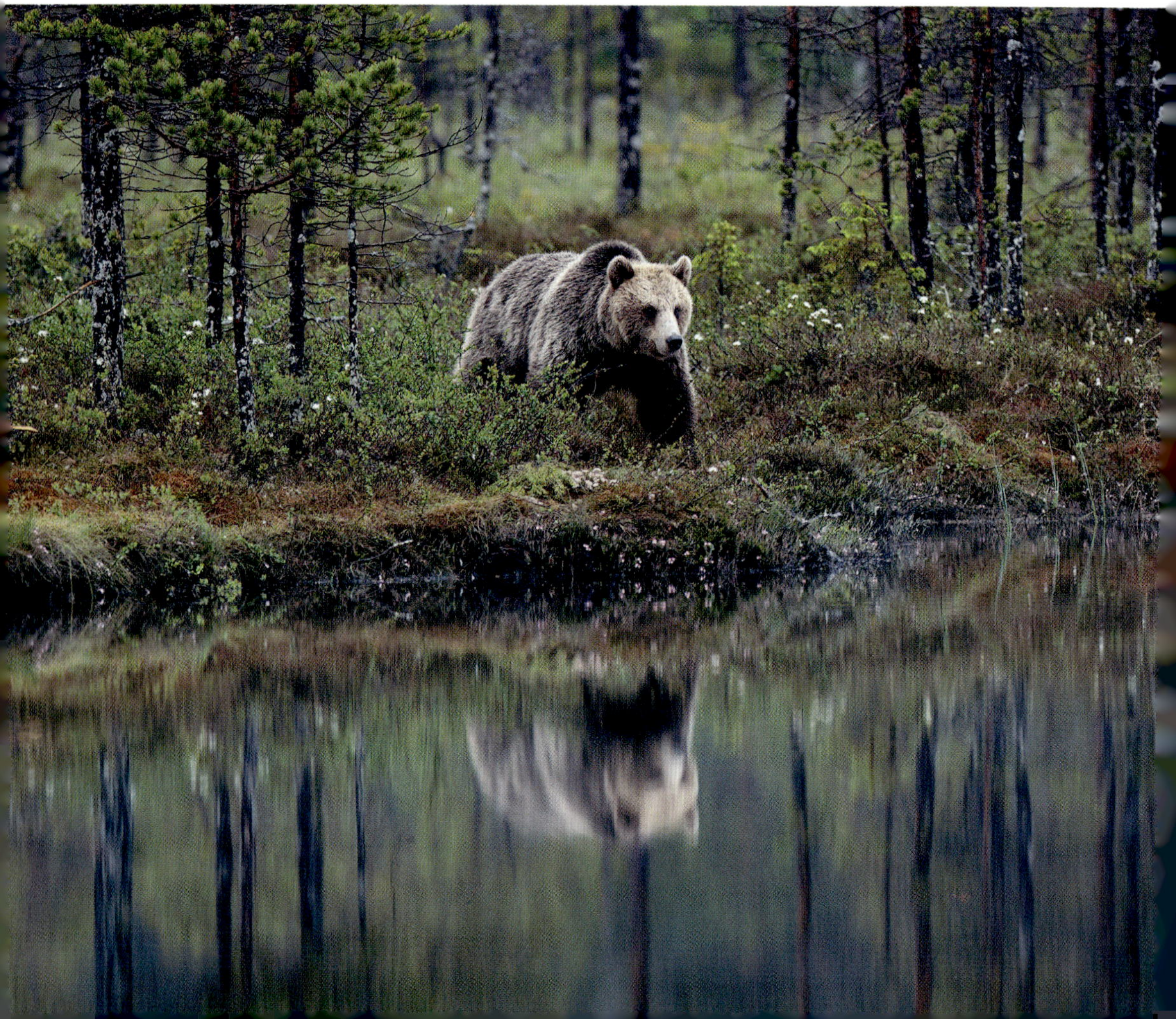

27th – posted donation to Green Party; donation to Gorilla Organization; Raffle stubs to B. Red Cross; and order to Galapagos Con. Trust

27 Wednesday

Received a voucher from Museum Selection
Received order from the Folio Society. – "Great Expectations", "Period Piece, A Cambridge Childhood", "A Room Of Ones Own", "Spring, A Folio Anthology". Did some shopping.

28 Thursday

Rang Evelyn Ellis to offer my sympathies about Helen's death
Received a new membership card for the Nat. His. Mus., and a culture vulture direct. Did some shopping.

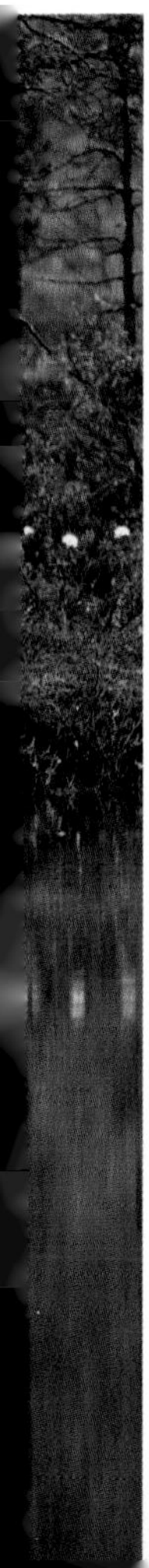

29 Friday

Yom Kippur (at sunset) (Jewish)

Received information from D. W. C. T. about gorillas; raffle tickets from Donkey Sanctuary; a ticket to ABA Chelsea Rare Book Fair. Julian and Pauline get married today. Pushed wedding card under their door. Received order from Owl Barn.

30 Saturday

Received a Bulletin from the N.S.S. Posted raffle stubs to D. Sanctuary and donation to N.S.S.

1 Sunday

Still reflection

by Anton Lilja

Anton and his father hired a hide for a day in Suomussalmi, Finland, hoping to see brown bears. They arrived just as a storm whipped up. But by dawn, the pond in front of the hide was as still as glass, and the rain had stopped. They put dog food out as bait, and they didn't have to wait long for a visitor. At four thirty in the morning, a bear came out of the forest and stood right by the pond.

October

WEEK 41

2 Monday

Received notification of renewal of membership of Z.S.L. Stuck 70th Birthday Cards in album, along with those for my 21st Birthday

3 Tuesday

Charged my M. Scooter.

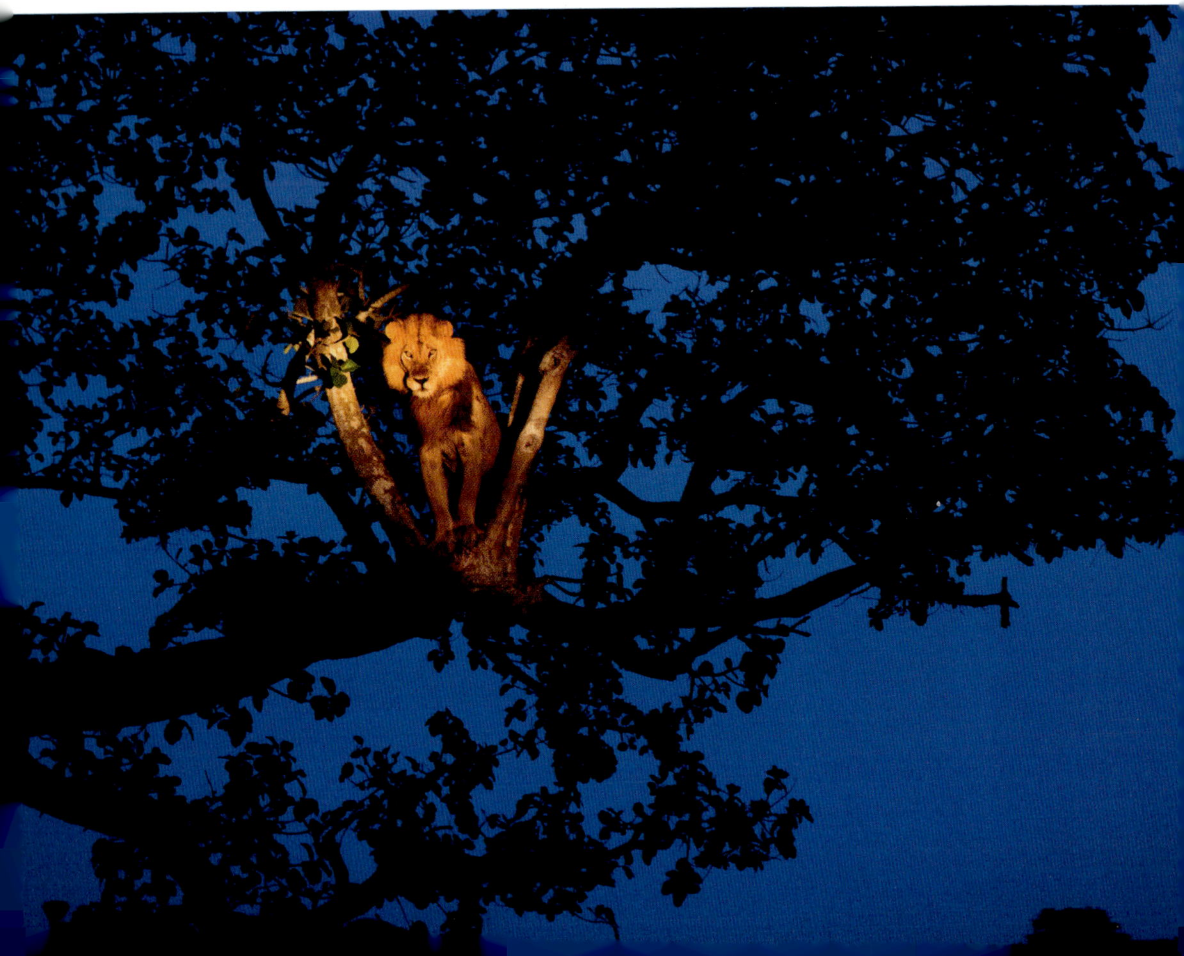

4 Wednesday

Received Annual review and other lit. from Butterfly Conservation; and an appeal from World Animal Protection. Did some shopping. Posted order to B.C.; donation to W. A. P.; and cheque for replacement. Collected some medication.

5 Thursday

Full moon ○

Received a card from Kew Gardens thanking me for being a legacy supporter, and sending me a badge. Had my hair cut.

6 Friday

Received raffle tickets from W.A.P. Pauline gave me some wedding cake. Had a flu jab. Posted raffle stubs for W.A.P. Booked ticket for Paignton, 19th December.

7 Saturday

Received a ticket for trip to Paignton.

8 Sunday

Lion in the spotlight

by Joel Sartore

Tree-climbing is not a normal lion habit, but lions in Queen Elizabeth National Park, Uganda, often take to the trees in the day, probably to cool off and escape the flies. This tree held two dozing brothers. 'It was dusk by the time the first young male woke from his nap,' says Joel. He was listening to a female calling in the distance. Joel was with the chief biologist studying the lions in the park, who spot-lit the male so it could be identified.

9 Monday

Columbus Day (USA)

Booked chiropody appt. for 20th Decem
Changed M. Scooter. Received thank you lette
from the Gorilla Org., and Gal. Con. Trust. Al
lit from L.A.C.S. Also a card to say there
a parcel for me. Did some shopping

10 Tuesday

Received a thank you letter from Humanis
U.K.; lit from the Green Party; and a Bulletin
from the Société Jersiaise. There is a page in
Hackney , about Charles Bradlaugh.

11 Wednesday

Received the Ethical Record for
October – December (It is now quarterly);
a cheque from Aviva; and a calendar
from Butterfly Conservation. Posted
votes to Green Party.

12 Thursday

Received a statement from Nat. West
Bank; Kew Magazine; and lit from the
Folio Society. Phoned an order to Folio
Society.

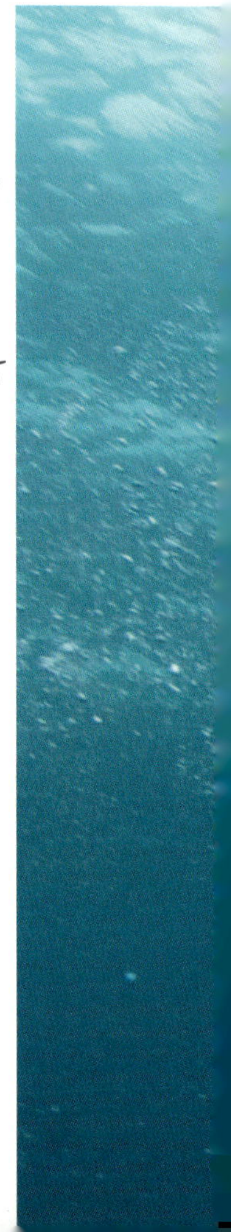

Dive robbers

by Jean Tresfon

For five days, Jean had been trying to photograph the feeding frenzy that develops when sardines and herrings migrate off South Africa's Wild Coast. His luck finally changed in clear water a few miles off Port St Johns. 'Activity was intense, with dolphins herding the fish into a ball from below, while Cape gannets rained down from above,' says Jean. 'In this picture, the gannet is desperately trying to swallow a herring as a gang of cormorants gives chase.'

13 Friday

Received magazine from Z.S.L., and Museum Selection magazine. Ordered two books from Museum Selection.

14 Saturday

Received two Puzzler Magazines, and a thank-you letter from W.A.P..
Charged M. Scooter.

15 Sunday

Did some shopping.

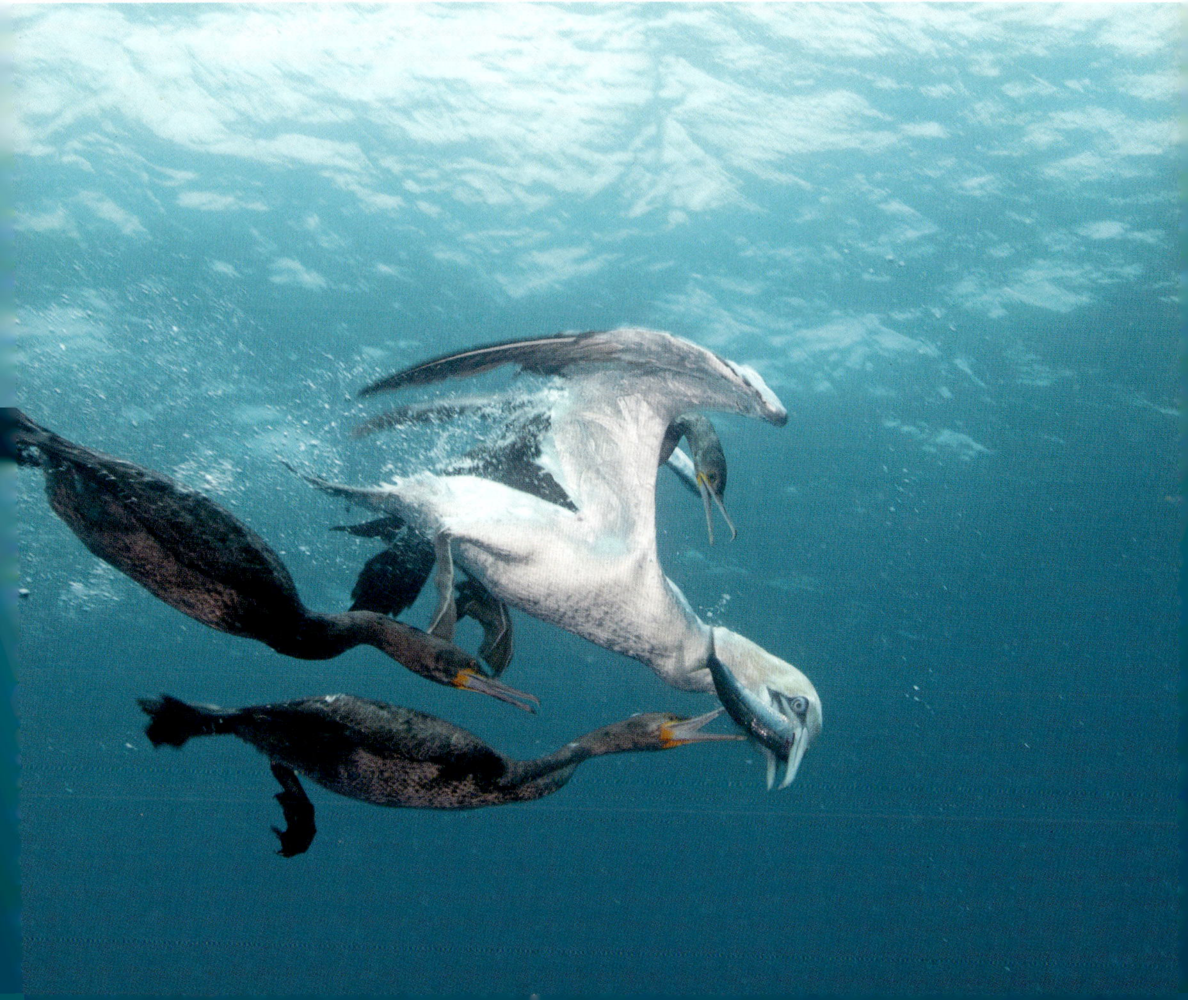

16 Monday

Received a letter from W. A. P., thanking me for buying raffle tickets.

17 Tuesday

18 Wednesday

Received four books from Museum Collection. Also received 2 tea-towels from M. Collection; a telephone bill; and an invitation from D. W. C. T., to attend the Durrell Lecture.

19 Thursday

Diwali (Hindu, Sikh)
New moon ●

Charged M. Scooter. Ordered some medication.

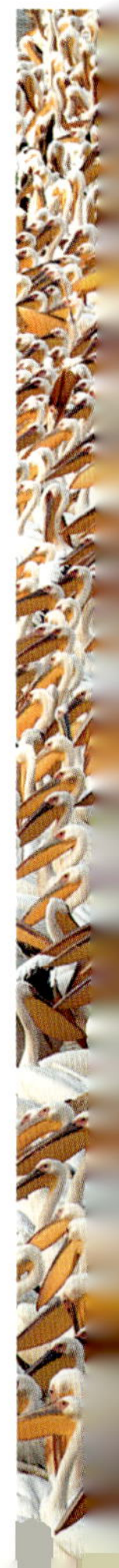

Feeding of the five thousand

by Yossi Eshbol

Each autumn, thousands of great white pelicans on migration from Europe to Africa rest and refuel in Israel. The fishponds at Ma'ayan Zvi in northern Israel are a favourite meal stop. The pelicans usually stay a few days at the most, but on this occasion, much to the fishery keepers' chagrin, 5,000 of them stayed a whole month. A lot of expensive fish were eaten, and the pond guards had their work cut out trying to chase the pelicans away.

20 Friday

Received literature from British Red Cross, and Freedom From Torture. Ordered book and diary from Nat. His. Mus. Did some shopping. Posted reply to D.W.C.T.

21 Saturday

Received a new Nat. West Bank Book; R.S.P.B. Magazine for Winter; another Owl Barn Mag.

22 Sunday

Posted donation to F.F. Torture. Did some shopping. Serena's Mum thanked me for the post cards.

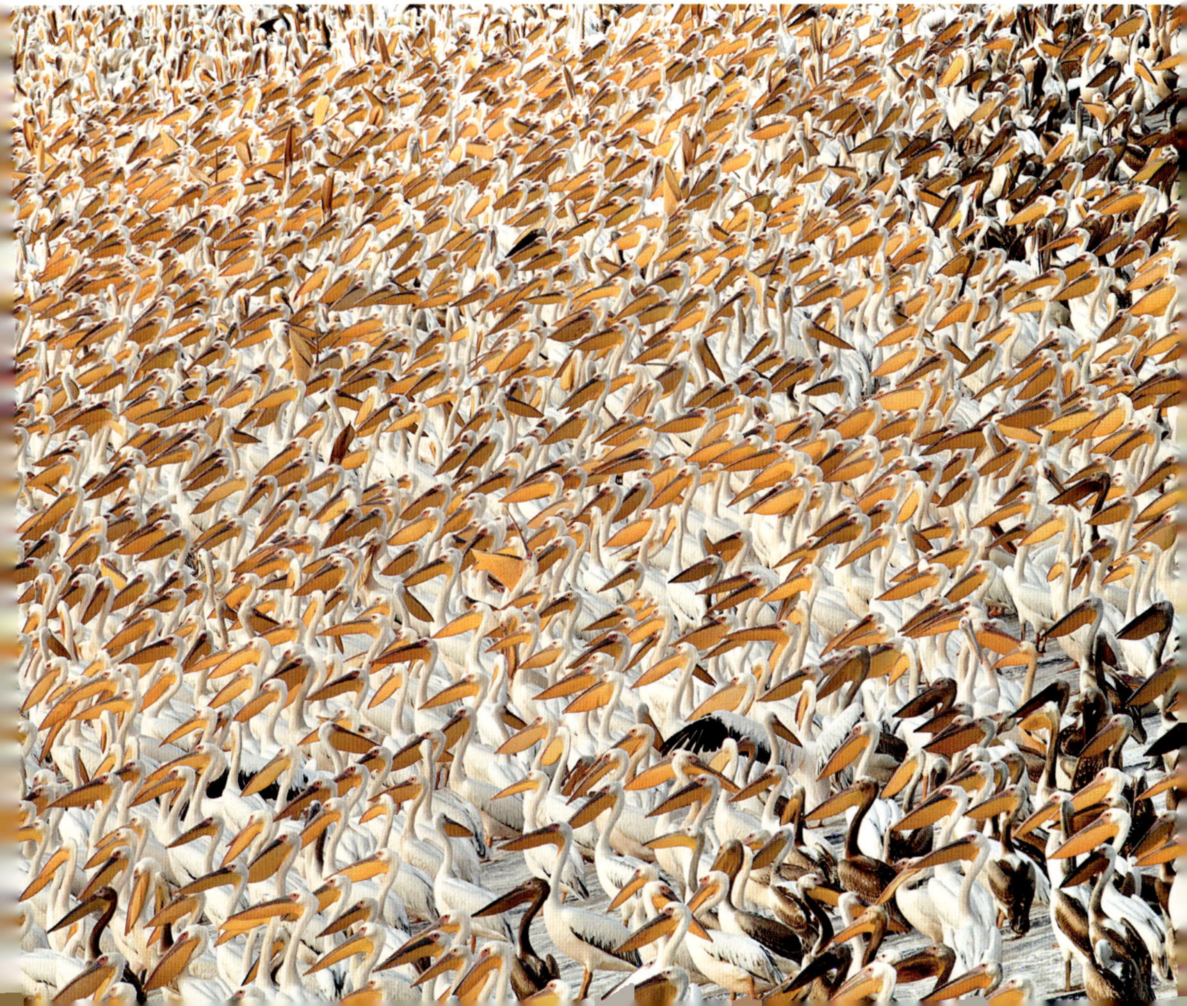

October

23 Monday

Labour Day (New Zealand)

My hot water and radiators are not working. Rang Folio Society. My order should arrive today. Julian came and fixed my boiler. Folio books did not arrive.

24 Tuesday

Received Wildlife Photographer Of The Year - NO 27, and 2018 diary from Nat. H.S. Mins and agenda for A.G.M. from Ethical Society. Folio Society say they tried to deliver order yesterday and will redeliver tomorrow.

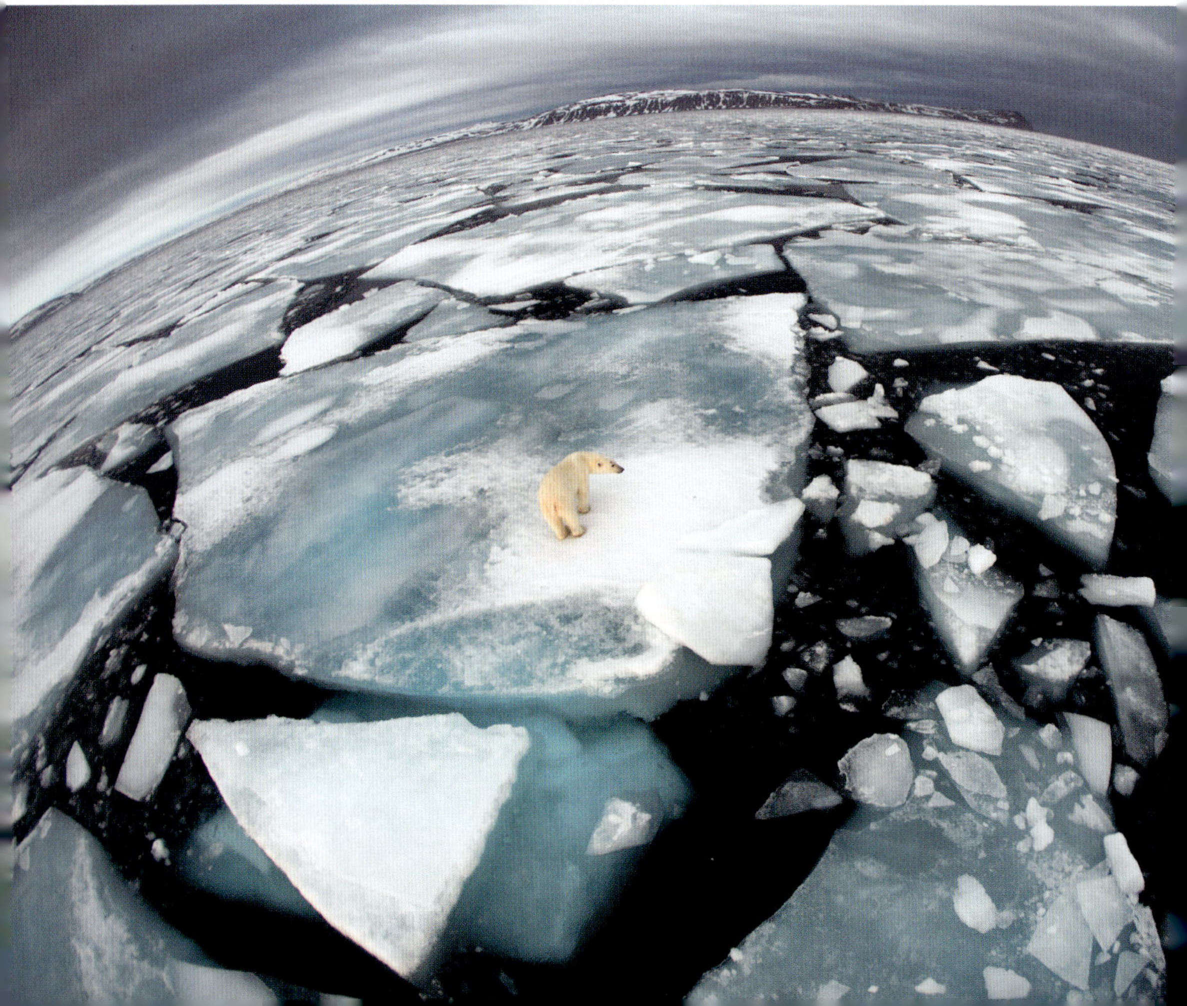

25 Wednesday

Received Fellows' News, from the R.S.P.B. Charged M. Scooter. Folio books have still not come. Posted donations to R.S.P.B. and B. Red Cross. Did a little shopping.

26 Thursday

Rang Folio Soc. They are going to send my order tomorrow. Received raffle tickets from Butterfly Conservation. Charged my M. Scooter. Collected medication. Did some shopping. Folio order arrived while I was out. Rang Folio I am to ~~order~~ refuse tomorrow.

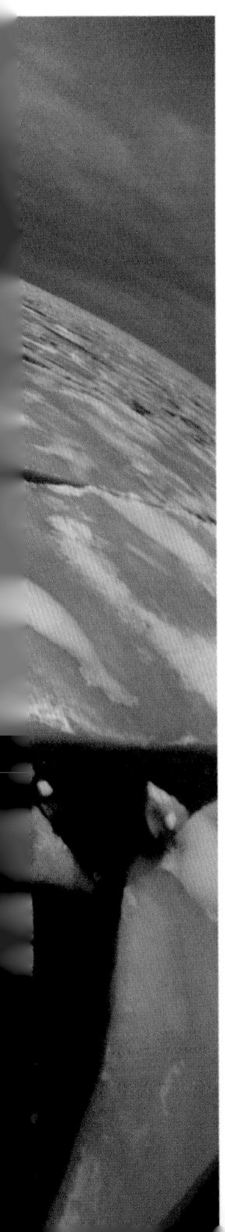

27 Friday

Received from Folio Soc. details of books from other publishers, and the R.S.P.B Annual Review. Ordered 5 books from Folio Society. It is 24 years ago today since dad died.

28 Saturday

Received literature from the Orangutan F. I am mentioned as a donor.

29 Sunday

British Summertime ends, clocks go back

Ice matters

by Anna Henly

Anna was on a boat in Svalbard – an archipelago midway between mainland Norway and the North Pole. It was October, and around four in the morning when she spotted this polar bear walking on broken-up ice floes, tentatively, not quite sure where to trust its weight. Polar bears rely almost entirely on the marine sea ice environment for their survival, and year by year, increasing temperatures are reducing the amount of ice cover and the amount of time available for the bears to hunt marine mammals.

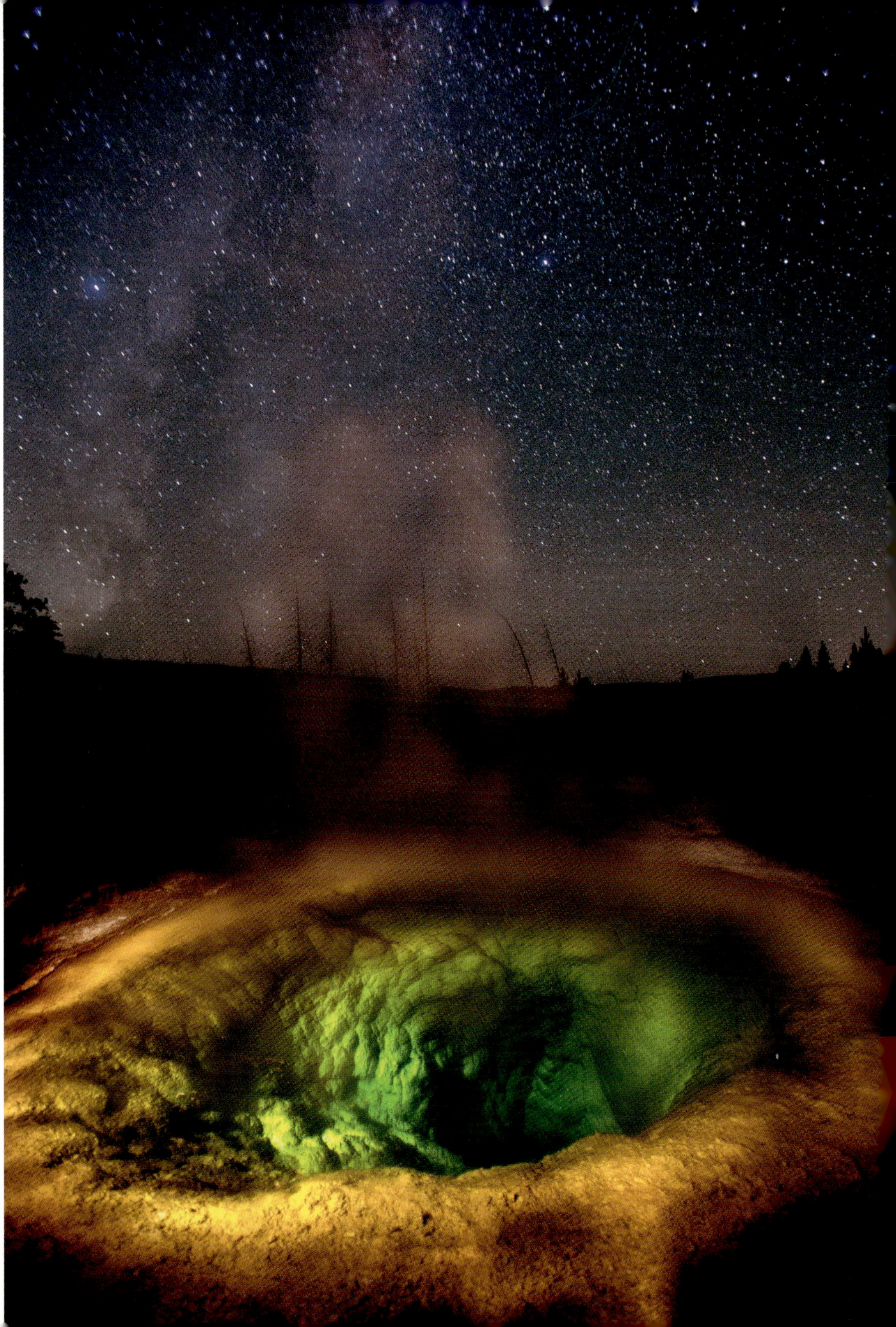

Tuesday – Rang bookcase shop. They should receive b. case on Friday.
3 Fri – charged M. Scooter

30 Monday

October holiday (Republic of Ireland)

Received lit. from W.A.P. Charged M. Scooter. Posted raffle stubs to Butterfly Conservation. Did a little shopping

31 Tuesday

Halloween

Received literature from the Donkey Sanctuary; literature, including A.G.M. agenda from N.S.S.; calendar, xmas cards and book from Galapagos Conservation Trust.

1 Wednesday

All Saints' Day (Christian)

Received news from D.W.C.T. about my adopted hornbill

2 Thursday

Received, from D.W.C.T., a thank you letter for donation, and information about a ring-tailed lemur. Pauline invited me to a bonfire party on Sunday.

3 Friday

The bookcase people rang. My case should arrive tomorrow evening. It is 21 years ago today since I arrived in Madagascar. Received order from Folio Society.

4 Saturday

Full moon ○

Posted a donation to the Donkey Sanctuary. Did some shopping. New bookshelves delivered this evening.

5 Sunday

Guy Fawkes night

Moved old bookshelves nearer to the kitchen. Went to bonfire party next door

Morning Glory by night

by Robert Sinclair

Some seven metres in diameter, the thermal Morning Glory Pool in Yellowstone National Park, USA, is home to thermophilic bacteria that thrive in the heat and give the pool its extraordinary colours. To capture the scene in a new and dramatic way, Robert waited for a warm autumn night and then carefully positioned two flashlights to illuminate the details of the inner walls beneath the star-filled sky.

6 Monday

Placed new bookshelf into place.
Put books into shelves.

7 Tuesday

Received literature from the Mary Ann Evans Hospice; and notification to renew my adoptions at D.W.C.T. Charged my M. Scooter.

8 Wednesday

Posted donation to Mary Ann Evans Hospice; and payment for renewal of D.W.C.T. adoptions. Collected some medica[tion] and did some shopping.

9 Thursday

Received news of my adopted Radiated Tortoise, and blue poison-dart frog at D.W.C.T., and a cheque from Aviva and literature from L.A.C.S. Posted donation to L.A.C.S., and did some shopping.

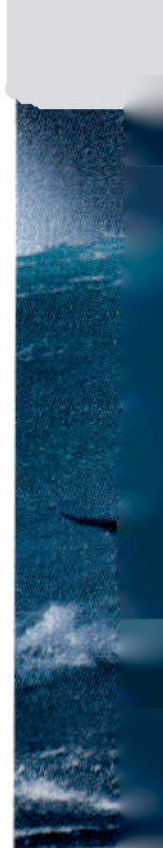

Surfing delight

by Wim van den Heever

Wim began to regret setting out in such a small boat that day. The heavy swell off Port St Johns, South Africa made it a challenge to balance. 'I had to concentrate hard', Wim says, 'on keeping the dolphins in the viewfinder while not falling out of the boat.' But the moment the mass of bottlenose dolphins exploded in unison, he knew it was all worth it. The perfect backdrop for such a serendipitous moment was the backlit curtain of sparkling spray.

10 Friday

11 Saturday

Armistice Day

Received literature from Butterfly Conservation and B. Red Cross; and two Nat. West Bank statements.

12 Sunday

Remembrance Sunday (UK)

Charged my M. Scooter

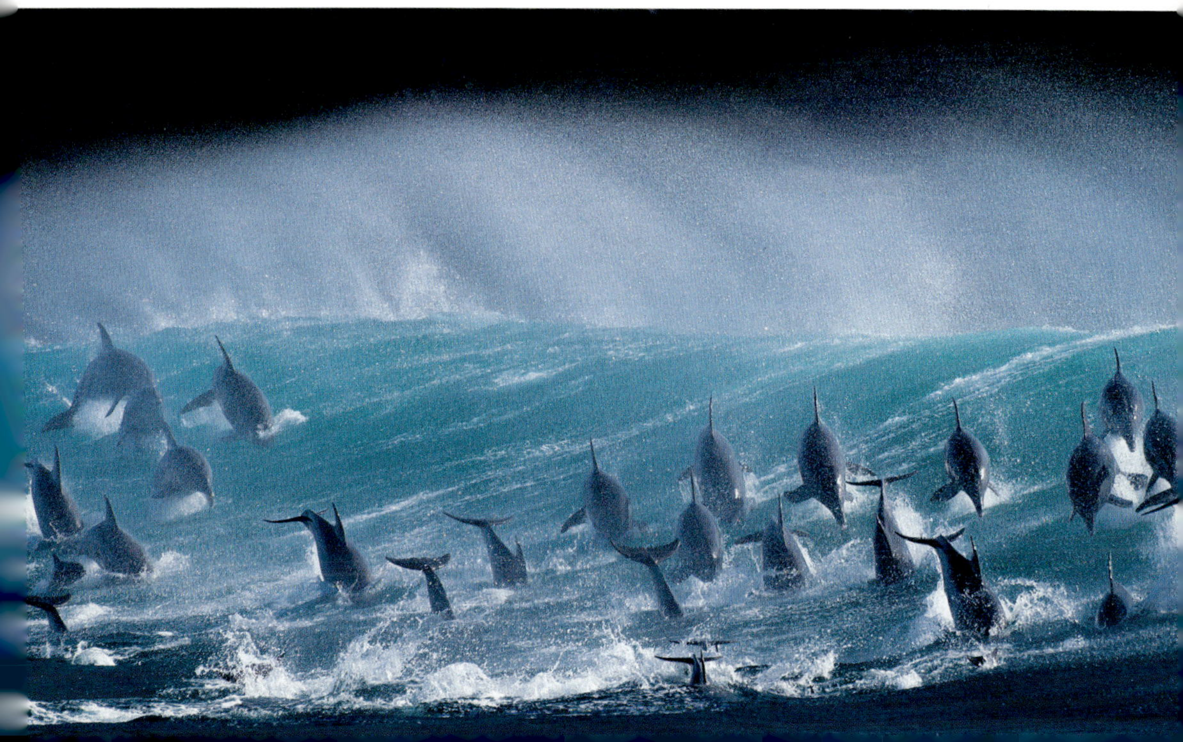

13 Monday

Ordered some more books from Folio Society. Did some shopping. Received two Puzzle Magazines, an Owl Barn Magazine, and a Museum Selection Magazine. Ordered more medication.

14 Tuesday

Had my hair cut. Did a little shoppin

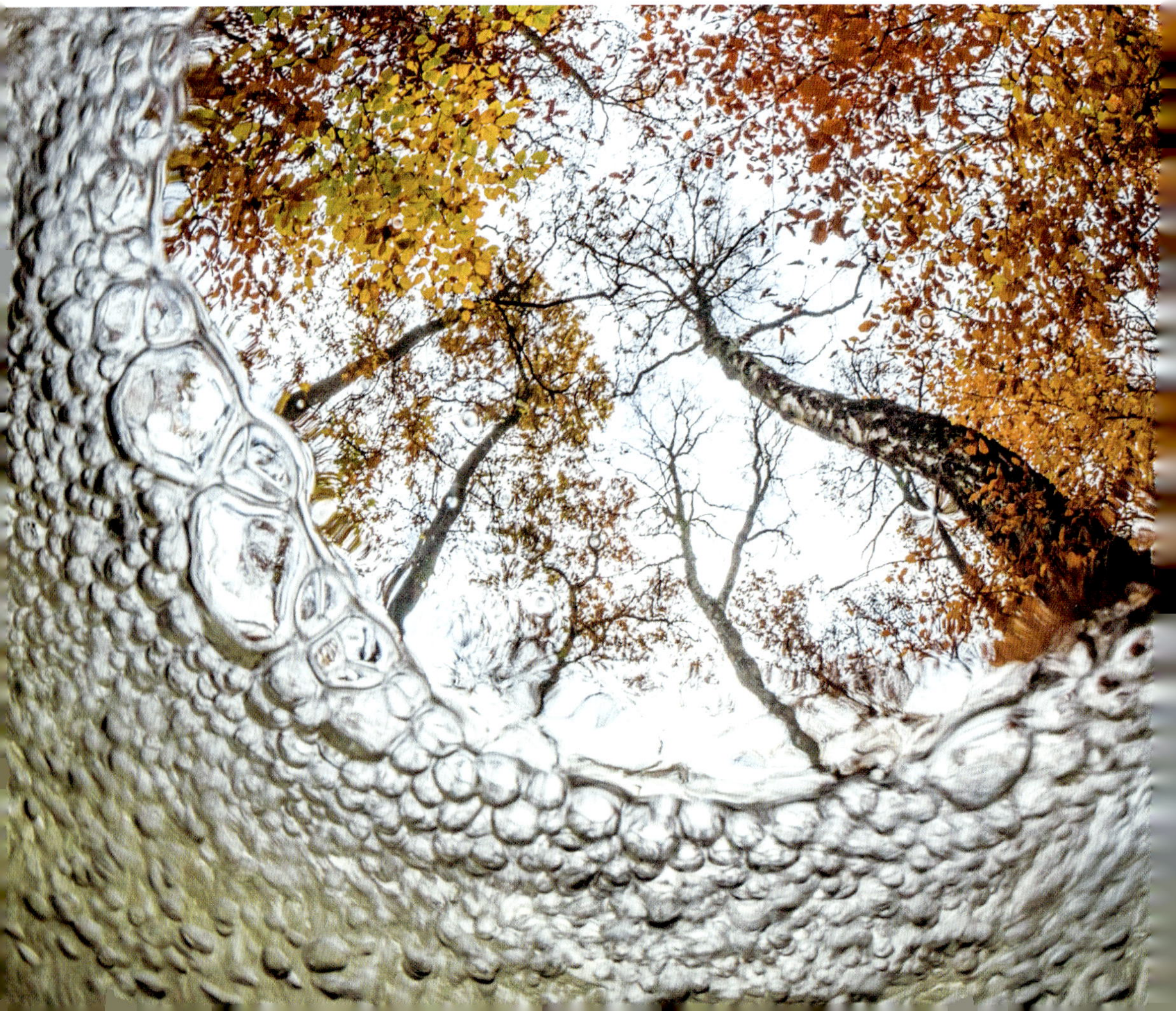

18th Posted donations to ~~L.A.C.S.~~, Freedom From Torture, and G.al. Con. Tru and B. Red Cross.

15 Wednesday

Received literature from Freedom From Torture.

16 Thursday

Washed some clothes.

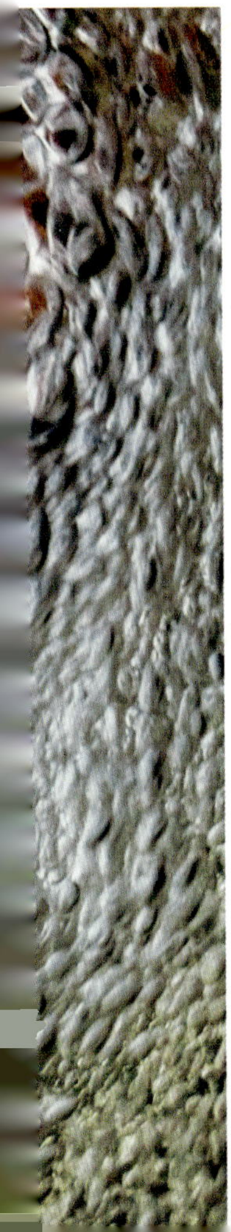

17 Friday

Received literature from G.C.T.; a telephone bill; the New Humanist; a thank-you letter from ZSL for renewing; and literature from the Folio society. Received box of books from Folio Society. Charged my M Scooter.

18 Saturday

New moon ●

Collected medication. Did some shopping. Received two lots of lit from D.W.C.T., lit from L.A.C.S., and the Gorilla Organization.

19 Sunday

Fish-eye view

by Theo Bosboom

Miniature, underwater landscapes fascinate Theo, particularly ones in fast-flowing streams and brooks. On the day he took this picture, he was experimenting with effects under a small waterfall in a brook near his home in the Netherlands. Kneeling in waders and holding his camera under water, he shot looking up through the effervescent surface below the fall, using the bubbles to frame the scene of autumn trees. 'I love taking pictures that show a fresh perspective on nature,' says Theo.

20 Monday

Received an RSPB catalogue, and an appeal from Kew Gardens. Charged M. Scooter

21 Tuesday

Posted donation to Gorilla Organizatio[n] and to Kew Fund. Did some shopping.

22 Wednesday

Received a 'phone call from the Folio Society. Rang Norman Bocvac. He will take me to the N.S.S. A.G.M. Told me that Beaty has died

23 Thursday

Thanksgiving (USA)

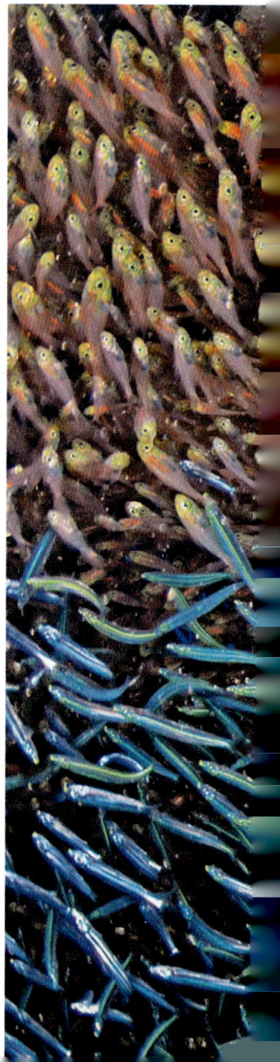

Lionfish bait

by Alex Tattersall

The wreck of the SS *Thistlegorm* has lain in the Red Sea at the southern tip of the Sinai Peninsula since 1941. She now attracts many thousands of divers each year, and a host of fishes. In one of the huge holds, Alex discovered more than 20 common lionfish, attracted by a copious supply of prey. Here a lionfish is attacking a huge shoal of silversides and cardinalfish swirling in a huge baitball. 'The synchrony was mesmerising,' says Alex.

24 Friday

Received another Culture Vulture direct magazine. Still can't book return ticket from Paignton. Rang Blue Waters Lodge, and Jean London.

25 Saturday

Norman Balrac took me to C. Hall, to the N.S.S. A.G.M..

26 Sunday

Charged M. Scooter Did some shopping.

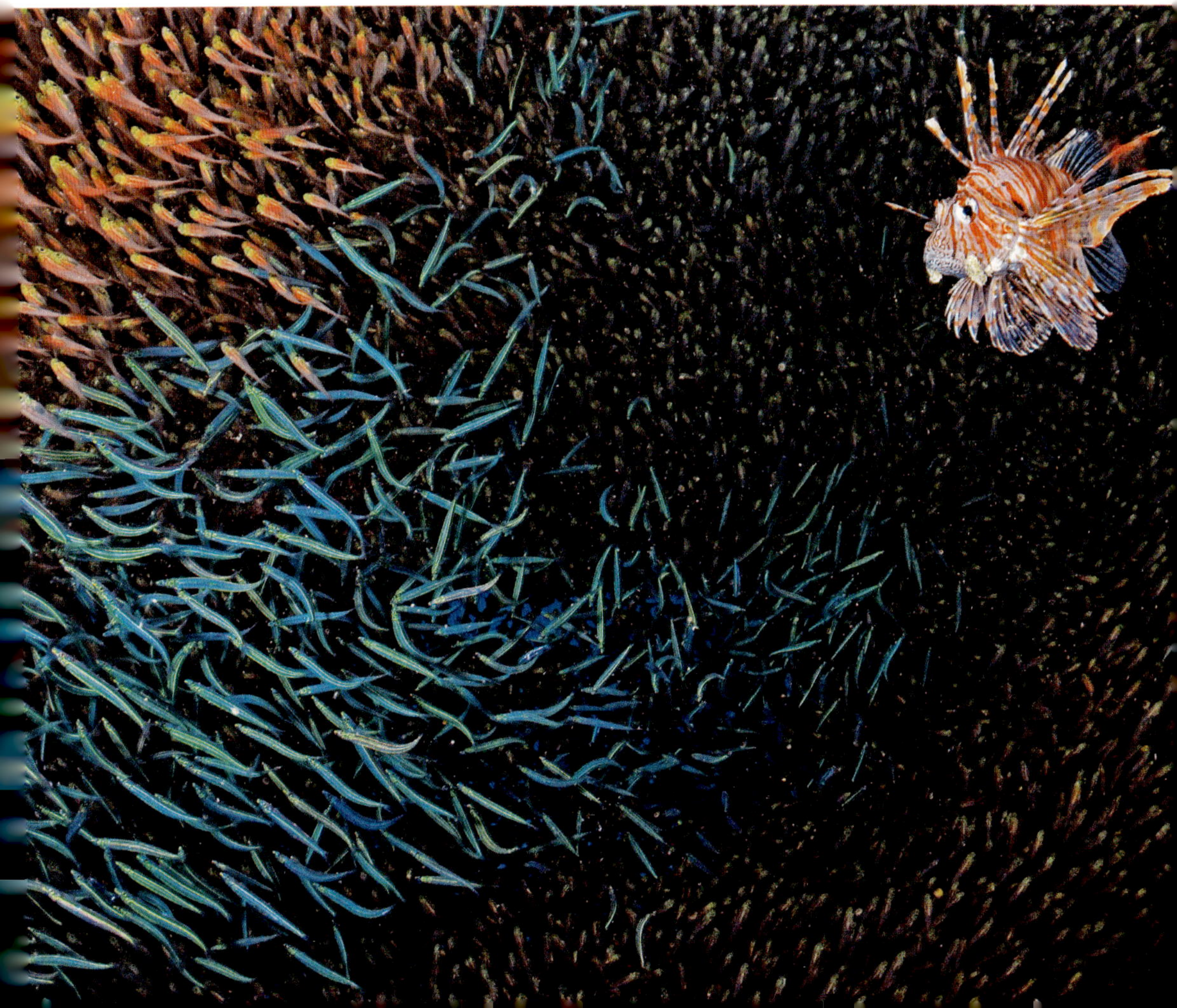

November – December WEEK 49

27 Monday

Received appeals from D.I.D; HUMANISTS U.K; and World Animal Protection. Charged M.Scoot Collected medication. Posted donations to Huma U.K. Did some shopping. Rang Wild Sounds. next book is due in January.

28 Tuesday

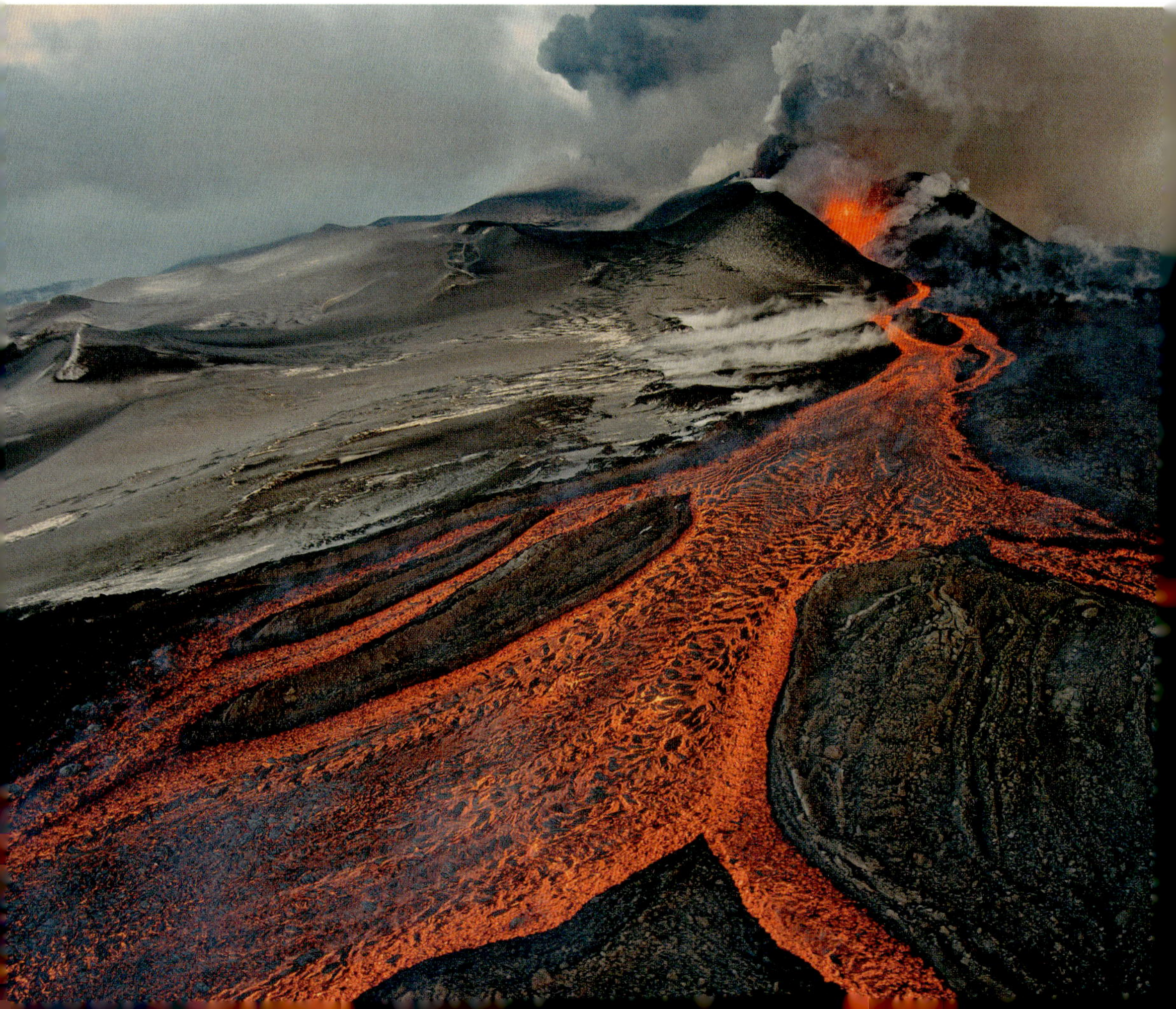

2ND Saturday – my kichen kettle has stopped working.

29 Wednesday

Charged M. Scooter. Received renewal forms for scooter, and literature from the Orangutan Foundation. Did some shopping. Collected medication.

30 Thursday

St Andrew's Day, holiday (Scotland)

Received advertising literature from the R.S.P.B.

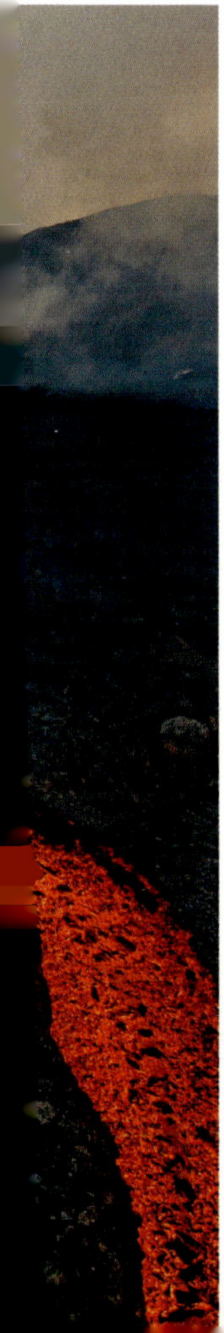

1 Friday

Finally managed to book return ticket from Paignton. Rang Collin at Blue Waters Lodge

2 Saturday

Received tickets to return from Paignton; a thank you letter from the Gorilla Organization; and an Owl Barn Magazine.

3 Sunday

Full moon ○

Charged M. Scooter. Began Packing

The cauldron

by Sergey Gorshkov

On 29 November 2012, Plosky Tolbachik – one of two volcanoes in the Tolbachik volcanic plateau in central Kamchatka, Russia – erupted after 36 years. 'So I dropped everything and went,' said Sergey. The only way to approach it was by helicopter. As gusts of hot air buffeted the helicopter, Sergey worked fast, strapped to the open door. 'I just kept shooting ... knowing I had this one chance, hoping that I'd take one image that might do justice to what I was witnessing.'

4 Monday

Received a Museum Selection Magazine. Posted a donation to F. F. Torture. Bought a new electric kettle. Put £20-00 on my mobile phone. Did some shopping.

5 Tuesday

Received information from British Telecom. Ordered two books from Museum Selection.

6 Wednesday

Received a Puzzler Magazine, and A Xmas Card. Did a little shopping. Wrote Xmas Cards. Rang. M. Greenleaf.

7 Thursday

Received another Puzzler Magazine, and a Xmas card, and a letter from the N. S. S. charged M. Scooter.

Arrangement of swans

by Stefano Unterthiner

Stefano spent six weeks at Lake Kussharo, in Hokkaido, Japan, before he found the perfect conditions to portray the winter gathering of whooper swans. 'I wanted the swans to look as though they'd been "painted" on top of the snow,' says Stefano. One night, wind swept the snow across the surface of the frozen lake. The resulting snow crust was so hard that, though the 150 or so swans had walked all over it, their footprints could barely be seen.

8 Friday

Received another cheque from AVIVA, and literature from Folio Society. Posted donation to N.S.S. and cheque to holiday Insurance, and calendar to Margaret Greenleaf. Went to Rushmoor School Xmas fair, but didn't buy anything. Gave Folio Diary to Linda Brewer.

9 Saturday

Received a Xmas card from Ann and Michael Davison.

10 Sunday

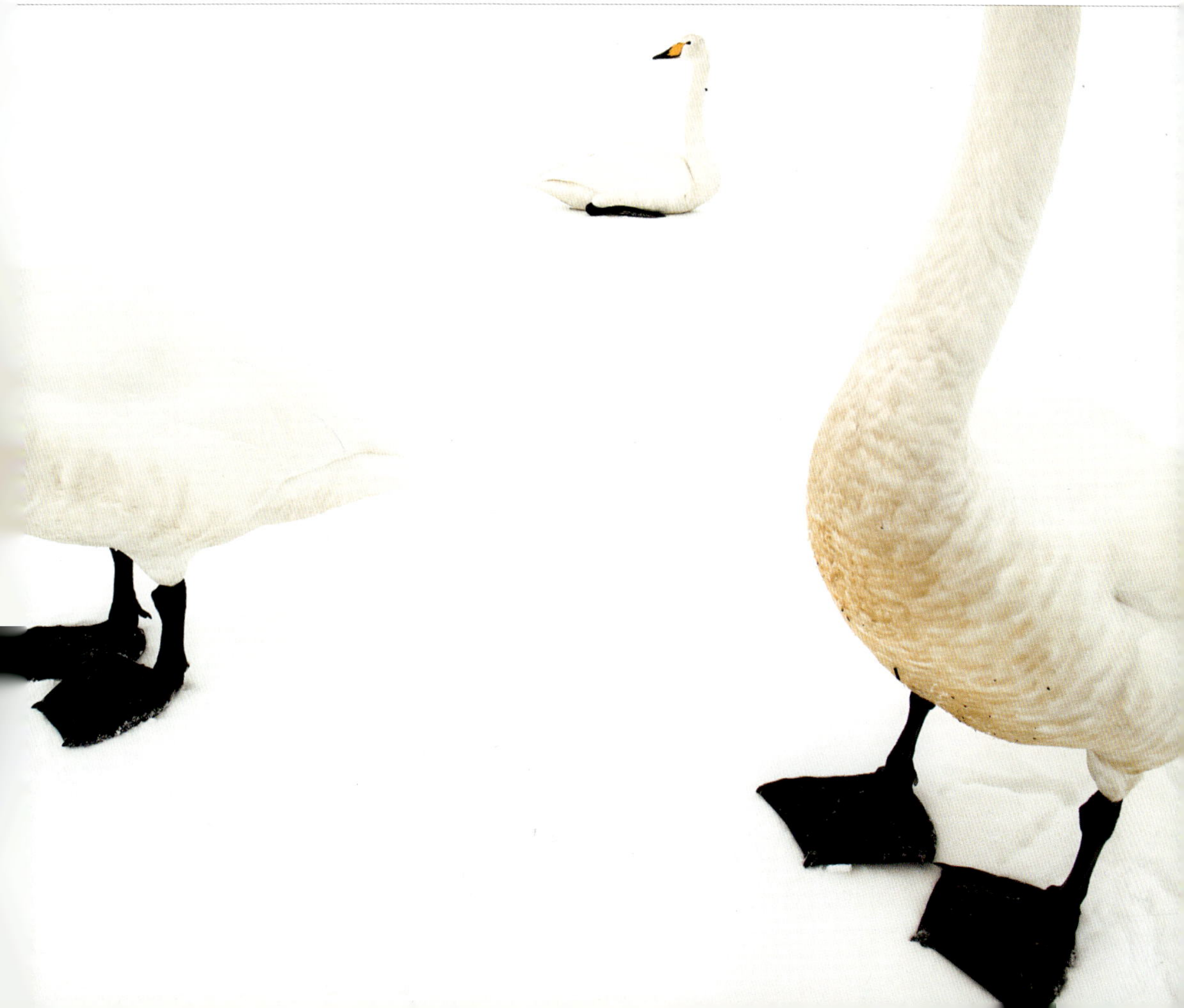

Monday – posted all X mas cards. Ordered more medication. Did some shopping.

11 Monday

Received two Nat. West Bank Statements; a card and gift voucher from J. and B. Reynolds; and a calendar and x mas card from Margaret G. Received two books by L. da Vinci, plus mags. from Museum selection.

12 Tuesday

Hanukkah (at sunset), Festival of Lights begins (Jewish)

Received a x mas card from Kew Gardens and a thank you letter from Humanists U. Rang Shaldon Zoo, but Nick Dunn is in Brazil. He will be back on Thursday. Part of my curtain rail has fallen

13 Wednesday

Collected medication.

14 Thursday

Received x mas cards from the R.S.P.B., and John and Jennifer, and a Shavian Magazine. Rang Shaldon Zoo, but Nick Dunn is busy today.

Squabbling jays

by Liina Heikkinen

It was winter in Kouvola, Finland, and Liina set off with her father to their hide to take pictures of birds. 'It was still completely dark,' she says, but soon the early morning light revealed a group of around six jays close by. 'There was a lot of squabbling.' This was her favourite shot because of the angle of the birds and the way their feathers are spread apart. The low light also helped bring out their beautiful colours.

Saturday – Charged M. Scooter.
Rang Mary. Told her about Shaldon Zoo.
Rang Stephen Norley. His mother has cancer.

15 Friday

Received Humanists UK NEWS, for December. Donated to Humanists U.K. Made enquiries about organ donation.

16 Saturday

Received a telephone bill; Insurance literature, and a Xmas card from Mary and Jim. Julian invited me to go round tomorrow.

17 Sunday

Did a little shopping. Went next door. Was given presents and a card.

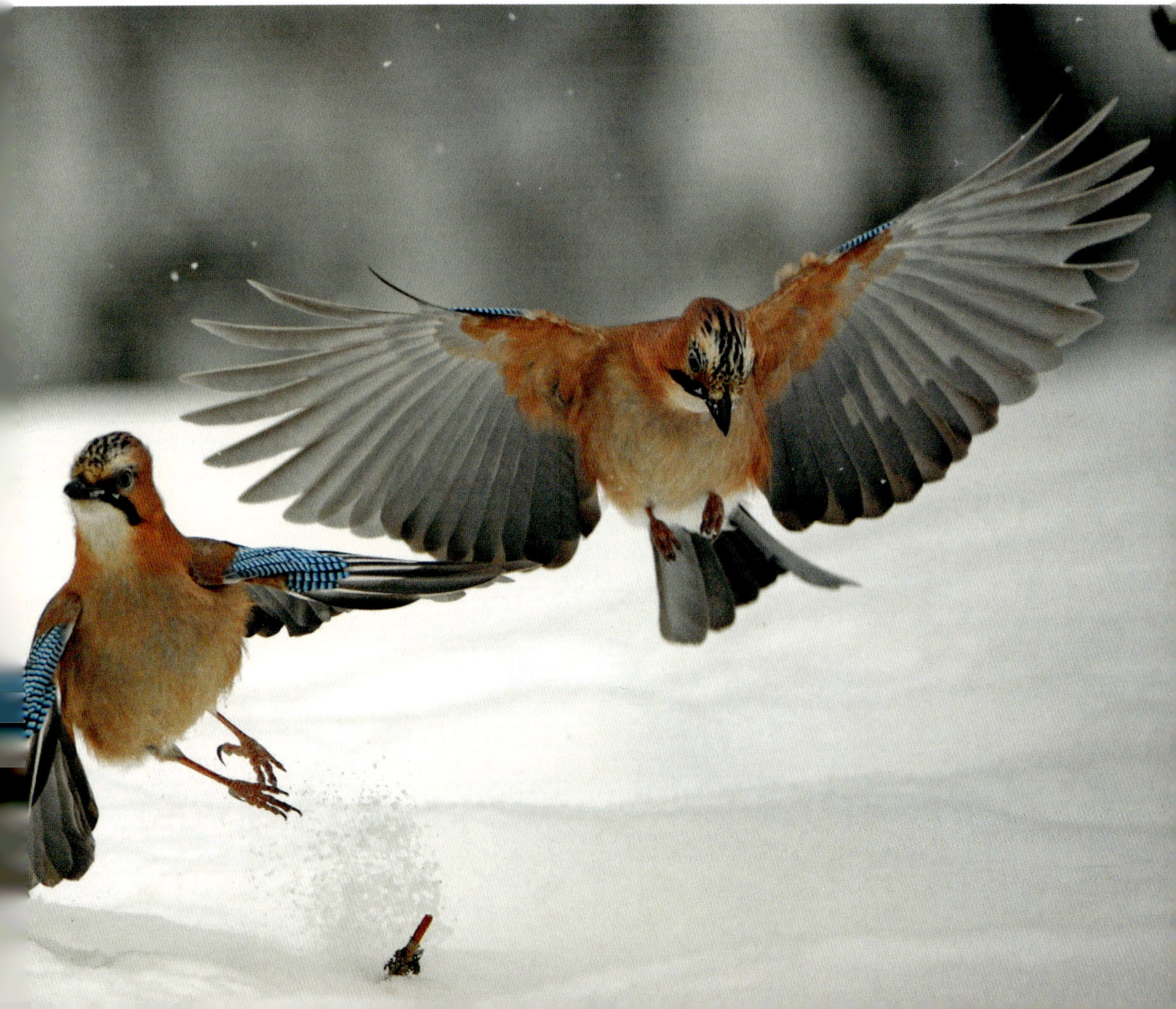

December

WEEK 52

18 Monday

New moon ●

Finished Packing. Booked taxi for Tomorrow. Received a letter from D.W.C.T., outlining their aims for the future and information about body donation.

19 Tuesday

Travelled to Paignton, and to Blue Waters Lodge.

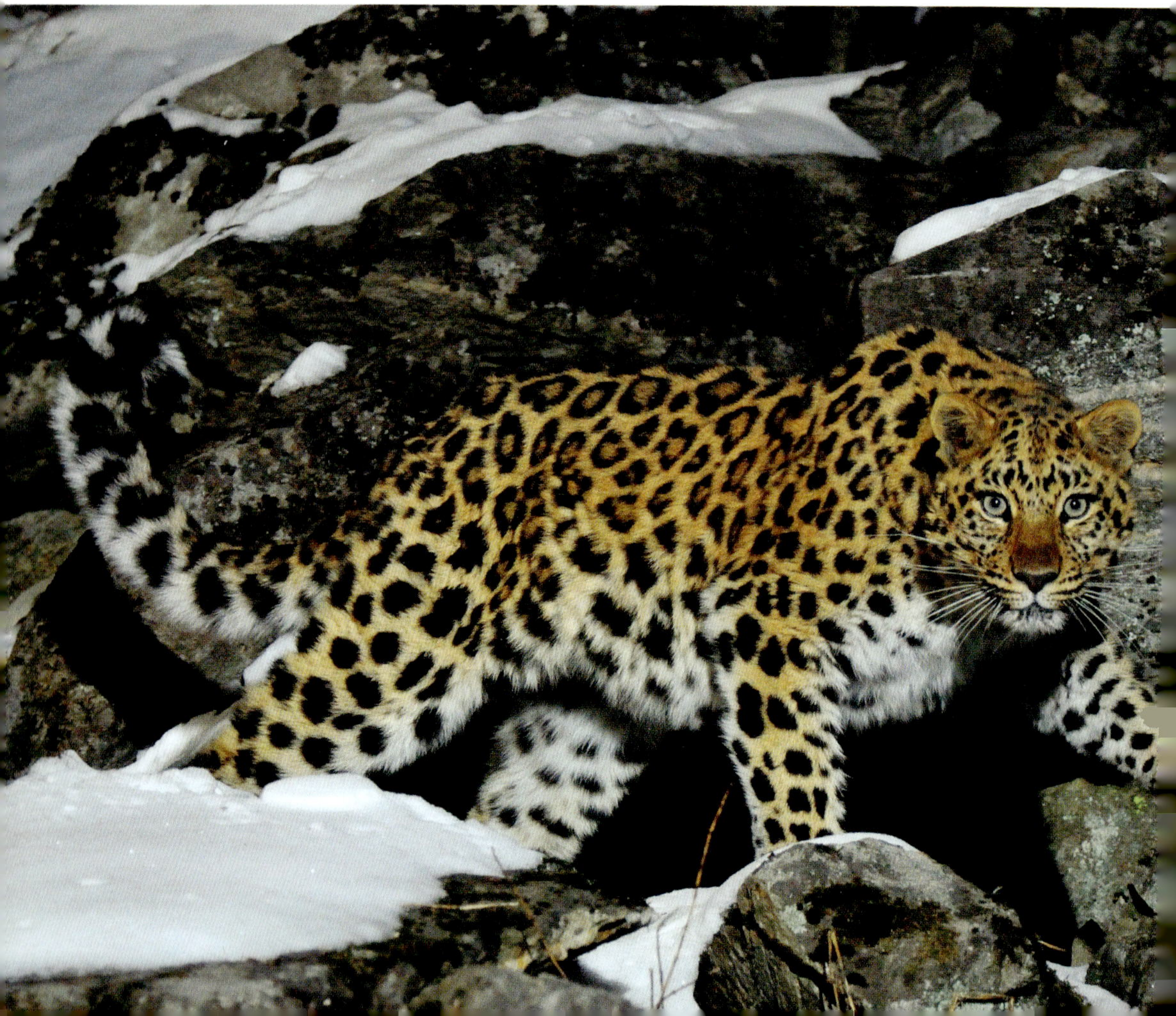

20 Wednesday

Hanukkah, Festival of Lights ends (Jewish)

Posted card to Susan, and donation to B. Red Cross. Banked 3 cheques, and changed 4 old £1-00 coins. Had foot treatment and bought foot cream. Bought second-hand book by Bill Bryson. Booked scooter for P. Zoo for tomorrow. Bought a flannel.

21 Thursday

Winter Solstice

Went to Paignton Zoo. Rang Shaldon Zoo, but no response.

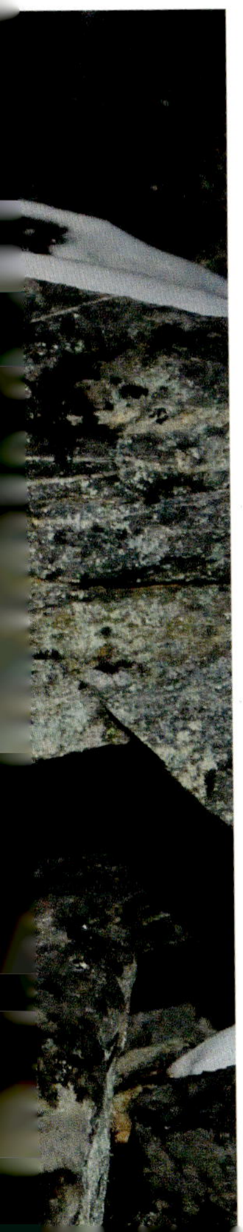

22 Friday

Bought a book, "Africa", from a charity shop, for 50P.

23 Saturday

Bought another book from charity shop. "Himalaya", for 50P.

24 Sunday

Christmas Eve (Christian)

Last look

by Vladimir Medvedev

Vladimir has spent many years in Kedrovaya Pad Nature Reserve in the Russian Far East tracking Amur leopards. He became familiar with the territory of this female (one of only about 40 leopards remaining) and built a hide in a tree overlooking a regularly used path. Two months of waiting were worth it. 'I'll never forget looking into the leopard's eyes only a few metres away,' says Vladimir. 'To let this leopard go extinct in the wild would be an unthinkable tragedy.'

25 Monday

Christmas Day, holiday (Christian)

Present from Julian and Pauline – a British Wildlife Calendar. Received chocolates and card from Colin and Jackie. Had a nasty turn at breakfast. Had lunch at Inn On the Green.

26 Tuesday

Boxing Day, holiday (Christian)

Attended a pantomime at the theatre and had dinner at Inn On the Green.

27 Wednesday

Had my hair cut. Posted five post cards. Dined at the Spinning Wheel. Booked a scooter at P. Zoo for tomorrow. Rang Nick Dunn. I will probably not be able to go to Shaldon Zoo.

28 Thursday

Went to Paignton Zoo again.

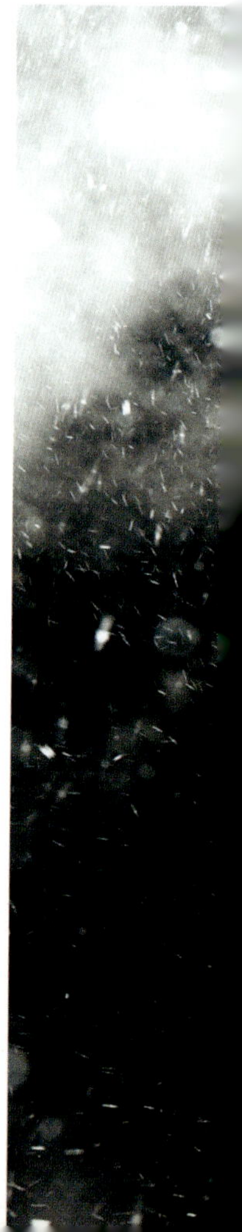

Snow moment

by Jasper Doest

When photographing the famous Japanese macaques around the hotsprings of Jigokudani, central Japan, Jasper had become fascinated by the surreal effects created by the arrival of a blast of cold wind. If it was snowing, the result would be a mesmerising pattern of swirling steam and snowflakes, which would whirl around any macaques warming up in the pools. But capturing the moment required total luck – for Jasper to be there when the wind blew and for the monkeys to be in the pool.

Sunday – A tree has fallen in the lion enclosure.

29 Friday

30 Saturday

Drew some more money from Nat. West Bank. Booked a M. Scooter for tomorrow at P. Zoo. Bought some talc.

31 Sunday

New Year's Eve
Hogmanay (Scotland)

Went to P. Zoo. Renewed memberships. Bought a book, "Life Story".

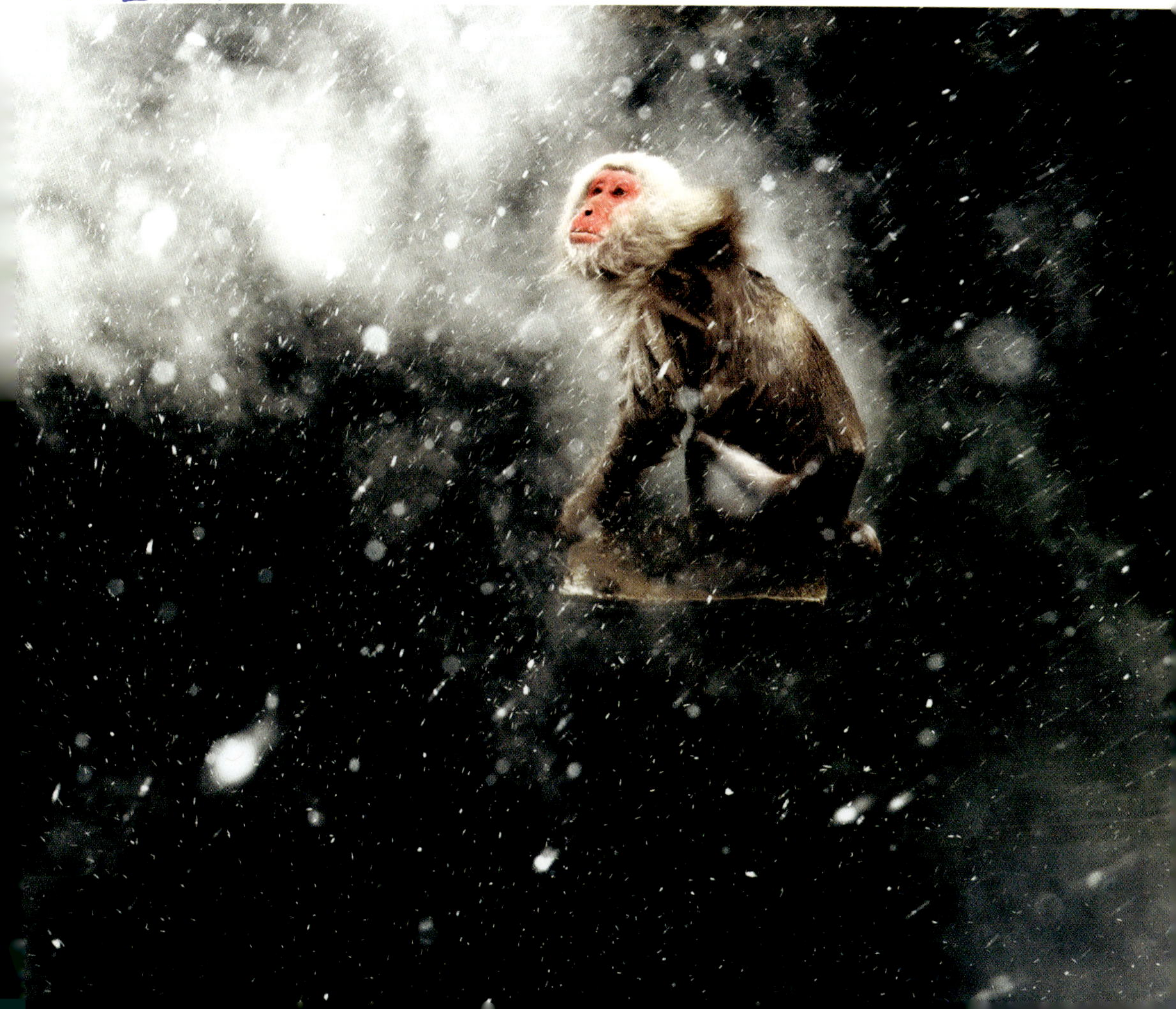

Index of photographers

Week 3
Ice aurora
Ellen Anon
USA
ellenanon@mac.com
Canon EOS 5D Mark III + 14mm f2.8 II lens; 36.2 sec at f3.5; ISO 1600; Gitzo GT2531 tripod + Really Right Stuff ballhead.

Week 15
Grand raven
Chris Aydlett
USA
aydlettphoto@gmail.com
www.chrisaydlett.com
Nikon D1X + 15-30mm f3.5 lens; 1/90 sec at f22; ISO 320.

Week 25
Flowerbow
Olar Barndõk
Estonia
olar.barndok@gmail.com
Canon EOS 5D Mark II + Canon TS-E 24mm f3.5 II lens; 1/200 sec at f11; ISO 100; Velbon tripod; Jue Ying wireless shutter remote.

Week 20
Simplicity
Valter Binotto
Italy
binoval@alice.it
Nikon D300 + Meyer Gorlitz Trioplan 100mm f2.8 lens; 1/1600 sec at f2.8; ISO 160; Gitzo tripod; reflecting panel.

Week 17
Battle colours
Gergely Bíró
Hungary
geryb4@yahoo.com
Canon EOS 5D Mark III + 300mm f2.8 lens + 1.4x III extender; 1/1250 sec at f7.1; ISO 3200.

Week 47
Fish-eye view
Theo Bosboom
The Netherlands
info@theobosboom.nl
Canon EOS 5D3 + 8-15mm f4 lens; 1/100 sec at f22; ISO 1600; Nauticam housing.

Week 11
Eye of a toad
Lukasz Bozycki
Poland
kontakt@bozycki.pl
www.bozycki.com
Nikon D80 + 70-300mm f4.5-5.6 lens + extension tube; 1/125 sec at f9 (-2.3 e/v); ISO 100; built-in flash.

Week 28
The shy crocodile
Jordi Chias Pujol
Spain
jordi@uwaterphoto.com
Canon 5D Mark II + 15mm f2.8 lens; 1/60 sec at f11; ISO 100; custom-built housing; x2 INON strobes.

Week 35
The golden hour
Lou Coetzer
South Africa
lou@cnpsafaris.com
Nikon D4 + 600mm f4 lens + 1.4x teleconverter; 1/4000 sec at f8 (-1.7 e/v); ISO 800.

Week 53
Snow moment
Jasper Doest
The Netherlands
info@jasperdoest.com
Nikon D4 + 24-70mm f2.8 lens at 55mm + polarising filter; 1/100 sec at f11; ISO 1600; Nikon SB-800 flash.

Week 43
Feeding of the five thousand
Yossi Eshbol
Israel
yossi.eshbol@gmail.com
Nikon D3 + 600mm f4 lens; 1/200 sec at f18 (-1.3 e/v); ISO 640; Gitzo tripod.

Week 36
The magical kokerbooms
Uge Fuertes Sanz
Spain
chavaldelapetra@hotmail.com
Canon 7D + Tokina 12-24mm f4 lens; 95 sec at f4; ISO 320; Manfrotto tripod; Tank007 TK-737 torch.

Week 9
The enchantment
Adam Gibbs
UK/ Canada
adam_gibbs@icloud.com
Nikon D800 + 24-120mm f4 lens at 50mm; 1/3 sec at f16; ISO 100.

Week 22
The duel
Sergey Gorshkov
Russia
gsvl@mail.ru
Nikon D300S + 600mm f4 lens; 1/2000 sec at f5; ISO 640; Gitzo tripod.

Week 49
The cauldron
Sergey Gorshkov
Nikon D4 + 16-35mm f4 lens; 1/40 sec at f8; ISO 800.

Week 2
Great tit poised
Corentin Graillot Denaix
France
corentin.graillot.denaix@wanadoo.fr
www.naturels-declics.com
Canon EOS 40D + 300mm f4 lens + 1.4x extender; 1/500 sec at f7.1; ISO 400; tripod; hide.

Week 16
Land of fire and ice
Erlend Haarberg
Norway
erlehaar@frisurf.no
Nikon D700 + 500mm f4 lens; 1/160 sec at f7.1; ISO 200; Gitzo tripod.

Week 30
The encirclement
Thomas Haider
Austria
office@thomashaider.at
Nikon D300 + Tokina 10-17mm f3.5-4.5 lens at 10mm; 1/60 sec at f8; Subal housing + domeport; 2x Subtronic Nova strobes.

Week 51
Squabbling jays
Liina Heikkinen
Finland
liina.heikkinen@hotmail.com
Nikon D700 + 200-400mm f4 lens; 1/4000 sec at f4; ISO 1000; Manfrotto tripod; hide.

Week 44
Ice matters
Anna Henly
UK
anna.photography@btinternet.com
www.annahenly.com
Facebook: Anna Henly Photography
Canon EOS 5D + 15mm f2.8 lens; 1/100 sec at f3.5; ISO 400.

Week 29
Life in the balance
Pål Hermansen
Norway
palhermansen@hotmail.com
Canon EOS 5D Mark III + 300mm lens; 1/3200 sec at f2.8; ISO 2500.

Week 21
Dive buddy
Luis Javier Sandoval
Mexico
javier_uyuyuy@yahoo.com
Nikon D7000 + 10-17mm Tokina fisheye lens at 17mm; 1/125 sec at f10; ISO 100; Sea & Sea YS-120 DUO strobes; Aquatica housing + TLC Arm Set.

Week 27
Exposed
Gerard Leeuw
The Netherlands
gmjleeuw@hotmail.com
Nikon D800E + 70-200mm f2.8 lens + cable release; 137 sec at f22; ISO 50; Gitzo tripod.

Week 40
Still reflection
Anton Lilja
Sweden
antonlilja@live.se
Nikon D2X + 300mm f2.8 lens; 1/160 at f3.5 (-1 e/v); ISO 400.

Cover & week 32
Curiosity and the cat
Hannes Lochner
South Africa
hannes@lochnerphoto.com
Nikon D3 + 16-35mm f4 lens; 1/60 sec at f16; ISO 3200; Nikon R1C1 strobe; Pocket Wizard wireless remote.

Week 1
Ice birds
eanine Lovett
USA
eanine@lovettphoto.com
Nikon D200 + 80-400mm f4.5-5.6 lens at 370mm; 1/1000 sec at f6.3; ISO 250.

Week 6
Fluff-up
John E Marriott
Canada
johnemarriott@gmail.com
Canon EOS-1D Mark IV + 500mm lens; 1/1250 sec at f7.1; ISO 1600.

Week 12
Pelican perspective
Bence Máté
Hungry
office@matebence.hu
Nikon D300S + Tokina 10-17mm f3.5-4.5 lens; 1/160 sec at f16; ISO 500; Subal housing; three linked SB-800 flashes; floating remote-control system.

Week 52
Last look
Vladimir Medvedev
Russia
vladbear@mail.primorye.ru
Nikon D300 + 80-400mm lens; 1/80 sec at f4.8; ISO 2800; 2x 6500K Xenon studio lamps.

Week 39
Gobi oasis
Alessandra Meniconzi
Switzerland
alex.photo@mac.com
Canon EOS-1Ds Mark III + 70-200mm f2.8 lens; 1/20 sec at f8; ISO 100; Giotto tripod.

Week 5
Giant with sunbeams
Alexander Mustard
UK
alex@amustard.com
Olympus OM-D E-M5 + Panasonic 8mm fisheye lens; 1/250 sec at f8; ISO 200; Nauticam housing.

Week 7
A swirl of flamingos
Klaus Nigge
Germany
klaus.nigge@t-online.de
Nikon D3 + 70-200mm f2.8 lens at 200mm; 1/1600 sec at f5.6; ISO 250.

Week 10
The greeting
Richard Packwood
UK
nantyr@btinternet.com
Nikon D3s + 500mm f4 lens + 1.4x teleconverter; 1/125 sec at f5.6; ISO 400; Gitzo tripod.

Week 38
Magic mushrooms
Agorastos Papatsanis
Greece
agorastospap@yahoo.gr
Nikon D700 + 70-200mm f2.8 lens; 1/60 sec at f2.8 (-0.3 e/v); ISO 100.

Week 18
Beavering
Louis-Marie Préau
France
photo@louismariepreau.com
www.louismariepreau.com
Canon EOS 5D + 16-35mm lens; 1/125 sec at f4; ISO 800; Ikelite housing.

Week 8
True love
Steve Race
UK
steve.race@yorkshirecoastnature.co.uk
Canon EOS-1D Mark III + 500mm f4 lens; 1/800 sec at f6.3 (+0.7 e/v); ISO 400.

Week 19
Twin hope
Diana Rebman
USA
dianarebman@aol.com
Nikon D7000 + 70-200mm f2.8 lens; 1/160 sec at f5 (-0.3 e/v); ISO 1600.

Week 31
Perilous pickings
Jenny E Ross
USA
jenny@jennyross.com
www.LifeOnThinIce.org
Canon EOS-1Ds Mark III + 100-400mm lens at 275mm; 1/800 sec at f5.6; ISO 800.

Week 14
Cold embrace
Cyril Ruoso
France
cyril.ruoso@wanadoo.fr
Canon EOS 5D + Sigma 14mm f2.8 HSM lens; 1/160 sec at f20; ISO 200; custom-made housing; Inon D2000 S + Canon 580EXII + Nikon SB-24 strobes; hide.

Week 41
Lion in the spotlight
Joel Sartore
USA
sartore@inebraska.com
Nikon D3 + 24-70mm f2.8 lens; 1/125 sec at f2.8 (-1.3 e/v); ISO 4000.

Week 24
Travelling companions
Douglas Seifert
USA
douglasseifert@mac.com
Canon EOS 5D Mark II + 16-35mm f2.8 lens; 1/200 sec at f11; ISO 640; Seacam housing; two INON z-220 strobes.

Week 45
Morning Glory by night
Robert Sinclair
USA
rob@sinclairimages.com
Canon EOS 5D Mark II + 16-35mm f2.8 lens at 16mm; 45 sec at f2.8; ISO 100; Gitzo tripod + Canon remote shutter release.

Week 37
Salmon swipe
Paul Souders
USA
paul@worldfoto.com
Canon EOS-1Ds III + 16-35mm lens; 1/250 sec at f10; modified housing; radio remote-control.

Week 26
Lucky pounce
Connor Stefanison
Canada
connor_stef@hotmail.com
Canon EOS-1D Mark IV + 500mm f4 lens at 500mm; 1/2500 sec at f8; ISO 500.

Week 23
Badger dream scene
Marc Steichen
Luxembourg
photo@marcsteichen.com
Canon EOS 5D Mark III + 300mm f2.8 lens + Meyer Gorlitz Trioplan 100mm f2.8 lens; 1/250 sec at f2.8; ISO 400; in-camera multiple exposure.

Week 48
Lionfish bait
Alex Tattersall
UK
info@uwvisions.com
Nikon D7000 + Tokina 10-17mm fisheye lens + 1.4x teleconverter; 1/100 sec at f11; ISO 320; two INON z-240 strobes; Nauticam housing; Zen 100mm mini-dome.

Week 42
Dive robbers
Jean Tresfon
South Africa
jtresfon@iafrica.com
Nikon D300 + 12-24mm lens; 1/250 sec at f7.1; ISO 400; Subal housing; two Sea&Sea strobes.

Week 50
Arrangement of swans
Stefano Unterthiner
Italy
info@stefanounterthiner.com
Nikon D3 + 24-70mm lens; 1/320 sec at f16; ISO 1000.

Week 13
Rhino in charge
Wim van den Heever
South Africa
wim.vandenheever@gmail.com
Nikon D3X + 200-400mm f4 lens; 1/320 sec at f7.1; ISO 400.

Week 46
Surfing delight
Wim van den Heever
Nikon D4 + 200-400mm f4 lens; 1/3200 sec at f8 (-0.7 e/v); ISO 1000.

Week 4
Resurrection
Marsel van Oosten
The Netherlands
marsel@squiver.com
Nikon D4 + 24-70mm f2.8 lens; 15 sec at f8; ISO 400; Gitzo tripod + Markins ballhead; Surefire UB3T Invictus flashlight.

Week 34
On top of the world
Jérémie Villet
France
jeremievillet@gmail.com
Canon EOS 7D + 28-75mm f2.8 lens; 1/160 sec at f2.8 (-0.7 e/v); ISO 320.

Week 33
Hare in a landscape
Robert Zoehrer
Austria
aon.912782458@aon.at
Canon EOS-1D Mark III + 500mm f4 lens; 1/640 sec at f11; ISO 250.

First published by the Natural History Museum, Cromwell Road, London SW7 5BD.

Text based on original captions used in the Wildlife Photographer of the Year exhibitions.
ISBN: 978 0 565 09385 3

A catalogue record for this book is available from the British Library.

THE TURQUOISE COAST OF TURKEY

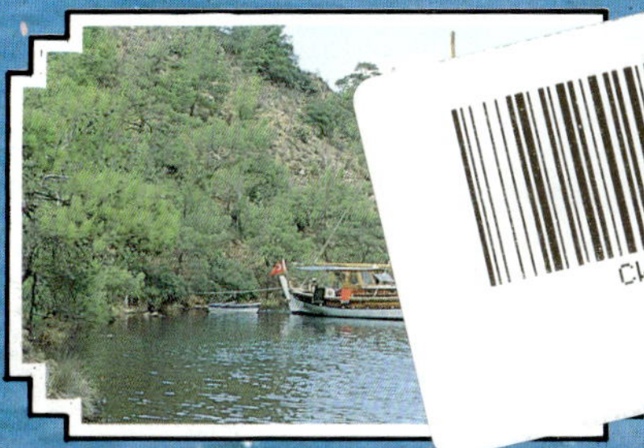

ROD HEIKELL

NET
TURİSTİK YAYINLAR
SANAYİ VE TİCARET A.Ş.

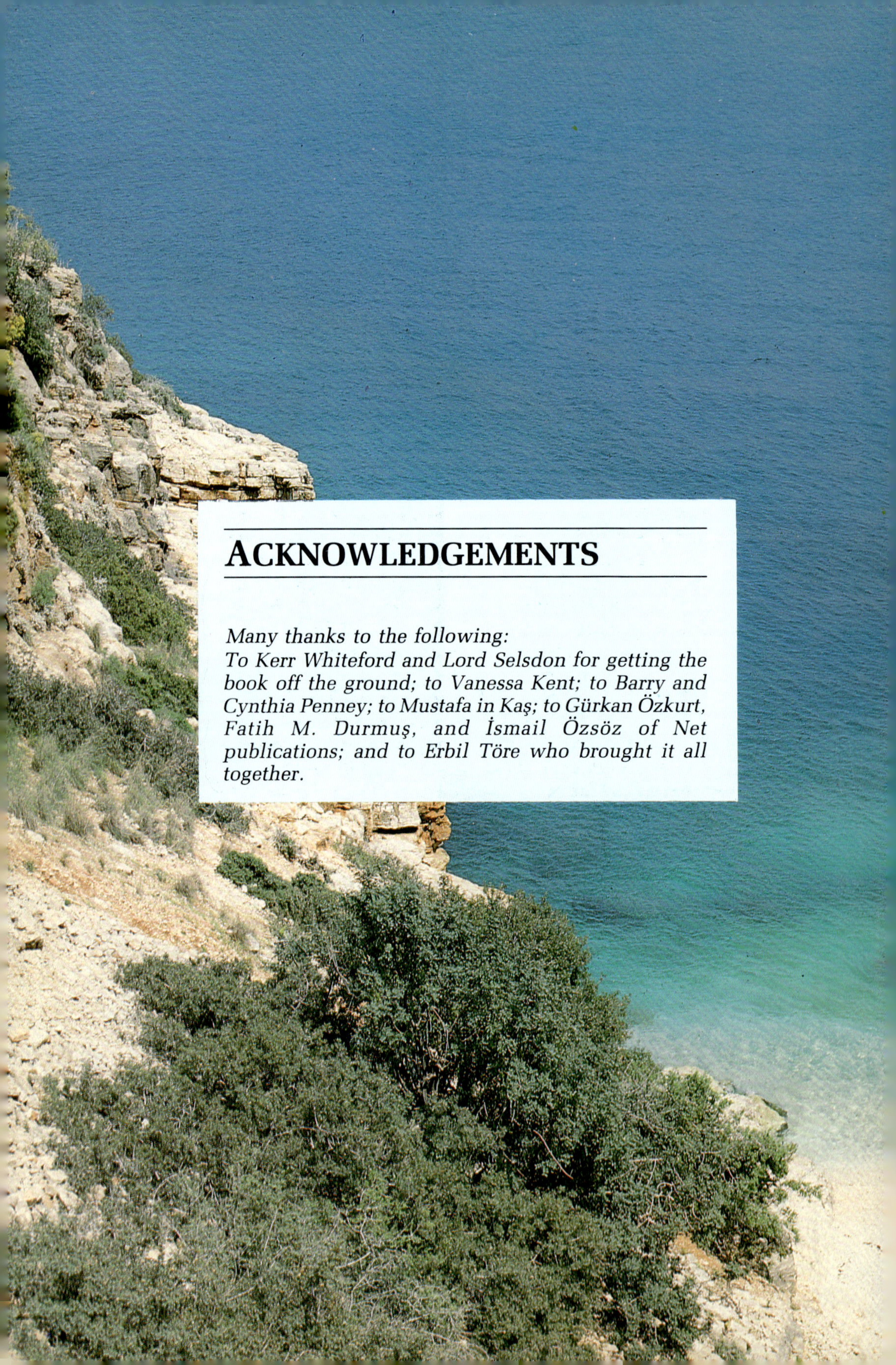

ACKNOWLEDGEMENTS

Many thanks to the following:
To Kerr Whiteford and Lord Selsdon for getting the book off the ground; to Vanessa Kent; to Barry and Cynthia Penney; to Mustafa in Kaş; to Gürkan Özkurt, Fatih M. Durmuş, and İsmail Özsöz of Net publications; and to Erbil Töre who brought it all together.

PREFACE

Turkey is rapidly attracting growing numbers of tourists, particularly to the Aegean coast, and a book was needed that covered the coast from Bodrum to Kekova in more detail than did the other travel guides available. Rod Heikell has travelled the length of the Turquoise coast described in this book in his own yacht and by road, not once, but several times. He has stopped in little known spots along the coast seldom visited by others and certainly never visited by other travel writers. He has a knowledge of the coast and of things to see and do ashore that needed to be set down on paper, and here it is. To it all he brings a wide breadth of knowledge on things ancient and modern in Turkey.

With this book as a companion you will find much to see and do along the coast. The important Graeco-Roman sites are described along with plans to guide you around them. Comment is made on Byzantine and Ottoman influences. Modern concerns such as the plight of the turtles at Dalyan and the life-style of the Yörüks are included. It is all spiced with anecdote and tales of the colourful characters along the coast.

It is with great pride and care that we offer our Turquoise Coast to yachtsmen and women from all over the world. While enjoying this unique natural and historical beauty and the hospitality of its friendly people, please bear in mind that it belongs to you as well and help us to keep the waters always clean and unpolluted.

Barlas Küntay
Vice-Chairman
Net Group of Companies

Cover photograph by Amil KUNT

THE TURQUOISE COAST OF TURKEY

Published and distributed by:

NET TURİSTİK YAYINLAR A.Ş.

Yerebatan Caddesi, 15/3, 34410 Cağaloğlu, Istanbul-Turkey
Tel.: (90-1) 520 84 06-527 42 70 Telex: 23264 acı tr

1363. Sokak, 1, Kat: 5, 35230 Çankaya, İzmir-Turkey
Tel.: (90-51) 12 30 01-25 38 61

Deniz Mahallesi, 126. Sokak, Çöllü Apt., D.2-4, Antalya-Turkey
Tel.: (90-31) 11 43 14-17 31 05

Yenimahalle, Nev-Yap Sitesi, 5. Blok, D.1, Nevşehir-Turkey
Tel.: (90-4851) 30 89

Text: **Rod Heikell**
Photographs: **Rod Heikell, Net Publication archives**
Layout: **Not Ajans (Fatih M. Durmuş)**
Typesetting: **AS Dizgi**
Colour Separation: **Asır Matbaacılık Ltd. Şti.**
Printed in Turkey by: **Asır Matbaacılık Ltd. Şti.**

ISBN 975-479-059-0

1st edition, 1988

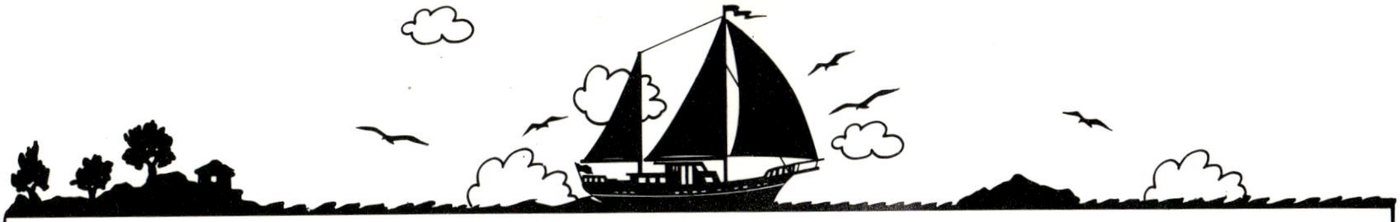

CONTENTS

BOXES

INTRODUCTION

ABOUT THE COUNTRY I: BACKGROUND

HISTORY

Turkey has a history which can be traced back to the Stone Age and to the first incipient agriculture when crops were first planted and reaped. From these early settlements major civilizing forces have moved in and out of Asia Minor culminating in the Ottoman Empire, the last vestiges of which disappeared with the formation of the Turkish Republic in 1923.

STONE AGE

A Stone Age city dating back to 7000 BC has been discovered at Çatal Höyük near Konya, and numerous wall-paintings including what are the earliest known landscape paintings have been uncovered. Around 5000 BC a city existed at Hacılar near Burdur where early copper implements as well as crude pottery have been discovered.

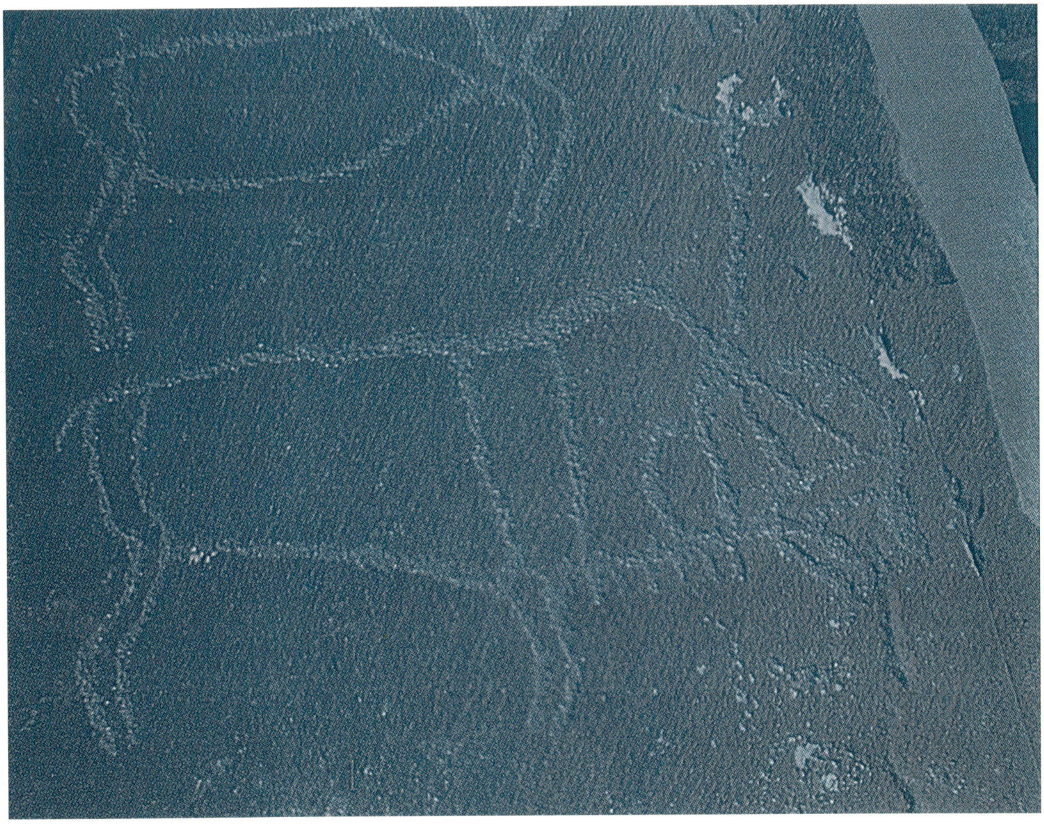

THE BRONZE AGE

A people known as the Hatti built cities near Kayseri and Boğazkale near enough in the dead centre of Turkey. This was a Bronze Age culture and the cities were sizeable places producing bronze weapons and fine pottery. The earliest occupation of Troy near the Dardanelles has been dated to 3000 BC. Around 1900-1600 BC the Hittites moved into Anatolia and built a large city in Hatti territory at Boğazkale. The Achaean Greeks attacked Troy in 1250 BC as related by Homer in the *Iliad* and *The Odyssey*, and following this Greeks pushed out of their lands by the Dorians, colonised the Mediterranean coast of Turkey.

IRON AGE

The arrival of the Greeks along the coast of Turkey beginnng around 1200 BC heralded the tentative beginnings of some quite spectacular civilizations and the flowering of art, music, philosophy and science. The Ionians, clustered in the cities around what is now Lake Bafa south of Izmir, produced notable philosophers, scientists, and artists who in many respects were way ahead of their times. In Caria and Lycia the indigenous populations merged and adopted Greek culture. These Greeks laid the foundations of the Hellenic Age to come.

Cult standard symbolizing the cosmos. (Hittite Periode)

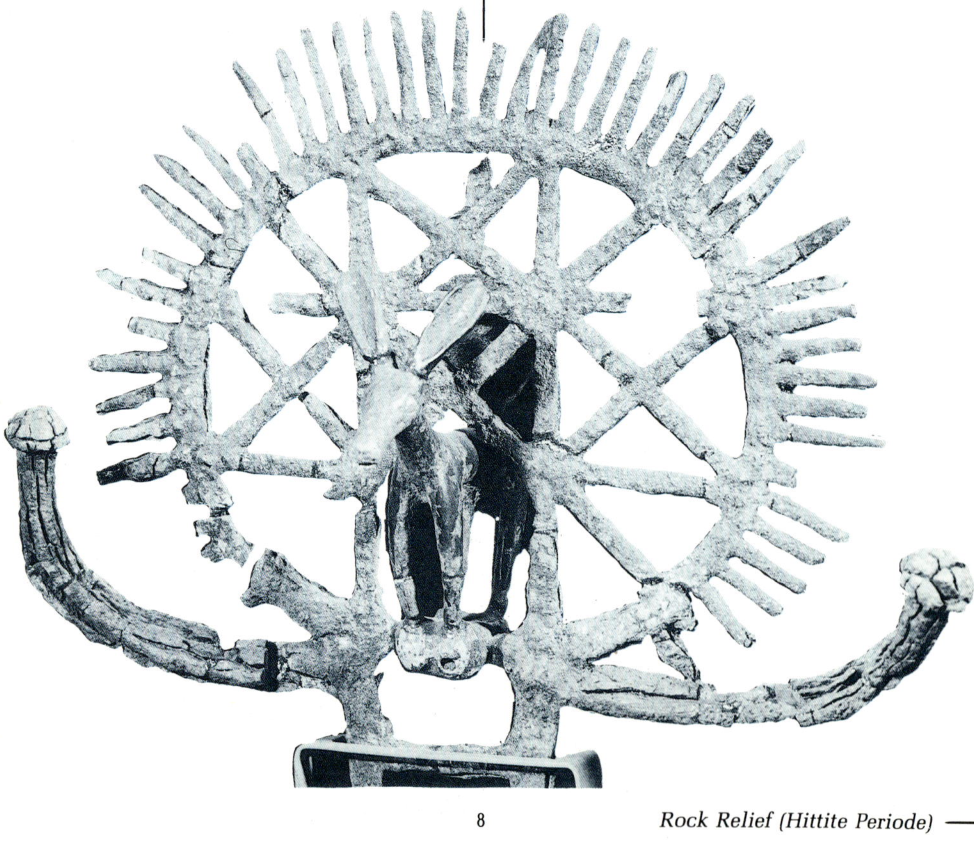

Rock Relief (Hittite Periode) ⟶

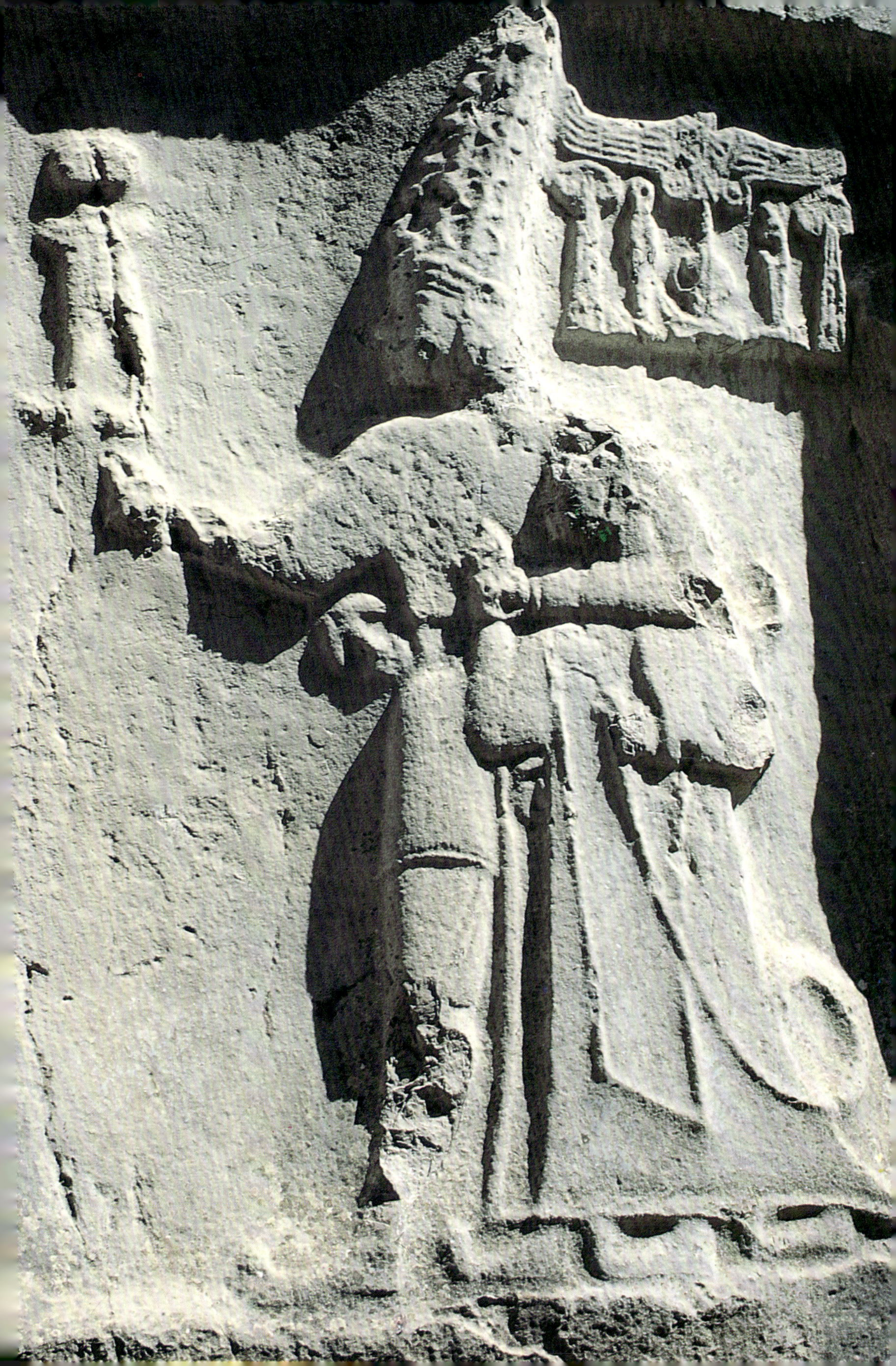

The Persians And Alexander

The Persians under Cyrus (500-530 BC) conquered most of Anatolia though the inhabitants of the coast were to give them constant trouble. For a while it looked as if the Persians would overrun Greece, but the defeat of Xerxes at Salamis (480 BC) put a stop to that. In 334 BC Alexander the Great crossed the Hellespont into Asia Minor and proceeded to conquer it at a breath-taking pace. Alexander was a confirmed Hellenophile and his campaign fully Hellenised the coastal cities. His death at the early age of 33 in 323 BC threw Asia Minor into turmoil as various groups struggled for power. Small city-states attempted to enlarge their territory or were in turn snapped up by others. Pergamum was an important city-state along the Turkish coast and for a while in the 2nd century BC controlled a large part of the coast.

The Head of Alexander.

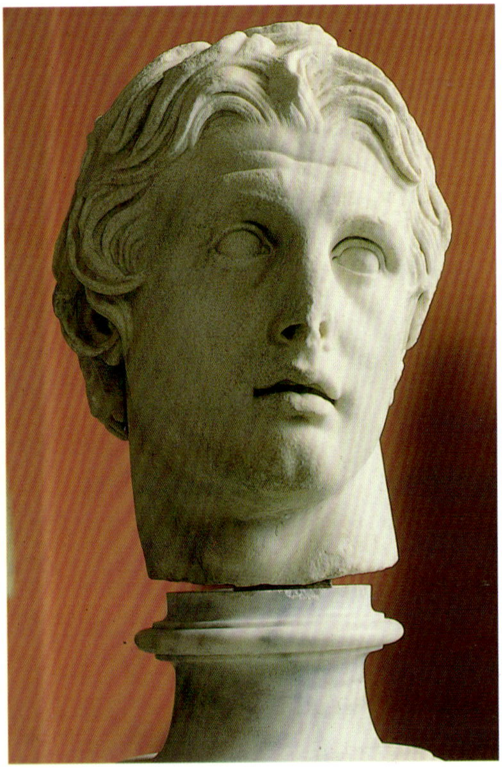

The Head of Eros.

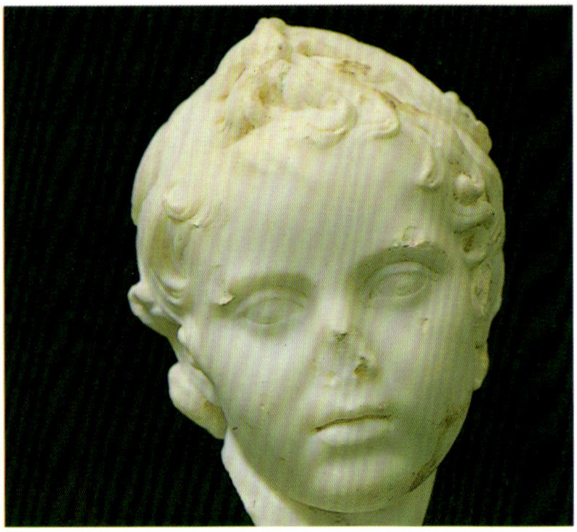

The Romans

In 129 BC the Romans established the Roman Province of Asia and appointed local governors to rule the province. They were content to leave things pretty much alone as long as taxes were remitted to Rome. Intervention only occurred when local rulers challenged the Romans and attempted, like Mithridates, to take over the Asian provinces. Under Augustus (27 BC-AD 14) the region enjoyed great prosperity and stability.

Christianity

The Romans were remarkably tolerant to the early christians and churches were established all over Asia Minor and particularly along the coast. By the 3rd century AD the Romans perceived the enormity of the threat and the Emperor Decius started the first wholesale persecutions of the christians. In the 4th century AD the Roman Empire was under threat from the Goths and the Persians, but under Constantinople, established in 330 AD on the site of Byzantium. Constantine became a Christian on his death-bed in 337 AD. In the sixth century AD Rome itself was under threat from barbarian invasions from the north and while it declined, Constantinople in the east grew in power and importance.

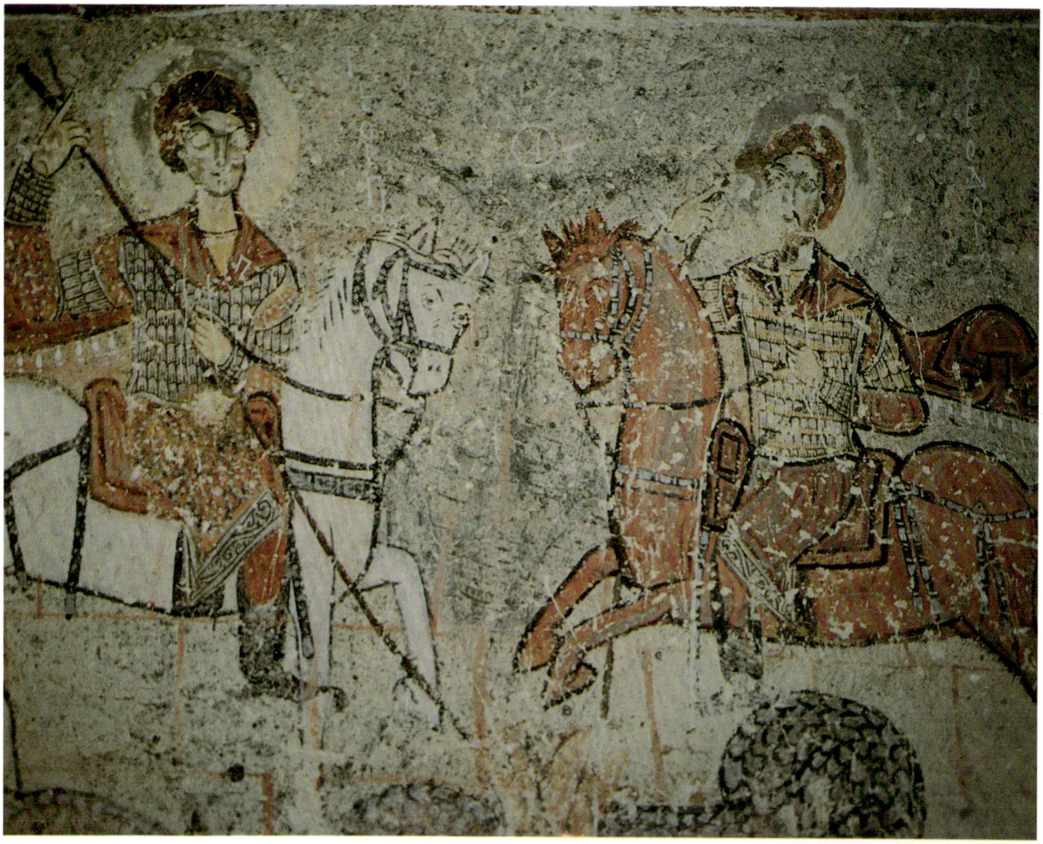

BYZANTIUM

Under Justinian (527-565 AD) the Eastern Roman Empire, Byzantium, flowered and acquired not only a civilized life-style, but much territory as well including Anatolia and the coastal regions. The Byzantine Empire was to last until the fall of Constantinople to the Ottomans in 1453, but much happened in between.

ISLAM

In 612 Muhammed was given his revelations in Mecca and before his death some 30 years later, Islam had become a major force to be reckoned with. The Arabic Empires adopted the new faith and by the end of the 7th century had forcefully spread it right up through Anatolia.

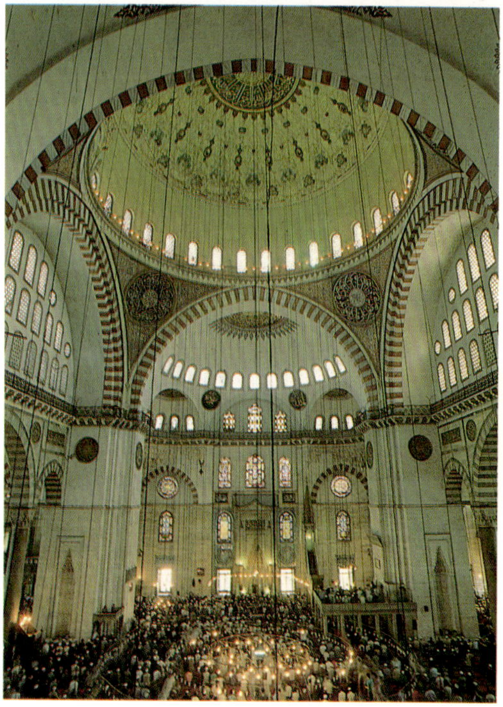

THE SELJUKS

Around 800-1000 Turkoman tribes were forced down into Anatolia by the Mongol tribes pushing west from the steppes. In 1071 the Seljuks defeated the Byzantines at Malazgirt and then proceeded to occupy much of Anatolia. The Seljuks built numerous fine cities and some of their graceful architecture remains such as the Fluted Minaret in Antalya. The Seljuks also gave us Omar Khayyam and his wonderful poetry. In 1243 the first Mongol invasion of Anatolia effectively destroyed the Seljuks.

Yivli minare - Antalya.

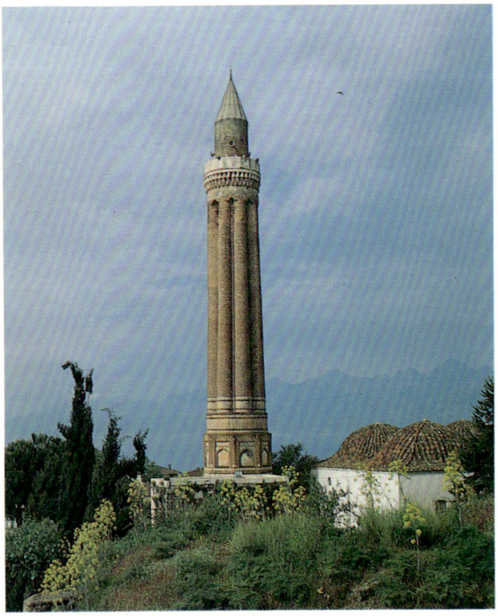

CRUSADERS

The crusaders travelled through Anatolia en route to the Holy Land and the knights, soldiers, and general hangers-on brought havoc, for friend and foe alike, to the region. The Holy Land and Jerusalem was briefly occupied, but no lasting change was effected and Islam was only briefly stemmed. In 1204 the fourth crusade sacked Constantinople, their allies in the cause, weakening already declining Byzantium.

THE OTTOMANS

The decline of the Seljuks and Byzantium left a power vacuum that was filled by bands of Turks migrating from the east into Anatolia. Near Bursa one of these groups was lead by Osman, son of Ertuğrul, and Osman was to give his name to one of the greatest empires to rise in Turkey - the Osmanlı, later Ottomans. In a short time the Ottomans had expanded and acquired territory and in 1453, under Mehmet the Conqueror, they took Constantinople. The height of Ottoman power was under Süleyman the Magnificient (1520-1566), also called the 'Lawgiver'. The Ottomans advanced through the Balkans and Hungary to the gates of Vienna and on the sea their fleet ruled the eastern Mediterranean under Süleyman's admiral, Barbarossa. This was the height of the Ottoman Empire and after this the period from 1578-1666 is known as 'The Rule of the Women' when ineffective sultans gave up decision-making to the Viziers and influential wives in the harem. The empire began to appreciably shrink after 1666 and by 1832 nearby Greece became independent. When the First World War broke out Turkey joined the Axis powers. With the Allies victory in 1918 things looked bleak for Turkey.

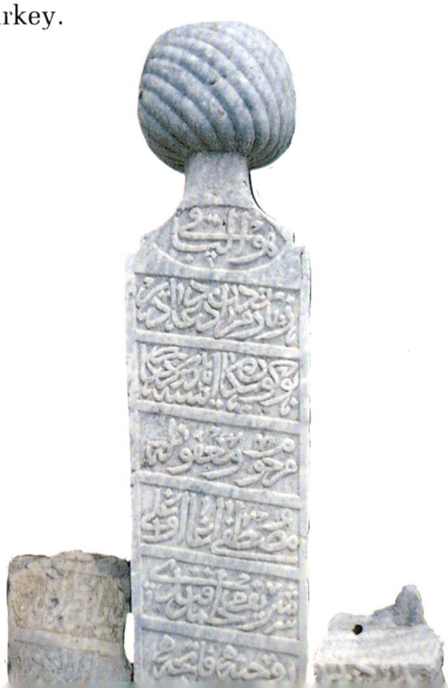

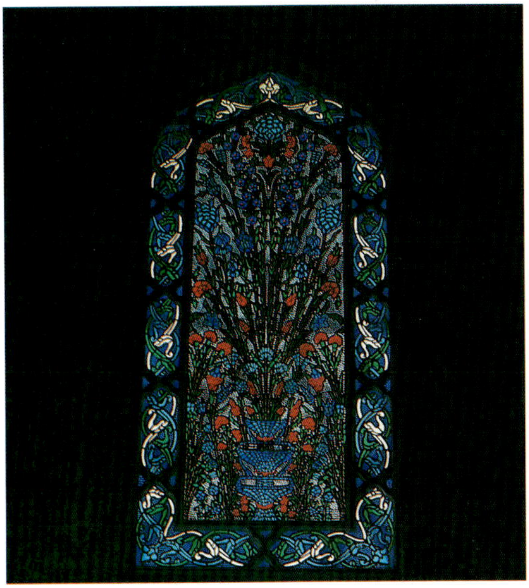

ATATÜRK AND THE TURKISH REPUBLIC

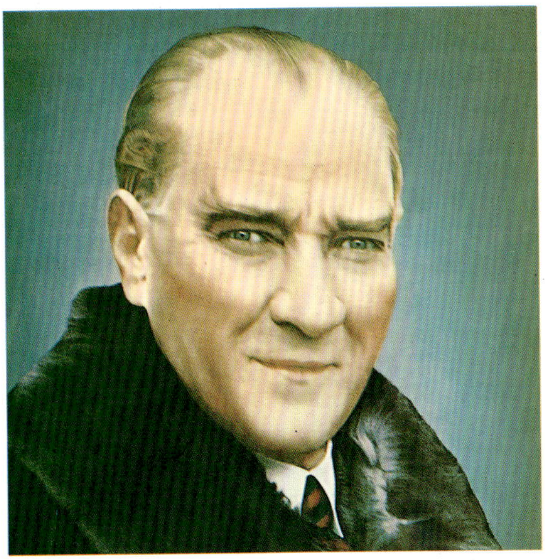

After the war the misguided Allies had promised various countries slices of Turkey, and one of these recipients was to be Greece. In 1919, encouraged by Britain, the Greeks invaded Smyrna (İzmir) and then pushed inland. They didn't reckon with Mustafa Kemal, an Ottoman general who had begun organising a new government to take over from the pathetic last sultan. The Greek invasion caused large numbers of Turks to flock to his cause and after two years hard fighting he decisively defeated them. Mustafa Kemal became a national hero and he set about organising the Turkish Republic which was declared in 1923. He insisted on major reforms of just about every institution. One of these was the adoption of surnames and Mustafa Kemal took the name 'Atatürk', 'Father of the Turks', to become Kemal Atatürk. Amongst his reforms were the abolition of polygamy, the removal of Islam as the state religion and the adoption of a secular code, the abolition of Arabic and the introduction of the Roman alphabet, the introduction of educational reforms and compulsory schooling for children, and the introduction of the vote for women. More than this he gave the Turks a pride in themselves and their country after years of debilitating rule by weak and corrupt sultans. He died in 1938.

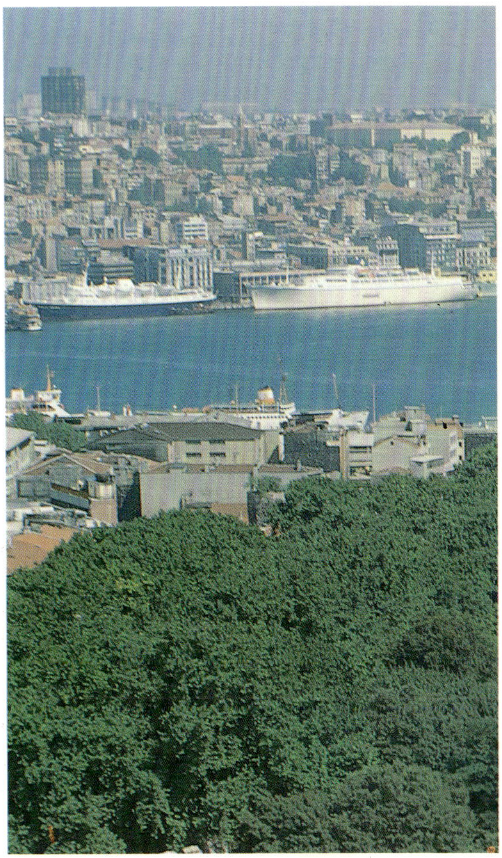

The Bosphorus Bridge.

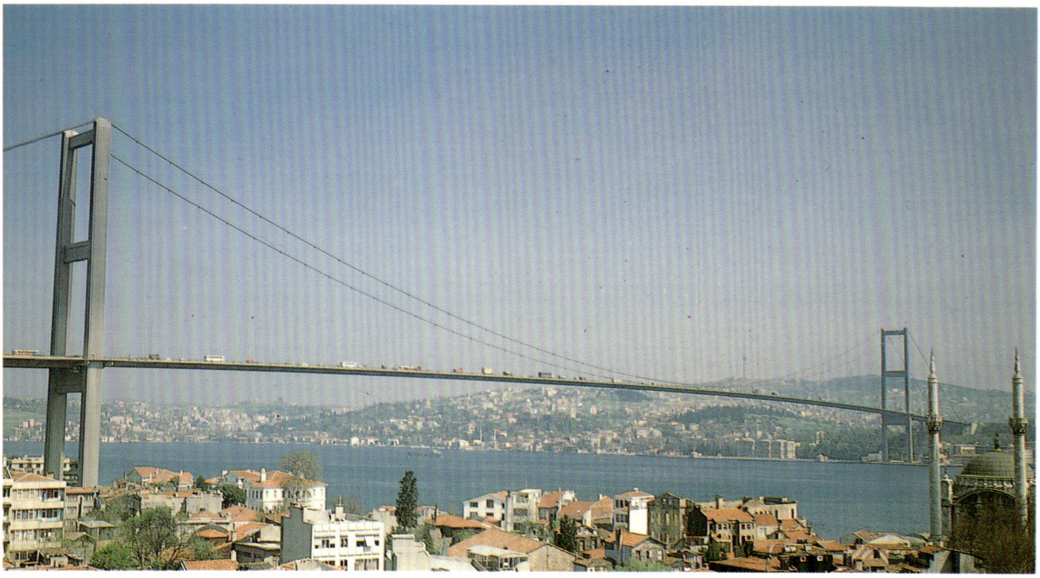

To this day Atatürk is revered throughout Turkey. He can be seen everywhere in portraits hung in offices and shops, in busts and statues in public squares and gardens, on stamps and on lira notes. In an age of pretty nasty dictators, Atatürk was an autocrat of a distinctly benevolent mould and there can be no doubt that Turkey would not be the same without him. His status as a national hero should not be challenged by the visitor. Apart from the fact that there is a law against defaming his name, on the whole Turks genuinely regard him, even today, as the saviour of their country and they are right to do so.

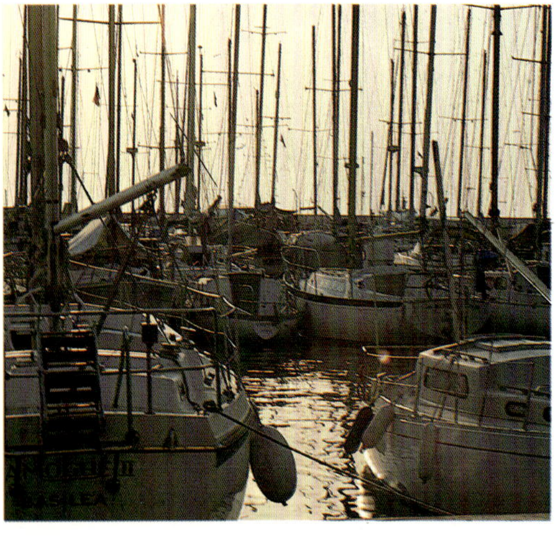

Islam And Mosques

Although Turkey has been a secular state since Atatürk's reforms, 99% of Turks are Muslims, though some are not all that devout and Islam in Turkey is a much gentler religion than the fundamentalism in Iran next door. Muslims believe in everything in the Bible, particuarly the Old Testament, except that Jesus is regarded as a prophet and not the son of God. After Jesus came Muhammed who was the last and greatest of the prophets and to whom God communicated the final revelations, which are written down in the *Koran*. The word Islam means 'submission to God's will', and at the beginning of daily prayers the call from the minaret is: 'there is no god but God, and Muhammed is his prophet'. To be a Muslim you only need say this phrase, (and understand what it means), pray five times daily at the set times, give alms to the poor, observe the fast of Ramazan, and make a pilgrimmage to Mecca if possible.

A Muslim must not eat pork or drink wine. The latter is normally interpretted as a prohibition on alcohol in general though the less devout say Muhammed said nothing about raki and beer. No image can be worshipped and images that might

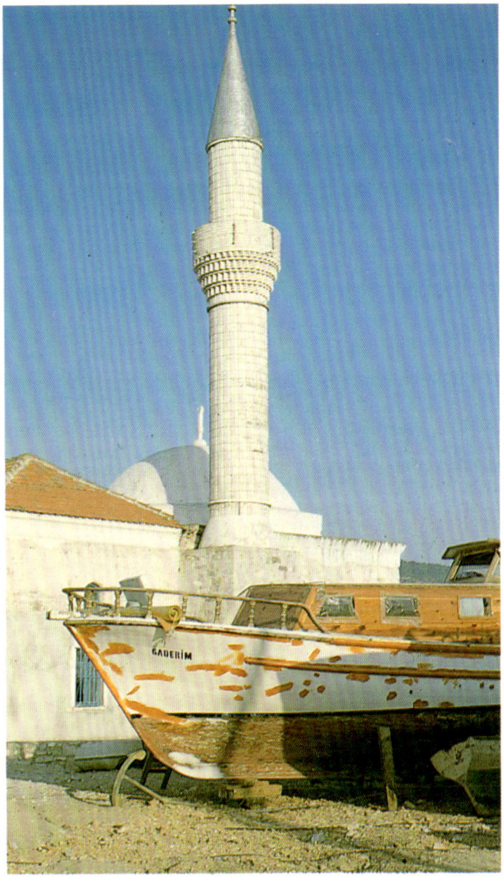

Mosque. Bodrum waterfront

possibly be venerated have been vigorously destroyed by the faithful. This accounts for the general paucity of portraits in Islamic art.

Unlike many Muslim countries, visitors can enter a mosque in Turkey, so long as the proper etiquette is observed. While the Turquoise coast has no grand mosques like those in Istanbul, Bursa, and Konya, there are interesting examples in İzmir, Milas, Muğla, and Fethiye. You should remove your shoes before entering a mosque, a purely practical rule designed to keep the carpets inside clean for worshippers. You should be modestly attired, no shorts, short skirts, tatty clothes, and women should cover their hair and shoulders with a scarf. Do not take photographs using a flash or talk loudly. Avoid visiting a mosque on Fridays which is the Muslim holy day.

FESTIVALS

Though Turkey uses the Gregorian calendar for most things, Islamic festivals are fixed using the Islamic calendar based on a lunar month and thus eleven days shorter than the Gregorian year. Consequently the dates of Islamic festivals reckoned on the Gregorian calendar change from year to year. There are two major Islamic holidays.

The first is Kurban Bayramı, the 'Feast of the Sacrifice', which remembers Abraham's willingness to sacrifice his son. Most families buy a sheep which is paraded around before the big day when it is ritually slaughtered and the feast takes place. Meat is distributed to the poor who cannot afford to slaughter a sheep. There is much celebration and everything usually closes down for it. The second festival is Şeker Bayramı, the 'sugar festival', celebrating the end of Ramazan and a month of fasting for the faithful. At these times the coast is packed with Turks on holiday celebrating the festivals and if you are land-based, you may have difficulties finding accomodation.

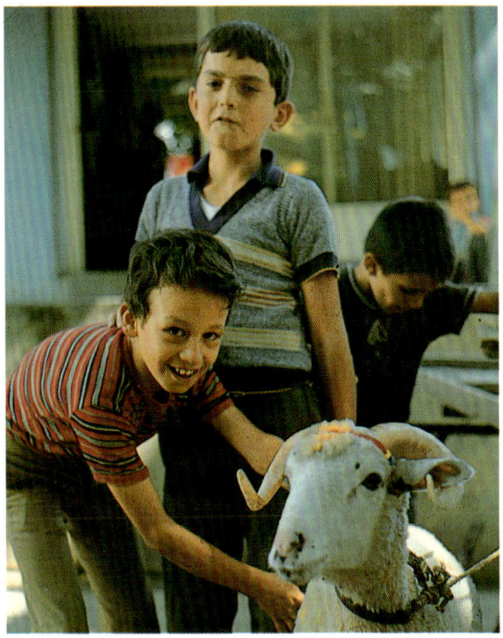

Sacrificial sheep for Kurban Bayramı. Bodrum

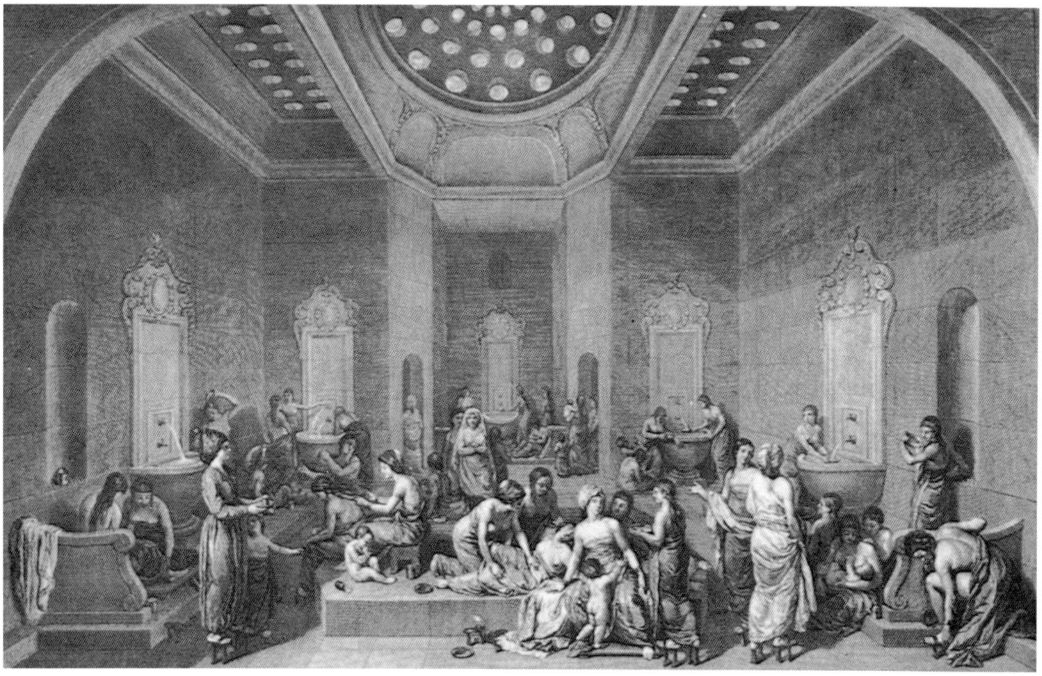

Hammams

The Turkish steam bath or hammam was an essential part of every Turkish community. The Ottoman hammam developed from the Roman bath but with the number of chambers reduced to two instead of four. The central bath-house has a dome over it studded with thick bottle glass which lets smokey hafts of light into the misty atmosphere of the baths. In the middle of the bath-house there is a circular marble platform on which you sit or lie or where the brave are pummelled with a Turkish massage. The latter are fairly violent affairs compared to the gentler European-type massage, though recipients always feel good afterwards. Around the edge of a hammam are cubicles with hot and cold running water where you wash dirt and grime off before relaxing on the central platform.

A hammam leaves you feeling wonderfully relaxed and often quite sleepy. There are different times for men and women, with men getting the lions-share of the time available in male dominated Turkey. In the main towns around the coast, in Bodrum, Muğla, Marmaris, and Fethiye you will find hammams - ask where they are located at the Tourist Information Office.

Language

Turkish is a language that shares its roots with few others, Azerbaijani being one if you are interested, though it may also be connected to Hungarian and Finnish. When Atatürk did away with the Arabic script he got a group of prominent linguists together to adapt it to the Roman alphabet and to simplify it. The result is a language that is basically phonetic and if you follow the rules for pronouncing a letter and say a word, you have a good chance of getting it right. Many modern terms have been borrowed directly from English and French and expressed in a Turkish form. Thus a '*bufe*' is a buffet, a '*otel*' is a hotel, a '*bira*' is a beer, '*viski*' is whisky, and so on. In the appendix at the back of the book there is a guide to pronounciation of the Turkish alphabet. For vocabulary the Berlitz *Turkish For Travellers* has everything the visitor needs.

About The Country II: Information For Visitors

Getting There

You can get to Turkey and the Turquoise coast by air, sea, or road.

By Air

From Britain and Europe there are numerous charter flights in the summer to İstanbul, İzmir, Dalaman, and Antalya. There are also scheduled flights to İstanbul and İzmir and internal flights connecting İstanbul with the other airports. The most convenient airport for the Turquoise coast is Dalaman. From here it is 20 minutes to Göcek, under an hour to Fethiye, about 1½ hours to Marmaris, and around 4 hours to Bodrum. From İzmir it is around a 4 hour transfer to Bodrum. Internal flights are regular and not expensive. From İstanbul there are daily flights to İzmir and three to four flights a week to Dalaman and Antalya in the summer.

By Sea

Daily ferries run from the Greek islands to Turkey: from Rhodes to Marmaris, Kos to Bodrum, Samos to Kuşadası, Khios to Çeşme, and from Lesvos to Ayvalık. If you arrive on a charter flight in Greece and spend more than one day in Turkey you may be prevented from using the return portion of your ticket in Greece. On a scheduled flight to Greece you will have no problems in this respect. Most of the ferries can take three or four cars so it is possible to drive down to Greece, take a ferry down through the Greek islands, and then a ferry across to Turkey.

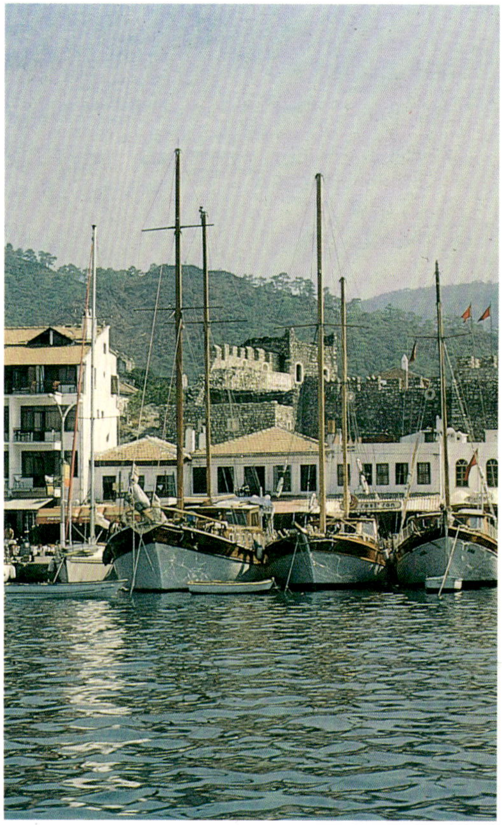

By Rail

The train from England and Europe is a long drawn out journey with stretches where there is not even a dining car. The train that now follows the fabled Orient Express route is not to be confused with the luxurious restored coaches of Wagons-Lit, a trip which costs upwards of seventeen times the return air fare, for a one-way ticket! The trip from London to İstanbul takes four days and the discomfort is such that it has little to recommend it.

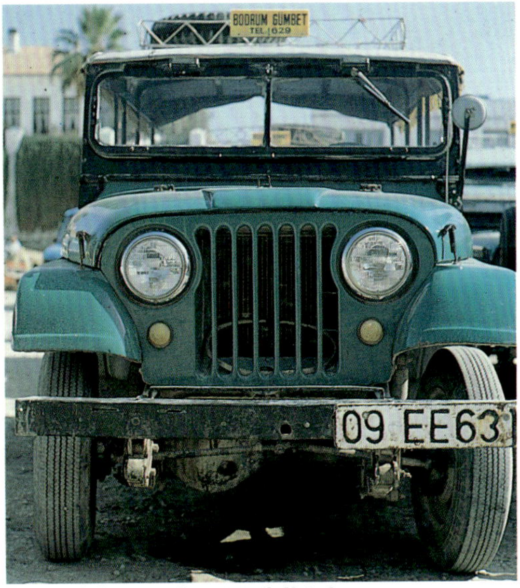

Jitney dolmuş: when it's full it leaves.

BY ROAD

You can drive down to Turkey and depending on the time available it can be done in four days from Calais or at a more relaxed pace, the latter is much recommended as there is a lot to see and do en route. You will need a transit visa for Bulgaria which you cannot obtain at the border.

GETTING AROUND

BY BUS

Bus and minibus (*dolmuş*) are the most widespread form of public transport in Turkey. Different companies run scheduled trips to most parts of the Turquoise coast and to the smaller villages you can get a *dolmuş*, small minibuses that leave when they are full or nearly so. The buses are all fairly modern, mostly Mercedes 0302's assembled in Turkey. You can book a seat on the bus in advance and on popular routes it is worth doing this. Some of the driving is a little aggressive so it is best to sit towards the back where you cannot see what is happening on the road up ahead. On board there will be bottled water courtesy of the bus company, ask for '*su*', and lemon cologne is liberally distributed at intervals to keep you smelling nice on the journey. The bus will stop every two hours or so for the toilet, snacks, and *çay*.

The larger towns will have a central bus station (*Otogar, Otobüs Terminali, or Otobüs Garajı*) that buses leave from. As you get further down the coast, buses get less frequent, and from Fethiye around the coast to Antalya, there are only a few scheduled services. *Dolmuş'* fill in where the larger buses leave off. To get to many of the smaller villages there will only be a *dolmuş* service and you must squeeze in with locals, bags of fruit and vegetables, sacks of flour, and whatever else has been purchased in town. As these depend on demand, they will not run if there are not sufficient people to fill them.

BY CAR

This is the best way of exploring many of the more remote inland places mentioned in this book. You can hire cars at İzmir, Kuşadası, Bodrum, Marmaris, Fethiye, and Antalya. Hire-cars are not cheap in Turkey and the extra charge for the kilometres travelled can add a substantial amount to the basic hire charge - try to get a deal with unlimited mileage. It may be that you can get a better deal before you leave with a Fly-Drive package which usually works out substantially cheaper than buying the flight and hiring the car separately. You require only a license from your own country to drive in Turkey. If you take your own car to Turkey you can keep it there for three moths before you must take it out of the country to avoid customs duty.

There are few cars on the roads along the Turquoise coast and for the most part driving is a pleasure. However there are a few pointers for the newcomer driving in Turkey for the first time. Trucks and cars cannot be relied upon to turn in the

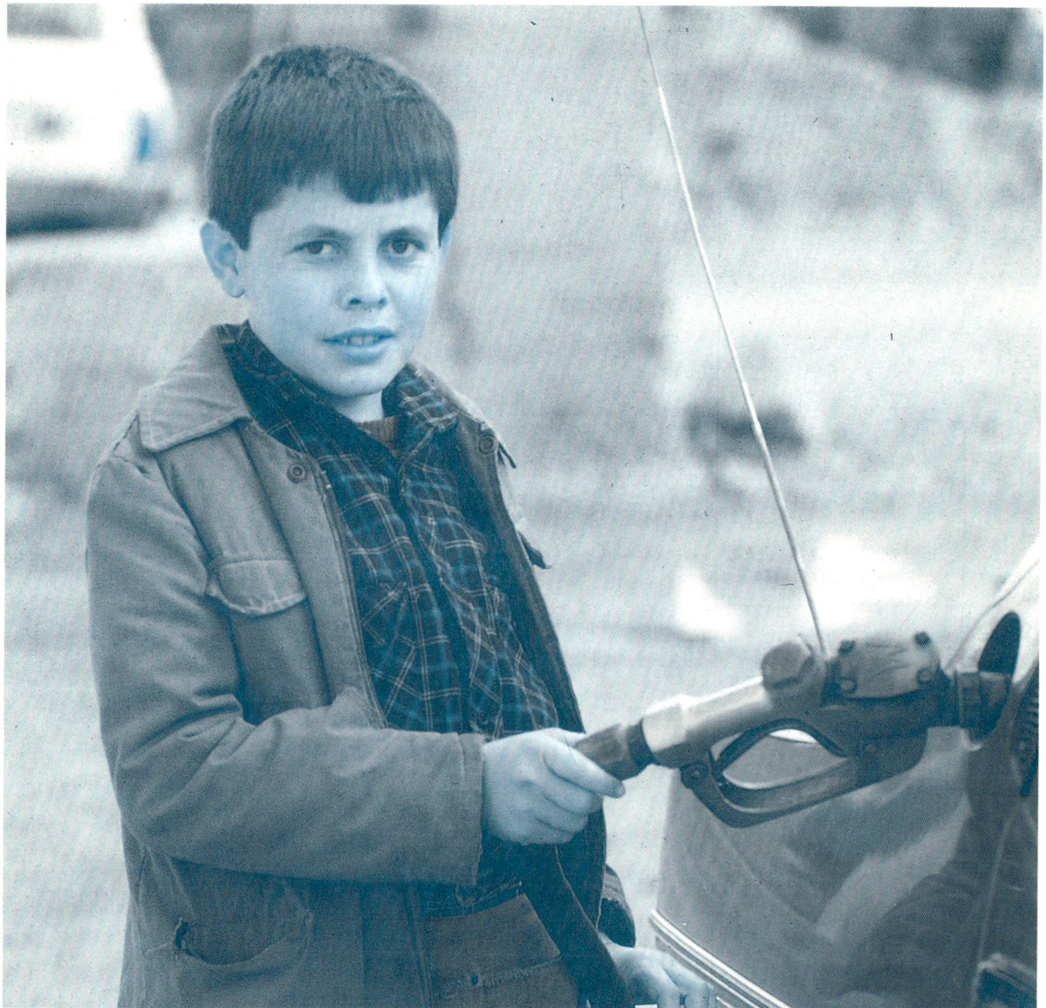

Petrol mister? Fethiye

direction they are signalling. A vehicle turning left will usually indicate left and then pull over onto the hard shoulder until the road is clear. It is not normal except where marked to pull into the middle and turn left. Driving at dusk and at night is not recommended. Apart from herds of sheep or goats or the odd cow or donkey on the road, there are also unlit vehicles - horse and carts, tractors and trailers, motorbikes, and the odd truck and car. Sometimes a tractor and trailer or a cart exhibit a single white light at the rear which can be confusing. The main roads along the Turquoise coast are good well-paved affairs though there are not any stretches you could call a motorway. However some of the minor roads are very rough ill-made affairs, often a single lane with just gravel and a lot of pot-holes and at worst dirt or clay tracks which are passable in the summer, with due care and attention, but are often impassable after heavy rain in the spring and autumn. One thing you will have to get used to is using the horn to warn pedestrians, cyclists, and other drivers of your presence before overtaking. Likewise anyone overtaking you will give a toot on the horn to let you know he is there. Driving in Turkey, especially in towns and cities, is a much more raucous business than in comparatively sedate Europe.

TAXIS

Taxis are all metered and you should make sure the meter is on to avoid exorbitant demands at the end of the trip. If there is no meter or the driver says the meter is broken, agree on the fare for the trip first. There are agreed tarif rates for intercity and intracity journeys and a tarif card should be available. Overall, taxis are cheap and the service polite and good-humoured. Incidentally Turks do not tip taxi-drivers unless some extra service has been provided, so there is no need for you to do so.

BY BOAT

A quick glance through this book will leave no doubt in your mind that not only will a boat let you see a lot of places along the coast that cannot be reached by land, but that you will see the Turquoise coast best from a boat. Whether you are in charge of a yacht or reclining in a deck-chair on a skippered charter, there is nothing but nothing to beat the approach to a town or a deserted bay from seaward. You don't have to be a nautically inclined old salt to do this. On a charter *gulet* all you have to do is sit and watch the scenery glide by while the the skipper and crew do the work. This is gin and tonic cruising at its best, on a boat small enough to get into tiny coves, but with the comforts needed to enjoy the voyage and none of the anonymity of a large cruise ship. Those who enjoy sailing their own yacht can potter around some of the most beautiful coastline in the eastern Mediterranean. Since the introduction of simplified paperwork a few years ago, getting around by yacht is much easier. You can arrange to charter a yacht or a skippered *gulet* in Britain and most countries in Europe, France, Germany, Italy, and Scandinavia, and this is the best thing to do if you want to be sure of getting a boat, especially in high season. Britain offers the most choice and the majority of yacht companies are British owned and operated. There are a number of options available.

On a charter gulet all you have to do is sit and watch the scenery glide by while the skipper and crew do the work.

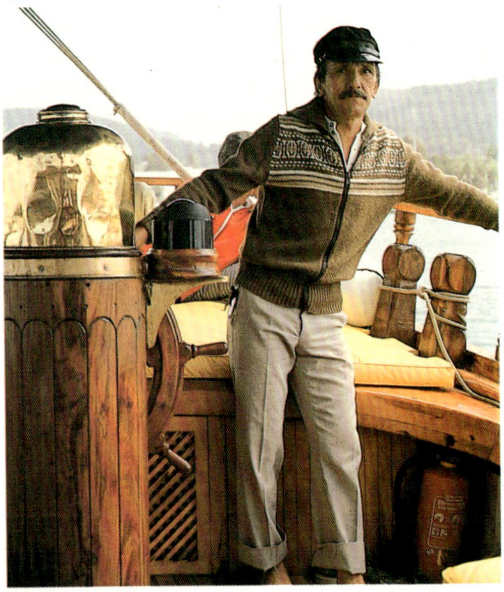

(i) Flotillas: On flotilla you sail in company with other identical boats and a lead boat to look after you. A number of flotilla companies operate around the Turquoise coast with bases in Bodrum, Marmaris and Fethiye. The holidays budget for a fair amount of free sailing time so don't feel you will be just tagging along with the rest of the fleet. For beginner and experienced sailor alike, flotillas are a good way of getting around the coast. You have the security of the lead boat with an experienced skipper whose local knowledge gives you a valuable head-start, an engineer to make sure things mechanical dont't bug your holiday, and a hostess versed in the ways of life ashore and just where you can buy this or that.

(ii) Bareboat Charter: A number of companies run bareboats from Bodrum, Marmaris, Göçek, Fethiye, and Kemer. It is best to book in advance to be sure of getting a boat in high season though there maybe one spare if you are lucky. You will need to have some sort of certificate attesting to your ability, such as the RYA Yachtmaster or Overseas Helmsmans

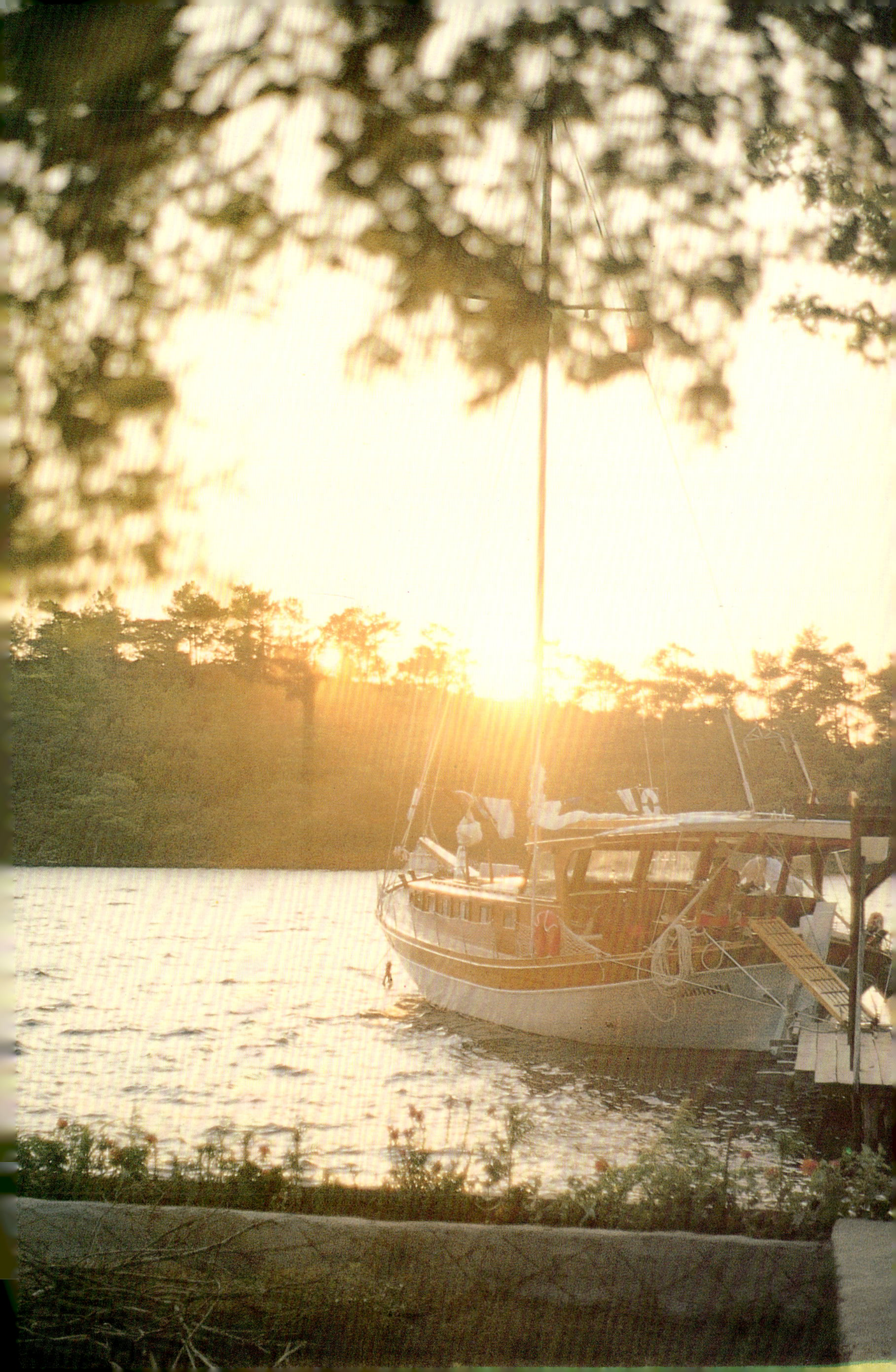

Certificate. How many miles you intend to cover will of course depend on your inclination, your crew, and the time available; but generally most bareboat charterers make plans that are too ambitious so most of your time is spent at sea and too little time is spent ashore. It is a travesty to sail around a beautiful coastline with lots of interesting things to see and do ashore, and then to spend most of your time at sea.

(iii) Skippered Yachts: There are large skippered yachts for charter from Kuşadası, Bodrum, Marmaris, and Fethiye, and others come over from the Greek islands, principally Rhodes. Most of these charters are arranged from Britain and Europe, though you may be able to pick up a charter in Turkey if there is a slot free. This type of charter is the most expensive, but then a luxury yacht with every service on board doesn't come cheap anywhere in the world.

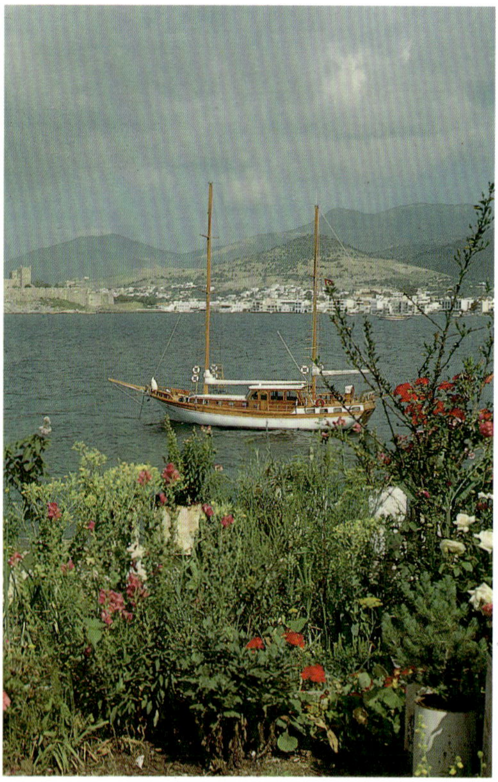

(iv) Charter *Gulets*: *Gulets* are traditional Turkish boats that have been specifically built for charter and come complete with skipper and crew. Some fill up berths on board on an ad hoc basis, others have to be chartered as a complete boat and then as many berths, or as few, are filled by the charterer(s). Amongst the crew will be a cook who will produce breakfast, lunch, and dinner if needs be. You pay for the boat to be stocked up with food and provisions of the liquid variety, but not for the cook's services. Most gulets are chartered for a one or two week trip, but a few do two or three day trips from Bodrum and Marmaris.

(v) Day Trips: From many places around the coast day-trip boats will run you to places of interest that you cannot get to by land or that are easiest to get to from the water. Most of these boats are small open boats with a canvas canopy, though one or two larger gulets do day-trips. The trips vary from short hops to nearby beaches, to round trips to ancient sites, and a beach or two for a swim, lasting all day.

Accomodation

You will find hotels, motels, pensions, and village rooms. Unless you are staying in an up-market hotel, the categories mean little. There are many pensions (*pansiyons*) which are really up-market hotels and some hotels which are inferior to a room in a house. Always inspect the room as a grand façade can hide grubby rooms and likewise a modest exterior may conceal delightful rooms. You will have little difficulty finding somewhere to stay in all but the smallest villages, though Bodrum and Marmaris get very full in the high season and you may end up expending a fair bit of shoe leather to find a bed for the night. Prices vary from rock-bottom for the cheapest pensions with few facilities to European prices for the up-market hotels. Prices must, by law, be exhibited at the desk and on the back of the room door.

In most hotels and pensions you will be promised that there is hot water, there may even be a large sign out front advertising the fact, but often there will be none. Most of the places along the coast use solar water heaters and by the time four or five people have showered the water will be cold, that is until the sun can heat up the water again. In the morning there will not, of course, be any hot water until the sun has had time to heat it up. In the hot summer months this is not a problem and a tepid shower is welcome, but in spring or autumn it can be a niggling problem. In some cases a paraffin heater or a wood-burner will be called into action, or in the up-market hotels electric immersion heaters boost the water temperature when the sun fails.

Camping

There are several camping sites scattered around the coast, but the Turks are not really into camping and for visitors, accommodation is so cheap it is not really worth it. It is unwise to camp outside of the official sites.

Customs And Immigration

Visitors from most countries and that includes Britain, Western Europe, Australasia, and the USA, do not require a visa and will automatically get 3 months on entry into Turkey. At the entry point customs will make a cursory check of your baggage and sometimes a body-check. If you arrive in your own car or yacht, the customs check will be more thorough and valuable items will be listed in your passport or in your transit log in the case of a yacht. When you leave you will have to produce these items to show you have not disposed of them in Turkey.

One thing to note is that you cannot export antiquities from Turkey. In the case of ancient Greek or Roman artifacts this is quite straingtforward - they cannot leave the country under any circumstances. However Ottoman artifacts and carpets of museum quality are also included in this category. If you purchase an expensive carpet or *kilim*, you are required to have a statement from a museum or other authority stating it is not of museum quality. Customs can ask for this statement and if you don't have it you may be required to get one before you can export the piece. I should stress that for the vast majority of pieces on sale, this statement is not required and you will have no problem taking a carpet or *kilim* out of Turkey.

Food

Turkish cuisine has been praised as the best in the eastern Mediterranean, and so it is. The traditional cuisine scores from combining a wealth of basic raw ingredients in novel ways to make dishes which often have novel names. The most

Open air köfte seller

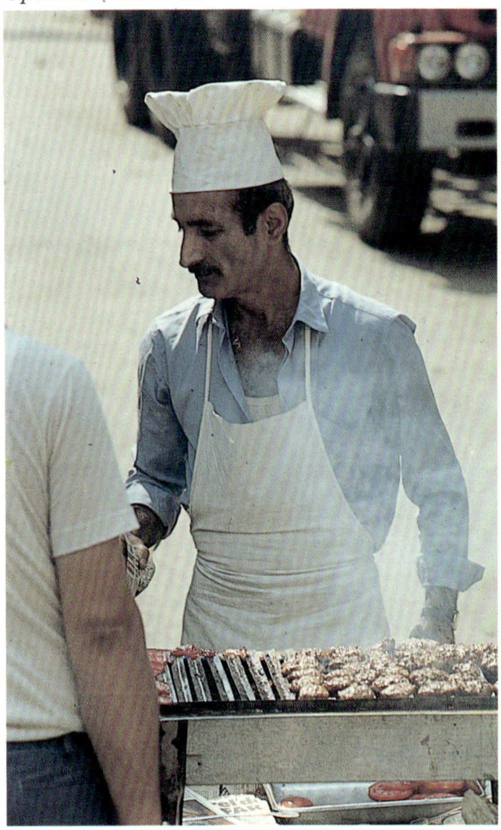

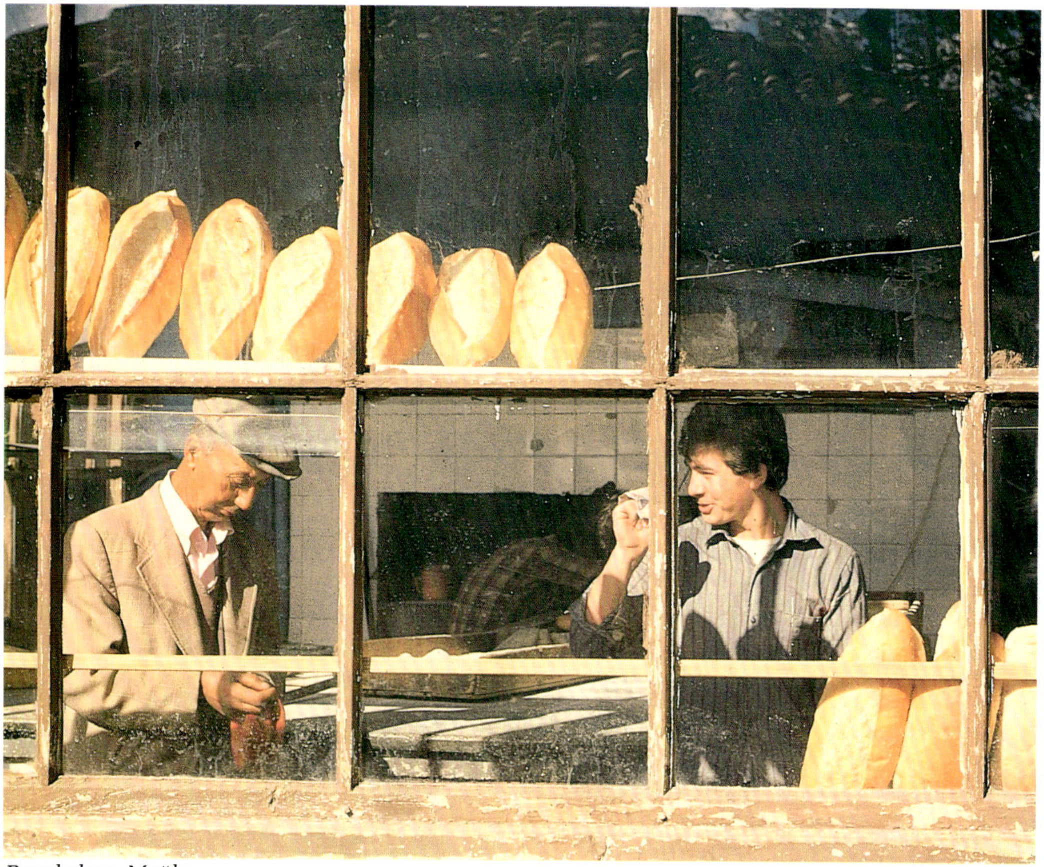

Bread shop. Muğla

memorable of the names are aubergine with tomatoes and onions called *'İmam bayıldı'*, 'the *Imam* fainted', and a sweet pastry soaked in honey called 'lady's navel'. Aubergine figures a lot in Turkish cooking and it was said that in Istanbul you could tell when the aubergine season started from the fires that swept through the city, fires caused by the hot oil from fried aubergine dishes spilling over and igniting. Over forty dishes are attributed to this purple vegetable. Females also figure a lot in the naming of dishes, particularly desserts, with names like 'lady's thigh', 'lady's breasts', 'lady's fingers', and so on through most of the anatomy.

Mezes are superb in Turkey and can make a meal in themselves. Commonly you will come across *cacık*, yoghurt with cucumber and garlic, *patlıcan salata*, pureed aubergine mixed with yoghurt, *taramasalata*, red fish roe with yoghurt and garlic, *pilaki*, white beans in a vinaigrette sauce, *dolma*, stuffed vine leaves, *börek*, white cheese or mincemeat wrapped in *filo* pastry and deep-fried, *Amerikan salata*, potato salad with mayonnaise also called Russian (Rus) salad, *çoban salata*, a mixed salad meaning literally 'shepherds salad', and many more depending on the chefs inclination and ability such as fish salads, pickled octopus, fiery tomato and onion purees, and the celebrated *imam bayıldı*. Soups are usually on at lunchtime and the most popular are lentil and rice soups, meat broths, and vegetable soups. Special shops serve only *İşkembe çorbası*, tripe soup, which is a sovereign remedy for hangovers in the eastern Mediterranean. Friends who live in Turkey swear by it, but however bad my hangover I've steadily refused to believe that tripe soup could cure it.

Cooked dishes like stews and oven dishes are prepared at lunchtime and kept hot until the evening, so the best time to have them is at midday when they are fresh. Most of the dishes combine meat, usually lamb, with vegetables to produce dishes like *salçalı köfte*, meatballs in a sauce with vegetables, or *patlıcan kebap*, a lamb and aubergine stew. This is usually accompanied by *pilav* rice or *bulgur*, (cracked wheat *pilav*). Some restaurants specialise in *kebaps*, of which there are several varieties depending on where they originated. The *kebap* itself is cooked on a slowly revolving vertical spit and the cook slices meat off it with a long knife. Usually the meat comes on a bed of rice with a salad garnish and a piquant tomato sauce or yoghurt according to your taste. *Adana kebap* is spiced with hot peppers, *Urfa kebap* comes with sliced onions and black pepper, and *Bursa* or *İskender kebap* comes on chopped *pide* bread with yoghurt and butter. Beef usually comes as *bonfile* or *biftek*, small steaks grilled over charcoal. *Şiş* kebap is grilled lamb on a skewer and *şiş köfte* is meatballs.

Fish is not cheap in Turkey and you should enquire about the price beforehand. It is sold by weight so before it is cooked the patron will weigh it and give you a price. Usually it comes fried or grilled, though in some places more ambitious dishes and sauces are prepared. Enquire to see if one of my favourites, a lemon and dill sauce, can be prepared. Usually your grilled or fried main course will come with French fries, a legacy of increasing tourism in this area. Instead you may like to order rice or *bulgur pilav*.

Sadly in some of the larger resorts the traditional cuisine is being subordinated to blander 'international' dishes that the restauranteurs think the tourists want. Unfortunately some of them do like their steak-and-eggs-and-chips. Fast food places have also sprouted in the resorts and the Turks have taken to these with a vengeance ensuring that they are here to stay. At least the hamburgers are made with real meat.

Desserts are not generally served in restaurants and for the traditional sweet sticky desserts you will usually have to go

'imit seller in Fethiye. Simits are ring-shaped rolls of bread covered with sesame seeds.

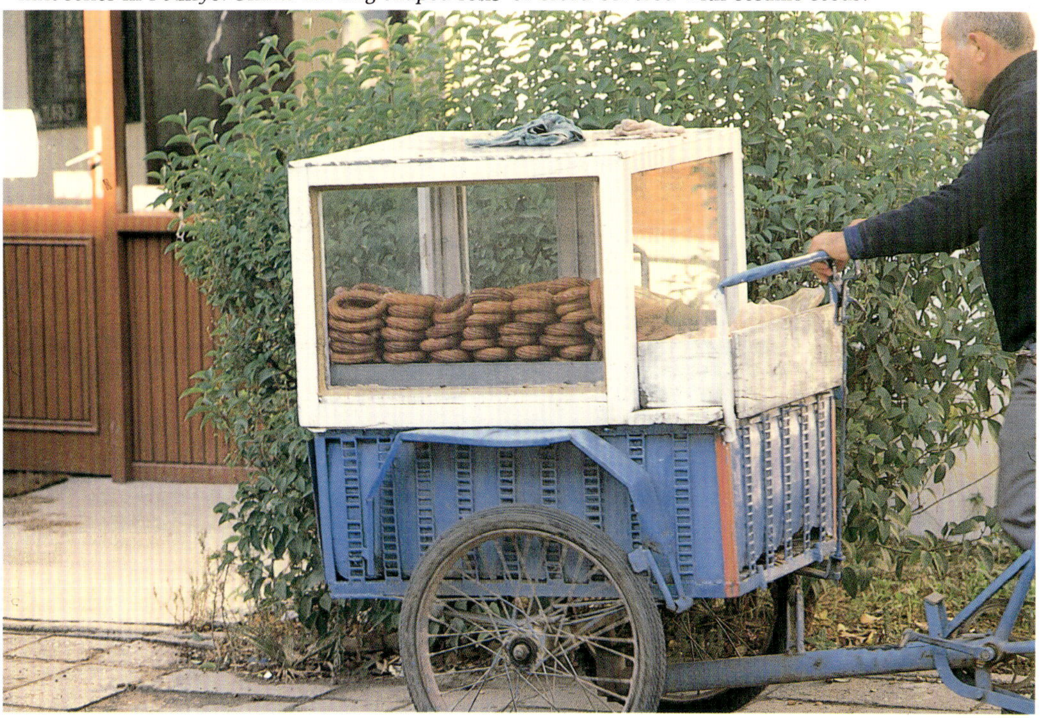

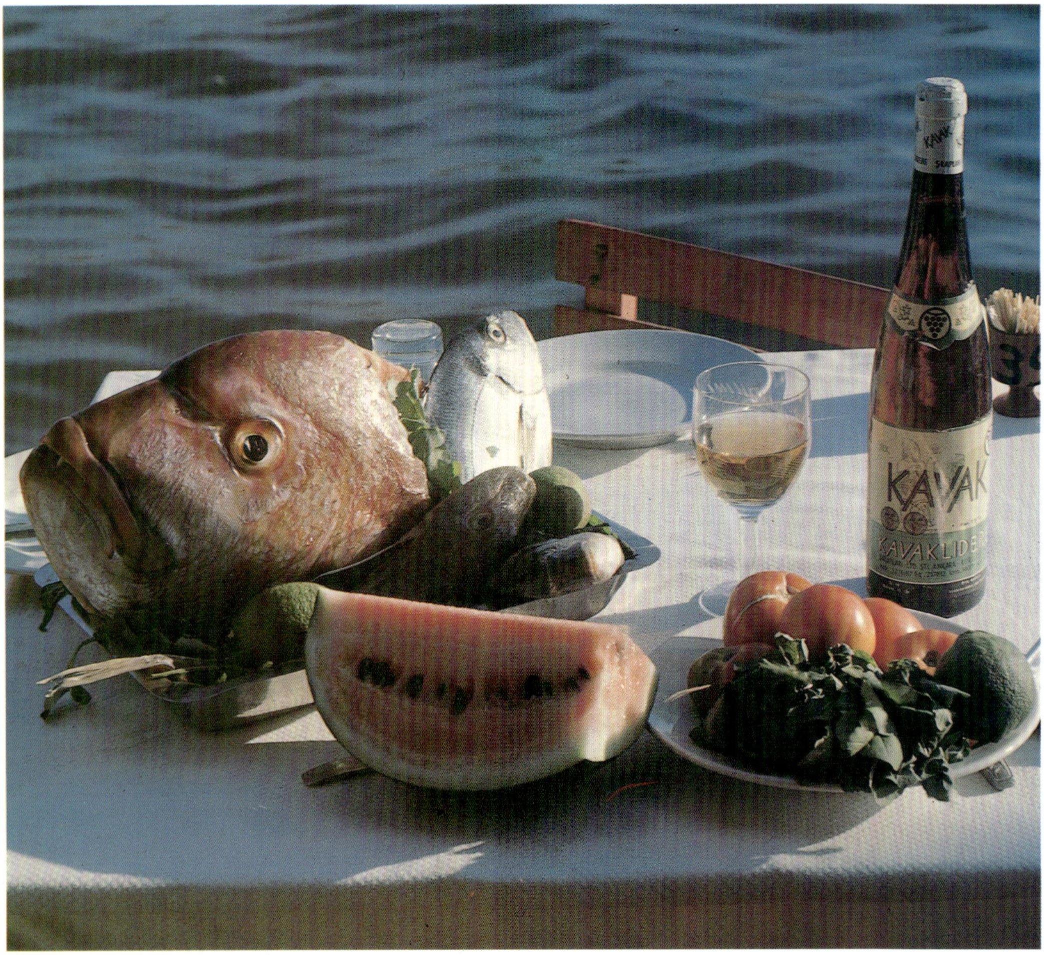

Döner Kebap restaurant

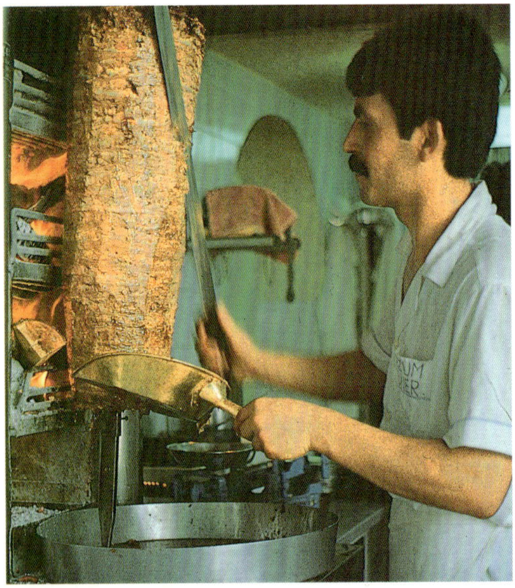

to a *Patisserie*. However a restaurant will usually have fresh fruit and depending on what is in season it may be peaches, apples, pears, grapes, oranges, or melon. As far as I am concerned a plate of honeydew melon beats sticky sweets anyday. The sticky sweets are almost identical to those found in Greece and parts of the Middle East: *baklava*, flaky pastry stuffed with nuts in a honey syrup, and *kadayıf*, shredded wheat with nuts in the same sweet syrup. Some of the *Patisseries* make a variety of chocolate and sponge cakes, but on the whole these are too sweet for my taste. *Dondurma*, ice cream, is also popular and is often sold on the streets by colourfully attired vendors who make a great show of their prowess at flicking scoops of ice cream into the cone.

DRINKS

Though the Turks introduced coffee to Europe, it is not the national drink. That privilege is accorded to *çay* and all over Turkey you will find *çay* shops serving the little tulip shaped glasses of strong amber tea. It is always drunk without milk and usually sweet, though the sugar lumps come separately so you can determine how sweet you want it to be. In some tea shops you can get 'apple tea' made with dried apples, and *ada çay*, 'island tea', made from sage and reputed to cure everything from a tummy upset to a cold. In most *çay* shops you can get *Türk kahve*, Turkish coffee, a small cup of concentrated brew with the grounds in the bottom of the cup. Nescafe is also obtainable in some cafes and *çay* shops in the larger and more cosmopolitan spots, a reflection of the demands of tourism on the coast.

Beer is brewed in Turkey with '*Efes*' and '*Tuborg*' the two most common brands. The beer is a light, slightly bitter pilsener, eminently drinkable on hot summer days. Wines are surprisingly good when you consider that Turkey is nominally a Muslim country. Good reds are *Villa Doluca, Dikmen,* and *Buzbağ*. Good whites are *Villa Doluca, Çankaya,* and *Kavak*. Though they are good quaffable wines, consistency is not always what it should be and the bottle that follows, of the same brand and vintage, may not be as good as the first.

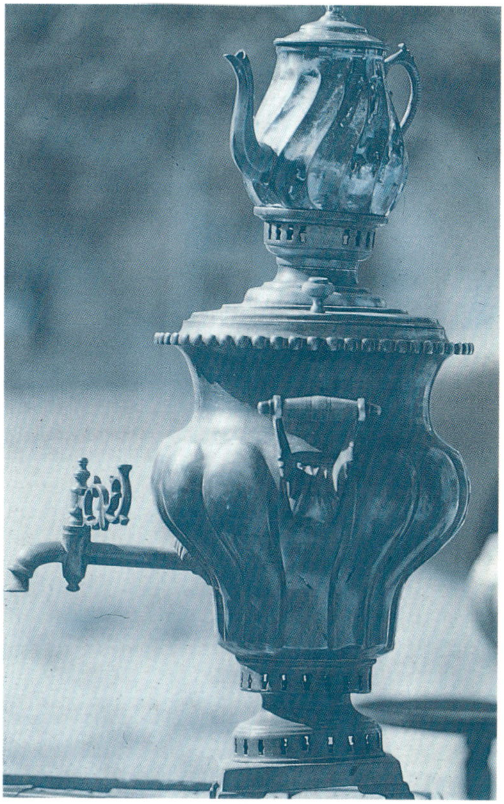

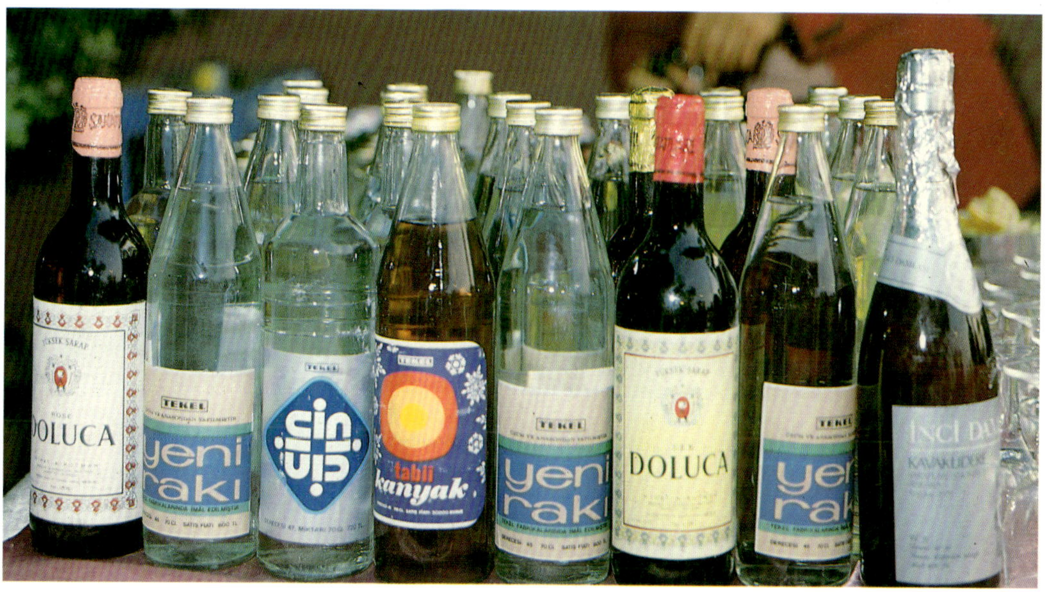

If there is a national drink after *çay*, it is *rakı*, the clear aniseed flavoured spirit similar to Greek *ouzo* and French *pastis*. With water it turns a milky white colour. Some Turks drink prodigious quantities of the stuff, but newcomers should beware of the kick hiding behind the pleasant aniseed flavour. Other hard spirits such as gin, vodka, and brandy are also manufactured in Turkey by the state distiller *Tekel*. The brandy is terrible, more akin to cough mixture than brandy as we know it. Imported spirits are available but expensive.

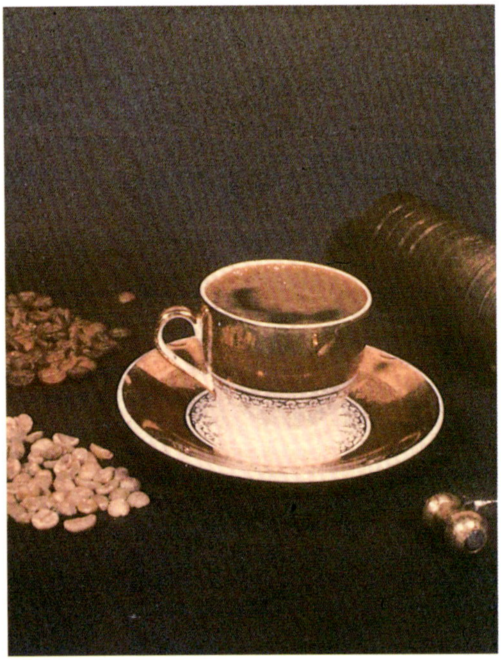

Apart from all this alcohol, caffeine, and tanin, there are excellent fruit juices. Most of the good brands are concentrated 100% juice and are excellent. Cherry, peach, and apple are commonly available. Spring water (*su*) is available everywhere and will often be put on the table in a cafe or restaurant as a matter of course. If you want fizzy mineral water ask for *maden sodası*. One other drink you will come across is *ayran*, yoghurt mixed with water. Though I love yoghurt, and Turkish yoghurt is good stuff, *ayran* is something I can't get on with. Turks drink a lot of it, but most foreigners try it only once.

Doctors And Dentists

Although medical and dental services are adequate in the large cities, in the burgeoning resorts along the coast medical and dental services have not kept pace with the summer populations. In the towns, in Bodrum, Muğla, Marmaris, Fethiye, and Kaş, there are doctors and dentists, but for anything major I recommend you go to İzmir or if possible return to Europe. For minor ailments it is quite normal to go to the chemist (*eczane*) who will advise you on what to take. Sign language suffices for most minor ills. Medicines normally on prescription in Europe are readily available over the counter in Turkey and this includes antibiotics, sulphur drugs, and the contraceptive pill.

Toilets

Though the newer hotels, pensions, and restaurants have western style commode toilets, there are still a lot of the eastern style foot-pad toilets around. Most public toilets are of this type and it takes a while to get used to them. They are actually a more ergonomic design than the commode type, as apparently the squatting position is better for you. A few pointers may help. Be careful to remove loose change and other items from your trouser pockets or it is likely to fall out. Always carry some toilet paper with you as there will often be none, especially in public toilets. A sign will usually ask you not to put paper down the toilet, Turkish plumbing is not designed for it, and a basket will be provided. While hygiene is usually good in hotels and restaurants, in public toilets it is more often not - just hold your nose and think of roses.

Tourist Information

Tourist Information Offices can be found in Bodrum, Marmaris, Köyceğiz, Fethiye and Kaş. As well as information on local attractions and places of interest, these offices can also supply lists of hotels, details of organised excursions, information on hire-cars and rates, and routes and timetables for buses and *dolmuş'*. The staff in these offices are invariably helpful and will have brochures and maps for the region and often for other parts of Turkey as well. If you have any complaints about anything, take them to the Tourist Office staff who will contact the local police or other relevant authority.

Money And Banks

Turkish *lira* is the currency and mostly you will be dealing with 500, 1000, 5000, 10.000 and 20.000 *lira* notes. Turkey has an inflation rate of around 40% per annum, so for the tourist with hard currency costs remain about the same from year to year, though some charges, hotel and pension room rates and marina fees for instance, are now priced in one of the stable hard currencies such as deutschemarks or sterling.

Along the coast there are banks in the larger towns and resorts, in Bodrum, Muğla, Marmaris, Köyceğiz, Fethiye, and Kaş. There are also exchange offices at the airports in İstanbul, İzmir, Dalaman and Antalya. Banks are open from 8.30 am to midday and 1.30 to 5.00 pm. You can change money in the form of Eurocheques with a Eurocheque card, Travellers cheques, or hard cash. In some banks you can get cash with a credit card, Visa being more common than Access, but this may take some time and it is best not to rely on it. Credit cards such as Visa and Access, and charge cards such as American Express and Diners Club, can be used in the more up-market shops, especially leather and carpet shops, hire car companies, and in up-market hotels and restaurants. Often you will be asked to pay 5% to 7% over and above the cost of an item if you use plastic money, as this is what must be paid by the vendor to the card company. There is a black market for hard currency in Turkey, but apart from the fact it is illegal, the rate is in any case not much above the bank rate, perhaps 10% at best, so it is not worth dabbling in. If you are buying expensive souvenirs, such as *kilims* or carpets, keep your currency exchange slips to prove you have legally exchanged money to purchase them.

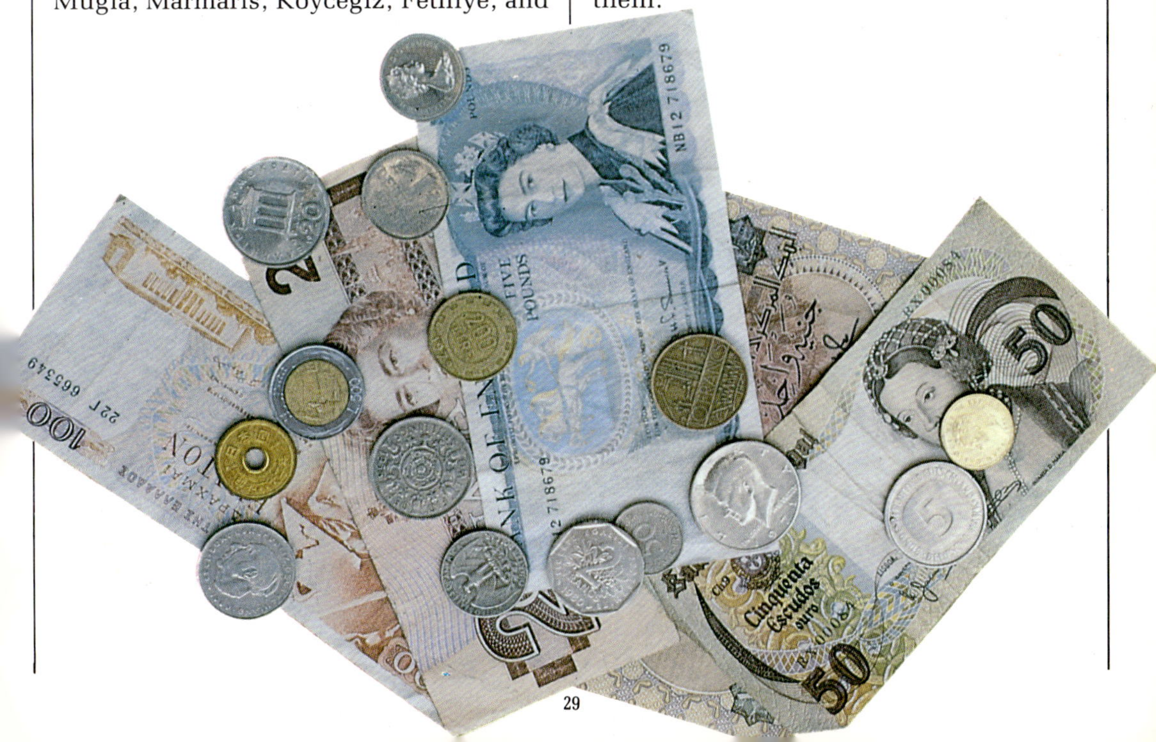

Post And Telecommunications

This all takes place at the PTT, '*Posta, Telefon, Telgraf*', where you can buy stamps, post letters, buy telephone tokens (*jetons*), and make telephone calls. In the large towns and resorts there will be a telephone kiosk and post-boxes. Telephone calls are best made using jetons which can often be purchased in a shop near telephone kiosks as well as the PTT. Using *jetons* (large/*büyük*, small/*küçük*) you can dial international direct, though you may have to pop *jetons* in at a fast rate for calls to Britain or the USA. The telephone lines are often busy and you just have to be patient dialling national or international. Going through the operator is even slower, often a matter of hours, so it is best to persevere with direct dialling and a handful of *jetons*.

Shopping

Is a delight. From the array of fresh produce, herbs and spices, and cloths in the market to the array of carpets and *kilims* in carpet shops, it is a feast for the eyes. Turkey has a lot to offer the souvenir hunter, and there are few who don't come back with something to remind them of the country. Some of the things you will find are...

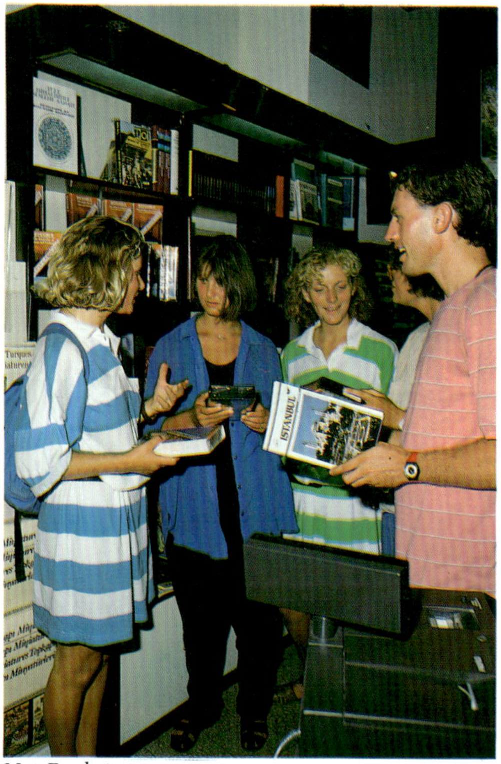

Net Bookstore.

The Grand Bazaar.

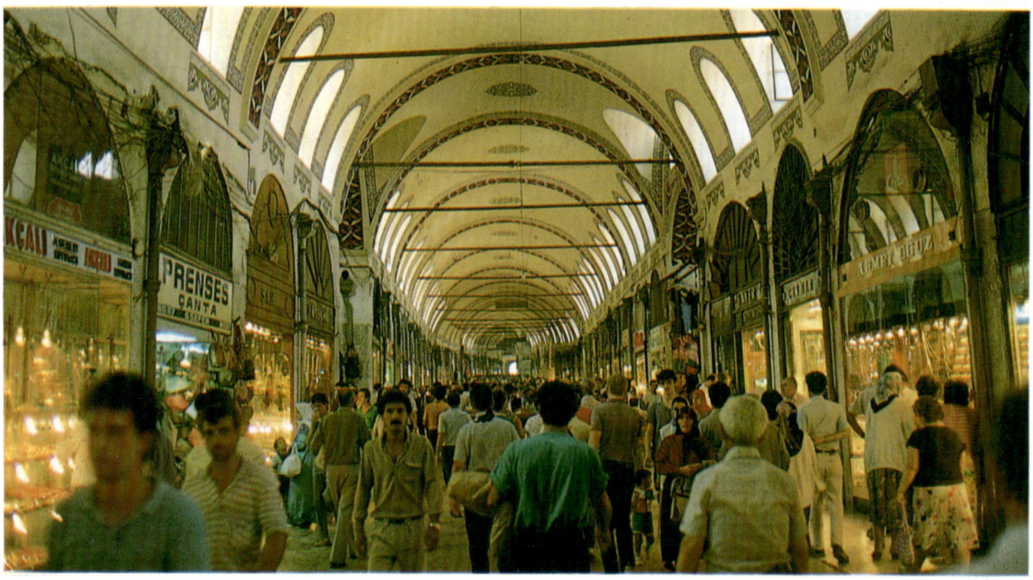

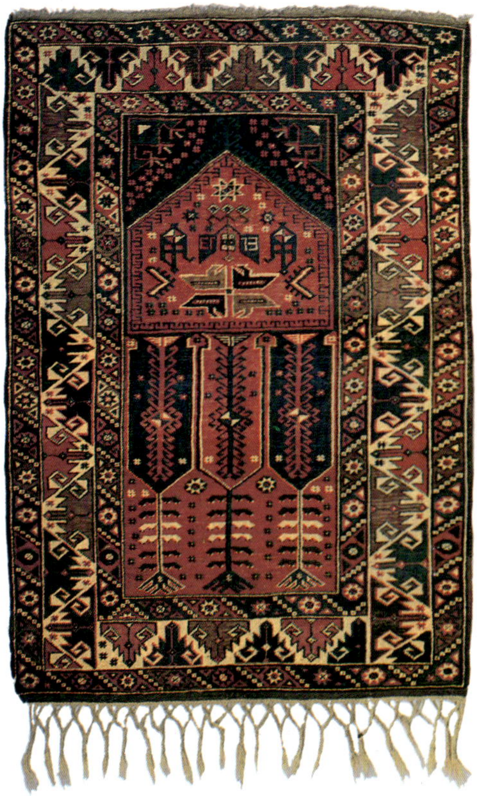

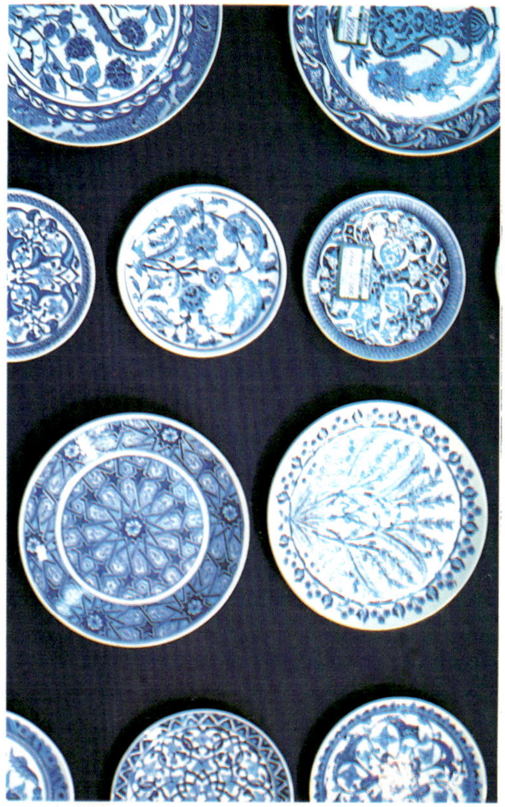

CERAMICS

Plates of different sizes and other assorted pottery are hand-painted in bright and attractive colours and patterns. The firing is not always the best and the pottery often has cracks under the glaze, but is still worth having.

MEERSCHAUM

Most of the meerschaum in the world is found in Turkey and the ardent pipe-smoker will know all about Turkish meershcaum pipes. The white soapy stone is carved into all sorts of shapes for the bowl, mythical creatures, old men, turbanned heads, and abstract patterns, some of it of great artistry and worth buying even if you are not a pipe-smoker. For pipe-smokers, meerschaums are a bargain in Turkey compared to prices in Europe.

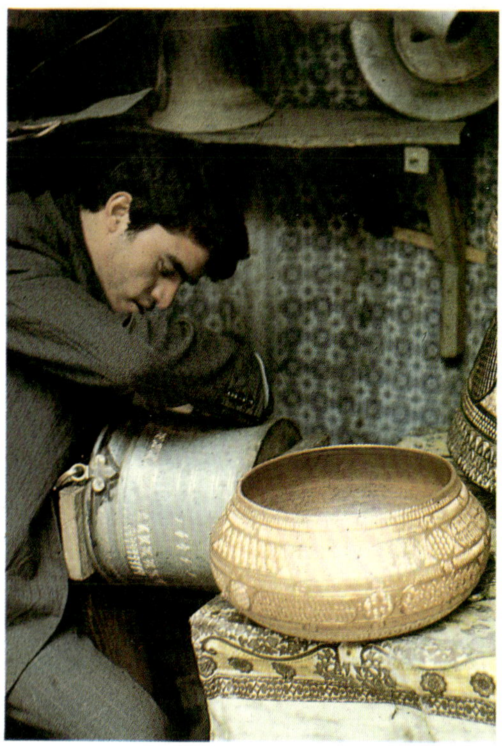

Galeri İstanbul.

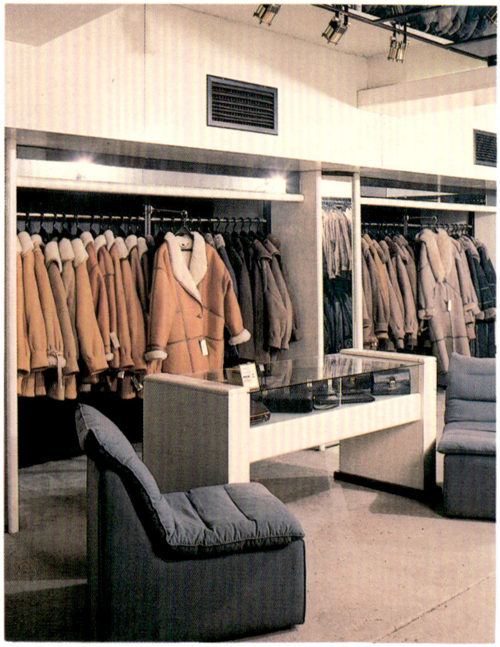

LEATHER AND SUEDE

These are excellent value whether you are buying the latest leather fashion gear or more traditional garb. However take your time over buying an article, make sure it fits properly, and check to see that it is well-made as there is a lot of badly made gear using poor quality left-overs, as well as nicely executed sturdy stuff.

JEWELLERY

There is old and new and sometimes a combination of the two. Ottoman jewellery is quite elaborate often fussy stuff and so a jeweller may re-work it into several less ornate pieces. Depending on your taste, there are good bargains to be had in gold, but go to a reputable goldsmith and check the hallmark carefully.

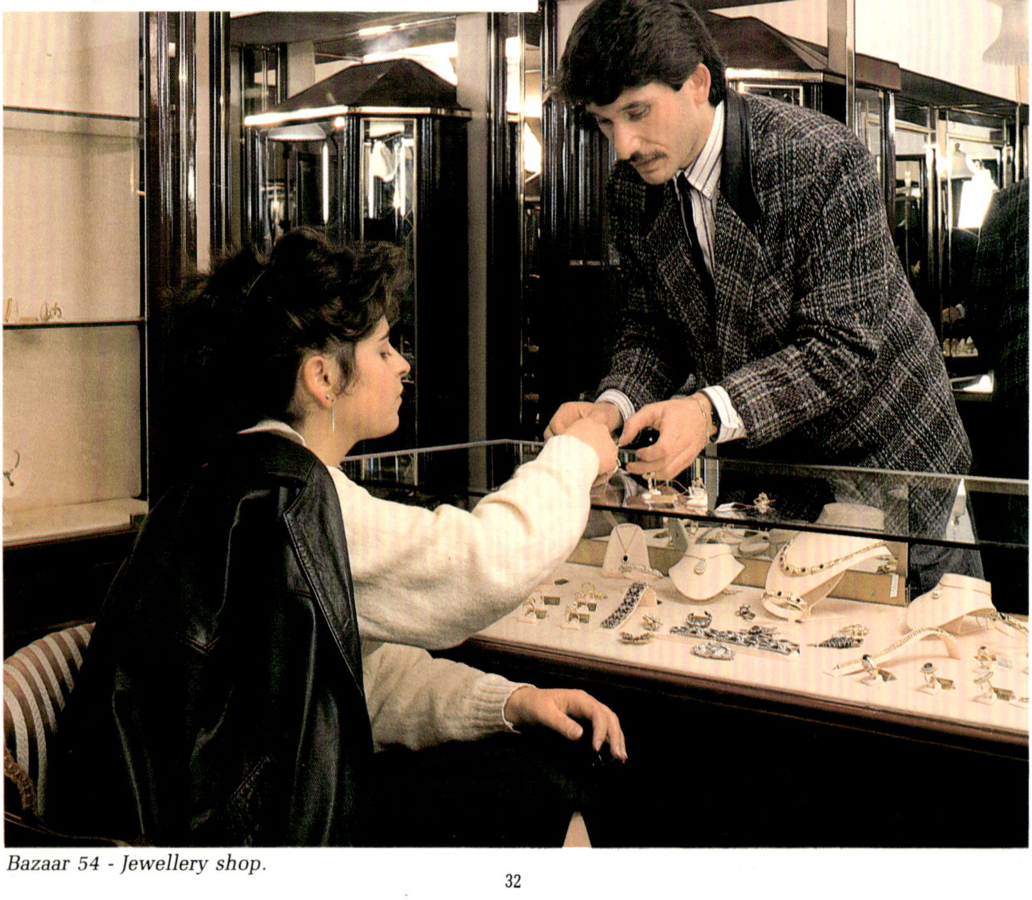

Bazaar 54 - Jewellery shop.

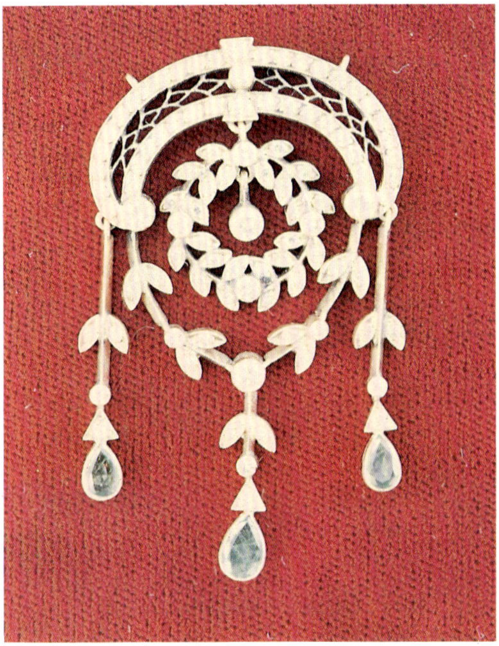

COPPER

Large copper pots and pans and other vessels are commonly available and are good value if you have room in your baggage to carry them home.

CARPETS AND KİLİMS

To give a run-down on buying a carpet or *kilim* is impossible and in the end you should not be concerned with whether or not you have obtained a bargain, but whether you like the piece. Good carpets and *kilims* are not cheap, not even for Turks, and for exceptional pieces you will be looking at thousands of pounds. But for a substantially lower sum you can buy a good carpet or *kilim* at less than the price in Europe, though only at around one third off European prices. Buy a carpet or kilim because you like it and have a place to put it in your home, and not in the mistaken belief that you can sell it on and make money in Europe or elsewhere. Carpet and *kilim* wholesalers buying in bulk get a bigger discount than you can.

There are a number of pointers to help you on your way to getting a good piece. Examine the carpet to determine how close the weave is. The finer the weave, that is the more knots there are per square centimetre, the better the quality and the higher the price. Examine the colours on the surface and then part the pile and look

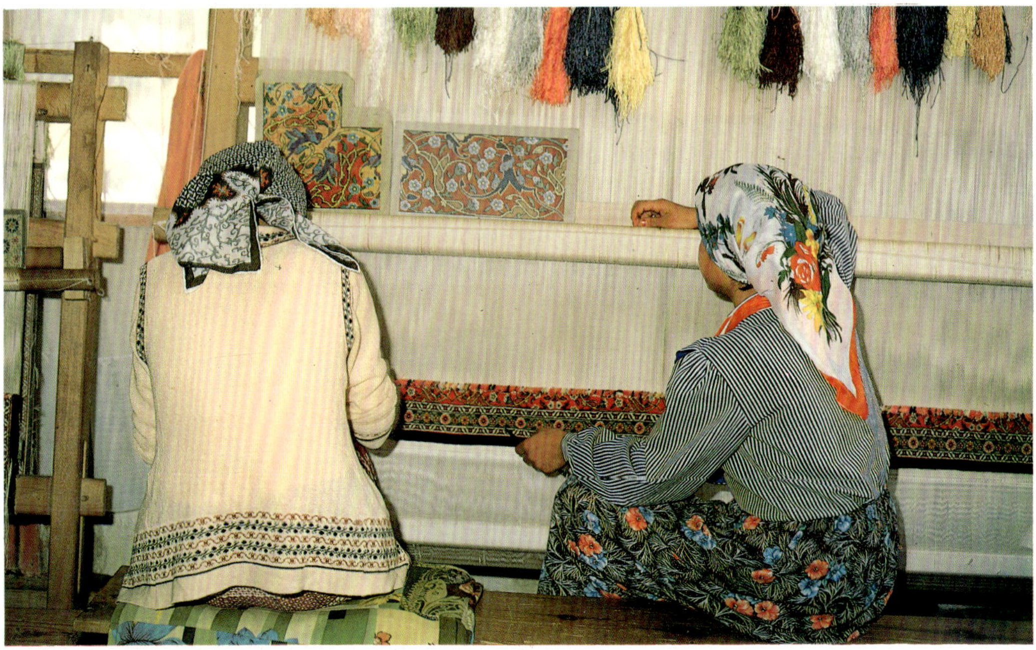

Bazaar 54.

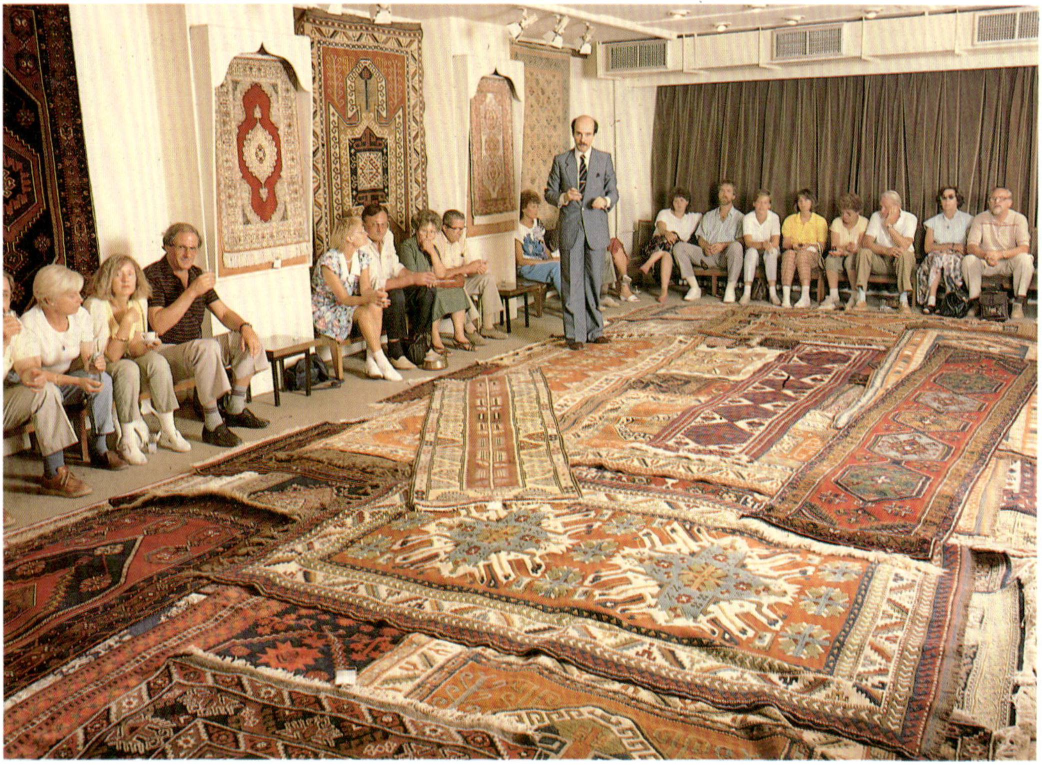

at the root of the fibres. If the colour is darker at the roots there is a good chance the piece has been acid-washed to look older - this shortens its life by weakening the fibres and decreases its value. Genuinely old pieces that have faded have an even gradation of colour through each fibre and a different feel to the coarseness an acid-wash gives.

Take the piece outside to look at it in daylight which will give you a better idea of the colours than the soft lights in the shop. Artificial dyes have been used since the 1890's and despite the salesman's assurance that the piece has 100% vegetable dyes, this is unlikely. Take a handkerchief or a bit of cloth of some sort, preferably white, and dampen a corner and drag it across the carpet. If the artificial dyes have not been fixed properly you will pick up colour on the damp cloth. Pre-1890 pieces are very expensive indeed and are nearly all collectors items. The carpet should have a different shading when looked at from opposite ends as the pile is always orientated one way or the

Flat-weave kilims come as rugs, camel bags, and cushion covers.

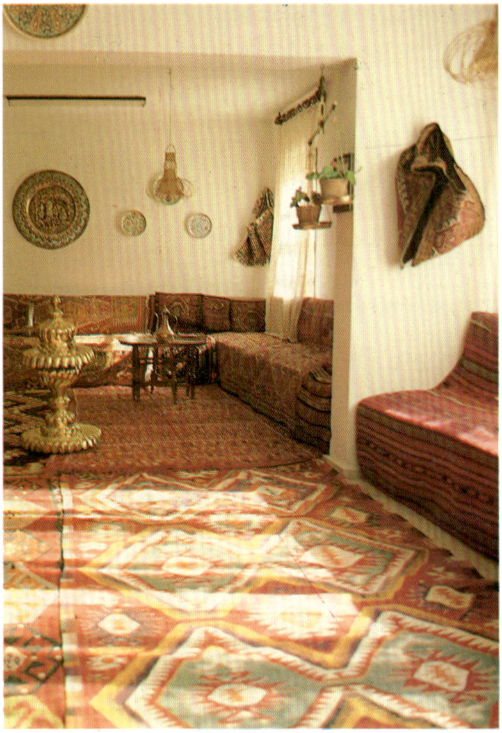

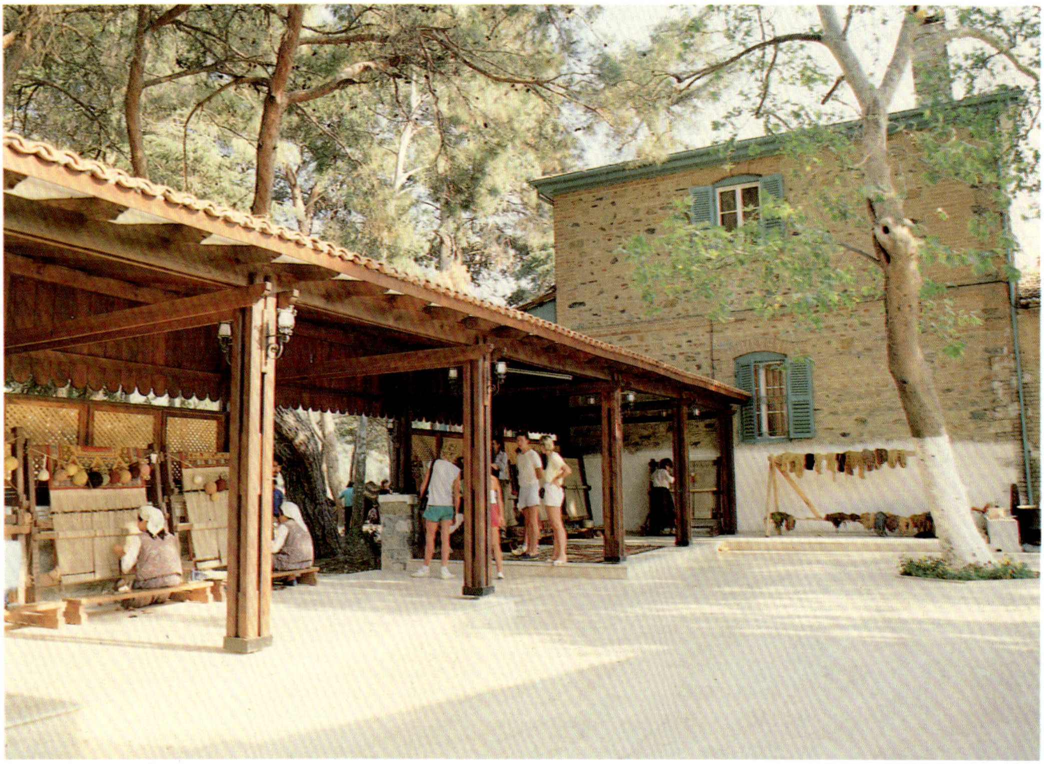

Sultanköy Handicrafts Production Centre.

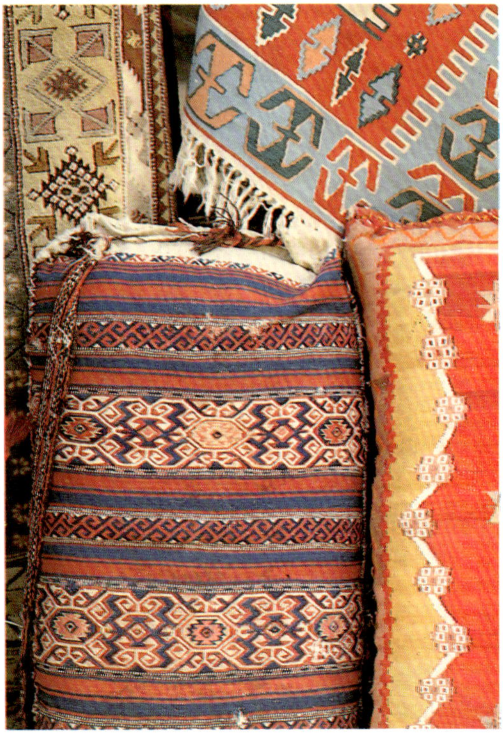

other. It is not a bad idea to get hold of one of the small books on carpets for sale in Turkey, to get some idea of regions and colours and patterns, but it won't make you into an expert and the carpet dealer will know this.

Haggling over the price is ritual and you should never pay the asking price. Go around a number of shops to see what sort of price you can get down to for similar pieces and to get an idea of patterns and colours and the 'look' of a carpet. *Kilims*, the flat woven rugs, are a different ball-game again and it is mostly a matter of comparing like pieces and prices. It's worth spending some time over buying a piece and the time spent looking is enjoyable in itself. Usually the dealer will offer you *çay* or coffee, but don't feel obliged to make a purchase because of this. All this bother is well worth it. You will be buying something which is hand-crafted, beautiful, and functional. A good Turkish carpet or *kilim* will most likely go on giving service after you have shuffled off.

CHAPTER -1-

BODRUM-TO-DATÇA

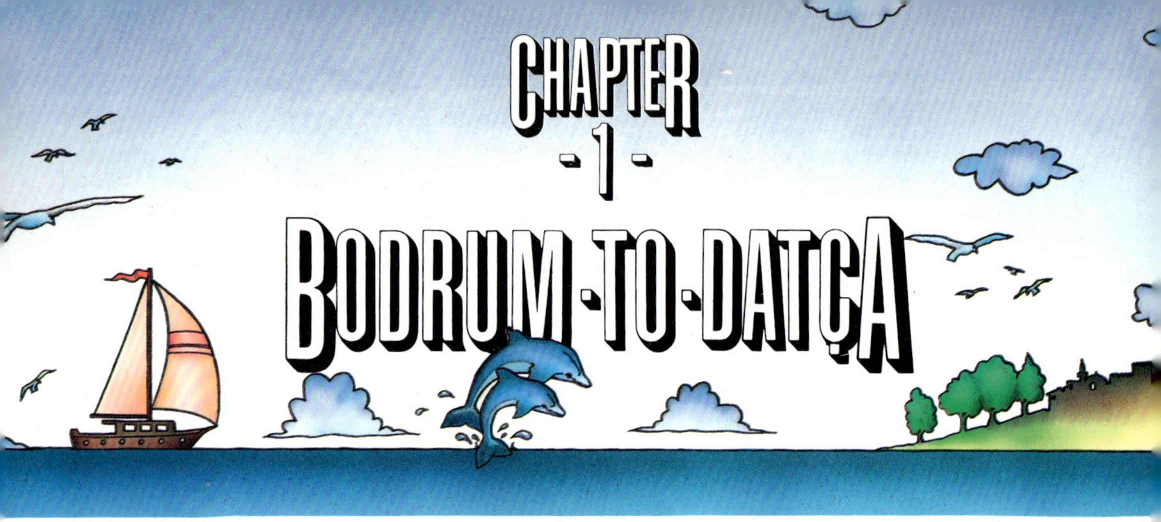

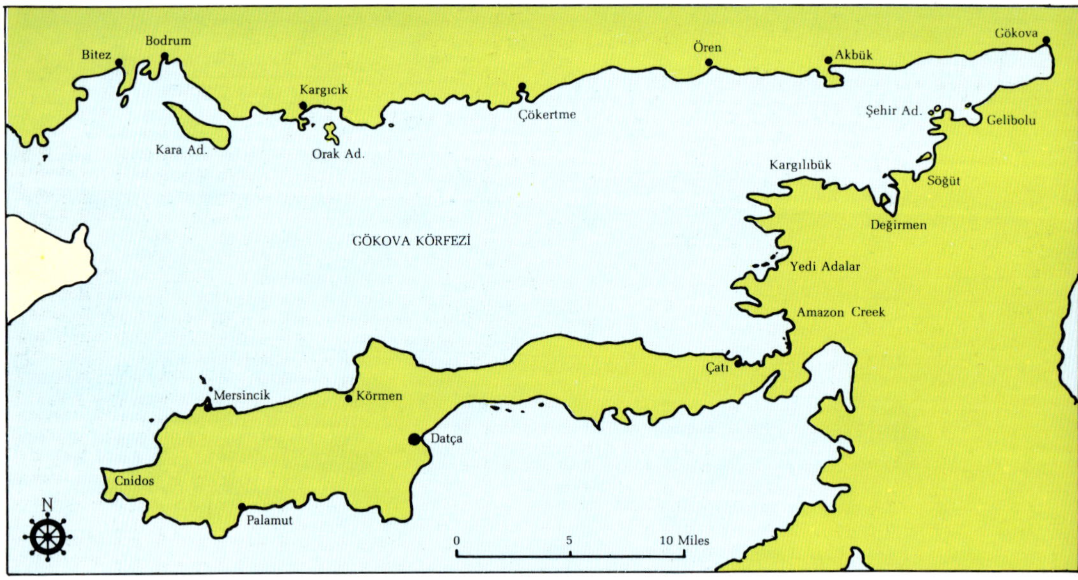

Ancient Caria
Bodrum
Halicarnassus
The Castle of the Knights
Local Boats
Around Bodrum: Kara Ada, Gümbet, Bitez, Ada Boğazı, Kargı, Bağla, Aspat, Karaincir, Akyarlar.
Excursions from Bodrum: Archaeological: Priene, Iassus, Didyma, Ephesus, Aphrodisias. Other: Mumcular, Milas, Pamukkale.
Gökova Körfezi
Pabuç and Kargıcık
Orak Adası
Çökertme
Around Çökertme
Ören
Akbük
Gökova İskele
Around Gökova: Idyma, Muğla.
Gelibolu
Şehir Adaları
Cedreae
Anthony and Cleopatra
Söğüt
Değirmen Bükü
Kargılıbük
Yedi Adalar
Amazon Creek
Çatı
Körmen
Mersincik
Cnidos
Palamut
Coast to Datça: Kalaboshi, Parmak, Kargı.

If you look at a map of Turkey and exercise a little imagination, in the southwest corner you will see what looks like a great gaping set of jaws snapping at the island of Kos just tantalisingly out of reach. This is the Gulf of Gökova, the ancient Gulf of Keramos, which with a part of the bottom jaw as far as the former fishing village of Datça, is the content of this chapter. In common with all of the area covered in this book, it is a mountainous region cut by deep gorges and ravines and until recent years an area as remote as any in the Mediterranean. Bodrum is the undisputed tourist hot-spot of the coast, an all-singing-and-dancing tourist resort in startling contrast to the simpler pleasures of the small villages and bays in the gulf. The only way to explore the gulf properly is by boat. It is quite simply impossible to visit many of the places by road though adventurous souls can get to some of them on newly constructed gravel roads carved through the hills to coastal villages. But to get the feel of the region there is nothing to touch the approach from seawards. Deep into the gulf the slopes are covered in pine forest down to the waters edge giving an almost improbable solid green covering to the otherwise dry rocky hills.

This region between Bodrum and Datça encompasses the greater part of what was ancient Caria. For the inland sites in

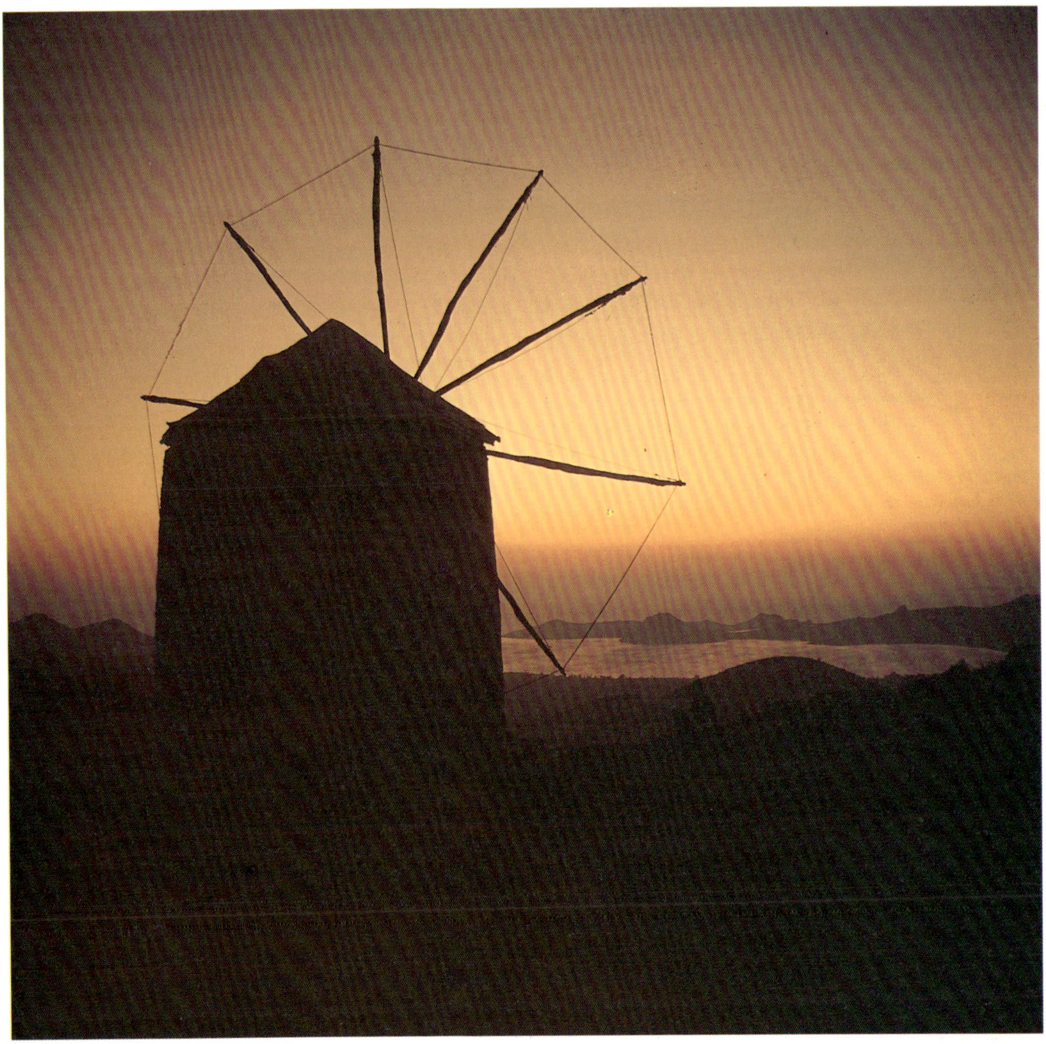

this area, excursions are best made from Bodrum where buses and *dolmuşes* can get you to most of them. Alternatively a hire car will let you cover more ground and offers greater flexibility so that you can spend as much or as little time at a site as you want. Many of the sites of the ancient cities are dotted around the coast and can be reached by a day boat trip. From Bodrum a *gulet* can be chartered for a two, three, or seven day trip around the gulf and the ancient sites. At most of them there is a sheltered anchorage or a harbour nearby and even if you are not interested in ancient bits of rubble or have suffered from a surfeit of Graeco-Roman remains, only the most hard of heart can deny the romance of sitting on deck and watching dusk settle on the skeleton of a Cedreae or a Cnidos.

Ancient Caria:

In ancient times the coast and the hinterland were divided into provinces that owed their origins to the indigenous population or to peoples who colonised it from other areas. In many cases it is difficult to determine whether an area was so named from the indigenous population or colonists, or as is often the case, a mixture of the two. Caria is one of those regions whose origins are unsure with conflicting evidence and ancient commentaries giving no definitive answer. Herodotus (484-425 BC) tells us that the Carians were originally from the Greek Islands, subjects of King Minos of Crete, that they were great seafarers and fighters who manned the Minoan fleets. They were then called Lelagians and when the Dorian and Ionian Greeks spread from mainland Greece down through the islands, the Lelagians were forced across to the coast of Asia Minor. Thucydides, the Athenian historian (460-396 BC), gives a variation of Herodotus' story. He claims the Carians were pirates throughout the Greek islands and that King Minos expelled them when their piracy got out of hand. Pausanias, that intrepid travel writer of the 2nd century AD, says that the Carians were a native race of Anatolia and that colonists from Crete had mixed with them and adopted their name. Archaeological evidence tends to the opinion that the Carians were an indigenous race with a long history of their own. Colonists from across the water most certainly arrived here and were absorbed into the local population along with new ideas and skills that were adopted by the native Carians. The brief mention Homer makes of the Carians in the 8th century BC is that they were 'barbarous of speech' and it is interesting that today the harshest dialect in western Turkey is still found in this region. Turks from Istanbul often comment that they cannot understand all that is said in Bodrum - Turks from Bodrum say that is just as well.

Right through the Greek and Roman periods the Carians preserved their own identity. Greek and Roman architectural ideas were adopted and presumably so were matters of dress, diet, and religion. One thing the Carians were long famous for was their seafaring skill. As far back as the 8th Century BC the Carian fighting fleet was a feared and respected force, though there is a curious tale told by Herodotus that rather confounds this apparent fame. When Xerxes was preparing his fleet for the invasion of Greece in 480 BC, Artemisia, queen of Caria, not only contributed ships to the expedition but also joined the fleet in person. At the Battle of Salamis when the Persian fleet was routed by the numerically inferior Greek fleet, Artemisia managed to escape in an unusual way. While her own ship was being pursued by an Athenian ship, by design or accident, she turned and bore down on a ship from her own side, a Calyndian vessel, and ramming it amidships sank it with all hands. The Athenian ship then left her alone presuming she must be fighting on the Greek side; Xerxes watching from a distant hill-side assumed the Calyndian ship to be one of the enemy and was full of praise for Artemisia's bravery. Apparently none of the luckless Calyndians survived to tell the real story.

*At it's greatest Carian territory extended from what is now Lake Bafa in the north to Lake Köyceğiz east of Marmaris. In the north were the ancient cities of Heracleia, Alinda and Alabanda. In the south Caunos represented the most southerly Carian territory and overlapped into Lycia. The area corresponds almost exactly to the modern administrative province (***'vilayet'***) of Muğla. Caria remained intact through the great invasions that swept through Asia Minor without losing it's identity although that identity took a few batterings along the way. When the Persians dominated Asia Minor under Darius and Xerxes', Caria was part of the greater Persian Empire. However with Xerxes' defeat by the Athenians and*

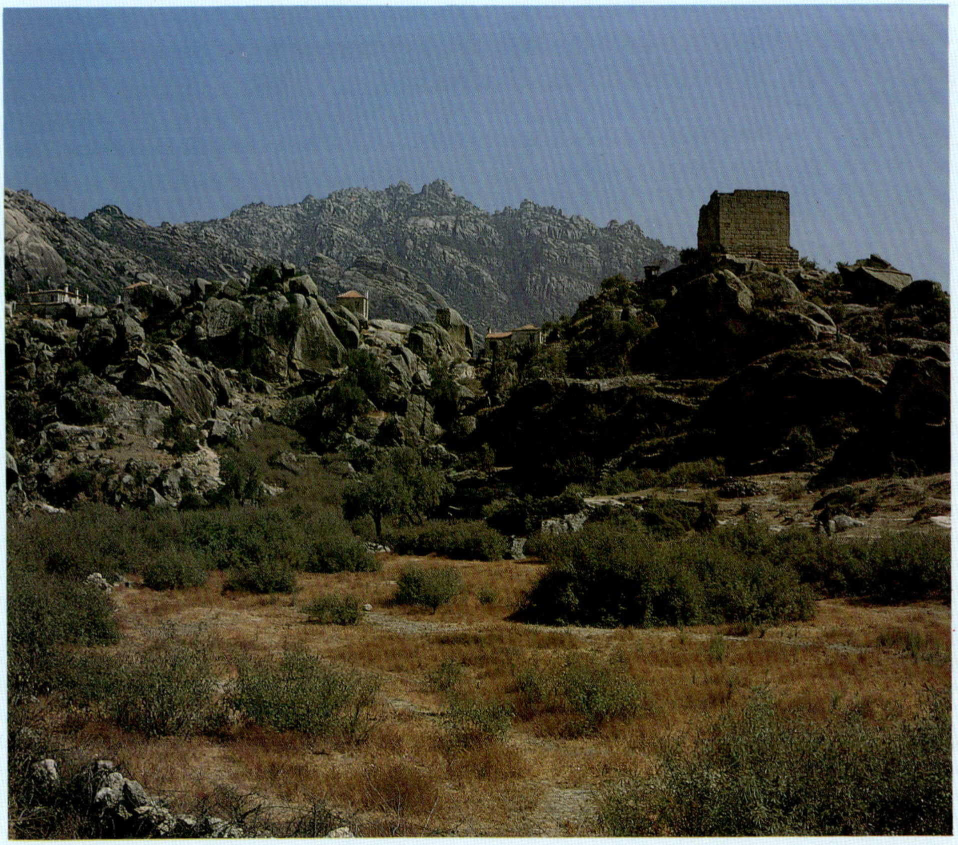

the formation of the Delian Confederacy, the Carian cities came under Athenian sway. With the Spartan victory over Athens in 405 BC the Carian cities were under Spartan rule, though only for a brief ten years until the Spartans were removed from power. The Persians now moved in again and divided their empire into satrapies, provinces ruled by a local governor who owed allegiance to Persia. In 377 BC Mausolus became satrap of Caria and he craftily developed Caria into an independent power without upsetting his Persian masters. Alexander the Great stormed through the region in 334 BC and with the aid of Queen Ada, an exiled Carian queen, soon had the region firmly under his control. Queen Ada was installed as ruler and appears to have become something of a mother figure to the eccentrically talented Alexander. The death of Alexander in 323BC left a power vacuum and like much of the then civilized world, Caria was fought over by various groups though none gained any lasting control.

The Romans finally sorted things out and with the defeat of the Macedonian King Phillip V in 197 BC, order finally returned to the region. There were political hiccups with the arrival of Mithriadates in 88 BC and Anthony's orgiastic rule a little later, but the defeat of Anthony by Octavius marked the beginning of an era of stable government and prosperity for Caria. Towards the end of the Roman Empire and the birth of Byzantine, Caria began to decline, the population moved away, and the once great coastal cities lost their former power and some of their splendour. What happened in the interior is difficult to know, certainly Caria could no longer be considered a region but rather a collection of coastal towns. On the whole antiquity had been kind to Caria. The centuries that followed were to be less so as Caria became more and more a remote and forgotten region.

BODRUM

Whether you enter Bodrum by land or by sea, two things immediately impress themselves on your senses. The first is the Castle of St Peter, a giant Medieval silhouette that dominates the town. From the sea it appears as a grey blob amongst the houses and as you close it, crennalated towers, battlements, and defensive walls gradually take form. In the harbour you are under the shadow of it's high walls. The other thing is the hustle and bustle and sheer energy of the town. There are yachts and *gulets* crammed into every available space. Cars and motorbikes hurtle around the waterfront narrowly missing pedestrians. Bodrum has been called the St Tropez of Turkey and if the panegyric is not quite accurate, it is a reflection of the feeling you get of a lot of people busily enjoying themselves. If you have come from some tranquil anchorage around the coast you will initially feel quite lost in the noise and confusion of the town. Once used to it the cosmopolitan feel of Bodrum comes as a welcome diversion to the more simpler pleasures of other places around the coast and for entertainment and a few nights out there is little to rival it nearby.

All of this is quite recent. Until a few years ago Bodrum was a remote fishing village that was easier to get to by sea than by land. Until the new road to Milas was built it used to take four hours to get there on the old road via Mumcular - a trip that now takes half an hour. In the 1950's Lord Kinross described what it was like trying

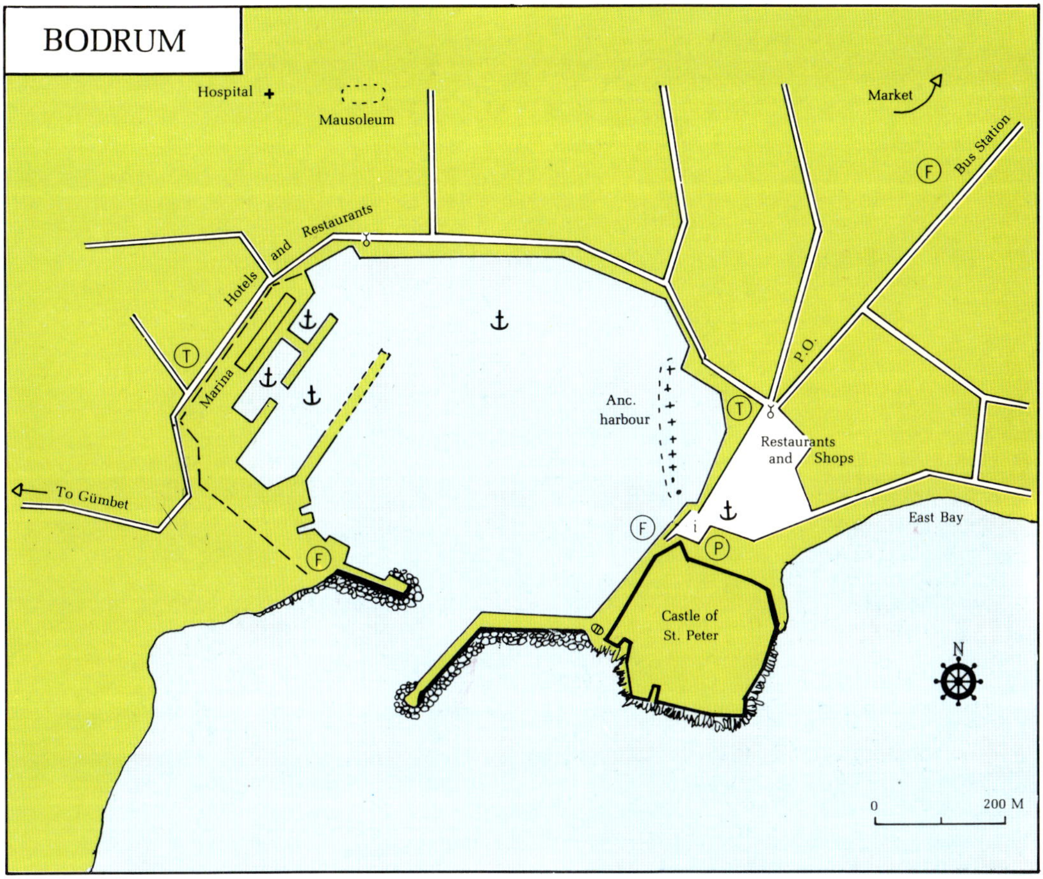

to get something to eat in Bodrum: "...no restaurant was open. They closed, I learnt, at 6.30 p.m. I dined off a biscuit and a bowl of yoghurt in a milk shop". Earlier on Bodrum was considered such a remote place that dissident writers and artists were exiled here. The most famous of them all was Cevat Şakir Kabaağaç, exiled here for his criticism of the Turkish Republic after it's formation in 1923. He acquired the title the 'Fisherman of Halicarnassus', a fisher of stories, and his tales of Bodrum and it's local characters became famous in Turkey, though sadly few have been translated into English. Others followed the 'fisherman' here and the village soon had a reputation for being a bit Bohemian, though evidently this was not enough to keep the restaurants open as Lord Kinross found out. In the seventy's the rich and those in the know from İstanbul and İzmir followed the writers and artists here and the village developed into a small resort that in recent years has grown and grown and looks like keeping on growing. Mercifully the foresight of the local council has restricted new buildings to the 'Bodrum-style' and to no more than three stories so that the town retains an architectural cohesion.

It also retains the character of a market town. On Friday, traditional market day because it is the Muslim equivalent of the Christian Sunday and the faithful could combine a trip to the mosque with their buying and selling, traffic is virtually brought to a stand-still by the stalls and customers thronging the streets. The taxi drivers get furious with the local farmers calmly wandering up the main street with a donkey laden with produce or half a

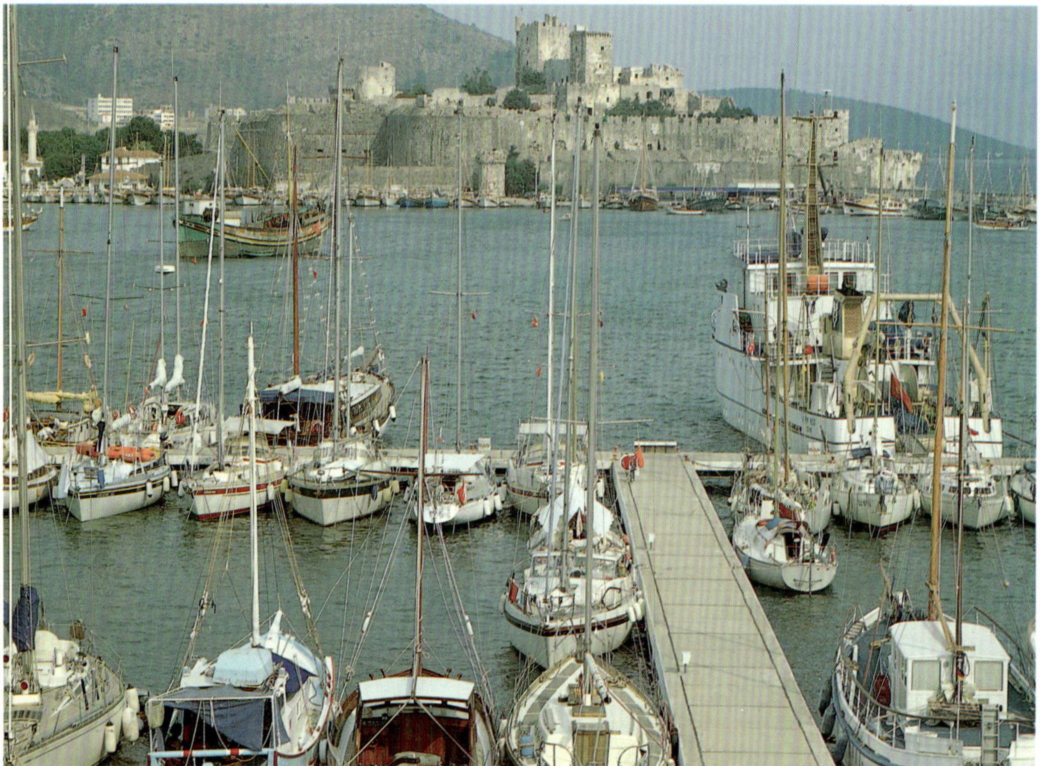

dozen sheep quite as at home on the street as they are roaming around the fields. All of the farmers, small-holders, tinkers, travelling merchants of every variety, anyone in the surrounding area, converges on Bodrum to buy or sell. Fresh fruit of every kind, oranges and tangerines, lemons, grapefruit, peaches, nectarines, water melons, honey and rock melons, plums, apples and cherries, can be found heaped up in huge piles according to the season. Tomatoes and more tomatoes, green peppers, hot peppers, aubergines, potatoes, carrots, green and red cabbages, cauliflowers, lettuces, onions and spring onions, fresh garlic and coarse Mediterranean parsley can be found in over-abundance. Not for nothing is Turkey called the market-garden of Europe. As well white village cheeses, green and black olives, nuts and dried fruit, herbs and spices, live chickens and ducks, sheep and cattle and the occasional camel, pots and pans, cloth and carpets are all displayed under cotton awnings in a scene straight out of a bazaar in the Arabian Nights. If you are in Bodrum for a few days only, contrive to be there on a Friday for market-day.

At night Bodrum throbs to the sound of amplified music and the babble of conversations from bars and restaurants. There are any number of good restaurants. Try 'Ibos' or 'Number 7' in an alley by the castle, the 'Gemibaşı' or the 'Amphora' close to the marina, or the 'Park' along the waterfront to the east of town. You can get chinese, well Turkish-chinese, by the marina, and in the main street behind the waterfront of the eastern bay is the 'Ahtapot' serving only octopus, but octopus as you have never tasted it before in a casserole, a stew, or a cold salad. Bars are littered all the way around the waterfront from the marina to the 'Halicarnassus' disco at the far end of the eastern bay. A few nights on the town will soon revive memories of the quieter places down the coast where your ear-drums and your liver can recover from the after-effects of too much Bodrum nightlife.

HALICARNASSUS

For somewhere that was the capital of Caria and the site of one of the Seven Wonders of the World, precious little remains in present-day Bodrum to remind one of it. The town itself is a collage of ancient bric-a-brac. You will find a section of column used as a base for a potted plant, blocks of ancient marble built into houses and the castle, part of a frieze used as a doorstep, a capital serving as a garden table, reliefs and pediments built into the walls of houses, everything that could be used has been. All of the ancient marble and stone has been recycled in some way or another and while this may offend the classical sensibility, it pleases the senses.

Halicarnassus was established as a Dorian city by colonists from the Peloponessus around the beginning of the tenth century BC. In 484 BC Herodotus, the 'father of written history', was born here and much of what we know about the origins of Halicarnassus and Asia Minor in the fifth century, we owe to him. Herodotus stands apart as an early writer because of his ability to arrange his material systematically and to look critically at his sources. He was surprisingly free of racial prejudice and his appreciation of the personalities he wrote about and his awareness of the foibles of human nature elevate his writings over and above most earlier and many later writers. After travelling throughout the known world he returned to Halicarnassus, but he

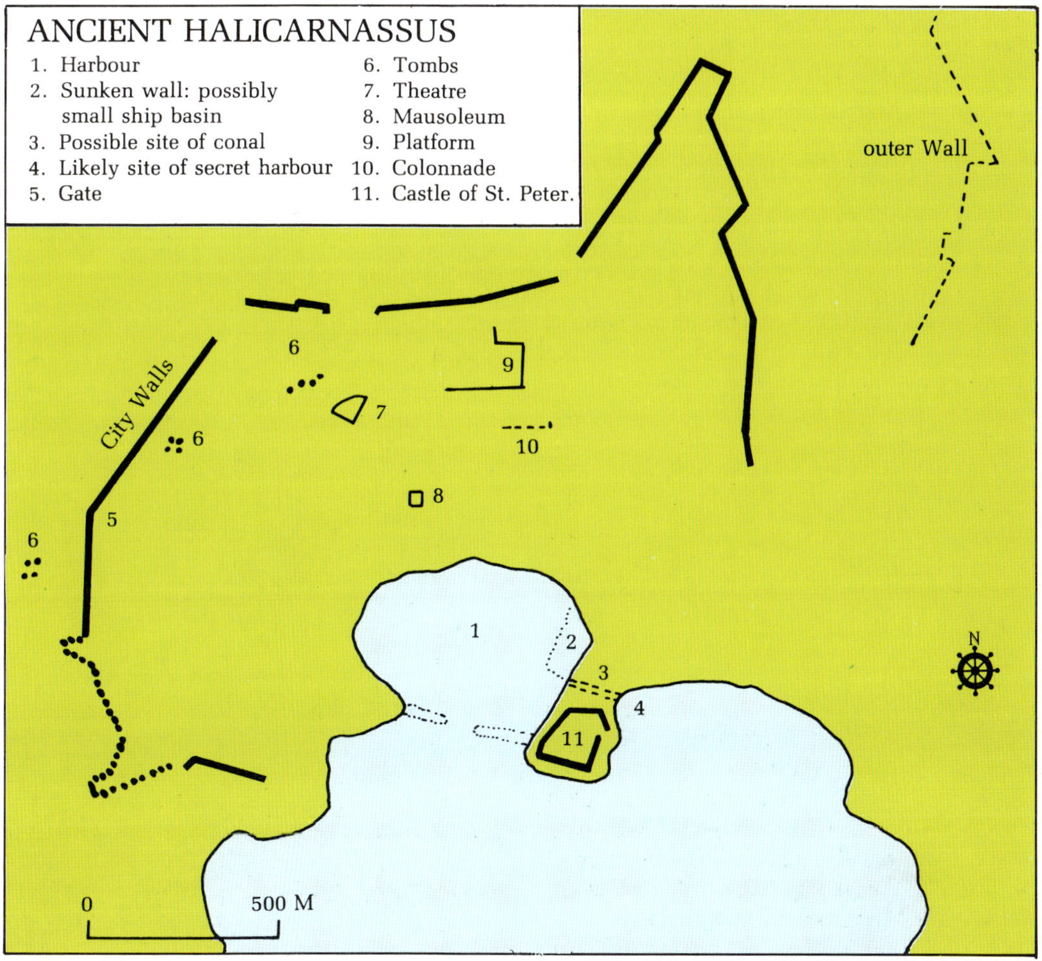

to stay long. He left after disagreements with the Dynasts and spent the last years of his life in Thuria in Italy.

It was the Dynasts who were to put Halicarnassus squarely on the map of the ancient world. In the fourth century BC the region was in Persian hands and ruled by local satraps. In 377 BC Mausolus took over and he set about making Halicarnassus the capital of Caria. He cannot be accused of mean ideas: he constructed three and a half miles of fortified city walls, the remains of which can still be traced on the western side of the town; he enclosed the harbour we see today and had a canal dug across the isthmus that now connects the castle to the mainland; he built temples and the theatre that remains today on the hillside above the main road to Gümbet; and for himself he built a large palace of sun-dried bricks decorated with marble from the Sea of Marmara, though the site of this edifice is not known with any certainty.

When Mausolus died he was succeeded by Artemisia, his sister and wife, it being common practice for a king to marry his sister as the Pharoahs did in Egypt. In his memory she constructed the magnificient tomb which became one of the Seven Wonders of the World. It also gave us the word 'mausoleum'. Today little remains apart from a hole in the ground where it stood, a few foundations and odd bits of marble. The small museum on the site at least has a reconstruction of what this huge tomb-monument looked like, but the site itself is disappointing. The mausoleum was reported to be still standing in the 12th century, but when the Knights of St John arrived in 1402, it was in ruins, presumably destroyed by an earthquake. The knights found the large quantity of marble a useful source of building materials for the castle and you can see bits and pieces of marble in the walls.

Although she ruled for just three short years, Artemisia proved to be a formidable successor to her brother and husband. When the Rhodians learnt that a woman now ruled Halicarnassus, they decided the city would be easy meat for their forces to take. When the Rhodian navy entered the harbour Artemisia led her fleet out of the canal and counter-attacked from the rear, routing the Rhodians and capturing their ships. Not content with simply defeating the Rhodians she sailed the ships back to Rhodes and those left behind, believing their triumphant fleet was returning, put up no resistance. She captured the city and the Rhodians, over-awed as well as overwhelmed by this Amazon-like Queen, erected a statue in her honour.

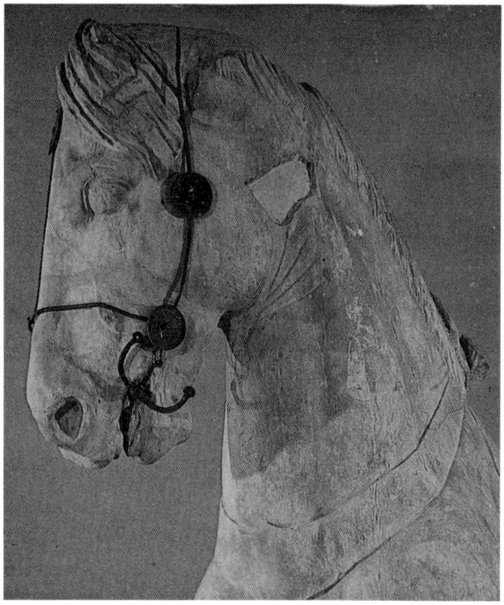

Marble horse from the Mausoleum at Halicarnassus, now in the British Museum.

Halicarnassus got it's come-uppance in 334 BC when Alexander arrived on the scene. The Halicarnassians declined to surrender so Alexander in his methodical way invested the city and after a long and fierce siege, the defenders fired the city and retreated to two strongholds on the east and west of the harbour. Alexander sacked the city and left a detachment of troops to blockade the defenders, who surrendered a short time after. Between the fire and Alexander's troops sacking the town much of it was destroyed and it never really recovered. Thereafter it's fortunes followed the ups and downs of other more important cities along the coast until it's decline in Byzantine times.

The Castle Of The Knights

While most of ancient Halicarnassus has disappeared, the castle the Knights of St John built has remained virtually intact since it's construction in the early 15th century. The Order of St John of Jerusalem was born in the 12th century in the dust of Jerusalem and the blood of the Holy War. Originally the order was purely a nursing brotherhood providing hospitals for the sick and wounded. Later it's duties were extended to the defense of pilgrims visiting Jerusalem and it is from here that it's military side appeared. In 1291 the knights were compelled to leave Palestine with the collapse of the last Christian stronghold and they went first to Cyprus and then to Rhodes. In Rhodes they developed new military skills and became sailors. In their swift galleys these Christian corsairs became a respected and feared fighting force along the coast of Asia Minor. After Rhodes the knights established a string of castles on the islands of the Dodecanese and then turned their attention to Asia Minor. The site at Bodrum, where an earlier Seljuk castle had stood, was perfect, and construction began in 1402.

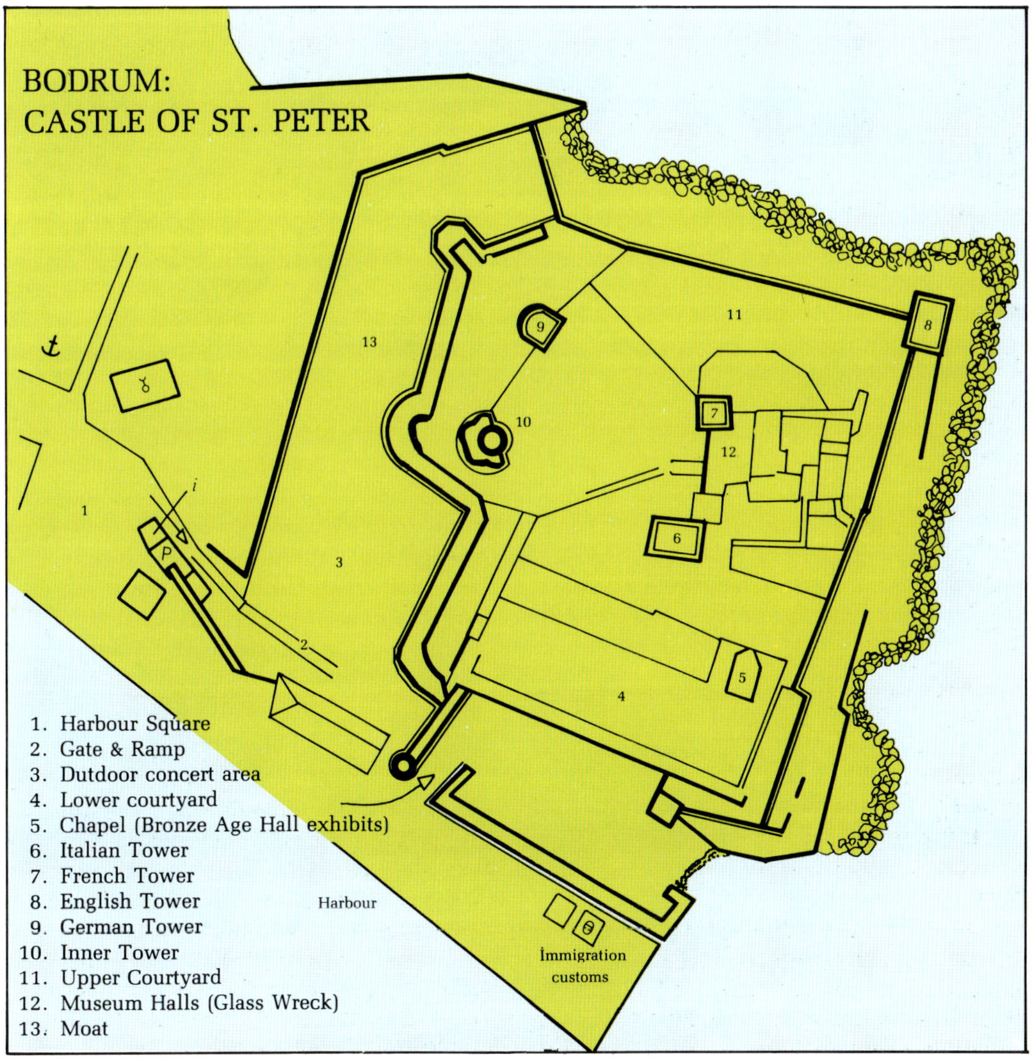

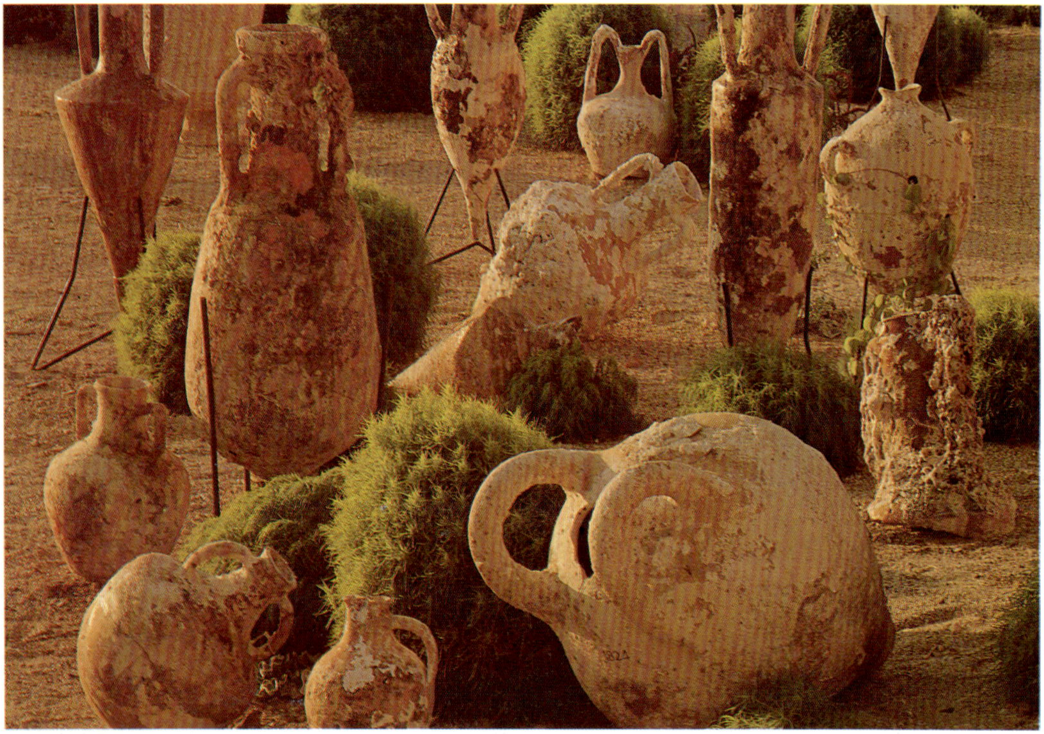

The layout of the castle roughly followed the divisions of the order into eight Langues or tongues, the eight European nationalities from whom the knights were recruited. These were Auvergne, Provence, France, Aragon, Castile, England, Germany, and Italy. In the Castle of St Peter there are four towers: the Italian, French (incorporating Auvergne and Provence), German, and English towers. I presume Aragon and Castille were accomodated in one of the towers or were not represented in the castle at Bodrum.

The knights of the order were all men of noble birth from the great houses of Europe. To be recruited the noble blood had to be traced through four generations and any possibility of illegitimacy or common blood in the line barred a man from joining. Once accepted the novice knight served on the military side for a year, usually in the sleek galleys. One year of duty in the galleys was called a 'Caravan' and after three 'Caravans' the knight had to reside for a further two years in the order, in somewhere like the Castle of St Peter, before he was a fully fledged Knight of St John. After this many would return to their estates in Europe, but on being summoned by the Grand Master in times of crisis, it was their duty to return. There were lower orders with no restrictions on birth, the Chaplains and Brothers, who served in the hospitals and with the soldiers on the military side, all of them along with the knights bound by those Medieval dictates of Chastity and Obedience. At their best these knights probably came as close as any to the ideal knight imagined by romantics, what Chaucer called the 'verray parfit gentil knight', but they were also a skilled fighting machine as brutal and cruel in battle as any foe they fought against.

The knights occupied the Castle of St Peter until the fall of Rhodes to Süleyman the Magnificient in 1523. Süleyman allowed the Knights of Rhodes to leave, he considered them gallant adversaries whose lives should not be wasted and is reputed to have said of the Grand Master '...it is not without some regret that I oblige this old Christian to leave his home'. The knights

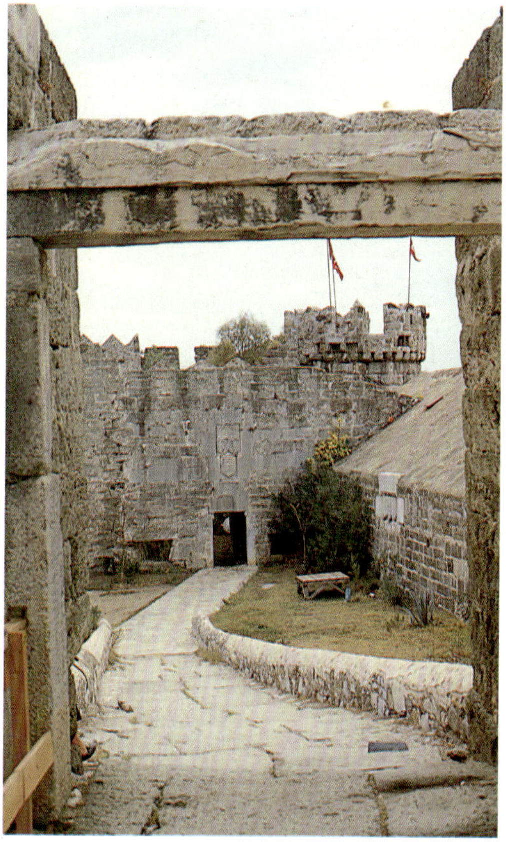

Gateway to the Castle of the Knights of St. John.

in Bodrum left soon after. The Castle of St Peter is a wonderful example of Medieval military architecture now partially restored to house a Museum of Underwater Archaeology.

In the museum finds from the numerous wrecks excavated along the coast are imaginatively displayed. Peter Throckmorton got the museum off the ground in the early 1960's and the work has been continued by Dr George Bass and the Institute of Nautical Archaeology. Finds ranging from the contents of a Bronze Age ship that sunk off Cape Gelidonya around 1200 BC, 6th and 7th century AD wrecks from Yassıada, an island at the tip of the Bodrum peninsula, and an 11th century AD Levantine trading ship loaded with exquisite glassware that foundered in Serçe Liman, are all exhibited along with models and drawings showing how the delicate and dangerous job of underwater archaeology is carried out. The finds are arranged in different rooms and halls so that you get to wander around the gardens and towers and along the galleries of the castle to see the different exhibits - a visit is as much a promenade through the castle as a tour of the museum.

Coat of arms on the gate into the castle and an inscription by Jacques Gatineau, master of the castle from 1512-1513, warning that anyone who spied on the castle would be punished.

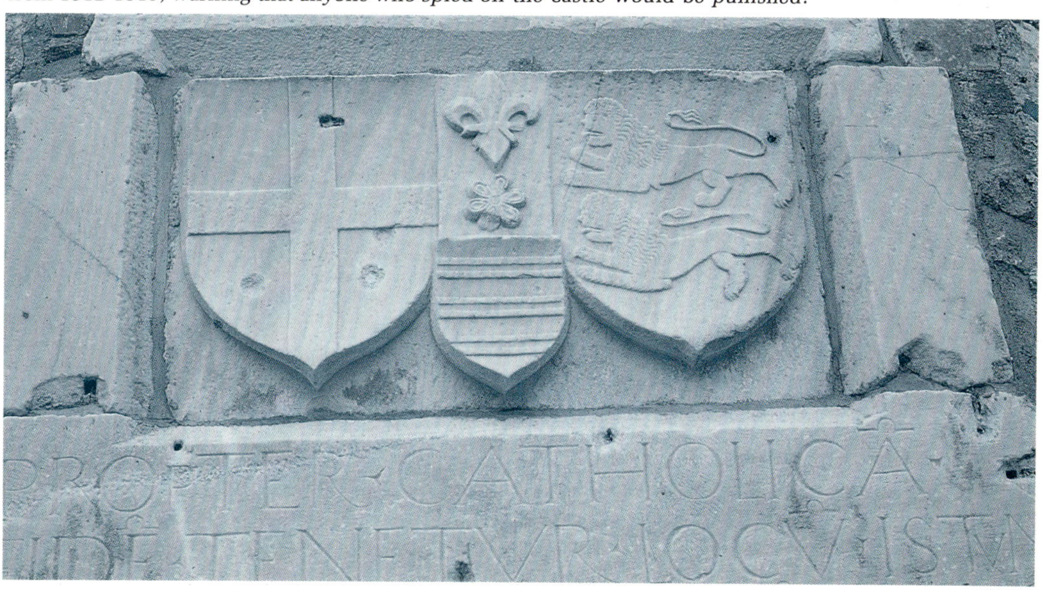

LOCAL BOATS

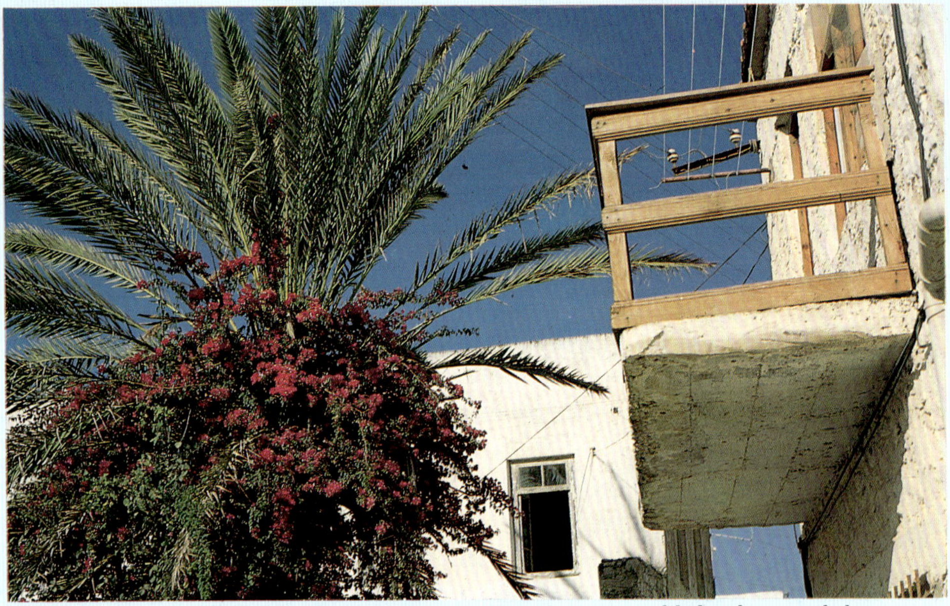

Gulet under construction in Bodrum. Some are built in the most unlikely places and then precariously carted overland to the sea.

On the outskirts of Bodrum, along a gravel road to the southeast, are the principal boatyards building the traditional Turkish boats that line the town quay. The boats are still built using traditional methods though modern materials have imposed some new techniques on the builders. Some are built using plans but the majority are built by eye using forming pieces to get the shape of the hull right. The keel is laid first and then the ribs are attached to give the skeleton of the boat. It is then planked up, the cabin built and the deck laid, before the interior is completed. The hull is then caulked and painted and varnished. Many of the metal fittings are made up locally and in a country where yacht fittings are few and far between, ingenuity is the key-word. Though the finished article tied up to the quay looks impressive, the timber used is often of poor quality and the wood-working skills that put the boa together are not always what the should be. Most of the boats are buil of local pine that has not been properly seasoned and is full of knots. This is reflected in the life expectancy of these boats which is reckoned at best to be 30 years and for many not much more than 20 years. A properly constructed yacht built of quality hardwood has a life expectancy three times this.

*There are numerous myths about the boats, the **'gulets'** and **'tirhandils'**, now built and being built for chartering. Ten years ago there was virtually no local boat-building except for a few boats for private owners and a few new fishing and sponge boats. The most popular type of boat, the **'gulet'**, with a clipper bow and a wide counter over the stern, is an extension of a traditional Italian design known as the 'varkalas' in Greece and related to the Arab 'baggala'. They have been* *used for trading in the Aegean for several centuries though the hull has evolved considerably in that time. In earlier designs the counter was not as large nor did it overhang the stern as much as it now does. The reasons for making it larger on modern* ***'gulets'*** *was simply to get more room on deck and to accomodate a permanent table for that all important 'al fresco' life. The beam of the boats increased considerably as well, again an expedient measure to fit more spacious accomodation into the traditional hull shape. The rig has changed as well, not that it matters today as few* ***gulets*** *rely on sails for motive power when there is a big diesel below. Originally a low aspect lateen rig and later a gaff rig was used. With high aspect bermudan rigs fitted the gulet is top-heavy and later versions have a ballast keel bolted on the bottom in an attempt to counteract this tendency.*

The ***'tirhandil'*** *is closer to the traditional boats of the area. This double-ended sweet hull form is found throughout the Aegean and the Turkish name is almost identical to the Greek name for it, the* ***'trehandiri'****. It is a more seaworthy boat than the* ***'gulet'*** *and properly rigged it is a*

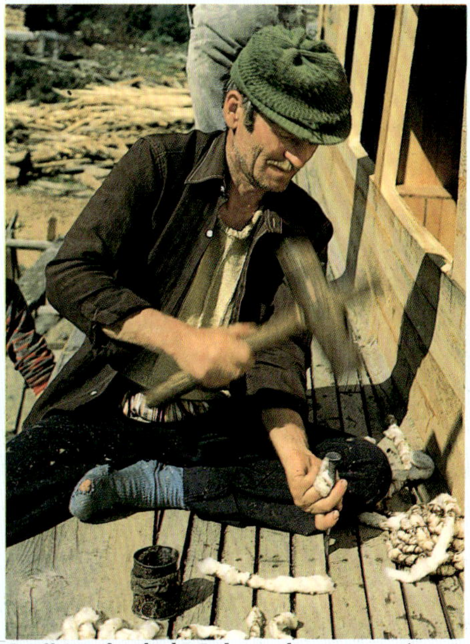

Caulking the deck. Gulet under construction at Torba near Bodrum.

better sailing boat. It is not as popular as the ***'gulet'*** *for charter simply because it is difficult to distort the hull lines too much to get more deck space and volume down below. You will find few of the* ***'gulets'*** *or* ***'tirhandils'*** *actually sail. They are motor-sailers and rely principally on a big engine to get around, the few scraps of sail that are hoisted are to steady the boat or to save a few litres of diesel.*

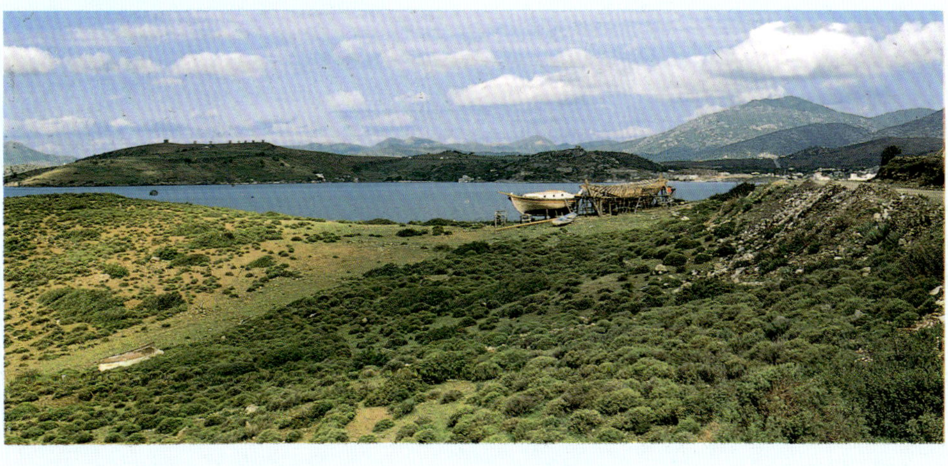

Recently boat-building techniques have improved and with more care and attention to detail and better quality wood, some wonderful new boats have been built. The design is not only ideal for a charter boat, with lots of space above and below deck, it is aesthetically pleasing to the eye as well. Many of the charter skippers are great characters and the crew look after your every need including preparing meals. For those who enjoy gin and tonic cruising it is hard to beat a charter on one of these local boats.

AROUND BODRUM

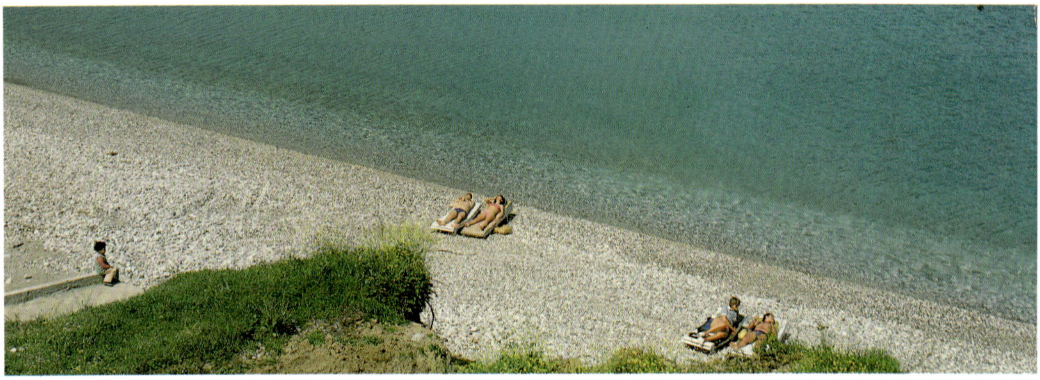

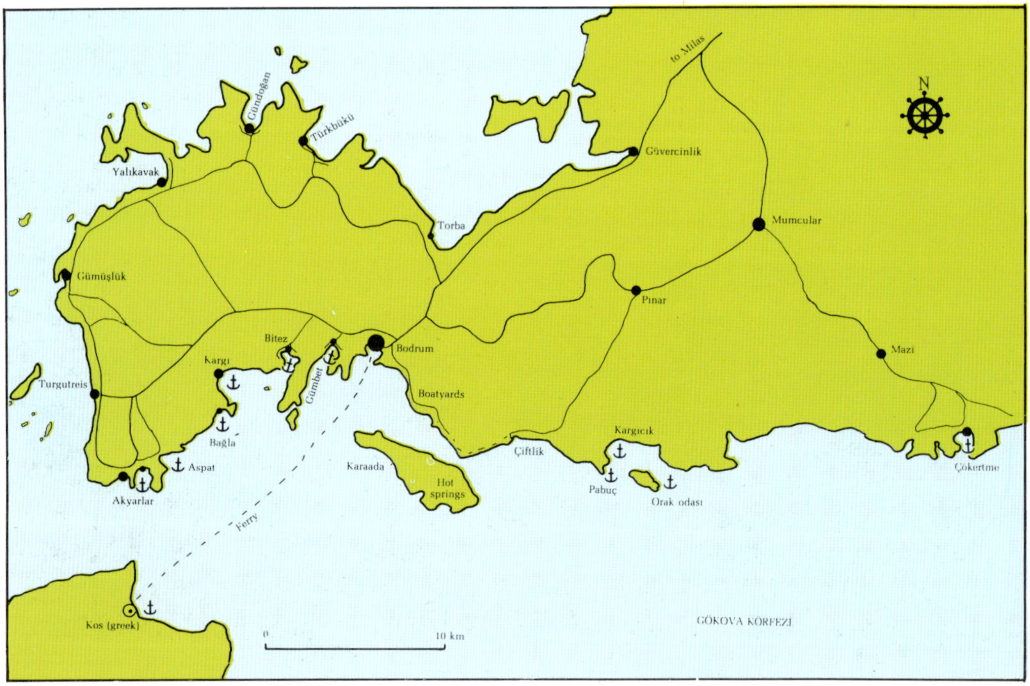

Kara Ada

Kara Ada, Black Island, is the large hump-backed island lying across the approaches to Bodrum. In calm weather you can anchor off the few dilapidated buildings on the north side where a hot spring bubbles up into a sea-cave in the rocks. The water is said to have therapeutic qualities and the fine grey mud in the immediate vicinity is reputed to be used by Elizabeth Arden for those very expensive facial mud-packs - get yours here for free!

Gümbet

Just to the west of Bodrum and virtually a suburb to it is Gümbet. Gümbet is the local dialect for the domed water cisterns that dot the peninsula and provide water through the summer for this rocky peninsula. It is popular, some would say too popular, as the nearest beach to Bodrum and consequently hotels, restaurants and bars line the foreshore to accomodate and refresh the summer invasion of tourists.

Bitez

Around the corner to the west of Gümbet is Bitez, a more sedate beach although still popular in the summer. The bay has a number of hotels and numerous restaurants around the shore. Dinghy sailing and board-sailing holidays are run from here and you can usually negotiate the hire of a sail-board for the day. Behind the hotels and restaurants on the waterfront are acres of citrus orchards and those with a keen nose will be able to smell the sweet sticky citrus perfume from the beach.

Ada Boğazi

The headland dividing Gümbet from Bitez has a series of coves between the tip and a small island, an area known as the 'Aquarium' or less imaginatively as 'Paradise Bay'. The clear turquoise water is a favourite stop for tripper boats from Bodrum, but yachts should not attempt to negotiate the narrow winding channel between the headland and the island.

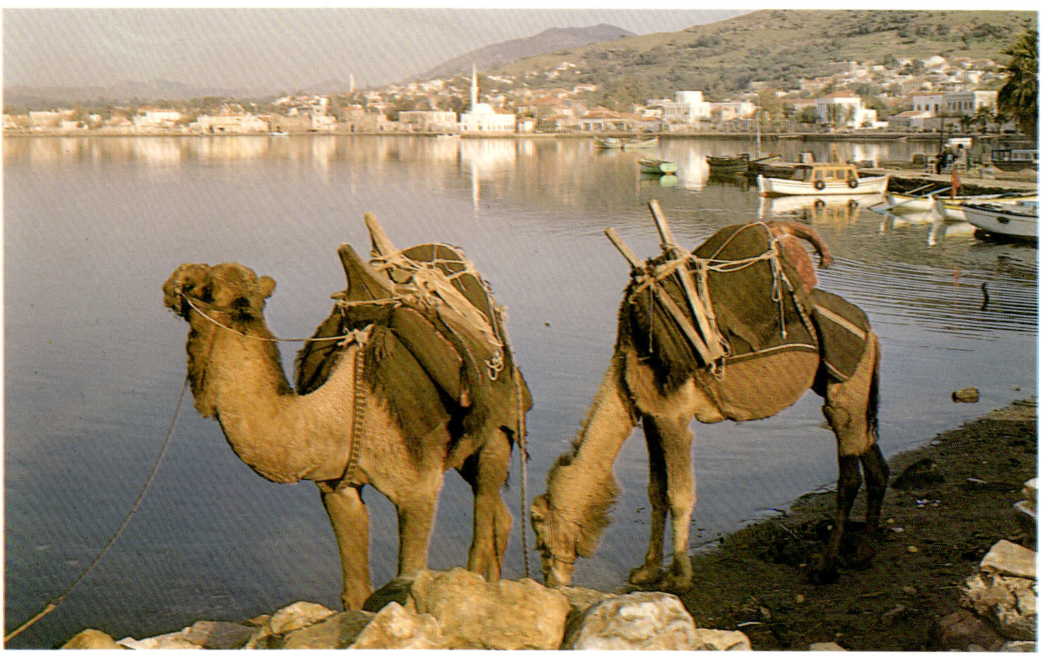

KARGI KOYU

A small bay about 3 miles west of Bitez that is little frequented other than by water-borne visitors. A small restaurant on the beach and crystal clear water.

BAĞLA KOYU

Lies directly south of Kargı under a short headland. Just one excellent restaurant and like Kargı, a lot of peace and quiet.

ASPAT & KARAİNCİR

To the south of Bağla a steep crag by the water has an ancient fort on the very top. Around the corner from the crag are the twin bays of Aspat and Karaincir, popular stops for the trip-boats and charter gulets in the high season. A holiday village and restaurants ashore and for the very energetic a superb view from the top of the steep crag if you make it - the climb is not to be undertaken lightly.

AKYARLAR

Just before you turn the corner to go north around the Bodrum peninsula, the white houses of Akyarlar can be seen tucked into a little bay. Before 1923 this was a summer resort for the Greeks and several Greek houses and a church can be seen in the village. There are several small restaurants and with a bit of luck the local fishermen will have caught something fresh for lunch or dinner.

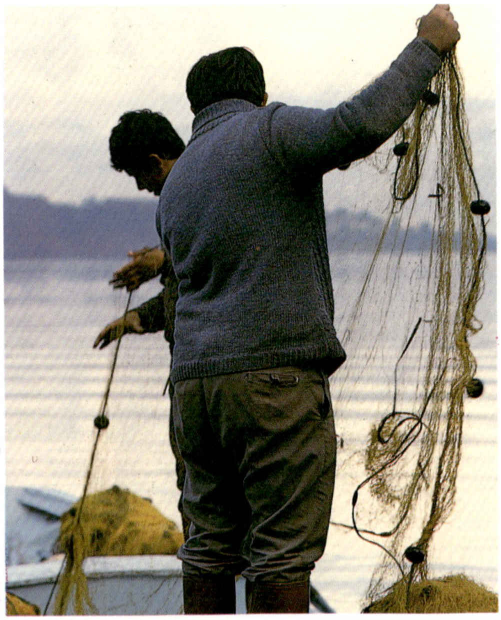

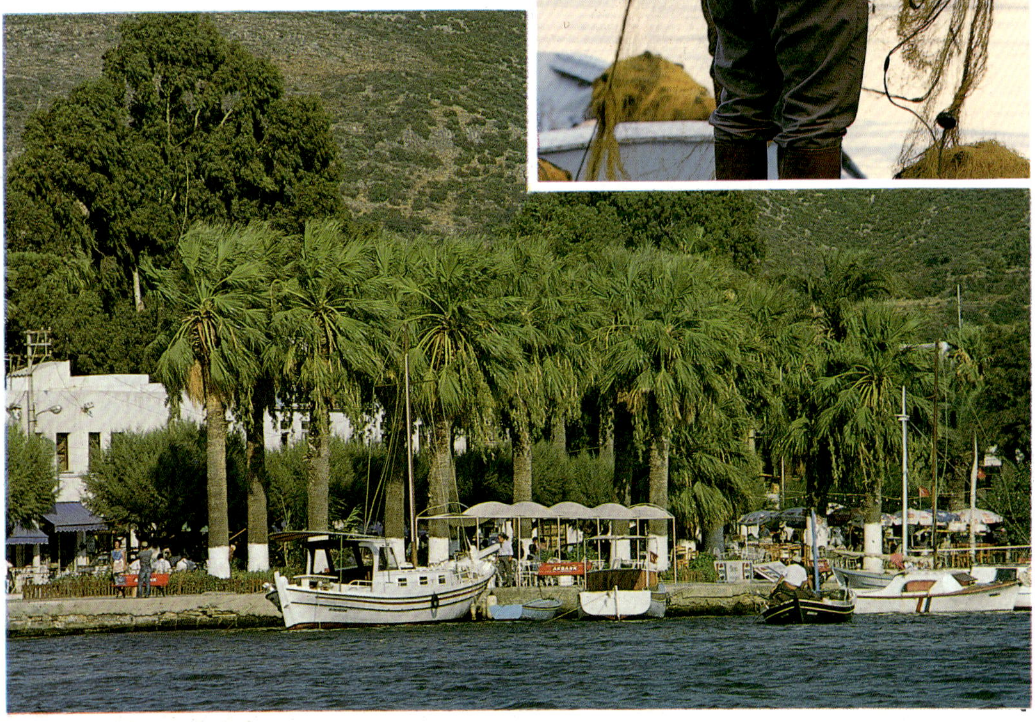

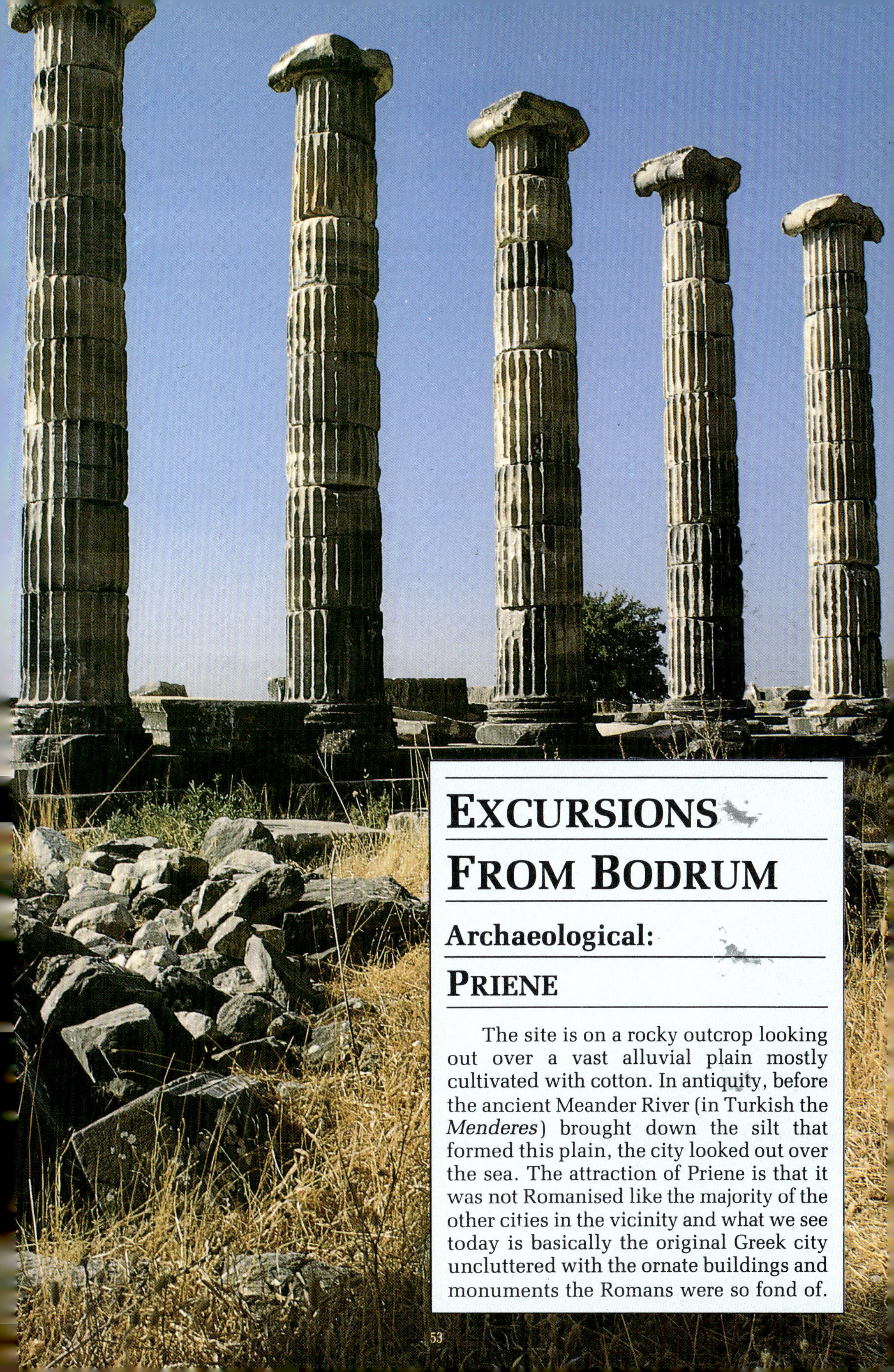

EXCURSIONS FROM BODRUM

Archaeological:

PRIENE

The site is on a rocky outcrop looking out over a vast alluvial plain mostly cultivated with cotton. In antiquity, before the ancient Meander River (in Turkish the *Menderes*) brought down the silt that formed this plain, the city looked out over the sea. The attraction of Priene is that it was not Romanised like the majority of the other cities in the vicinity and what we see today is basically the original Greek city uncluttered with the ornate buildings and monuments the Romans were so fond of.

The site is comparatively small compared to Ephesus or Aphrodisias, but no less interesting for that. There remains the Temple of Athena, a paved street and the agora, a group of private houses around a courtyard, the gymnasium, and a fine theatre with a number of carved stone thrones in the front row. Little remains of the acropolis on the summit though there is a quite stupendous view over the plain to the now distant sea. From Bodrum you can take an organised coach tour or a bus to Söke and a taxi or *dolmuş* from there to the site.

Iassus

The site of this ancient city is sprawled over a steep ridge on the side of a small fjord-like inlet that once provided perfect shelter for ships and galleys. Much of the site is planted with olive trees and you may be challenged by the odd goat or cow grazing amongst the ruins as you make your way around. There are numerous Greek buildings, Roman additions, and a tower and a fort built by the Knights of St John that look clumsy in comparison with the older structures. In the hamlet of Kıyıkışlacık at the head of the inlet there are several tavernas where you can take a relaxed lunch after your exertions around the site. From Bodrum there are organised coach tours or take the bus to Karakuyu and a taxi or *dolmuş* to Kıyıkışlacık.

Didyma

Not an ancient city, but a shrine to Apollo - and what a shrine. The Temple dedicated to Apollo is the largest Ionic temple still standing, or at least partially standing. The Temple to Artemis at Ephesus was larger, but only one column remains of it. At Didyma the temple was begun in 300 BC and 500 years later was still not completed. In the 19th century only three columns remained standing with shattered columns lying all around, but extensive reconstruction by a team of French and German archaeologists has restored some of it's former glory. From Bodrum there are organised coach tours or take a bus and *dolmuş* to Altınkum and go by taxi from there to the site.

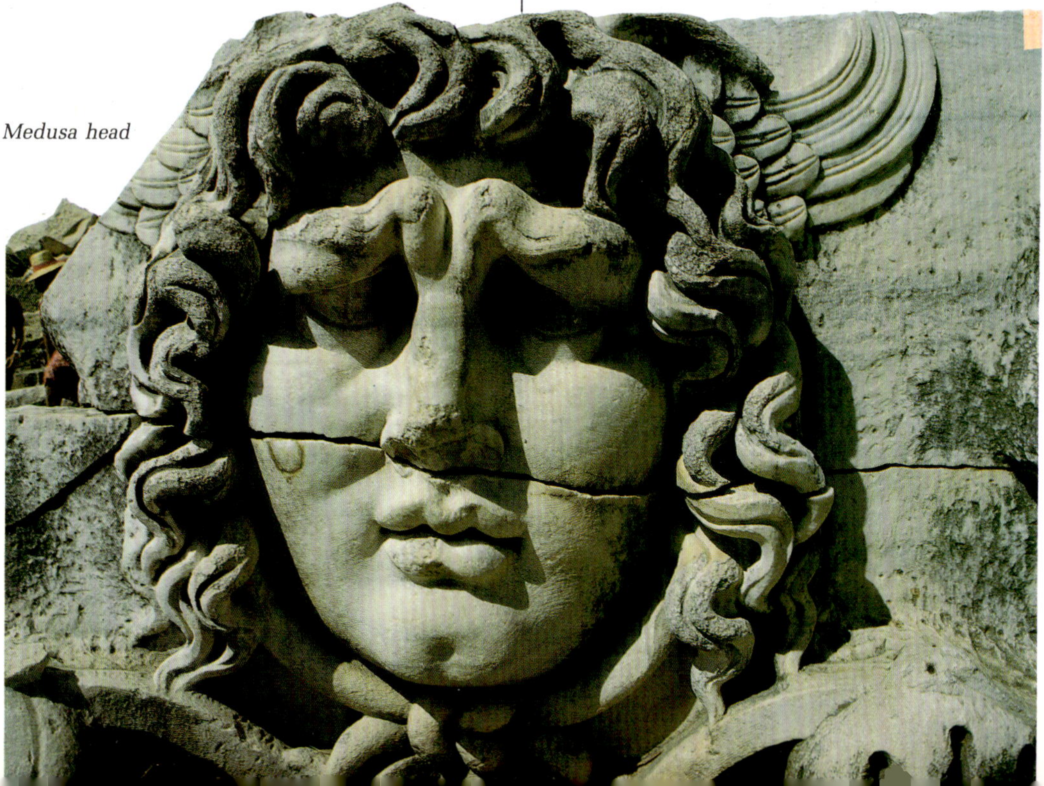

Medusa head

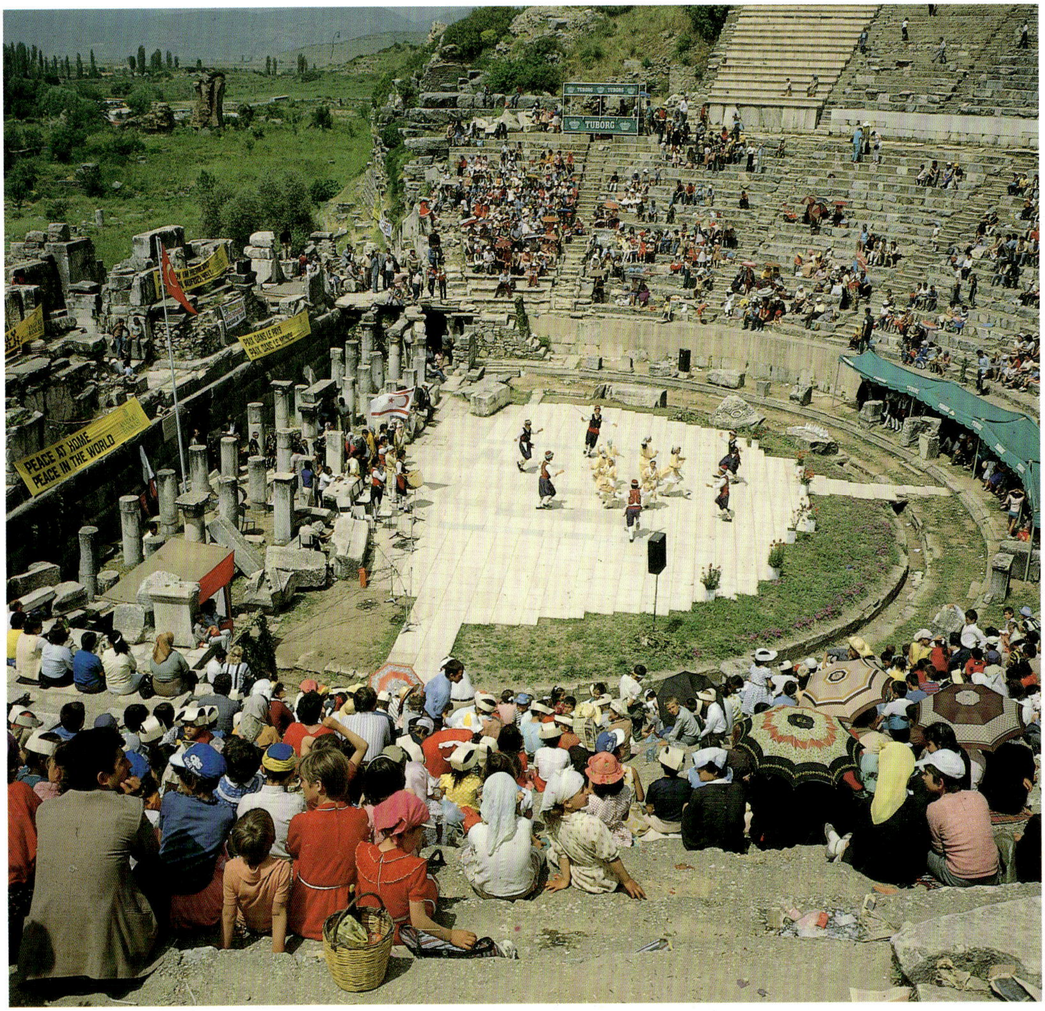

EPHESUS

Of all the sites this is the most well known - and deservedly so. The city was of Greek origin, founded in the 11th century BC, but it had been a place of worship to the 'Earth Mother' long before this. Though it was an important Greek city, it was the Romans who really made it what we see today. They chose the city to be the Roman capital of their Asian provinces and for 200 years it enjoyed great prosperity and power. Most of the grand buildings and monuments we see today date from this period and the scale and ornateness are a reflection of the importance of the city. There is much to see here: the theatre with seats for 25,000; the much embellished facade of the Colsus Library; the marble street with ruts from the chariots, and the buildings, including rich merchants' houses and a bordello, lining it; the Temple of Hadrian; the city walls and gates from where you can view the silted harbour that ultimately led to the demise of Ephesus; and scattered up the hillside the ongoing excavations that reveal more and more of the extent of the city. The impact of Ephesus is it's completeness and it's size. From Bodrum it is best to take an organised coach tour, it is over 200 kilometres to Ephesus; or you can take a bus to Selçuk and a *dolmuş* from there.

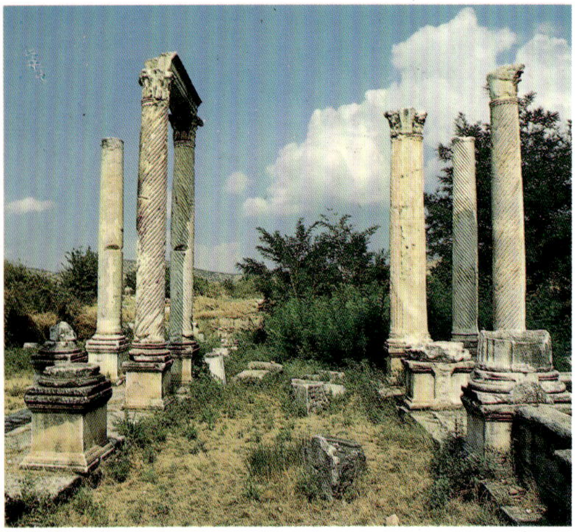

APHRODISIAS

Less well known than Ephesus, but in many ways more impressive, a visit to the site of this ancient city is best combined with an overnight trip to Pamukkale. Though there is still much reconstruction to be done, the site has been much excavated in recent years and there is more than enough to see here. There is a wonderful 30,000 seat theatre with a colonnaded area beyond it; an odeon with a chess-board cavia and a small sunken pool in the centre; a huge temple to Aphrodite; and just beyond the city a vast stadium virtually intact.

Other:

MUMCULAR

A small agricultural village to the east of Bodrum on the old road to Milas. The first thing you will notice about Mumcular is that for such a small place it has an over-abundance of carpet shops. The area around here is noted for it's carpets and it is well worth the excursion to take a look at what is on offer, usually for less than is asked for in Bodrum. Even if you don't buy a carpet, the drive alone through thick pine forest and small hamlets and farms makes the excursion worthwhile.

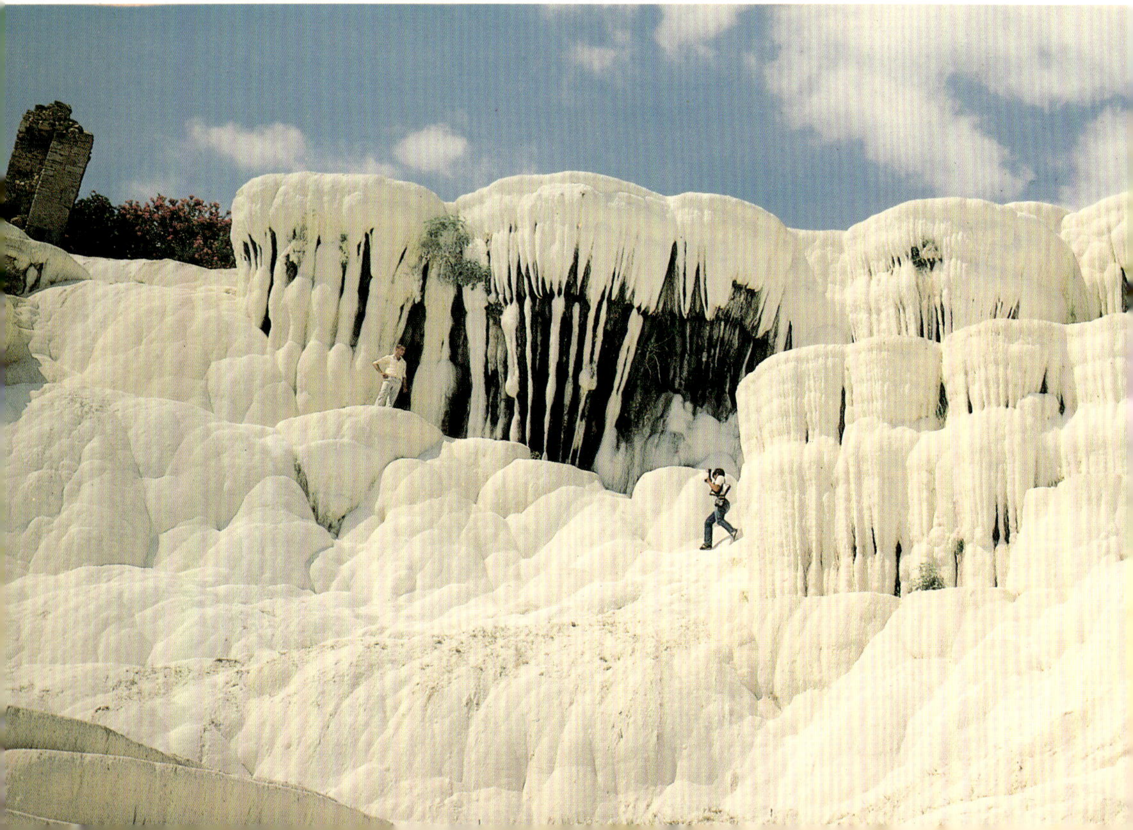

MİLAS

Milas stands on the site of ancient Mylasa, one time capital of Caria until Mausolus moved it to Halicarnassus. Little remains of the ancient city except for a Roman mausoleum and an ornamental gateway. What Milas does offer are a number of fine Ottoman mosques dating from the 14th century: the Orhan Bey Camii, the Ulu Cami, and the Firuz Bey Camii with a pink marble façade. There are also numerous old Ottoman houses with typical wooden balconies mostly dating from the 19th century. Just outside Milas on a steep hill are the remains of a fortified castle, Peçinkale, a stronghold of the Menteşe Turks who ruled this area just prior to the Ottomans. Milas is also known for it's carpets, more so than Mumcular. In particular it is famed for some of the browns and greens it gets from vegetable dyes and for patterns particular to the area. From Bodrum regular buses run to Milas, about a 30 minute trip.

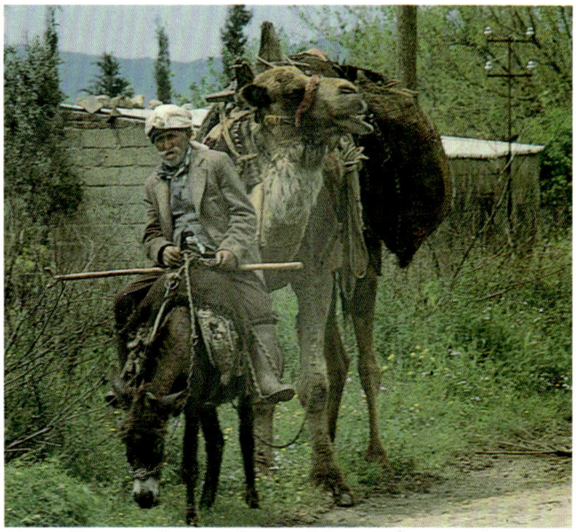

Traveller on the road near Mumcular.

PAMUKKALE

The name means 'Cotton Castle' and refers to the white calcium terraces and curtains of white stalactites deposited by the warm springs trickling down the hillside. It is a long haul from Bodrum and it is best to stay overnight - that way you

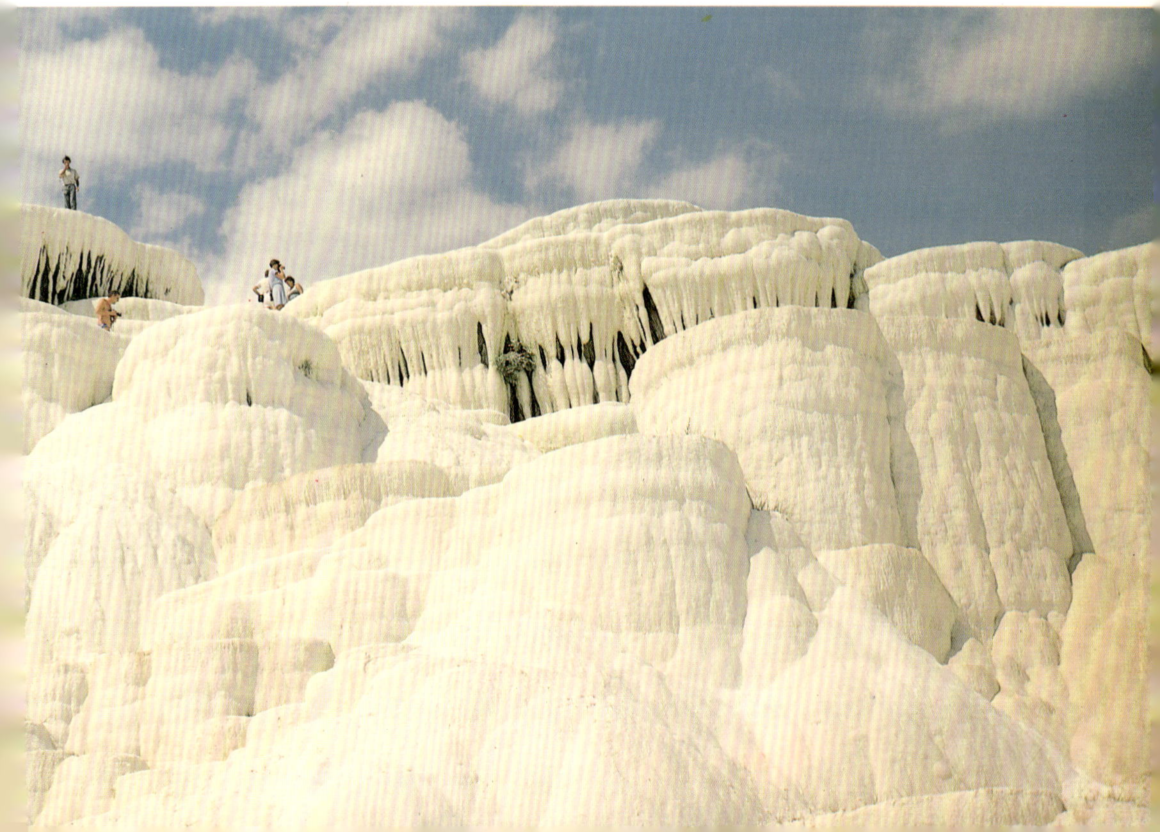

get to spend some time relaxing in the hot pools at the top of the terraces. It was popular with the ancients as well and the ruins of the spa town of Hierapolis are scattered around the plateau on the summit. Some of the sacrophagi on the edges of the terraces have been partially encased in white calcium and in some of the pools bits of column and other ancient debris lend a delightfully decadent pagan feel to the place. You get the feeling that somewhere around the corner a Roman noble is cavorting in a pool full of nymph-like maidens. There are numerous hotels and pensions around the summit for an overnight stay.

GÖKOVA KÖRFEZİ

The Gulf of Gökova extends in a great jagged gash for over 40 miles from Bodrum to the small village of Gökova at the eastern end. On the northern side of the gulf high mountains rise abruptly from the sea and until recently no roads connected the villages along this shore to the towns and villages in the interior - the only communication with the outside world was by boat or by donkey over rough paths through the mountains. The south side of the gulf is lower, but just as remote and wild as the north side. The gulf takes it's

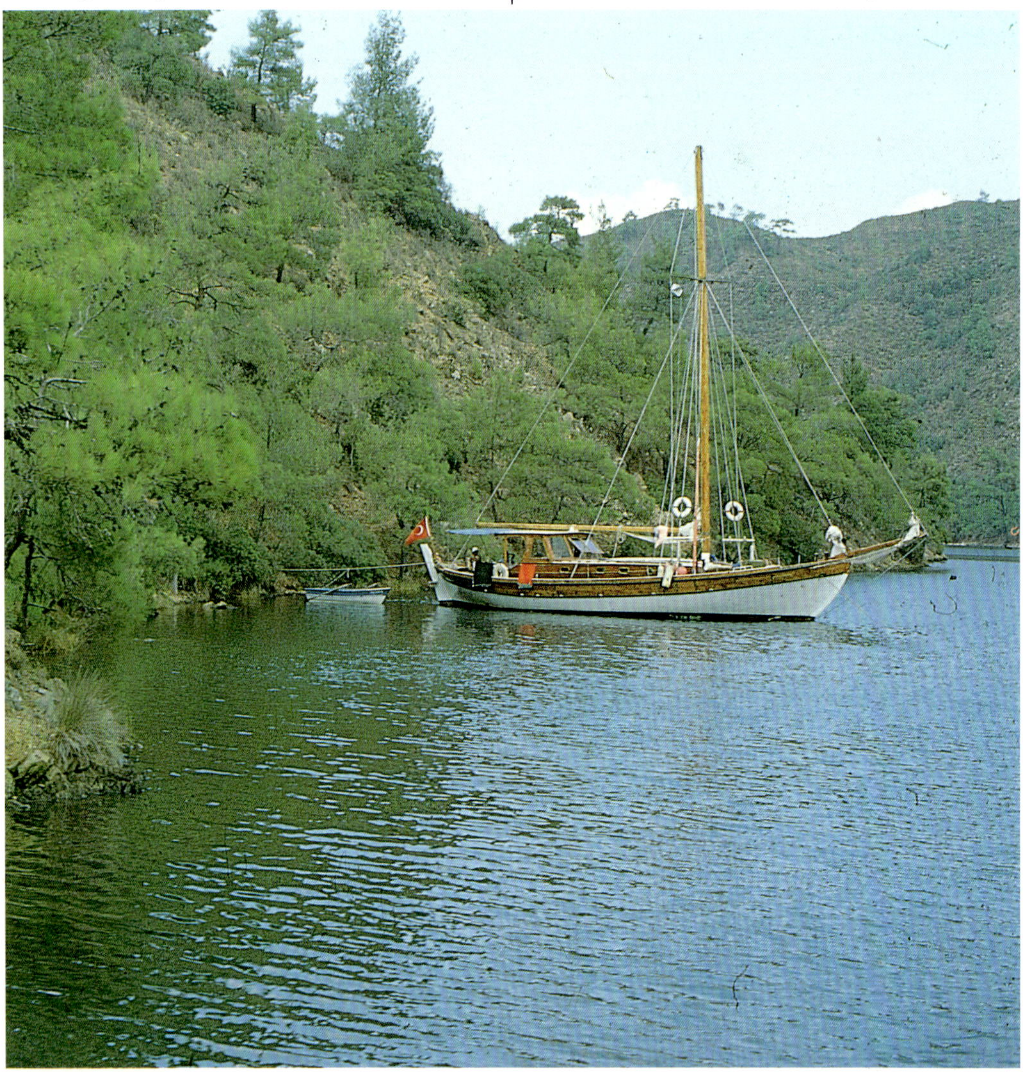

name from the hamlet of Gökova on a marshy plain at the head, but in times past it had a number of other titles.

On the British Admiralty charts surveyed in the late 19th century by Commander Graves in H.M.S. Beacon it is called the Gulf of Kos after the Greek island that sits in the open mouth of the gulf. In the Graeco-Roman period it was known as Sinus Ceramicus or the Gulf of Keramos, after the important port and city of Keramos on it's northern side near the present day village of Ören (Ören means ruins).

Today the gulf is popular with yachts and gulets based in Bodrum offering an enclosed area ideal for a one or two week cruise. For some time there has been an attempt to declare the gulf a national park

Leafy cove. Değirmen Bükü.

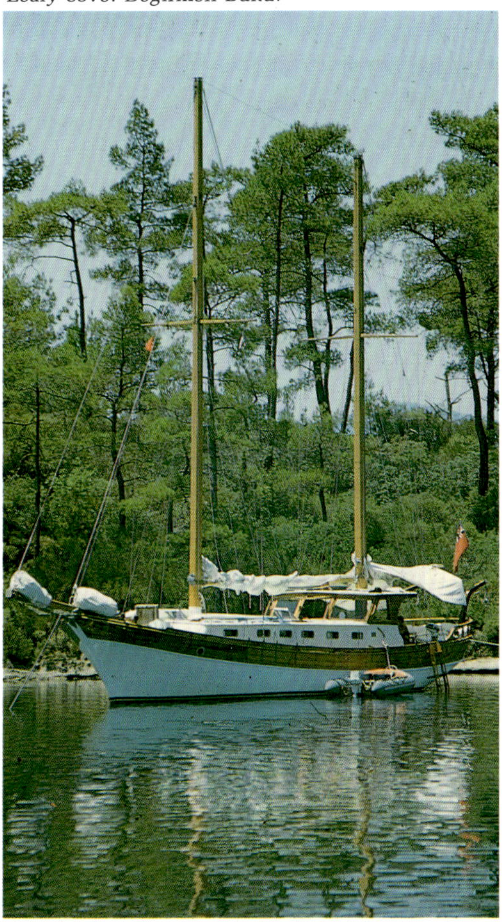

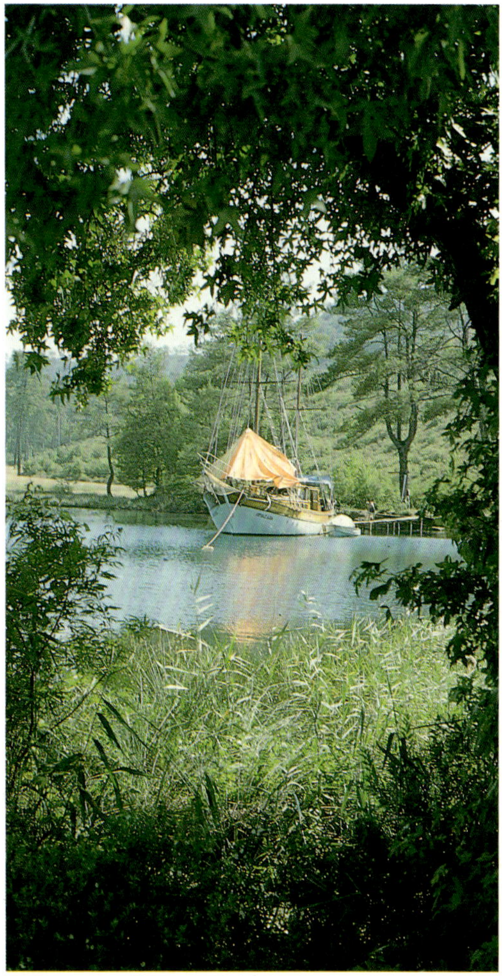

Leafy cove. Değirmen Bükü.

and forbid the construction of hotels or any buildings that would detract from the natural beauty of the area. Unfortunately nothing has yet happened and some parts of the area have hotels planned or built, though nothing really detrimental yet. Worse than hotels is the construction of a coal-fired power station behind Ören where there is a coal mine to supply the fuel for it. Hopefully something will be done in the future to save the area from development or at least to put a stop to the sort of environmentally unsympathetic buildings that blight some Mediterranean coastlines. Water-borne visitors should be aware of the fire risk to the pine forests in the summer and take every care with barbecue fires and cigarette ends.

Pabuç And Kargicik

Two bays immediately northwest of Orak Adası. Both bays make ideal lunch stops although there is no reason why you cannot stay overnight.

Orak Adasi

A stark rocky island lying a short distance off the coast. There is a cove on the north side suitable for a lunch stop when the *'meltem'* is not blowing and a more sheltered cove on the eastern side. The attraction of this little island is it's seclusion and the remarkably clear water around it's shores - ideal for snorkeling.

Çökertme

Çökertme is a popular first night stop for yachts bound into the gulf. After a night of revelry in Captain İbrahim's restaurant it is often a last night stop as well. From Bodrum the entrance to the bay is difficult to make out until you are nearly upon it - a copse of spindly trees on the eastern entrance are the only distinctive objects. Most yachts anchor in a cove near to the hamlet although some anchor off the coastal flat the hamlet is built upon. The setting is spectacular with the mountains rising from the shore in layered folds and tucks enclosing steep gorges and gullies. The gentler slopes around the bay are planted in olives and a few crops while the higher slopes are covered in pine - a landscape that will be repeated many times down the coast. The only flat land is the sandy patch by the waters edge where the houses of the hamlet are built.

Towards evening one of Captain İbrahim's sons will row around the anchorage to see how many people want a lift to the restaurant. The raffish Captain İbrahim, looking not unlike a latter day corsair from the Barbary coast, is a well known character in the gulf. The evenings entertainment starts after dinner with İbrahim bringing out his *nargile* and offering everyone a puff - a sort of Çökertme peace-pipe. The tobacco is placed in a bowl on the top with a live coal to keep it burning and the smoke is sucked through the water to the coiled pipe and mouthpiece. The smoke is cooled as it bubbles through the water and has none of the harshness of cigarette or cigar smoke. Then the music starts and the dancing follows soon after. The evening runs on *rakı*. Some evenings are like something out of Boccacio's *Decameron*, bawdy almost Medieval evenings that seem removed not only from the 20th century, but from Turkey as well. If you participate it is best to leave your dinghy behind and get one of İbrahim's sons to row you back to the boat as the *rakı* will more than likely have stacked the odds against you finding your own way back.

In the morning, in a more sober light, you can see carpets being woven on hand looms in the village. The carpets from Çökertme and the surrounding region as far as Mumcular are distinctive and pleasing pieces and here is as good a place as any to get one if you happen to find one you like.

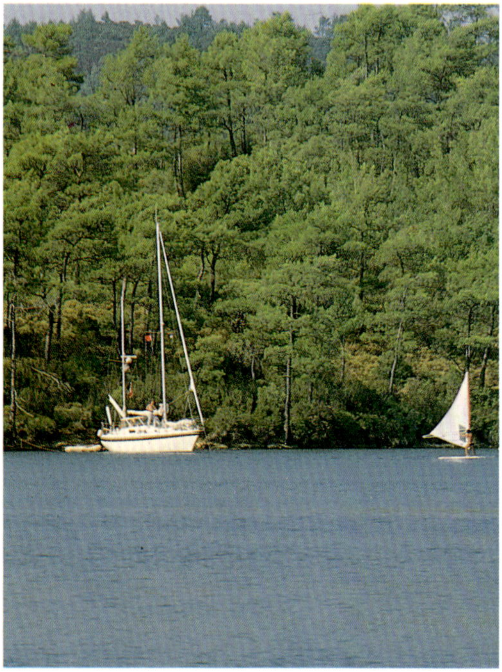

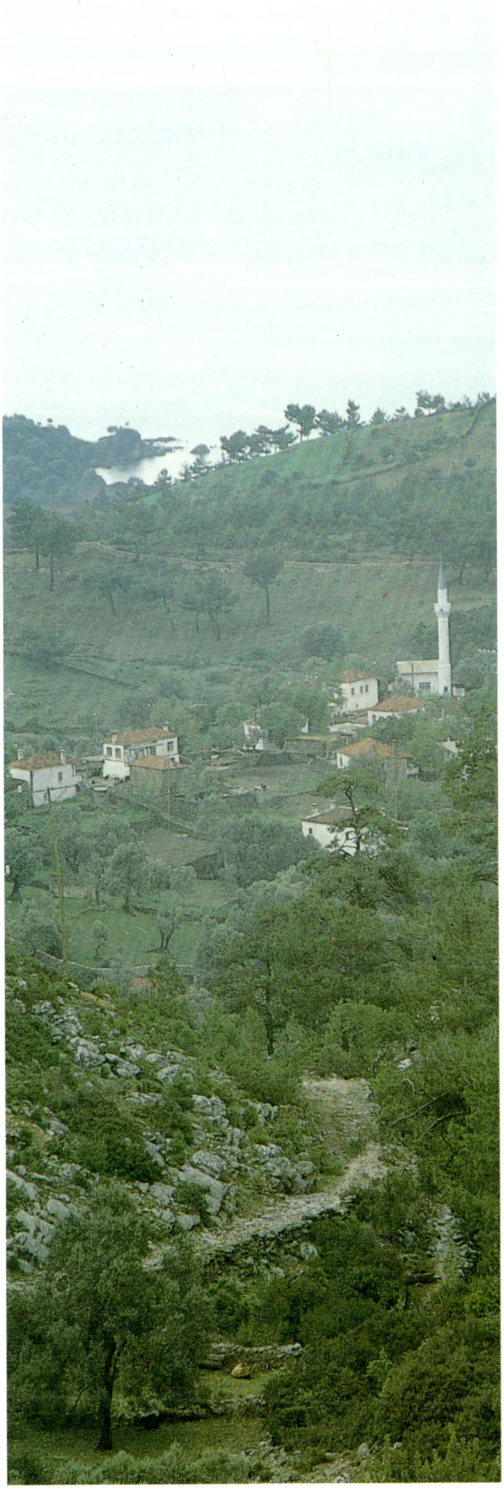

The village of Mazi perched on the slopes above the Gulf of Gökova.

AROUND ÇÖKERTME

To the west of Çökertme are a number of coves that make ideal lunch stops and depending on the weather, can be used as overnight stops. These should be explored with caution as there are numerous rocks and reefs off the coast. One of my favourite places is below the village of Mazı where a fish restaurant sits on a rocky bluff by the shore with steps cut into the rock to get up to it. You can anchor immediately west of the restaurant off the beach although it can be a bit rolly from the swell that curves around the headland. From the restaurant you have an uncluttered view out over the bay and the gulf to the Dorian Promontory ten miles away on the other side.

ÖREN

From Çökertme the coast is fairly straight with the mountains rising abruptly from the sea to 600 metres (2000 ft) and more. Ören sits on the only flat bit of land along the coast, a narrow strip of land under Kıran Dağı, a sheer curtain of rock between Ören and Akbük. In calm weather a boat can anchor off Ören or in a bight to the east, but it is not a safe place for an overnight stay.

The very forces that formed the coastal plain Ören is built upon are the same forces that spelled the end of the ancient city of Keramos. A river cuts its way down through the mountains behind Ören and although it only runs above the ground in the winter, (in the summer the smaller volume of water runs in underground channels), it brings down sufficient silt to build up an alluvial plain. Keramos originally stood by the sea, an important port in antiquity, but today the ruins are a mile from the sea and the city walls are partially buried in the silt brought down over time. For the city that the gulf was named after, remarkably little is known about it. The walls and remaining masonry indicate a Carian city that was Hellenised and was evidently of some size and importance. The name is identical to the Greek word for 'pottery' or 'tile', from which we get the word 'ceramic', and although George Bean states that this is only a coincidence, is it also a coincidence that a small trading boat carrying pottery was excavated by George Bass and his team from Bodrum Museum a short distance along the coast. This and other finds in the area have lead to the conclusion that there was a pottery workshop somewhere in the gulf and what better place than the city called Keramos. The city survived into the early Roman period, but declined soon after that, probably because the port became completely silted.

AKBÜK

From Çökertme to Gökova at the head of the gulf there are no real indentations in the coastline except for a short headland which shelters the bay of Akbük. From the distance the low line of the headland stands out prominently against the rock face of Kıran Dağı behind. Once around the headland you enter a wide bay that slopes gently up to the foot of the mountains, much of it covered in pine. The surprise of the place is the small restaurant near the shore where in discriminating surroundings excellent food is served,

Small cove near Gökova İskele

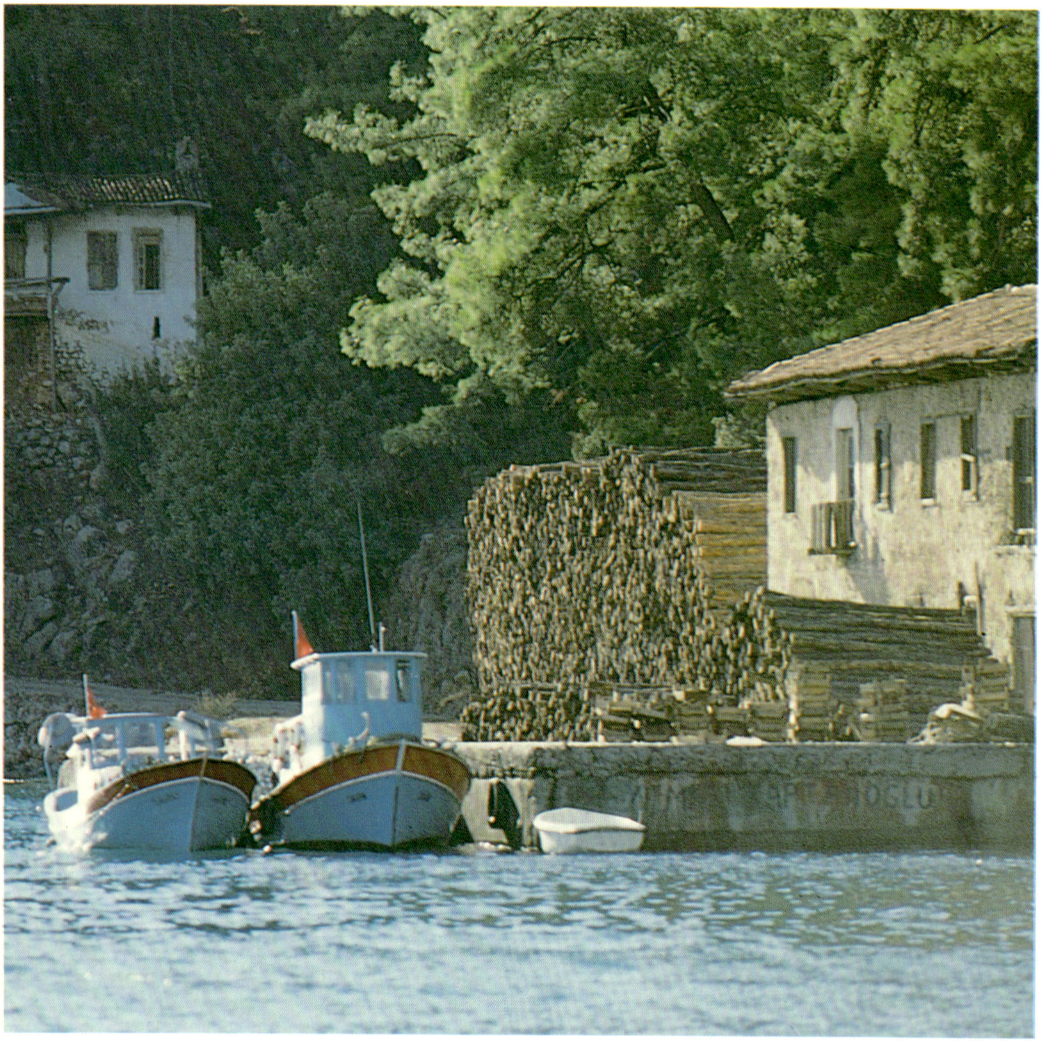

much of it of a sophisticated and varied nature that somehow seems at odds with this stark and lonely place.

Gökova İskele

The small village at the head of the gulf. The anchorage is not the most secure and in any case the village is a drab place with a number of depressing barrack-like buildings in the centre. It is a useful place if you want to get to Muğla or Marmaris although Söğüt is a better anchorage even if it is further away. Close to Gökova there is a small rocky cove a few local fishing boats use and you can anchor here. Ashore there is a good fish restaurant, a pleasant lunch stop but not really suitable for an overnight stay.

Small cove near Gökova İskele

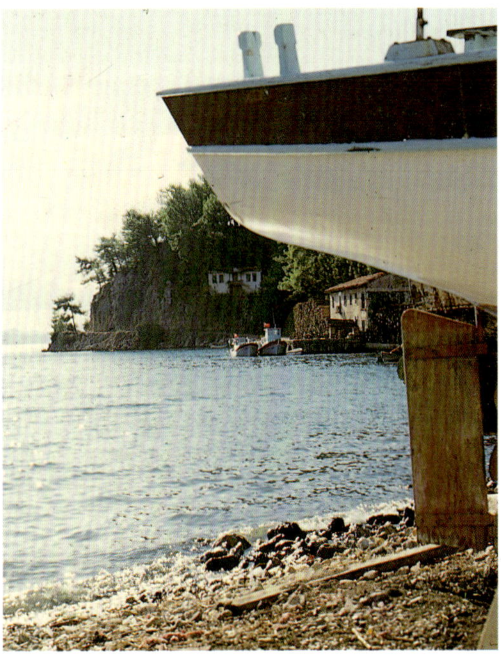

Around Gökova

Idyma

Idyma was an important city of the Rhodian Peraea, but little remains of it. The fertile alluvial plain at the head of the gulf would have been cultivated by the inhabitants of Idyma though the acropolis was built high up, in a better defensive position, on the hill above Gökova. It is a long and steep climb from Gökova and a pointless one since little remains of it.

Muğla

Muğla is the capital of the *'Vilayet'*, the modern administrative province covering most of what was ancient Caria. The town is largely a modern one, but has an old Ottoman core with numerous examples of fine old Ottoman houses. The market on Thursdays and Fridays is a lively and thoroughly authentic one and well worth visiting with everything from saddles, agricultural implements, copper pans and aluminium ones as well, iron stoves and tin chimneys, caged birds, as well as fruit and vegetables in abundance.

Washing day in Muğla

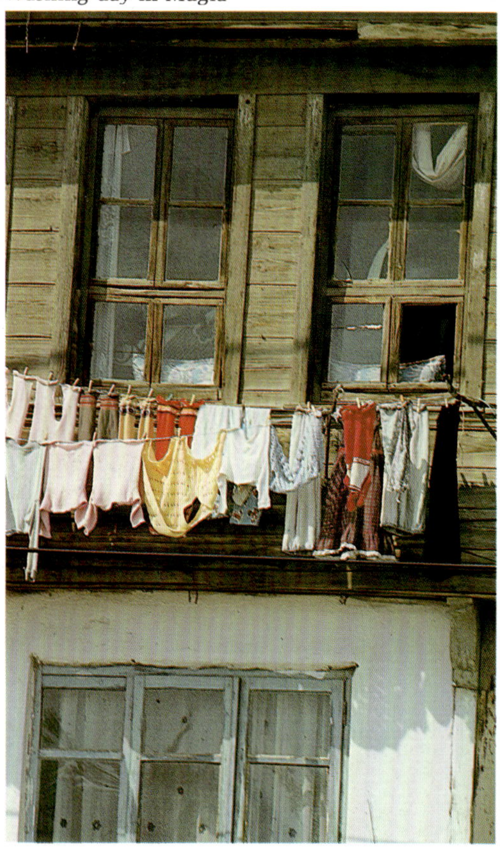

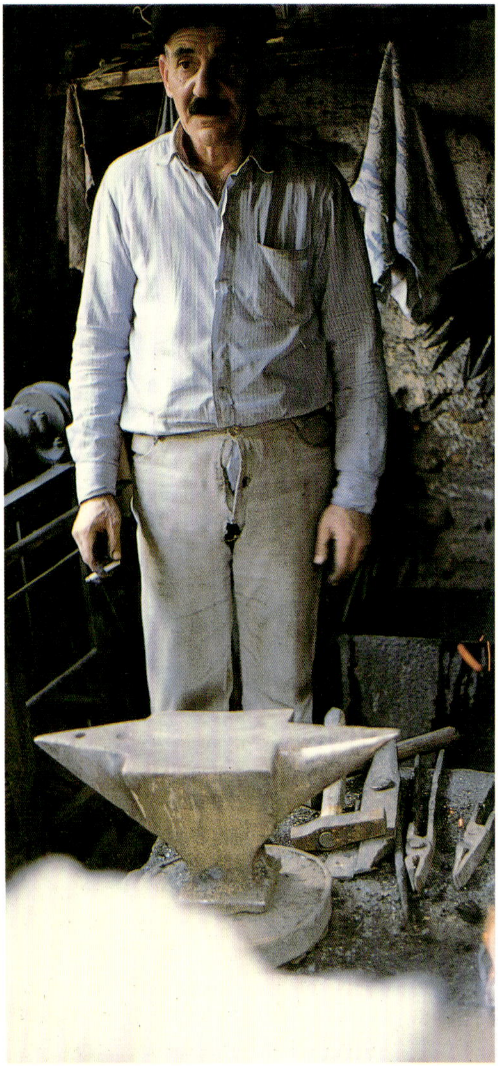

Blacksmith. Muğla.

GELİBOLU

Going west from Gökova the first anchorage you come to on the south side is Gelibolu. At the head of the bay there is a flat marshy area and on the high ground to the north and south are a few ancient ruins. Gelibolu is probably a corruption of Callipolis, an ancient city situated six miles inland to the east. The site on the coast was probably the port for the city proper and somehow retained the name when the inland site declined in the early Middle Ages.

ŞEHİR ADALARI

It has numerous names. In Turkish it is called Şehir Adaları, Şehirlioğlu and Sedir Adası meaning variously the 'Island city' and the 'Island of cedars'. In ancient times it was known as Cedreae, the name of the 'cedar tree' though none are to be seen today. On Admiralty chart 1533 the islands are called rather theatrically the 'Snake and Castle Islands': the 'Castle' bit is easily derived from the ancient ruins of Cedreae and the 'Snake' bit comes from a symbol found on a tomb on the smaller island. More recently it has been dubbed Cleopatra's Island and the tale behind the name is fascinating. When the Roman Empire was divided up between Anthony and Octavius, Anthony and his mistress Cleopatra spent a great deal of their time

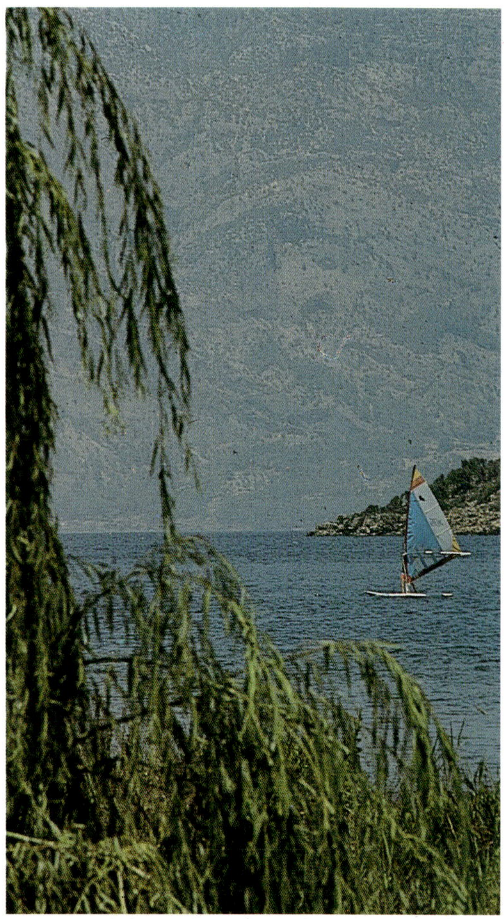

in the Roman provinces of Asia Minor. Evidently Cleopatra spent some time in Cedreae, but was distressed by the lack of a sandy beach to cavort upon. In an age when anything seemed possible and frequently was, she ordered sand to be brought by ship from the Sahara and had the perfect little beach on the west side of the island constructed. Is it just an apocryhal tale? The sand has been examined by a geologist, Professor Tom Goedike, and pronounced to be untypical of the region and to conform to the type of sand found in the Sahara.

The approach to the islands and the anchorage on the north side of Castle Island is a beguiling one. Tombs litter the slopes of Snake Island. In the passage between the islands the water shallows to a sandy turquoise that is so clear you can see the bottom 5 metres (16 ft) below as if you were standing on it. From the anchorage little can be seen of ancient Cedreae apart from a section of the city wall and a few piles of masonry. The city proper was situated on the eastern half of the island and to get to the theatre, the temple, and the city walls you will have to pick your way through the olive trees and thick undergrowth. The small theatre is romantically sited in a dense thicket and is well preserved though much overgrown. Once it would have had a view out over the anchorage but today the dense thicket shuts out the sky and the sea. Other buildings are scattered around the undergrowth and as you come across a building here or there, it is a bit like being let loose in an archaeological toyshop, discovering one new treat after another.

On the northeast tip of the island the remains of an ancient breakwater now partially submerged can be seen. Galleys and trading ships would have used either the anchorage on the north now used by yachts and *gulets* where they could beach the vessels at the head, or this small harbour tucked under the city walls. Further to the east of the ancient harbour, the walls of the city, some of it in perfect condition, can be traced for much of their length.

On the mainland opposite a necropolis and parts of an ancient wall can be seen. To the south of the necropolis is the bay of Taş Bükü with a few houses and a restaurant and a recently built holiday village at the southern end. In recent years numbers of land-based visitors have been attracted to Taş Bükü and from here small boats run them across to Castle Island. Two small cafe-bars opened on the island to cater for the summer visitors and visiting yachts and *gulets*. The inevitable despoiling of the islands from rubbish thoughtlessly discarded by visitors has recently had a stop put to it with the appointment of a warden and the provision of containers for litter. Water-borne visitors should know better than to dump non-biodegradeable rubbish, especially plastic, in the sea; but even biodegradeable litter such as orange peel or vegetable matter should not be thrown overboard in a bay like this where the prevailing wind will blow it onshore. Would that the holiday village in Taş Bükü could be removed as easily as the litter on Castle Island.

ANTHONY AND CLEOPATRA

In 44 BC when Julius Caesar was stabbed to death by an aristocratic clique including Cassius and Brutus, the Roman Empire was left without an obvious successor. Two figures emerged as likely candidates: Octavius, Caesar's nephew, and Anthony, Caesar's best general. The two came to terms with one another and quickly quelled the aristocrats and any other candidates they thought might pose a threat. The Empire was divided between Octavius and Anthony, with Anthony taking the east including Asia Minor. The difference between the two could not have been more marked. Octavius was a sickly youth, a methodical and careful ruler who was planning for the future of the Roman Empire and his succession. Anthony was more in the mould of Caesar, a devil-may-care general, albeit a brilliant one, who led his men into battle and was popular with them. He drank heavily and was notorious for his womanising. When Caesar had tamed Egypt he took Cleopatra as mistress and Anthony followed him in this. Cleopatra's fatal beauty did not appear to have dimmed over time and she exercised a hold over Anthony that ultimately led to his death.

In the period Anthony ruled over the eastern Roman provinces he spent a good deal of his time with Cleopatra enjoying himself in the cities around the coast of Asia Minor. The partying was on a scale seldom seen before or since. Plutarch described one such event in Samos like this: "While nearly the whole world was filled with groans and lamentations this one island for many days resounded with the music of flutes and harps. The theatres were filled, and choruses competed against one another. Every city sent an ox for sacrifice and kings vied with one another in entertainments and gifts. Everywhere men began to ask how on earth the conquerors would celebrate their victory when their festivities at the opening of the war were so expensive." As Anthony spent more time with Cleopatra his popularity with the legions declined. His popularity in Rome declined as well and it was all but inevitable that a showdown with Octavius was in the offing.

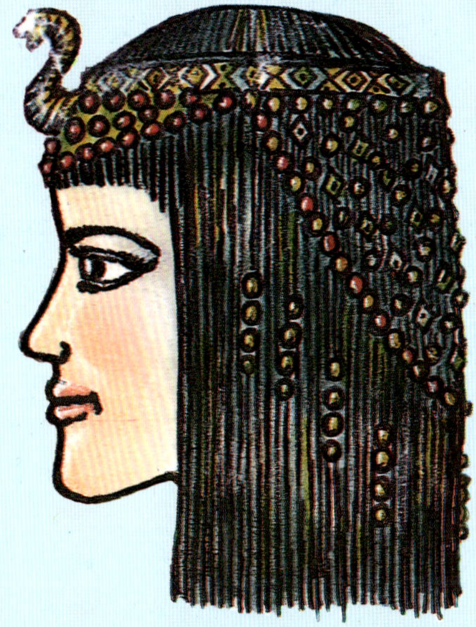

Octavius had to take action against Anthony when he declared Cleopatra joint ruler of Egypt and her offspring, including her illegitimate son by Caesar, the heirs of the Eastern Roman Empire. Octavius gathered his forces against Anthony and the two rivals met at Actium in western Greece. The outcome was decided almost before the battle began. Anthony's legions and generals deserted to Octavius and when the fleets came out to do battle, Octavius' superior forces quickly routed Anthony's fleet. The story of Cleopatra fleeing the battle in her purple-sailed galley and Anthony deserting his men to follow is well known and a sad finale to his brilliant life. Shakespeare catches the shame and despair of it all in this passage:

She once being loofed
The noble ruin of her magic, Anthony,
Claps on his sea wing, and like a doting mallard,
Leaving the fight in height, flies after her.
I never saw such an action of such shame.
Experience, manhood, honour, ne'er before
Did violate so itself.

The conclusion to it we all know. Anthony committed suicide as did Cleopatra soon after her capture. The illegitimate son of Caesar was quietly disposed of.

Inevitably the liasion of Anthony and Cleopatra and their pursuit of pleasure along the coast of Asia Minor has spawned a whole host of apocryphal tales of what went on where. Many of the ancient Graeco-Roman ruins have had a tale and a name tacked onto them - Cleopatra's Island, Cleopatra's Beach, Cleopatra's Bay, Cleopatra's Baths, and so on - poor old Anthony hardly gets a mention. There may be some truth in some of the tales and even if there is not, there should be.

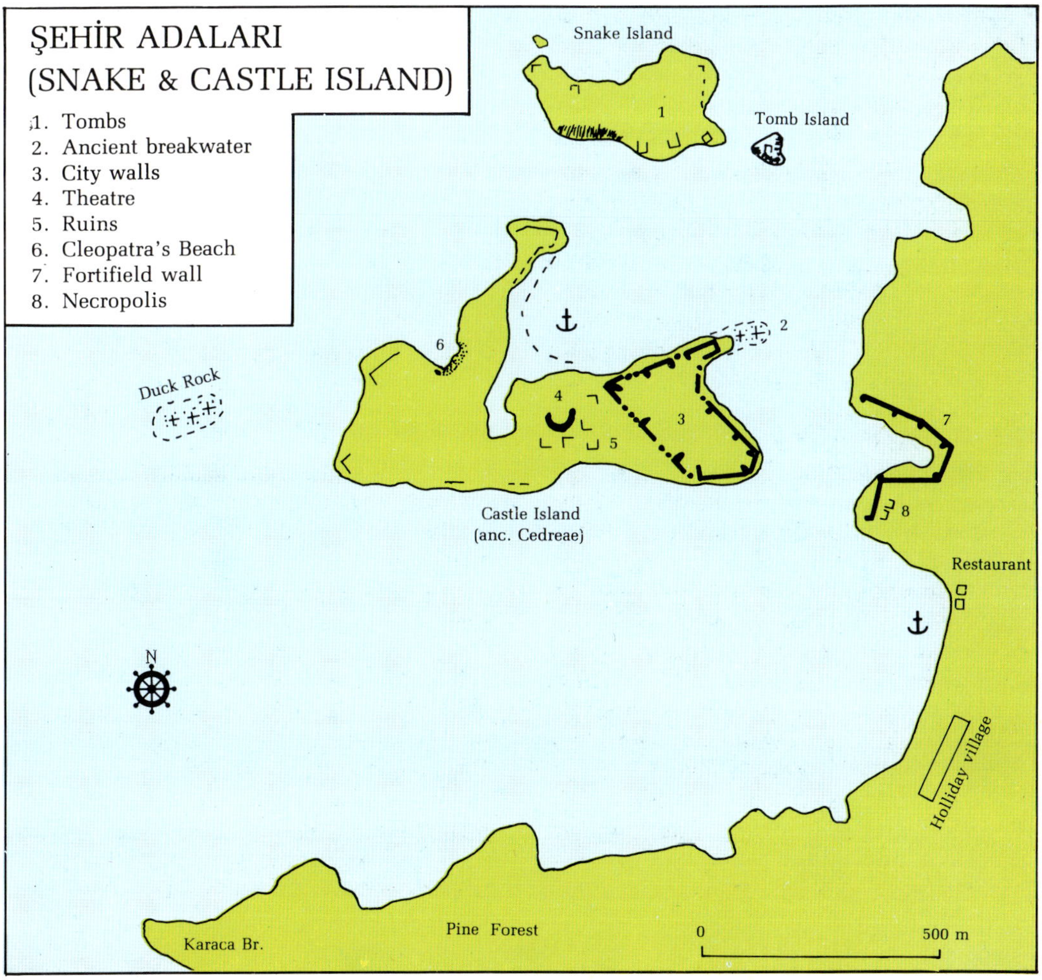

Duck Rock

Care needs to be taken of this razor-backed reef just to the west of Castle Island. It has claimed several yachts and one can only wonder if a slight phonetic mistake was made by the midshipman surveying it for the Admiralty, but one that couldn't be printed on a chart.

Söğüt

From Şehir Adaları it is a short passage around Karaca burnu and Karaca Island to Söğüt (pronounced 'Soyut'). The approach to Söğüt from behind Karaca Island is a gently pleasing one with the slate-coloured cliffs of the island in contrast to the wooded foreshore. In calm weather you can anchor in the cove on the shore for a swim and lunch; but be prepared to move out when the wind gets up. Söğüt is an enclosed bay surrounded by thick pine forest. A holiday village has been built on the flat land at the head of the bay. Most yachts and *gulets* anchor with a long line to one of the pines on the western side and this is the best place to be. There are several restaurants around the bay with jetties off them where you can berth, but these can be noisy at night if the evenings entertainment goes on for a while. However it is worth going onto the long jetty off the village when a space is free to fill up with water. A spring favours this spot with water renowned for it's purity, so much so the place has been dubbed 'honey water bay' by some. A *dolmuş* runs into Marmaris if you feel you want to sample some town-life after the simple life in the gulf.

A short distance to the west of Söğüt is the T-shaped inlet of Kesr. A yacht can anchor in the eastern arm of this mini-fjord. The western arm is obstructed by a fish farm.

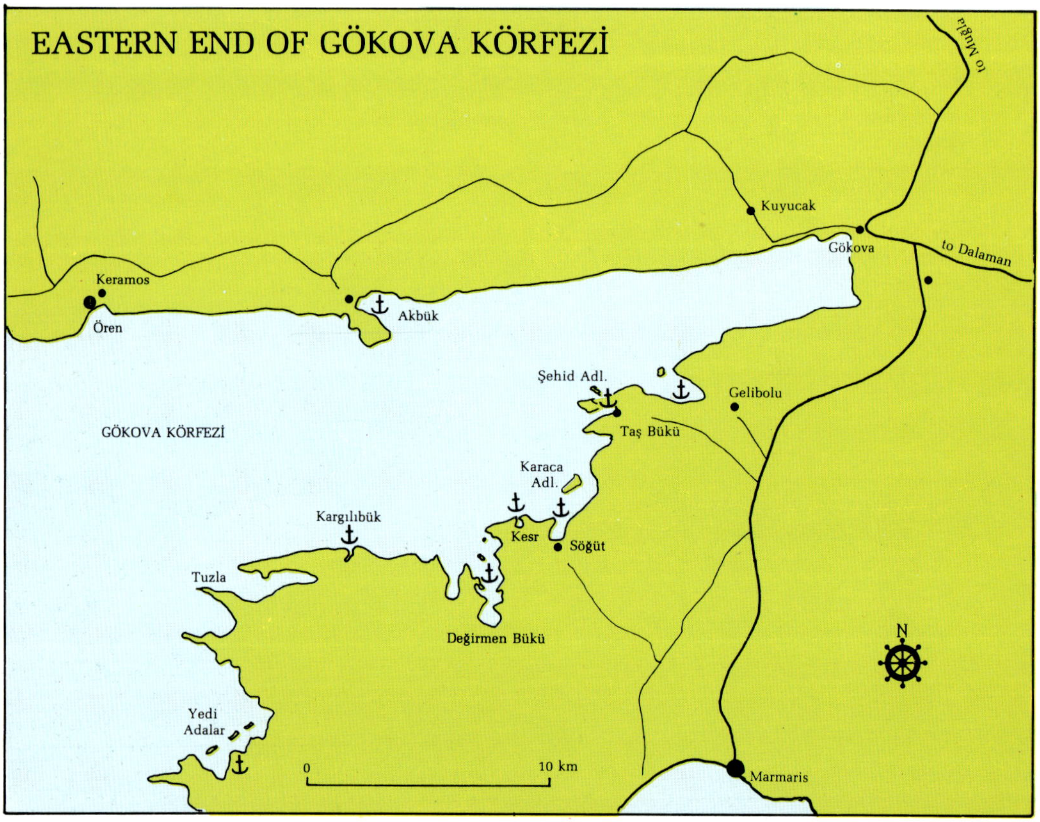

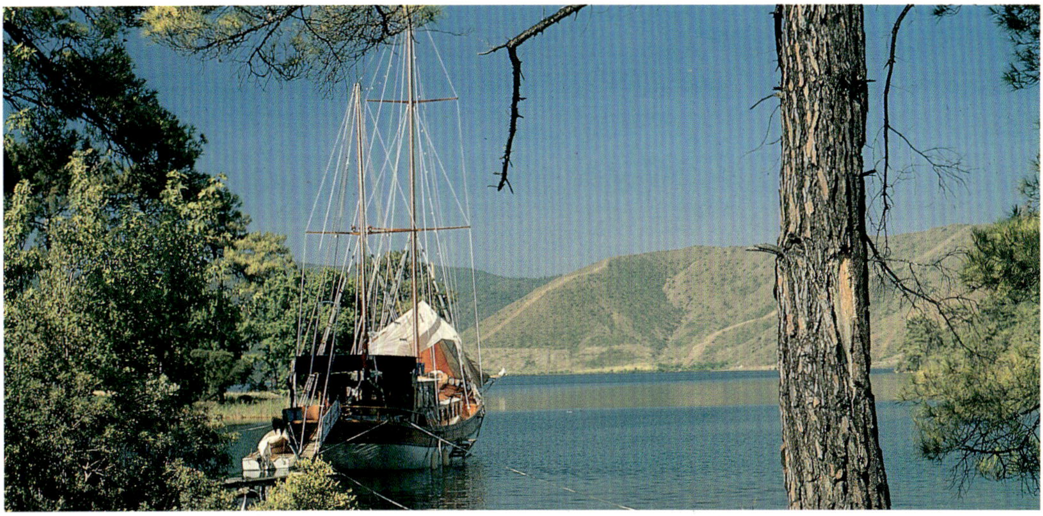

Leafy cove. Değirmen Bükü.

DEĞİRMEN BÜKÜ

A large deeply indented bay with a number of coves and inlets dotted around the edge. Most yachts and *gulets* head for the cove on the eastern side where you can anchor with a line ashore to a tree or to the pier off a restaurant. Alternatively there is English Harbour on the western side or an anchorage under the spit of land enclosing the head of Değirmen Bükü.

On the eastern side of the bay the slopes are covered with thick pine forest and the eastern cove is a little gem with pine on the slopes and a few deciduous trees near the shore. The slopes around English Harbour have recently been replanted with pine after a fire sadly destroyed the mature forest - a salutary reminder to us all of the fire risk from a cigarette carelessly discarded or a barbecue fire. At the head of Değirmen Bükü there is a stand of fragrant amber trees which are

Restaurant with minstrel. Değirmen Bükü.

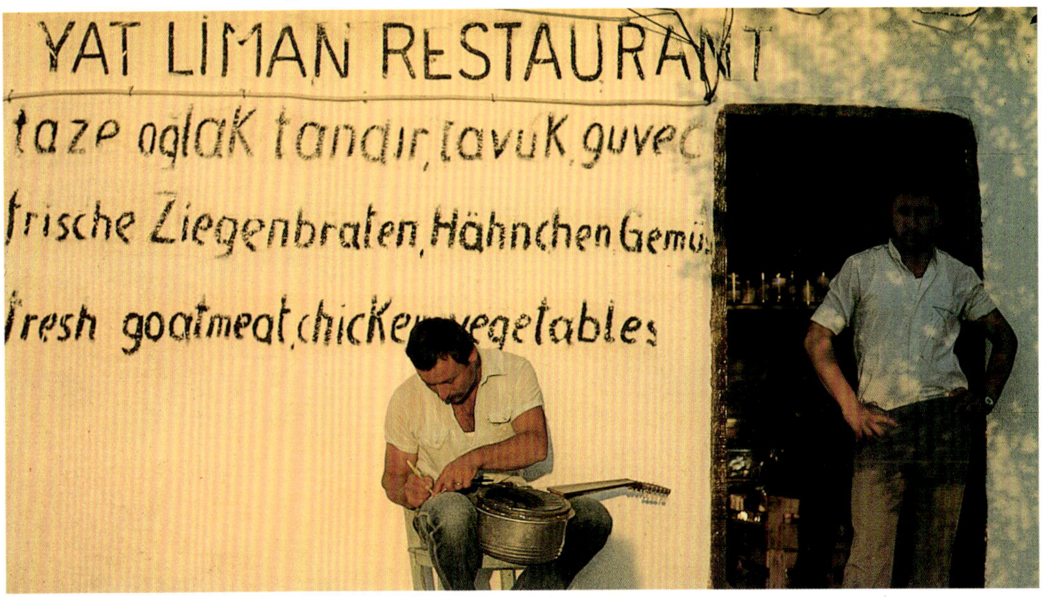

tapped for their resin. Gashes are cut in the trunks and a tin nailed to the tree collects the resin in much the same way natural latex is collected from rubber trees. The resin from the fragrant amber is used as a base for incense and perfumes. From the eastern cove it is a pleasant if longish walk over the hill to the head of the bay and the stands of fragrant amber. At one point a spectacular rocky bluff rises sheer from the flat land. In Autumn when the leaves are turning, the surroundings are reminiscent of parts of northern Europe. In the eastern cove you will find the only facilities here: two restaurants, one of which advertises roast goat as a speciality and very good it is to. A hose from a nearby spring supplies water nearly as good as that from Söğüt.

English Harbour, the inlet on the western side of the bay is so named from the Second World War when English torpedo boats are reputed to have holed up here during daylight hours before venturing out at night. The name and the tale are difficult to relate to the Turkish situation in the war which was to take a neutral stance with non-agression treaties towards both the Axis and the Allied powers. Turkey did not declare war on Germany until February 1945 by which time it was evident that Germany's fate was sealed and surrender was not far off. It may be that England illegally used this remote cove to harbour torpedo boats or that there was some other complicity no doubt sealed in a War Records office somewhere.

KARGILIBÜK

A long narrow inlet a few miles west of Değirmen Bükü. The inner half is shallow and only small boats will be able to get into it. Most yachts and *gulets* anchor half way inside at the dog-leg and take a line ashore to a pine.

YEDİ ADALAR

The name means the seven islands, but as there are only five easily recognised as such, whoever named the place must have counted a detached rock or two. The area has a wilder and more rugged aspect to it than the softer pine covered slopes further east. Here the trees are stunted and twisted by the prevailing westerlies that howl over the islands and adjacent coast in the summer months. The islands are lumpy rocky things bereft of any vegetation and the waters around them are spiked with razor-back reefs and jagged pinnacles of rock. There are several anchorages around the coast with the best being in the creek where with care a yacht can get right inside and take a line ashore to a tree. The creek is used by a few fishermen and is a little oasis for water-birds — heron, cormorant, curlew and the electric blue kingfisher.

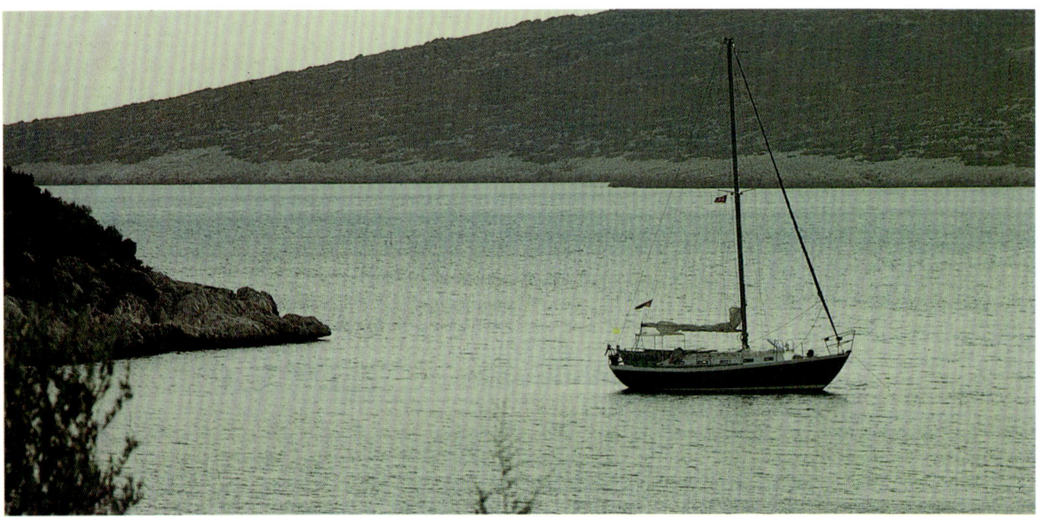

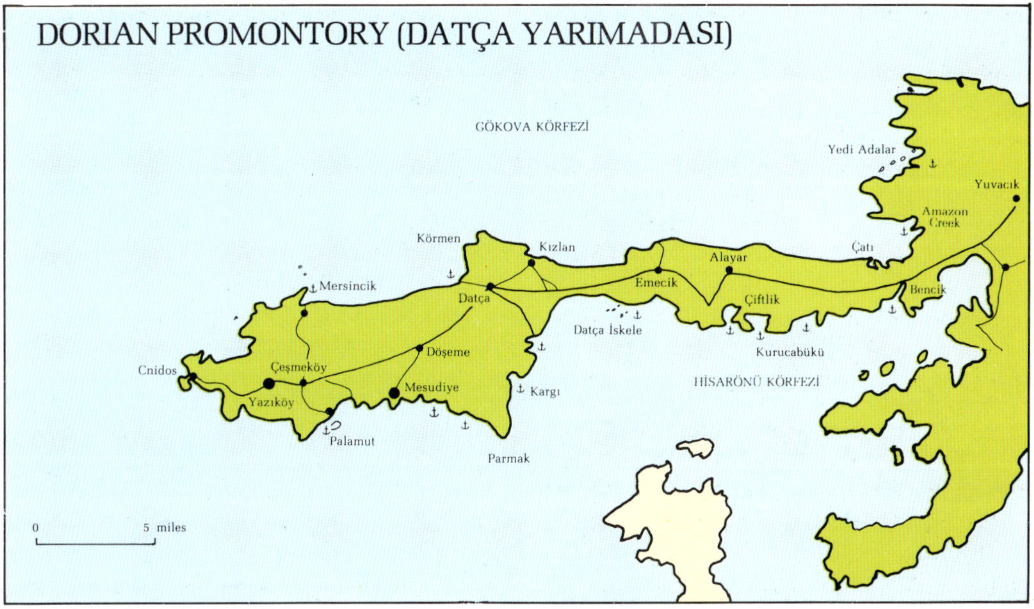

Amazon Creek

Normally I abhor the renaming of bays and islands along the lines of 'Dream Bay', 'Paradise Island', and others of the same mould, but in the case of Amazon Creek the name fits the surroundings. Most yachts must anchor in the entrance to the creek as inside it is too shallow, but small yachts and *gulets* with local knowledge can get right inside where the trees and undergrowth hang thickly out over the water and give the place the appearance of a jungle river. There is a camping ground and a small restaurant here where the owners make yachts welcome. Fresh bread, the unleavened round loaves of 'village bread', is cooked daily and good food is served in the restaurant.

Çati

This is the last anchorage on the southern side of the gulf before a long straight stretch of coast to Körmen and Mersincik. Çatı is a small land-locked cove offering all-round protection and solitude

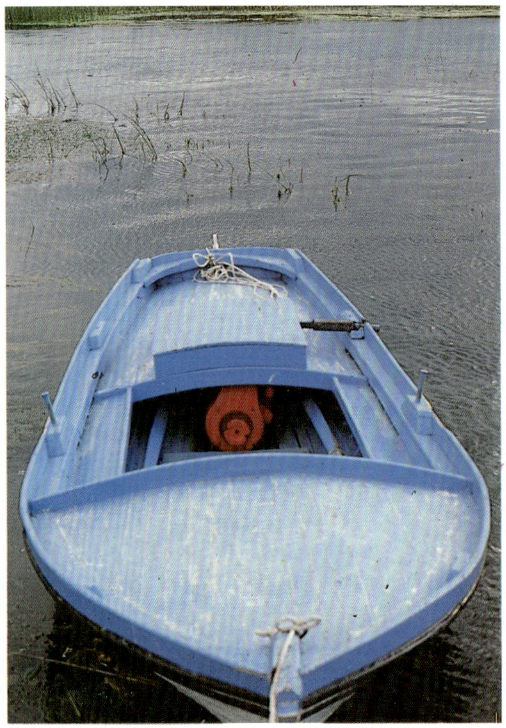

as well. The latter may be disturbed by an intruder according to a tale from a friend of mine. They were awakened in the night by a lot of noise on the shore and with a spotlight picked out the shape of a brown

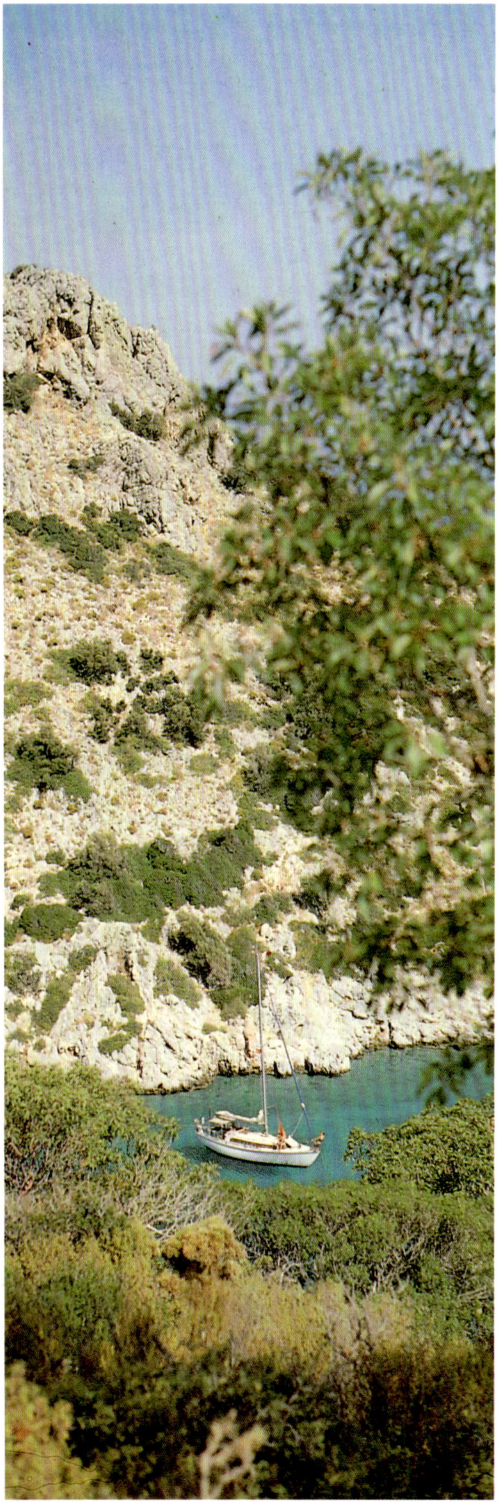

Mersincik

bear scavenging along the waters edge. Apparently there were two bears in the area, probably mates, until one was knocked down and killed on the road. The other has remained and seems to have made the area around Çatı part of it's territory.

KÖRMEN

Most of the Dorian Promontory is mountainous except for the coastal plain at Körmen. A rough stone breakwater shelters a harbour occasionally used by small coasters and the crescent shaped 'caiques' (*'mavna'* in Turkish) to load produce from the farms on the plain. Körmen is one of those places that is initially disappointing. It seems somehow ordinary, the harbour a bit scruffy, after the other anchorages in the gulf. But the place grows on you and the surroundings, the steep northern slopes of the promontory and the fertile plain, are really quite grand. The locals are friendly and the restaurant and pension by the harbour has simple but good fare.

In antiquity a harbour existed here although virtually nothing remains of it. George Bean discovered a capital built into the village mosque that has been reused as a boundary stone and is inscribed in letters of the fourth century "Boundary of the Harbour". He also traced the route of an ancient road, the modern road has been built along much of it's course, to Triopium (*Palamut*) on the other side of the peninsula.

MERSİNCİK

Mersincik is the most westerly bay suitable for an overnight stay on the south side of the gulf before you turn the corner to Cnidos and Datça. The anchorage off the hamlet is rather exposed and most yachts and *gulets* make for a small cove north of the hamlet. The cove is an idyllic little spot surrounded by steep pine-covered slopes except for the pebbly beach and flat land at it's head.

CNIDOS

When the energetic Charles Newton, British Consul to Turkey in the mid-nineteenth century, discovered a massive stone lion at Cnidos, all eleven tons of it, he wrote afterwards that 'the lion seemed made for the scenery, the scenery for the lion'. The scenery on the rocky promontory is just like this. Indeed the scenery has altered little since the city was deserted sometime in the Middle Ages and apart from the modern lighthouse on the cape, not at all since Newton visited it and shipped off tons of antiquities, including the lion, to the British Museum. The view from seaward is that which small trading ships would have seen 2000 years ago and more as they approached the harbour.

Cnidos at the extremity of the Dorian Promontory sits on tiered rocky slopes dominated by the slab-sided Cape Krio. It was the second city to bear the name Cnidos. The original site was near Datça, but the inhabitants soon realised the strategic advantages of a city on the end of the promontory and subsequently established new-Cnidos there. Martime commerce was on the increase in the fourth century BC and the inhabitants of old-Cnidos, halfway along the Dorian Promontory, must have watched enviously as trading ships sailed by and around Cape Krio heading for Halicarnassus and points further north. All through the summer the *meltem* blows from the north and often the traders would have to anchor in the lee of Cape Krio to wait for the wind to die down before they rounded the cape. In the summer you can wait some time for the northerlies to drop as any yachtsman in the area knows and the Cnidians were onto a good thing when they moved to the end of the promontory.

The move from the old site near Datça to the new site occurred sometime in 360 BC. The craggy Cape Krio was then an island, so the Cnidians laid a causeway to it and constructed harbours on either side.

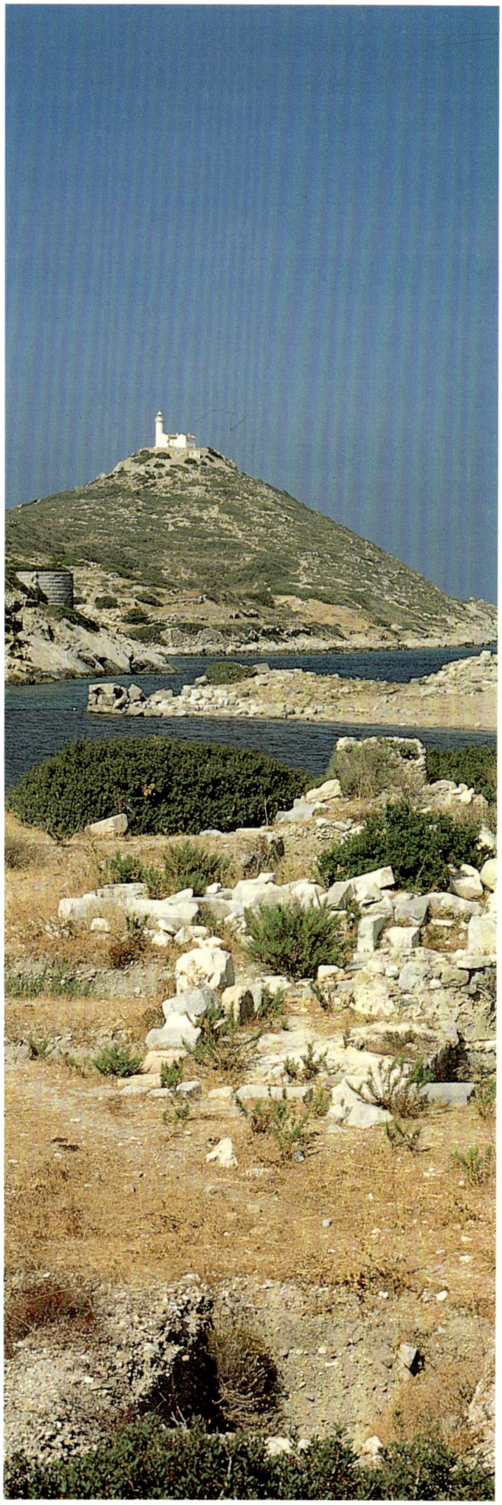

Cnidos. Looking out over the ancient harbour from the city.

The island was largely used for private residences while the public buildings were laid out on a generous scale on the flatter mainland opposite. From the skeleton that remains the size and scale of the city is easily visualised, mostly because no modern buildings obscure it and little grows on the dry rocky ground to conceal the ancient streets and buildings. The city walls, the small theatre by the harbour, several temples including the temple of Aphrodite, patron deity of the city, the agora, the streets, the large theatre, and the acropolis on a bluff above the city are all easily identified. It is the isolation and size of the site which is impressive, not it's completeness. If you sit for a while in the upper part of the city you can mentally reconstruct it from the jumbled pile of stones and get a fair idea of what it must have looked like.

If Cnidos captured wind-bound ships in it's harbour, Praxiteles captured the hearts of the Greeks with what was apparently the most beautiful statue of the era. Men literally fell in love with his statue of Aphrodite and they came from far and wide to look at it. In this Cnidos had some of the earliest tourist trade, long before the English deserted their own damp climate for the Cote d'Azur or more recently jetted around the skies looking for sun, sea, and sand. The statue was a source of some contention. It was modelled on Phryne, the most famous and beautiful hetaera of the age, and it was sculpted nude, a revolution in an age where only men had been sculpted nude. Praxiteles first offered the statue to the citizens of Kos who had also recently moved their city from a site inland to the site of present day Kos. The prudish citizens of Kos are said

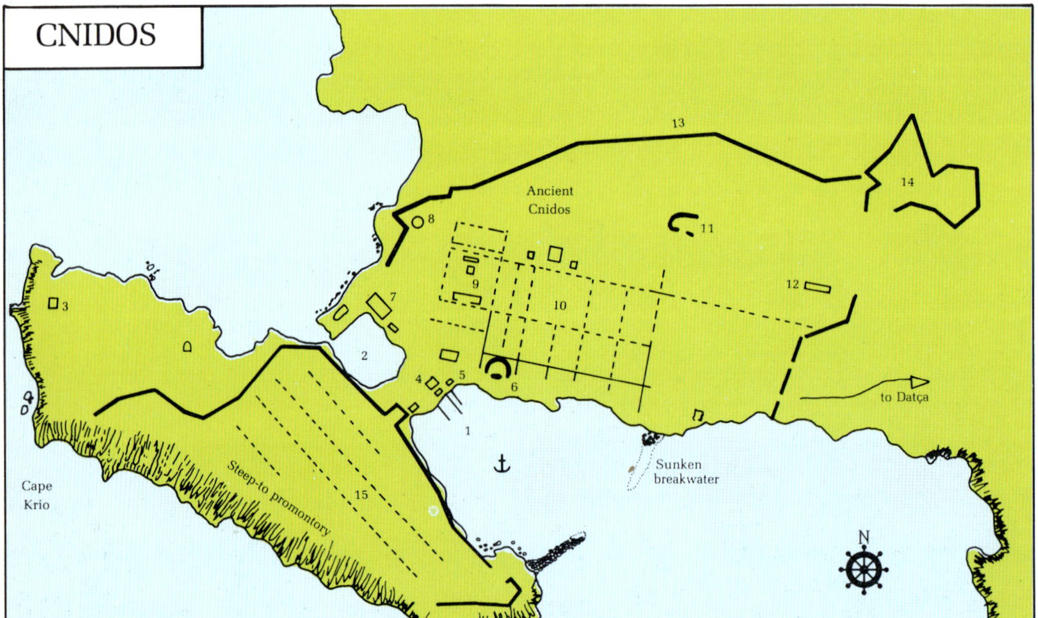

1. Southern harbour (Büyükliman)
2. Trireme hasbour
3. Lighthouse
4. Gendarmarie
5. Restaurants
6. Lower theatre
7. Agora
8. Temple of Aphrodite
9. Corinthian Temple
10. Terraced Streets
11. Upper theatre
12. Sanctuary of Demeter
13. City wall
14. Acropolis
15. Ferraces

to have refused the nude Aphrodite and ordered another with cloth chipped into the marble for modesty. So the Cnidians got the nude Aphrodite which they mounted on a circular platform in a temple on the northern slopes. The temple base is still there, but badly Aphrodite is not.

Many stories are told of the beautiful statue. Lucian relates that the shrine had a back as well as a front door so that the posterior of Aphrodite, said to be as lovely as the front, could be seen. With the old woman who held the key to the vital back panel, Lucian viewed Aphrodite from the rear and pronounced that she was indeed as lovely behind as she was in front.

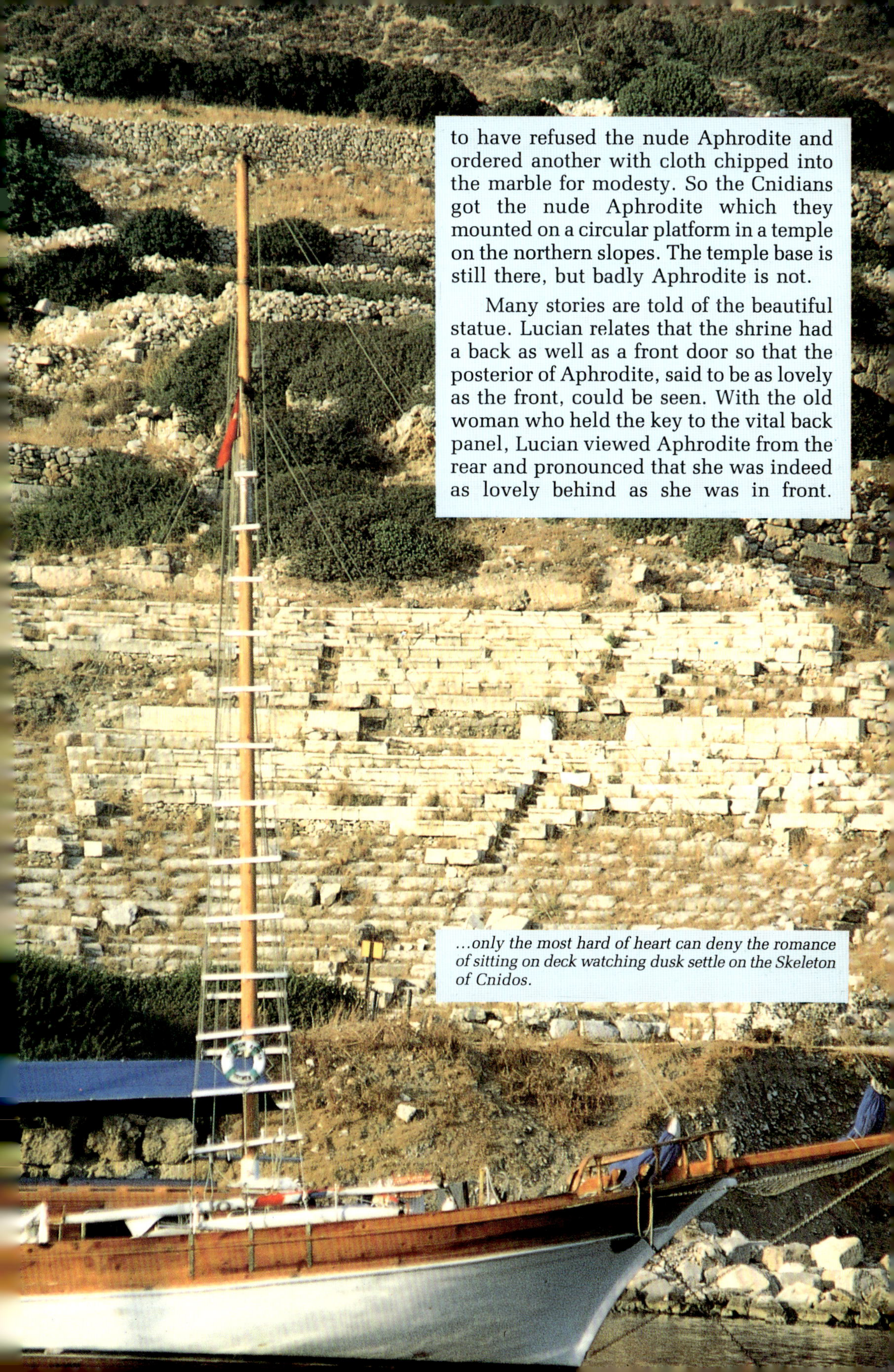

...only the most hard of heart can deny the romance of sitting on deck watching dusk settle on the Skeleton of Cnidos.

During his tour of inspection he noticed a dark mark on the inner thigh and asked the old woman whether it was a flaw in the marble. She replied that it was not. A love-sick admirer, unable to control his desire for her, contrived to hide inside the shrine and so have her to himself for the night. In the morning the statue was discovered to have a dark stain on the inner thigh, the mark of the young man's passion, that proved impossible to remove from the marble. Another tale relates how the King of Bithynia offered to pay off all of the city's debts, a not inconsiderable amount, if he could have the statue in exchange. The good citizens of Cnidos quite rightly preferred the beauty of Aphrodite to a clean slate in the city's financial affairs.

What happened to the statue is uncertain. One source says it was taken to Constantinople and later destroyed there in a fire. Iris Love, who excavated here under the American School, believes she found the head in the cellars of the British Museum, shipped back in 1859 by the entsiastic Newton. The museum denies the head came from Cnidos and the fate of the statue is still very much clouded in mystery.

The paradox of Cnidos is why it went downhill. It is easy to understand why ancient cities such as Ephesus and Caunos expired as the rivers their harbours were built near silted up. The traders just couldn't get their ships in despite dredging. Since trade was almost exclusively by sea this spelt death to a city. Up until twenty years ago most trade between the small villages and towns along this coast was still carried out by sea. But the harbour at Cnidos did not silt. It's still there and is now called Büyük Liman, 'Big Harbour'. Yachts and *gulets* use it as a convenient stop-over when going north or south, or as in the days of old, as a refuge from the northerlies. The ancient breakwaters are still in place, though the eastern arm is now just under the water and a danger to craft unaware it is there. The western arm is virtually intact, it's extremity in water some thirty metres deep. Around the inside of the harbour large sections of the ancient quay are still in place, though the sides have crumbled making it unsafe to go alongside. The smaller northern harbour is the one Strabo called the 'Trireme Harbour' and it held around twenty of these warships. It is open to the north and has consequently silted from the sand deposited in the entrance by the waves pushed down onto it by the northerlies, but otherwise it is essentially intact. So why did Cnidos decline? By Roman times it was no longer a major city and in the Byzantine era it is barely mentioned. There is no evidence of a great calamity like a fire or an earthquake destroying it. There is no good answer to the question. It just gradually went downhill until it was no more than a provincial town, finally abandoned in the Middle Ages.

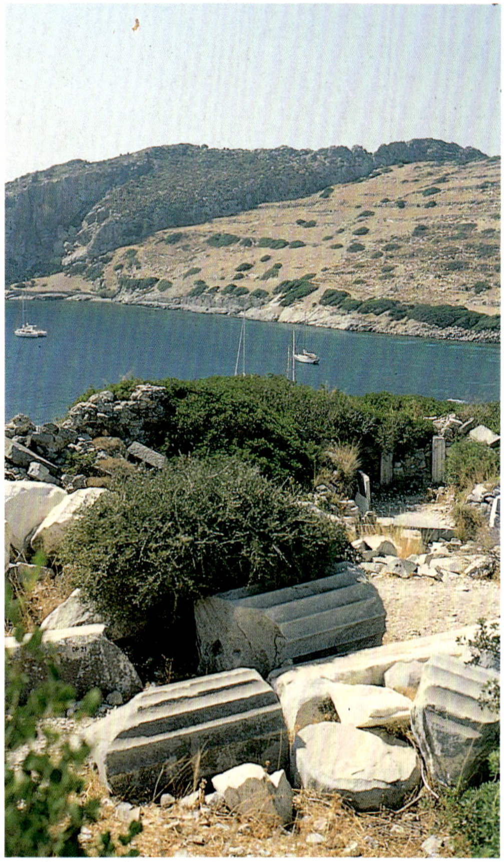

Cnidos. Looking out over the ancient harbour from the city.

It never regained it's former importance and glory. Today there are a few small fish restaurants, a modest pension built by one of the locals, and a small gendarmarie post, but these are recent additions to the landscape. The gendarmes guard the ruins and will sometimes want to check your bags after a visit to see if you have any ancient bric-a-brac in them, and to take the opportunity to request cigarettes and whisky. The restaurants often have good fresh fish, sometimes lobster, and drinkable local wine. Perhaps the wine is similar to Cnidian wine of two millennia ago that was described as 'nourishing, enriching the blood and promoting easy movement of the bowels, but relaxing the stomach if drunk in excess' (Bean). Come to think of it, that describes todays wine pretty well.

PALAMUT

The southern side of the Dorian Promontory is for the most part bare rock where little grows except stunted and thorny bushes and pungent thyme. Palamut is one of the few spots where the green of trees and crops relieves the dull grey limestone, though from seaward you can easily miss the hamlet tucked into the corner of the bay with the island of Baba Adası shielding the view. Getting into the small harbour is a hair-raising business as you must head straight for the beach before making a sharp turn to port through the narrow entrance. The exceptionally clear water makes the approach look far worse than it is. You will swear there can't be any depth under the keel, that you can reach down and touch the bottom, that any second the boat will come to a standstill. It is deeper than it looks.

Palamut is one of a group of villages known as Betçe, the 'five villages'. The others, little huddles of white houses and trees and patches of cultivated land, are scattered over the hill-side between Palamut and Datça. It is a little visited area that relies on agriculture and fishing to keep the village economies turning over.

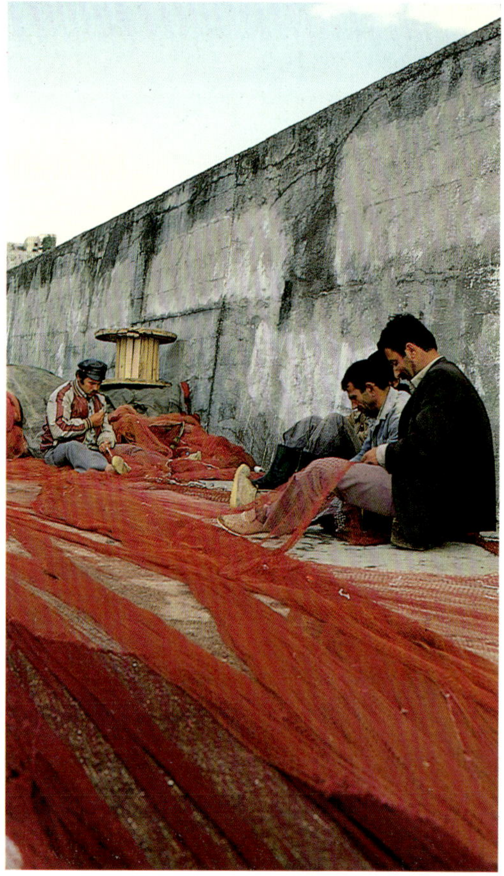

In Palamut the fishermen are a raffish piratical looking lot, but immensely friendly despite their appearance.

The little hamlet is the most likely site of ancient Triopium, a city that was once the equal of Cnidos. Thucydides mentions how a Spartan fleet sheltered in the harbour at Triopium between new-Cnidos and old-Cnidos at Datça. In 1984 while investigating the harbour at Palamut by yacht I very nearly came to grief on what I first assumed to be a short reef running out from the coast on the west side of the bay. Later on when I snorkeled over it, it turned out to be the remnants of an ancient breakwater which probably enclosed a small harbour slightly larger than the present day one. George Bean has theorised that breakwaters extended from the end of the island across to the shore to enclose a large harbour. While there are no reasons why a harbour of this size could not have been constructed with the technology of the age, it is unlikely a harbour on so grand a scale would have been needed and it would surely have been much commented on as a maritime wonder of the world. It was not and Thucydides mentions it as one of several harbours along this stretch of coast.

Triopium was a place of some importance early on. It was a meeting-place for the Dorian states and the festival of Triopian Apollo, a sort of early Olympics with athletics and running races, even horse-races we are told. Probably the stadium and the temple of Apollo stood on the level ground around Palamut, but today there is no trace of them. Up above Palamut are the remains of a sizeable town and an acropolis and this is the likely site of the city. The walk up to the site is a pleasant one, but don't go expecting to find anything like the ruins at Cnidos. For the more indolent traveller it is far better to sit in the simple restaurant on the beach and contemplate what the harbour of Triopium may have looked like over a glass or two of rakı.

Coast to Datça

KALABOSHI

A small cove close inside Kalaboshi Point. There is a small hamlet and restaurant nearby and a Gendarmarie post to keep an eye on Symi across the water.

PARMAK

A delightful cove with pine forest down to the waters edge. Ashore there is a small hotel and restaurant.

KARGI

A bay just around the corner from İnce Burun before you get to Datça. It is a windy barren place with a number of houses around the shore.

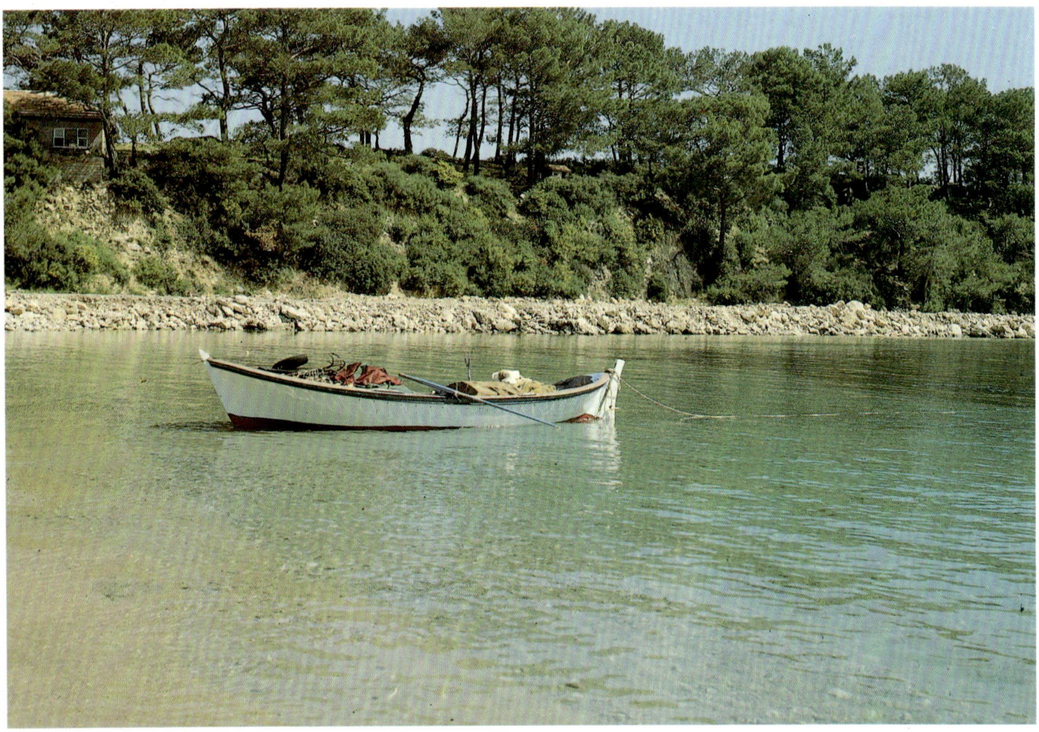

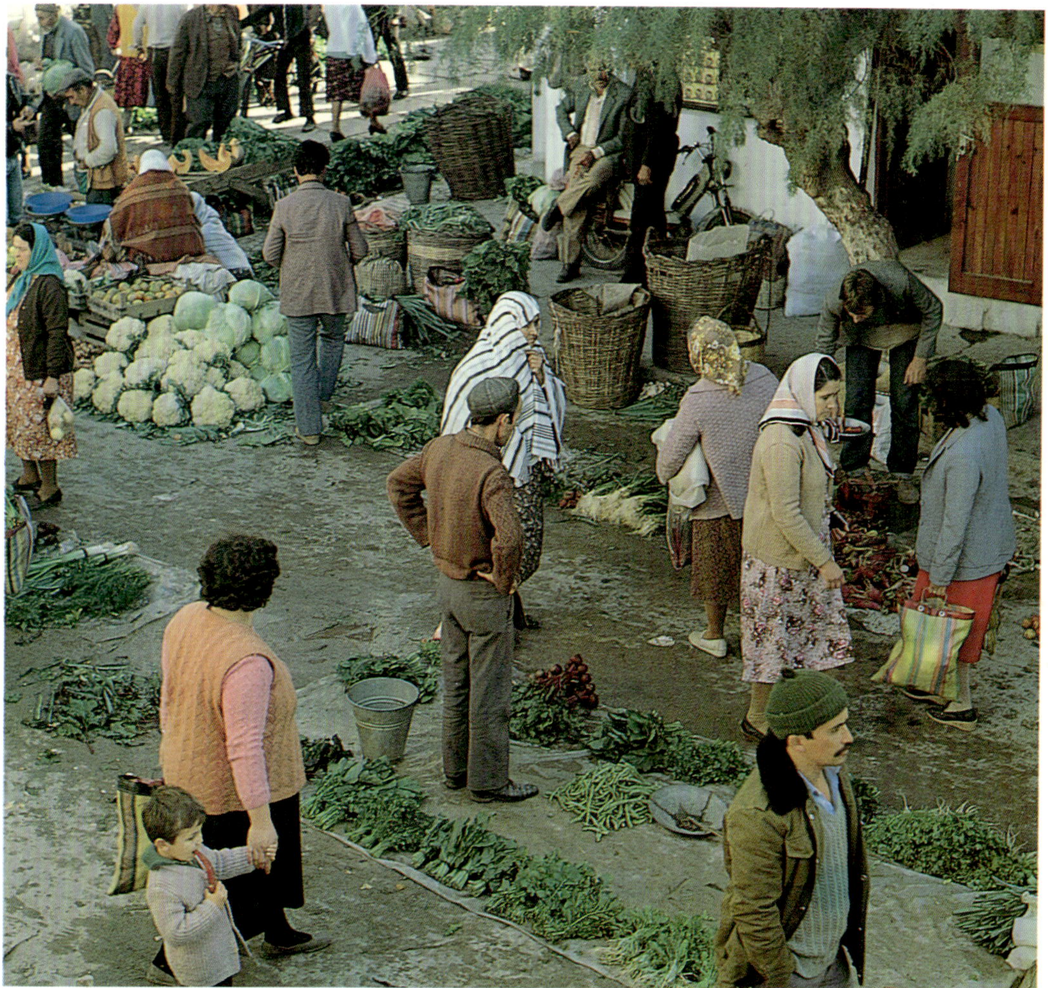

Bodrum

FACILITIES

Bodrum: Restaurants, hotels & pensions, telephone, P.O., Banks, Doctor, Dentist, Laundry, Showers, Toilets, fuel, water, ice, gas, provisions, engineer. Officials: Health, Immigration, Customs, Harbourmaster, Police, Tourist Information office.
Gumbet: Restaurants, hotels & pensions, telephone, showers, toilets, water, provisions.
Bitez: Restaurants, hotels & pensions, telephone, toilets, water.
Kargı: Restaurant.
Bağla: Restaurant.
Aspat: Restaurant.
Karaincir: Restaurant.
Akyarlar: Restaurant.
Çökertme: Restaurant, pension.
Ören: Restaurant, water, provisions.
Akbük: Restaurant.
Gökova İskele: Restaurants, pensions, water, provisions.
Şehir Adaları: Restaurants, pension.
Söğüt: Restaurants, pension, toilets, shower, water, ice, provisions.
Değirmen Bükü: Restaurants, water.
Amazon Creek: Restaurants, pension, water, provisions.
Cnidos: Restaurants, pension, Gendarmarie.
Palamut: Restaurant, water.
Kargı: Restaurant.

CHAPTER 2

DATÇA TO MARMARİS

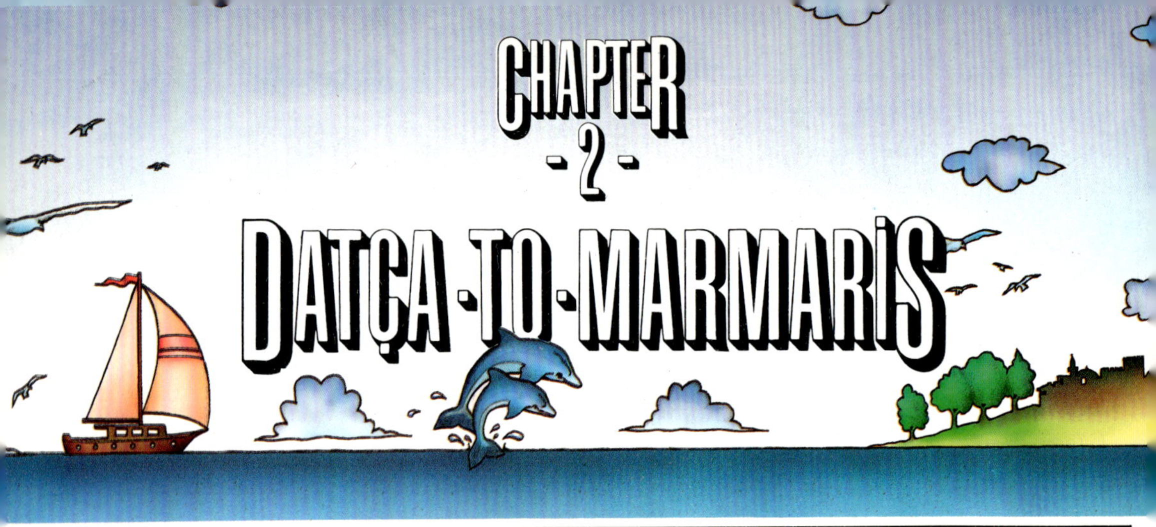

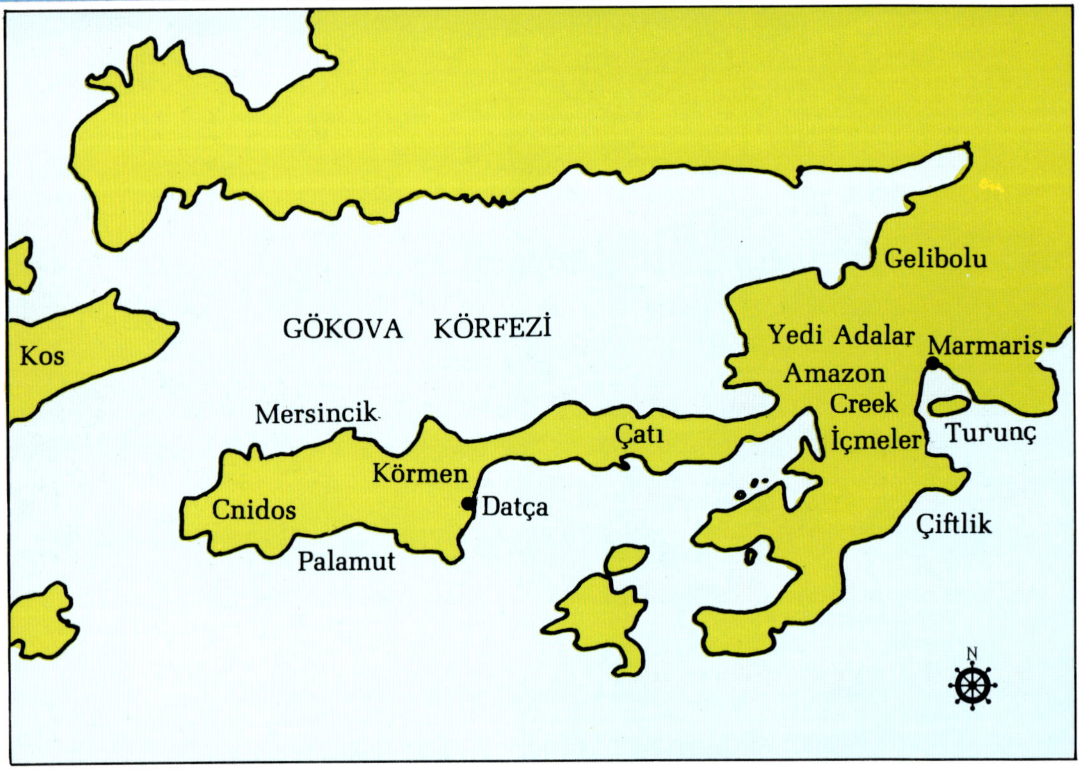

This chapter continues the description of places along the under-belly of the Dorian Promontory and then around the Loryma Peninsula to Marmaris. Even more than the Gulf of Gökova, this is a remote bit of coast and the only way to get to many places on the Loryma Peninsula is by boat - there are no roads, not even dirt roads. Land-based travellers are best advised to take a gulet from Marmaris if they want to explore this region. The one road that does run into the Loryma Peninsula, to Bozburun, is perilous in places and you are certainly ill-advised to try it after heavy rain.

DATÇA

Datça, or to give it's proper name, Datça İskele, *İskele* meaning a landing place for an inland village, is a fishing village which in recent years has developed into a small tourist resort. It lies around the waters edge on either side of a small isthmus and straggles in a higgledy-piggledy way inland. The village and especially the new buildings cannot be described as attractive, but somehow it works as a pleasing and happy place that I have grown attached to over the years. The small harbour is invariably packed

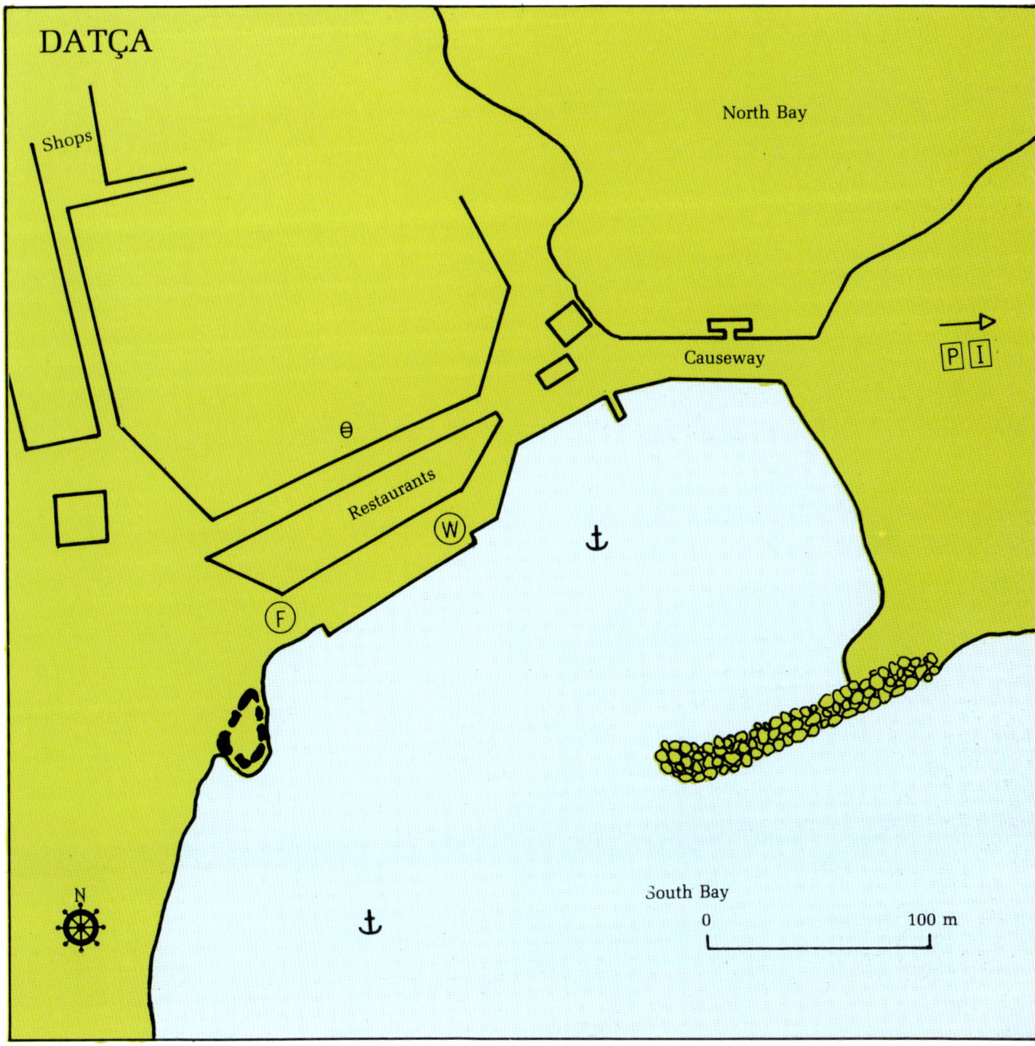

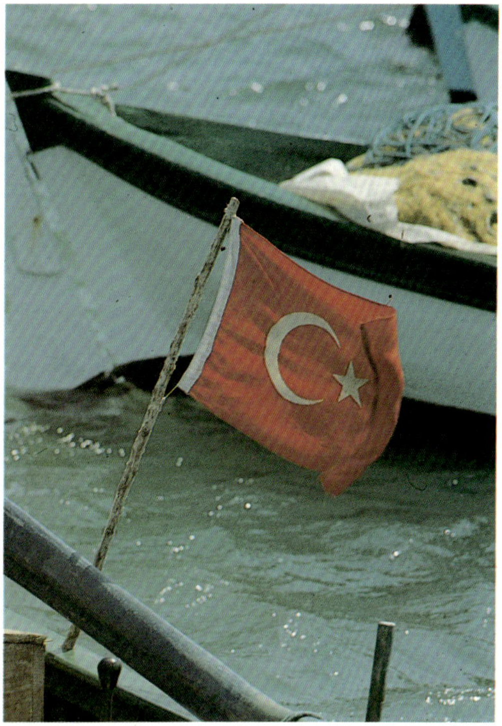

Local boats. Datça

with yachts and *gulets* and if a yacht arrives late in the afternoon it will have to anchor off outside the harbour. Just above the harbour on a low rocky outcrop are several restaurants with views out over the bay to the Greek island of Symi seven or so miles across the water. In one or other of these restaurants you can watch yachts and *gulets* beating up against the *meltem* towards Datça and competing for space in the harbour - good sport if you have already arrived and found a space.

Datça İskele is on the southeastern side of the only good fertile land on the otherwise barren and rocky Dorian Promontory. This precious fertile plain, remarked upon by Spratt in the 19th century as having "fine groves of olive and valonia (Mediterranean oak), and of almonds and other fruit trees", was more than likely the reason for siting old-Cnidos here. The city was founded by Dorians sometime in the 11th-12th century BC, though the site is mentioned earlier than this date. From the 7th century the city rose to some prominence and embarked on some colonisation of it's own. A band of colonists from old-Cnidos settled on Sicily, but problems with the locals forced them to move to the Lipari Islands off the northeast coast of Sicily. One of this group of islands is Stromboli, the still active volcano dubbed the 'lighthouse of the Mediterranean' as the dull red glow when it erupts can be seen from many miles away at night, and finds from these early colonists have been discovered there. Trade with Egypt was also an important ingredient of old-Cnidos' wealth and the city helped to establish Naucratis, a Greek-Egyptian trading colony on the Nile delta.

Today little remains of old-Cnidos and compared to new-Cnidos on the end of the promontory, it hardly warrants looking for the old bits of rubble left behind. Near the harbour there is a large platform with terrace walls and this was probably a sanctuary. The acropolis lies to the north

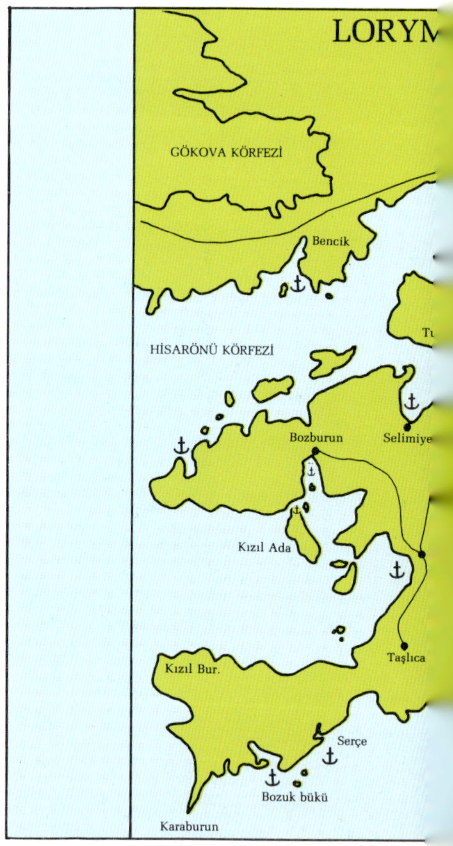

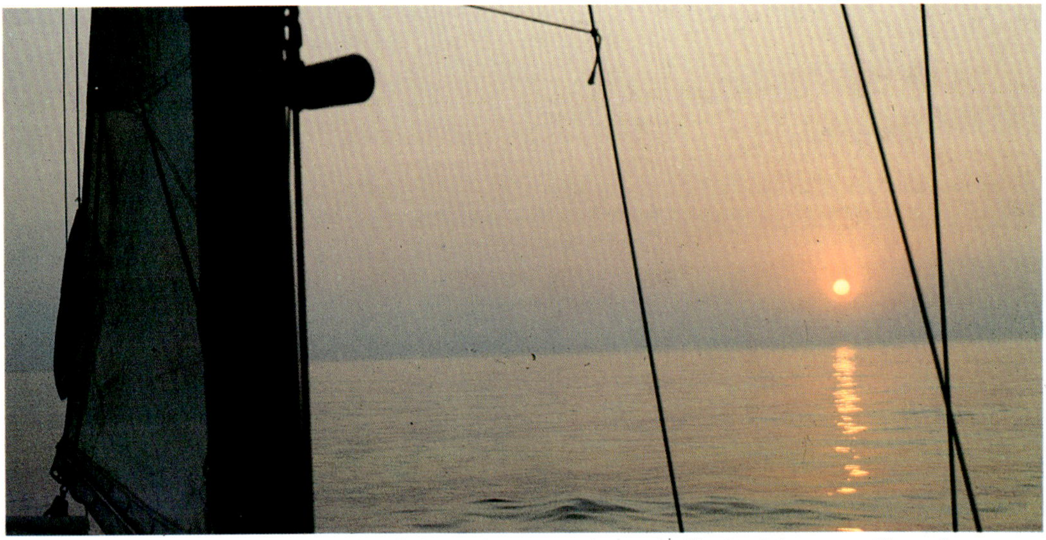

...not only will a boat let you see a lot of places that cannot be reached by land, but you will see the coast best from a boat.

of the present village and from the extent of the city walls, some of it submerged in the sea either because the land has sunk or the sea level risen, it has been calculated that there was an enclosed area of over two square miles. The move to new-Cnidos occurred sometime around 360 BC, but the old site was not abandoned. Probably it continued as a small client town producing the crops that could not be grown on the barren ground at the end of the promontory. According to George Bean the name was later recorded by Pliny as Stadia and this name survives in the modern Turkish name of Datça, though I can't make the connection between the two.

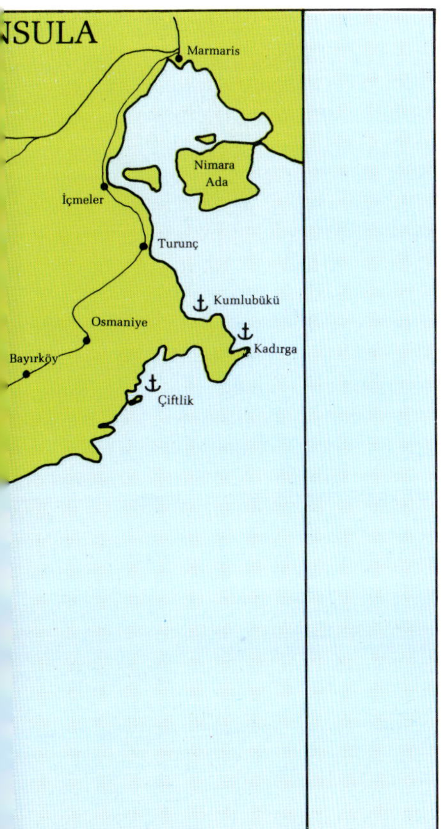

HİSARÖNÜ KÖRFEZİ

The small gulf at the southeastern end of the Dorian Promontory is as wild and beautiful as it's larger counterpart on the northern side. Many of the places around it's shores are easiest reached by boat, the road around the south side from Hisarönü to Bozburun is particuarly bad in places, especially in the spring and autumn when there has been a lot of rain. Like the shores of the Gulf of Gökova it's shores are extensively covered in pine forest and there are a number of ancient sites, though none of them measure up to Cnidos or Cedreae.

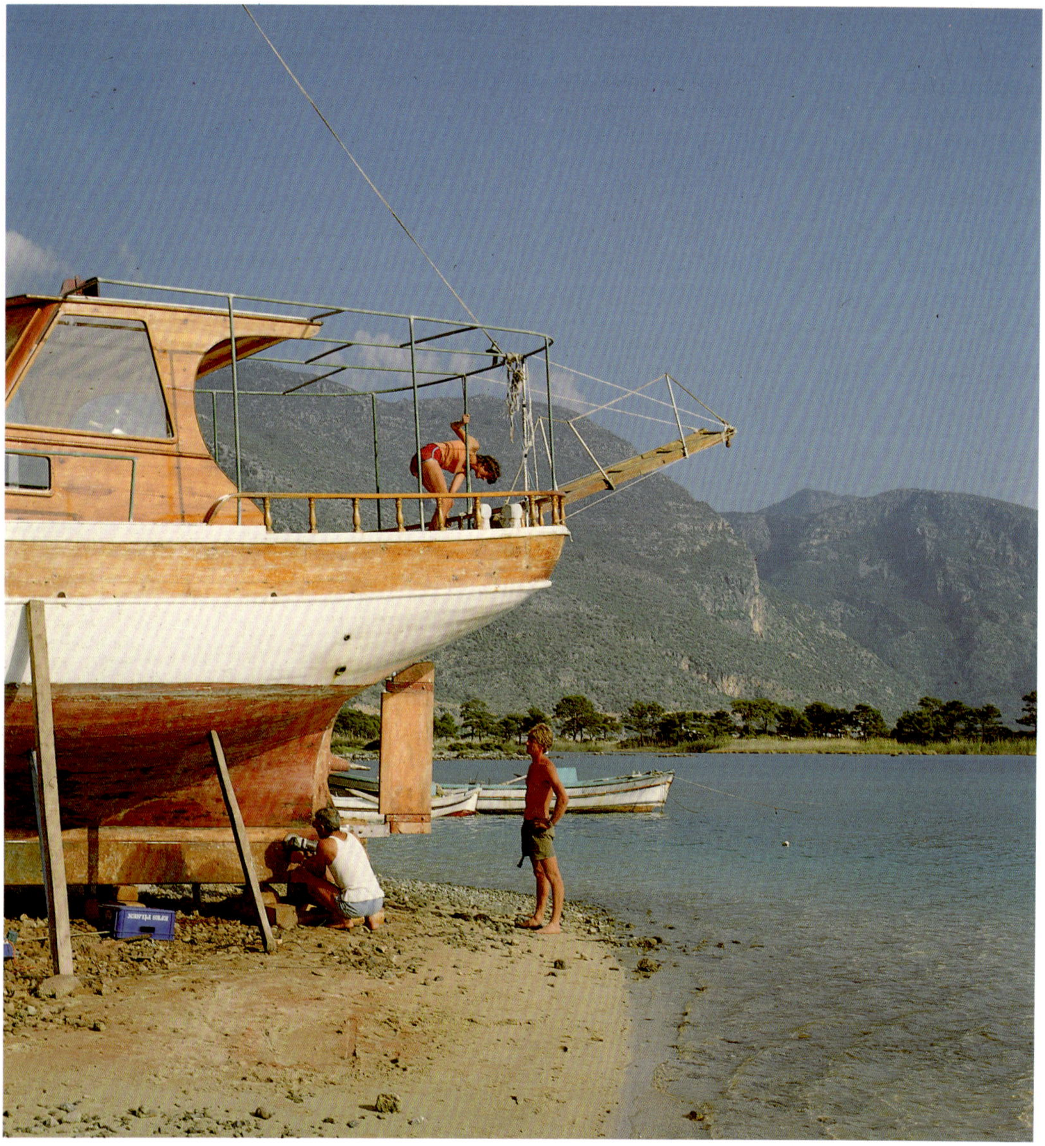

From Datça to Bençik

Değirmen

From Datça the shoreline runs in a shallow curve until you get to a group of jagged rocks and islets at the eastern end of the bight. On the east side of a jagged headland, (with 'ancient ruins' marked on the Admiralty chart, though I have never explored them), there is a cove and a holiday village nearby.

Kuruca

A bay with a large holiday village sprawled around the shores. The rocky landscape now changes to thick pine forest again, corresponding to the pine forests on the Gökova side (Kuruca Bükü). The holiday village is said to be popular with the elderly and an amusing anecdote is told to account for this. Just before construction of the holiday village began in the early 1970's, seven old and useless donkeys were turned out to pasture in Kuruca. Two years later when the construction team turned up to begin work, they found a healthy family of 28 donkeys grazing peacefully around the shores. What Kuruca can do for the virility of a donkey it can do...

BENÇİK

At the narrowest part of the Dorian Promontory a long inlet runs into it so that only a short neck of land, about half a mile wide, joins the promontory to the mainland. The local Turkish name for it is 'Balıkaşıran' which means 'the place where fish jump across' and neatly sums up the size of the neck. This narrow neck of land figured prominently in the history of old-Cnidos. In the 6th century BC the Persians were rapidly mopping up the Greek cities in their conquest of Asia Minor. The Cnidians realised they were threatened and hit upon the idea of turning the promontory into an island by digging a canal from Bençik to the other side. Work proceeded slowly and the rock tended to shatter and splinter a lot, injuring the workmen. If you enter Bençik from seawards one of it's outstanding features is the knobbly red rock that makes it look not unlike a mini-Grand Canyon. It certainly looks dangerous stuff to work with though I have not tried to imitate the Cnidian workmen and see if it does splinter when hit. The difficult nature of the job gave the city elders cause to consult the oracle at Delphi and the reply was unequivocal:

'Dig not nor fence your isthmus: Zeus himself
Had made your land an island, had he so wished.'

The Cnidians stopped work and the Persians encountered no resistance when they arrived. When Spratt explored the area in 1838 he believed he found evidence of work on the canal, but nobody since has.

ORACLES

Time and time again, as with the Cnidians asking whether or not they should continue to dig their canal across the Dorian Promontory in the face of the Persian invasion, the matter of oracles comes up. Whether it was going off to start a war, whether or not to build a new city in in a chosen spot, whether to fight an invader or submit, or on a more mundane level whether it was going to be a boy or a girl, or whether to pursue a romance, one of the oracles was consulted. The oracle at Delphi was pre-eminent and known all over the civilized world, but other oracles of lesser fame existed. The oracle at Didyma in the gulf above Halicarnassus was one such. Others were situated in Crete, at Paphos in Cyprus, at Mycenae and Epidavros, at Colchis at the eastern end of the Black Sea, at Ammon in Libya, in Athens, and for a short time even in unbelieving Rome.

An oracle was the answer of a god or demi-god to an inquiry about the future. Apollo was the preferred god for prophecy and the sanctuary at Delphi dedicated to him the preferred oracle. The oracle was delivered by a priestess, the Pythia, who was said to sit astride a chasm from which intoxicating vapours issued. Alternative accounts state that laurel leaves were burnt and the fumes from these caused the priestess to fall into a trance. The answers the priestess gave were always interpreted, in some cases the answers were apparently unintelligible gibberish; but the interpreters at the temple always managed to get something down, usually in hexameter verse, and it must be supposed the real power of the oracle lay with these poet-interpreters. The oracle was frequently ambiguous and some of the ambiguities had tragic consequences. When Phillip of Macedon was about to set off against the Persians he asked the Delphic oracle what the outcome would be and received this answer:

The ready victim crowned for death
Before the altar stands.

Assuming the victim to be the King of Persia, Phillip went ahead with his campaign. Unfortunately for him he was the victim. The ambiguity of the responses meant the oracle had, de facto, an excellent success rate. When the Greeks asked if they would succeed against the Persians, this cryptic answer was given:

Seed-time and harvest, weeping sires shall tell
How thousands fought at Salamis and fell.

Whether it was to be the Greeks or the Persians who fell in their thousands it did not say.

The oracle was not above being partisan or even above being bribed. When the Cnidians asked the oracle whether or not to continue digging the canal, the Delphic oracle was in a pro-Persian period despite being under Greek control. Possibly the priests thought the temple would be under Persian management in the near future when they looked at the success rate of the Persian army against the Greeks. Yet despite the often partisan nature of the oracle, despite bribery and wars over who controlled Delphi and so controlled the prestigious oracle, it continued to be the most revered of all the sacred places. Delphi itself was considered to be the 'navel of the earth' and for those who have been to the precipitous mountain site on which the temple stood, it is not too difficult to understand why. The site is on one side of a great crack in the Parnassus mountain range, a crack that opens up to the plain of Itea and the sea a long way below. Delphi was more to the Greeks than just a fortune-telling enterprise, it was a focus for Greek civilization and a secure centre for a world constantly on the move and threatened by enemies without and ideas within. On the walls of the temple a number of precepts were inscribed, amongst them one that has survived in various forms down through the ages: 'Know thyself'. The Delphic oracle was a focus for Greek civilization to know itself.

One of the last oracles delivered from Delphi before it's destruction by the Goths in AD 396 captures something of the desolation and mystery of Delphi. It was to be an epitaph for the Roman world as well as the Greek, since Christianity and monotheism was ascendent in the world:

Go, tell the king - the carven hall is felled,
Apollo has no cell, prophetic bay
nor talking spring, the cadenced well is stilled.

KEÇİ BÜKÜ

From Bençik the Gulf of Hisarönü narrows as the Bozburun Peninsula pinches it tight until the flat marshy land at it's head. In the southeast corner a long inlet forks south and this is one of the loveliest places in the gulf. From seawards you enter the inlet with thick pine cover on one side and banks of tall reeds on the other. Halfway down the inlet a steep-sided islet blocks one side of the channel and on the top is perched a fortified structure. Towards the head the inlet opens out, but the eastern side is obstructed by a sand-bar and much of it is shallow with thick reeds around it. The

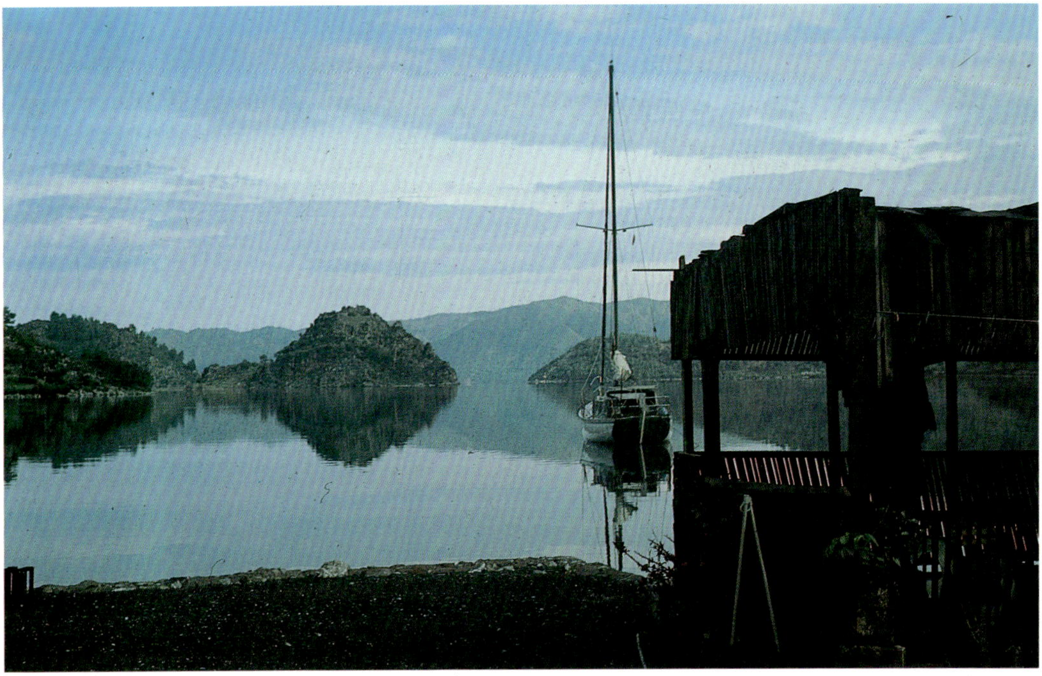

The anchorage off Kadir's restaurant. Keçi Bükü.

western side is the anchorage yachts and *gulets* use. The surroundings are nothing short of spectacular and a good sized handful of the adjectives commonly found in tourist brochures would not do Keçi Bükü justice. Whether you arrive by land or sea, the place is well worth tarrying in for a few days, or more.

Above the anchorage the small village of Orhaniye is shut in by vertical walls of rock. The gorge behind the village channels a stream down to the sea and this bubbles through the village and surrounding farms. On my first visit here a wedding was scheduled for the next day and I was invited to attend. It took place at the farm of the bride's parents and a more beautiful setting is hard to imagine. A brook bubbled through a yard hemmed in by the farmhouse and outbuildings and conveniently supplied crystal clear water for the farm. It was springtime and the yard was covered in peach and almond blossom. Dogs, chickens, goats, and a donkey puzzled by all the commotion wandered about the tables set up for the occasion. The wedding party was segregated into a reception party for the males and another for the females, each party with their own separate band of musicians, this being the correct way to stage the wedding I was told. Only the groom, the father of the bride, and a few village elders were allowed to attend the reception for the bride and the women; a local 'sheriff' with a stout staff kept the local lads from creeping up to watch the women dancing. As a foreigner I was an honoured guest and one of the few males allowed to watch the women. The formal part of the ceremony and the signing of the register was brief, most of the afternoon was taken up with drinking *raki*, eating, dancing, and drinking more raki while the musicians, principally the clarinet player, wailed for all they were worth. My memory of the latter part of the reception is clouded by a raki induced fog, but I remember making my way back to the boat with the help of several men from the village, the clarinet player tootling away in the lead, and none of us very co-ordinated.

The area around Keçi Bükü and Orhaniye has some interesting ancient associations. To the north on the flat plain

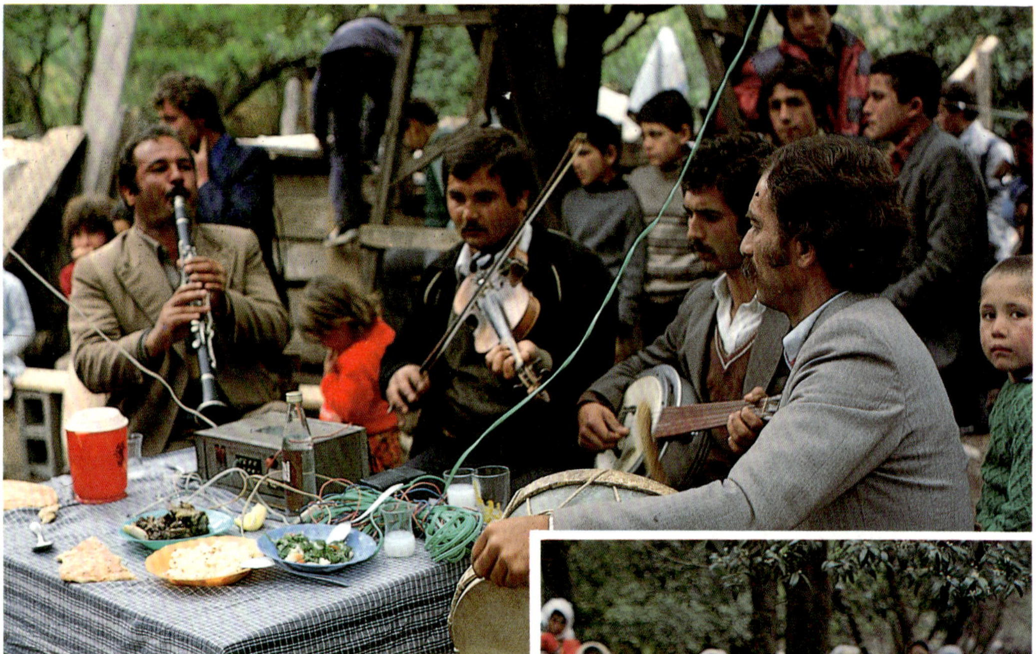

The wedding party. Orhaniye.

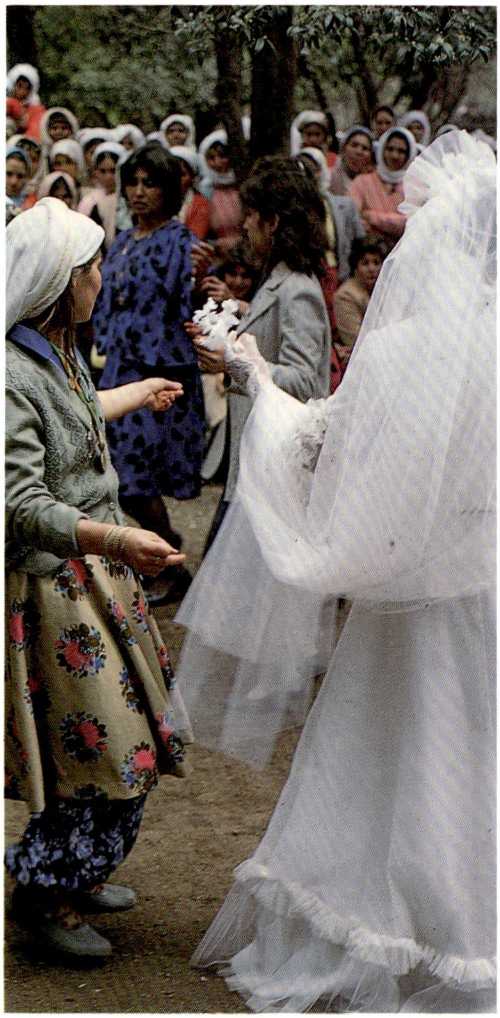

at the head of the gulf lies the village of Hisarönü, from which the gulf takes its name. In antiquity it was called Bybassus and on a rocky outcrop nearby the remains of the acropolis can be seen, but little else remains. Like the other cities in this area, Bybassus was part of the Rhodian Peraea and was important for it's association with a temple complex to the south (and to the east of Keçi Bükü). It is likely that Keçi Bükü was the ancient harbour for Bybassus and a landing place for those making a pilgrimage to the temple.

The temple was dedicated to Hemithea, literally the 'demi-goddess', who was revered for her healing powers, particularly for women in childbirth. The method used is described by George Bean as incubation, a method in which the goddess stood over the sick woman and cured her in her sleep. It is speculation on my part, but it occurs to me that all these references to incubation and curing people in their sleep, the method was also practised at Epidavros and by Hippocrates in Kos, could refer to hypnosis. It is common knowledge that hypnosis can act as an analgesic and that pain can be almost

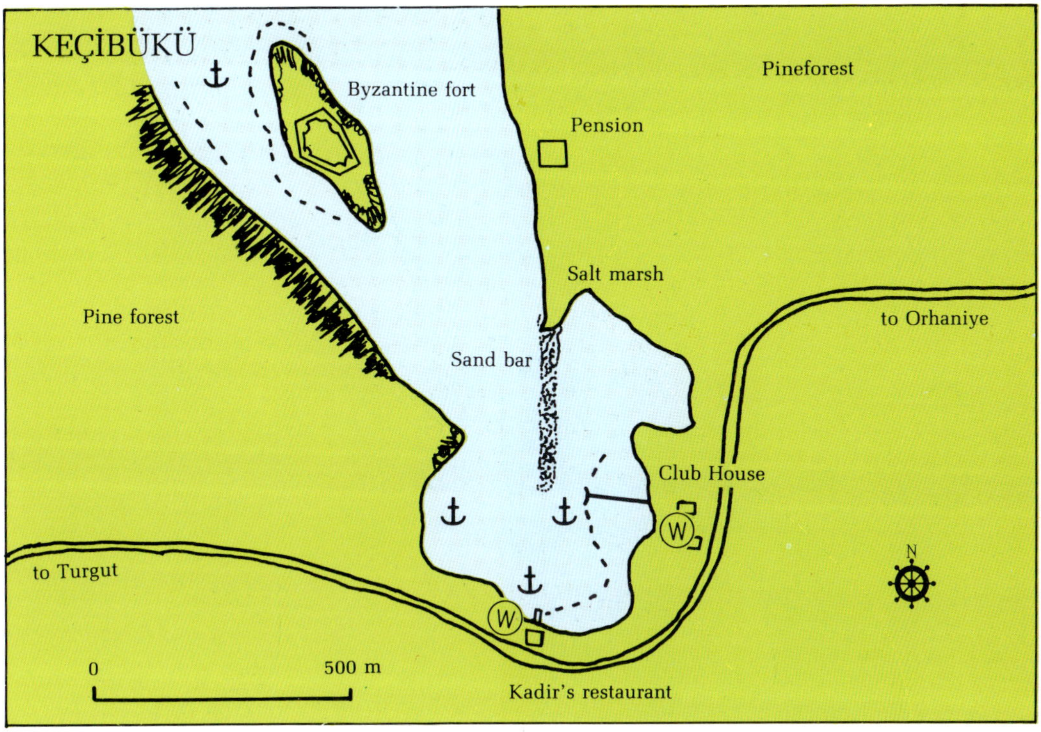

entirely eliminated under a hypnotic suggestion, or at least that consciousness of pain can be eliminated. I have no concrete references, but I have seen statements to the effect that major open-body surgery has been conducted with the patient under hypnotic suggestion. Certainly hypnosis would make childbirth relatively pain-free and it may be for this that Hemithea was famous.

However cures were effected, the temple was popular for some 200 years from the 4th to the 2nd centuries BC. A festival, the Castabeia, was held here at intervals, and so crowded did it get that an inscription on the site records how accomodation could not be found for the numbers attending and there were worries that revenue was being lost. The historian Diodrus relates that the temple was honoured throughout the Rhodian Peraea and even further afield. Votive gifts were showered on the site from pilgrims who came from far and wide. To get to it today, (it is called *Pazarlık*, 'the market place', in Turkish), entails a fair hike and then a stiff climb some 270 metres (900 ft) to a ridge on Eren Dağı. Little remains apart from the platform of the temple and a small theatre in poor condition; and the curious tale relating the strange healing powers of Hemithea.

Around Keçi Bükü itself there are a few ancient ruins on the eastern side of the inlet and the fortified structure on the islet. The latter may have had ancient foundations, but is more than likely of Medieval origin. Of more recent origin is Kadir's restaurant at the foot of a small jetty in the inlet. Kadir cooks simple but delicious fare, he often has fresh fish, and the view over the anchorage from his secluded restaurant is alone worth the visit. Water from a nearby spring has been analysed in İzmir and found to be just about as uncontaminated as you can get, so yachts and *gulets* often fill their tanks here. To the east of Kadir, on the way to the village, a new restaurant and bar known as the 'clubhouse' has been built. The village of Orhaniye is about two kilometres away - a pleasant walk around the bay and through farmsteads to the foothills of Eren Dağı.

SELİMİYE

Immediately south of Keçi Bükü a large bay loops back on itself and fans out into two arms. At the head of the southern arm is the small hamlet of Selimiye, the only habitation in the area apart from a few farms scattered around the shore. The bay is a remote place, yet in antiquity a small city flourished here, either near present day Selimiye where there are a number of ancient ruins or on the northern side of the bay where there is an ancient acropolis with a fort from the Middle Ages built on top of it. The bay was called Sinus Schoenus, the 'Bay of Reeds', in antiquity and the city, most likely near Selimiye, was called Hyda or Hyla.

SELİMİYE TO BOZBURUN

From Selimiye the steep coast is a wild and rugged landscape with little sign of habitation. A chain of islands, two of them quite large and three smaller ones, lie just off the coast. Once around the corner into Sömbeki Körfezi the landscape changes dramatically to barren rocky hillside and a rubbly coastline, a harsh glaring landscape hard on the eyes after the green pine of Hisarönü.

THE MEDITERRANEAN LANDSCAPE

Around the coast the thick pine forests provide welcome shade from the sun and a welcome green vista to relieve the otherwise harsh and barren landscape. But this 'christmas tree' landscape is not at all a typical Mediterranean one and the pine forests we see are man-made affairs, an artificially produced landscape using a fast growing tree that thrives on the poor coastal soil. In some of the well-watered valleys and coastal flats there are small stands of deciduous and broad-leaf species that more closely approximate what the Turkish coastline would have looked like less than a thousand years ago. Some of the names of ancient places also hint at a different landscape. Cedreae in the Gulf of Gökova means 'cedar' and presumably there were extensive stands of these trees where now there are none. Ancient writers talk of the coast and islands as fertile places with abundant forests where now there is nothing but baked earth and rubbly barren hillsides. What happened to this landscape?

Most of it, contrary to popular opinion, disappeared in comparitively recent times, as little as 500 to 600 years ago when the forests were cut down to build the great galley fleets of the Ottomans and the merchant fleets that transported goods around the Ottoman Empire. All over the Mediterranean whole forests were felled to provide the wood to build ships for the Venetians, the Genoese, Spain, the Moors, and the Ottomans. Some idea of the scale of tree-felling that went on can be garnered from recent estimates of how many trees it took to build a large fighting galley. In the Battle of Lepanto in 1571 where the combined Christian fleets took on the combined Ottoman fleet, the Christain flagship was a large galley called the 'El Real'. Recently a replica of the 'El Real' was built and the following figures are quoted in David Attenborough's ***The First Eden*** *for the timber used in her construction: "Fifty beech trees were required for her oars, three hundred pines and firs for her planks and spars, and over three*

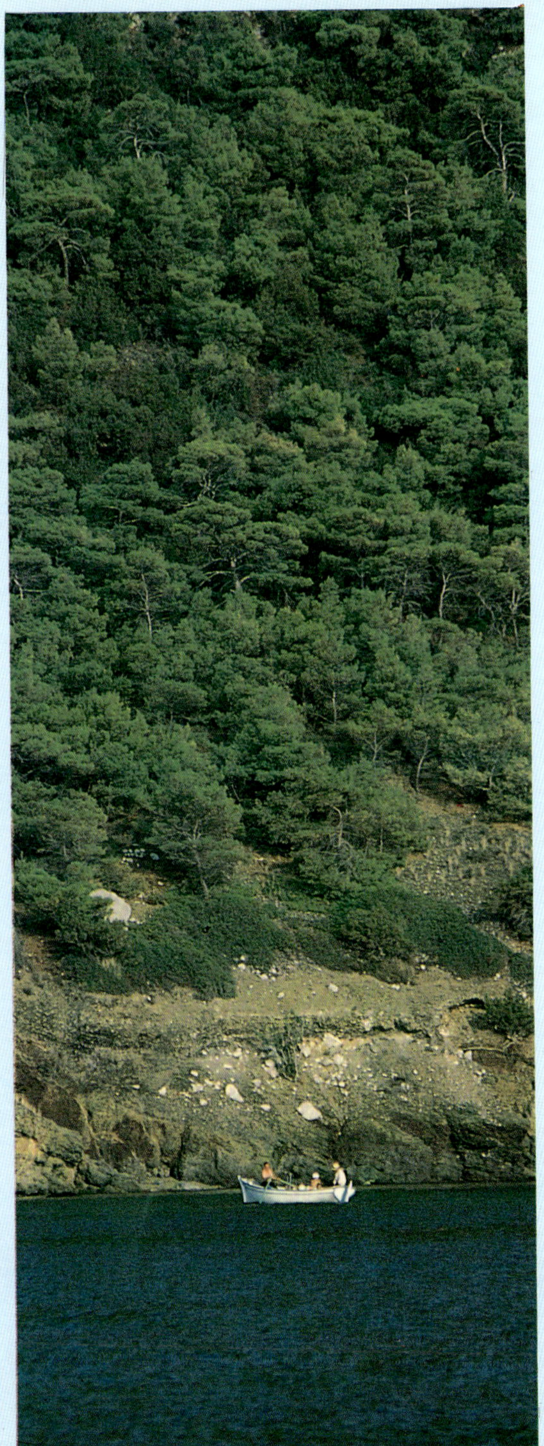

'Christmas tree' landscape in the gulf.

hundred mature oaks for the timbers of her hull.'' In the Battle of Lepanto the Christain fleet numbered over 250 ships and the Ottoman fleet slightly more. To build this number of ships would have required over a quarter of a million mature trees.

It was not long after the Battle of Lepanto that ship-building moved away from the Mediterranean to the great northern European forests around the Baltic. In the Mediterranean most of the coastal forest and much of it for a good way inland had been felled and there was quite simply no timber to build ships with. In 1600 no forest of any consequence existed along the coast of Asia Minor though some still remained in inland areas where access made it impossible to get the cut timber to the centres of boatbuilding. What man had started, the domestic goat finished off. The Turks brought large herds of goats into Asia Minor and when they were let loose on land where forests had been felled there was no chance of regeneration. The goat will eat just about anything and newly sprouting shoots and sapling leaves are a delicacy. The same story was re-enacted all over the Mediterranean. David Attenborough succinctly sums up the whole sad story:

''The woodlands and forests that had once ringed the entire Mediterranean and provided a home for a rich population of animals had now largely gone. They survived only in places for which no soldier bothered to fight, where no forester found it possible to haul out timber, and no farmer thought it worthwhile to make a field. Now the macquis and the garrigue, which had once grown only on the rockiest and most impoverished stretches of the coasts,

*spread all around the Sea and dominated what were once among the most fertile lands in the world." David Attenborough/**The First Eden** 1987.*

In the few places where the original forest cover still exists we can get some idea of what the shores of the Mediterranean would have looked like. Holm and cork oak, Aleppo pine, juniper, and cypress would have been commonly found in the forest. In the spring in that short period when nature seems to have gone berserk and there are wildflowers everywhere, pockets of indigenous flora abound: orchids in a profusion of types and colours, cyclamen and crocus, varieties of chrysanthemum, lupins, toadflax, and vetch. Anyone seeing Turkey in the spring would not recognise it as the sun-baked brown country they see in the summer.

Between the tall trees and the wildflowers there were three species of plants that were to have a profound effect on the Mediterranean landscape when man discovered how useful they could be to him. The wild grape vine, a common creeper in the forest; the wild fig, a small bushy tree; and the wild olive. It appears that from early on man understood the principles of grafting a good bearing variety to a hardy variety so that the two characteristics were combined in one. It's difficult to assess which had the biggest impact on life in those far-off times. The olive was eaten as a fruit, but far more important was the oil it yielded when crushed. Olive oil was used for lamps to provide light, to anoint the body and sooth sunburnt skin, for cleaning when it was rubbed over the body and then scraped off along with the dirt, to seal amphoras, and of course in cooking. The grape could not compete with all these uses, but it did produce a beverage when fermented that if drunk in sufficient quantity, meant you couldn't give a damn if it didn't have any other uses. It seems the ancients were just as fond of this agreeable beverage as we are.

ATABOL KAYASI
(Age Latha)

Not a place but a rock. Just off the northwestern corner of Sömbeki Körfezi, this rock lying just under the water seems to have a magnetic attraction for boats. When the *meltem* is blowing it is all but impossible to see it lurking just under the surface. A number of yachts and motor-boats have hit it and the razor-sharp rock has simply sliced a hole in the bottom of the boat and it has toppled over the other side and slid down to rest in deep water.

BOZBURUN

The end of the Loryma Peninsula divides into two ragged headlands which look like the jaws of a snake on a chart. The inside of the jaws is Sömbeki Körfezi, the ancient Gulf of Symi after the Greek island a short distance offshore. Bozburun sits in a cavity where the upper molars should be. The approach between a number of islands and the rubbly hills of the peninsula is quite different to the landscape further north - the land around is baked hard by the sun and the few strips of cultivated land do little to relieve the starkness of the vista. It is no wonder that the inhabitants of Bozburun, like the inhabitants of the equally parched and rocky island of Symi, turned to the sea for their livelihood. Bozburun has long been a sponge-fishing village, although as elsewhere, fewer of the young men contract to carry on the arduous and often dangerous work when the pickings of a bar or restaurant job is so much easier.

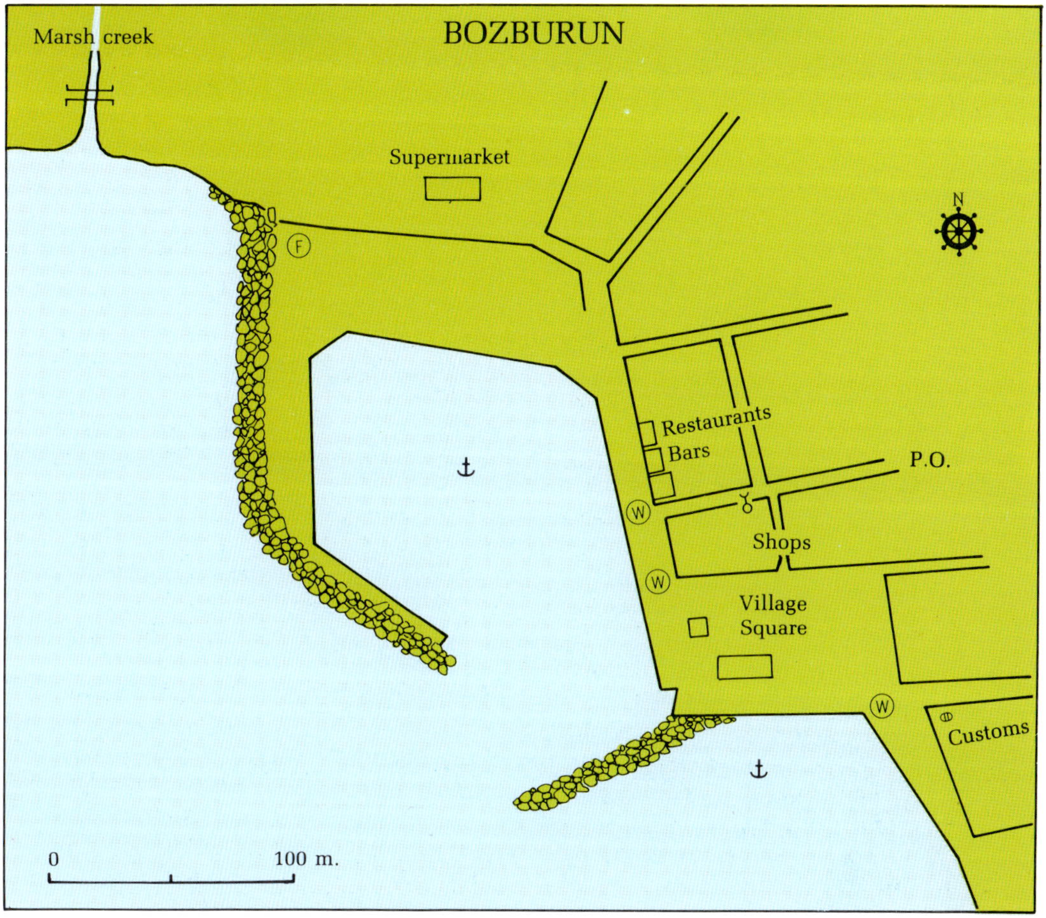

The sponge-fishing boats leave for their annual voyage in May or June and slowly cruise the coast until October. Aboard one of these small boats, often only nine or ten metres (around thirty feet) long, will be five or six men, living and sleeping sponges until the winter. The sponges are found in anything from ten to seventy metres (30 to 230 feet) of water and a diver will spend about an hour underwater doing his stint. The equipment is often antiquated and makeshift and would give a professional diver the horrors. A wet-suit is worn to keep warm and air is supplied along a long hose to a simple mask and regulator. The sponges are cut off their rocky beds and loaded into nets to be hauled on board where they are washed.

The sponge that comes up from the bottom looks and smells nothing like the honey-coloured articles tourists buy in the shops. It is a brown, sometimes nearly black animal, often with bits of seaweed and other marine growth encrusted on it, and after a couple of hours in the sun it smells abominable. After the sponges have been left in the sun to dry they are squashed to break up the fibres and the marine growth on them and then washed in seawater for a day or so. The sponges don't yet look like the finished article, but they are beginning to smell better. To get them looking as we know them they are bleached to remove the pigmentation and then washed again. It seems the real thing will never be out of favour because despite the development of artificial sponges, chemistry cannot imitate nature and only the real thing has that almost creamy feel to it.

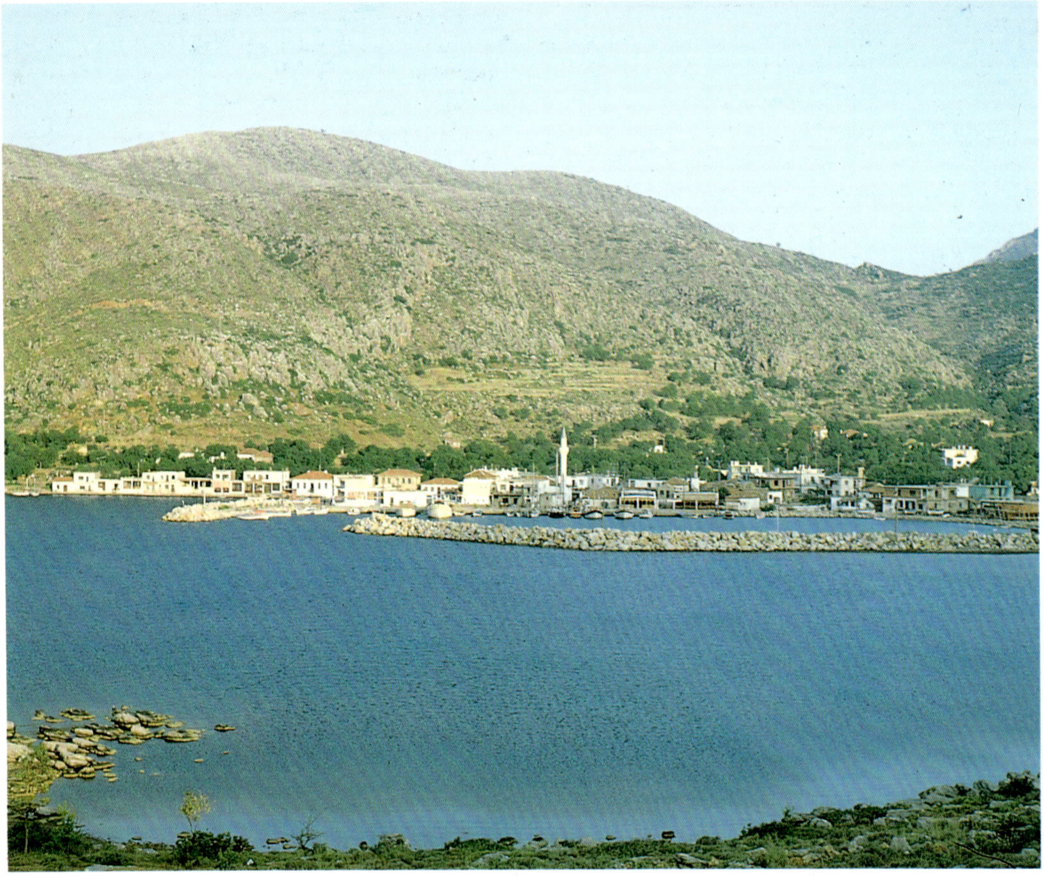

In Bozburun you are unlikely to see any of the sponge-fishing boats in the harbour during the summer, but you might see them around the coast. Bozburun has developed into a small resort in the last few years, relying on charter boats for much of the custom. The road around the peninsula is a rough and ready affair and it is still much easier to get here by boat than by land. The village council has improved the harbour and the locals have been quick to build a few restaurants around the quay to cater for water-borne visitors. After the harsh and glaring landscape encountered in the approaches to Bozburun, the cool shade of the awnings and a cold beer are a bit like paradise. On the outskirts of the village and in a bay to the east the local boat-builders have found a new trade building *gulets* for charter boats. A few years ago the boatyards were struggling to make ends meet building and repairing the sponge-fishing boats, but now the yards are populated with the half-finished hulls of *gulets* for the charter market.

AROUND BOZBURUN

KIZIL ADASI

The normal approach to Bozburun from the south between Kızıl Adası and Zeytin Adası can be short-circuited by going around the north end of Kızıl Adası, but only in calm weather and with a bit of local knowledge. In the gap between the north end of Kızıl Adası and the small island of Kibeli Adası there is an anchorage reminiscent of the Caribbean except for the Byzantine arch on Kibeli. The water is that clear blue and emerald green that a white sandy bottom gives. Shore-based visitors can hire a local boat to get them over to this idyllic spot. On the southeastern side of Kızıl Adası there is another appealing anchorage you can try if the northerly one, popular in the summer, gets over-populated.

Söğüt

On the eastern side of Sömbeki Körfezi lies Söğüt Liman. A small hamlet sits on the shore under craggy slopes. In the summer a simple restaurant opens, but there is not a lot else to the place. On a rocky headland are the remains of the acropolis to ancient Amnistus, an important deme of the Rhodian Peraea. Some of the wall and a gate are in good condition and at the waters edge there is a section of ancient quay in good condition, but unless you have the stamina of a Hercules for exploring under the hot summer sun, you are better off cooling down in the clear waters of the bay and looking for any sponges that might have been overlooked in the rocky shallows.

The Rhodian Peraea

The Dorians moved down from northern Greece into the Greek islands and Asia Minor between 1200 and 1000 BC. They brought with them the iron slashing sword and quickly overcame any resistance from tribes equipped with mere bronze weapons. In the southeast corner of the Aegean the Dorians took the island of Rhodes for their principal settlement and in 408 BC founded the city of Rhodes on the site it still occupies today. With the foundation of this new site the Dorians set about managing the cities in Asia Minor which had hitherto only been loosely under Rhodian dominion. Not surprisingly, the Loryma Peninsula, a short eight miles away, formed the power base of Rhodian territories in Asia Minor, an area known as the Rhodian Peraea.

Though the Loryma Peninsula as far as present day Hisarönü and Marmaris formed the heart of Rhodian territory, at times it included a much larger region. The area at the end of the Gulf of Gökova, including Idyma, Callipolis, and Cedreae, was part of the Peraea and control extended as far north as Stratoniceia for a while, an area near the ugly open-pit coal mine at present day Yatağan. In 190 BC Caunos was bought from the Egyptians and added to the territory. A year later the whole of Lycia was given to the Rhodians by the Romans, though this was a nominal gift only since no real Roman control was exercised over much of Lycia, and certainly the Rhodians did not control it.

The cities in the Peraea were governed by officials from Rhodes though the majority of the citizens were native Carians. It is strange to think of this now isolated and wild Loryma Peninsula as a bustling landscape with towns dotted around it. Important demes such as Physcus at Marmaris near the sea can be comprehended, but it is difficult to think of Söğüt or Syrna or Thyssanus, now isolated ruins in a rocky wilderness and little known outside of fusty academic libraries, as important and busy places at centre stage of life in this region. The Rhodian Peraea declined in the second century AD and the cities dotted around the peninsula were never revived.

Bozuk Bükü

Getting around Kızıl Burun and Karaburun to the underside of the Loryma Peninsula can be a rough and windy business when the *meltem* is blowing, and the anchorage at Bozuk Bükü, like that of Cnidos on the end of the Dorian Peninsula, has been used since antiquity by boats waiting for the wind to drop before heading north. So it is not surprising that the first thing you see on approaching the bay is a perfectly preserved fortification on the headland enclosing it. The best anchorage in the bay is a small cove just

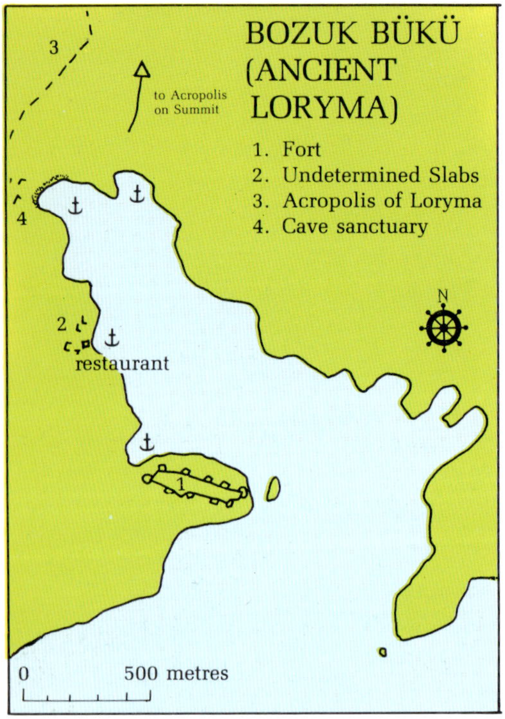

around the north side of the ancient fort where you are out of the gusts of wind which blow down at the head of it. Besides which, this is the closest anchorage for exploring the fort which apart from a few scattered stones around the bay, is the only recognisable structure remaining from ancient times.

Bozuk Bükü was formerly called Loryma and the measure of it's importance was that the peninsula was named after it. It was primarily a harbour of refuge and not a trading harbour, the acropolis for the city being situated at the head of the bay. It was used at various times to assemble naval fleets, most notably in 395 BC by Demetrius Polioketes before his attack on Rhodes. Polioketes is remembered for the gargantuan siege machine he had constructed for the assault on Rhodes, a huge catapault estimated to be nine stories high and weighing around 125 tons. The bits and pieces of this contraption would have sat in Bozuk Bükü on transports before the short voyage across to the island. The attack failed, but Polioketes,

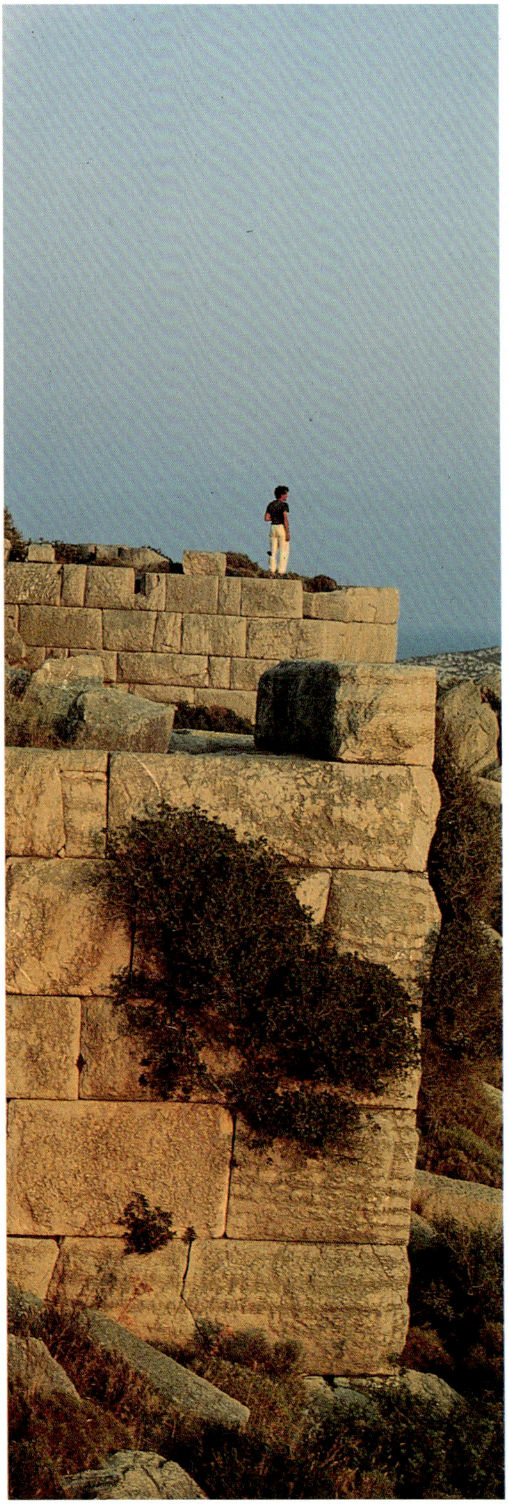

Massive stone blocks of the ancient fort at Bozuk Bükü.

ever magnanimous in defeat, sold his siege machine and donated the money to the Rhodians to build a statue to commemorate the battle. The result was the huge bronze statue of Helios, the sun god, that stood astride the harbour at Rhodes and one of the seven wonders of the ancient world. Later in Byzantine times the bay was called Aplotheka from the Greek 'hoplotheke', meaning an arsenal, from the ancient fort standing at the entrance. On British charts it is still called by this name. It is well worth the short climb up to the fort for a brief inspection; some of the stone blocks are over five metres (17 feet) long and more than a metre (3 feet) square, all of them fitting perfectly together without mortar. There is also a fine view across to Rhodes. In the west side of the bay are several restaurants, but apart from that no modern population has bothered to move in after the ancients left.

SERÇE LİMANI

Before you can see the entrance to Serçe it looks as if you are headed for sheer cliffs with no obvious gap in them. Then just when you think the chart must be wrong or the skipper has made a glaring mistake in his navigation, the entrance to Serçe opens up between the cliffs and you sail into a completely land-locked natural harbour. The narrow entrance opens up into a large bay with two arms running north and west - you may feel a bit like Alice disappearing down the rabbit hole and discovering a whole new world on entering Serçe. Most yachts anchor in the western arm where Osman, the proprietor of the small restaurant ashore, usually rows out to take a line ashore for you. By the time you have spent an evening with the roguish but thoroughly likeable Osman you may well feel a bit like Alice. In this isolated harbour where no road or village intrudes, Osman entertains with a band of musicians from his village high in the hills above and according to the latest reports even had a belly-dancer in attendance on occasions. It used to be that you only got fish or chicken here. Chicken took a little longer to come since it was 'on the hoof' and had to be caught and plucked first.

Serçe has no ancient remains and it is a puzzle to me why such a perfect natural harbour was not utilised by the ancients in what was a populated and busy region. However it was known as a port of refuge. In several of the rooms in the castle museum in Bodrum there are extensive exhibits of Islamic glass, exquisite pieces with delicate designs and hues. One

Osman. Serçe.

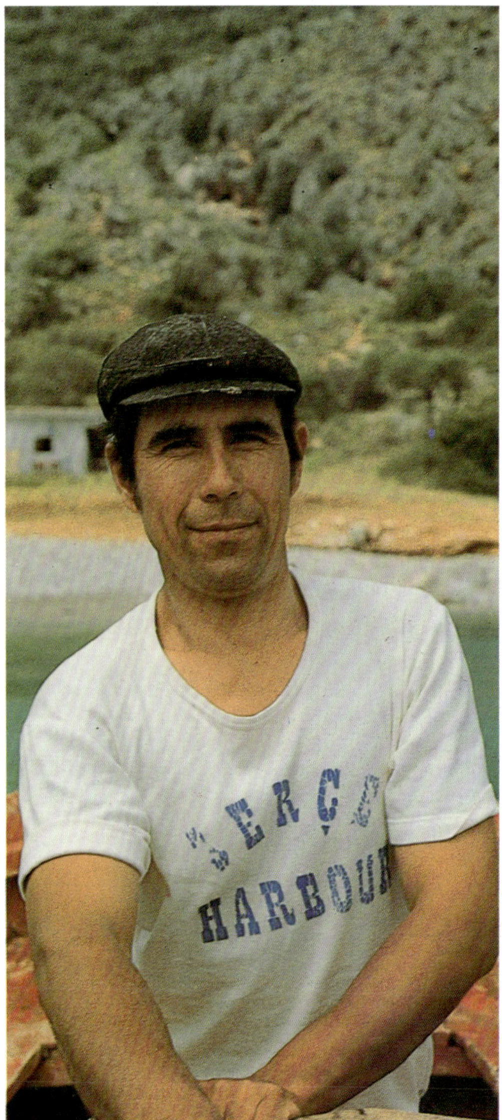

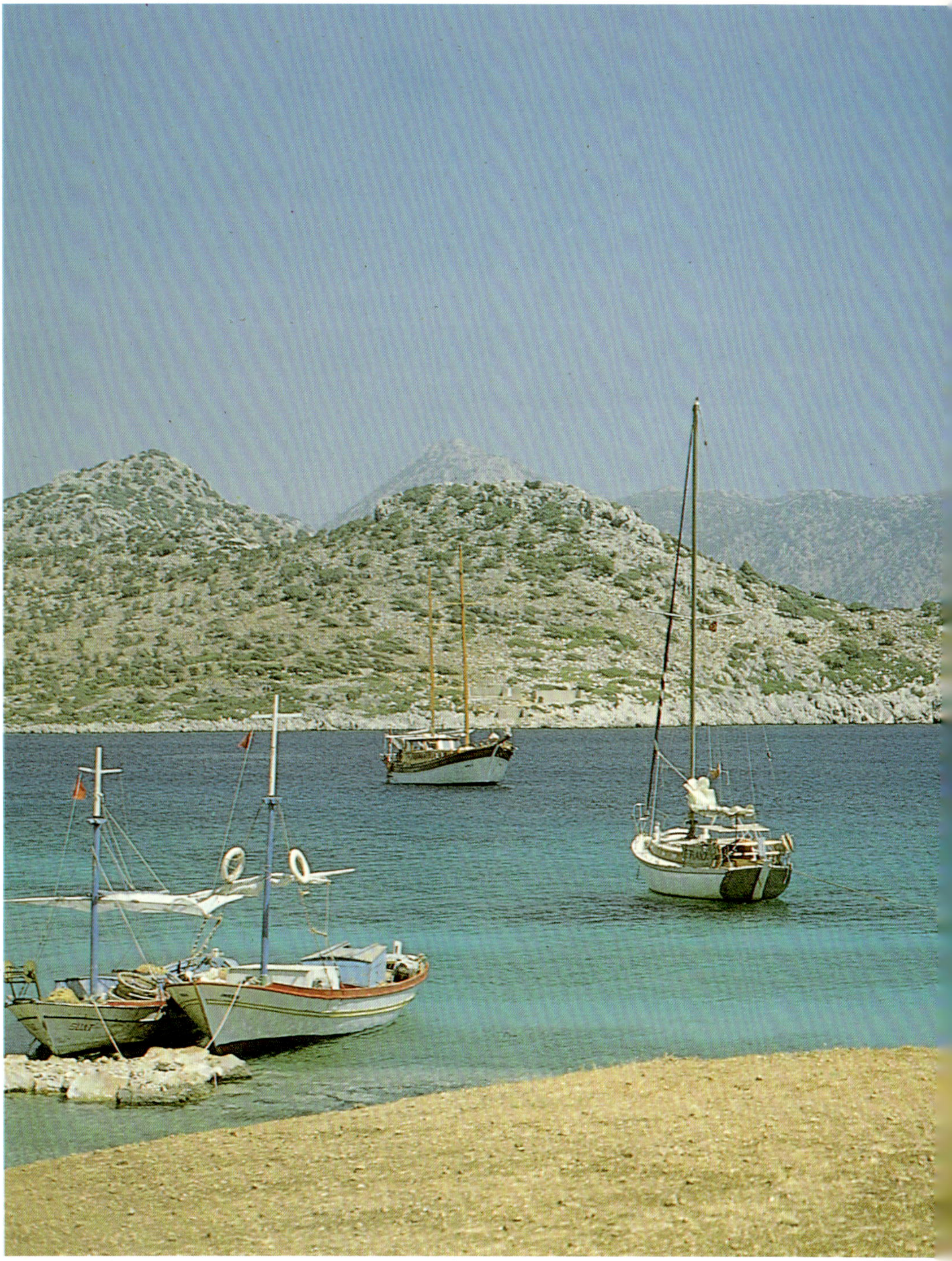

Serçe.

outstanding exhibit is a very thin glass beaker with a fine design of lions chasing each other. The glass beaker and many other artifacts were excavated from the wreck of a small eleventh century trading ship that sank in the entrance to Serçe. The wreck was excavated by Dr George Bass and his underwater archaeological team in 1977 and from the remains of the wreck and the artifacts found a reasonable picture of what happened can be built up.

It would appear that the ship, a

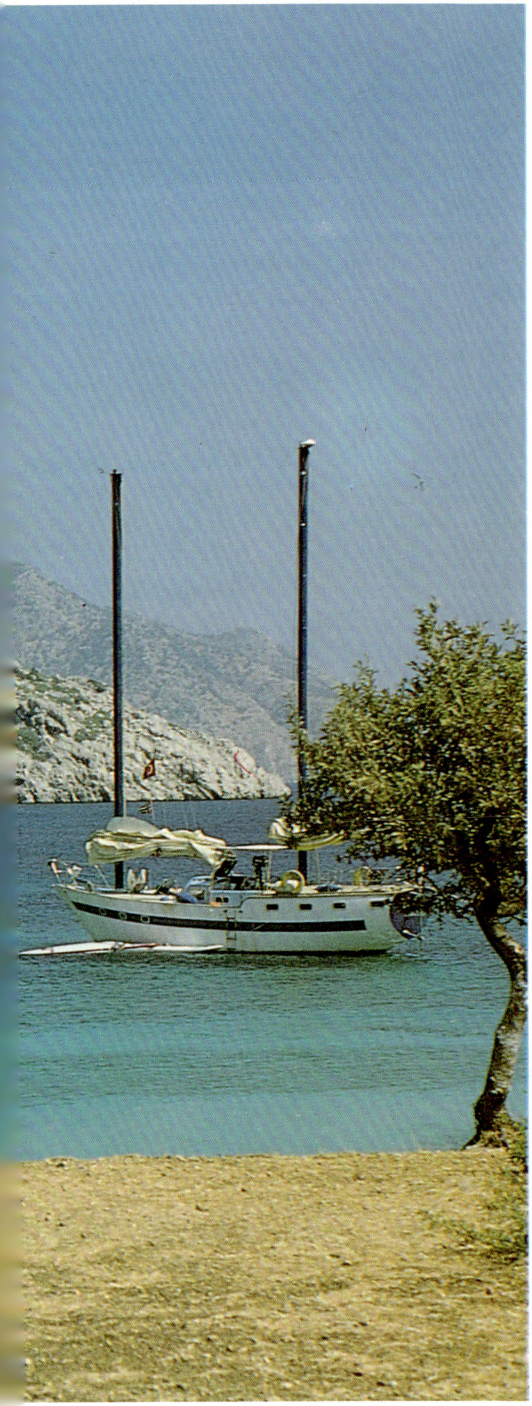

wooden trader of about 15 metres (50 feet) overall length, was voyaging along the coast from a Fatimite port somewhere in the east. Curiously enough it appears to have been a Byzantine ship carrying a cargo of Islamic glass and not an Islamic ship. Amongst the artifacts fish and pork bones were found, the remains of the crews last meal. The strict Islamic orthodoxy of the time meant no Muslim, however lax, would touch pork. In addition Byzantine coins, official seals, and lead weights were found adding to the evidence for the wreck being a Byzantine ship. Most likely the ship was heading for Loryma, but was encountering difficulties with the *meltem* which blows up this stretch of coast, and so decided to put into Serçe to wait for more favourable winds. While attempting to sail through the entrance the ship hit a rock and sank instantly in 32 metres of water near the north side of the entrance.

Fisherman. Serçe.

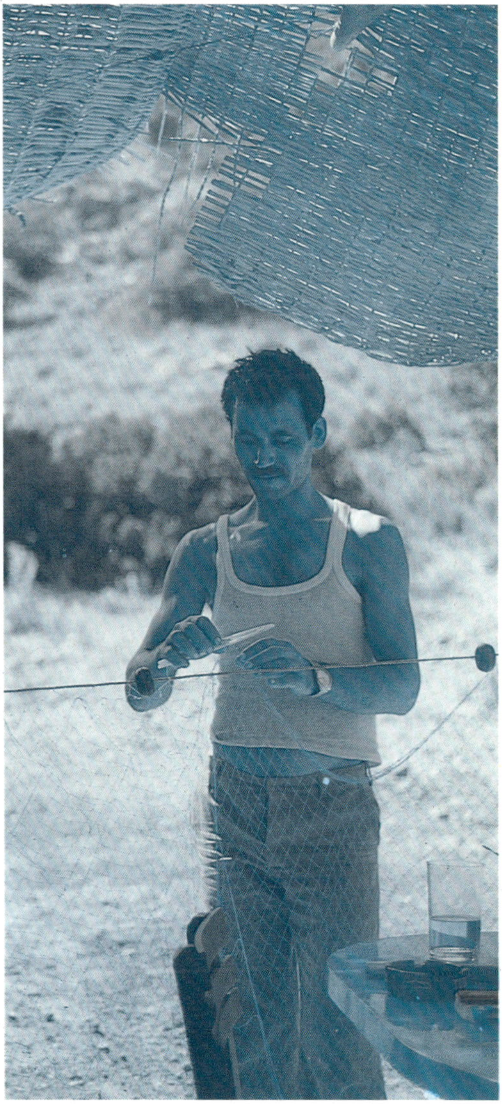

By one of those strange coincidences I discovered the difficulties the Byzantine ship would have encountered. The engine on my yacht refused to start as I approached Serçe in 1984 and so I decided to sail in. In the entrance the wind constantly changes direction so that one minute it is behind, the next in front, and for a minute or two I thought my yacht might join the Byzantine ship on the bottom. Compared to the Serçe ship, my modern yacht and rig gave me far more manoeuvrability than it had and yet I experienced some difficulty negotiating the entrance under sail. The difficulties of the Byzantine ship with it's tubby hull and clumsy rig would have been immense. Herein lies a clue as to why Serçe was not developed as a harbour by the ancients - the entrance is too narrow and the shifting wind in the entrance makes it too difficult for a sailing ship to enter or leave. Better that an ancient harbour should have a wide entrance like Bozuk Bükü with fairly constant winds blowing down on it. From the personal belongings and valuables found it appears the skipper and crew had no time to rescue their personal effects and had to immediately jump overboard and swim ashore, fortunately not far away in this instance. One interesting fact about the ship is that it is the oldest known example of a ship built in a 'modern' way. The ancient method of building a ship was to build up the planks of the hull and then fit strengthening ribs and floors inside. The 'modern' method is to build a skeleton of ribs and then plank over it. Despite it's 'modern' method of construction, externally the ship looked not unlike merchant ships of 1500 years earlier.

GEORGE BEAN

Throughout this book there are references to George Bean and his books on the Graeco-Roman sites in Turkey. At many of the sites I have come across locals who remember him with great affection and in one out of the way spot I had no choice other than to donate a copy of one of his books to a local who had known him. George Bean became something of a legend as he criss-crossed the Turkish coast looking for little known sites and identifying and translating the inscriptions he often found on ancient material transplanted from it's original site to a Turkish village. In the 1950's and 1960's when he collected most of his material, travel was not as easy as is now and most of the sites could only be reached after a long and arduous hike on foot. George Bean was a big man, he stood at least six foot six inches tall and was broad of shoulder, and as Professor Cook has related in a memoir to the man, this made for a problem or two in a country where most things were designed for smaller men:

"George put up with a good deal of hardship; in a Turkish bus the luggage rack at the back was often the only place he could he fitted into, and in hotels he never found a bed that didn't confort him. As he said, things were not made for a full-grown man."

Professor Cook goes on to tell of George Bean's method of finding out from the locals where old bits of rock might be lying around. He spoke perfect Turkish and on arriving in a village would sit down over coffee and talk to the locals about the crops, the weather, events in the outside world, eventually getting around to the matter of ancient sites in the area. Professor Cook, who accompanied him on some of his travels, admits that he used to get annoyed with this apparent time-wasting until he realised that unless the villagers accepted them, they were not going to get anywhere. While other archaeologists whizzing around in jeeps found little that was new, George Bean confirmed and named many sites and discovered a number of new ones.

George Bean spent over twenty five years travelling the coast of Asia Minor from the Sea of Marmara in the north to Mersin and İskenderun near Turkey's border with Syria. He published numerous scholarly papers and in 1964 started on the series of archaeological guides to the Graeco-Roman sites that he is most well known for: ***Aegean Turkey; Turkey Beyond the Maeander; Lycian Turkey;*** *and* ***Turkey's Southern Shore****. These are the best of any guides to the sites and as a bonus you get Bean's pithy asides and witty comments on all sorts of aspects of life in ancient times. He is still known in some of the villages as Bin Bey - a larger-than-life character in the mould of those 19th century adventurers like Spratt and Newton.*

GERBEKSE

Tucked into the north side of Gerbekse Burun is a small cove with room for a few boats to get into it. The cove is often called Byzantine Creek after the ruins of a Byzantine trading station ashore. Around the shore and overgrown by bushes and trees are the ruins of several Byzantine churches and other buildings belonging to what was a sizeable settlement. Quite possibly the 'glass-ship' that foundered at Serçe had visited here before it's disastrous voyage south.

ÇİFTLİK

Behind Çiftlik Adası there is an anchorage out of the prevailing winds. On the island there is a military observation post and on the shore a small holiday village and several restaurants. The barren terrain at the bottom of the Loryma Peninsula here gives way to pine and macquis making this a greener place, softer on the eyes, and yet lacking the wild beauty of the anchorages further down the coast.

Cove. Loryma Peninsula.

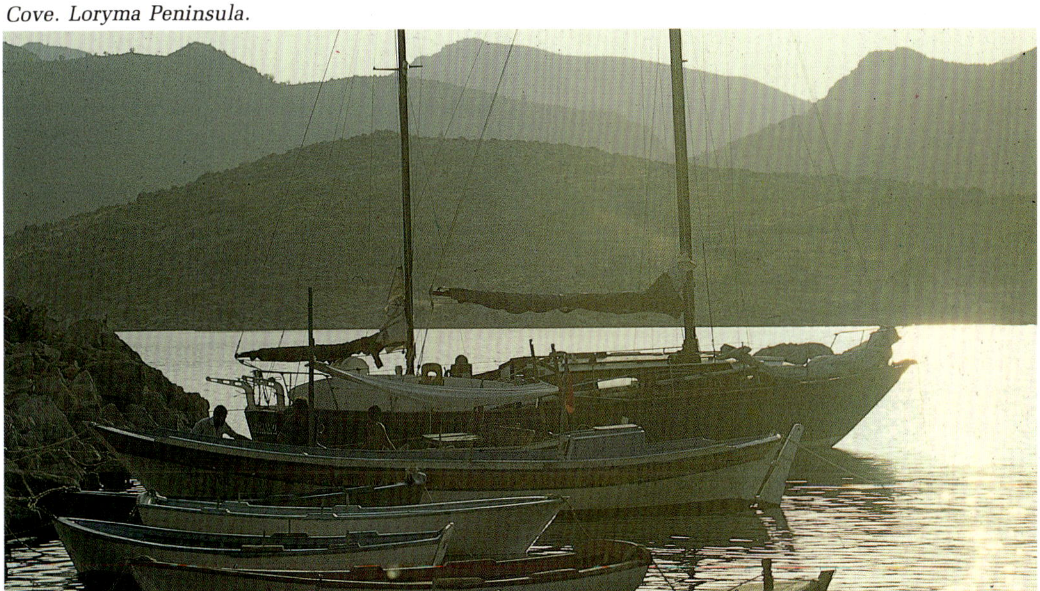

KADIRGA

On the north side of Kadırga Burun there is a large bay surrounded by low cliffs and this is sometimes used by charter *gulets* as a lunch stop.

KUMLU BÜKÜ

A mile above Kadırga lies the bay of Kumlu Bükü. The development spreading around the coast from Marmaris has touched here and there are a number of new villas and small hotels built or being built. In the southwest corner there is the 'Yacht Club', a restaurant with laid moorings off it and most yachts and *gulets* stop here.

On the north side of the bay, atop the headland, are the ruins of ancient Amos, a member of Rhodian Peraea. Parts of the acropolis walls and towers and a gate remain as well as the platform of a small temple and a small theatre. The site has either subsided or, as the locals alledge, it was damaged by an earthquake, though whether this was long ago or moie recently is difficult to know. Eliciting information on ancient ruins from the locals can sometimes be an amusing experience. After struggling in my bad Turkish to get some information on Amos from a local, he was eventually able to assure me that the ruins were very old, they had been there at least since his grandfather's time. Amos yielded some interesting information when George Bean visited it in 1948. He discovered a number of tablets inscribed with the terms of land-leases from around 200 BC, and it is surprising just how explicit and detailed these leases were: "(The leases had) ...precise instructions for the payment of rent, provision of guarantors, and development of the property; the tenant must build a minimum number of sheds, plant a minimum number of vines and figs, with a minimum space for corn between, and dig a drainage trench. Penalties are fixed

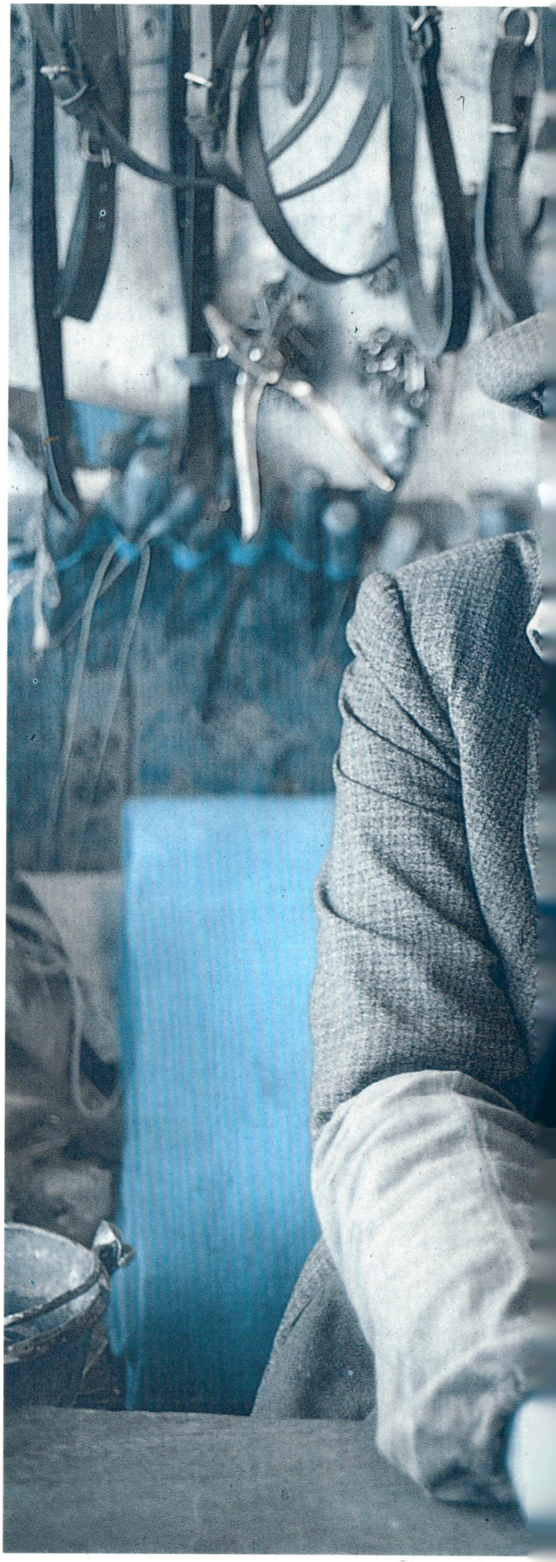

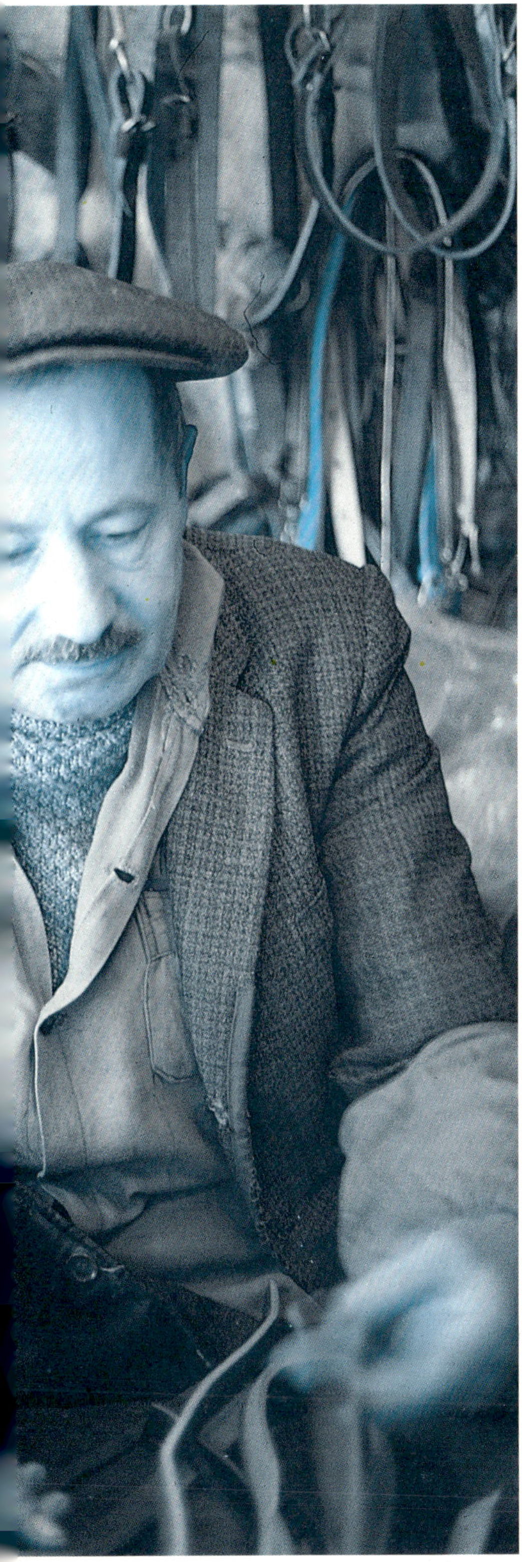

for failure to observe these conditions, and also for cutting wood on the property, burying a corpse in it, or encroaching on the public roads.''

George Bean/*Turkey Beyond the Maeander*. 1980

TURUNÇ BÜKÜ

A small bay just before the island passage into the huge Bay of Marmaris. Villas and hotels line the shore, a visual reminder that you are close to the tourist hub of this section of the coast.

FACILITIES

Datça: Restaurants, hotels & pensions, telephone, P.O., Banks, Doctor, toilets, fuel, water, ice, gas, provisions, engineer. Officials: Immigration, Customs, Harbourmaster, Police, Tourist Information.
Değirmen: Restaurant.
Kuruca: Restaurant, hotel, water, provisions.
Bençik: Water.
Keçi Bükü: Restaurants, pension, water, provisions.
Selimiye: Restaurant.
Bozburun: Restaurants, hotel & pensions, telephone, P.O., Bank, toilets, fuel, water, ice, provisions. Officials: Police, Gendarmarie.
Söğüt: Restaurant.
Bozuk Bükü: Restaurant.
Serçe: Restaurant.
Çiftlik: Restaurants, hotel, gendarmarie.
Kumlu Bükü: Restaurants, pension, showers, toilet.
Turunç Bükü: Restaurants, hotels & pensions.

Saddles, bits, girth straps, and reins.

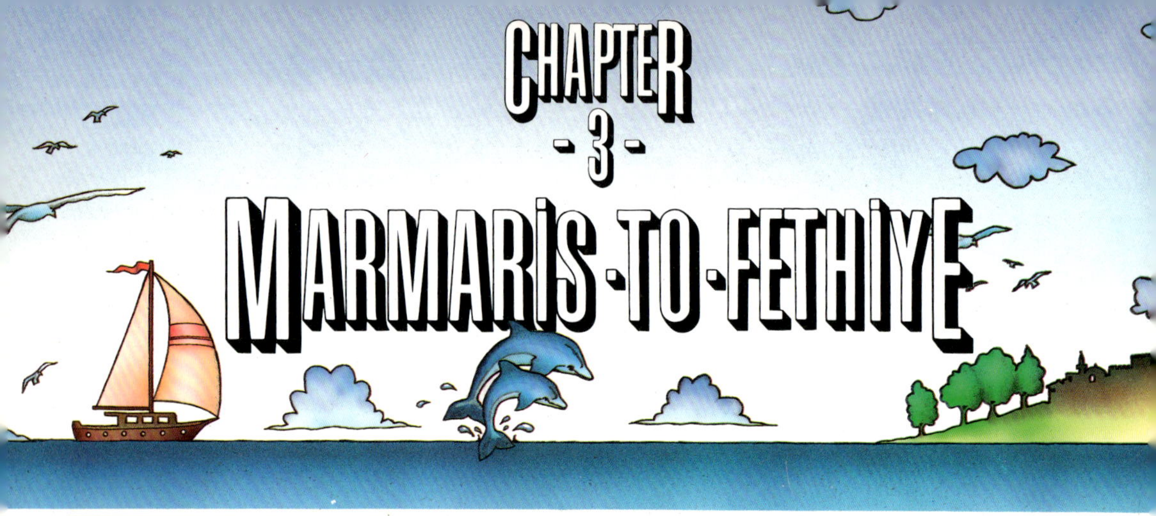

CHAPTER - 3 - MARMARIS-TO-FETHIYE

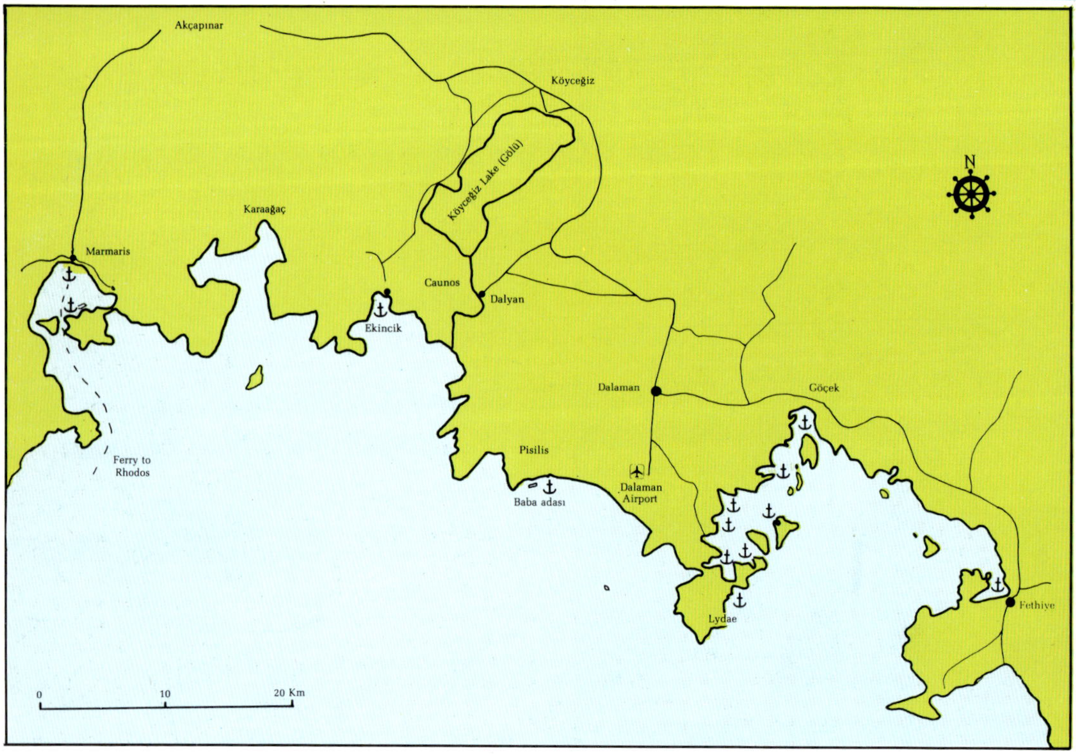

From Marmaris the coast turns south towards the huge rocky hump sticking out of Anatolia into the sea, a region known in ancient times as Lycia and a region as inhospitable as any in Asia Minor. Close to Marmaris is ancient Caunos, sited on the delta of the Dalyan River, a sort of halfway house between ancient Caria and ancient Lycia. In common with the coast described in the previous chapter, much of it is inaccessible by road and though you can touch at points along the coast with diversions off the main road, for the most part the places described here can only be reached from the sea. *Gulets* can be chartered from Marmaris to make the trip down to Fethiye, it can take three days or ten depending on your inclination, and then the return trip made by road if it is necessary to return. From Fethiye excursion boats make daily trips into the Gulf of Fethiye, though necessarily only to a few chosen places. To dally longer in the gulf you will have to charter a yacht or a *gulet*.

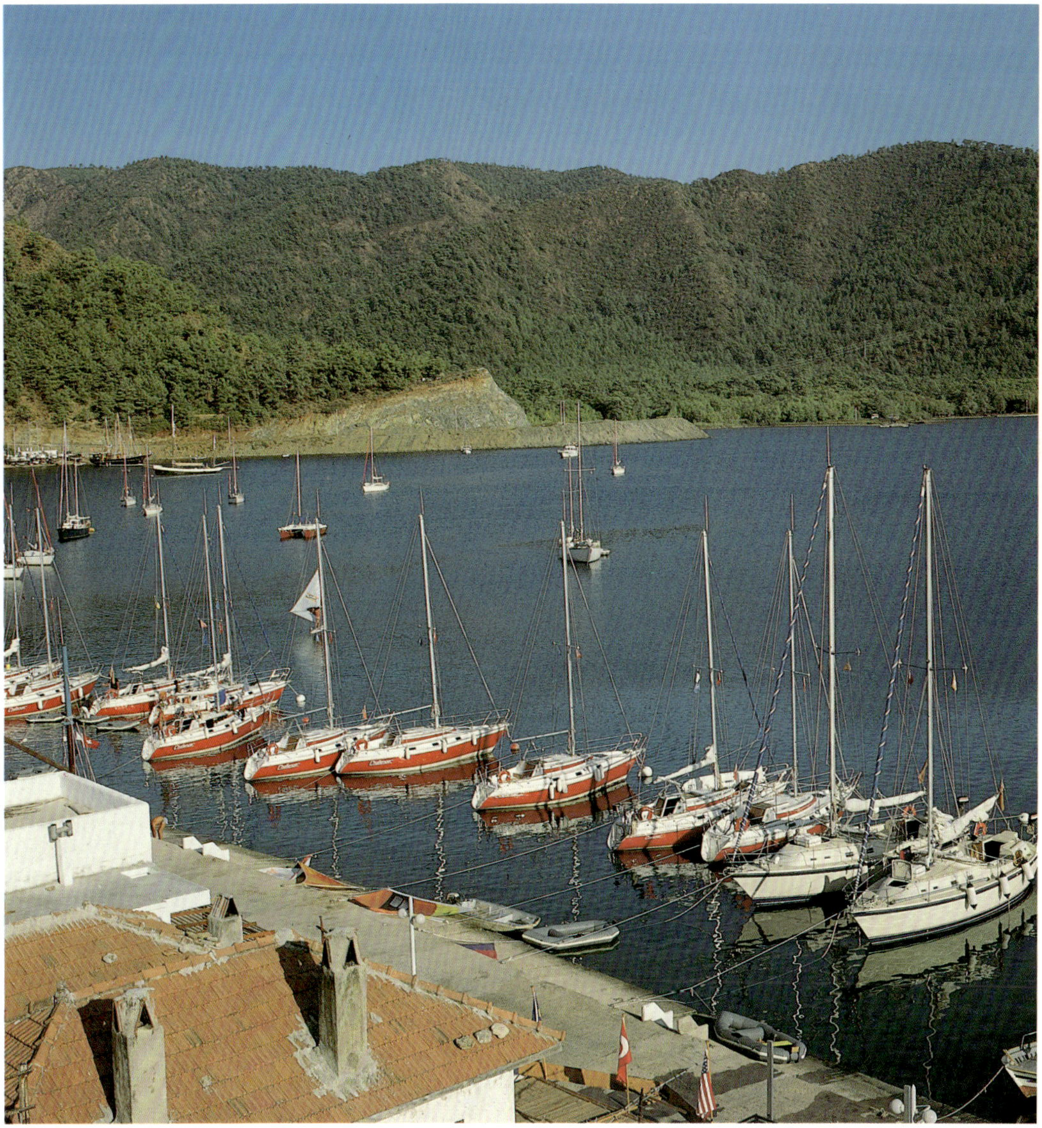

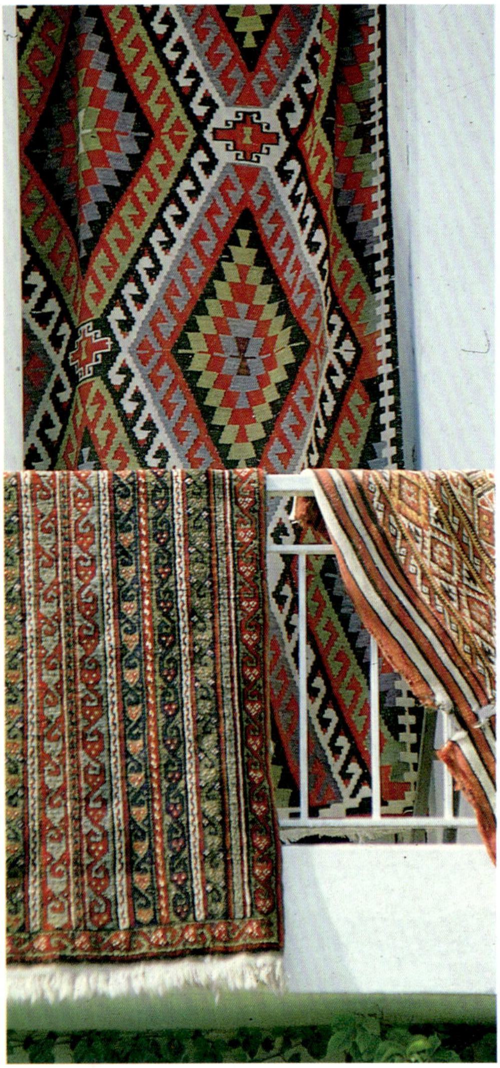

Airing carpets. Marmaris.

MARMARİS

When Nelson was pursuing Napoleon and the French Fleet around the Mediterranean in 1798, he put in at Marmaris to make some repairs and give his long-suffering sailors a short respite from the hectic business of keeping up with Napoleon. Nelson thought Marmaris the best fleet anchorage in the eastern Mediterranean and thereafter the Admiralty recommended it as "...suited to the various purposes of airing stores, stretching rigging, repairing boats, erecting tents for carpenters, armourers and coopers, and for unloading and carrying transports and prizes." The Admiralty's prose never did stretch to much more than the utilitarian. It is not difficult to see why Nelson and the Admiralty thought Marmaris an excellent fleet anchorage. From seaward you pass through a narrow passage between two islands and enter a huge land-locked bay. Pine forest (useful to the carpenters and coopers) carpets the slopes of the hills and islands enclosing the bay. In the northeast corner the white houses and red rooves of Marmaris town can be seen. Today it is not the lofty masts of ships-of-the-line that will be seen, but a thicket of yacht masts advertising that Marmaris is the hub of yacht charter along this section of the coast.

What was the small village of Marmaris sits in one corner of the bay. Around it large hotels line the foreshore reflecting the new found prosperity of the place. Marmaris village was largely destroyed by an earthquake in 1958 and though much of the re-building does not have the rustic charm of the older buildings, it all works as a friendly and thoroughly Turkish place.

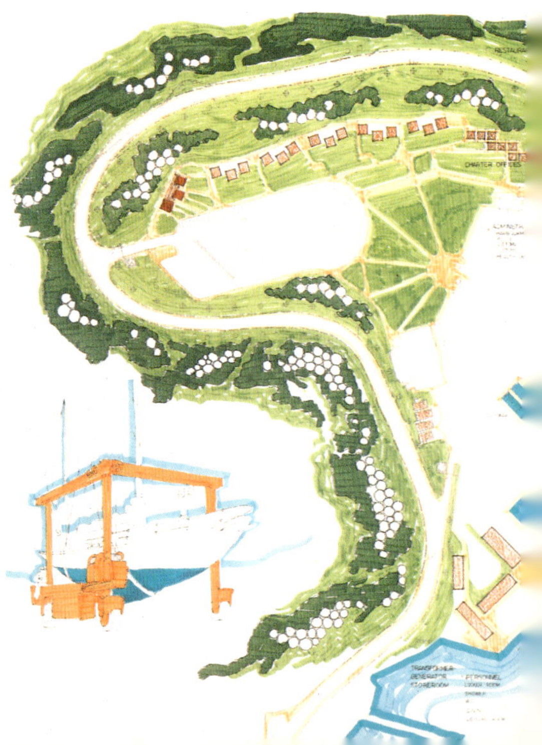

On a low rocky spur by the shore a partially ruined castle will be seen with some of the older houses built into and against the walls. The castle was built by Süleyman the Magnificient in 1522 as a base for his assault on Rhodes against the Knights of St John.

The quay and esplanade is the centre of life in Marmaris and whether you are dining out, having a quiet drink, or just strolling around the waterfront, this is the place to be. Here there are all the restaurants and bars you could desire. The attraction is the boats berthed stern-to the quay and there seems to be an eternal fascination with watching people messing about in boats. The boats themselves vary from battered but loved cruising boats to the giant gin-palaces of millionairres. And of course there are rows of the traditional wooden *gulets* waiting to whisk charterers off around the coast. Those that have not managed to get a place on the quay are anchored off in the bay. Immediately east of the town centre a large marina is nearly

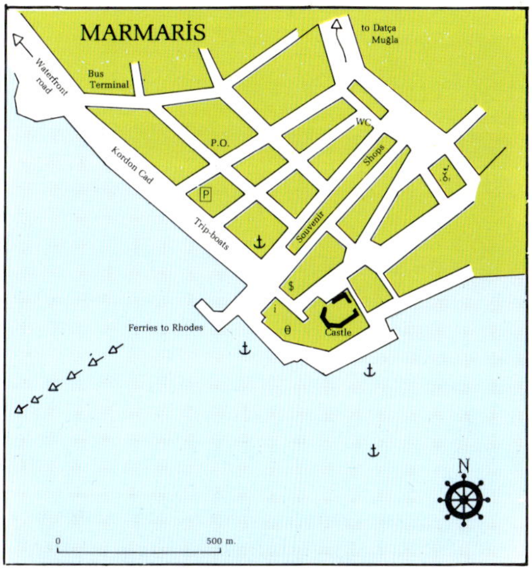

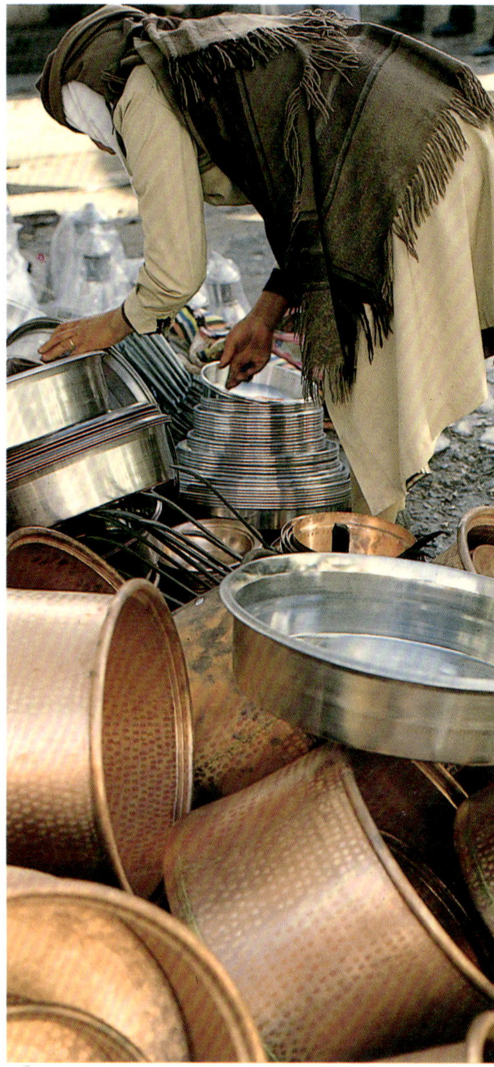

Copper wares. Marmaris.

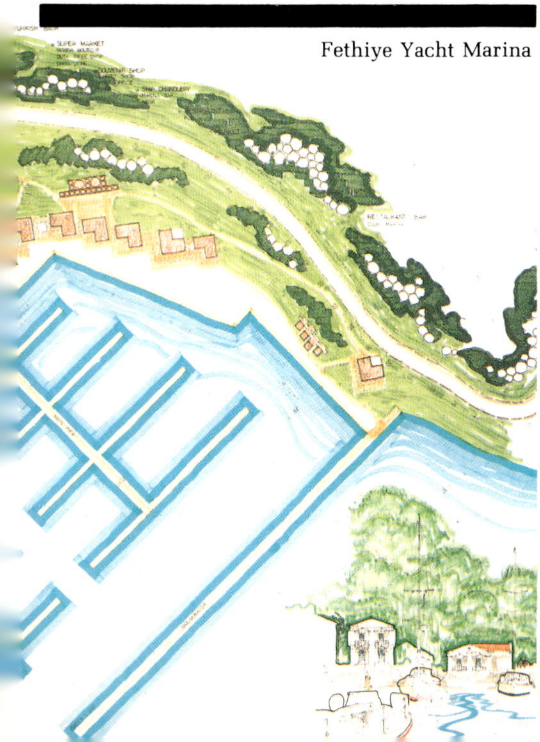

Fethiye Yacht Marina

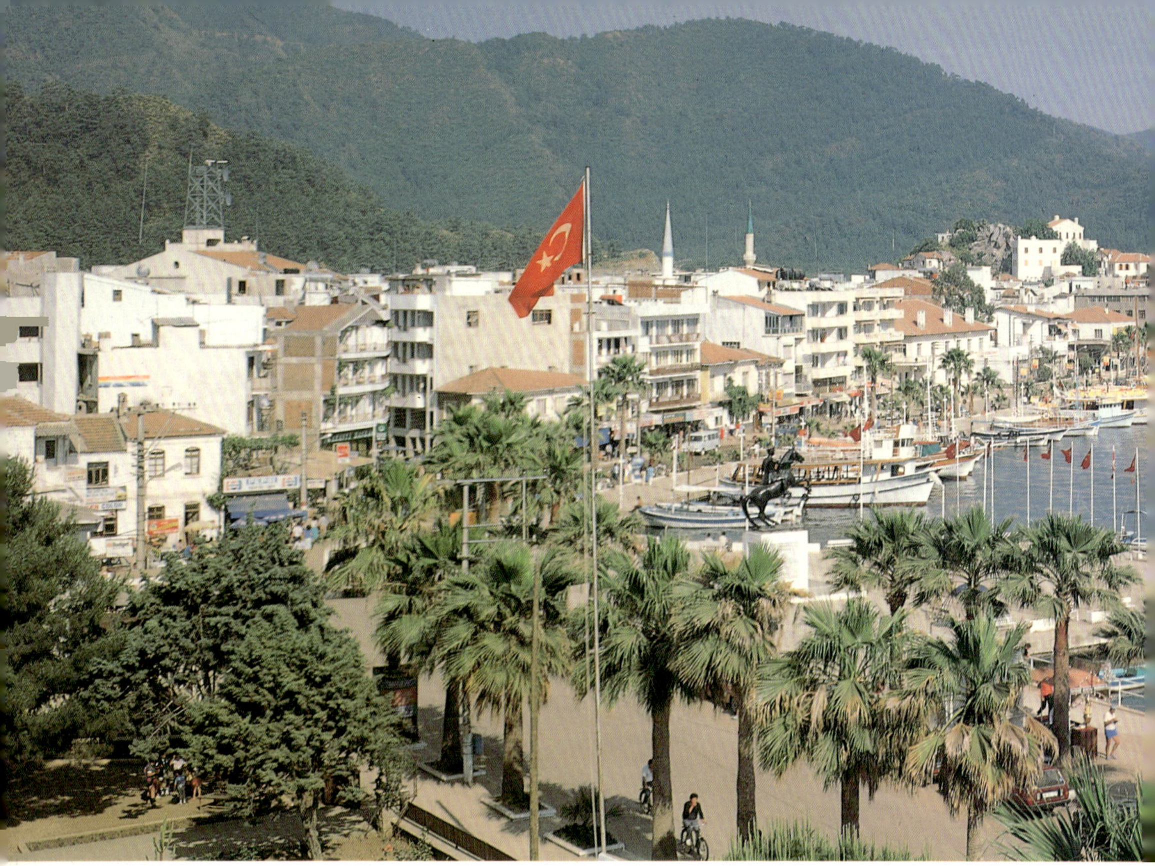

complete and when it is finished the numbers of yachts in Marmaris is expected to increase dramatically. Nelson would have gazed enviously at such luxury.

Behind the quay lies the old quarter of the town with shops selling everything and anything that visitors to Marmaris might want: fashionable leather goods, carpets, *kilims*, brass and copperware, beach-wear, lace, ceramics, not to mention more mundane things like film for your camera and freshly-made fruit juice to quench your thirst. Recently the local town council banned vehicles from many of the narrow streets and from the road around the quay, which makes walking around much more pleasant than it used to be when one had to dodge cars and motorbikes trying to force a way through hordes of pedestrians.

Marmaris is the site of ancient Physicus, a deme of the Rhodian Peraea, but virtually nothing remains of this ancient city. The acropolis was sited on a hill to the north of the present town, but there is little to see and an excursion is not worthwhile for the ruins. It is worthwhile for the delightful walk up a rocky gorge hemmed in by pine and kept cool by a stream. It is strange that so little should remain of ancient Physicus when it was

ANCIENT CARIA AND THE RHC

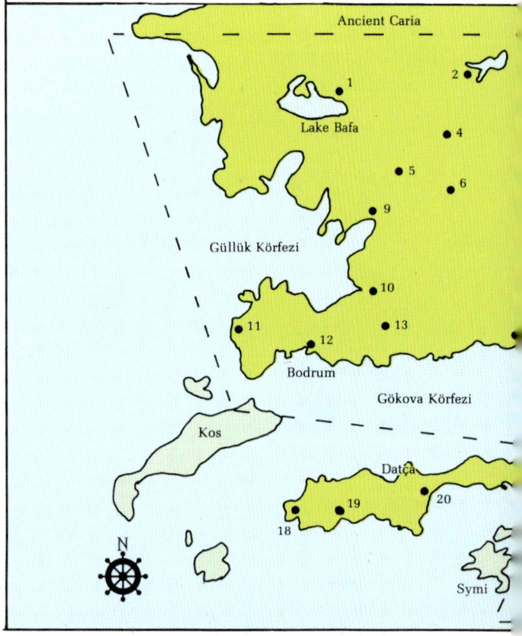

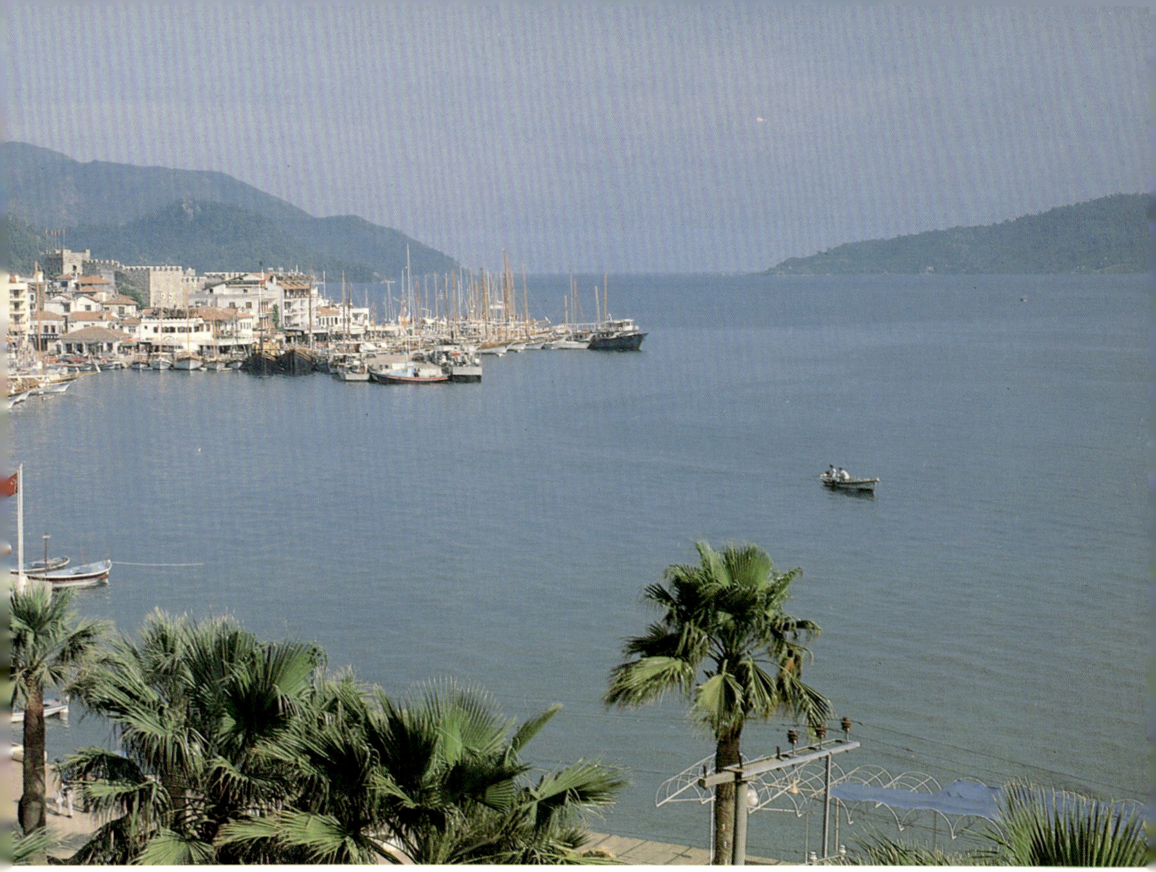

considered to be the most important of all the cities in the Peraea, the only one to be named separately according to George Bean, and a city that enjoyed a special relationship, presumably commercial, with Lindos on Rhodes. In all likelihood the city was carried away piece-meal by ships for building projects elsewhere, or perhaps just as ballast; the accessibility of the site and the safe anchorage denying it the longevity of the other less accessible sites on the Loryma Peninsula.

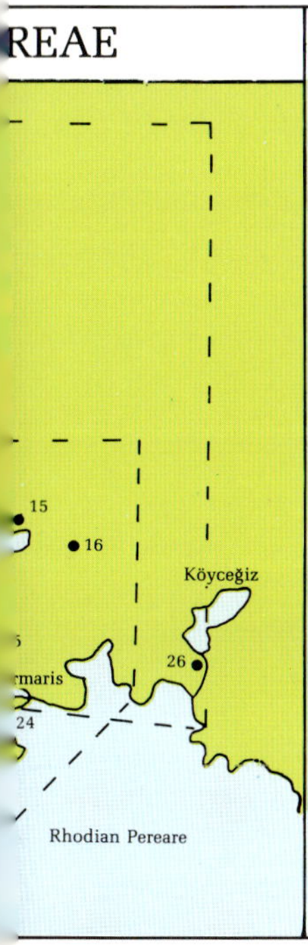

1. Heracleia
2. Alinda
3. Alabanda
4. Labraynda
5. Euromos
6. Mylasa
7. Stratoniceia
8. Lagina
9. Iassus
10. Bargylia
11. Myndus
12. Halicarnassus
13. Theangela
14. Keramos
15. Folyma
16. Callipolis
17. Cedreae
18. Cnidos
19. Triopium
20. Old Cnidos
21. Bybassus
22. Thyssanus
23. Loryma
24. Amos
25. Physcus
26. Caunos

Around Marmaris

Most excursions from Marmaris are by trip-boat to the bays and coves around the coast as far as Kumlu Bükü, or across to Nimara Island, the large island blocking off the south side of the bay. Nimara Island along with the small island of Bedir Adası lying close off it is a popular destination with a number of attractive wooded coves around it's northern side. A couple of restaurants open in the summer on the island. On the south side of the island the locals tell of a phospherescent cave.

In the pine forests behind Marmaris it is common to see rows and rows of beehives. It puzzles me what the bees feed on in the hot summer, but somehow excellent honey is produced in this area, and indeed throughout the area covered by this book, local varieties of which are on sale in the town. It is excellent stuff and excellent value, with different varieties available for the conoisseurs of nature's amber nectar. Royal jelly can also be found for those who suscribe to it's apparently miraculous qualities.

Land-based visitors to Marmaris who want to visit those places on the Loryma Peninsula accessible by road can either hire a car or go by *dolmuş. Dolmuş'* run infrequently through the summer to Orhaniye and Bozburun and points in between. From Marmaris several ferries, capable of taking cars, run daily to Rhodes and you can make a day-trip of it or stay over and return the next day.

Camel Wrestling

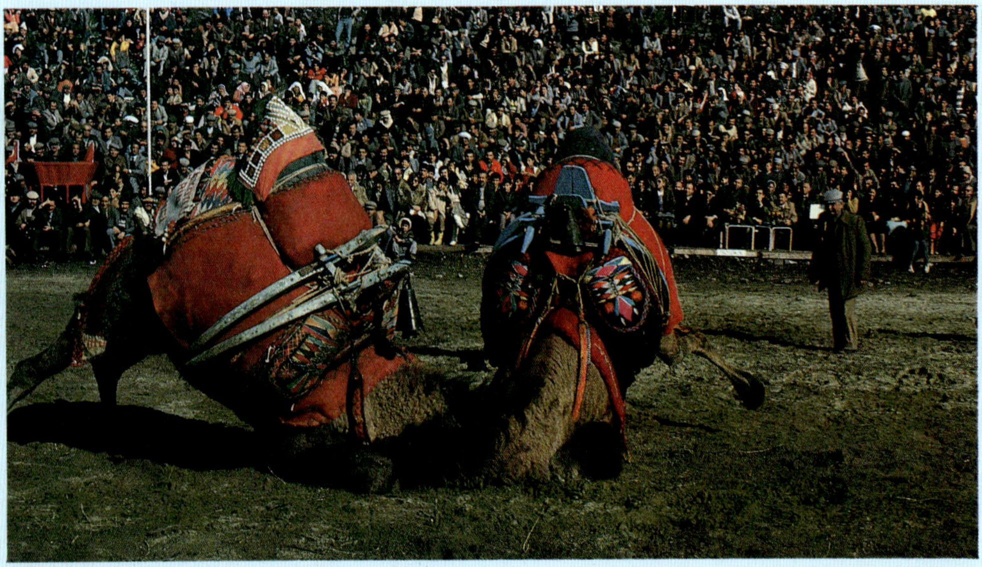

While the Spanish have bullfights, and the Italians cockfights, and the English go hunting with hounds— the Turks have camel wrestling. Camel wrestling is now mostly restricted to the Muğla region though it was once more widespread. In the winter you will see elaborately saddled camels being paraded through the villages with the owner extolling just how his camel is going to make mince-meat of anyone rash enough to challenge his beast. The camels are all fully grown bulls specially fed to increase their bulk further, and the sight of them wrestling one another would seem to promise some spectacular action.

In reality it doesn't happen and camel wrestling is more akin to comedy than to blood-sport. Bull camels normally wrestle and butt one another in a knock-out contest for precedence in a herd, and more importantly, precedence in mating. In the arena two bulls are led out and then a young cow is paraded around to get them excited. It's very easy to know when a bull is excited as streams of viscous milky saliva issue from his mouth and nostrils. Mostly the two bulls will half-heartedly butt each other and lean on the other until one of them gives in and runs away. This is the really exciting bit as the bull will often charge off towards the crowd, with the conquering bull in pursuit, and the spectators must scramble hurriedly out of the way. The antics of spectators trying to avoid a thousand kilograms (nearly a ton) of camel running towards them can lead to pure comedy and is the best part of camel wrestling. Miraculously there are few accidents. Occasionally two bulls will get down to it and actually try to wrestle one another, feinting in here and there, eventually locking a fore-leg inside the leg of the opposition and leaning on him to topple him over in a dromedary's version of a wrestling fall and pin.

The sport is a declining one as the cost of keeping, feeding, and training a camel solely for competition doesn't come cheaply, and only a rich man can afford to do it. Large bets are wagered by owners and spectators alike, though how you tell just which camel won can be difficult to determine. What happens when they both run away? — it happens. It's worth going once just to see and it's quite nice to know that there isn't a lot of blood and gore involved in the sport — it's really quite gentle.

KARAAĞAÇ

A large bay to the east of Marmaris, but unfortunately a naval area to which access is prohibited.

EKİNCİK

A well-protected bay tucked into the northeast corner of the coast before it curves south. Ekincik is a popular first night stop-over for boats heading out of Marmaris and consequently it is crowded in the summer. It's also the place where water-borne visitors can hire a local boat to go up the Dalyan River to the ruins of ancient Caunos and this further adds to the congestion in Ekincik. Crowded though it may be, it is well worth the visit both for the magnificient surroundings and the visit to Caunos.

The bay is hemmed in by pine-clad slopes with a spectacular flat-topped red rock outcrop on the eastern side. At the head of the bay there is a pebbly beach and a short walk away the small village of Ekincik. There are several restaurants, the one on the eastern side of the bay being justifiably popular for the view over the anchorage and it's good food. A flotilla of small boats is permanently stationed in the bay for excursions up the Dalyan River to ancient Caunos - hire rates are more or less standardised for the trip.

İZTUZU AND THE TURTLES

Though the title may sound like something out of a Japanese morality tale, İztuzu is a beach and the turtles in question are the beleagured loggerhead turtles who lay their eggs on that beach. To the east of Delikada Islet and the mouth of the Dalyan River, a long fine sandy beach known as İztuzu runs around the shore, the sort of place that photographers for travel brochures drool over. Apart from a few shacks and the locals, little else intrudes on the peace and quiet of this beach, certainly not sun-starved northerners frying their bodies in the heat of summer. There is, however, another visitor to the beach and that is the

Loggerhead Turtle, Caretta caretta, which comes ashore to lay it's eggs here. There are few places left in the Mediterranean where the right conditions, a south-facing beach, fine uncompacted sand, and the abscence of noise and bright artificial lights, remain for the loggerhead to breed. One of these is İztuzu.

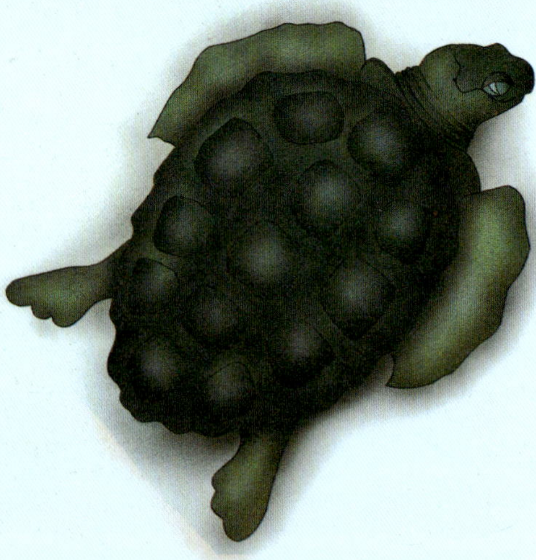

Now it appears that İztuzu may be threatened by tourism. It is planned to build accomodation providing 3000 beds on the beach, a hotel and holiday village complex. Foundations have been laid for a 600 bed hotel. Tourists en masse will compact the sand making it difficult for the female to excavate a pit in which to lay her eggs. Noise will drive her away from the beach. And if, somehow, baby turtles are born, the bright lights of the hotel will dis-orientate them and cause them to head inland instead of towards the sea and relative safety. If a newly born turtle doesn't make it to the sea in time, and is not picked off by predators, it fries in the sun - an irony that may have escaped the hotel developers.

In the eastern Mediterranean there are known to be two principal breeding spots for the loggerhead: in Zante in the Ionian Sea, and at İztuzu. Hotel development has already occurred along Laguna Beach in Zante and has significantly affected the breeding population of loggerheads using the beach. Now, on hindsight, the Greeks have restricted further development and the beach is patrolled during the breeding season to minimise disruption to the turtles. At İztuzu the development of a hotel and holiday village complex would seriously disrupt the numbers of turtles using the beach during the breeding season and it is only to be hoped that sense prevails and precautions are taken to minimise disruption. A solution to one of the problems would be to use 'black-out' screens to hide the lights of the hotels during the period when the baby turtles emerge and make their way to the sea. These are used in Australia on beaches where turtles breed and would offer a partial solution. In addition the beach could be made off-limits during the breeding season, but that would probably be an almost impossible position for a hotel advertising sun, sea, and sand, to take. And in a country that as yet has no Ministry of the Environment, it seems an unlikely possibility.

CAUNOS

Caunos is usually remembered as much for the experience of getting to it as for the site itself. The boat-trip from Ekinçik takes you along a rocky coast with small inlets and craggy headlands covered in pine to the mouth of the Dalyan River. The small islet of Delikada protects the mouth of the river and a sand-bar across the mouth prevents all but shallow-draught boats from proceeding up it. Once into the river tall reeds shut out the scenery and divide it up into countless different channels. You could be on the Norfolk

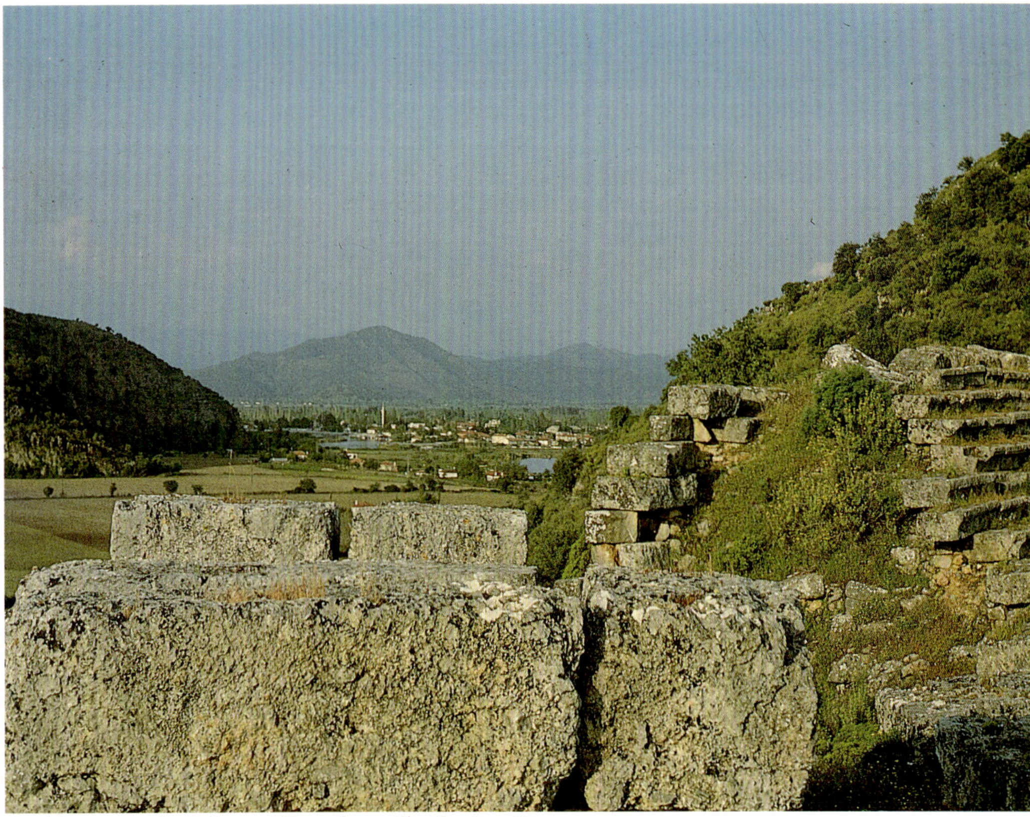

Looking towards Dalyan village from the theatre, Caunos.

Broads or some other northern European river delta until you turn a corner and see several imposing rock-tombs carved out of the cliff-face. If you have come by road to Dalyan village you take a boat from there to the site and the approach from up-river is much the same sort of riverscape as from down-river. After chugging through the reedy channels you come to a landing stage on the western side of the river and the track that leads to the site of ancient Caunos. Improbably a small kiosk sits in this reedy waterland, selling cold drinks to thirsty tourists on their way to and from the ruins.

The track winds through low land with a steep rocky hill prominent from afar. This is the acropolis hill, about 150 metres (500 feet) high, but appearing to be more when looking up at the sheer cliffs from below. At the base of the acropolis hill are a theatre in good condition, a large Roman bath-house with the heating cavities intact, and a smaller building thought to be a library. A Byzantine church also stands nearby. Down towards the ancient harbour a temple and agora have been uncovered in the excavations. Close to the harbour a quite fascinating structure has been excavated and restored, fascinating because it's precise function is still somewhat mysterious and the likely function makes it unique. Two concentric pools are ringed by low walls and columns with a circular platform in the middle pool. Notches in the columns were probably there for an attached screen around the pool. Leading away from the pools is an enclosed garden that was also partly screened off from full public view. The pools may have been purely ornamental with a fountain in the middle, but then why are there steps down into the pool and why was it all screened off. The Turkish excavators have suggested that it was used as a shallow swimming pool and the flat platform in the middle was purely for sitting on. The existence of an outdoor bathing pool as luxuriantly appointed as this, an enclosed arbour leading off it, and a prominent site close to the harbour and the centre of the city, leads to pleasant sybaritic musings on the life-style enjoyed by the inhabitants of Caunos. The idea of young Caunian maidens in diaphonous silk cavorting in the shallow pool by the harbour brings to mind those wonderfully naive drawings in children's books of everyday life in ancient Greece and Rome, where nothing as nasty as disease or ugliness touched the inhabitants of the drawings.

Disease is something we know the Caunians suffered dreadfully from - the Greek and Roman writers and commentators tell us so. Stratonicus (4th century BC), renowned for his scathing tongue, visited Caunos and commented on the greenish complexion of the inhabitants by saying he now knew what Homer had meant when he said: "As are the generations of leaves, so are the generations of men". The Caunians thought it unkind of him to call their city unhealthy to which Stratonicus replied he had meant no such thing, after all "how could I dare to call a city unhealthy where even dead men walk the streets". Strabo (63 BC - AD 21) remarked that although the city and it's territory were rich, the city was notoriously unhealthy because of the heat and the abundance of fruit. Over-indulgence of fruit was generally supposed to cause disease, a theory still prevalent throughout Europe until the 17th century. Dio Chrysostom (AD 40 - 115), the wandering philosopher, was especially caustic about the Caunians: "Their misfortunes are due to their extreme folly and rascality, and if they were all but wiped out by fever, it is no more than they deserve". From Stratonicus and his reference to the green complexion of the Caunians to Dio Chrysostom's desire that they all sucuumb to fever, it is not too difficult after looking at the marshy hinterland around Caunos to conclude that malaria was the scourge of the city. The

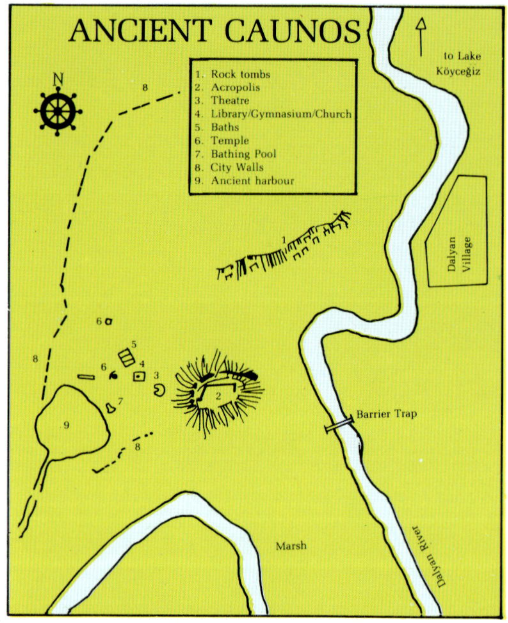

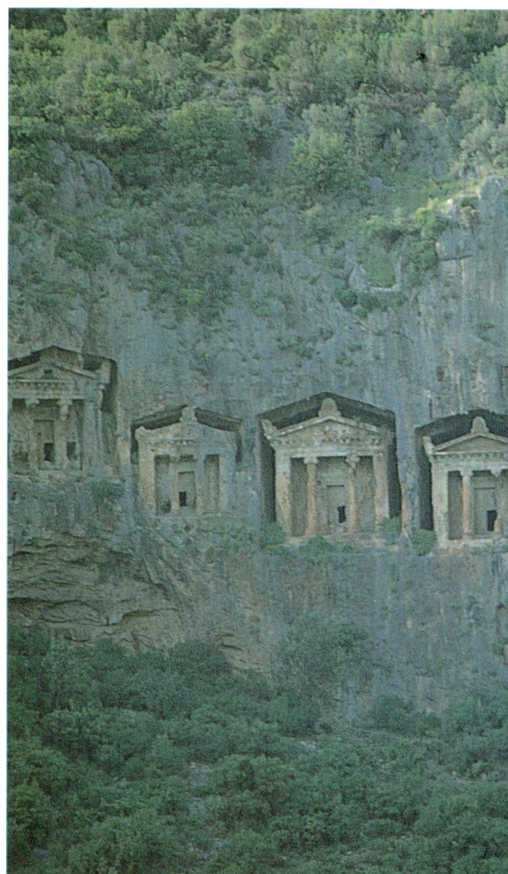

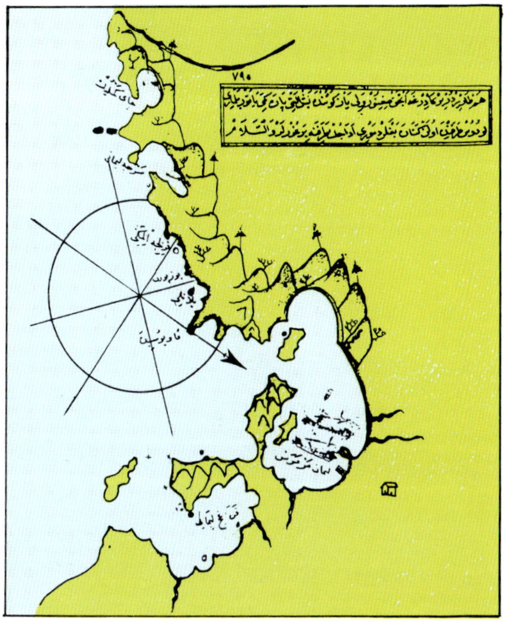

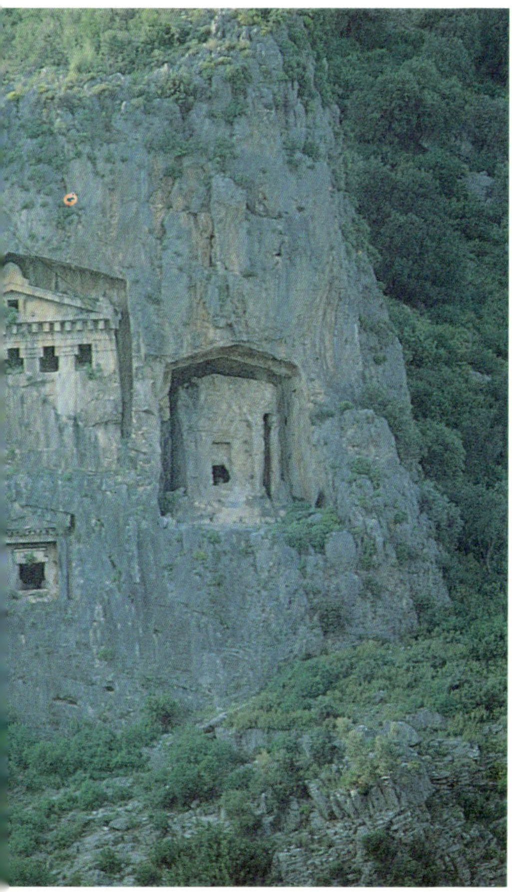

area is made for the mosquito to breed in and no doubt in antiquity Caunos throbbed to the irritating whine of the malarial Anopheles. In fact it was not until 1948 that the area around Caunos was sprayed and malaria brought under control. There are still mosquitoes in the Dalyan area, though thankfully not of the species that transmits malaria.

The climb up to the acropolis is not recommended for anyone short of breath. Although not very far, it is very steep, an ideal spot for an acropolis. Most of the walls and the tower are of Medieval origin, but on the summit the ruined fort is of ancient masonry. The climb up to the summit is worth it as much for the view out over the river to the sea nearly two miles away as for the ancient bits of rock. In antiquity it is likely that the sea came right up to the acropolis hill. The ancient harbour, now a small lake known as Sülüklü Gölü, was either right on the sea or connected to it by a channel and it suffered the same fate as other harbours situated at the mouth of a river such as Ephesus and Patara. It silted. From the acropolis hill you can see the vast swampy area knitted together by the reeds that now covers what was once sea. George Bean has surmised that an inscription found by the harbour detailing tax exemptions in the 1st century AD may have been an effort to encourage ships to use the harbour at Caunos and that these exemptions were necessary because the approaches to the harbour had already begun to silt up and consequently ships were avoiding it. Certainly the fortunes of the city had begun to decline by the 2nd century AD.

Caunos sits on the border between ancient Caria and ancient Lycia. It is mentioned as a Carian city, but it's culture evidently owed much to the Lycians. Herodotus tells us it was neither Carian nor Lycian and it is interesting that though inscriptions have been found in Carian script, there are sufficient different and unique characters for us to assume there was a Caunian language. While the language was largely Carian, the rock-tombs in the cliff-side are typically Lycian.

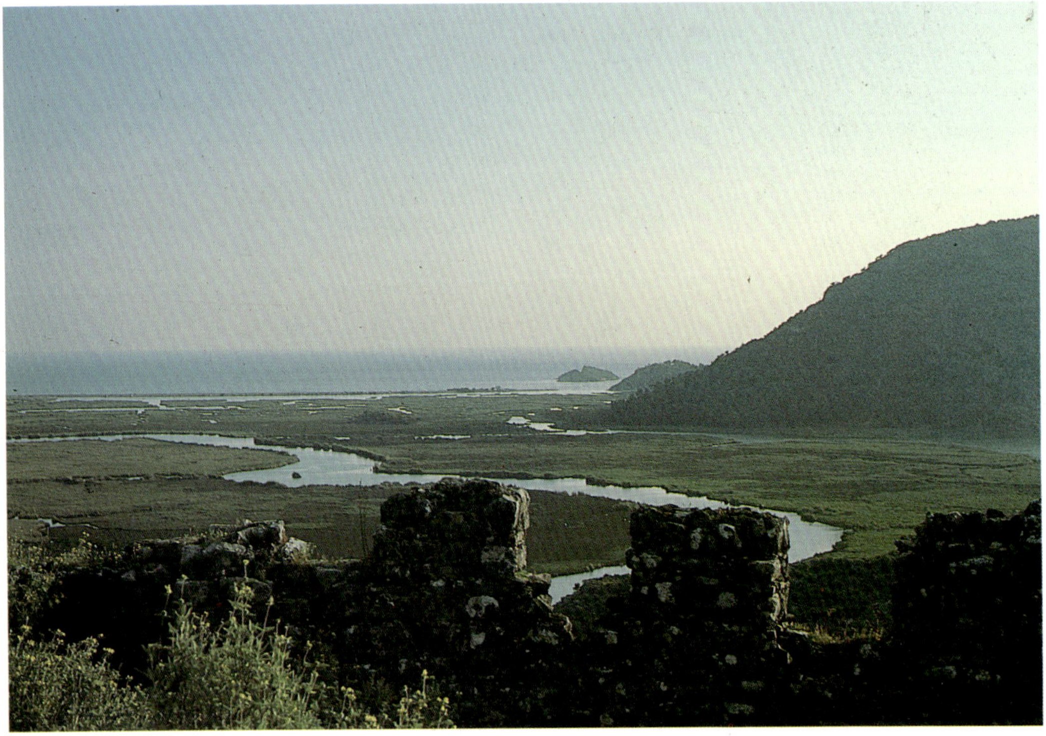

The exterior is hewn to look like the entrance to a temple with columns, friezes, and a pediment. Despite the grand exterior, inside there is only a small chamber with benches on which the dead were laid. The largest of these temple-tombs is incomplete and we can see how they were constructed. The roof, pediment, and the frieze are complete, but the columns have only been roughly shaped and work on the chamber had not started. With the arrival of Alexander the Great Caunos adopted Hellenic practices and by the 1st century BC Greek institutions and culture had entirely taken over. Though it was a prosperous city, Pliny mentions Caunian salt and slaves as it's principal exports, it was not well known outside of Asia Minor. No great artists or writers were claimed by Caunos and it seems the only thing the city was renowned for was it's unhealthy site. Rather than support artists and philosophers as other cities did, the profits from the city coffers were spent on a sybaritic lifestyle if the bathing pool by the harbour is anything to go by.

DALYAN AND THE RIVER

If you visit Caunos by road then it is to the village of Dalyan you must go before hiring a boat to get there. Dalyan sits on the east bank of the river and it's name literally means a 'fish-trap'. Mullet and bass (*kefal* and *levrek* in Turkish) swim up the river to Lake Köyceğiz to spawn and on their return are caught in a trap stretched across the river. The barrier fish-trap used to be situated at the village of Dalyan, but now it is sited a kilometre downstream. Basically it is a great mesh barrier across the river with enclosures in it from which the trapped fish can be taken. Excursion boats are locked through one side of the barrier to ensure that as few fish as possible escape. In Dalyan village there are several restaurants by the river specialising in mullet and bass dishes - either fish is excellent eating.

It is likely that the ancient Caunians also employed a fish-trap across the river to catch mullet and bass, in ancient Greek *kephalos* and *labrax*. George Bean has identified an inscription regulating catches of fish in the river and we know that Caunos produced salted fish for export. In an age where salting fish was just about the only way of preserving them, salted fish was a valuable commodity. Even today you can get salted cod throughout the Mediterranean where it is known as '*baccala*' or a variation on that name. Today the '*baccala*' mostly comes from Scandinavia and one of it's advantages over frozen fish is that it weights less, as much as one fifth the weight of frozen cod, and so costs much less to transport. One of the other things the Caunians would have made was garum, an essence of fish much valued by Roman epicures, but which sounds revolting. It was made by filling a barrel with fish entrails and salt and drawing off the liquid which formed from this evil mixture. The 'pissalat' still used in Provence is probably a direct descendent of the Romans' garum and in the Sea of Marmara, an essence made from mackerel livers soaked in brine, is also probably descended from ancient garum.

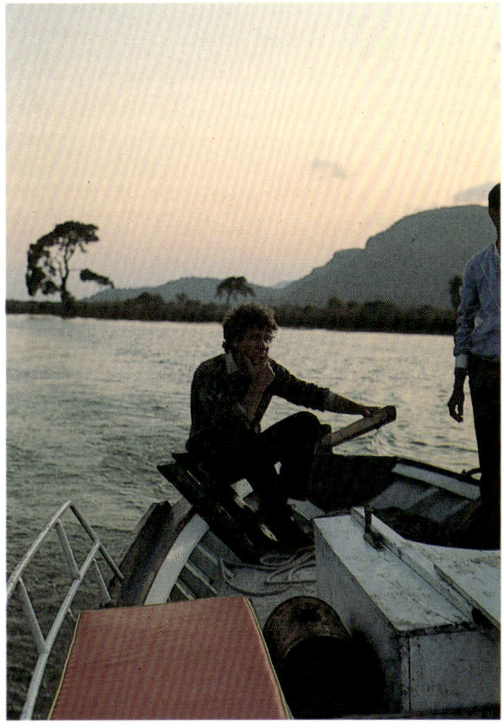

River-trip. Dalyan.

The river delta looking from the acropolis. Caunos.

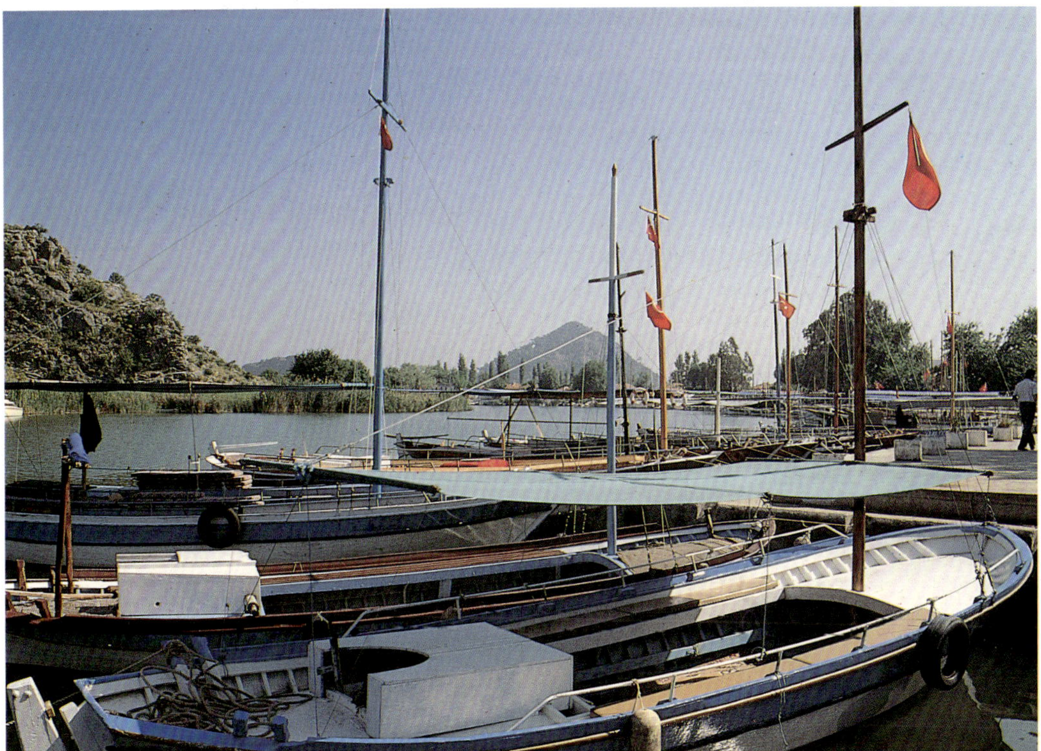

A river delta such as at Dalyan attracts all sorts of wild-life, especially water-birds. The marshy channels and pools supply food for the kingfisher, grebe, herons, bittern and snipe. Birds of prey such as kestrels and hawks circle overhead. Large numbers of terrapins sun themselves on the banks and it may be that the kestrels and hawks are keeping an eye out for a slow fat terrapin. Or maybe it is for one of the snakes said to be common in the area, though I have never seen one here.

KÖYCEĞİZ AND THE LAKE

By road from Marmaris you have to retrace your steps to Akçapınar near the head of the Gulf of Gökova before proceeding east again. The road passes through a large central plain and gently

Harbour at Köyceğiz.

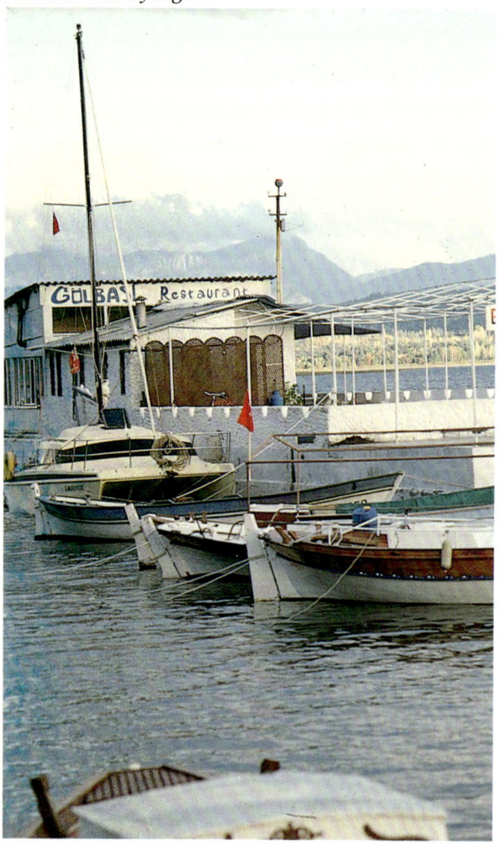

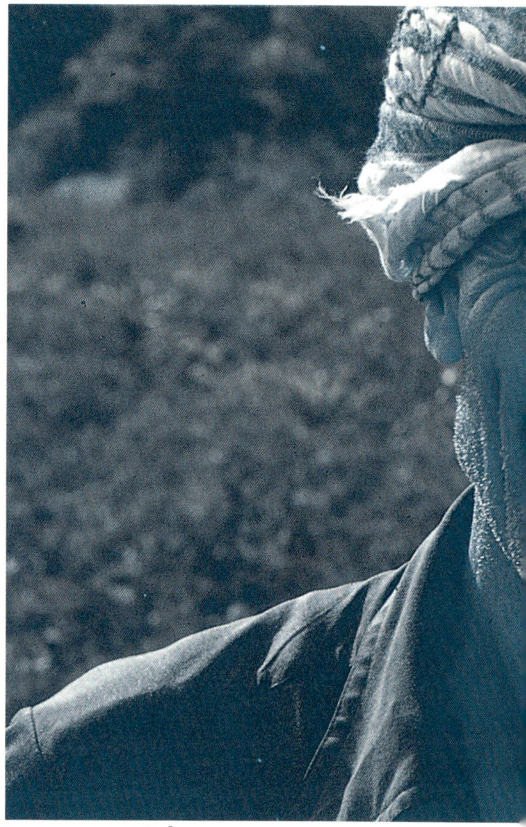

Local farmer. Dalyan area.

rolling countryside, skirting the precipitous coastal mountains. About 30 kilometres from Akçapınar you reach Köyceğiz on the northern end of Lake Köyceğiz (Köyceğiz Gölü), the Lake that feeds the Dalyan River. Köyceğiz itself is a pleasant little place, unpretentious to a fault, with a most helpful Tourist Information Office. There are several hotels and pensions and good restaurants with fresh mullet and bass from the lake. From Köyceğiz you can hire a boat to go to Caunos and/or to the Sultaniye hot springs in the southwest corner of the lake, though this is a much longer trip than from Dalyan.

The Sultaniye hot springs were described to me as a thermal establishment with rooms for hire and luxuriantly appointed baths. In 1984 it was nothing like this. The buildings and baths were in a dilapidated condition and the only visitors appeared to be the shepherds and

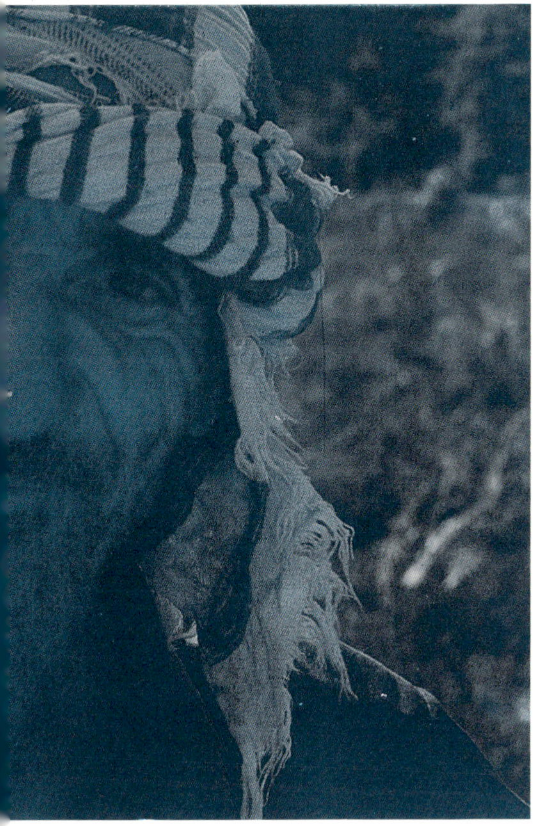

springs are said to be the most radioactive in Turkey and the second most radioactive springs in the world — post-Chernobyl I'm not sure whether this is really the way to advertise them. The Tourist Office hand-out goes on to say that the hot springs are beneficial for: rheumatism, neuralgia, neuritis, gall-bladder disorders, mental disorders, liver complaints, and women's diseases. Since I was suffering from none of these I declined to try the baths, a reluctance encouraged by the absence of people in the vicinity who perhaps knew more about the effects of radioactivity than I did. Apparently the establishment has now been tidied up and is not the tumble-down place I looked at.

The boat-man who took me across was upset I hadn't tried the thermal baths, (neither did he though), so he took me to a spot on the banks of the Dalyan River where after a short walk we came to another thermal pool amongst the trees. Despite the prescence of strange algae-like growth in the pool, which earned it the title of 'the slime pool' from a companion, this time I went in. In these pools, or any hot pool for that matter, never put your head under the water. There are sufficient cases of meningitis contracted from immersing the head and all it's orifices in a hot pool to make it an unnecessary risk to take.

From Köyceğiz the road continues inland through lush countryside until it winds up a gorge and down to Göçek on the northeast end of the Gulf of Fethiye. The turn-off to Dalyan is a few kilometres on from Köyceğiz. A little further on the main airport for this region at Dalaman is clearly sign-posted from the non-descript village of Dalaman. After Göçek the road continues along the coast to Fethiye.

Lake Köyceğiz

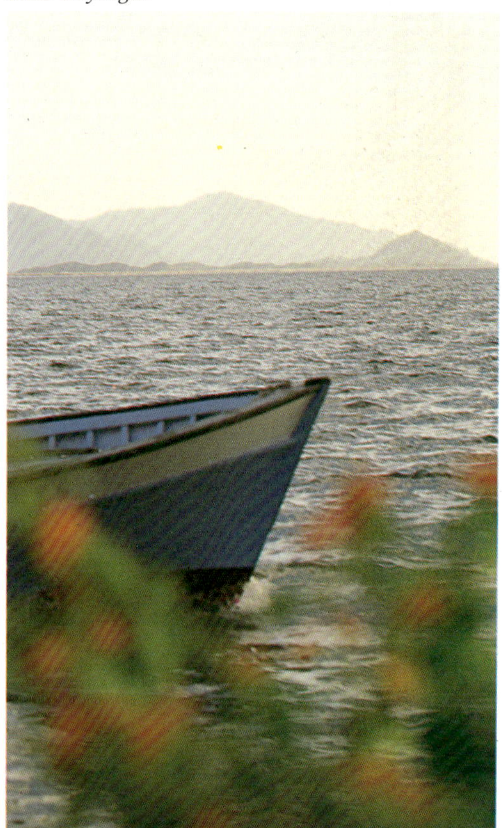

THE LYCIANS

Ancient Lycia encompasses the sea-girt bulge that runs from EkinÇik and ancient Caunos around as far as Antalya, a semi-circle of some of the most mountainous and wild landscape to be encountered anywhere in Turkey. During the Ottoman period it was called 'Uch', the 'Frontier', a name that conjures up the nature of the landscape. It is a region hemmed in by mountains. On the west and east two high mountain ridges, the tallest peaks standing well over 3000 metres (10,000 feet) high, cut off Lycia from neighbouring Caria to the west and Pamphylia to the east. In the north a lower but no less rugged range and a great plateau cut Lycia off from central Anatolia. Around the coast a series of mountain ranges drop precipitously into the sea and though the peaks are not as high as those in the interior, the aspect from seaward is of an inhospitable coast. Right into early summer the highest peaks in Lycia, Akdağ in the west and Bey Dağı (ancient Mt Solymnus) in the east, are covered in snow on the highest slopes.

As the landscape is wild, so were the men who lived here. The Lycians enjoyed a reputation for independence and fought for it tooth and nail, often to the last man. This last statement is not a cliché tacked on for effect, on at least two occasions we know it to be fact. In 546 BC the Persians defeated Croesus, the last Lydian king, and advanced upon Lycia. On the Plain of Xanthos the Lycians met the much superior forces of the Persians, to no avail. Herodotus tells us of the tragic finale to the battle:

"When Harpagus advanced into the plain of Xanthos, they met him in battle, though greatly outnumbered, and fought with much gallantry; at length, however, they were defeated and forced to retire within their walls, whereupon they collected their women, children, slaves, and other property and shut them up in the citadel, set fire to it and burnt it to the ground. Then having sworn to do or die, they marched out to meet the enemy and were killed to a man."

Five hundred years later in 42 BC it all happened again when Brutus besieged Xanthos. Against a superior force the Lycians fought to the finish, and when they saw there was no hope of victory, they once again slew their women and children and burnt the city down. Plutarch recorded Brutus' feelings on this second mass suicide:

"It was so tragical a sight that Brutus could not bear to see it, but wept at the very mention of the scene. Thus the Xanthians, after a long space of years, repeated by their desperate deed the calamity of their forefathers, who after the very same manner in the Persian Wars had fired their city and destroyed themselves."

Such was the feeling of the Lycians towards independence that they were the last region to be incorporated into the Roman provinces in Asia Minor.

Who were these Lycians and where did they come from? They are mentioned in Homer's **Iliad** *where they fought on the side of the Trojans in defence of Troy, a gallant force from 'distant Lycia and the eddying Xanthus'. Herodotus fills us in on the details. The Lycians, he says, came from Crete after 'Sarpedon and Minos, fought for the throne, and the victorious Minos expelled Sarpedon and his party'. They were then called the Termilae, and only adopted the*

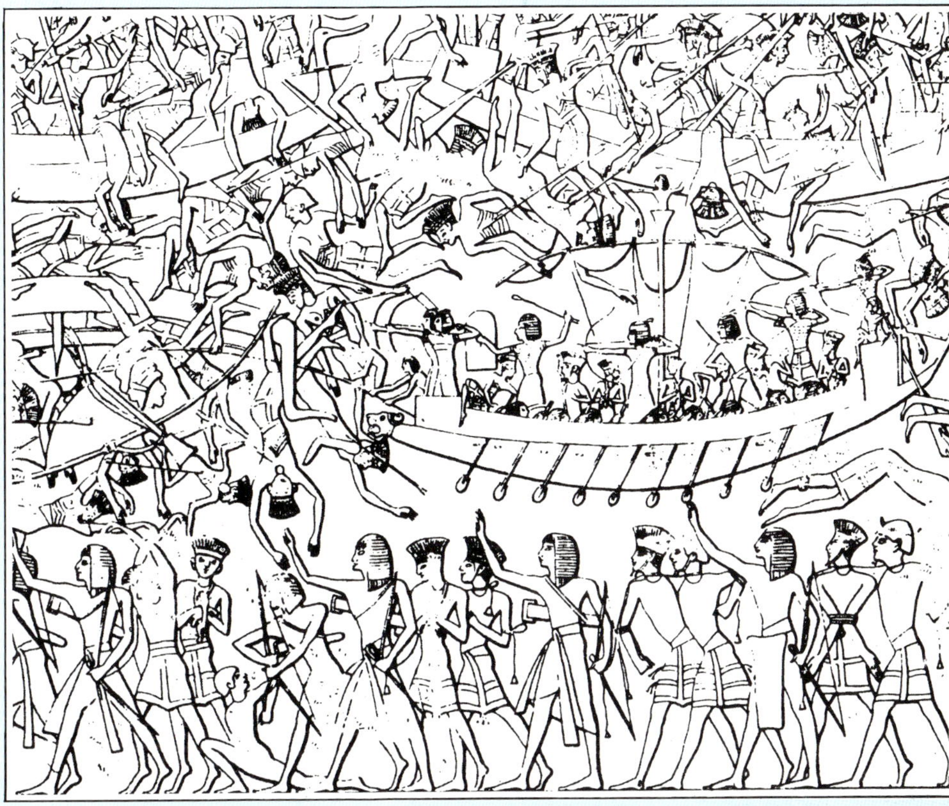

name Lycian when the noble Lycus, son of King Pandion, was expelled from Athens and came to join Sarpedon. From Lycus they adopted the name Lycian. It's all a bit tortuous and not as interesting as the light Hittite and Egyptian references throw on the origins of the Lycians. The Hittites record that a maritime people called the Lukka lived here sometime in the 14th century BC. Egyptian records mention a people called the Lukki living here, a people feared as sea-raiders. This latter reference makes a good deal of sense on later evidence.

The Lycian coast has often been referred to as the 'pirate coast', and with it's many strategically sited coves and islands where these sea-raiders could lie in wait for plump merchant ships tramping up and down the coast, it deserves the epithet. Numerous campaigns were mounted to clean up the coast from as early as 1194 BC right up until the 19th century. A relief at Medinet Habu in the Nile delta records how Ramses III put together a great fleet to take on the Lukki and decisively defeated them, leaving the coast free of piracy for a while. When Xerxes assembled his huge force for the invasion of Greece in 480 BC the Lycians contributed fifty ships and Herodotus gives us this tantalising description of the piratical bunch that manned them:

"They wore greaves and corslets; they carried bows of cornel wood, cane arrows without feathers, and javelins. They had goatskin slung round their shoulders, and hats stuck round with feathers. They also carried daggers and rip-hooks."

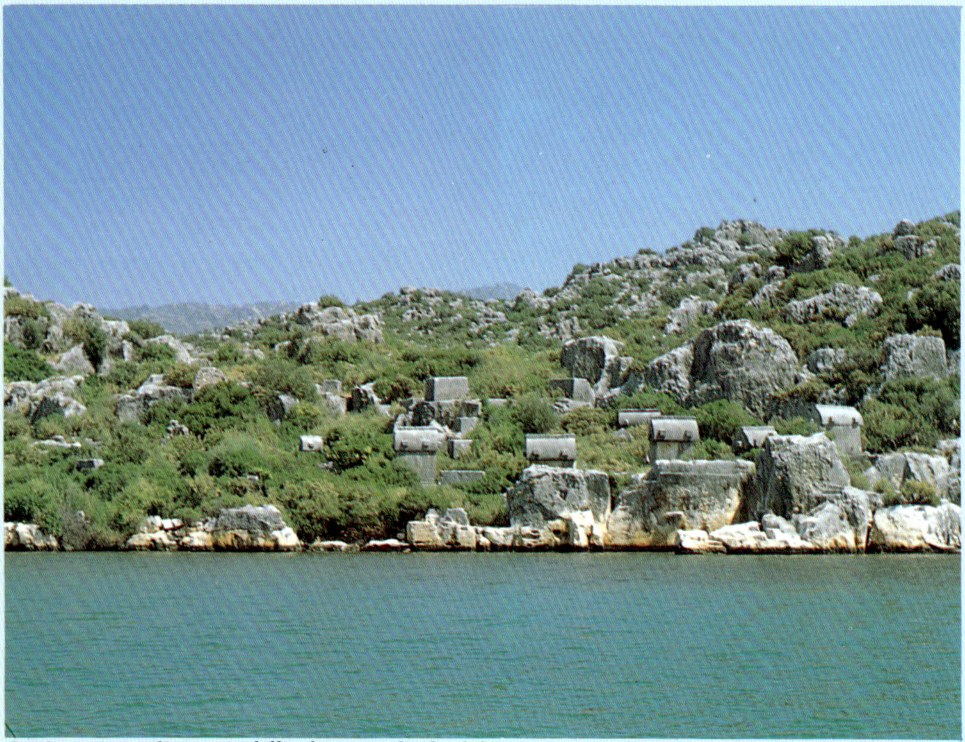

Lycian necropolis ...it is difficult not to think of the region as a vast necropolis peopled with the shadowy figures of Lycian nobles. (to go with BOX: The Lycians)

Piracy is again mentioned in the 5th century BC, but it is not until the Roman occupation of Asia Minor that attempts were again made to bring it under control. In 78 BC a campaign was mounted by Servilius Vatia, governor of Cilicia, and though he had moderate success, it did little to check it. In 67 BC Pompey, an able and intelligent admiral, was given wide-ranging powers and almost unlimited resources to tackle the piracy problem, which he did with total success. However Pompey was reluctant to give up his power and his ships and became himself something of a thorn in the Senate's side. After the fall of Rome the Lycian coast once again became a haven for pirate fleets and not until the 18th and 19th centuries and the presence of the British Navy was the piracy problem again tackled and the Lycian coast cleaned up.

In this remote region the sites of over forty cities have been found and much remains to identify the culture of the Lycians. The most obvious features of the Lycian landscape are the tombs and sarcophagi left behind. They are everywhere and it is difficult not to think of the region as a vast necropolis peopled with the shadowy figures of Lycian nobles and warriors. Ancestor-worship was evidently important to the Lycians and the tombs are extravagant affairs, the more grandiose decorated with a frieze and inscriptions placing a curse upon anyone tampering with the tomb. Five distinct types of tomb can be distinguished: pillar-tombs, temple-tombs, house-tombs, pigeon-hole tombs, and the ubiquitous sarcophagi. Pillar-tombs are specific to Lycia and consist of a long tapering pillar set on a stone base with the grave chamber at the top. These were for important dynasts and the best examples are at Xanthos. Temple-tombs are to my mind the most impressive of the Lycian tombs and consist of a temple facade with a grave chamber behind it. Those at Caunos are the most romantically sited while those at Fethiye the most accessible. House-tombs were modelled on the wooden houses of the Lycians and so give us some idea of what everyday accomodation was like several thousand years ago. They are smaller than the temple-tombs, though often several stories high, and the stone has been hewn to imitate wooden roof beams and the doorway and portico. The house-tombs were sometimes decorated with reliefs and painted as at Myra where fragments of a painted relief have miraculously survived. Pigeon-hole tombs were the down-market version of temple and house tombs, small unadorned chambers cut into a cliff-face. The best examples are at Pınara where the cliffs are literally pock-marked by these tombs. Sarcophagi are found everywhere: scattered over hill-sides, on the summits of hills, by the shore, and in the sea where the land has subsided. The older sarcophagi are the largest with massive stone bases, grave chambers, and heavy lids often with a peaked 'gothic' look to them. In Roman times the sarcophagi became smaller and less ornate, perhaps as the importance of ancestor-worship declined.

With the decline of the Roman Empire, so too Lycian fortunes declined. In Byzantine times there were small settlements around the coast, a number of Byzantine churches will be seen in isolated spots, but the interior was not heavily populated as in Lycian times. In the late Middle Ages this region was viewed as a wilderness, the region of 'Uch', the 'Frontier' of the Ottomans, and the coast was the haunt of pirates who had semi-permanent settlements ashore. The Lycians and Lycian culture faded into vague folk-memories of a proud and independent people who had built great stone cities and buried their dead in magnificient tombs. Not until those intrepid travellers of the 19th century, Francis Beaufort, Charles Newton, Thomas Spratt and Edward Forbes, was the existence and extent of Lycian culture to be brought to the notice of the West.

EKİNCİK TO ANCIENT CAUNOS

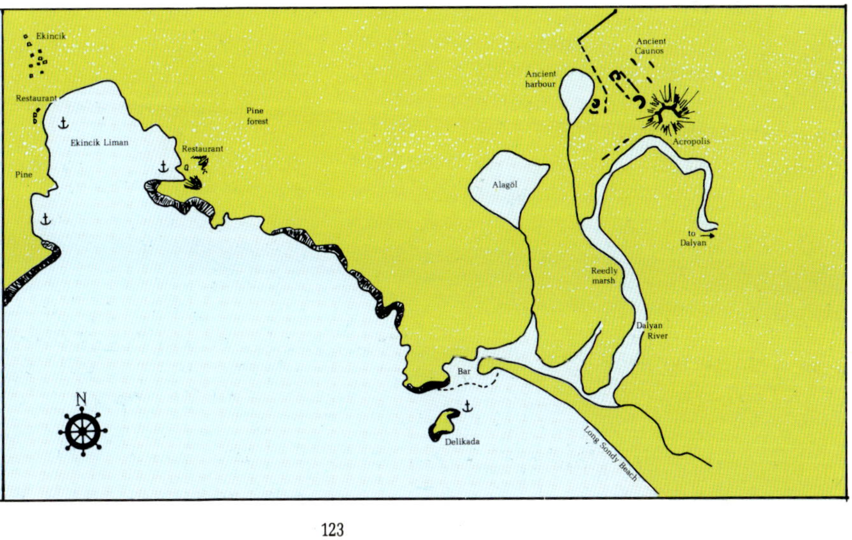

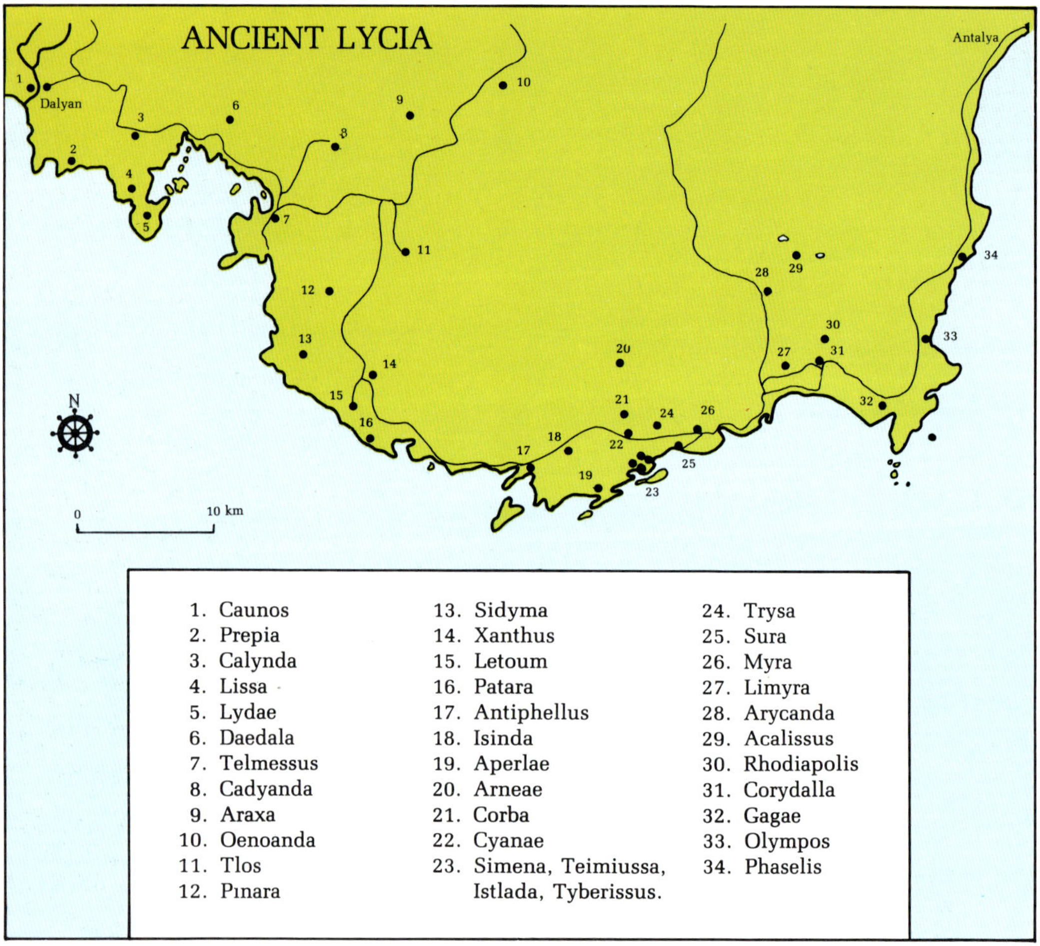

CALYNDA

After Dalaman the road passes close to the site of Calynda, an ancient city that had declined almost into obscurity by the 1st century AD. There is not much to see here and it's one claim to fame is that it supplied the ship to Xerxes' fleet that Queen Artemis sank at Salamis, a strange tale I have related in the section on ancient Caria. The locals tell of vast hordes of gold buried here, but like many of these tales they are probably based on the assumption that archaeologists couldn't possibly be looking for bits of old rock as they say, they must surely be looking for gold and treasure with all the effort they put into an archaeological dig. Then again, there may be gold here.

BABA ADASI

From Ekinçik and Dalyan there are several rocky capes before the slab-sided island of Baba Adası can be seen close off a long sandy beach. On the summit of the island there is a remarkable pyramidal structure built in brick, the purpose of which has been disputed. It has been variously described as a mausoleum, a monument, and a lighthouse, the general consensus being that the latter was the most likely purpose. There is a fair-weather anchorage behind the island from where you can visit the ruins of a sizeable town near the shore. Most of the ruins to be seen are of a Medieval town, probably of Prepia, a place in this vicinity mentioned in Medieval Italian Sailing

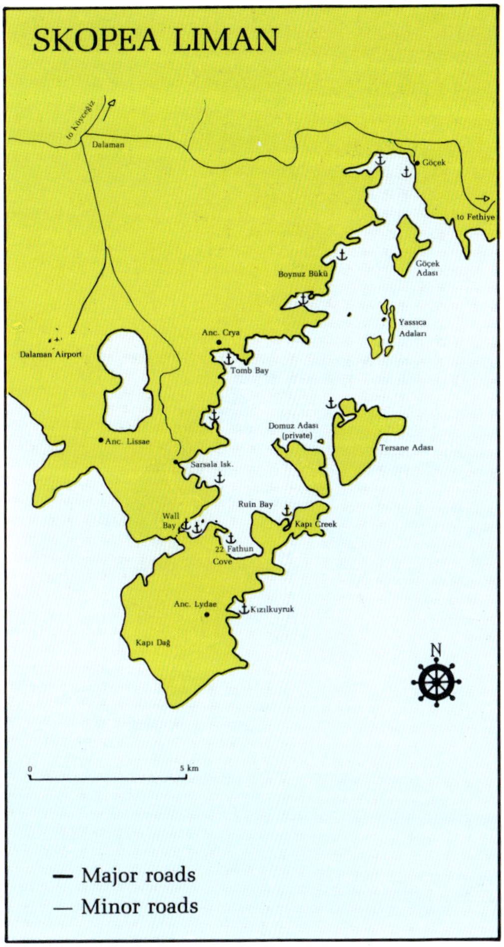

Directions (the 'Portolans'). Evidence of a more ancient settlement, probably the town of Pisilis, are also scattered around the site and incorporated into the Medieval buildings. It may be that a harbour was situated on the Dalaman River that flows into the sea near here, that in antiquity and the Middle Ages the river's course was different to what it is today and formerly it flowed close to Pisilis/Prepia, and that the harbour silted as at Caunos. The fact that Prepia was mentioned in the Portalans does not mean it necessarily had a harbour, but thc existence of the lighthouse, if that is what it was, indicates it had an importance over and above simply being there.

By land it is difficult to get to Prepia as the road is very rough and only really suitable for four-wheel drive vehicles. From Dalaman there is a reasonable road to Kızılyurt, but it deteriorates rapidly after this.

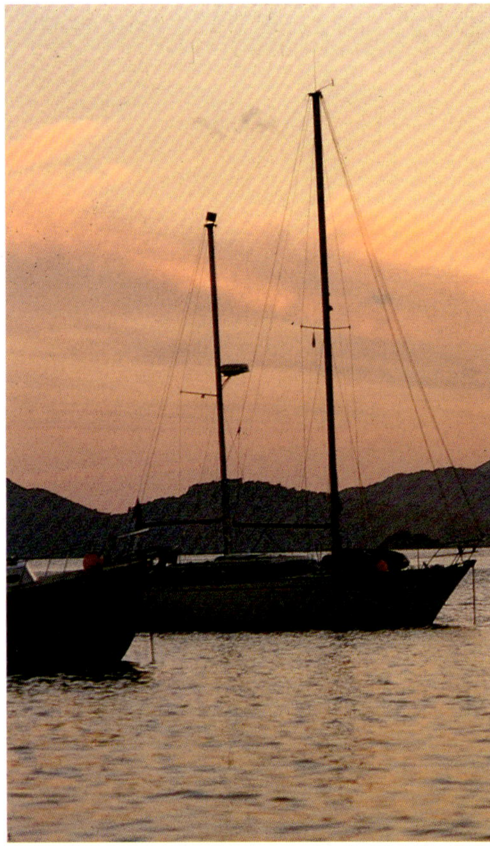

Göçek.

FETHİYE KÖRFEZİ

From Baba Adası the bold silhouette of Kapı Dağı, the headland at the western entrance to the Gulf of Fethiye can be seen. The gulf is a jagged bite out of the mountains of Lycia with a number of small islands scattered around the perimeter. The locals call it the Gulf of Twelve Islands, though that is counting some fairly small ones to get to that number. It takes it's more well-known name, Fethiye Körfezi, from the town of Fethiye tucked into it's eastern corner. In ancient times it was called Sinus Glaucus, Glaucus being one of the Lycian generals mentioned by Homer in the *Iliad*.

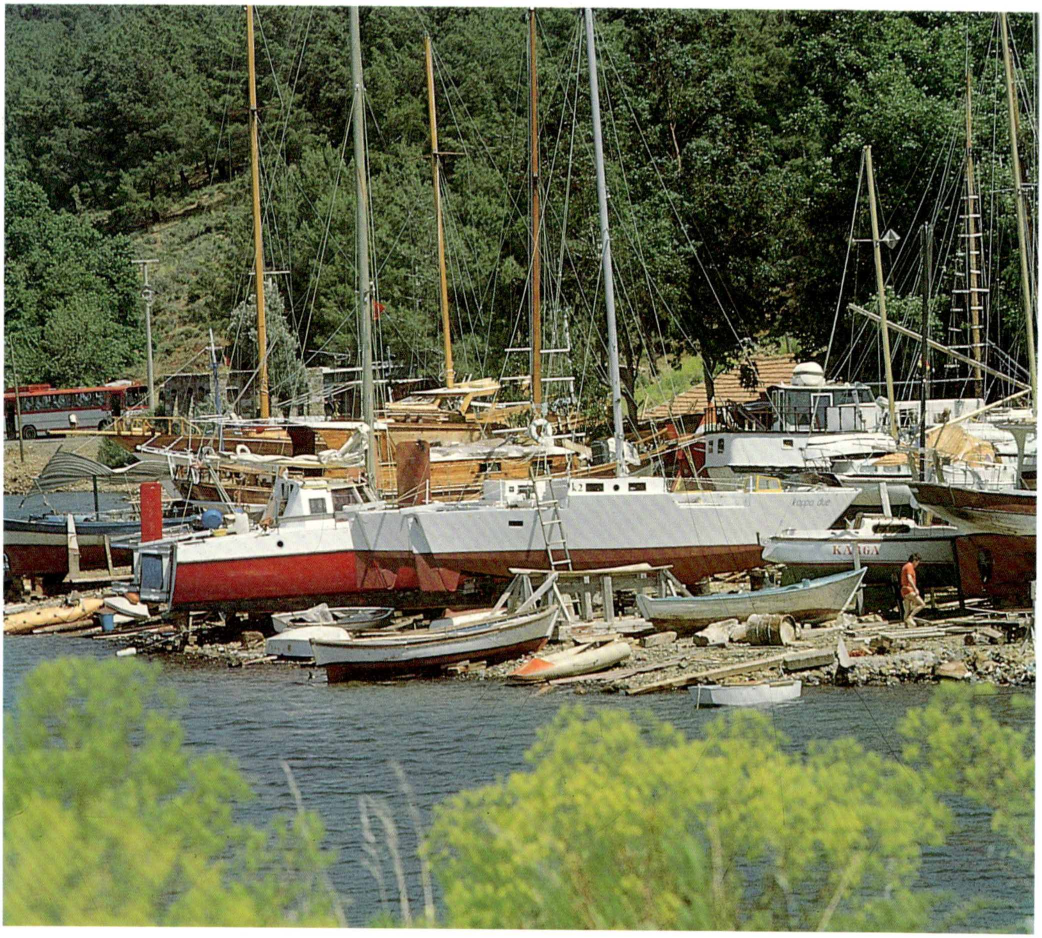

The main road from Köyceğiz touches the gulf at Göçek and then skirts the northern shore until it touches again at Fethiye. To get anywhere else in the gulf, particularly to the islands and coast on the western side, there is no alternative but to go by boat. These islands and the much indented coast on the western side, called Skopea Liman on the Admiralty chart, are a popular cruising ground for yachts and *gulets* offering sheltered waters behind the islands and attractive coves and bays within short distances around the coast. Formerly the shores were virtually deserted, but in recent years with the increasing numbers of yachts and *gulets* about, small restaurants have sprung up in the more popular bays. From Fethiye there are day-trips into the gulf to a number of the places mentioned.

KIZILKUYRUK KOYU

A bay just inside the western entrance to the gulf that can be easily recognised by the prominent red cliffs around it. The anchorage is a delightful one in peaceful surroundings and it was probably known and used by the ancients. From the bay a path leads to ancient Lydae, about an hours easy walk to the west, with some of an ancient path evident along the way. The site is set in splendid isolation and there are the remains of the agora, several indeterminate buildings, part of a colossal statue, and the remains of other buildings scattered about; but the most striking feature of the site is two large mausoleums in reasonable condition. The ruins are of Roman and Byzantine origin and little is known about the city at this time and virtually nothing of it's existence in pre-Roman times bar a brief mention in the 'Stadiasmus' and later by Ptolemy in his 'Geography'.

To the north of Lydae, near the narrow neck joining the headland of Kapı Dağı to the mainland, are a few ruins and a fort belonging to Arymaxa, a deme of Lydae. A wall runs right across this neck of land from the cove on the east side to the sea on the other. Whether the wall is of recent origin or has older antecedents is uncertain, but it would have made an effective defensive wall cutting the whole headland off from a land attack.

KAPI CREEK

Between Domuz Adası and the northern tip of Kapı Dağı there is a narrow channel leading into Skopea Liman. Just around from here an inlet, barely visible until you are at the entrance, runs in. There are a few old houses around the shore and a restaurant on the eastern side, but otherwise there are just olive groves and pine on the higher slopes. It is an idyllic spot and not surprisingly it is popular with yachts and *gulets*. The restaurant serves simple but good fare and will often supply 'village bread', the huge round loaves of unleavened bread cooked in an outdoor oven.

On the west side of the bay there is a triple vaulted house, at least I have been assured it was simply a house, of unusual design and with no obvious explanation for it's complex construction. A short walk over the ridge behind the inlet you come to the sea again and here there is a delightful rocky cove, shaded by pine, just right for a secluded dip.

Kapı Greek. Gulf of Fethiye.

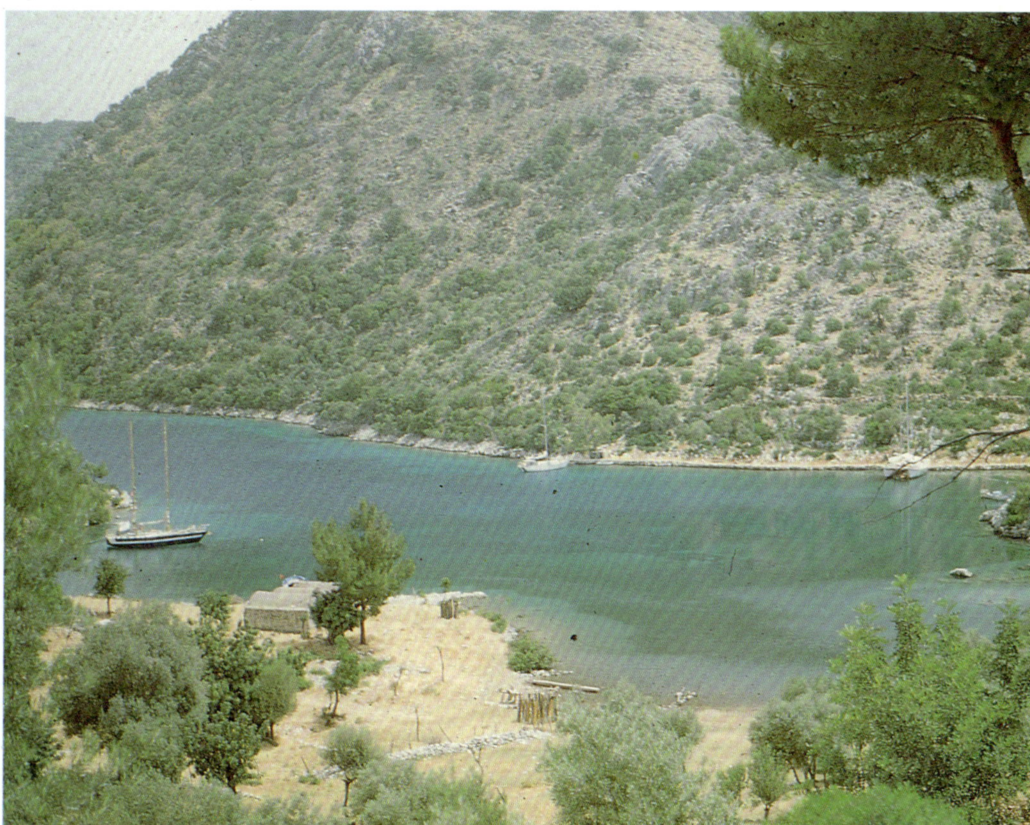

Twenty-Two Fathom Cove

A small cove just across from Kapı Creek. It's name comes from Admiralty chart 1986, surveyed, incidentally, by Commander T Graves as far back as 1840, which has a 22 fathom sounding shown at the entrance of the cove. Ashore there is a restaurant. On the eastern arm of the cove the rock has weathered into jagged and weird columns to create a curious landscape.

Manastir Koyu

Directly west of 22 Fathom cove lies Manastır Koyu, a large bay with two stunningly beautiful anchorages in it.

Ruin Bay

Lies in the south of Manastır Koyu and is so named from the ruins, now partially underwater, at it's head. Local knowledge claims these as Cleopatra's Baths, but it is unlikely they were built until after Cleopatra was long gone. Whatever story attached to the place, it is enchanting with clear turquoise water and pine overhanging the shore. Several restaurants open in the summer.

Wall Bay

At the far western end of Manastır Koyu there is a cove with several places to anchor around it's perimeter. A remarkable square rock sits in the water near the head of the cove. Like Ruin Bay, thick pine forest overhangs the water except on the northern side which is planted in olives. Several restaurants open in the summer. At the southern end of Wall Bay, a solid stone wall crossing the isthmus can be seen, from which the bay takes it's name. This is the same wall mentioned in connection with ancient Arymaxa, the deme of Lydae.

Sarsala İskelesi

A large bay on the coast opposite Domuz Adası. It is one of the few places on this side of the gulf you can reach by road, though the track described thus can barely be classified as a road. The best anchorage here is not in the large bay itself but in a cove on the south side where the slopes plummet dramatically down to the sea. As you enter the cove you will see an old marble column on the point. In the bay proper there is a small hamlet whose inhabitants make a living from agriculture and fishing.

Village beauty.

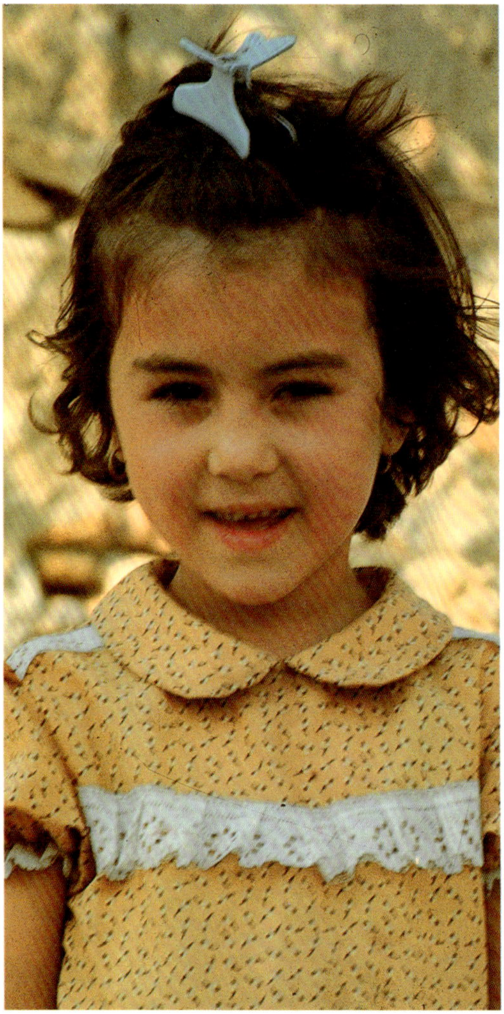

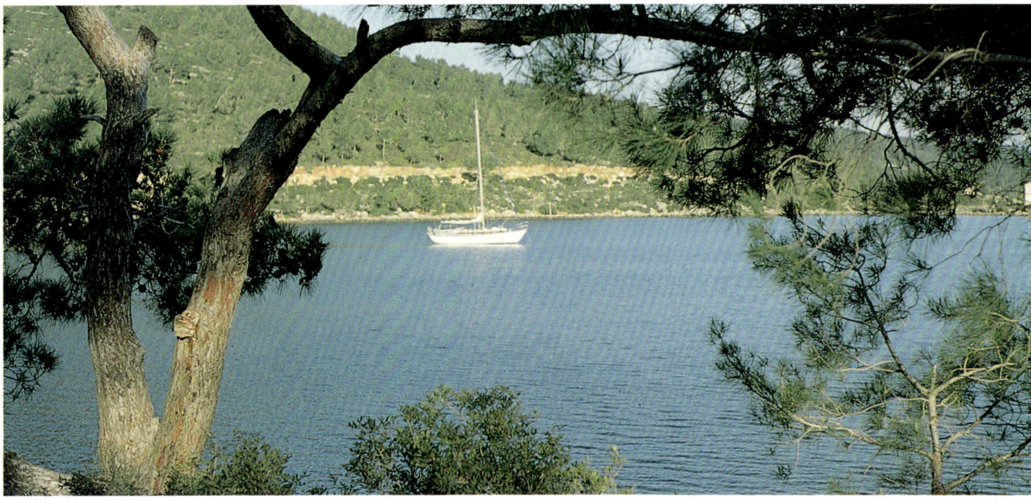

...not only will a boat let you see a lot of places that cannot be reached by land, but you will see the coast best from a boat.

Tomb Bay

(Properly Taşyaka). This bay lies to the northwest of Domuz Adası and Tersane Adası, under the prominent headland of Topburnu. The bay is a delightful anchorage under wooded slopes with a small restaurant ashore. On the north side of the bay there are several temple-tombs and pigeon-hole tombs and steps cut into the rock leading up to a minature acropolis. The site has been identified by George Bean as Crya which Pliny called by the evocative name: 'Crya of the fugitives'. There is no explanation for this strange apellation and little is known about this small city other than the fact she controlled two islands, Carysis and Alina, presumably the two largest islands now called Domuz and Tersane. To the east of the tombs there is a painting of a fish on the cliff, most likely a later Byzantine addition.

Domuz Adasi

The southernmost of the chain of islands strung through Skopea Liman and one of the largest along with Tersane Adası. Part of the island is privately owned, apparently by the owners of *'Hürriyet'* (Freedom), one of the largest Turkish daily newspapers. A large residence and ancillary buildings have been built on the northeastern side of the island with a quayed area nearby, but it should come as no surprise that yachts and *gulets* cannot use it and landing on the island is not permitted.

On a charter gulet all you have to do is sit and watch the scenery glide by while the skipper and crew do the work.

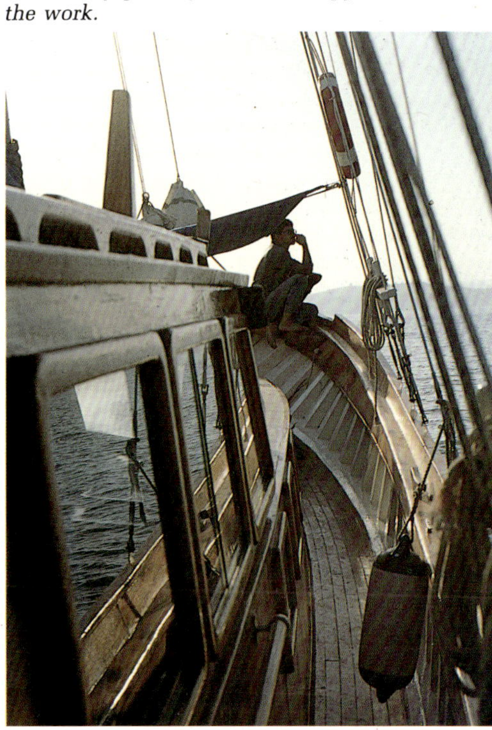

Tersane Adası

The largest island in the gulf lying immediately east of Domuz Adası and separated from it by a narrow channel. On the northwest side of the island a narrow inlet opens up into a T-shaped cove, an almost totally enclosed anchorage providing a safe haven in all weather. Tall palms around the shore give the place the feel of a tropical anchorage. Ashore there are numerous buildings, now deserted and partially ruined, of what was evidently a sizeable community. A number are older Byzantine buildings with more recent additions, but most date from after this period.

Apparently there was a prosperous Greek village here until the exchange of populations between Greece and Turkey after World War I. Now there is a solitary family who farms the surrounding land and a restaurant which opens in the summer. Tersane means a 'boat-yard' and it is likely that before the village was abandoned the inhabitants were engaged in building and repairing boats. There is a poignant atmosphere about this deserted village and it is a pleasant irony that once again boats visit Tersane, though for a pleasure-seeking purpose rather than the utilitarian purpose of days gone by.

Yassica Adalari

A group of islets to the north of Tersane Adası with a number of dangerous off-lying rocks and reefs. There are several anchorages around the group, suitable in settled weather, that make attractive lunch-stops.

Boynuz Bükü

A large bay on the coast directly opposite Yassıca Adaları. A river flows into it at the head and it is thus well-watered through the summer and consequently a green and shady place. A stand of deciduous trees and oleander grow around the river mouth with pine on the rocky slopes around. Reeds grow in the choked mouth of the river giving it the appearance of a mini-Dalyan. A restaurant opens in the summer.

Tersane. The enclosed natural harbour on Tersane Island.

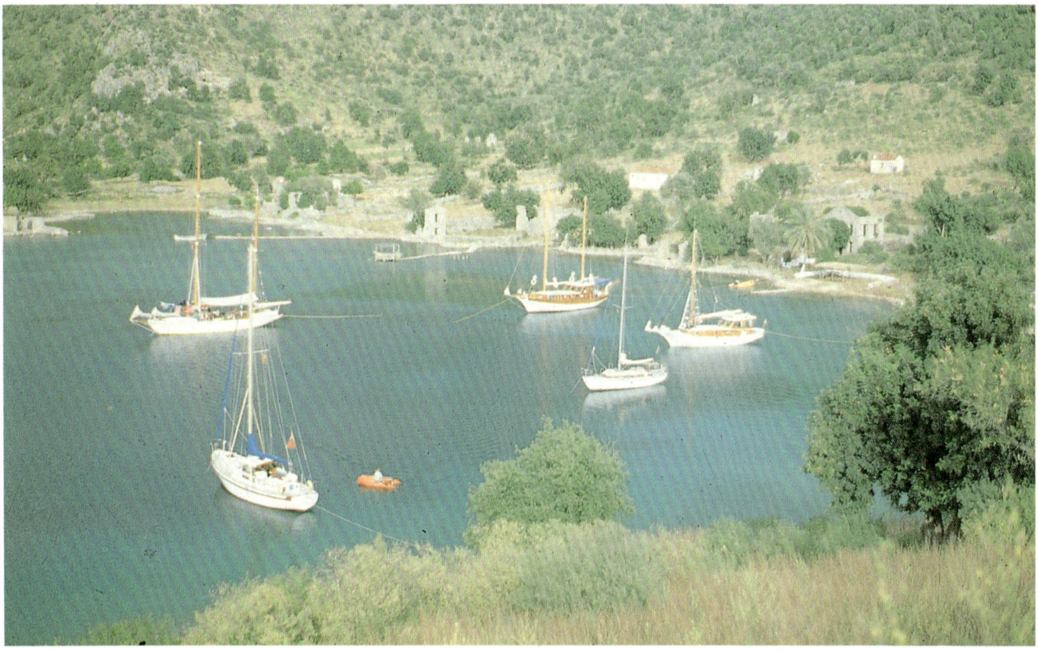

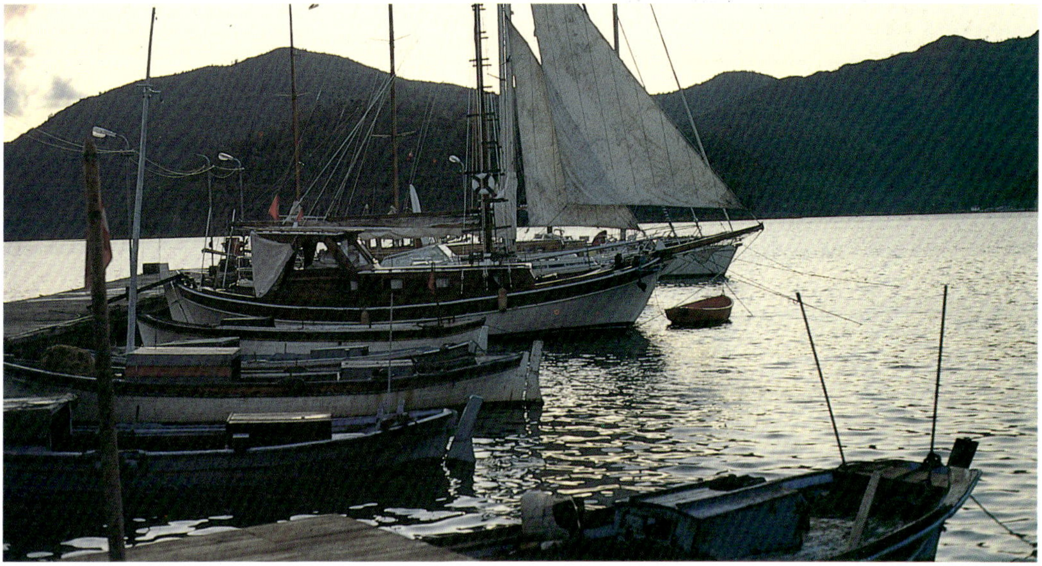

Göçek.

GÖÇEK

At the very northern end of the gulf there is a large bay with the village of Göçek strung around the shore. On the western side there is a wharf and oil storage tanks that rather mar the otherwise beautiful bay. The wharf is marked on early charts as 'Patersons Wharf' and the modern name, the 'Turkish Chrome Company Wharf', doesn't convey the same tone as the old name. Turkey has extensive workable deposits of chrome ore and exports much of Europe's requirements of the stuff, essential for making hardened steel.

The village of Göçek, formerly a small agricultural centre, has blossomed in recent years with the increased numbers of charter yachts around. It possesses the important advantage of being a mere twenty minutes from Dalaman Airport, so charterers can be off the plane and on the boat in half an hour. As a consequence it is becoming a charter boat base for the area. It is a pleasant little village that has grown sympathetically to satisfy the needs of the boats based here. Ashore there are good restaurants, some serving excellent fresh fish, and good shops for provisioning before a trip around the gulf. Land-based visitors may be able to hire a boat here for excursions into Skopea Liman.

FACILITIES

Marmaris: Restaurants, hotels & pensions, telephone, P.O., Banks, Doctor, Dentist, laundry, showers, toilets, fuel, water, ice, gas, provisions, engineer. Officials: Health, Immigration, Customs, Harbourmaster, Police, Tourist Information.
Ekinçik: Restaurants, pension.
Dalyan: Restaurants: hotels & pensions, telephone, P.O., Bank, toilets, fuel, water, provisions.
Köyceğiz: Restaurants, hotels & pensions, telephone, P.O., Bank, Doctor, toilets, fuel, water, provisions. Police, tourist information.
Kapı Creek: Restaurant.
Twenty-Two Fathom Cove: Restaurant.
Ruin Bay: Restaurants.
Wall Bay: Restaurants.
Sarsala: Restaurant.
Tomb Bay: Restaurant.
Tersane: Restaurant.
Boynuz Bükü: Restaurant.
Göçek: Restaurants, hotel & pensions, telephone, P.O. Bank, laundry, toilets, fuel, water, ice, gas, provisions. Police.

CHAPTER -4-
FETHİYE-TO-KEKOVA

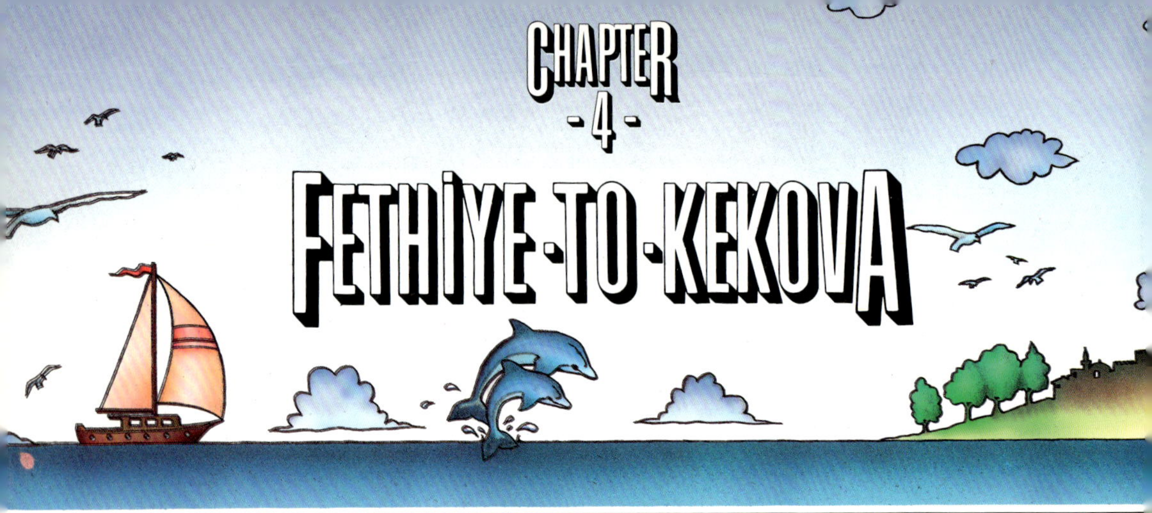

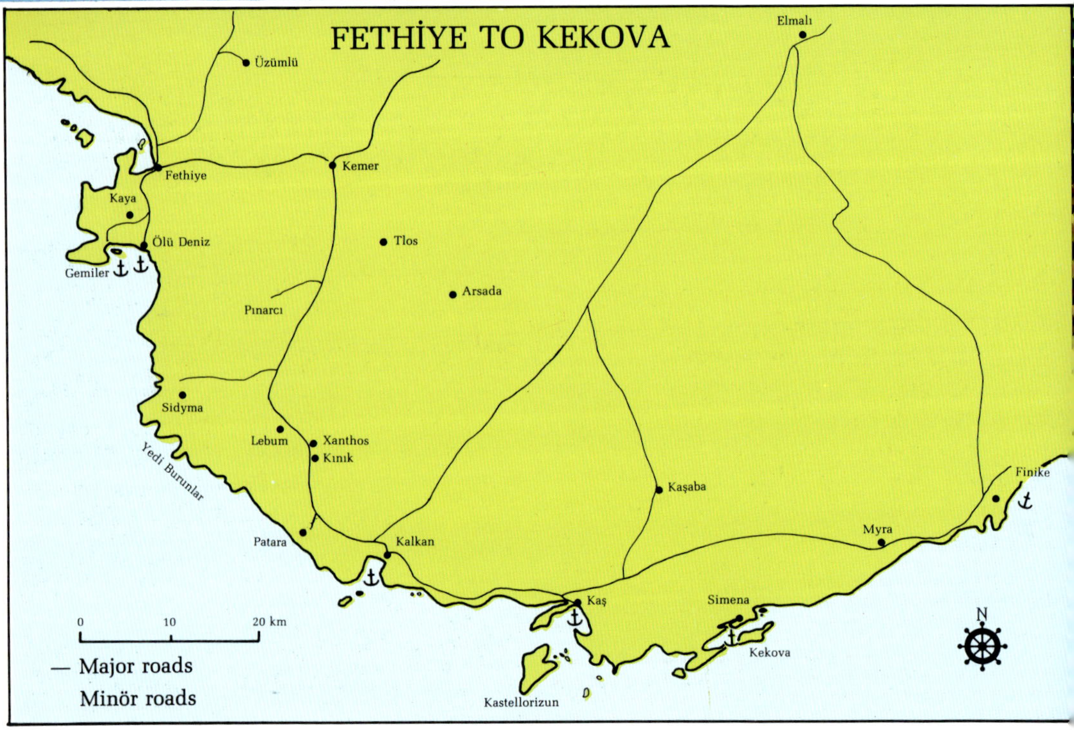

From Fethiye the coast curves around in a mountainous bulge to Antalya. It is a rugged region that like the rest of the coastline described in this book, is difficult of access by road for much of its length. There are sideroads leading off to some of the places described, but some of these, such as the road to Gemiler from Kaya, are rough affairs that are hard on vehicles. Conversely the waterborne visitor must take to the roads to visit some of the ancient sites in the Xanthos valley, and to see what the interior, cut off from the sea by rugged mountains, is like.

This region was the heartland of ancient Lycia and some of the ruins here are quite simply spectacular. Some of them like Patara have not been excavated and the sight of a once great city half-buried by sand dunes is an evocative one. Some like Tlos are in a wild and savage setting in the mountains. All of them are worth a visit, as much for the landscape along the way, as for the sites themselves.

Fethiye from seawards

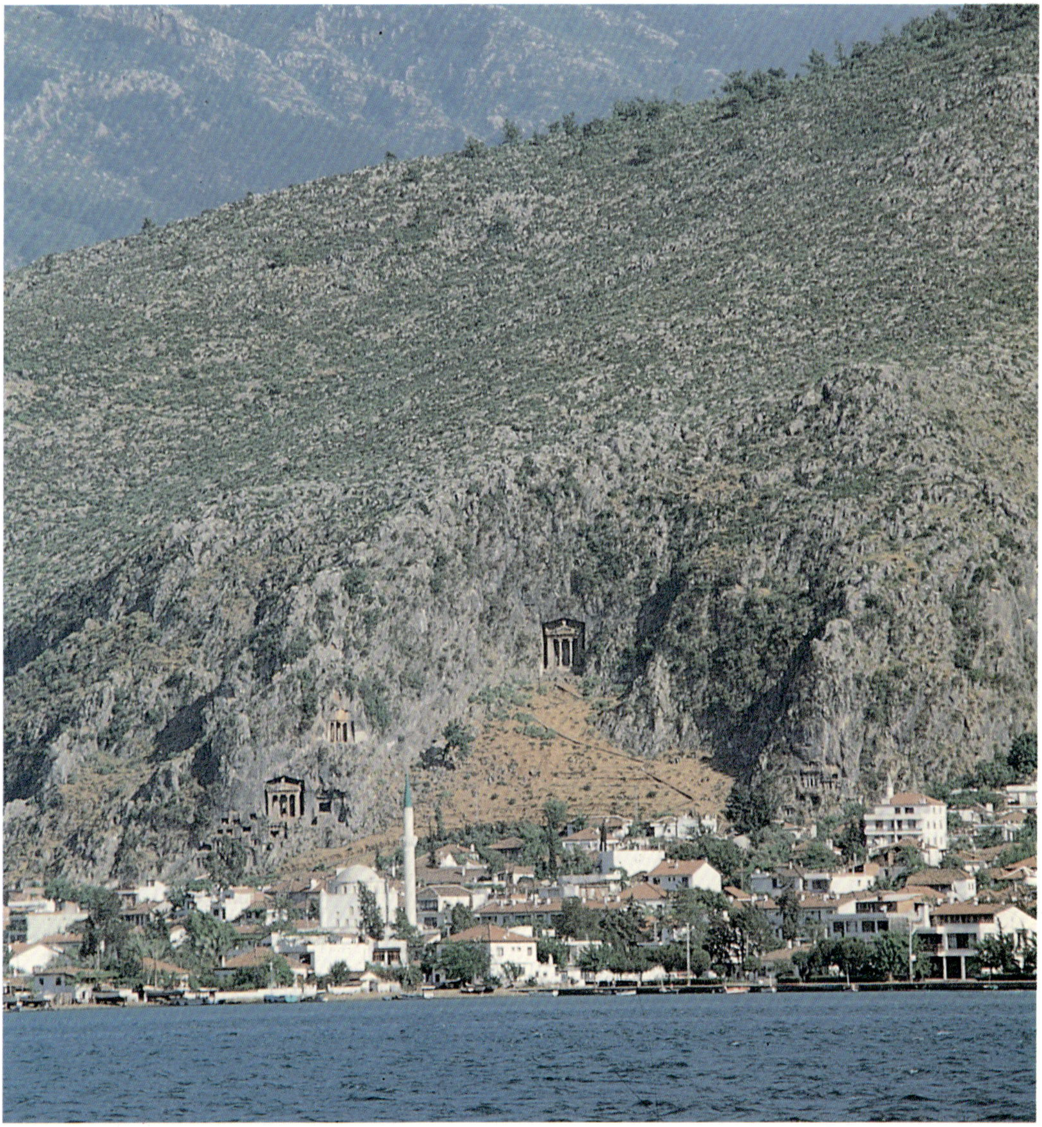

FETHİYE

As you come into Fethiye by road you pass along a long cobbled street lined with shops selling anything and everything to do with the land, and workshops for servicing and maintaining agricultural machinery. Tractors and trailers compete with cars and buses for space on the roads. Mo-peds with baskets of produce on the back bounce over the cobbles towards the town centre. This is one face of Fethiye. As you approach Fethiye from seawards you pass between the headland of Belen Dağı and Fethiye Island, between shores covered in villas, into the almost land-locked bay of Fethiye where a forest of masts at one end of the town identifies the other face of Fethiye. Somewhere between the tractors and trailers and the hotels and yachts is Fethiye.

Whether you arrive by land or sea, it is to a comparitively modern town. Like Marmaris, Fethiye was progressively flattened by a series of earthquakes in the 1950's, that of 1957 doing most of the damage. The rubble from the collapsed buildings was pushed down into the sea to provide flat land around the waterfront for re-building and most of the buildings in Fethiye date from this time or later. You cannot call Fethiye an attractive town, there is just too much reinforced concrete everywhere, but it has a bustling work-a-day charm to it that grows on you. The market on Fridays behind the waterfront is as good as anywhere with stall upon stall of fruit and vegetables brought in from the rich agricultural land around Fethiye. There is a covered fish market with more variety than elsewhere along the coast, perhaps because the fishing grounds here are not hemmed in by offshore islands as they are further north. And there are stalls selling all manner of agricultural impedimenta from scythes, a tool probably seen here two thousand and more years ago, to rolls of clear polythene for covering greenhouses.

The town has not always been called Fethiye. It was given it's present name

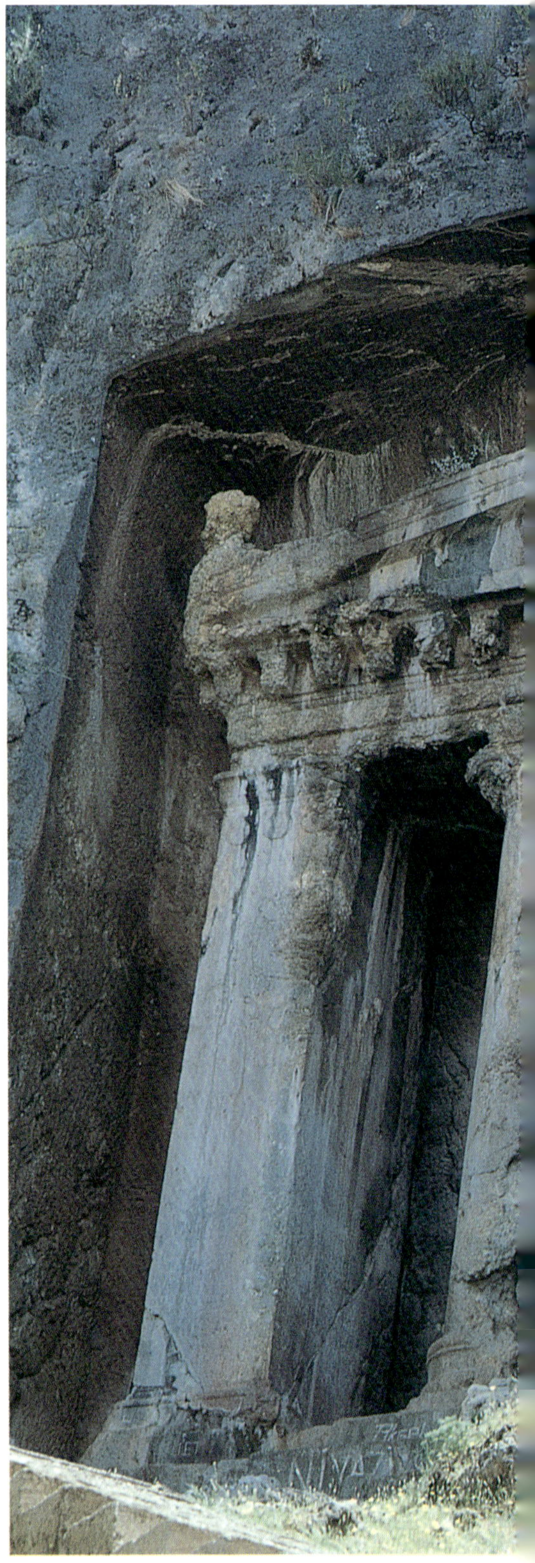

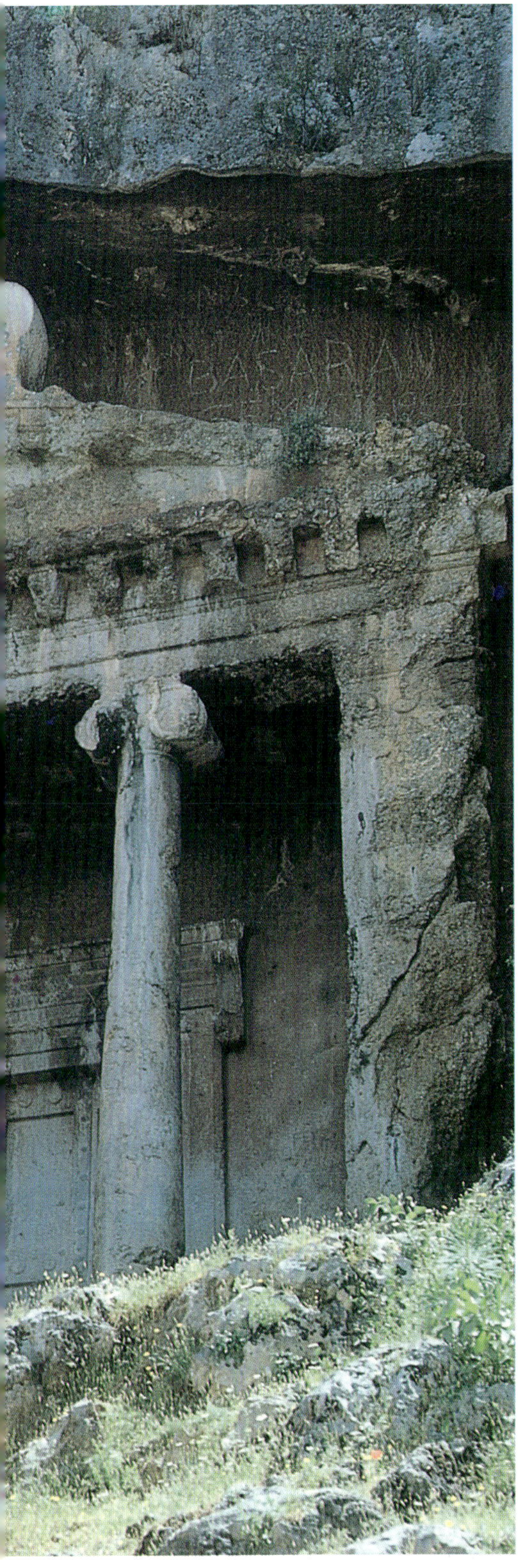

from a famous Turkish aviator, Fethi Bey, who was killed in a crash in the early years of the Republic. Prior to this it was known as Makri, 'the far-off land', and it didn't get very good write-ups from 19th century travellers to it. Dr Clarke recorded in his *Travels in Europe, Asia, and Africa* (1817) that most of the crew on the ship he was travelling on succumbed to malaria at Makri and that he himself "...soon became a striking example of the powerful influence of such air, not only in the fever which then attacked him, but in the temporary privation of the use of his limbs, which continued until he put to sea again." (quoted in Lord Kinross: *Europa Minor*). In the 8th century the place was called Anastasiupolis after the Byzantine emperor Anastasius II, so it must have been of some importance in Byzantine times. As a safe natural harbour it was used to ship timber, valona oak and pine, from the interior, a trade that continued right up into the 20th century. In ancient times it was Telmessus, 'the City of Light', a name that evocatively captures the varied and subtle pastel shades of the setting sun on the mountains around Fethiye.

Of ancient Telmessus virtually nothing remains except a number of rock tombs and sarcophagi. The rock tombs cut into the cliffs that rise up behind the town stand out clearly from seaward. To get to them you must climb up a lot of steps clearly sign-posted from the town. The largest of the temple-tombs is that of Amyntas, an unknown citizen who must have been rich or famous or both to deserve such a grand tomb. It is a temple-tomb in the Ionic order built in the 4th century BC and embellished with a frieze and imitation iron studs on the door to the main chamber. Inside is a chamber with three benches for the dead - as always the interior is a bit of a let-down after the imposing exterior. To the left of this tomb are two other temple-tombs and below them some house-tombs and pigeon-hole tombs.

To the west of the tombs is a Medieval castle, thought to have been built by the

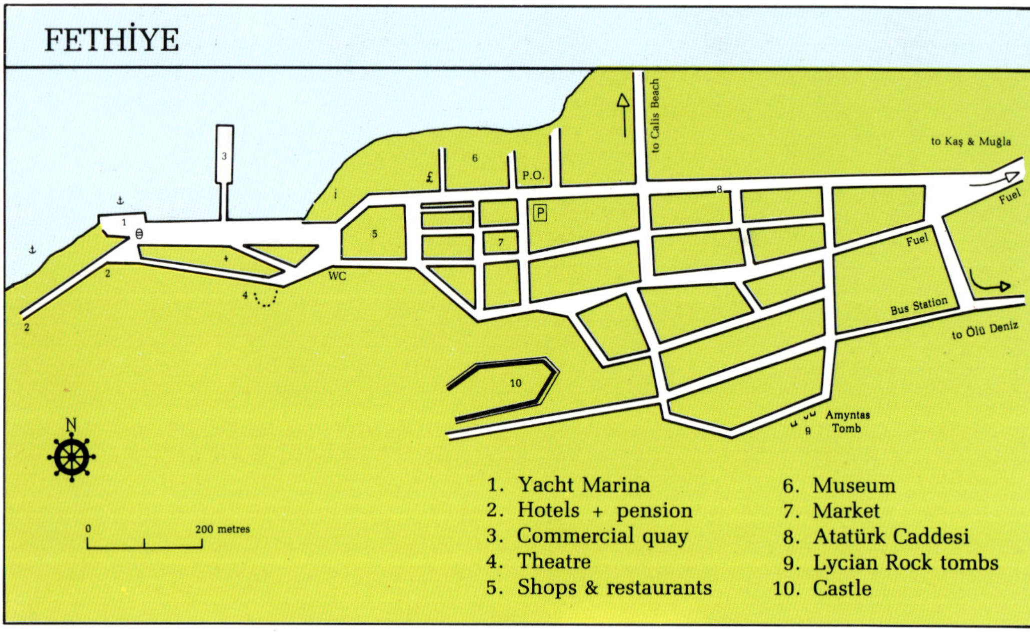

Knights of St John, and possibly modified later. Around the town are numerous sarcophagi with a superb example in front of the town hall. It stands on a heavy stone base and has been carved to represent a two-storey Lycian house with a curved 'Gothic' lid adorned with a relief of rows of warriors. It says much for the Lycian artisans that when the 1957 earthquake flattened most of Fethiye, the lid on the sarcophagus moved slightly, but otherwise it was unaffected. Apparently the sarcophagus used to sit in the sea so the sea level must have risen since antiquity and then receded again. There is literally nothing else to see of ancient Telmessus. Charles Newton in 1838 and Thomas Spratt a little later mentioned a theatre in good order on the west side of the town, but little is left of it today except a depression in the ground. Ancient Telmessus, along with Physicus at Marmaris, was no doubt carted away bit by bit by ship or used by the locals for building materials.

Telmessus seems to have been an independent city in Lycia for some of the time. In the 4th century BC the Lycians besieged it and brought it into the Lycian League. George Bean relates a curious tale of it's recapture in the time of Alexander the Great when it had been taken over by a certain Antipatrides. Nearchus, appointed satrap of the region by Alexander and coincidentally an old friend of Antipatrides, asked a favour of him. "...Nearchus asked permission to leave in the city a number of captive women singers and boys that he had with him. When this was granted, he gave the women's musical instruments to the boys to carry, with daggers concealed in the flute-cases; when the party was inside the citadel, the prisoners' escort took out the weapons and so seized the acropolis. This is described by the historian as a stratagem; others might call it sharp practice." (George Bean: *Lycian Turkey*) Telmessus has been described as a place where divination was practised and Telmessian seers were well known in ancient times. However as George Bean points out, it is likely that these seers came from another city called Telmesssus in Caria, above present day Bodrum, and not from the site at Fethiye. Further down the coast at Patara there was an oracle famous throughout the ancient world.

The Bay of Fethiye, once used to sheltering small coasters and fishing boats, now shelters large numbers of yachts and *gulets*. From Fethiye there are the islands and bays in Scopea Liman a short distance across the gulf, and to the south after the Seven Capes, there is Kalkan, Kaş, and Kekova. Land-based visitors can take day-trips from Fethiye to Scopea Liman. The numbers of yachts in the Fethiye area have prompted the building of a large marina on the western side to the bay and construction has begun on this. The project, modelled on marinas in the south of France and Italy, will provide all facilities and add a touch of class of the bay. With Dalaman Airport less than an hour away it is likely that Fethiye could soon rival Marmaris as a charter boat base when the marina and facilities are complete. For the water-borne visitor Fethiye is the place to organise trips inland to a number of sites otherwise inaccessible from other places along the coast. There are some organised coach tours or local buses can be taken to some of the places. A number of sites like Tlos and Pınara can only be reached by hire-car or jeep.

Around Fethiye

Calis Beach

On the east side of Fethiye Bay, a wide sandy beach stretches for four kilometres around the shore. This is the 'resort' part of the town where wealthy Turks on holiday would come before tourists from overseas arrived. There are numerous hotels and pensions around the beach, but you can still find a patch of sand all to yourself.

Paçariz And Batikkaya Bükü

On the headland forming the west side of Fethiye Bay there are several attractive bays. Paçarız is the bay on the northeast tip. Batıkkaya is a little further around, tucked under a rocky headland with a small islet in the entrance. The latter is entrancing with a good beach and a

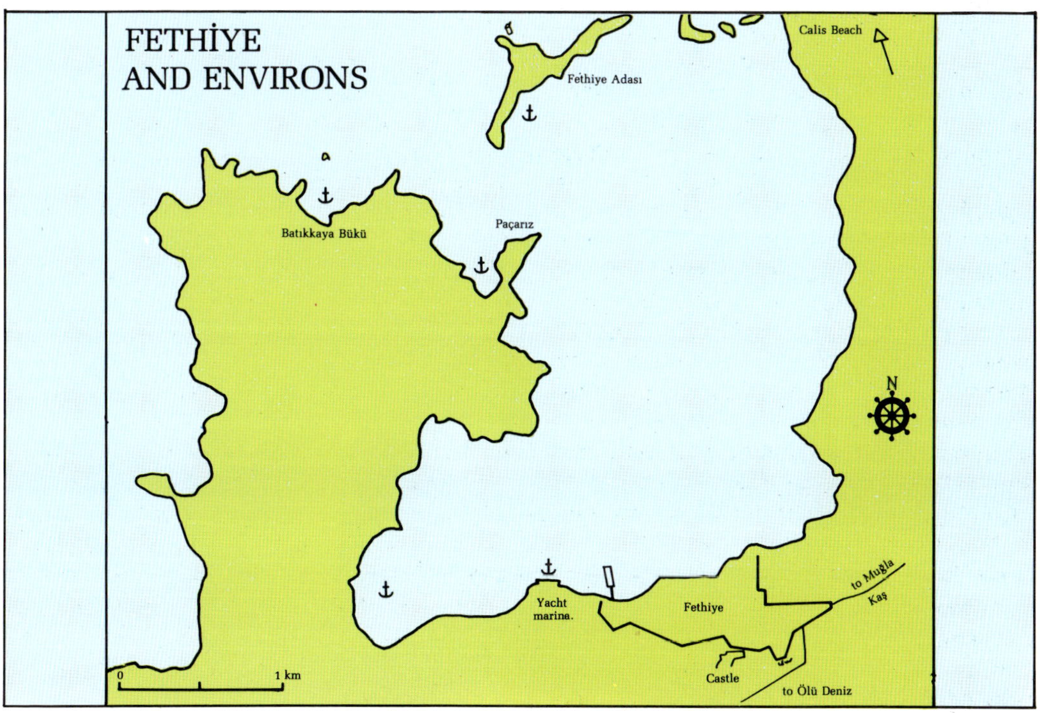

wooded foreshore. Recently a whole villa complex has been built here, a somewhat overpowering development on the simple landscape.

Fethiye Adasi

Across the entrance to Fethiye Bay lies the long skinny island of Fethiye Adası. A boat can be hired to go across to it or a yacht can anchor off on the lee side. There are sandy beaches, around which a number of villas have been built.

Excursions From Fethiye

Tlos

Tlos lies high up on a rocky promontory in the Lycian hinterland. From Kemer the road is sign-posted to the site. The city is unexcavated but there is much to see and the wild setting only enhances the site. From the acropolis hill with a more recent Turkish fort built on top of it you get a view right over the Xanthos valley and towards the mountains to the east. There are numerous rock-tombs cut into the cliff-face including a magnificient temple-tomb with a relief of Bellerophon on his winged horse Pegasus. Bellerophon was the son of King Glaucus of Corinth who was wrongfully exiled, accused of murder and rape, to Lycia. (From Glaucus' blindness to his sons innocence we get the word 'glaucoma'.) In Lycia Bellerophon was set a number of Herculean tasks; to kill the Chimaera, and to do battle with the savage Solymi and the Amazons, which he successfully accomplished with the aid of his winged horse, Pegasus. Thus vindicated, he married the daughter of King Iobates of Lycia and ruled happily ever after. Tlos claimed descent from Bellerophon, hence the relief over the temple-tomb.

Around the flat area below, now cultivated, are the ruins of a stadium,

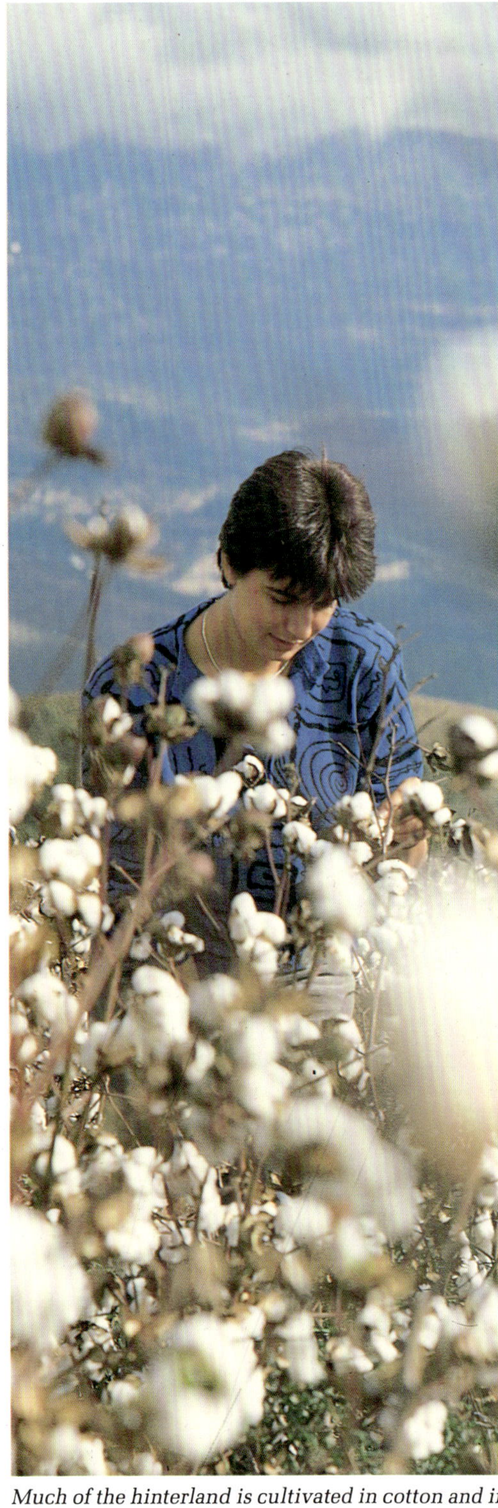

Much of the hinterland is cultivated in cotton and in the late summer and autumn the fields are busy with cotton pickers.

gymnasium, a baths complex, and a theatre with carved actors masks on the stage building. It is a long trip from Fethiye to Tlos, a five hour return journey, but well worth it to see this once grand city in a now remote and wild landscape.

PINARA

Pınara lies off the main road south from Fethiye, but the road to the site itself is a rough one. The main attraction of the place is the site, a rocky promontory some 600 metres (2000 feet) high with nearly perpendicular cliffs which are literally honey-combed with rock-tombs. Of the city itself little remains except a well-preserved theatre and the foundations of numerous buildings. The rock-tombs in the cliffs, nearly all of which are pigeon-hole tombs, are inaccessible and must have been constructed by workers dangling on ropes from above. A number of house-tombs lower down can be reached from the base of the cilff.

SIDYMA

Further along the main road through the Xanthos valley there is a turn-off to Sidyma. Like the road to Pınara, this road is also very rough. The Turkish village of Dodurga now stands in and on the site of ancient Sidyma and some of the ancient material has been used in the construction of the village. Virtually all the ruins here are of Roman origin: a baths complex, a small temple, a stoa, part of the theatre, and the inevitable necropolis with rock tombs and numerous sarcophagi. The city remained important into the Byzantine era as evidenced by a substantial Byzantine fort on the acropolis hill.

XANTHOS

Of all the Lycian cities, Xanthos was always pre-eminent and indeed the term Xanthian was often synonomous with Lycian. It was the capital of Lycia, the richest and most powerful of the cities, and

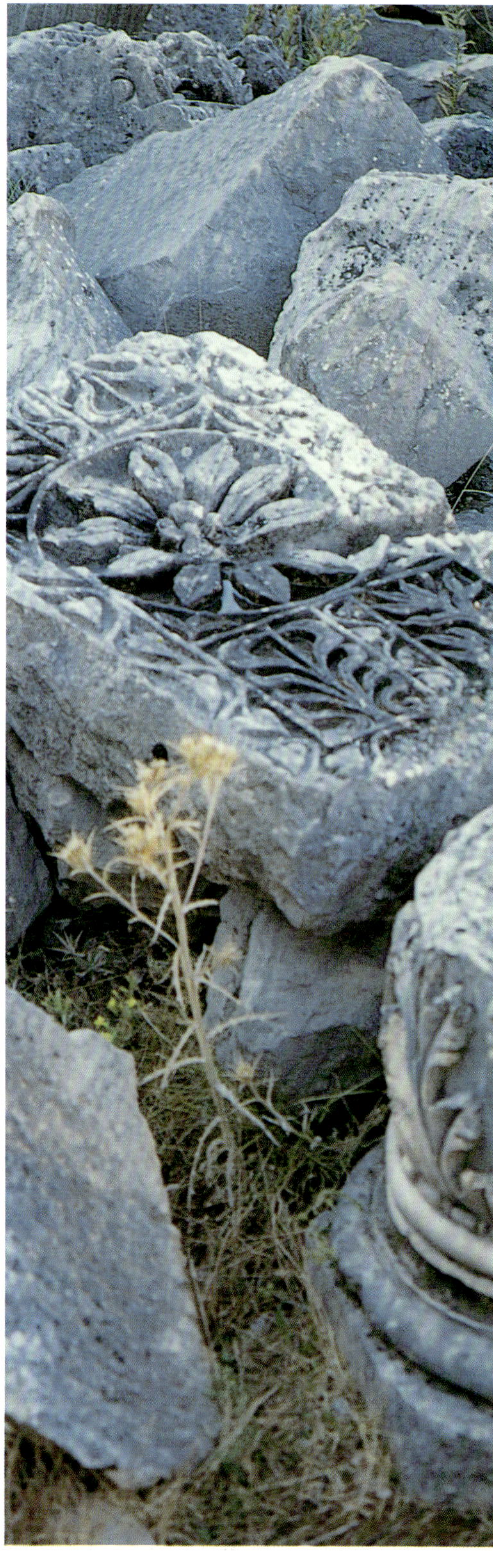

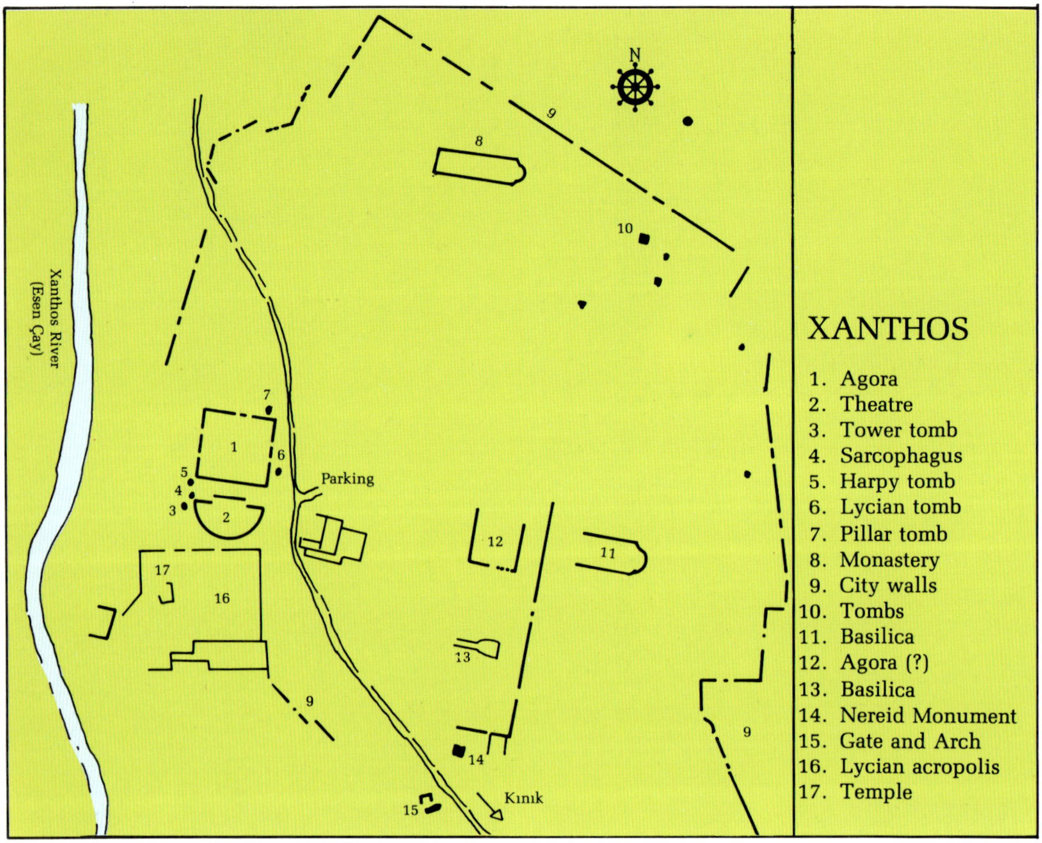

a city with a tragic history. It lies right on the main road through the Xanthos valley at the little agricultural village of Kınık. A gravel road leads up to the site where you can park opposite the Agora. The custodian of the site will probably wander out to sell you a ticket to see the ruins and then retreat to the shade to snooze off again.

The site of the city on a low hillock is not as impressive as at Pınara or Tlos, but has the advantage of a view out over the flat land of the Xanthos valley on all sides. The Xanthos River, now the Eşen Çay and the largest river in Lycia, flows close to the city on the west side providing ample fresh water. Xanthos means 'yellow', and is the Greek name for the river and the city - in Lycian it was called Arnna, but was not generally called by this name. The city is mentioned by Homer in the *Iliad* and by Herodotus and later by Appian and Plutarch who relate the details of the two tragic mass suicides I have already described in the section on the Lycians in the last chapter. How any Xanthians remained after committing mass suicide twice in 400 years and burning the city to the ground is a mystery, but there were evidently a few survivors and no doubt an influx of new Lycian blood to rebuild and re-populate the city for it to again resume it's role as capital of Lycia.

The site itself is much damaged, largely as a result of Sir Charles Fellows and the British navy's wholesale export of some quite remarkable friezes and sculptures in 1842, much of which can now be seen in the Xanthian Room of the British Museum. No doubt the locals also helped themselves to the building materials so conveniently left behind by the Lycians. Despite the damage done by Fellows and the navy, there is still much to see. Most of the buildings are of Roman origin, but dotted all around the site, as if carefully preserved by the Romans, are Lycian monuments. Opposite the car-park is the theatre and the Agora. Just above the theatre are two Lycian tombs. The one on the north is called the Harpy tomb, from a relief on it showing bird-women carrying off children in their arms, interpreted by Fellows as the screaming Harpies described by Homer. This interpretation is now thought to be incorrect and the figures probably represent those other bird-women, the Sirens, carrying off the souls of the dead in the form of children. The original friezes were carried off by Fellows, but plaster casts have been made by the Turkish authorities and it is these that can be seen today. The other tomb is a sarcophagus standing on a stunted pillar, the pillar itself being hollow and a tomb. On the other side of the Agora there is a tall obelisk, covered in Lycian script and the longest Lycian inscription known, though exactly what it says is not known as the Lycian language has not been properly deciphered yet. The obelisk is yet another tomb, though again of a novel type, underlining the importance of this city.

The dead of Xanthos and locals from Kınık.

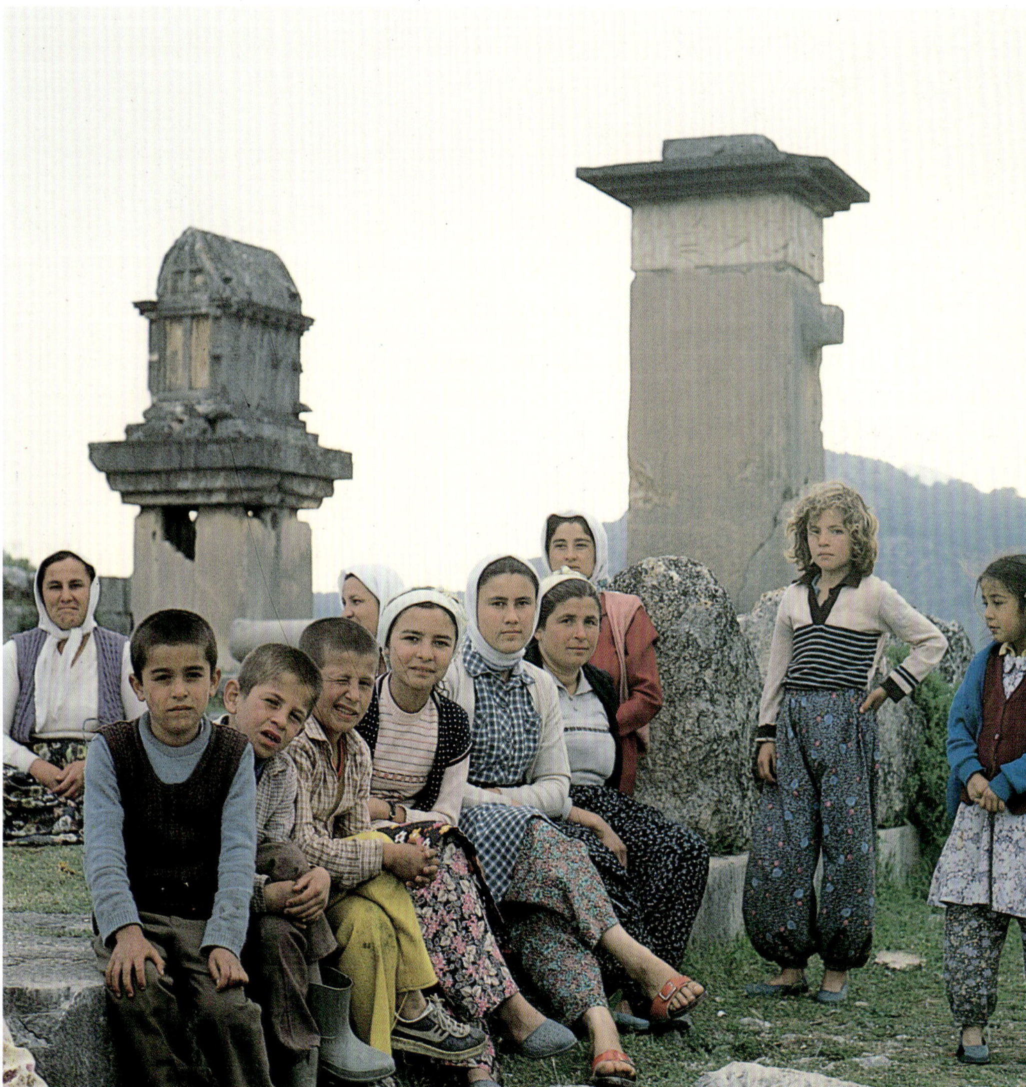

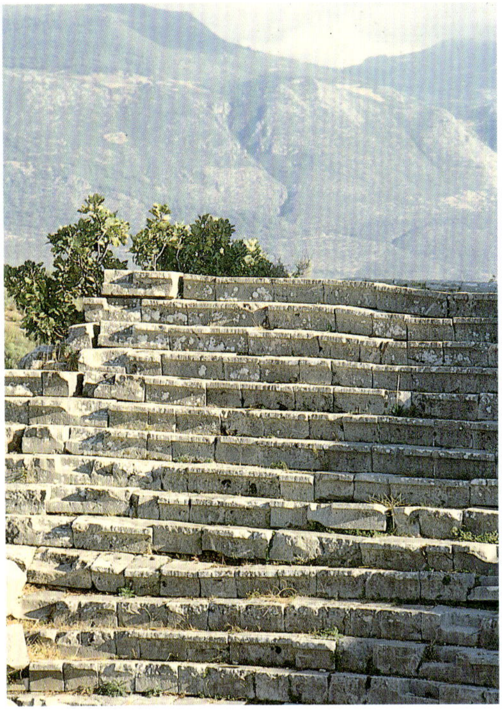

Theatre. Xanthos

Further up the hill the remains of a Byzantine monastery built over a large Roman temple can be seen. Close to the car-park another Byzantine basilica, with extensive mosaics, was built over what was the residential area. Scattered over the hillside are numerous rock-tombs and sarcophagi, enough to keep your average tomb enthusiast happy for days.

On the road down to the village from the car-park are the remains of the southern gate to the city and a Roman arch. Just above here sat the Nereid Monument, the one that now graces the British Museum courtesy of Fellows and the British navy, though it is likely, as with the Elgin Marbles, that the British Museum and the British government have not heard the last of it yet. Xanthos is easily reached from Fethiye and there are organised excursions to the site. Alternatively you can take a bus or *dolmuş* to Kınık from Fethiye or Kaş. The rather ramshackle village doesn't offer a lot, though there is one excellent *kebab* restaurant, so long as you don't expect any choice, on the main road.

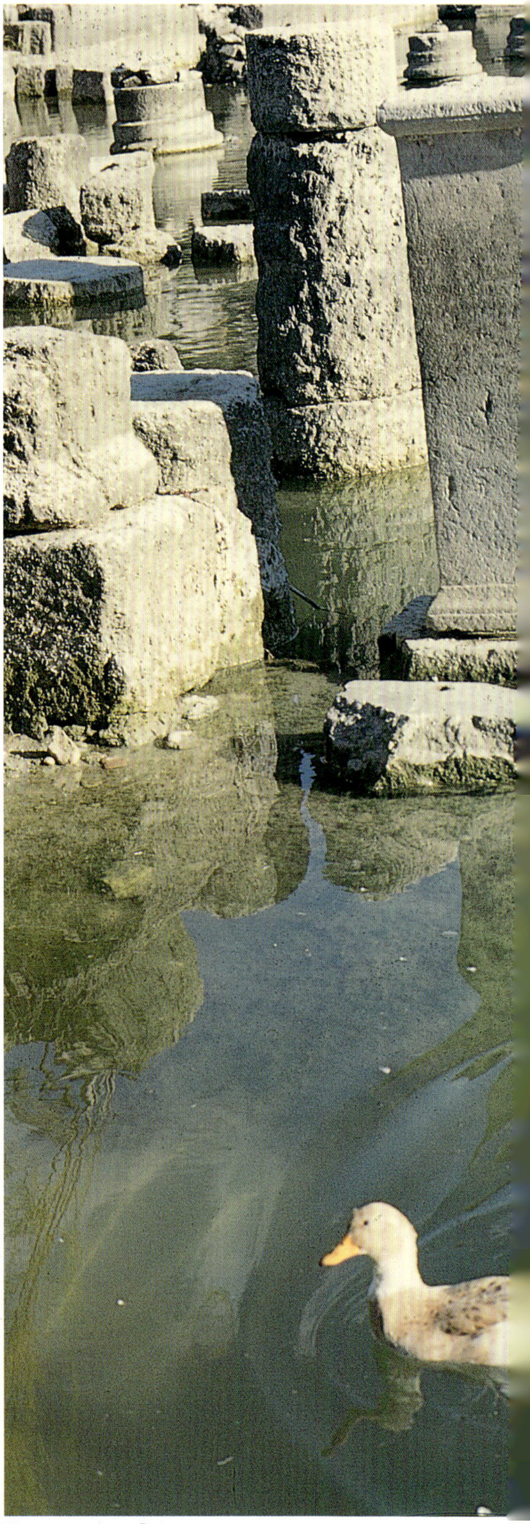

Watery ruins. Letoum.

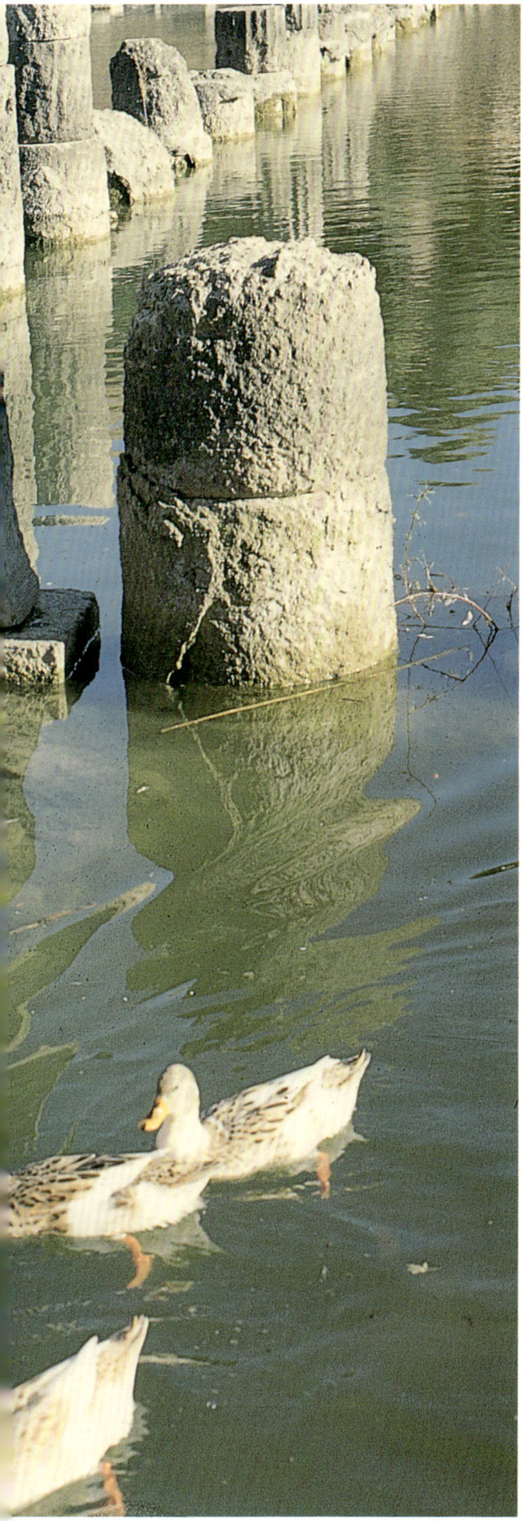

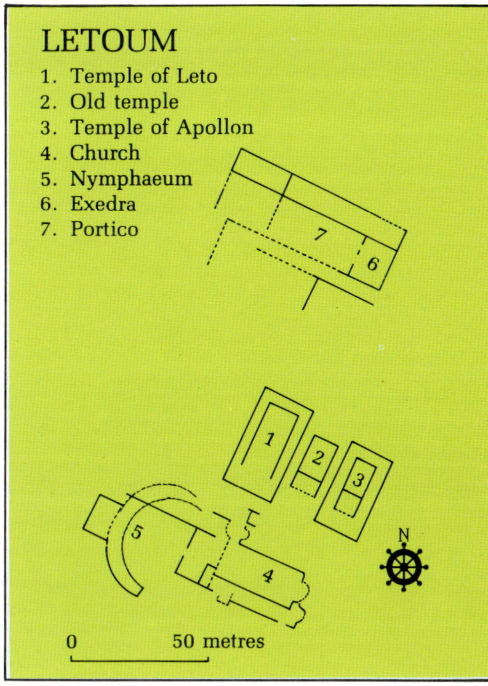

LETOUM

Just before you get to Kınık and Xanthos on the main road from Fethiye, there is a turn-off sign-posted to Letoum (Letoon). A short drive along a good road you come to a small village with plastic-covered greenhouses covering every square metre of ground. After zig-zagging through the greenhouses you come to one of the most delightful sites in Lycia. Letoum was a sanctuary precinct and not a city as such, though it did have a settlement around it. This was the spiritual heart of Xanthos and of Lycia, the federal sanctuary to the Lycian League and the place where national festivals were held. The sanctuary was dedicated to Leto, the national deity of Lycia, and several tales tell of how and why she came to this place. Leto was loved by Zeus, one of the many who put a fire-cracker up his skirt, and one of many hated by Zeus' wife Hera for doing so. Leto was driven out by Hera and exiled. She wandered far and wide, including Asia Minor, and finally arrived on Delos where she gave birth to Apollo and Artemis. During her travels in Lycia, she went to quench her thirst at a fountain, but before she could drink local herdsmen came and drove her away. After the birth of Apollo and Artemis it is said she returned and turned the churlish herdsmen into frogs - certainly there are a lot of frogs in the sunken ruins of Letoum. Another tale tells of how she was guided by wolves to the Xanthos River to assuage her thirst. From the Greek 'lykos' for wolf, the name 'Lycia' evolved.

There is no doubt that Letoum was a major sanctuary. There are no less than three temples side by side. The site was not excavated until the 1950's and most of the foundations are now partially underwater, lending a watery tranquility to the site. Frogs happily croak away, terrapins sun themselves on the steps of the portico, and a family of ducks paddle around the submerged northern stoa. Of the three temples, only the foundations remain, while to the south there is a large nymphaeum, partially underwater, and to the north a stoa, also underwater. Over the back is a theatre in good condition. In the centre of the Temple of Apollo, one of the three temples, there is an unusual Lycian mosaic of a lyre, the sun, and a bow and arrow - the only surviving Lycian mosaic known. If, as is normally the case, the custodian seeks you out when you arrive, he will show you where to find the mosaic.

KAYA

This ruined town is an entirely different beast from the Lycian ruins as it dates not from thousands of years ago, but from a mere hundred. The ruined town built over the sides of a valley away from the sea was populated by Greeks until the 1923 exchange of populations between Greece and Turkey which left Kaya deserted. It is a poignant reminder of those troubled times, all the more so for being deserted now when it was so obviously once a prosperous large town. A few crops are grown around the town and the

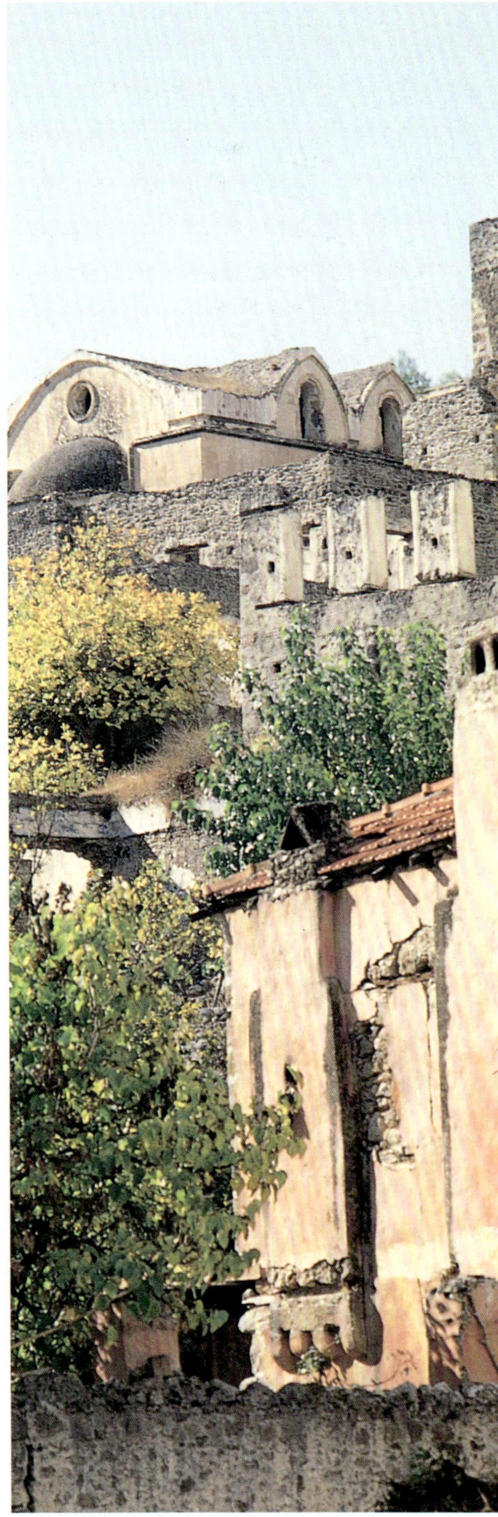

Kaya. Deserted since 1923.

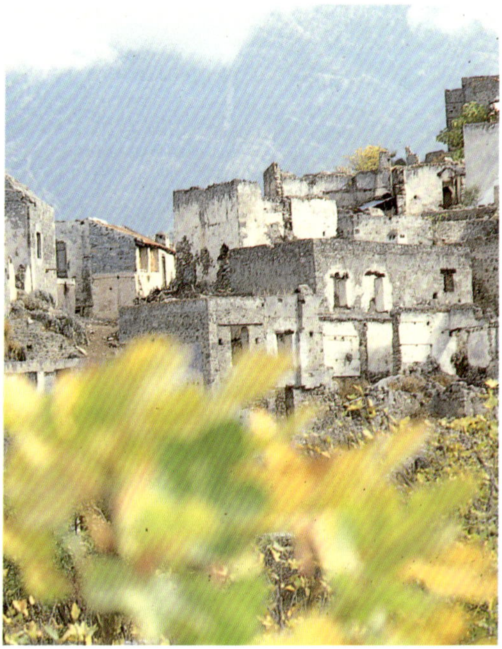

decaying buildings make handy ready-made folds for sheep and goats, but the small Turkish village nearby is a poor relation to what Kaya once was. There are two large churches though the murals are sadly defaced. It is interesting that the town is entirely hidden from the sea, a legacy of the piracy that afflicted this coast even in the 19th century.

You can reach Kaya by taking the road to Ölü Deniz, a road sign-posted but not easily spotted on the road out of Fethiye, and then continuing for a short distance until a turn-off sign-posted to Kaya. The track, adequate for a car, runs through the forest until the valley of Kaya is seen below. Coach excursions run from Fethiye. A more precarious but passable road continues on from Kaya to Gemiler. By contrast the road to Ölü Deniz is a good paved road, despite it's somewhat pot-holed start from Fethiye; the trip to Ölü Deniz taking around twenty minutes.

19th CENTURY TRAVELLERS

In the early 19th century a remarkable group of British travellers explored this part of Asia Minor and identified many of the sites scattered around the wild landscape. These early travellers had to cope not only with inhospitable terrain over which they rode or walked when it got too rough for the horses, but also with bands of brigands, wily pashas, malaria, smallpox, and cholera. Thomas Spratt and Edward Forbes were accompanied on their trip through Lycia by E.T. Daniell, a young clergyman who was to study the antiquities of the area. Daniell stayed behind after Spratt and Forbes left to rejoin the 'Beacon', and fell ill and died. Spratt himself fell ill of the same disease en route to his ship and nearly died; the disease left him debilitated for years. Captain Beaufort while surveying the Cilician coast in 1812 was severely wounded when some Turkish soldiers opened fire on the ship's boats. A midshipman was killed and for a while it was thought that Beaufort would have to go to Malta for treatment. Fortunately he recovered. That he and others did survive is remarkable given some of the cures of the time for the maladies. For diarrhoea ***The Travellers Medical and Surgical Guide*** *of 1888 advises the use of a lead and opium mixture and for boils Baker suggests the use of a paste made of gunpowder and sulphur. On a lighter note Lord and Baines in their* ***Shifts and Expedients of Camp Life*** *(1876) suggest the following treatment for blisters:*

"It not unfrequently happens that the feet of those not thoroughly accustomed to hard tramping will

become blistered. When the eggs of either poultry or wild birds are to be obtained, it is a good plan to break one or two, according to their size, into each shoe before starting in the morning."

The thought of these carly travellers tramping over the countryside with eggy shoes is an amusing one.

Between 1810 and 1812 Captain Francis Beaufort was engaged in surveying harbours and anchorages along the Turkish coast for the Admiralty. On todays Admiralty chart 241, 'Anchorages on the South Coast of Turkey', most of the plans are from Beaufort's original survey and apart from obvious man-made changes, the construction of roads, hotels, houses, chimneys, and a number of artificial harbours, his meticulous surveys are still accurate. Beaufort, in the mould of the times, was an amateur historian, archaeologist, and naturalist, and while on his tour of duty he explored the interior and wrote an entertaining book on the region: **Karamania**, *'...or a brief description of the south coast of Asia Minor and of the remains of antiquities collected during a survey of that coast in the years 1811 and 1812.' He had an eye for detail and for a good tale, and the book is packed with interesting description and anecdote. After his tour of duty Beaufort went on to become Hydrographer for the Admiralty and was largely responsible for re-organising it and making hydrographic surveys and charts an important part of the Admiralty's business. He is of course the same Beaufort that invented the Beaufort wind scale for wind and sea conditions that still bears his name and that is used to this day.*

Sir Charles Fellows, Thomas Spratt, and Edward Forbes together

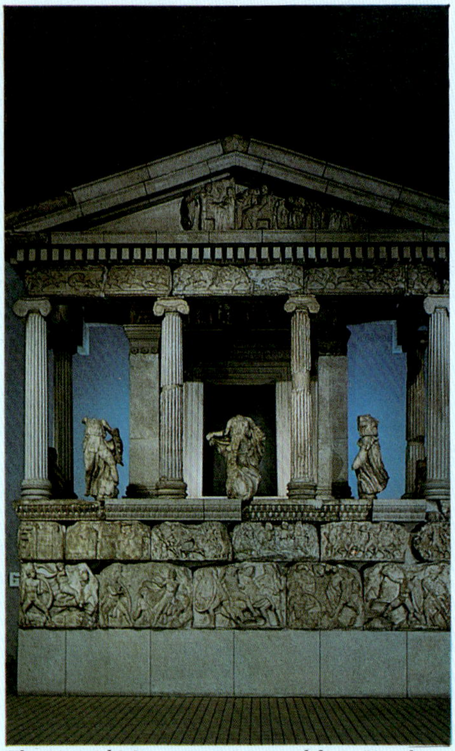

The Nereid Monument removed from Xanthos by Sir Charles Fellows in the 19th century (BOX: 19th Travellers).

'rediscovered' Lycia in the 1840's. Charles Fellows was the British Consul in Asia Minor in the 1830's and 40's and during his time there he explored and examined a large number of ancient sites. He was largely responsible for revealing the splendours of Ephesus and Cnidos to the interested western world, but his greatest accomplishment was the rediscovery of Lycia. On horse and foot he visited many of the sites of Lycian cities and proved beyond doubt that Lycia as a separate entity and culture existed. With the help of the British navy he carried off many fine pieces of sculpture and entire friezes to Britain, most of which are in the British Museum. He didn't mess around and even the huge lion, all eleven tons of it, at Cnidos, was crated

up and shipped off. In Lycia his prime objective was Xanthos and here, with the help of British sailors under the command of Spratt, he dismantled and removed some of the finest Lycian monuments known and shipped them on the navy's ships to Britain. The most well known is the Nereid Monument displayed in the Nereid Room of the British Museum. Freya Stark, musing on the thought of British sailors in this remote part of the world wonders whether they played cricket here in the camp they set up under the ruins of the ancient city, and if so was this the first time cricket was played in Asia Minor. At any rate it didn't catch on in the way football has in modern Turkey. Fellows travels in Turkey resulted in a number of volumes on his discoveries, much of which was collected together in an abridged edition: **Travels and Research in Asia Minor** *(1852).*

After the statues and friezes from Xanthos had been loaded on the 'Beacon', Spratt, Edward Forbes, a naturalist on board the ship, and E.T. Daniell, a young clergyman, remained behind for a journey into the interior. This was not as unusual as it might seem. The commander of the 'Beacon', Thomas Graves, actively encouraged his junior officers and surveyors to look beyond the coasts they surveyed and to take an interest in the interior, in the history and culture of a region, and especially in ancient history. The trio of Spratt, Forbes, and Daniell visited many sites inland and their travels are recorded in a book Spratt and Forbes wrote: **Travels in Lycia, Milyas, and the Cibyratis** *(1847). As I have mentioned, Daniell died of fever in Antalya and Spratt very nearly died on his journey back to rejoin his ship. They were an eccentric bunch, these early travellers. Edward Forbes, the naturalist, is recorded in a later memoir as a colourful character roaming 'like a native' around the countryside on his forays:*

"In these rambles it was his delight to encase himself in an old shooting-jacket, full of pockets; his long hair, surmounted by a "Jim Crow" hat, hung down to his neck; his feet were shod with a pair of primitive country boots, into which he tucked the loose ends of his trousers; a botanical vasculum was slung across his shoulders, and a stout hammer supplied the place of a walking stick. Thus attired, he wandered over the hills and valleys... dined and danced with the natives, pitched his tent on the hill-sides, dredged among the bays and inlets, and plied his hammer along its shores". **Memoir of Forbes** *Wilson & Geikie.*

These travellers are not as well known as the likes of Byron, Lord Elgin, Hobhouse, or Edward Lear, but in their own fashion they were more adventurous and contributed much to

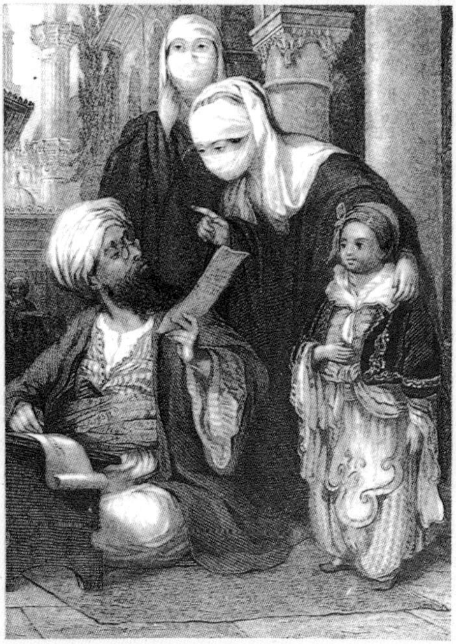

our knowledge of Asia Minor and ancient civilizations, even if on hindsight we can criticise their scavenging of ancient sites. There were other later travellers and in the 20th century the redoubtable Freya Stark travelled around Lycia by jeep, on horseback, and by foot exploring Lycia and following in the footsteps of Alexander the Great to give us that travel classic ***Alexander's Path*** *(1958). Likewise George Bean, who I have already talked about in chapter 2, explored and recorded sites in Lycia to give us the definitive books on the Graeco-Roman sites along the Turkish coast. Today the region is comparitively easy of access, at least to the major sites, though there are still small demes tucked away in the mountain fastness of the interior or perched away from the main roads on the rocky coast. Beaufort might have envied those on board yachts and gulets with reliable engines and Fellows would have certainly envied the good roads and new pensions. In his journal he offered this advice to future travellers:*

"A tent is the first requisite, the old cities and places of the greatest interest being frequently distant from the modern towns or khans; and a good tent makes the traveller quite independent of the state of health of the town. It is desirable that the tent should be of waterproof material".

Journal 1839 *Sir Charles Fellows*

GEMİLER

On the south side of the great craggy lump that forms the eastern side of the Gulf of Fethiye, lies the island and anchorages of Gemiler. This reef-strewn place could only be reached by boat until the new road was cut around the sides of Karadağ from Kaya, and given the state of the road, the trip by boat is still much the easiest way to get here. The attractions of Gemiler are two fold. It is an isolated wild place with a number of small coves just right for swimming and relaxing in. Several restaurants have opened around the shores, but these detract little from the place - plans for more large-scale development may not be so benign.

The other attraction of this spot is Gemiler Island lying a short distance off the coast. On it are the remains of a sizeable Byzantine settlement and though many of the buildings are in ruins, there is still sufficient to see, including some marvellous mosaic floors, to make a ramble ashore worthwhile. According to local folk-lore the island was a pirate stronghold at some time and given it's location on this

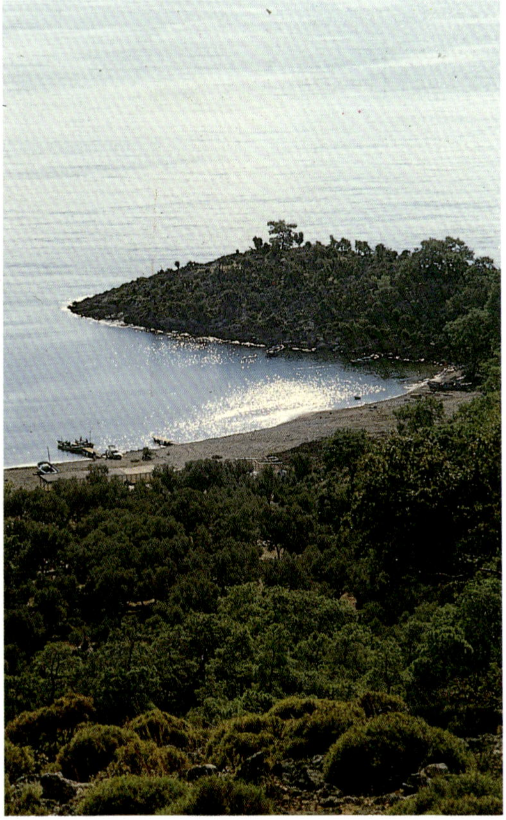

Cove. Gemiler.

lonely bit of coast, where a look-out on the high hills above could signal the approach of ships going north or south, it would seem a likely location for the thinking pirate to base himself at (Gemiler). At one time the island was said to be ruled by a queen who had skin extremely sensitive to the sun. An albino perhaps? A covered road was built from her palace on the top of the island down to the sea so she could walk out of the sun to the waters edge for a swim. Parts of an arched road still exist so perhaps there is some truth in the story. Land-based visitors can take a local boat from Ölü Deniz for a trip to Gemiler, a better choice than the road. Charter yachts and *gulets* can stay longer and sample the delights of the place at leisure.

Ölü Deniz

Ölü Deniz means the 'Dead Sea', not because it is dead like it's namesake in Israel, but because it is so enclosed and protected from the sea that no swell penetrates inside. There may be a storm in the sea just outside while in Ölü Deniz it will be comparitively calm. The setting is spectacular with mountains rising sheer from the sea to a 1000 metres (3300 feet) and more. A narrow strip of blinding white sand lies between the sea and the mountains. Thick pine grows wherever it can get a hold on the rocky slopes, often growing out at precarious angles, and along the narrow coastal strip, providing welcome shade from the sun. A number of hotels and restaurants have been built around the shores, but someone somewhere with some pull has restricted development so it does not violate the magnificient surroundings.

Ölü Deniz, the 'Dead Sea'.

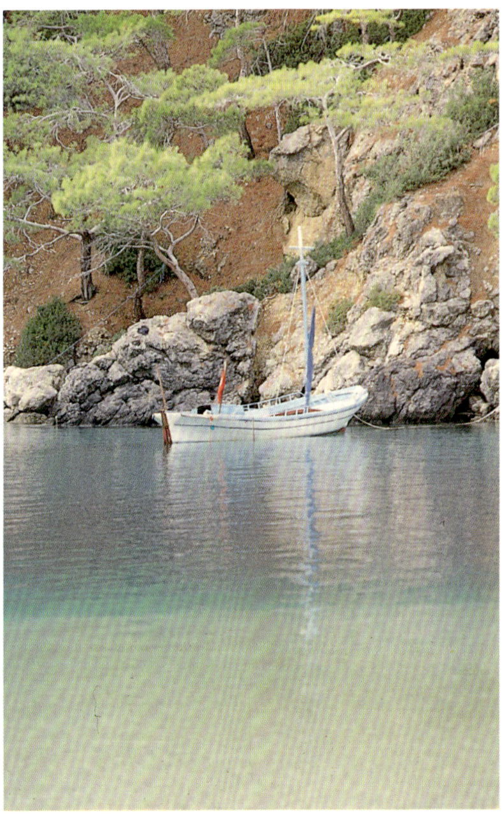

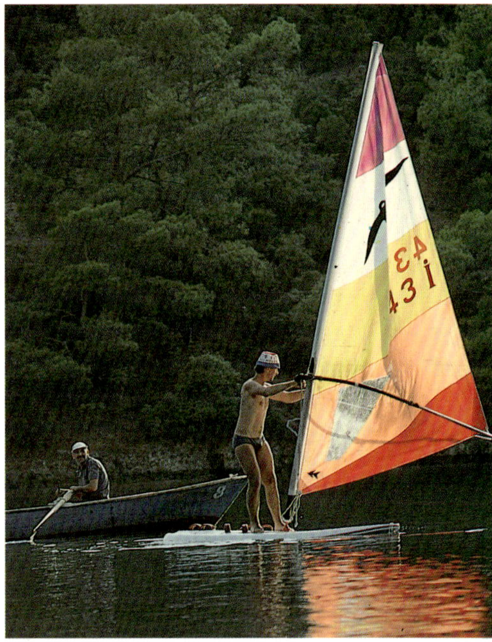

Ölü Deniz, the 'Dead Sea'.

Until 1984 yachts and *gulets* could anchor in Ölü Deniz, but since then entry has been prohibited and the only anchorage allowed is outside the entrance in a relatively unsheltered and sometimes dangerous bight on the rocky coast. This stern injunction on the use of Ölü Deniz was imposed by the Ministry of Culture and Tourism to stop the bay being polluted. Being a virtully land-locked bay

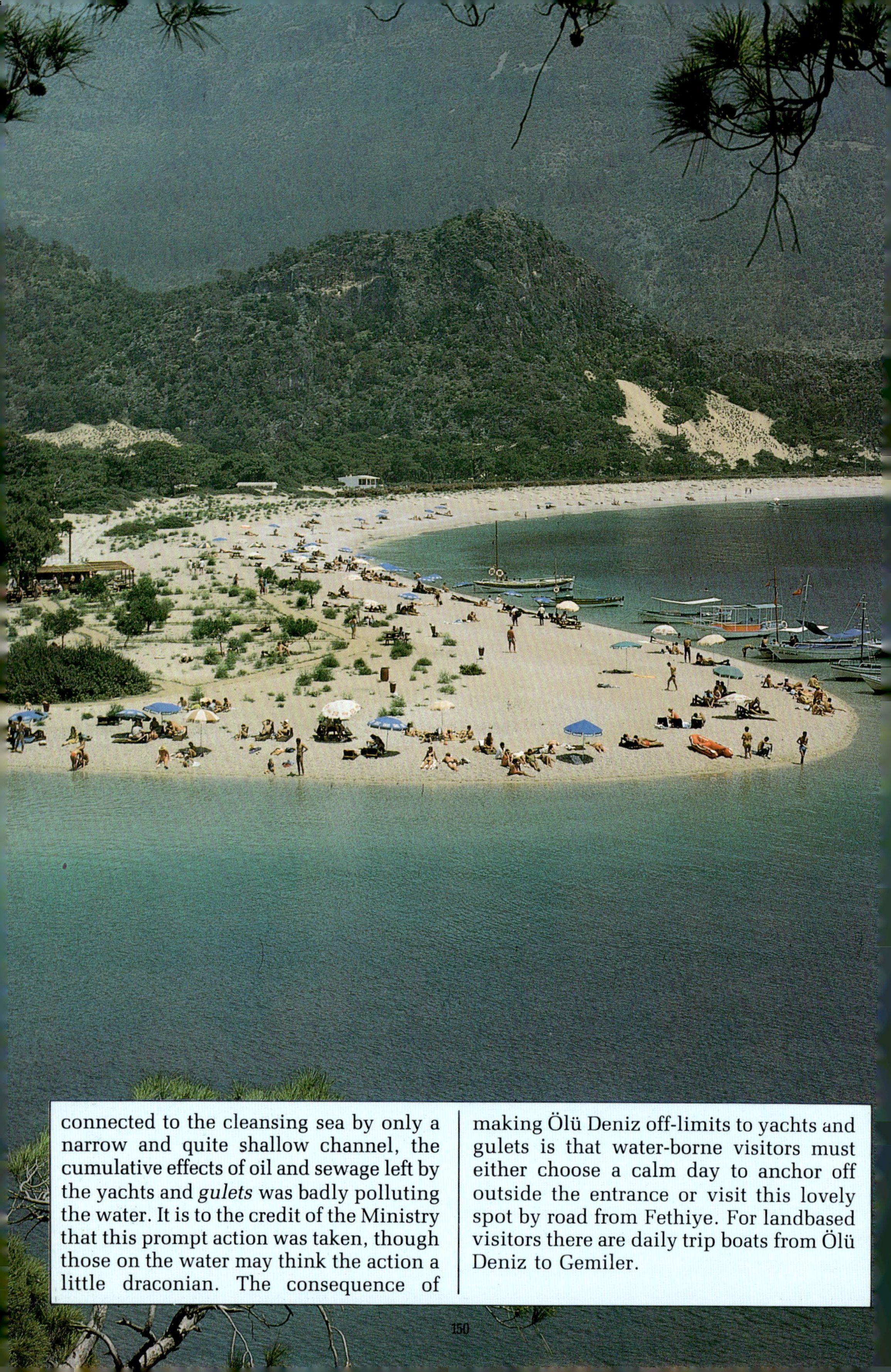

connected to the cleansing sea by only a narrow and quite shallow channel, the cumulative effects of oil and sewage left by the yachts and *gulets* was badly polluting the water. It is to the credit of the Ministry that this prompt action was taken, though those on the water may think the action a little draconian. The consequence of making Ölü Deniz off-limits to yachts and gulets is that water-borne visitors must either choose a calm day to anchor off outside the entrance or visit this lovely spot by road from Fethiye. For landbased visitors there are daily trip boats from Ölü Deniz to Gemiler.

YÜRÜKS: THE NOMADS

Throughout the coastal region of Turkey you will come across groups of nomadic herders, the yürüks, who in the winter come down to the pastures by the coast and in the summer, when the sun shrivels the vegetation on the coast, travel up into the mountains to the yaylas, the high mountain plateaus and valleys where there is sufficient grass and fodder for the animals until the autumn rains again regenerate the pastures on the coast. In Lycia you will see a few of the traditional black goat-hair tents, usually covered in plastic sheets nowadays, of the truly nomadic yürüks, though many now have more permanent houses on the coast and in the mountains. In other parts of Turkey there are larger numbers of these nomads, who carry everything with them on donkeys and camels along with their flocks of sheep and goats. In the Xanthos valley I remember seeing a donkey loaded down with a tent and kitchen utensils, the whole caboodle including the family cat which was installed in one of the saddelbags and getting a free ride to the next camp. To control the large flocks of sheep and guard their property, a large breed of dog is employed and these animals can be ferocious beasts - I for one keep well clear of them. They are said to have been bred in the east to take on the wolves that used to, and sometimes still do, attack the flocks, and I can believe these large dogs could successfully take on a wolf.

Though the life of the yürüks is becoming less nomadic in modern Turkey and they are losing many of their traditions, they still make superb kilims with patterns and colours particular to the clan and region they

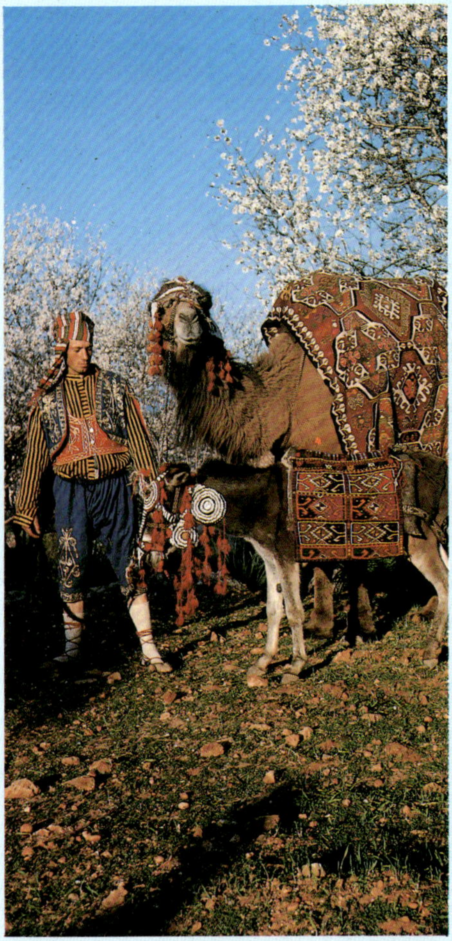

belong to. Some vegetable dyes are used, but in common with carpets and kilims woven elsewhere in Turkey, synthetic dyes have been used for a long time now. The dress of these nomadic herdmen has changed and though you still see some in the black shaggy goats-hair capes, more and more have adopted western style dress. The women more traditionally wear 'şalvar', the baggy trousers and short jacket, usually in a floral material, and on their heads a scarf cleverly arranged and knotted so it looks almost like a hat.

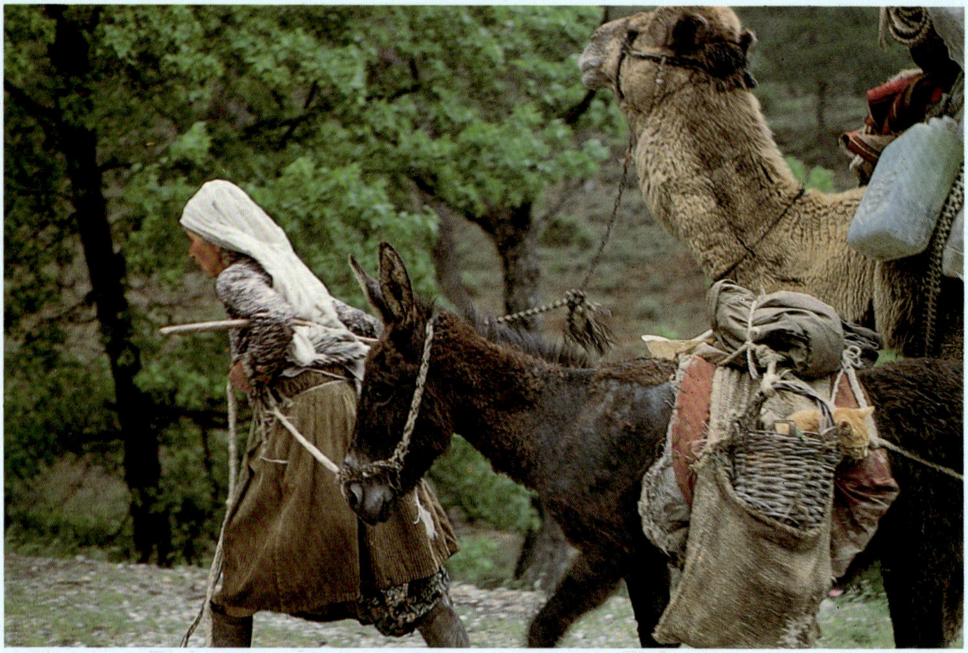

Yürük household, complete with cat, on the move (BOX: Yürüks)

The yürüks are not gypsies as is sometimes suggested. Their origins are probably from the indigenous peoples of Anatolia and it is likely they were here before the Turkoman tribes migrated down from the north. They do not wander the length and breadth of Turkey, but have definite routes and areas in the lowlands and highlands bordering the coast. They are a proud people who have to some extent been left behind in rapidly modernising Turkey and their traditional routes and rights would appear to have been overlooked as roads are cut through the country and property is snapped up by developers.

YEDİ BURUNLAR

The name means the 'Seven Capes' and refers to the series of high bold capes that jut into the sea south of Ölü Deniz. The mountains here drop spectacularly into the sea, effectively cutting off the interior and the Xanthos valley that the main road passes through until it meets the sea again at Kalkan. These capes have a nasty reputation, a sort of Turkish 'Cape Horn' for this stretch of the coast, and yachts and *gulets* going north will often leave Kalkan early in the morning to get past them before the *meltem* starts blowing around midday.

Looking out across the sand dunes to the sea at Patara.

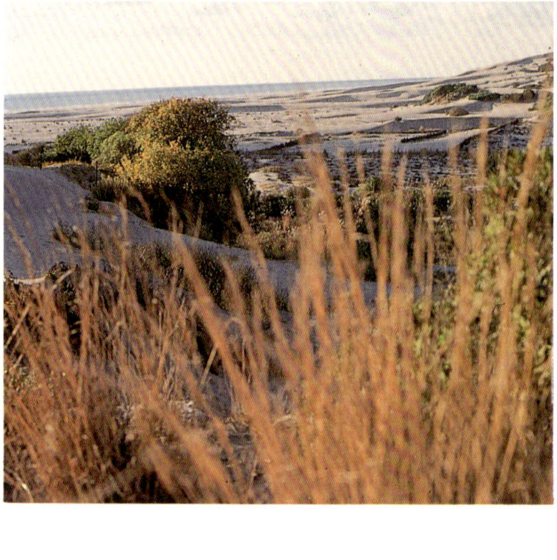

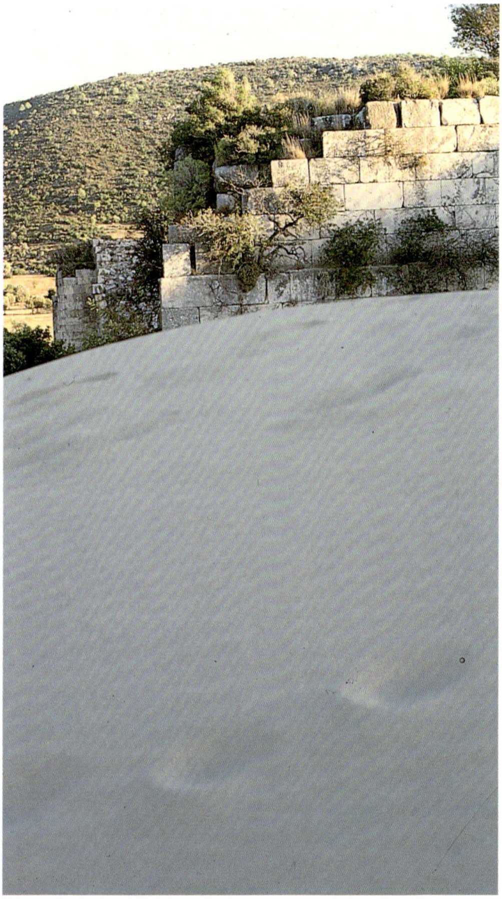

Sand dunes half covering the theatre at Patara.

After the seven capes there is a long sandy beach with sand dunes extending inland for some distance. At the southern end of the beach lies Patara near the mouth of the Eşen Çay, the ancient's Xanthos River, with much of the site covered by the shifting sands.

PATARA

The ruins at Patara are some of the most evocative in Lycia. Sand dunes cover most of the site, half-filling the theatre cavea, heaped up over massive stone blocks, and totally burying the harbour entrance and moles. What was the most important harbour in Lycia is now covered in sand and more than Caunos or Ephesus, it illustrates the fate of a harbour built at the mouth of a river and thus prone to silting, and the inevitable demise of the city attached to the harbour.

Patara was Lycian in origin, it's Lycian name of 'Patara' has been found on inscriptions and coins, and was probably founded around the 6th century BC. Herodotus mentions it in connection with the Oracle of Apollo that was practiced here and which was said for a time to rival that at Delphi - at least in Asia Minor. The origin of the oracle was attributed to Danaus, King of Argos, who was told by Apollo to search the world until he found a bull and a wolf fighting each other. He was to build a temple to whichever was the victor; a temple to Poseidon if the bull won or a temple to Apollo if the wolf won. The wolf was victorious and Danaus built a Temple to Apollo at Patara. In truth this and other eponymous founders were probably later inventions for a small harbour-city that grew as Xanthos prospered. Patara was in effect the port of the capital and it's importance only overshadowed Xanthos and other inland cities when it was made the seat of the Roman provincial governor during the last years before the birth of Christ. Later it was at Patara that the Apostle Paul, that intrepid traveller and fervent evangelist, changed ships en route to Jerusalem at the end of his third missionary journey. Later in the 4th century AD Patara was honoured as the birthplace of Bishop Nicholas of Myra, the saint who was metamorphised into our Father Christmas.

From seawards little can be seen of the ruins as rolling sand-dunes have formed between the sea and the site of the city. It can be visited from Kalkan by taxi or from Fethiye. The road to it is clearly sign-posted off the main road and you follow it, over a bridge across the present course of the Eşen Çay, through a ravine-like pass until you get to a parking area by the theatre. Before this you pass an arch with an inscription to Mettius Modestus, governor of Lycia-Pamphylia around 100 AD. At the turn-off to the theatre the road leads on to a restaurant by the beach. From the theatre, half-filled with sand, you can

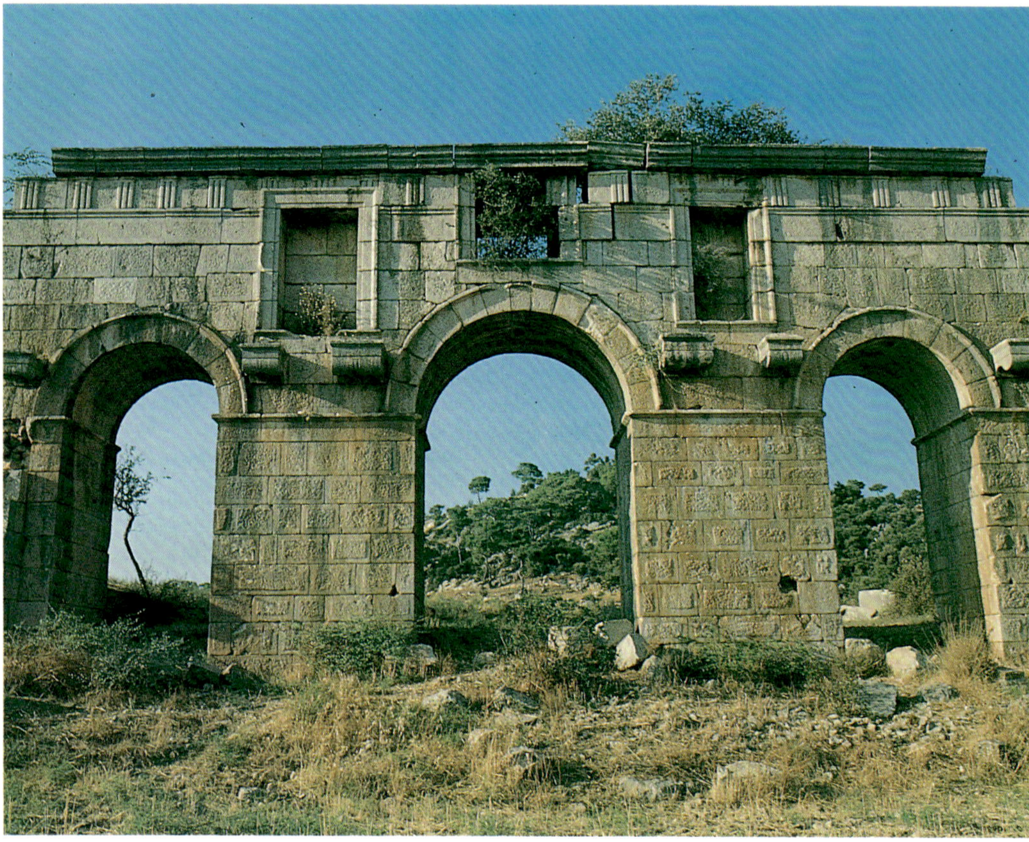

look out over the site of the city which in it's hey-day covered a sizeable acreage. The harbour is now a marshy area cut off from the sea by at least half a kilometre of sand. On the top of a low knoll by the theatre is an unusual round structure with steps cut around the inside and which was probably a cistern, though of unusual design. Nearby are the ruins of what may have been a lighthouse. Down from the theatre are parts of the city wall. After Brutus had witnessed the mass suicide of the Xanthians, he gave the inhabitants of Patara the chance to submit and not repeat the tragedy of Xanthos. After pleading with the Patarans for several days, Brutus eventually persuaded them to give in peacefully and true to his word, spared all the inhabitants. Despite his part in the murder of Julius Caesar, Brutus seems to have been an honourable man with no appetite for needless blood-letting. Around the east side of the harbour are two bath complexes and a small temple. On the other side of the harbour is the massive Granary of Hadrian, some 60 metres (200 feet) long and 24 metres (80 feet) wide, still virtually intact. Nearby are the remains of the agora and a tomb.

There can be no doubt that under the sands much remains of Patara. No trace of the Temple to Apollo, famous for it's oracle, has been found. To date no systematic excavation of the site has been carried out. Sitting in the theatre and looking out across the sand dunes calls to mind those well known lines of Shelley's on the impermanence of man's constructions:

My name is Ozymandias, King of Kings,
Look on my works, ye Mighty, and despair!
Nothing beside remains. Round the decay
Of that colossal wreck, boundless and bare
The lone and level sands stretch far away.

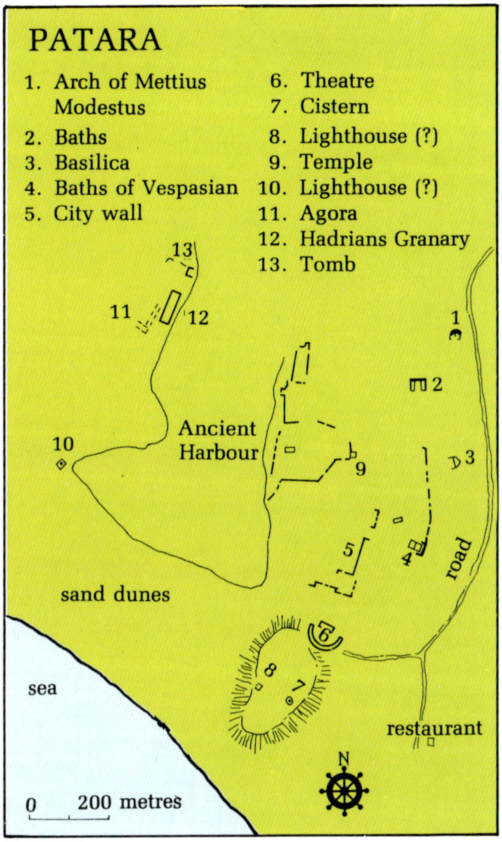

KALKAN

To the east of the long sandy beach off Patara is the large bay of Yalı Liman with the village of Kalkan in it's northeast corner. A steep road leads off the main road to the village, but check your brakes before heading down. Kalkan was devastated by the same earthquake that flattened Fethiye and the government of the day decided not to repair the houses of the old village, but to build an entirely new village above it. In the 1980's a number of rich entrepeneurs bought up most of the old village and many of the old houses have been restored. With the addition of a small yacht harbour Kalkan has prospered and today it is a pleasant little resort village with a number of good hotels and pensions and some quite excellent restaurants.

The attractions of the place are simple.

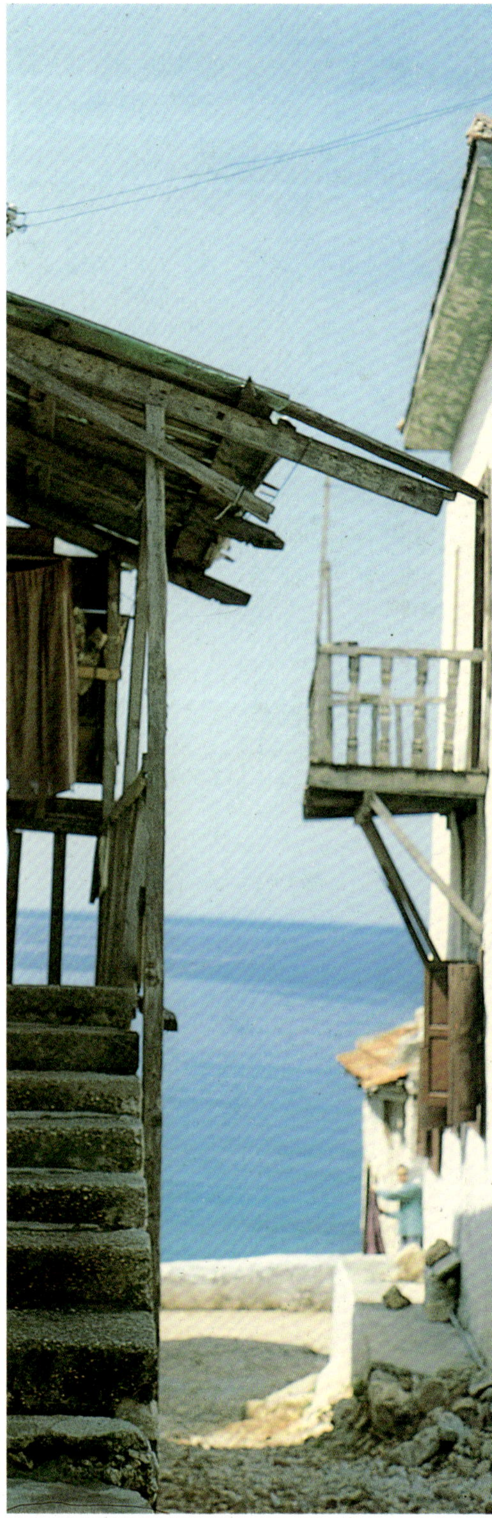

Old village houses. Kalkan.

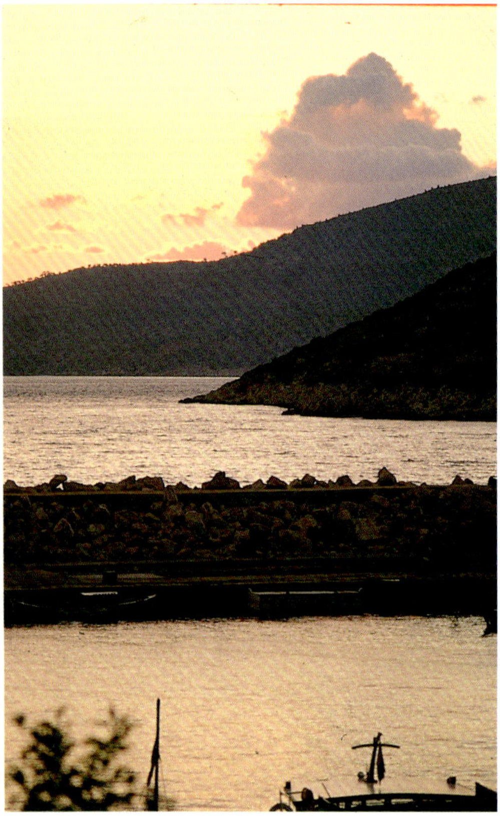

Kalkan

It is small enough to be comfortable but big enough to offer some variety for eating out. Amongst the old houses of the village are some good examples of traditional architecture with wooden balconies jutting out over the streets. Bougainvillea and jasmine clothe the old plaster through the summer making the village a green oasis amongst the otherwise rocky mountain slopes. In the back-streets, Kalkan has one of the jolliest tailors around who will whip up a shirt, a pair of trousers, or the traditional baggy pantalons, usually black, still commonly worn in rural Turkey. These baggy trousers, so I have been told, are designed to accomodate a lot of bits and pieces in their voluminous pockets because when a muslim dies, he goes to paradise with only the clothes on his back. You can take a lot with you to paradise in a pair of these trousers. On a practical level they are surprisingly cool to wear in hot weather.

For water-borne visitors Kalkan is the nearest safe harbour after Fethiye and yachts and *gulets* going north stop here before tackling the trip past the seven capes. For those with a few days to spare it is a pleasant spot to tarry in and a trip to Patara and Xanthos can be arranged from here if you feel like a bit of a wander around some ancient ruins.

Kaş

East of Kalkan lies a maze of islands and reefs with the largest island, Kastellorizon (in Turkish 'Meis'), the lonely easternmost outpost of the Greek archipelago. On the shore opposite lies the village of Kaş, formerly Greek until the exchange of populations in 1923. It looks like a Greek village with a cluster of white-washed houses around the harbour. Even the mosque was formerly the village church only now it sprouts a minaret instead of the Orthodox cross. Kaş is the only place of any size between Fethiye and Antalya with the exception of Finike. Because of it's situation in the 'middle' of the Lycian coast it has become a centre for land and water-borne visitors, though in a thoroughly pleasing and modest fashion.

Sarcophagus by the harbour. Kaş.

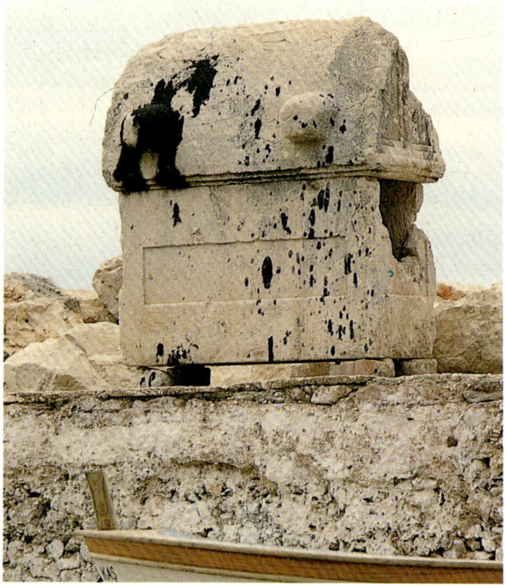

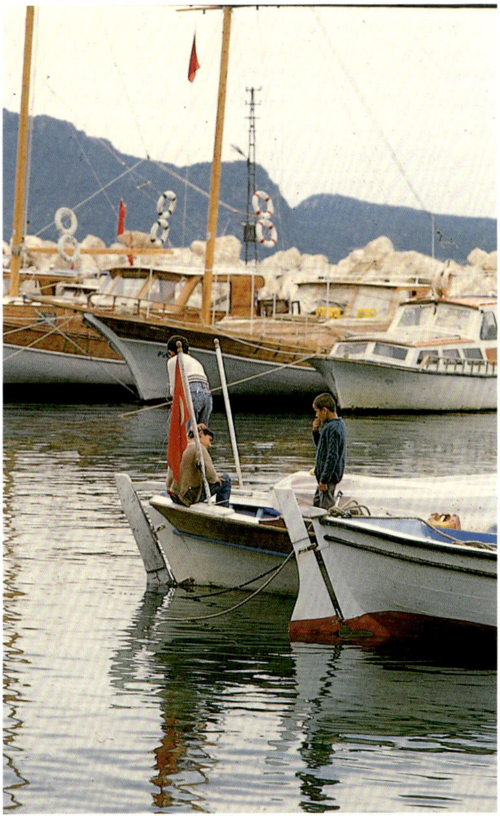

Kaş Harbour.

Kaş is a recent name for the town that was known as Andifli until last century. Formerly a small town to the north, Kaş Kasaba, was the administrative centre for the region, but when it declined the centre was moved to Andifli and the name Kaş came with it. The port, and particularly Buçak Limanı, formerly Port Vathy, on the western side of the isthmus, was used for shipping timber from the interior. Kaş has been identified as the site of Antiphellus, a Greek name in which 'phellos' means 'stony ground', an epithet as true today as it was then. The 'Anti' refers not to an opposite as might be supposed, but to an associated or sister-city geographically removed from the other. Antiphellus was the harbour-city for for Phellus, a city on a site in the mountains near the village of Çukurbağ. However during Roman times when sea-power and a safe harbour were important, Antiphellus prospered while Phellus declined. Apart from Buçak Liman, it is likely there was a small artificial harbour on the eastern side of the isthmus where the small harbour of Kaş is sited today.

Little remains of ancient Antiphellus except for a number of sarcophagi and a delightful little theatre on the peninsula. It is well worth a wander around here to watch the sunset over the sea and islands. Once dusk has fallen a number of rock tombs in the cliffs behind Kaş are illuminated with concealed lights like ancient giant glow-worms bringing the Lycian dead into the 20th century. There are a number of sarcophagi around the town and one at the harbour, but the numbers are considerably less than when Spratt was here in the 19th century. He counted over a hundred lying around the site. Most have probably been broken up and used as handy building materials by the locals. One of the spin-offs of tourism in Turkey and indeed in the eastern Mediterranean generally, is that it has made ancient bits of stone of value since tourists come to see them, and thus they are something to be valued and cared for, since tourists spend money and keep the local economy going.

Old balconied house near the waterfront. Kaş.

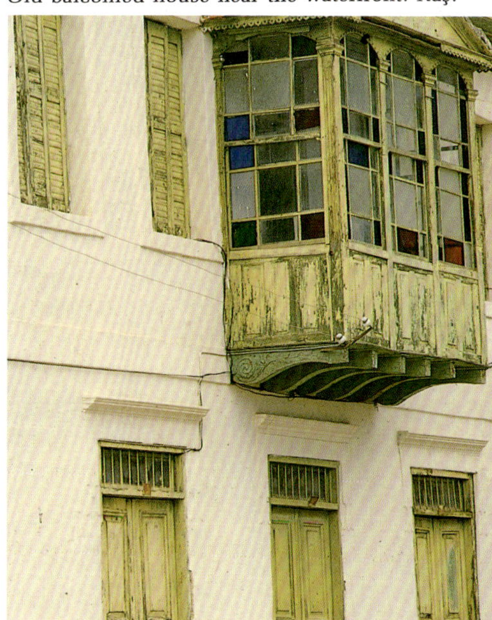

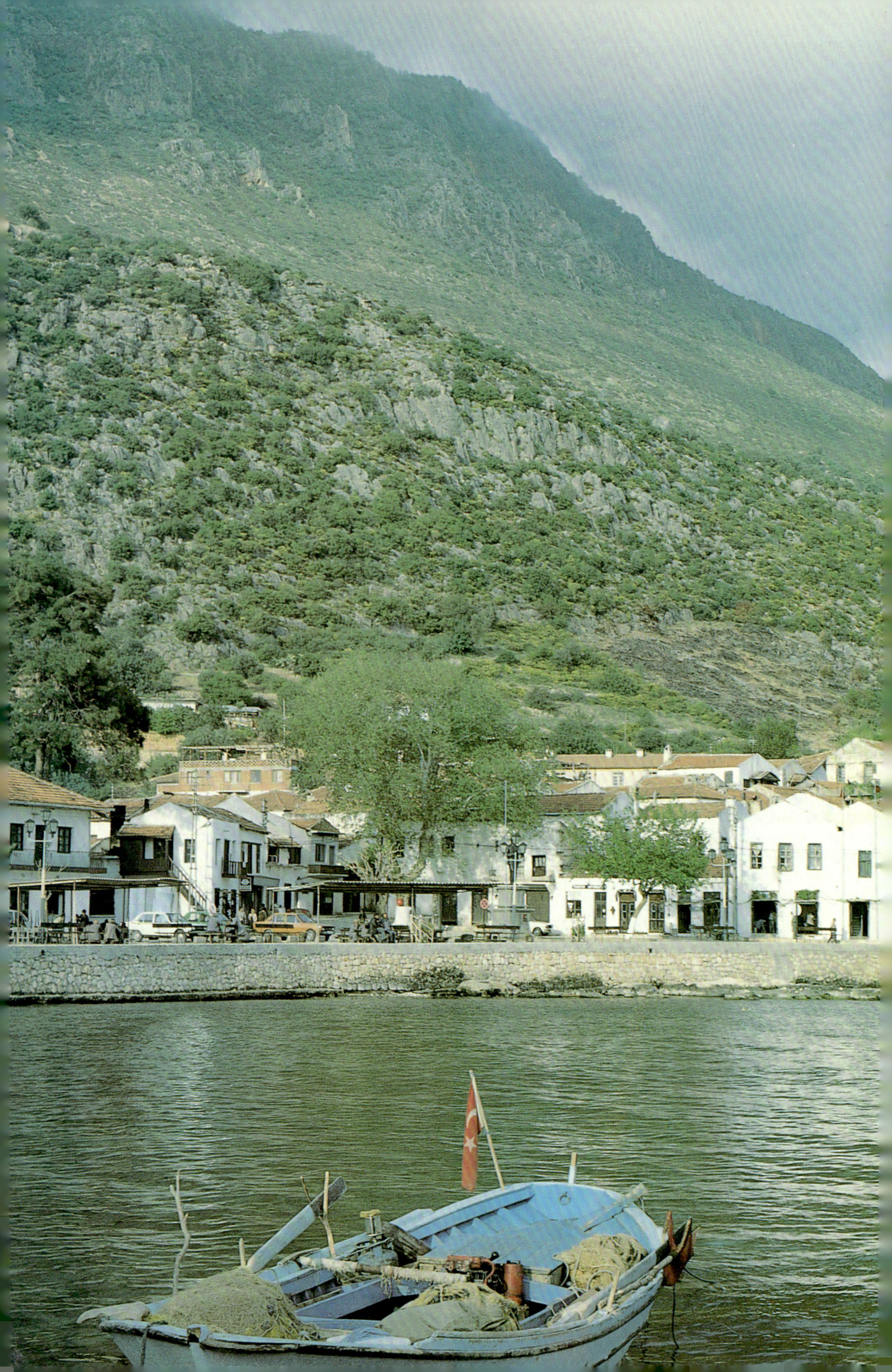

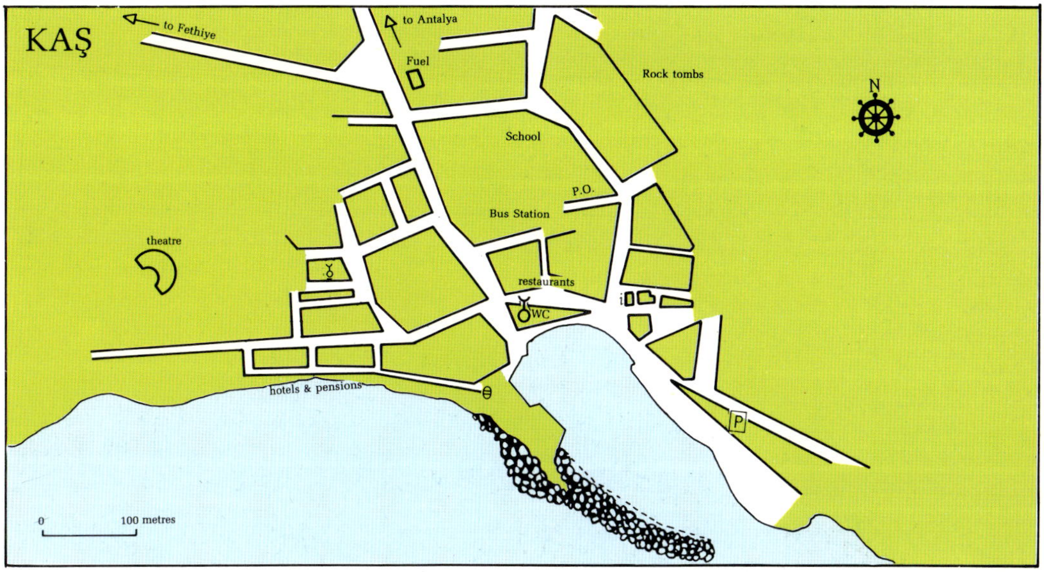

I have spent many happy days in Kaş and I always enjoy returning here. There is something very comfortable about the place that invites you to stay - not doing anything in particular. If you are interested in *kilims*, Mustafa in 'Magic Orient' near the tourist office has a good selection from all over Anatolia. In fact Kaş is not at all a bad place to buy carpets and *kilims*, though you still need to haggle a bit. For land-based travellers there are daily boat excursions to Kekova and the ancient sites of Aperlae, Simena, and Teimiussa. It is a long day, the boats usually leave at 9:00 in the morning and return at 6:00 in the evening, and it can be wet on the return trip if the *meltem* is blowing; but the excursion is well worth it as much for the trip and scenery around Kekova as for the sites themselves. The road to the village of Üçağız on the coast near Kekova is a precarious road and the boat trip is much to be preferred.

The Oldest Known Shipwreck

Off Ulu Burun a short distance to the southeast of Kaş, Dr. George Bass and the underwater archaeology team from INA, the Institute of Nautical Archaeology, have been excavating and recovering artifacts from what is now believed to be the oldest known shipwreck. Since 1984 a team of divers have been at work mapping and photographing the layout of the wreck and then systematically removing item by item, in a carefully scheduled way, the artifacts below. It has not been easy to work on the wreck which lies more than 45 metres (150 feet) down. Divers could spend only a maximum twenty minutes working on the wreck because of the danger of a nitrogen build-up and the risk of narcosis, or worse, 'the bends'. To complicate matters the wreck off Ulu Burun is in an exposed and windy spot and the dive-ship 'Virazon' had to be securely anchored on four sides to keep it in place. The members of the expedition established a camp on the bare rocky slopes of Ulu Burun itself and live at the camp throughout the summer while diving is taking place.

The wreck was located by a Turkish sponge diver in 1982 who noticed a pile of copper ingots on the sea-bed. Investigations by INA divers based in Bodrum soon established that this was a wreck of some importance and in 1984 excavation began in earnest. It wasn't long before some of the finds from the wreck established it as one of the most important excavated yet. Two bronze swords with inlaid hilts have been found. A gold chalice. Cobalt blue glass ingots. A gold pendant with a nude goddess grasping a gazelle in each hand. Silver bracelets. Ivory. A carved rock crystal cylinder seal with gold caps. A solid gold scarab. While these may be the sort of finds which make the headlines, for the archaeologists working on the wreck the most exciting finds are of a more mundane nature.

Stone anchor(s) of the type found in the Ulu Burnu wreck.

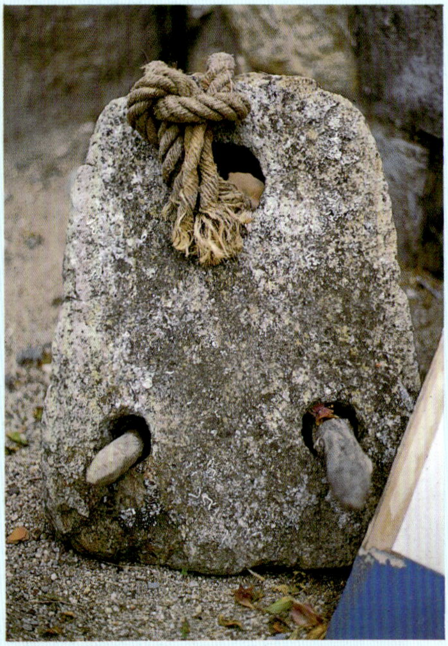

Parts of the keel and planking of the wreck itself have been discovered and from this the construction method, using mortice and tenon joints, pushes back the known period when this method of boat-building was used by some 200 years. From the pottery found on board the date of the wreck can be established to be around the 14th century BC. The copper ingots that originally betrayed the prescence of the wreck came to a staggering total of 200, each of them weighing in at around 27 kilos (60 pounds). There is an interesting coincidence here. George Bass relates how months later he came across a passage on an Egyptian tablet of the time mentioning a promised gift of 200 talents of copper from the King of Cyprus to an Egyptian pharoah. As it happens, a talent weighs in at around 27 kilos, and George Bass wondered if it was just possible that this cargo... but the coincidence is probably too great. However the boat was evidently bound to or from Egypt as evidenced not only by the gold scarab bearing the name of Nefertiti, incidentally the only gold scarab ever found naming the mysterious Nefertiti, but also a large quantity of yellow resin stored in amphoras. This yellow resin is probably from a tree related to the Pistacia nut tree and was used in Egyptian burial rites. It was probably used as a base for perfumes and incense, thus its use during burial to disguise the smell of mortal flesh in a hot climate.

The vessel itself was around 15 metres (50 feet) long and the valuable nature of its cargo indicates it was no ordinary trading ship. The diversity of the origins of the cargo is staggering. The copper ingots probably came from Cyprus. The glass and the amphoras from the Canaanites in what is now Israel and the Lebanon. Tin ingots

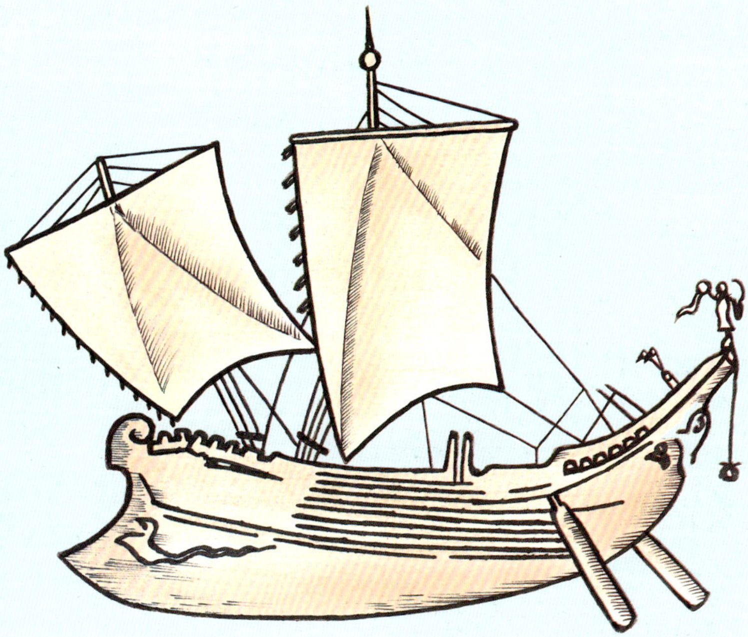

found on board may have originated in Afghanistan. A vase is of Mycenean origin. Unworked ivory may have come from Syria or North Africa. Most incredibly of all, amber beads found on board are of a type of amber originating in the Baltic. From wrecks like this it is necessary to revise the limits of the known trading world and accept that goods travelled greater distances, more frequently, than was previously thought. The Ulu Burun ship carried a cargo from the four corners of the ancient world and quite possibly a crew of mixed nationalities. As the excavation continues it is likely that we will learn much more about the extent of trade in the ancient world more than 3300 years ago, as well as about the ships and the men and the cultures of the times.

Bayindir

In the southeast corner of the Bay of Kaş there are a number of rock-tombs and a few ruins on the summit of the hill above the anchorage. Land-based visitors will have to get a local boat to take them across while yachts and *gulets* can anchor in the bay. Be warned that the climb up to the summit is difficult and in places dangerous. George Bean identifies the site as Sebeda, a small settlement of no consequence and hardly mentioned by ancient writers. Until recently the bay was still called Port Sevedo on Admiralty charts, a name that reflects the ancient name of the place.

Asar And Aperlae

On the west side of Kekova a long peninsula juts out and it's name, Sıcak Yarımadası, meaning the 'hot peninsula', adequately reflects the temperatures here in the summer. At the head of the long inlet on the western side of the peninsula are the ruins of ancient Aperlae. It was never a great city in ancient times, but it

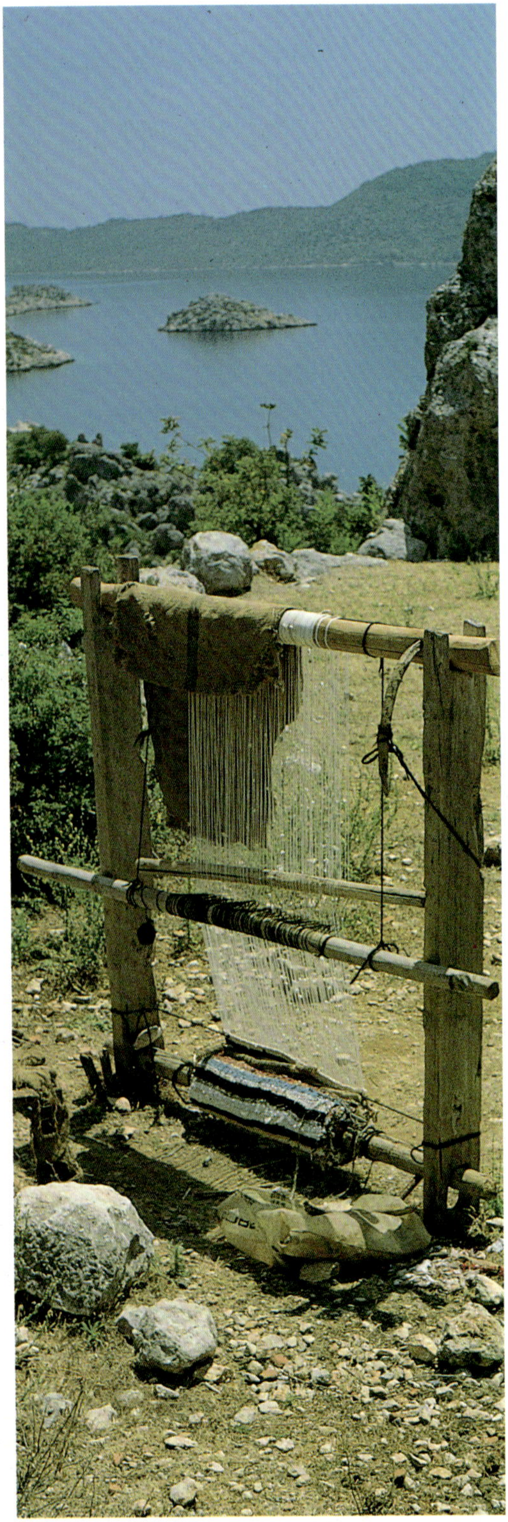

View from Kale Köy out over Kekova.

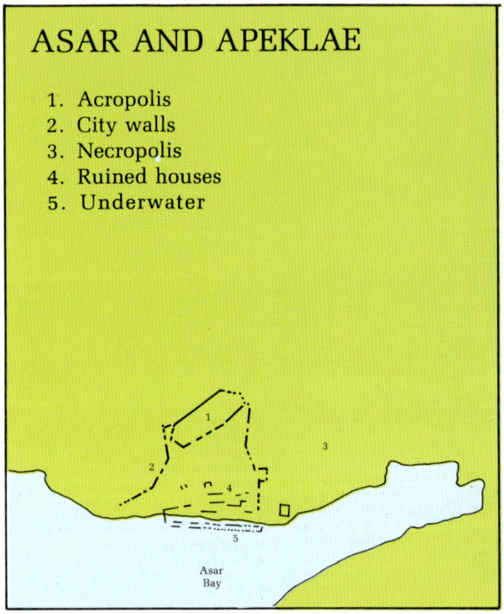

was of some consequence as the leading city of this region. Part of the interest in the place is that the quay and harbour streets are now underwater. Either the sea level has risen or an earthquake caused this part of the city to subside. Ashore there are parts of the city wall and the ruins of buildings, and a number of sarcophagi. The ruins of Aperlae in this deserted landscape have a great deal of appeal. The excursion boats from Kaş make a brief stop here while those in a yacht or *gulet* can make a longer visit. The anchorage in Asar can become uncomfortable and even untenable with the *meltem* so for peace of mind it is best to go to the western end of the bay enclosed by Kekova Island and anchor in Pölemos Bükü. It is a half mile hike across the isthmus from this anchorage to the site - wear sturdy footwear and take some drinking water with you.

KEKOVA

Kekova Adası is the long thin island enclosing a stretch of water between it and the much indented mainland coast. It takes it's name from Kakava, in Greek 'the island

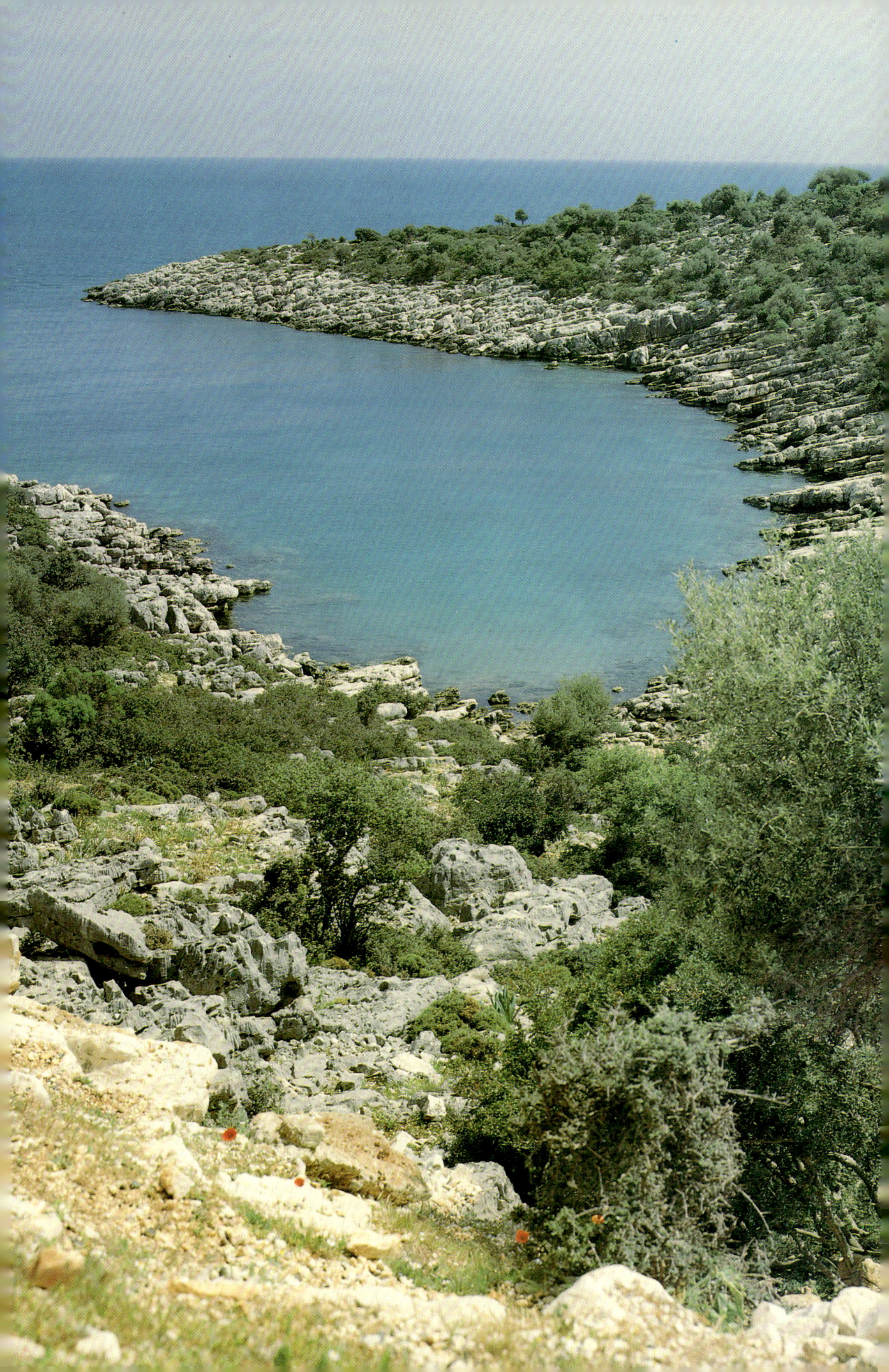

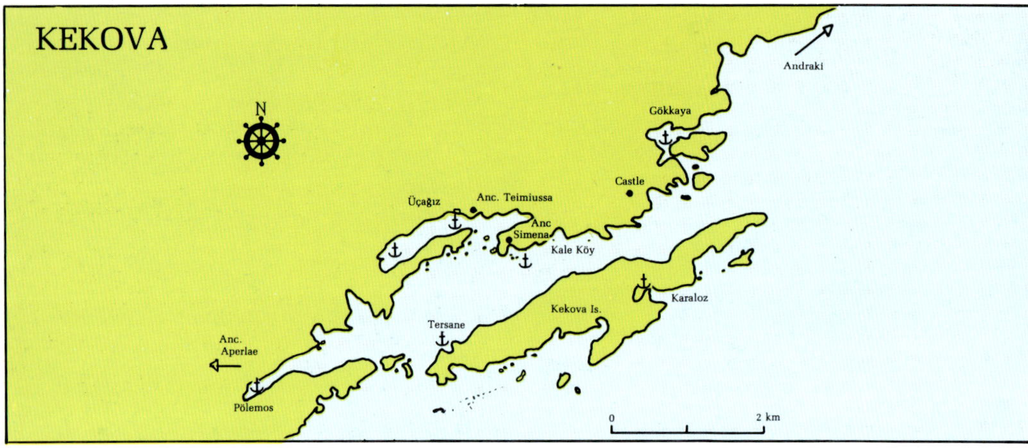

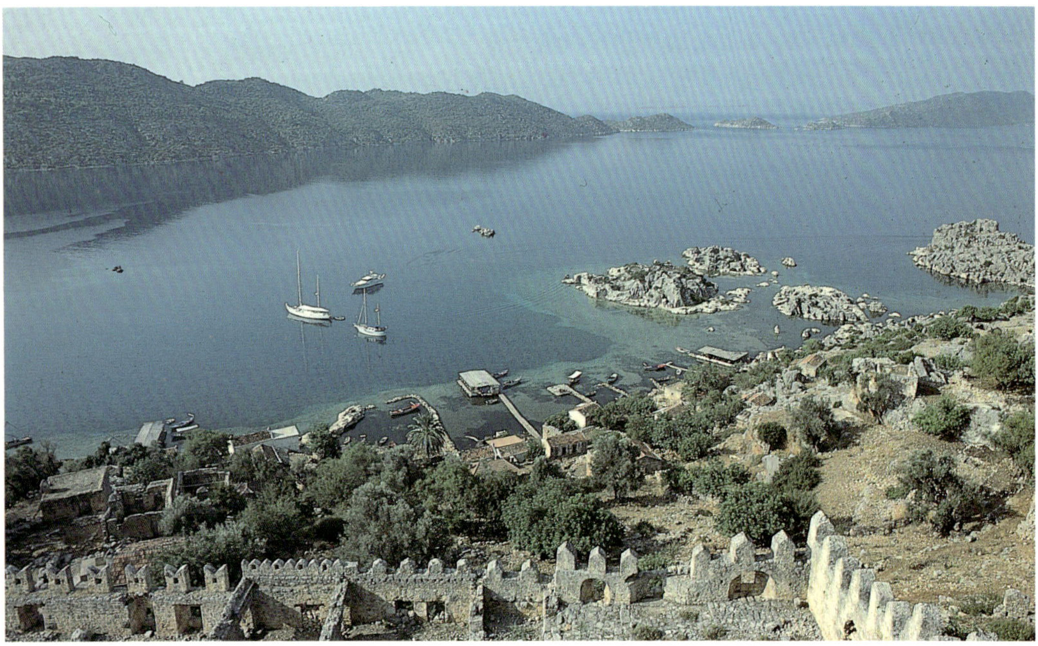

of the partridges', though whether there are any still there I don't know. The island has popularly given it's name to the whole area which is referred to as simply Kekova. The Greek name for the area was Tristomo, 'the three mouths', so called from the three entrances: one at either end of Kekova Island plus the one into the bay with the village of Üçağız on the shore. The Turkish name Üçağız itself means 'the three mouths' echoing the Greek Tristomo. The area enclosed by Kekova is also known as Ölü Deniz like it's namesake further north, 'the dead sea', because it is so calm inside.

Within the area enclosed by Kekova Island there are many anchorages and coves and a number of appealing sites of ancient and more recent habitation. When Beaufort visited here during his survey of the coast in the early 19th century he recommended it as a fleet anchorage: "... its great extent, its bold shores, and the facility of defense, may hereafter point it out as an eligible place for the rendevous of a fleet." Unlike Marmaris it was never used as such though local folklore tells of a Turkish submarine that evaded the Allies in World War I by hiding in here.

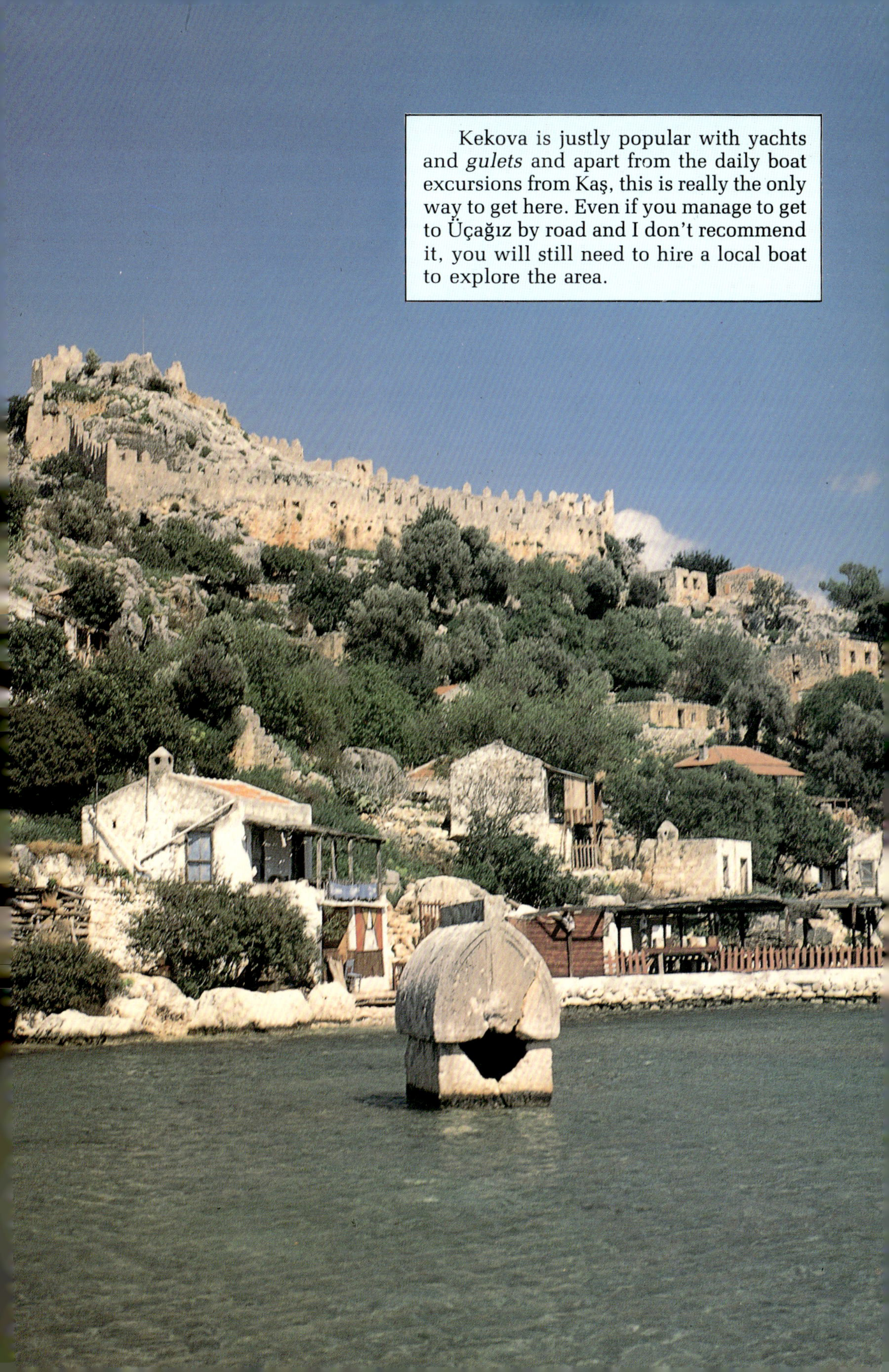

Kekova is justly popular with yachts and *gulets* and apart from the daily boat excursions from Kaş, this is really the only way to get here. Even if you manage to get to Üçağız by road and I don't recommend it, you will still need to hire a local boat to explore the area.

Pölemos Bükü

The bay at the western end of Kekova. There is only macquis and olive trees ashore and blessed peace and quiet, but a half mile over the isthmus are the ruins of Aperlae.

Tersane

At the western end of Kekova Island itself there is a miniature cove with the apse of a church standing on the beach. Around the shore and partially underwater are the ruins of other buildings of what was a small Byzantine settlement. Like it's namesake in the Gulf of Fethiye, Tersane means a 'boatyard', so presumably the inhabitants were engaged in building and repairing boats. The settlement was deserted by the early 19th century if not earlier, as Beaufort mentions a deserted village with a small chapel on Kekova Island which Greek sailors used for their devotions. Today the lonely apse on the beach gives the place a haunted quality, a reminder of the long forgotten souls and the busy little community that once existed here. The excursion boats from Kaş usually stop here to let everyone cool off with a swim in the turquoise waters of the cove. Yachts and *gulets* frequently use it as well, the anchorage being a safe one as well as enchanting.

Kale Köy and Simena

Once into the calm waters between Kekova Island and the mainland, the most conspicuous object is the Medieval castle above the hamlet of Kale Köy (Castle Bay). It's castellated ramparts are silhouetted against the blue sky on the ridge above the ramshackle houses of the hamlet, and even the most unromantic cannot help being captivated by the romance of the castle in this rocky wilderness. It gets better. As you pass into the bay between rocks and reefs on either side, what appeared to be a craggy rock reveals itself to have steps cut into it and the top levelled off flat. The general explanation for this is that the rock was quarried for construction purposes, and although other islets around the coast have been quarried for this purpose, why should this small lump of rock be worked when there is rock more easily accessible on the hillsides nearby. Given that the sea level has risen, or the land subsided in this region, as evidenced by the submerged harbour precinct here at Kale Köy and elsewhere such as at Aperlae, it is likely that this structure was a watch-tower or a defensive structure, or possibly a purely frivolous platform for diving and swimming off. There is no reason to suppose the ancients did not go swimming to cool off in the heat of summer just as we do.

Rock with steps cut into it. Kale Köy.

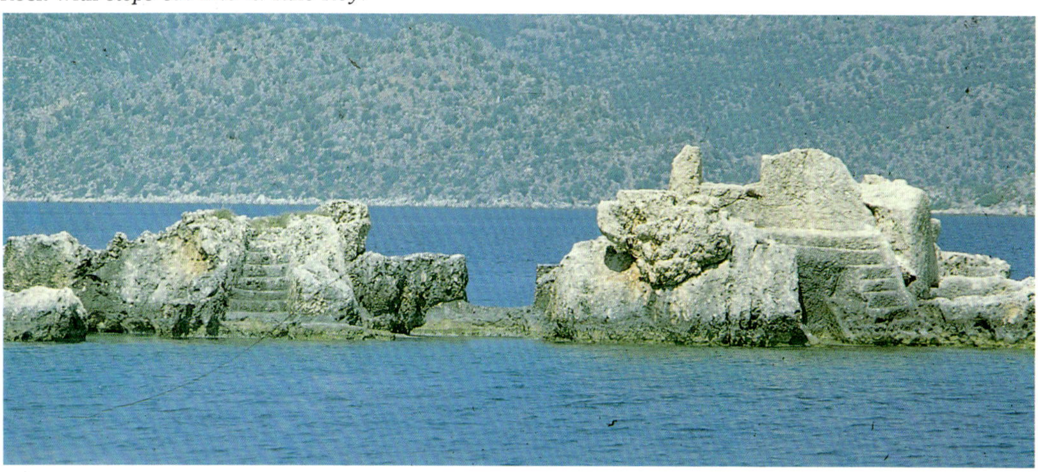

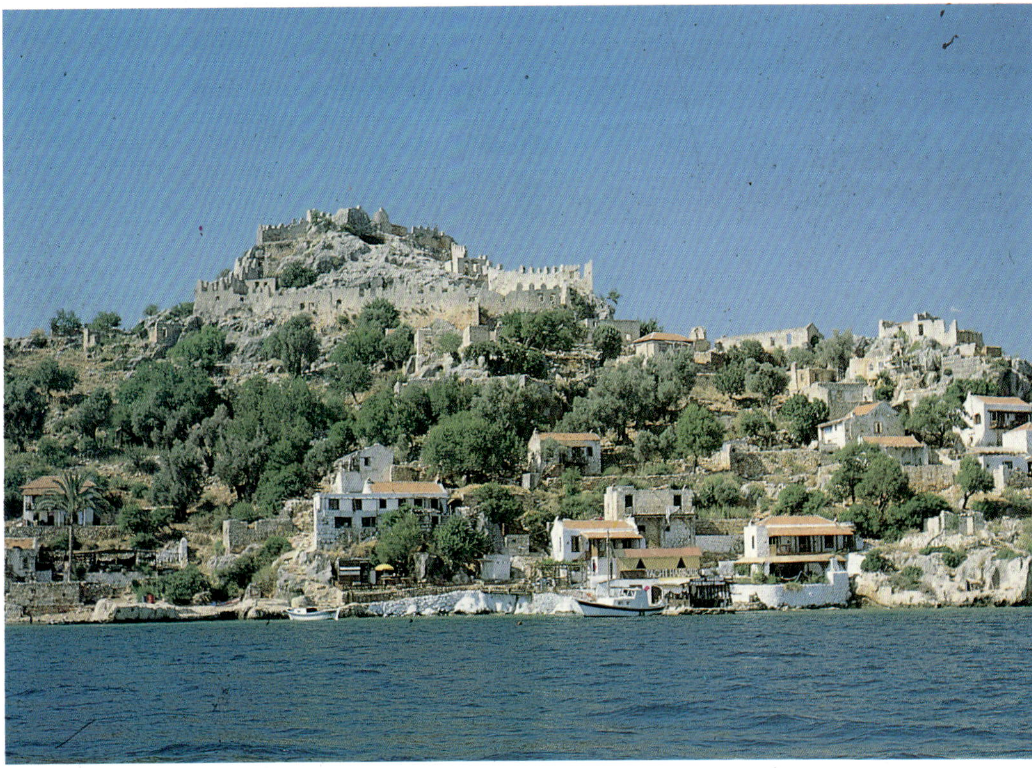

Kale Köy.

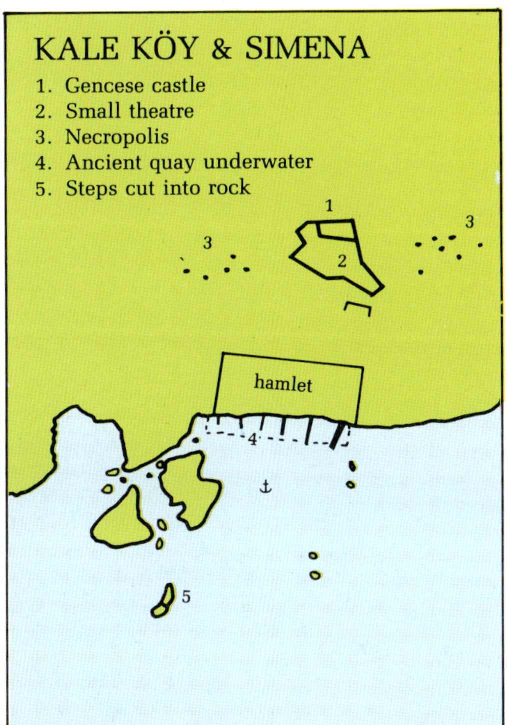

Part of the attraction of Kale Köy is the mixture of Ancient and Medieval on the one site, with the houses of the hamlet tucked in between and on top of the site. The buildings of the hamlet are a sort of architectural palimpsest with a bit of ancient stone here, a bit of Medieval masonry there, and the family livestock safely tucked up in a rock-tomb. Along the waterfront are numerous, for such a small place, restaurants, with jetties out over the now submerged quay and streets of ancient Simena. In the shallow water to the west a sarcophagus sits in the water like an elegant man-made dinosaur basking in the sun. From the shore it is a steep though short walk up to the castle. It is thought to be largely of Genoese origin with later Turkish improvements, but it undoubtedly sits on the site of a more ancient structure. Inside the walls is a small theatre with just seven rows of seats entirely hewn from the rock of the hill. It probably held around 300 people with a squeeze, a reflection on the modest population of ancient Simena.

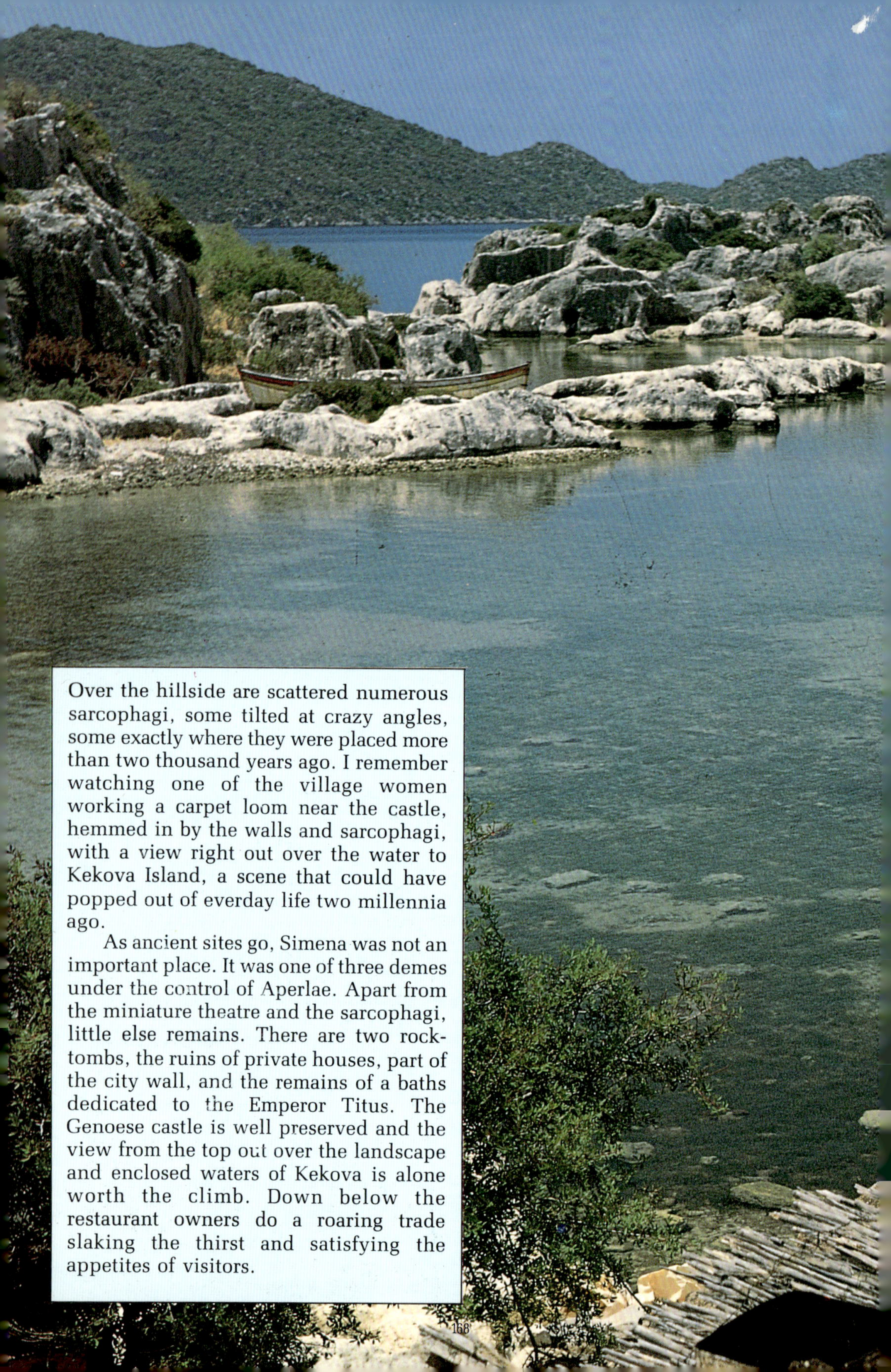

Over the hillside are scattered numerous sarcophagi, some tilted at crazy angles, some exactly where they were placed more than two thousand years ago. I remember watching one of the village women working a carpet loom near the castle, hemmed in by the walls and sarcophagi, with a view right out over the water to Kekova Island, a scene that could have popped out of everday life two millennia ago.

As ancient sites go, Simena was not an important place. It was one of three demes under the control of Aperlae. Apart from the miniature theatre and the sarcophagi, little else remains. There are two rock-tombs, the ruins of private houses, part of the city wall, and the remains of a baths dedicated to the Emperor Titus. The Genoese castle is well preserved and the view from the top out over the landscape and enclosed waters of Kekova is alone worth the climb. Down below the restaurant owners do a roaring trade slaking the thirst and satisfying the appetites of visitors.

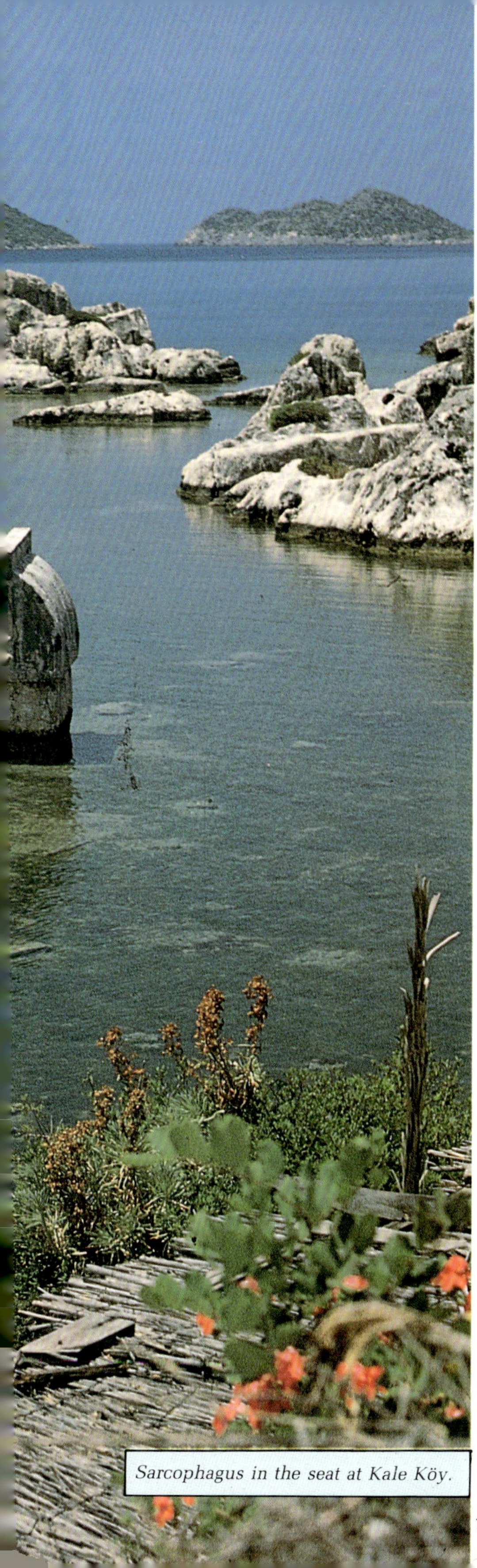

Sarcophagus in the seat at Kale Köy.

Üçağız And Teimiussa

From the waters enclosed by Kekova a narrow channel, with an islet and reefs in the middle, leads into another large and totally enclosed bay. On the shore stands the hamlet of Üçağız, a small farming community where on my last visit, I was chased off by a villager for trying to take a photograph of his young daughter. It is worth remembering that permission should sometimes be asked before a photograph! Livestock roam at leisure through the hamlet which until recent times was only inhabited in the winter. In the summer the villagers retired to a '*yayla*' in the mountains to escape the summer heat and where there is grass and fodder for the livestock.

Immediately east of Üçağız a number of sarcophagi are scattered in gay abandon over the low slopes of the coast. This is the site of Teimiussa, a small settlement under the control of Aperlae. Little remains except the numerous sarcophagi and a couple of rock-tombs, the remains of a fort that is really no more than a fortified tower,

Main street. Üçağız.

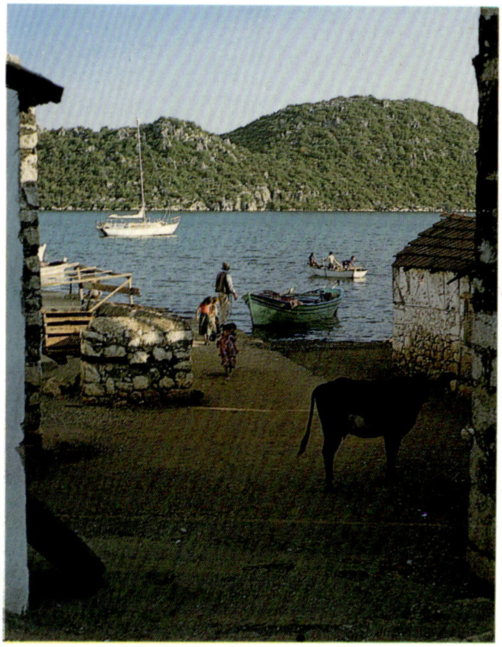

and part of a quayed area. The latter is quite remarkable being hewn from the rock with a narrow track at the back separated by a rock gateway from the quay.

AROUND KEKOVA

GÖKKAYA LİMAN

At the eastern end of Kekova lies a group of islands and above water rocks with channels winding in and out of them. Gökkaya is a fascinating place to explore from the water and in a yacht you can find your own little place to anchor in. Ashore there is a restaurant, but otherwise it is uninhabited. There are a few ruins ashore and on the mainland a short distance to the west there is another Genoese castle guarding the eastern approaches to Kekova. The Genoese seem to have wrested this bit of coast from the Venetians. They controlled Kastellorizon up the coast, and in fact it's name is a corruption of Castello Rosso, the 'Red Castle', after the Genoese castle on the island. The struggle between Genoa and Venice to control this important trading route bringing valuable commodities from the east to the west, the humble peppercorn being one of the most important items, was a long and hard struggle with Venice now controlling one part of the coast, Genoa another; and not until the impending hegemony of the Ottomans did the Genoese and Venetians begin to co-operate - a little.

MYRA

Approximately two miles to the east of Gökkaya is the beach of Andraki, an open anchorage formerly the port for the city of Myra. In calm weather a yacht or *gulet* can anchor off and ashore you can get a taxi to the site of Myra, about 5 kilometres away. However as the anchorage is uncertain it is better to do the trip from somewhere like Kaş or Finike.

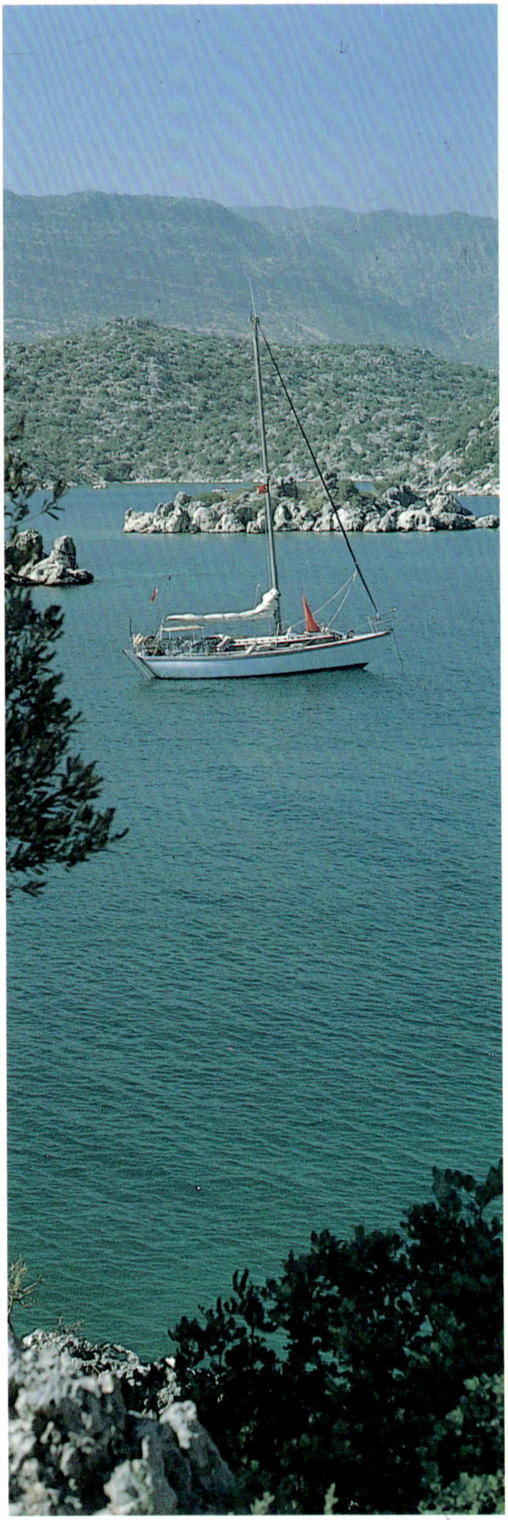

Gökkaya.

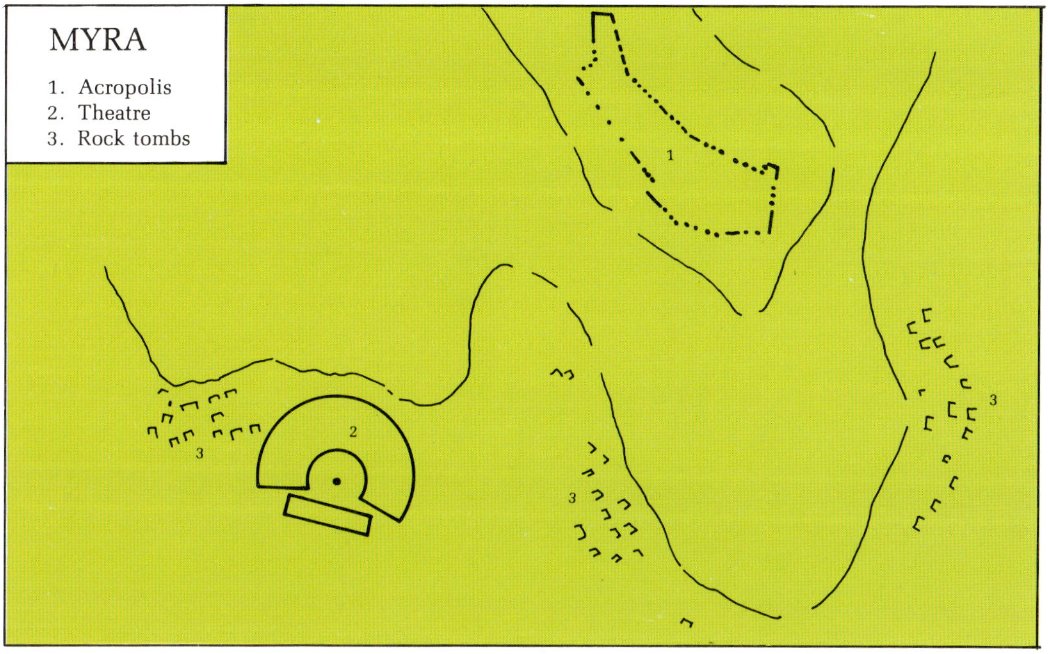

A trip to Myra is well worth the effort. The theatre here is well preserved and there are a group of easily accessible rock-tombs behind it. The area around is a sea of plastic-covered greenhouses growing early tomatoes in the rich alluvial soil for export and the home market. The theatre is partially buried by alluvial soil and is an excellent example of just how a river not only silts up a harbour, but can bury a city. As you go into the theatre there is a stall space with an inscription above it reading 'Place of the vendor Gelasius', where friend Gelasius would have sold whatever the inhabitants of Myra munched on as they watched the show. Close to the theatre are a group of remarkable house-tombs, the best examples around, and easily accessible up a narrow path. One of these has a series of interesting reliefs sculpted around the entrance showing (presumably) the man buried here, his wife and sons. Around the corner on the northeast side of the hill are another group of tombs and one of these has the remains of paint on the frieze. This frieze shows the indoor and outdoor life of the man and his family with servants in attendance and is quite one of the most remarkable rock-tombs in Lycia.

Down in the village of Demre through which you pass to get to Myra, is the church of St Nicholas of Myra. Nicholas was born in Patara around AD 300 and became famous in his own time and was duly made a saint. He is patron saint of an unlikely lot of characters: of sailors, merchants, pawn-brokers, scholars, and those wrongly imprisoned and by travellers everywhere. He is patron saint of Greece and Russia. His bones no longer lie in the church and indeed it is unlikely that the tomb the custodian shows you was in fact the final resting place of the saint. In AD 1087 his bones were stolen by sailors from Bari in Italy, and removed to that city where they now alledgedly rest. However the Venetians also claim to have the bones of the saint, as do the Russians, and the museum in Antalya. Wherever they are, the spirit of St Nicholas survives throughout the Orthodox world and has penetrated the young lives of most of us. From St Nicholas of the Orthodox world he has metamorphised into the Santa Claus of the secular world. When at Myra he is said to have provided dowries for the daughters of an impoverished citizen by dropping three bags of gold down the

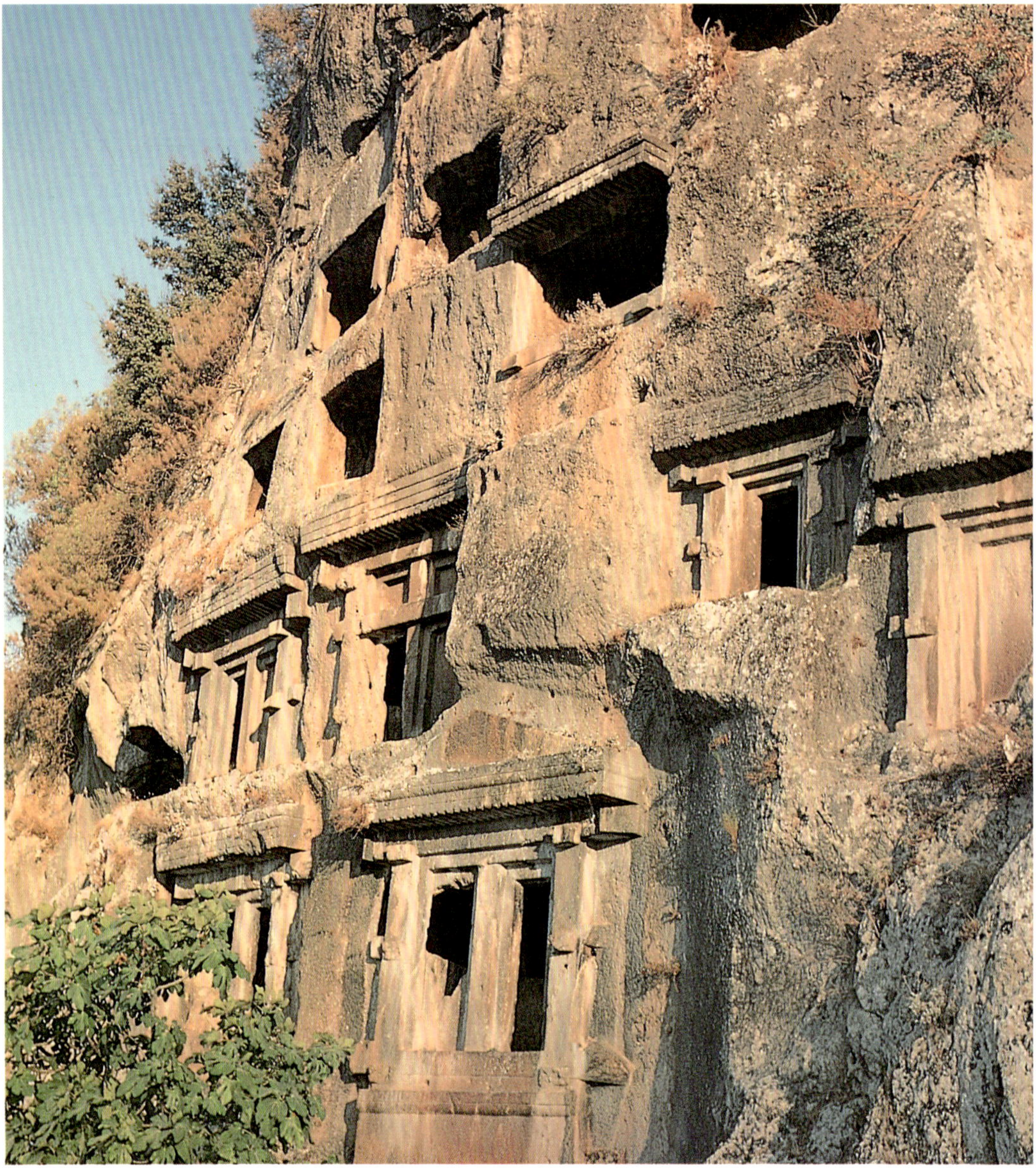

chimney at night. The daughters were drying their stockings by the fire and in the morning discovered the gold in each of their stockings - an innocent enough tale of a saint who seems to have only good attributed to him and who provides legitimisation for the tradition of putting stockings out for Father Christmas to fill on Christmas eve. Whatever the truth of the wondrous works and miracles attributed to him, he was well-loved in his own time and is still much loved as Santa Claus.

At Andraki, in ancient times Andriace, the port of Myra, there are a number of ruined buildings and a granary of Hadrian, much similiar to the one at Patara, but not as well preserved. It is here that the Apostle Paul, now a prisoner of the Romans, changed ship on his way to Rome and his trial. It was to be the last voyage this hardened traveller made, though there were many incidents and accidents along the way before the Romans finally had Paul safely locked up in Rome.

THE APOSTLE PAUL

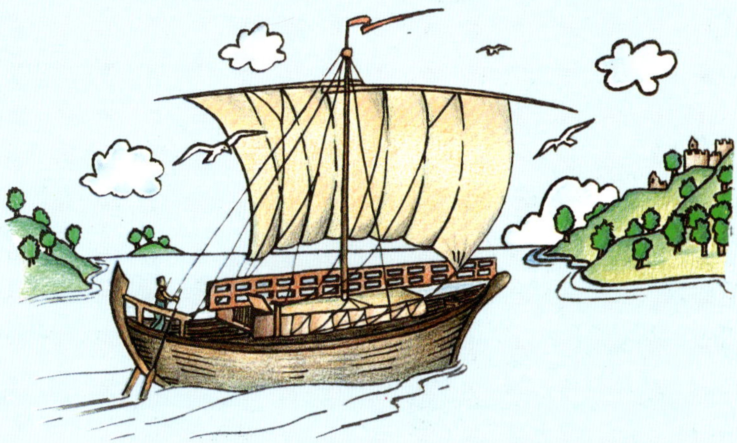

Of all the apostles, Paul stands out as the one who was the traveller par excellence. His journeys through the length and breadth of the ancient world are nothing short of remarkable and given the difficulties of travelling in these times, let alone the animosity and danger he faced trying to convert populations to the new faith, it is a credit to the endurance and tenacity of the man that he accomplished as much as he did. Paul, originally Saul, was born in Tarsus in what is now southern Turkey and changed his name after converting Sergius Paulus. He is traditionally represented as a stocky little man, with a bald head and a grey, bushy beard. He made three great missionary journeys before being arrested in Jerusalem and taken to Rome where he was beheaded in AD 62.

On all of his journeys he travelled along the coast of Asia Minor and there are many places along the coast I have described where he stopped and taught, or changed boats, or sheltered from the weather. The book of ***Acts*** *covers most of his exploits and journeys as well as his last voyage as a prisoner to Rome.*

One of the most well known incidents on Paul's travels is the riot of the silversmiths in Ephesus. On his third journey Paul stayed over two years in Ephesus preaching every day in the synagogue. He was a canny man and knew that he had to convert the old pagan centres of worship, and Ephesus was one of the oldest, if this new Christianity was to survive. Towards the end of his time there Paul preached that "...gods made by human hands are not gods at all", a

It was in Jerusalem after this third missionary journey that the authorities finally decided they could tolerate Paul's activities no longer and arrested him. He was put on a ship at Adramytium bound for the coast of Asia Minor:

"And putting to sea from thence, we sailed under the lee of Cyprus, because the winds were contrary.

And when we had sailed across the sea which is off Cilicia and direct jibe at the silverbmiths who made silver statuettes of Artemis and the temple for sale to pilgrims and tourists. Sales soon began to decline and one, Demetrius, a leader of the silversmiths, led a group of artisans against Paul saying "...the sanctuary of the great goddess Diana will cease to command respect; and then it will not be very long before she who is worshipped by all Asia and the civilized world is brought down from her divine pre-eminence." His speech caused an uproar and the band of silversmiths, and likely a number of merchants worried about the decline in business, rushed into the theatre shouting "Great is Diana of the Ephesians". Paul was not forced to leave the city by the authorities after this riot, but he evidently decided it was prudent to do so and set off for Macedonia.

Pamphylia, we came to Myra, a city of Lycia.

And there the centurion found a ship of Alexandria sailing for Italy; and he put us therein.

And when we had sailed slowly many days, and were come with difficulty over against Cnidus, the wind not further suffering us, we sailed under the lee of Crete, over against Salamone;

And with difficulty coasting along it we came unto a certain place called Fair Havens; nigh whereunto was the city of Lasea."

Acts *27: 4-8.*

It was by now the beginning of winter and the voyage onwards was beset with strong and adverse winds. From Crete a gale blew them down to Malta where the ship was wrecked in what is now called St Pauls Bay. Eventually a ship brought them to Rome and there Paul was tried and beheaded in AD 62. It is apocryphally told that when Paul was beheaded milk and not blood flowed from his body. However dubious this may be, few could have predicted what the result of Pauls work was to be as Christianity went from strength to strength to become the dominant faith in the very country where he met his end.

FACILITIES

Fethiye: Restaurants, hotels & pensions, telephone, P.O., Banks, Doctor, Dentist, Laundry, Showers, toilets, fuel, water, ice, gas, provisions, engineer.
Officials: Health, Immigration, Customs, Harbourmaster, Police, Tourist Information.
Calis Beach: Restaurants, hotels & pensions.
Gemiler: Restaurants
Ölü Deniz: Restaurants, hotels & pensions, telephone, showers, toilets.
Officials: Gendarmarie.
Kalkan: Restaurants, hotels & pensions, telephone, toilets, water, provisions.
Kaş: Restaurants, hotels & pensions, telephone, P.O., Bank, Doctor, Laundry, toilets, fuel, water, gas, provisions.
Officials: Health, Immigration, Customs, Harbourmaster, Police, Tourist Information.
Kale Koy: Restaurants.
Üçağız: Restaurants, pension, provisions.
Gökkaya: Restaurant.

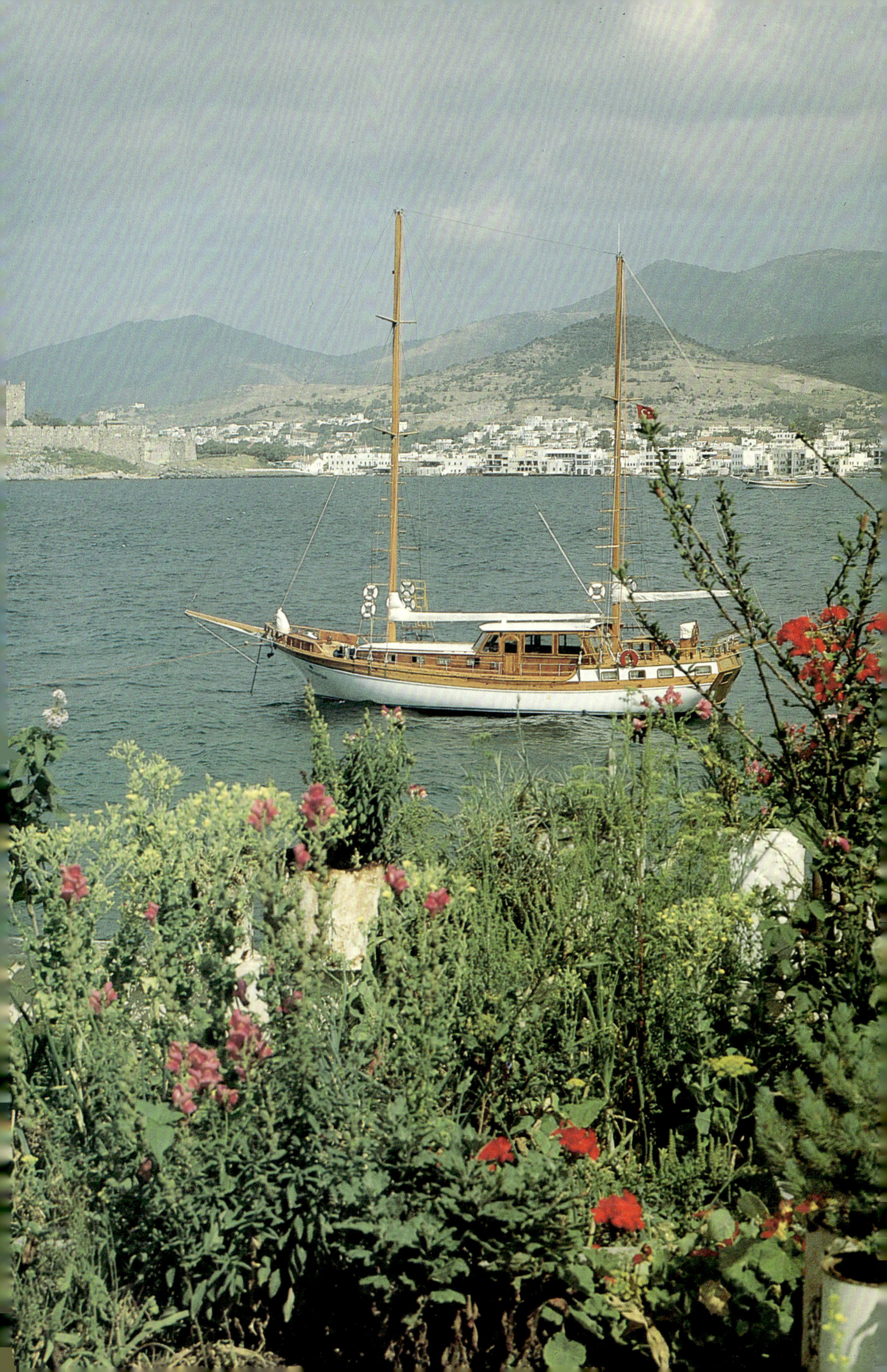

Appendix I: Useful Books

GENERAL

Discovering Turkey Andrew Mango Batsford Not a guide book but a good general introduction to things Turkish.

Companion Guide to Turkey John Freely Collins Entertaining guide to Turkey.

Turkey: A Travel Survival Kit Tom Brosnahan Lonely Planet Good useable guide.

Turkey: A Short History R.H. Davision Eothen Press Good concise guide to the history from Seljuks to Rebuplic.

Europa Minor Lord Kinross Travel Book Club Erudite and entertaining.

Atatürk: The Rebirth of a Nation Lord Kinross Weidenfeld & Nicholson. Tells of the birth of the Turkish Republic - a good read.

Stamboul Sketches John Freely Redhouse Press. As much about things Turkish as Istanbul.

ARCHAEOLOGY

Turkey Beyond the Meander & *Lycian Turkey* George Bean Benn/Murray. Much mentioned and lauded in this book, these are the guides par excellence to the Graeco-Roman sites. For the coast to the north there is *Aegean Turkey* and to the south *Turkey's Southern Shore. Ancient Civilizations and Ruins of Turkey* Ekrem Akurgal Haşet. Good compact guide.

Alexander's Path Freya Stark Murray. A travel classic around Lycia.

NAUTICAL

Turkish Waters Pilot Rod Heikell Imray Sailing directions and background for the Turkish coast.

The Jason Voyage Tim Severin Hutchinson. Follows the Jason voyage to Istanbul and along the Black Sea coast of Turkey.

Mariner in the Mediterranean John Mariner Adlard Coles. Visits to Turkey.

Appendix II: Pronounciation of the Turkish Alphabet

a as ah in father
b as b in bat
c as j in joke
ç as ch in choke
d as d in dote
e as eh in met or ay in stay
f as f in fat
g as g in get
ğ a soft g something like y or uh
h as h in hat
i as u in circus but also as uh, i, or oo depending on the sounds preceding it
i as i in sit or ee in meet
j as zh in measure
k as k in key
l as l in lot
m as m in me
n as n in nip
o as o in boat or aw in saw
ö as er in sitter
p as p in pay
r as r in bray
s as s in sea
ş as sh in shall
t as t in tea
u as oo in soon
ü as ew in pew
v as v in very
y as y in yes
z as z in zest

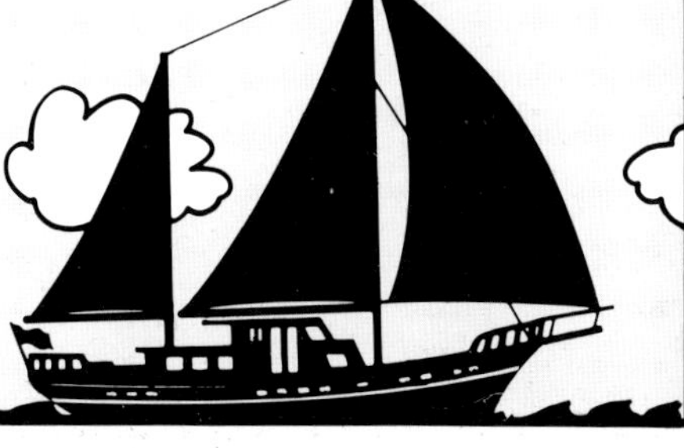

Appendix III: Common Turkish Terms Used In The Text

ada (adası): island
boğaz: strait, channel
burun, burnu: cape, headland
cami: mosque
dağ: mountain
deniz: sea
eski: old
göl: lake
hamam: Turkish bath
hisar: castle or fort
imam: cleric who presides over the prayers at a mosque
iskele: landing place
kale: castle
kapı: gate, pass
kara: black
kayası: rock or reef
kızıl: red
körfezi: gulf
köy: cove, creek
köyü: village
küçük: small
liman: harbour, port
muezzin: cleric who gives the call to prayer in a mosque
pazar: market
saray: palace
şehir: town
su: water
vilayet: province
yarımadası: peninsula
yeni: new

Appendix IV: Glossary Of Archaeological Terms

agora: the market-place
capital: topmost member of a column
cavea: auditorium of a theatre
cella: inner sanctuary of a temple
exedra: semicircular recess with a bench or benches
frieze: horizontal band of sculpture, usually surviving on tombs or tomb monuments
Hellenistic: period from Alexander the Great to Augustus, approximately 336 B.C. to the Birth of Christ.
odeum: small theatre for music and performances, oratory, etc.
orchestra: dancing-floor in a theatre
paradoi: side entrances to a theatre
pediment: triangular space over a colonnade or other feature
pronaos: front chamber of a temple
proscenium: front wall of a stage
stele: slab of stone set upright, like a grave headstone, bearing an inscription
stoa: covered portico

THE TURQUOISE COAST

A Guide to the Turkish Coast from Bodrum to Kekova.

TRANSPARENCIES:

Ignore any other markings on the transparencies except for those on the white dots. The order of the transparencies corresponds approximately to their order through each chapter.

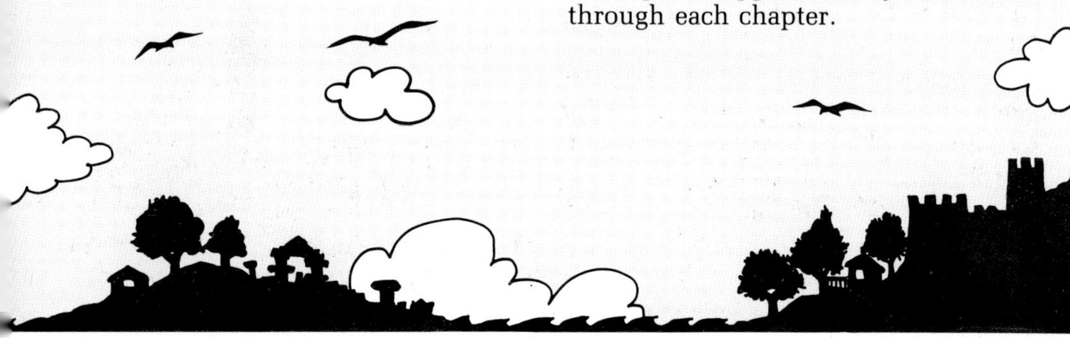

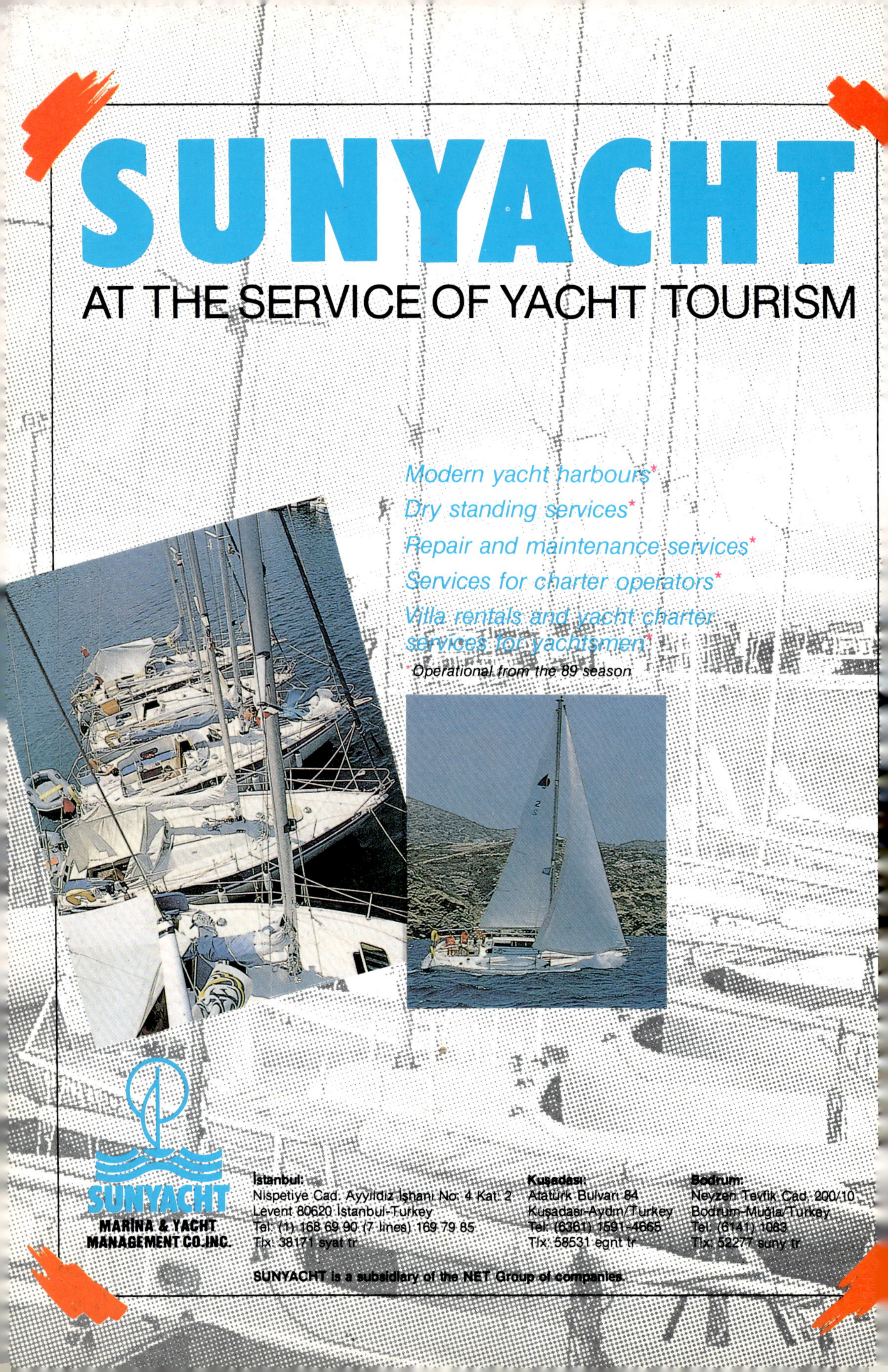
SUNYACHT
AT THE SERVICE OF YACHT TOURISM
Modern yacht harbours*
Dry standing services*
Repair and maintenance services*
Services for charter operators*
Villa rentals and yacht charter services for yachtsmen*
*Operational from the 89 season
SUNYACHT
MARINA & YACHT MANAGEMENT CO.INC.
İstanbul:
Nispetiye Cad. Ayyıldız İşhanı No: 4 Kat: 2
Levent 80620 İstanbul-Turkey
Tel: (1) 168 69 90 (7 lines) 169 79 85
Tlx: 38171 syat tr
Kuşadası:
Atatürk Bulvarı 84
Kuşadası-Aydın/Turkey
Tel: (6361) 1591-4665
Tlx: 58531 egnt tr
Bodrum:
Neyzen Tevfik Cad. 200/10
Bodrum-Muğla/Turkey
Tel: (6141) 1083
Tlx: 52277 suny tr
SUNYACHT is a subsidiary of the NET Group of companies.

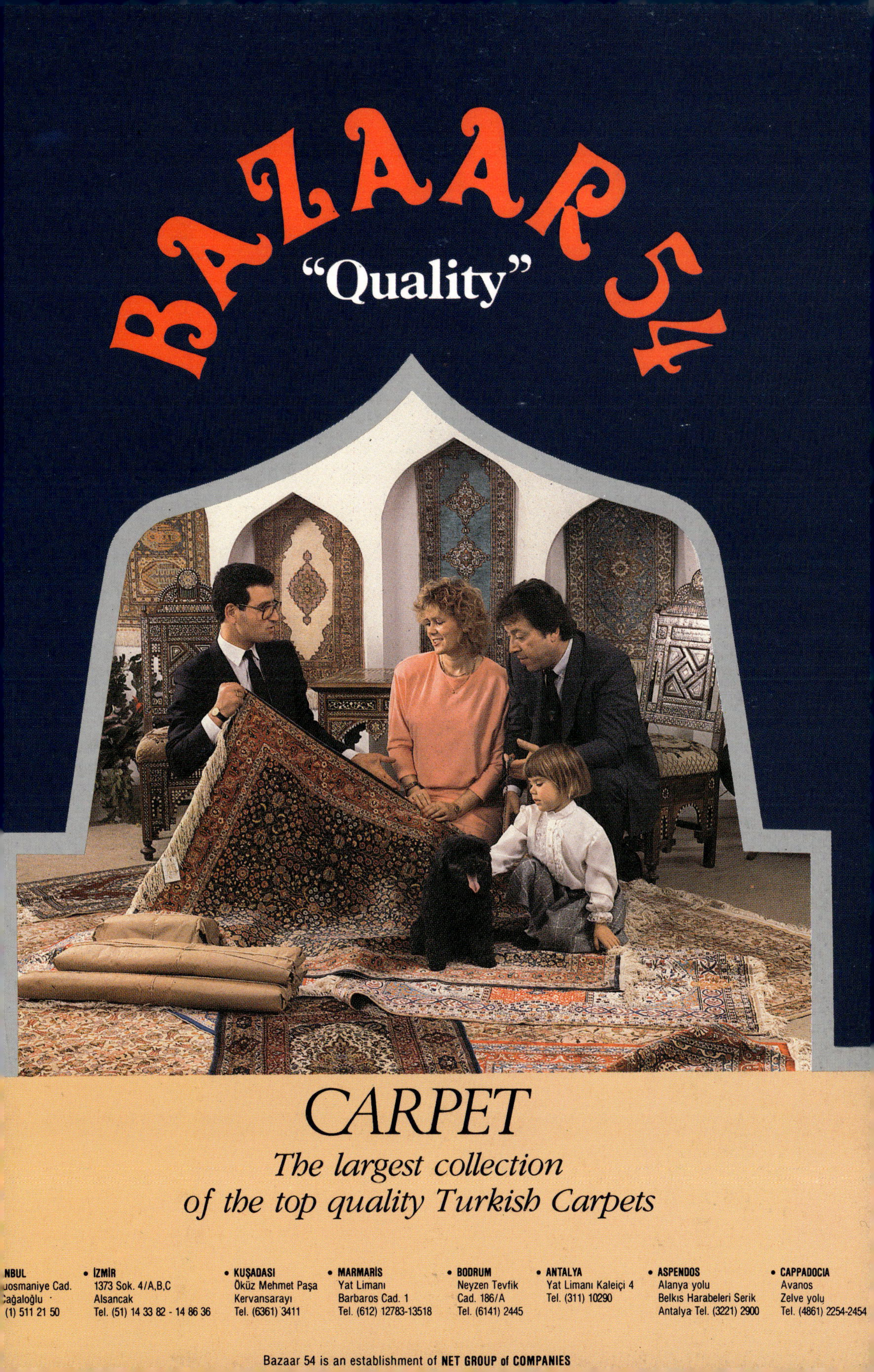
BAZAAR 54
"Quality"
CARPET
The largest collection
of the top quality Turkish Carpets
NBUL
uosmaniye Cad.
Cağaloğlu
(1) 511 21 50
• İZMİR
1373 Sok. 4/A,B,C
Alsancak
Tel. (51) 14 33 82 - 14 86 36
• KUŞADASI
Öküz Mehmet Paşa
Kervansarayı
Tel. (6361) 3411
• MARMARİS
Yat Limanı
Barbaros Cad. 1
Tel. (612) 12783-13518
• BODRUM
Neyzen Tevfik
Cad. 186/A
Tel. (6141) 2445
• ANTALYA
Yat Limanı Kaleiçi 4
Tel. (311) 10290
• ASPENDOS
Alanya yolu
Belkıs Harabeleri Serik
Antalya Tel. (3221) 2900
• CAPPADOCIA
Avanos
Zelve yolu
Tel. (4861) 2254-2454
Bazaar 54 is an establishment of NET GROUP of COMPANIES

THE TURQUOISE

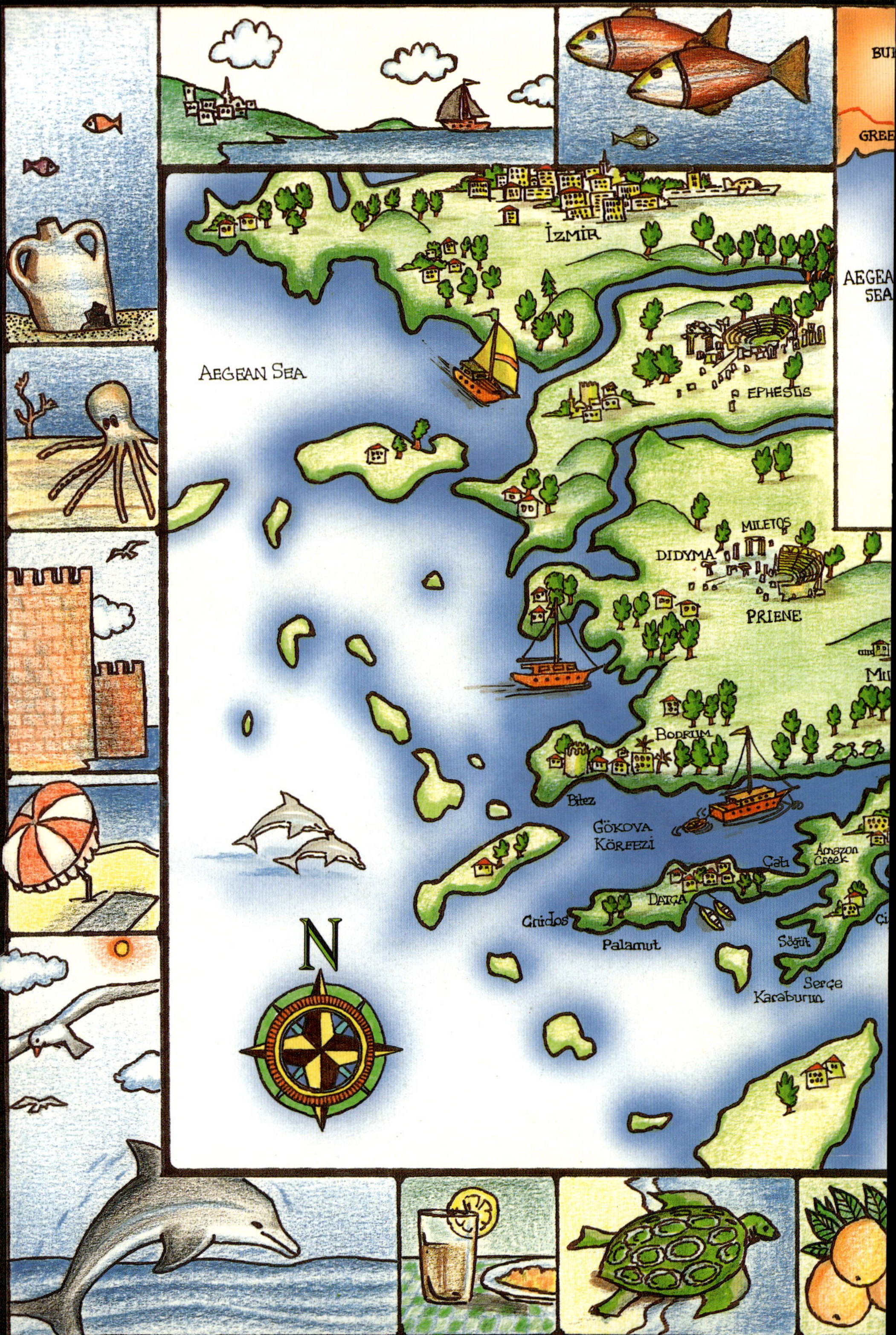

AST OF TURKEY

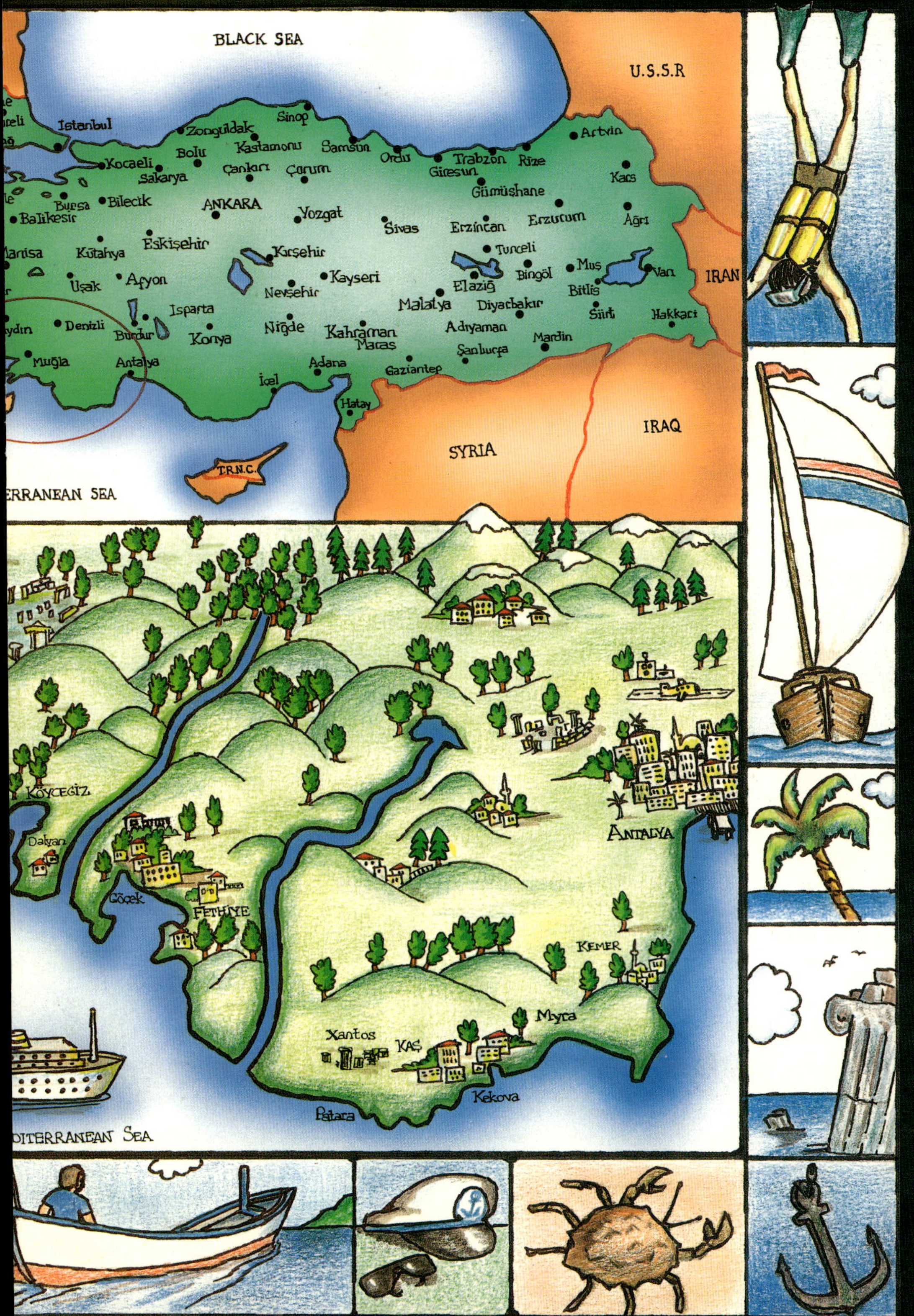

NET

PUBLICATION LIST

ISTANBUL (B)
(In English, French, German, Italian, Spanish, Arabic, Greek, Turkish)
ISTANBUL (BN)
(In English, French, German, Italian, Spanish, Japanese)
ISTANBUL (ORT.)
(In English, French, German)
CONTEMPORARY HANDMADE TURKISH CARPETS
(In English, French, German, Italian)
HAGIA SOPHIA
(In English, French, German, Italian, Turkish)
THE KARİYE MUSEUM
(In English, French, German, Italian, Turkish)
THE TOPKAPI PALACE
(In English, French, German, Italian, Spanish)
THE SACRED RELICS
(In English, French, German, Turkish)
THE SÜLEYMANİYE MOSQUE AND ITS ENVIRONMENT
(In English, French, German)
Unique CAPPADOCIA-The Göreme Region
(In English, French, German, Italian, Spanish)
CAPPADOCIA (BN)
(In English, French, German, Italian)
ANTALYA (BN)
(In English, German)
ALANYA
(In English, French, German, Turkish)
ASPENDOS
(In English, French, German)
PERGE
(In English, French, German)
TRABZON
(In English, German, Turkish)
PERGAMUM
(In English, French, German)
EPHESUS
(In English, French, German, Italian)
PAMUKKALE (HIERAPOLIS)
(In English, French, German, Italian, Turkish)
TURKISH CARPETS
(In English, German)
The Capital of Urartu: VAN
(In English, French, German, Turkish)
VIDEO CASSETTE-Istanbul (VHS-Beta)
(In English, French, German)
COLOUR SLIDES *(36 different sets, 12 slides in each sets)*
THE MAPS OF TURKEY AND ISTANBUL CITY PLANS

Publications distributed by NET

EPHESUS (AT)
(In English, French, German)
LYCIA (AT)
(In English, French, German)
KARIA (AT)
(In English, French, German)
NEMRUT (AT)
(German)
EPHESUS (T)
(In English, French, German, Italian, Spanish)
PERGAMUM (T)
(In English, French, German)
EPHESUS (İA)
(In English, French, German)
PAMUKKALE (İA)
(In English, French, German)
TURKEY (İA)
(In English, French, German)
ANTALYA (İA)
(In English, German)
CAPPADOCIA (İA)
(In English, French, German)
TOPKAPI (İA)
(In English, French, German)

NET BOOKSTORES

ISTANBUL,
1. Yerebatan Caddesi, Şeftali Sokağı, 10, 34410 Cağaloğlu
2. Ramada Hotel, Ordu Caddesi 226, 34470 Laleli
3. Ataköy Turizm Merkezi - Ataköy

İZMİR,
Cumhuriyet Bulvarı, 142/B, 35210 Alsancak

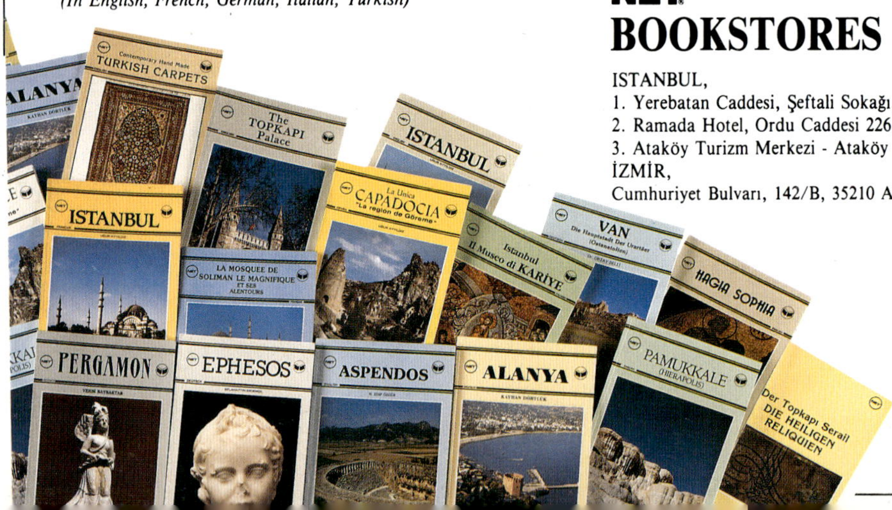

NOTES

NOTES